Managing the Environment, Managing Ourselves

A History of American Environmental Policy

Richard N. L. Andrews

Yale University Press   New Haven & London

Published with assistance from the Kingsley Trust Association Publication Fund established by the Scroll and Key Society of Yale College.

Designed by Rebecca Gibb. Set in Galliard type by Keystone Typesetting, Inc., Orwigsburg, Pennsylvania. Printed in the United States of America by Vail-Ballou Press, Binghamton, New York.

Library of Congress Cataloging-in-Publication Data
Andrews, Richard N. L.
Managing the environment, managing ourselves : a history of American environmental policy / Richard N. L. Andrews.
p.   cm.
Includes bibliographical references and index.
ISBN 0-300-07358-5 (cloth : alk. paper). — ISBN 0-300-07795-5 (pbk. : alk. paper)
1. Environmental policy — United States.   2. Environmental management — United States.   I. Title.
GE180.A53   1999
363.7'05'0973 — dc21
98-34987 CIP

A catalogue record for this book is available from the British Library.

The paper in this book meets the guidelines for permanence and durability of the Committee on Production Guidelines for Book Longevity of the Council on Library Resources.

10 9 8 7 6 5 4 3 2 1

S.D.G.

Contents

Preface

Since 1970, the natural environment has been one of the most visible and volatile topics of American public policy. In popular perceptions the "environmental era" began in 1970, with Earth Day, the coalescence of a broad "environmental movement," the signing of the National Environmental Policy Act, the creation of the Environmental Protection Agency, and the enactment of over a dozen sweeping new federal laws for environmental protection and ecological preservation. Much of the literature of American environmental policy deals only with this recent period and provides little sense of the historical origins or context of these policies.

In reality, American environmental policy has far older roots. It includes not only the recent burst of legislation intended to protect the environment, but *all* the policies by which Americans have used the powers of government to exploit, transform, or control their natural surroundings. These include nearly four hundred years' worth of policies establishing private rights, public restrictions, and economic incentives shaping human use of the natural environment, from colonial precedents and constitutional principles to subsequent laws, regulations, and other policies. Some recent policies are genuinely new, but far more are attempts to change or offset policies already in effect that reflect the environmental priorities and political power structures of previous generations.

Environmental policies are intricately interwoven with the broader forces and patterns of American history. The history of environmental policy is the history not merely of the Environmental Protection Agency, nor of the public lands, water resource, and wildlife agencies. It is all these things, but it is also the history of policies promoting transportation, industrialization, urbanization and suburbanization, trade, and other uses of environmental resources. It is a product not merely of specialized professions and interest groups, therefore, but of the country's dominant economic and political forces, shaped by elected officials, government agencies, business interests, and citizen demands. Some environmental historians would even argue that the history of human use of the natural environment is the *only* ultimately real or important history, underneath the distractions of more fleeting politics and "progress" (Martin 1992, 109–30). It is not, therefore, merely an isolated sector of interest to a few specialists and advocates, but an essential thread in the fabric of American historical understanding.

The purpose of this book is to provide a systematic account of how American environmental policy has developed, in the larger context of American history. It is in particular a history of environmental *policies* — of the actions of government that have affected the natural environment, and of the problems that motivated them and the consequences that followed from them — with particular attention to their implications for issues today. It is ultimately about the future of American environmental policy, in a world in which national environmental policies are increasingly under challenge not only by domestic critics — both for and against effective environmental governance — but also by the rising influence of global economic forces that are largely independent of national policy control.

Several themes run through this book. First, environmental issues are issues not just of science or economics but of governance. They concern problems that are not being solved by science and technology alone, nor by the "invisible hand" of markets or individual actions, and for which advocates therefore seek collective solutions through government action. They are debates as much about what government should do to solve environmental issues, therefore, as about the issues themselves. Some of these solutions have involved regulation, but others have involved public investments and subsidies, scientific research and technical assistance, information and educational programs, determination of property rights, and other government actions. Government policies themselves, moreover, are often causes of environmental problems as well as solutions to them.

Second, environmental policy includes not just what government says about the environment, not just what is labeled as environmental policy, but everything the government does that affects it. This is an important distinction. The term "environmental policy" dates back only to the 1960s, and some readers may wish to reserve it for actions explicitly taken under that label. Policymakers in other times and other policy arenas defined issues differently, one might reason, and had no conscious understanding of "the environment" as it is thought of today nor any meaningful intent to affect it by their actions toward other policy ends. Such a limited definition, however, would rule out even many current issues in which advocates of different priorities purposely describe them in rhetorics other than "environmental" in order to advance different political agendas. In reality, many of the impacts of government action on the natural landscape were evident and intentional in other policy sectors throughout American history (though not all, or always). Whether or not today's concept of "environment" and its full modern connotations were present, therefore, both the facts of those impacts and the ways in which policymakers characterized them are legitimate and essential raw materials for understanding the history and politics that have shaped American environmental policy.

Third, today's environmental policies have been strongly shaped, though not foreordained, by past policies and by their historical contexts. Policies are path–dependent: today's policies and issues in any society are strongly shaped by past issues and policy decisions, and by the political and economic forces associated with them, not merely by immediate political debates. American environmental policy reflects distinctive features of

American environmental conditions, and of the settlement patterns, technological infrastructures, economic and social dependencies, and political choices that have evolved in
interaction with them. To understand these conditions, and their interactions with social,
economic, and political choices over time, is essential to understanding American environmental policies themselves. These historical factors are also important considerations in
any proposal to use American policies as models for other societies — or, for that matter, to
consider adopting other governments' policy innovations in the United States.

Fourth, U.S. environmental policies have changed significantly and repeatedly over the
course of American history. Several of these shifts marked fundamental reversals in philosophy of environmental governance. Examples include the shift from nineteenth-century
privatization to active public management under Theodore Roosevelt's Progressivism,
from limited public management to massive federal investment in managed conservation
under Franklin Roosevelt's New Deal, from resource conservation to all–out industrial
exploitation during wartime, and from little or no federal responsibility for air and water
pollution control, waste management, and chemical hazards to detailed national regulatory authority in the 1970s. Most policy shifts, however, represented merely the cumulative addition of disparate pieces, whose inconsistencies were often left resolved. The result
is a patchwork legacy of conflicting policies with little coordination or integration, which
are contested again with each new issue, each new Congress, and each new administration.

This historical context affects every environmental issue today. Wetland protection and
endangered species preservation are severely constrained by constitutional doctrines establishing the primacy of private property rights, for instance, and by almost two centuries
of policies selling or giving away federal lands to private owners. Water pollution and
waste management policies are powerfully shaped by the fact that city governments, not
just private enterprises, have been responsible for these functions for almost a century. The
energy crises of the 1970s were founded on decades of public policies providing cheap
energy and thus promoting structural dependence on it. Public–lands policies today include century–old statutes promoting mining and other extractive uses with few requirements to prevent or correct their damage to the environment. Environmental administrators in government profess a hundred-year-old tradition of belief in using their science and
engineering expertise "in the public interest," while challengers from both businesses and
environmental advocacy groups point to forty years of literature rebutting such claims,
and advocate instead for more direct accountability of government agencies to citizens
affected by their actions. Federal pollution control regulations are now being whipsawed
between resurgent advocates of states' rights — the subject of a two-hundred-year-old
debate — and larger forces in the global economy, enlarged by five decades of policies
promoting world trade liberalization, which threaten to move economic activities and
their environmental impacts beyond any effective state or national control. The political
stalemate over environmental policy in the 1990s reflects the consequences of the very
policies put in place in the 1970s, at the height of the "environmental era," to provide for
effective protection and management of the natural environment. Today's policies will
shape tomorrow's as well, both by their effects and by their omissions.

Finally, environmental policy is not just about managing the environment, but about managing ourselves. Much of the history of American environmental policy reflects a primary emphasis on controlling, managing, and manipulating the natural landscape itself, as a supply of raw materials and energy, a site for human construction and development projects, a source of hazards to be controlled by human intervention, and occasionally, a source of amenity and human enjoyment. Protecting and maintaining that landscape requires restraining and moderating the impacts of human intervention in order to protect natural species, processes, and ecosystems for other purposes and to sustain their continued existence. Today and for the foreseeable future, in a world in which human population growth, technological capabilities, and material and energy consumption now impact the earth's natural processes on a global scale, managing the environment requires managing ourselves as well. In this task the perspectives of the social sciences and the humanities will be as important as the natural and engineering sciences, and both intellectual interaction and practical cooperation among all these fields will be essential.

No book could hope to do justice to all the significant events of American environmental policy, let alone the details of the policies themselves and the full stories of their establishment and implementation. I am painfully aware of how many of them I have had to mention only briefly if at all, and can only hope that readers unfamiliar with them will be inspired to read further about them, and that those who know them well will forgive my brevity and omissions. If this book at least conveys an informative and reasonably accurate account of the major lines of policy development, the contexts and forces that produced them, and their consequences for later and current issues, it will have accomplished what I can reasonably hope for it.

Any book of this scope owes many debts, both intellectual and personal. The first is to the distinguished group of scholars whose earlier work on the history of various aspects of environmental policy laid the foundations for it, including particularly Lynton Caldwell, William Cronon, Samuel Dana, Ernest Engelbert, Samuel Hays, Martin Melosi, George Rosen, Joel Tarr, and others cited in the bibliography. The second is to those who most directly inspired my own interest in the subject, particularly Maynard Hufschmidt and Blair Bower in environmental policy, Milton Heath and Joseph Sax in environmental law, and John Morton Blum in American history. Third, I have benefited greatly from my interaction with senior environmental policymakers who have shared thoughtful perspectives on their experience, particularly William Ruckelshaus, William Reilly, Alvin Alm, and Terry Davies, and from the excellent work of Dewitt John and the staff of the National Academy of Public Administration, whose efforts enriched the chapters on the Environmental Protection Agency.

I am also deeply grateful to a number of colleagues who were kind enough to read and suggest improvements in the manuscript, including Dan Esty, Donald Higginbotham, William Leuchtenburg, Michael Lienesch, Barry Rabe, and others including one anonymous reviewer, and to other colleagues whose ideas have influenced my own: in particular Otis Graham, Donald Hornstein, Michael Kraft, Robert Paehlke, Norman Vig, and others. I acknowledge with special thanks Jean Thomson Black of Yale University Press, whose enthusiasm and professionalism as well as her thoughtful comments provided valuable incentives to bring this to completion. Any remaining errors are mine alone.

Fellowships from Resources for the Future and the Rockefeller Foundation provided financial support for several stages of the research, which I acknowledge with thanks. I am also especially grateful to my students, whose critiques and fresh ideas have shaped my perspective in innumerable ways, and to the University of Michigan School of Natural Resources and the Department of Environmental Sciences and Engineering of the School of Public Health, University of North Carolina at Chapel Hill, for allowing and encouraging me to develop these ideas over some twenty-six years of teaching and research. Rebekkah Cote provided extraordinarily diligent secretarial assistance in various stages of the word processing of the manuscript, and Frederick Mullner provided valuable help in finding illustrations.

Finally, I am grateful beyond words for the personal and intellectual companionship of Hannah Wheeler Andrews throughout this project, and for her constant encouragement as well as her insightful questions and editing suggestions; and for the patience and support of all my family.

1 Environment and Governance

A belief in spontaneous progress must make us blind to the role of government in economic life. — Karl Polanyi, *The Great Transformation*

Every society develops particular patterns of relationships between its members and their natural environment. At a minimum, these patterns include acquiring the material necessities of life (food, water, heat, shelter), disposing of material and energy wastes, and protecting people from environmental hazards (fires, floods, predators, diseases). Beyond the minimum, they include attempts to satisfy additional human wants and aspirations: larger populations, material comfort and affluence, urban amenities, political and economic power, a sense of beauty or security, and monuments to religious values or human vanity.

These patterns differ greatly from one society to another. They differ in part due to the environmental conditions themselves — climate and weather patterns, hills and valleys and plains, minerals, vegetation and wildlife, rivers, estuaries and oceans — and the opportunities and constraints and hazards that these conditions present. They differ also with the characteristics of the society. Large and small populations make different demands on their environments. So do populations that have more or less powerful technologies for resource extraction and transportation, more or less elaborate systems for economic exchange, more dense or dispersed settlement patterns, and greater or fewer material aspirations. Different societies also see and value their environments in different ways: what is desired in one culture may be unrecognized, distasteful, or even feared in another.

The effects of these patterns may be more or less sustainable over time, both for the society itself and for its environmental conditions. They may also be more or less equitable in their impacts, more or less conscious and deliberate, and more or less influenced by the actions of formal governments.

Environmental Issues as Governance Issues

Human uses of the environment are matters of governance, not merely of individual choice or economic markets.

Some may disagree with this assertion. Strict libertarians might argue, for instance, that uses of the environment should be decided by autonomous individuals acting on their own preferences and values, without compulsion by governments. Free-market economists might argue that they should be decided by the sum of individual preferences expressed in market choices, and that government should intervene only to correct "market failures." Still others might argue that the only role of government should be to protect and enforce private property rights, leaving environmental choices to those who thus own the environment.

For at least seven reasons, however, government involvement in environmental issues is both necessary and inevitable.

First, *governments assign and enforce property rights, determining who has what rights to use or transform the environment and what duties to protect it.* When someone buys an acre of land, does she own the minerals underneath it and the water and wildlife that cross it as well, or may these belong to someone else or to the public? Does a commercial fisherman have the right to sell as many fish as he can catch, destroying an entire fishery and simply moving on to another, or is that right limited by a legitimate public interest in maintaining the fishery's survival? Does an upstream industry or city have the right to use a river for waste disposal, or does a downstream homeowner or community have the right to water free of contaminants?

Governments do not merely intervene in markets. They establish the basic operating conditions for them, affirming and enforcing principles regarding who actually holds the rights to produce or sell environmental assets — or to exclude others from them — in the first place, and who is liable for the costs of environmental damage. Even libertarians need governments to enforce their rights against environmental damage caused by their neighbors.

Second, *governments define and enforce the rules of markets themselves.* Governments enforce contracts and other rules of market honesty, for instance, so that both buyers and sellers can protect themselves against cheaters. Some of these rules involve environmental conditions: adulterated foods, contaminated or toxic products, businesses with unacknowledged environmental liabilities, false advertising claims for "green" products, and other misrepresentations. For that matter, modern corporations would not even exist without government statutes that allow people to pool capital assets in such organizations, to limit their personal liability for the corporations' actions, and to operate such corporations as "legal persons" with essentially the same legal rights as individuals. Markets do not operate without government enforcement of the rules of fair transactions, and environmental conditions are often elements of such fairness.

Third, *governments protect public health and safety.* Both infectious diseases and toxic agents are spread through environmental exposures against which people cannot fully protect themselves by individual actions or market choices: through air, water, and food contamination, insect vectors, and unwitting contact with infected individuals, for instance. Historically such hazards have killed and sickened vast numbers of people. Environmental hazards are also increased by the cumulative effects of individually logical choices: disposing of wastes as cheaply as possible, building more and more homes with septic systems around lakes, paving and building along rivers and thus increasing downstream floods. Governments are needed to enforce reasonable restrictions on individual behavior patterns that create hazards to public health and safety.

Fourth, *governments protect environmental assets from "tragedies of the commons."* Many valuable environmental resources are "open access" or "common pool" resources that can easily be captured and sold by competing businesses. Examples include ocean fisheries and large underground oil pools. Each commercial fisherman has an incentive to catch and sell as many fish as possible, and each oil company to pump as rapidly as possible, since otherwise the resource will be captured and sold by their competitors. National parks and public highways experience similar problems: the cumulative effects of individual choices can lead to overcrowding or even destruction of the common resource. Garrett Hardin described such problems as tragedies of the commons (1968). Such patterns of incentives and behavior, he argued, must be restrained by some governance mechanism — "mutual coercion, mutually agreed upon" — or the common resource will be destroyed by the cumulative results of individually rational choices.

Fifth, *governments provide collective goods that markets do not.* Many valuable environmental conditions are collective goods. Like national defense, clean air and public parklands benefit whole communities rather than just individual purchasers, and arable soils and sustainable fisheries benefit generations who are not yet present to make market choices. Markets undervalue or even fail to provide such goods: first, because it is impossible to organize payment by all the people who benefit from them, and second, because those who don't pay cannot be excluded from enjoying them as well. Acting as self-interested individuals, both businesses and consumers are tempted to "free-ride": to pay as little as possible for their share of collective goods from which everyone benefits.

Free-riding aside, individuals and markets also depend on governments to pool enough resources to finance projects that may be widely beneficial but require large investments for benefits that accrue over long periods of time. Examples include large multipurpose water resource development projects, building of transportation infrastructure, and space exploration. Not all such projects have been well justified in the past, but many clearly have been.

More generally, *governments provide environmental services that people prefer to have provided collectively,* acting as voting citizens of a community, state, or nation rather than as individual consumers. Examples include public water supplies and waste management services, community amenities, and parks and recreation areas. Governments also have the unique power to redistribute access to environmental amenities and economic resources based on votes rather than purchases. In societies more complex than small face-to-face communities, only governments can redistribute resources so as to provide at least minimal access to decent living conditions regardless of wealth. Also, only governments can moderate the inequities that markets tend to produce, both in general economic opportunity and in access to environmental resources and amenities. Governments do not always produce these results — often they are influenced by powerful economic interests to redistribute from the poor to the rich — but only governments *can* accomplish redistribution.

Finally, environmental issues are governance issues because *governments' actions have environmental impacts themselves.* Governments tax some uses and subsidize others, and they invest public funds in projects to transform the landscape for resource extraction, human settlements, transportation, food and energy production, and other uses. They preserve and manage some landscapes directly, regulate and restrict the use of others, and support research and professional expertise in areas of environmental knowledge that markets alone might not. Government actions both cause and correct environmental problems: government regulations and subsidies have been vital and effective tools for cleaning up pollution, for instance, but government incentives for Cold War military and industrial production also caused widespread contamination in the first place. Dealing with environmental issues therefore means dealing with the environmental effects of government actions themselves, not simply those of individuals and businesses.

In environmental policy issues, therefore, questions about the proper management of the environment are fundamentally intertwined with questions about the proper ends and means of governments themselves.

Environmental Policy

Environmental *protection* policy includes three elements of environmental policy that are explicitly intended to protect public health and ecological processes from adverse effects of human activities. The first element is *pollution control,* including prevention, safe management, and cleanup of waste discharges, accidental spills, and deliberate environmental dispersion of toxic materials such as pesticides. The second is *sustainable natural resource management,* including maintenance of naturally renewable resources (groundwater, forests, fish and wildlife, arable soils), regulation of rates of extraction and use of other resources (water, fuels, strategic minerals), and management of conflicting uses of landscapes for commodity production and recreation. The third is *preservation of natural and cultural heritage,* including areas of special beauty, historical and cultural significance, ecological functions, and landscape character.

Environmental policy as a whole, however, includes all government actions that alter natural environmental conditions and processes, for whatever purpose and under whatever label. Policies promoting transformation of the environment for mineral extraction, for agriculture or forestry or outdoor recreation, for urban or industrial development, or for transportation infrastructure are in their effects just as much elements of environmental policy as are pollution control regulations or habitat protection programs — whether or not they are called by that name. So are military operations, international trade agreements, and other policies with environmental impacts.

This broad definition of environmental policy has important practical implications. First, the "real" environmental policy of a government is not necessarily what its officials say their policy is, nor what the statutes and regulations say, but the cumulative effect of what government actions actually *do* to the natural environment. Many official statements of environmental policy, and even statutory mandates, are undercut by conflicting mandates or underfunded budgets, and others are ineffective in achieving their stated purposes.

Second, many of the most powerful instruments of environmental policy are lodged not in environmental protection agencies but in agencies that transform environmental conditions for other purposes. The policies of the Agriculture, Energy, and Transportation Departments, for instance, may affect the environment at least as much as those of the Environmental Protection Agency (EPA), and their budgets are far larger. Some of the most effective policy strategies for reducing pollution, therefore, might involve not adding new EPA regulatory programs, but changing or eliminating environmentally damaging programs administered by other departments.[1] More generally, the best way to achieve an environmental policy goal, such as reducing pollution or preserving ecosystems or landscapes, might often be to improve coordination of conflicting policies across multiple sectors, rather than merely to add a single new law involving one agency.

Environmental Problems as Public Policy Issues

Environmental problems share with other public policy issues a set of questions about what governments should and should not do, and how such decisions should be made. These questions are just as much a part of the debates about environmental problems as are the questions of environmental science, technology, and economics that often dominate such debates. They include the following:

Individual versus collective purposes. Which purposes should be pursued through collective decisions, and which should be left to individual choices? Some functions are intrinsically governmental and cannot be accomplished in any meaningful way by individuals or economic markets alone. Protecting public health has long been recognized as a government function, and sustaining the "commons" of environmental conditions necessary for the society's continuation and economic welfare is also such a purpose. Other functions, such as transportation, water and energy supply, waste management infrastructure, and other services, can be provided either collectively or individually.

Tradeoffs among public purposes. How should conflicting public values for uses of the environment be balanced? Even among legitimate public purposes, conflicts and tradeoffs are inevitable: among competing uses of environmental resources themselves, among competing allocations of limited budgets and staff expertise, and among different beneficiaries and victims. Which should be considered most important, by what criteria, and who should decide?

Proof versus prudence. How much evidence should be required to justify government actions? Government policies are collective actions, in which the good of society is asserted to override the rights or preferences of individuals. They must therefore be justifiable rather than arbitrary or capricious. In the United States in particular, this principle has led to elaborate requirements for scientific and economic justification of policy proposals. Uncertainty and conflicting judgments remain inescapable, however, so prudence must always substitute to some extent for proof.

As a result, policy decisions are not only decisions about substantive environmental problems but also about how much proof is necessary to justify a government action to correct them. This issue is important in itself, especially when costly or intrusive remedies are proposed for problems whose solutions are highly uncertain. It is also used by some advocates, however, as a tactic to slow or derail prudent policy proposals that they oppose for self-interested reasons: "paralysis by analysis."

Central versus local governance. At what level of governance—local, regional, state, federal, international—should environmental policy decisions be made? The principle of "subsidiarity" holds that policy decisions should be made at the lowest possible level: local decision-making provides the best venue for developing solutions tailored to specific conditions and communities. It is most accountable to those most directly affected, and most appropriate for maintaining the diversity of human cultures and communities.

By the same token, local governments also have more limited revenues and resources than those with broader jurisdictions, leaving poor communities unable to benefit from a broader base of economic support. Local decisions are also most likely to run counter to more general public values, whether pertaining to trade, environmental protection, or human rights. Granting autonomy to local governments also creates the risk that they will displace adverse effects onto other jurisdictions, and may pit local or even national governments against one another in using tax breaks, lower wages, and weaker environmental protection policies to attract or retain businesses.

More centralized governance, conversely, provides greater opportunities for setting general standards of acceptable behavior and competition, and can amass greater revenues with which to realize public purposes. Its risks, however, include greater bureaucratization, lessened accountability, dominance by powerful centralized interests, and standardization at the expense of local diversity. Policies must be designed to use the most appropriate combination of tools and levels of government to solve each problem.

Organization of government institutions. What sorts of government agencies, at any level, should be responsible for environmental protection? Should they be specialized independent agencies (for environmental regulation, for instance), or multipurpose departments encompassing both regulation and natural resource management? How can such agencies be coordinated with other agencies whose actions affect environmental conditions? There is no simple way of organizing all government purposes under one super-agency, but separate agencies have inherent tendencies to pursue their own missions at the expense of others.

Even individual units such as the EPA must be broken down into subunits that tend to focus narrowly on their own missions. Organizing by problem types such as air or water pollution, toxic chemicals, and waste management will lead to different results than organizing by problem sources such as industry, agriculture, and households or by administrative functions such as standard-setting, enforcement, and research. Conflicting perspectives and priorities must constantly be resolved.

Collective choice procedures. Who is to decide, and by what process, what environmental policies and priorities should be? Representative legislatures or appointed administrators? Experts or "the people"? Experts may be wise protectors of the society's future, or self-interested and arrogant elites. Members of Congress may be statesmen seeking the long-term good of the society, decent but parochial representatives of their constituents' wants, or merely self-interested incumbents selling themselves to interest groups to finance their own reelections. Ordinary people may be ideal citizens seeking the good of their society, or they may be just as self-serving or short-sighted as anyone else.

Each procedure for collective decision-making has strengths and weaknesses, both in principle and as a mechanism for determining what government should do.

Policy tools. What kinds of government actions are the best tools for achieving public policy goals? Regulations with civil or criminal penalties? Public expenditures, subsidies, and investments? Taxes and other economic incentives? Information disclosure requirements? Providing public services, or contracting for them? Some policy tools may be far more effective than others, either in general or for particular purposes. All have impacts on other goals as well, such as fairness, economic efficiency, and equitable distribution of the benefits and costs of the policy to particular communities. Policy choices must therefore be based on careful evaluation of their full consequences, and on experimentation and correction over time.

Intrinsic hazards of governance processes ("government failures"). Finally, governmental actions always involve complications intrinsic to collective decision-making (Wolf 1979). "Free-riding" describes each participant's temptation to try to avoid paying a fair share of the cost of collective services. "Rent-seeking" reflects the equally human tendency to seek excessive compensation for one's own property or services, or even one's vote. "Pork-barreling" describes the tendency of elected representatives to collude in allocating general public revenues to benefit their own constituencies.

Other complications stem from the *transaction costs* of reaching agreements. Collective decision-making is costly and time consuming. Collective decisions require vote-trading across issues important to individual participants but far removed from the merits of the matter at hand, and compromises — "splitting the differences" — that may distort or pervert the decision's outcome. Different voting rules have different consequences: the "tyranny of the majority" can marginalize minority viewpoints, but the tyranny of organized minorities can frustrate majority values. It is far easier to organize small but identifiable groups with personal economic interests to influence policy decisions than to mobilize larger and less identifiable constituencies that share a more general public interest in the outcome (Olson 1965). To many people, consensus seems intuitively the most desirable form of political decision-making. In practice, however, it rewards the most extreme form of minority tyranny by allowing holdouts to demand extra individual benefits ("rent-seeking") as the price of their approval.

Governments also tend to externalize the social and environmental costs of their decisions, just as businesses and individuals do. Government decisions are routinely designed to promote the short-term self-interests of public officials and powerful organized interests by providing concentrated and visible benefits while making costs and harms as widely dispersed and invisible as possible. The result is often that social and environmental impacts are displaced onto other agencies, onto other communities or countries, onto other levels of government, onto less-organized constituencies, or onto later legislatures and administrations and future generations. Examples include locating incinerators on downwind borders, imposing unfunded federal mandates on state and local governments, and subsidizing the extraction and use of natural resources at rates faster than can be sustained for future users.

Such jurisdictional externalities are in principle no different from the externalities sometimes produced by economic behavior, except that they represent government failure rather than market failure. Such problems arise whenever a government's jurisdiction and process do not include representation of all affected constituencies and responsibility for the full range of causes, consequences, and potential solutions. They are particularly common in environmental policy issues, for reasons discussed below.

In environmental policy no less than in other public policy debates, therefore, the fundamental issues include questions not only about technical and economic matters but also about the role of government, the costs and risks of its actions, and measures to minimize and correct harmful effects.

Special Characteristics of Environmental Issues

Environmental issues, however, also have characteristics that differentiate them from other policy issues. For example:

Environmental values, preferences, and power relationships. Environmental issues involve particular places with distinctive natural features and histories. People identify with such places and develop strong opinions about how they should look and be used: whether they should be kept as they are, used for established economic purposes, or altered to achieve some new vision. Moreover, the uses of particular places are interdependent. Unlike budget allocations, entitlement programs, and many other policy issues in which each constituency can lobby for a share of the outcome, each participant's use of the environment affects those of the other participants: hunters and hikers and loggers, fishermen and farmers and users of municipal wastewater treatment plants. Proposed changes, therefore, are often simultaneously good to some groups and bad to others.

Creating environmental policy, therefore, often involves negotiating conflicts among mutually exclusive preferences for the use of indivisible resources. Such conflicts are far less amenable to political compromise or compensation than other policy issues. Examples include conflicts over proposals for construction of mines, landfills, and other major facilities, logging of old-growth forests, damming of free-flowing streams, and development of beaches and lakeshores.

The physical and biological realities of environmental conditions also create one-sided relationships of economic and political power. Rights to use natural resources, such as forests and minerals, confer windfall economic benefits but also create resource-dependent interests and constituencies. Upwind or upstream users can always impose externalities on their downwind or downstream neighbors, but the latter have no inherent countervailing power to negotiate fair outcomes with the former. Hunters and fishermen benefit from capturing migratory animal species, but the reproduction and growth of those species depend on restraining people who use the ecosystems where the animals spend earlier stages of their life cycles.

All these conditions shape environmental policy debates in ways that make them distinct from political controversies based only on ideology, political party, social class, or other factors.

Public attitudes toward environmental risks. Environmental risks evoke strong public attitudes and preferences. Many people demand government action to prevent environmental risks that are far more remote than risks they voluntarily incur in their daily lives. Examples include risks of exposure to trace residues of man-made chemicals in comparison to such risks as driving a car, crossing a street, smoking, or even eating foods whose natural properties pose greater health risks than do their man-made additives (high fat, cholesterol, or natural toxins, for instance). This pattern appears to reflect greater aversion to risks that are perceived as more uncontrollable and more dreadful in their consequences than others. It may also reflect other values, such as a willingness to impose greater costs of risk prevention on other parties than on themselves (on "big business" or "big government," for instance). Whatever the reasons, fear of environmental risks represents a powerful and distinct force that is different from those motivating other policy advocates.

Tragedies of the commons. Many environmental conditions are by their nature open-access resources: available to everyone, and therefore difficult to protect from the cumulative effects of overuse. Examples include the atmosphere, water bodies (lakes, rivers, estuaries, and seas), underground aquifers and oil deposits, fisheries, and unmanaged public forests and grazing lands. Garrett Hardin's classic article "The Tragedy of the Commons" described as a model of such problems the case of self-interested sheepherders, each of whom adds animals to a common pasture until the cumulative effects of their individual decisions destroy it (Hardin 1968). Some open-access resources can be privatized, to be managed (though not necessarily protected) by a single owner. Some can be converted to government property or "common property" resources, in which either government or an association of the users manages and protects it.[2] But others are more difficult to protect. The users may be too numerous, too diverse, or too separated in space or time to create a viable regime, or the values to be protected may be too divorced from the interests of those causing the damage: as, for instance, when fisheries are destroyed not by other fishermen but by land developers or farmers.

Tragedies of the commons are not unique to environmental policy issues. Other examples include overpopulation (the cumulative effects of human childbirth decisions) and the politics of some other collective goods (for instance, the cumulative effects of individual legislators seeking "pork barrel" budget allocations). Environmental policy issues pose such dilemmas constantly, however, pitting long-term common interests against more immediate individual interests.

Scientific and technical premises. Environmental policy decisions are often framed by scientific and technical claims, including assertions about what is known and what options are technically possible, as well as assumptions, predictions, and uncertainties. This raises several problematic issues. First, it creates barriers to meaningful participation by people who do not understand the scientific and technical claims being made. Second, it makes the burden of proof a key issue in its own right: should governments be required to show strong scientific proof before acting to correct environmental problems, or should they act based on reasonable judgments about the risks or opportunities at stake even when significant uncertainties remain? Third, it raises questions about how much deference should be given to scientists in the policy process. Each discipline addresses only pieces of any issue, and individual scientists reach different conclusions based on the different bodies of evidence and criteria they use. Scientists are often overconfident of their judgments, and sometimes as self-interested as other policy advocates. Many scientific claims in policy debates — though by no means all — may therefore be just as political among conflicting groups of scientists as the policy decisions themselves are among conflicting public constituencies.

Irreversible damage to public interests. Finally, some environmental issues involve consequences far broader than the self-interests of particular advocates, some of which are potentially irreversible on any meaningful time scale. Examples include species extinctions, the exhaustion of nonrenewable resources and arable soils, and particularly the destruction of whole ecological systems that support living communities, such as forests, fisheries, wetlands, and estuaries. The potential for irreversible damage to irreplaceable natural conditions and processes — and more generally, to a healthful, productive, and attractive natural environment — is an important consideration in environmental policy. To the extent that claims of such damage are well founded, they deserve serious consideration.[3]

For all these reasons, environmental policy is worth studying not only as an example of public policy generally, but as an important and distinctive topic in its own right.

American Environmental Policy

Today's American environmental policies are the legacy of a long history. The label "environmental policy" was coined only in the 1960s (Caldwell 1963), and with it have come important changes in both understanding and policies. The existence of environmental policies, however, dates back not just the thirty years since the first Earth Day, but the two hundred-plus years since the establishment of the current constitutional regime, and the nearly four hundred years since European empires colonized North America. Today's environmental problems are shaped by the policies that previous generations created to address earlier environmental problems and opportunities. Environmental policy choices today, in turn, will shape the problems and opportunities of the future.

American environmental policy reflects distinctive American attitudes toward the environment. Examples include the nineteenth-century "cornucopian" perception of virtually infinite natural resources, and the more recent perception of industrial chemicals as insidious and ubiquitous cancer risks. It also reflects distinctive American attitudes toward governance, such as distrust of centralized power and authority, a preference for adversarial over authoritative decision-making, and shifting preferences for legislative, administrative, or direct popular decision-making. Both the goals and tools of environmental policy have changed greatly over the course of American history, as have the political processes by which it is made and implemented.

To the extent that the United States has a national environmental policy today, it consists not in any integrated or coherent whole, but in a heterogeneous patchwork of statutes, purposes, instruments, agencies, and levels of government. It resides in no single department comparable to the ministries of the environment in other countries. It lies in a multiplicity of agencies implementing a growing number of largely uncoordinated statutory mandates that affect the environment in conflicting ways. The Environmental Protection Agency, despite its name, has no single overall statute authorizing it to protect the environment. Even for a specific environmental policy issue such as pollution control, pollution of the air, water, and land are addressed by separate statutes, programs, policy incentives, and decision criteria. The United States in 1970 adopted a National Environmental Policy Act, but it has never translated this into any overall plan or strategy to guide its agencies toward common goals. Both the strengths and the weaknesses of U.S. environmental policy thus derive from a policy-making structure fragmented among diverse, mission-oriented programs and agencies.

Despite this lack of coherence, however, U.S. environmental policy has distinctive features that shape its results. One feature is the expansive deference it accords to private rights to transform the environment for economic gain, and the correspondingly weak powers it accords to public agencies to protect broader societal values. A second is the pervasive influence of federalism, in the form of constant renegotiation of the tension among national, state, and local governments. A third is the active role of an independent judicial branch, not only in resolving environmental disputes among individuals and businesses but in challenging the environmental actions of government agencies themselves.

In fact, perhaps the most distinctive difference between American environmental policy-making processes and those of many other governments is the broad rights of access and redress which U.S. laws and recent judicial precedents accord not only to business and labor organizations but to citizens in general. This vulnerability to judicial review has created a heavy burden of proof on public agencies to document and justify their decisions, both through elaborate environmental, economic, and risk analyses and through increasingly detailed documentation of consultation procedures.

Finally, American environmental policy has been overwhelmingly concerned with domestic issues, especially the environmental impacts of federal resource exploitation and development projects and, since 1970, the federal regulation of pollution and toxic chemicals. This preoccupation may become increasingly problematic in a twenty-first-century world in which both environmental impacts and the economic forces that cause them are increasingly global.

Plan of the Book

This book traces the development and impact of U.S. environmental policies through American history, in the context of the broader political and economic forces that shaped them.

Chapters 2 through 4 lay out the foundations and context for U.S. environmental policies. Chapter 2 frames the global context of the European colonization of North America and subsequent American history, including not only environmental policies per se — such as feudal land rights and worldwide European colonization for natural resource production — but also the broader changes in knowledge, technology, and social organization that have shaped much of American history, in particular the Scientific and Industrial Revolutions, the adoption of constitutional governance, and the rise of economic liberalism. Chapter 3 describes the environmental policies of the American colonies, focusing on the property rights they established — who had what rights to use land, water, fish and wildlife, minerals, and other environmental resources — and on how these policies evolved in American circumstances into policies different from those of the European colonizers. Chapter 4 sets out the constitutional context for environmental policy-making, especially the provisions that both established and limited the powers of the national government to make environmental policy — for instance, the commerce, property, treaty, and federal supremacy clauses on the one hand, and the requirements for due process, compensation for takings, and equal protection on the other. It then offers examples of how these principles continue to shape environmental policy issues today.

Chapters 5 through 7 trace the development of American environmental policy through the nineteenth century. The dominant policies of the early nineteenth century included the acquisition and exploration of western lands, the privatization and development of these lands for settlement and commodity production, and the use of both land grants and federal expenditures to subsidize the construction of a vast network of canals and railroads. Chapter 5 describes the development of these policies and notes the political failure to institute more protective policies even as the destructive effects of rapid land exploitation became widely evident. Chapter 6 traces the emergence in the late nineteenth century of policies that differentiated and classified lands by their resource values, and the emergence of new federal administrative agencies, developments that together laid the institutional foundations for public management of environmental resources. Finally, Chapter 7 recounts the concurrent development of environmental policy in American cities, examining the environmental and health impacts of urbanization and industrialization, the rise of the sanitation and public health movements, the expansion of municipal governments' responsibilities for public health and environmental services, and the unresolved conflicts among public health officials, municipal engineers, civic reformers, and industrial interests over urban environmental policy issues.

The turn of the twentieth century brought a profound shift in American environmental policy, with President Theodore Roosevelt's adoption of Progressivism as a philosophy of governance and natural resource conservation as a justification for federal environment management. Chapter 8 discusses the principles of Progressivism and conservation, their institutionalization in federal agencies for natural resource management and public health protection, and their enduring consequences for American environmental policy. Chapter 9 describes the maturation of these agencies into "subgovernments" during the interwar years, and the second major expansion and proliferation of them under Franklin Roosevelt's New Deal as responses to the human and environmental disasters of the Great Depression. This chapter also discusses the growing conflict between these agencies' Progressive self-images as apolitical expert institutions serving the public interest and the reality of their roles as political brokers among competing user interests.

World War II and the postwar era brought fundamental changes, in particular a period both of unprecedented industrial production and consumption and of rising public opposition to the environmental impacts of these actions: the rise of the modern environmental movement. Chapter 10 describes the joint effects of wartime, Cold War, and economic policies that promoted large-scale industrial exploitation of the landscape and its resources, and the concurrent incentives that moved the overwhelming majority of the American population into urban and suburban living conditions. Chapter 11 details the resulting changes in environmental conditions, in public awareness and political mobilization, and in policies that led to the emergence of a broad public movement for environmental protection out of previously fragmented constituencies and concerns.

The period since 1970 has been widely characterized as the "environmental era" of American public policy, and it does indeed represent a period of unprecedented political attention to the environment. It also has brought distinctive policy changes aimed at the control of pollution and the preservation of natural species and ecosystems. Chapter 12 recounts the creation and early history of the EPA and the implications of the country's unprecedented new policy of national regulation of pollution. It also describes the newly pivotal roles of citizens' environmental advocacy groups and of expanded citizen rights to obtain government information and to challenge government action or inaction in the courts. Chapter 13 then details EPA's continuing conflicts since 1980 among regulation, reform, reaction, and innovation, as the metaphorical "pendulum" of political power swung between advocates of environmental protection and of relief from regulatory burdens.

Chapter 14 moves beyond pollution control to the unfinished business of national environmental policy, including the National Environmental Policy Act, nature protection statutes, and policy reforms in agriculture, energy, transportation, and other sectors. It also documents the overall failure of the United States to implement coherent national environmental policy across the economic sectors and administrative agencies that most affect environmental conditions and resources.

Chapter 15 returns to the larger global context discussed in Chapter 2, and examines both the evolution of U.S. involvement in international environmental policy-making and the impacts of an increasingly global economy on American environmental policy and on the environment itself. Finally, Chapter 16 assesses the state of American environmental policy in the late 1990s and identifies key lessons of history and governance that will shape its future.

2 Historical Context: European Colonization and Trade

> [A]ll economic systems known to us up to the end of feudalism in Western Europe were organized either on the principles of reciprocity or redistribution, or householding; or some combination of the three. . . . In this framework, the orderly production and distribution of goods was secured through a great variety of individual motives disciplined by general principles of behavior. Among these motives gain was not prominent. . . .
>
> The transformation to [the market] system from the earlier economy is so complete that it resembles more the metamorphosis of the caterpillar than any alteration that can be expressed in terms of continuous growth and development. . . .
>
> The Industrial Revolution was merely the beginning of a revolution as extreme and radical as ever inflamed the mind of sectarians, but the new creed was utterly materialistic and believed that all human problems could be resolved given an unlimited amount of material commodities. — Karl Polanyi, *The Great Transformation*

The physical environment has been an underlying force in American politics and economics throughout the nation's history, and indeed since before America was a nation. The colonial period is often slighted in American policy studies, yet it encompasses a longer time span than the American nation has yet experienced since 1776. Generations of people immigrated and settled, lived and died, and used the American environment during that time. Important roots of American environmental policy were laid long before the American Revolution, in a context dominated by the colonial policies of European nations and the survival needs of European colonists. In fact, more emphasis may have been given to policies for managing the physical environment during the colonial period than during the first century following the Revolution (Engelbert 1950). It is worth attention, therefore, both for its own sake and for the precedents and patterns it established.[1]

The cultural context of American colonization was the laws, economies, and customs of the societies from which the colonists came, especially England. The colonial settlers came from Europe, with European ideas and traditions and upbringing, and they came for reasons based in European events. As colonial settlers, they were governed by policies made in the capitals of the European powers. Policies made in the colonies themselves therefore reflected either deliberate adoption, adaptation, or rejection of the European environmental policies that prevailed at the time.

American environmental policies today still reflect much of this basic structure, and many current issues in fact involve new battles over long-fought principles. To understand American environmental policies today, therefore, one must trace their roots back to the influences that formed them, and the contexts and concerns that have shaped American history more generally from the colonial period onward.

The Great Transformation

European society in the fifteenth century was in the process of a profound change — what Karl Polanyi has called the "Great Transformation" — from a feudal structure based on moral and personal obligations and land tenure to a market economy based on transferable wealth and commerce (Polanyi 1957 [1944]; White 1962). The High Middle Ages (circa 1100–1300) had been a period of dazzling accomplishment: it saw the invention of the compass, the mechanical clock, spinning wheel, windmill, and waterwheel, for instance, and the opening of trade routes to China by Marco Polo. The fourteenth century, however, had brought a "little ice age," crop failures and famine, corruption in church and government, and the Black Death — plague epidemics which killed twenty-three million people, literally one-third of the world's population from India to Iceland (Tuchman 1978). Feudal society in the fifteenth century was closely tied to the land and its resources, with relatively little commerce or technological innovation. Population was gradually increasing, and with it food production, but nourishment was poor and seasonal, since refrigeration was nonexistent and meat and vegetables could be preserved only by salting and drying. Open fires, tallow candles, and oilcloth windows provided light and heat; bad harvests, bad weather, and epidemics were regular causes of human misery. Infant mortality rates were high, and even the best-fed people generally died by about age fifty.

Under the feudal system, all authority and legitimacy emanated from the top. The king ruled by divine right, not by constitutional consent of the governed, but as the agent of God who came to that right by his birth. He delegated lesser authority and property to his vassals, barons, lords, knights and other free men who in return swore him their loyalty and military as well as economic support. All land and resources were ultimately owned by the king — hence the term "real estate" or "royal" property — and granted by him to his vassals as "fiefs" or "fee" for their services.

Land was the basis not only of subsistence and income, but also of people's social status and obligations. The land was held in major estates or "manors," each functioning as a relatively self-sufficient political and economic unit, a local agrarian state ruled by its lord — a "land lord." Though most lands of the manor were worked in common, individual families were sometimes given small plots of their own as part of their remuneration. The lord of the manor owed produce and service (especially military service) to a baron or bishop and on up, eventually, to the king. Common people were legally bound to the land as serfs, by obligations of grain and labor owed to the lord of the manor on which they lived. Most obligations had to be paid in kind, since money was scarce and common people had little access to it.

Property rights thus were always conditioned on grants from above, on the satisfaction of feudal obligations to one's superiors, and on strict adherence to customary law. The law of entail required that land could only be passed on intact to one's direct descendants, not divided into smaller parcels or sold. If there were no descendants, it reverted to the grantor. Primogeniture required that it be passed only to the oldest son. Annual payments ("quitrents") had to be made to the grantor in obligation for the grant. In short, all land ownership was derived from above and conditional.

The feudal society was organized for subsistence and stability, and its economy was governed by moral rather than market principles. Everyone had a proper role and function, assigned by their birth and defined by their land tenure. Each product had a traditional price and each form of labor a traditional wage, rather than one that fluctuated with supply and demand. From an ecological perspective, feudalism maintained a relatively stable set of relationships between human populations and their ecosystems for an extended period of time. Contrary to Garrett Hardin's example, common-land farming and grazing functioned for centuries without tragedy until fundamental economic changes disrupted the social system that regulated it (Hardin 1968; Buck 1985). The costs of this stability, however, included the maintenance of a rigid system of social classes, personal service obligations, and control of property that provided little opportunity for advancement based on merit, and discouraged or even prohibited innovation.

Feudalism and the manorial economy began to decline by the end of the twelfth century, but the transition to a market economy took several centuries. The key to the change was agricultural surpluses, which could be exchanged and marketed rather than consumed locally for subsistence. By the thirteenth century, regional markets had developed for foodstuffs, and international markets began to develop for such commodities as wool. From marketplaces and trade centers grew towns and cities, in which people supported themselves not by farming but by commerce. By the middle of the fifteenth century Europe had developed extensive trade links with China and the Indies. A new class of people developed in European society, a merchant class or bourgeoisie whose income came not directly from the land but from commercial exchange and sale. The rise of commerce included a major shift in emphasis from barter and direct exchange to monetary payments for products and services.

The socioeconomic system of the manor was fundamentally transformed by the combination of commerce, monetization, and falling agricultural prices resulting from surpluses. Wage labor was increasingly substituted for traditional peasant obligations, and cash crops for subsistence crops. The land itself gradually was partitioned and leased to professional peasant farmers for monetary rents. Market production gradually supplanted the manorial system. Many of the early enclosures were set aside for sheep grazing as the price of wool rose; later ones were used to grow food crops for the expanding cities. Peasant farmers producing for the market became the driving force of the agrarian economy, and with the incentives of legal leases and modest rewards, these farmers began to develop modern methods of intensive farming, such as crop rotation, seed selection, scientific cattle breeding, and the use of agricultural machinery.

In short, by around 1500 the emergence of a market economy had created strong pressures to commercialize agricultural land, to transform it from common subsistence use to enclosure and more intensive cash cropping, and to transform common people from land-bound peasants into tenant farmers and wage laborers. The effects on land and people were intimately connected. The transformation turned the land into a commodity, a factor of market production, and in the same process turned much of the agrarian population into a mobile labor force — freed from both the security and the obligations of serfdom — that had to seek employment wherever jobs and wages permitted. Rising commercial wealth, meanwhile, created steadily increasing demand for luxury consumer goods from distant lands (Kupperman 1995, 18).

This transition did not happen in a single stroke of policy, nor even in a single generation. But it represented a fundamental transformation of the relationships among people and between them and their physical environment.

Monarchy and Mercantilism

The economic changes of the Great Transformation paralleled equally profound political changes. Under feudalism, government revenues were constrained by the stable system of land obligations. The rise of commerce, however, shifted the basis of economic and political power from landholders to merchants, and with this shift came a centralization of royal power. Trade could be taxed more profitably than land, and cash taxes could be used to pay standing armies and government bureaucracies. Kings received revenues from merchants in return for official monopolies and other trade privileges. Merchants in turn benefited from the profitable business of provisioning armies, and armies provided a means of enforcing tax collection.

To increase their revenues from trade and tariffs, the monarchs of Europe took an increasing interest in promoting controlled trade. Their methods for encouraging such trade took three forms: incentives for exploration and colonization, grants of special privileges to enterprising merchants who were willing to take financial risks that might profit them personally as well as their monarchs, and protective taxes that benefited their own merchants over those of other empires.

Exploration was motivated at least in part by a combination of familiar economic impulses: to meet a rising demand for consumer goods, eliminate middlemen, and reduce transportation costs. In the mid-1400s the Turkish empire spread westward, blocking the overland routes to China and the Indies on which Europe relied. In the fifteenth century new scientific discoveries began to permit exploration of alternative routes by sea, which offered the economic benefits of waterborne transport for bulk cargoes. Better maps improved knowledge of shipping routes, the mariner's compass permitted more accurate steering, and the progress of astronomy — da Vinci and Copernicus in the fifteenth century, Galileo and Kepler in the sixteenth — led to improvements in the basic theory and methods of navigation, while the development of printing facilitated the spread of knowledge. Then as now, advances in science and technology played a critical role in converting environmental conditions into natural resources.

Portugal, Spain, and other countries thus began supporting explorers seeking sea routes to Asia, first around the southern tip of Africa and later westward across the

Atlantic. Diaz of Portugal reached India around the Cape of Good Hope in 1487, as did Vasco Da Gama in 1497–98 and Cabral in 1500. For Spain, Columbus reached the Americas in 1492 and 1497, Vespucci in 1497, and Magellan and Del Cano in 1519. Cabot of England reached Labrador in 1497, and Sir Francis Drake reached northern California in 1579. Verrazano reached North America from France in 1524, and Cartier in 1534–35. By the late 1700s George Vancouver had even reached the North Pacific, and New England's ships had explored Nootka Sound en route to Canton. Exploration led not only to the discovery of new trade routes, but to the discovery of new places with new stocks of resources: gold and silver primarily, but also fisheries, sugar and other commodities. The explorers claimed the places they discovered as possessions of their monarchs.

By the sixteenth and seventeenth centuries, exploration led to the development of an increasingly elaborate system of nationalistic trade policies known as mercantilism. The motivating force in this system was a convergence of interests between the nationalistic goals of the monarchs and the profit motivation of the merchants and entrepreneurs who made it work. Kings needed gold, silver, and other resources to feed and pay standing armies. Explorers were economic entrepreneurs willing to take large risks for large gains: Pizzarro and Cortez of Spain, for instance, and later Sir Walter Raleigh and Lord Baltimore of Britain. Some of the early explorers were financed by monarchs; later ones raised their own capital through "joint stock companies," antecedents of the capitalist corporation though lacking such features as limited liability. These corporations were chartered by the king and granted special privileges to whatever resources they might discover, or even quasi-feudal land grants. Examples included the British East India Company, chartered in 1600; the Dutch West India Company, in 1621; and the Virginia Company, chartered to settle the Virginia colony in America in 1606.

Colonization as Environmental Policy

For reasons rooted in European political and economic conditions, the nations of Europe thus reached out around the world in the sixteenth century (fig. 1). Each sought not only to explore, but to establish colonial empires. Each sought to find and capture new stocks of natural resources that were cheaper and more plentiful than those already available to them. In the Western Hemisphere, Renaissance Europeans saw not only economic opportunity but an imagined "New World," a romanticized Garden of Eden offering pristine landscapes, abundant natural assets, and innocent inhabitants — to which were soon added opposing images of terrifying natural forces and horrifying savagery (Jones 1965, 15–20, 70). These images produced a powerful and widespread belief in American "exceptionalism": a belief that for better or worse America was a radically different environment — and ultimately, society — from the "Old World" of Europe (Greene 1993, 5–7).

Colonization, then, was among other things an environmental policy. In the broadest sense, it was a policy of expanding the accessible environment of each empire — its physical resources as well as its economic and political control — to a larger and larger portion of the world. More precisely, it was an environmental policy to benefit the ruling political and economic classes of each empire. It provided them with natural resources they desired

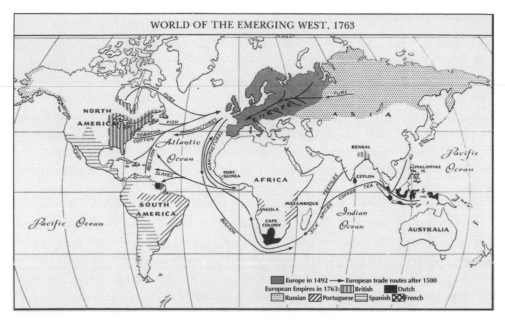

Figure 1. European global exploration and trade routes in the fifteenth and sixteenth centuries. [Source: Stavrianos 1988, 443. Reprinted by permission of Prentice-Hall, Inc., Upper Saddle River, N.J.]

on more favorable terms than previously, it relieved them of the urban concentrations of poor people displaced from the land by agricultural commercialization, and it gave them the financial prosperity they needed to maintain large standing armies.

European exploration and colonization also had unanticipated consequences that caused vast changes in the world's ecosystems. Living species previously limited to particular regions were disseminated worldwide. European stockyard animals (horses, cows, sheep, pigs), grain crops (wheat, rye, oats, barley), and fruits were transplanted to the colonies, and American vegetables — corn, potatoes, tomatoes, cassava, avocados, peanuts, and squashes — were brought to Europe and elsewhere, as were tobacco, cotton, sugar, drugs such as coca and curare (for anesthetics), and other products. Native populations were decimated by diseases to which they had not previously been exposed — smallpox, measles, scarlet fever, tuberculosis, and others — and syphilis in turn spread to Europe. The human races were interspersed worldwide, both by colonization and by the slave trade. The governance institutions and policies of the colonizing nations were imposed on different cultures and environmental settings. And not least, both localized ecosystems and the localized governance regimes that had evolved to manage them were subjected to powerful new external pressures for the benefit of distant markets and beneficiaries (Crosby 1972).

The overall result was to begin a vast, centuries-long process of reducing worldwide biodiversity, by promoting intensive specialized production of those few species that were most profitable in global markets and allowing others to be lost to extinction (Crosby 1972).

Freedom of the Seas

As European ships explored new seas and shores and their empires competed in the seaborne "carrying trade," several of the maritime powers sought to declare their sovereignty over the world's seas as well as its newfound shores. This practice began within Europe, in agreements which divided jurisdiction over the smaller European seas — such as the Baltic and Adriatic — among the various sea powers. Britain then asserted sovereignty over the North Sea to control Dutch fishermen off the coasts of Scotland. As explorers spread further, they claimed sovereignty over the new waters they found. The result was increasing conflict among the sea powers, often in the form of piracy against one another's ships.

This pattern of conflicts was broken by a Dutch legal scholar, Hugo Grotius, who set down basic new principles of the law of the sea that would endure for over three hundred years. In 1608 Grotius published *Mare Liberum* (Free Sea), a treatise which asserted that the seas were properly a common resource, free for use by all: what we would call today an "open access resource." Each nation was entitled to enforce its authority within a defensible perimeter of its coasts, but not over the high seas beyond: "imperium terrae finiri ubi finitur armorum potestas" [the dominion of land ends where the power of arms ends] (Christy 1975, 701). The sea-power nations gradually accepted these principles, and the boundary of each nation's seaward jurisdiction was said to be the limit of a cannon shot, or about three miles. The United States in 1793 explicitly declared a three-mile territorial sea, and most other nations did likewise. Not until the mid-twentieth century did the United States and several other nations, faced with new technologies for offshore fishing and mining, raise new challenges to Grotius's principles.

Constitutional Governance

From 1640 to 1688 — half of the seventeenth century, during which the English colonies in America were taking root and developing their social, political, and economic fabric — England was wracked by civil war. This conflict ended in England's "Glorious Revolution," in which William and Mary became rulers of England on condition that they swore to uphold a Bill of Rights guaranteeing Britain's governance by a representative constitutional government. This bill guaranteed not only religious toleration but also recognition of the legal powers of Parliament and of the rights of individuals. Most important, it established the principle that the sovereign was subject to the rule of law, no longer an absolute ruler.

England's civil war was a major influence on the development of policies and political attitudes in America. Most immediately, it preoccupied Britain with its own internal affairs for nearly fifty years, leaving the colonies both the hardships of developing on their own and the freedom to do so. Of necessity and opportunity, therefore, they developed their own institutions of self-governance and a system of export trade relationships with other ports and empires that was far more diversified than might otherwise have been permitted.

The civil war resulted in victory for the common people over the aristocracy, and led to policies that suppressed feudal privileges and replaced hereditary authority with principles of egalitarian liberty. The legislation establishing the commonwealth in 1649, for instance, stated explicitly that not the king, but "The People, are, under God, the Origin of all just Power" (Stavrianos 1971, 247). Conflict continued between those who defined "people" by universal manhood suffrage and those who limited them to property owners, but in either case the traditional principles of feudalism and the divine right of kings were rejected. In their place, the Commonwealth confirmed the "natural and inalienable rights" of each individual and the principle of popular sovereignty. These egalitarian ideas probably could not have arisen until the market economy freed common people from land bondage, and until they asserted their rights to equality by defeating the aristocracy. Once established, these ideas became an important basis for the American system of government and property rights, and for the rights demanded by many in developing nations today.

Finally, Britain's revolution established the principles of constitutional government, with the legislature rather than the king as supreme authority in matters of law, taxes, and the maintenance of armies, and it affirmed that the "natural rights" of individuals limited the authority of any government or king (Stavrianos 1971).

The Scientific Revolution

A dramatic transformation in people's understanding of their world occurred in Europe during the sixteenth to eighteenth centuries, a shift which laid the foundation for all modern western environmental policies. The change had many elements. One of the most important was the Reformation, which challenged both the sacred and the secular authority of Roman Catholicism, promoting the more democratic and humanistic Protestantism. A second was the Scientific Revolution, which replaced traditional theological philosophies of science with a belief in natural laws and in the value of learning through empirical observation and experimental methods. A third was the rapid spread of technological innovation, culminating in the Industrial Revolution. Finally, the fourth was the Enlightenment, or "Age of Reason," which popularized such ideas as belief in progress, critical reasoning, natural rights, utilitarianism, laissez-faire economics, and environmental relativism. These elements built on and amplified one another.

A common theme among these elements was a fundamentally altered view of nature, from the traditional view of nature as a divine mystery in which God acted through miracles, to a practical view of it as a complex but understandable mechanism — a clockwork on a cosmic scale — whose operations could be explained and predicted through human observation and reasoning. As Galileo put it, "I think that in discussion of physical problems we ought to begin not from the authority of Scriptural passages, but from sense experiences and necessary demonstrations. . . . Nor is God less excellently revealed in Nature's actions than in the sacred statements of the Bible" (quoted in Bronowski 1973, 209).

With this view of nature came a new and ambiguous view of human beings' relationship to nature. Humans were on the one hand a special species, possessing the newfound ability to understand nature's laws through their own reasoning powers and to manipulate its conditions to their advantage. On the other hand, humans were also a biological species of nature, themselves understandable — to an extent not yet even imagined — in terms of natural laws.

The basic discoveries of this period are well known. Nicholas Copernicus in 1543 described the planets as rotating around the Sun rather than Earth; Francis Bacon formalized the inductive method of scientific reasoning; Galileo Galilei in 1610 used telescopic observation to support Copernicus's theory; Johannes Kepler mathematically described the orbits and movements of the planets; Isaac Newton by 1687 postulated and mathematically proved the law of universal gravitation; Newton and Leibniz concurrently invented the mathematical method of the calculus.

The larger transformation, however, was far more profound than the particular discoveries. Newton's discovery, for example, was not just of gravity as an isolated event. It was the discovery of a universal law of nature which applied equally to an apple falling to the ground and to a planet in the heavens, and it was a demonstration of the power of empirical scientific method, combining reason and mathematics with observation and experimental proof. The calculus, in turn, was not just a new technique; it was a whole new conceptual method that made possible the study of continuous motion, and thereby of an uncountable number of other natural processes that we now take for granted and still study by its method. It also made possible the development of mechanical power in the following century.

The discovery of universal laws in nature, and of analytical methods for proving them, set off a wave of interest in the study of nature that has never abated since. Stated simply, people began taking a serious and scientific interest in how their environment worked. Those who could afford to collected and catalogued specimens of minerals, fossils, and forms of plant and animal life. Expeditions to foreign lands brought back specimens that further piqued public interest. In the 1770s, while Britain and America were fighting a revolutionary war, Captain James Cook was leading three scientific tours to the South Pacific to observe the transit of Venus, explore and chart the islands of that region, and conduct descriptive studies of natural history and ethnography. George Louis Le Clerc published the thirty-two-volume *Natural History* between 1749 and 1789; his *Theory of Earth* (1749) and *Ages of Nature* (1778) established a basic theory of geological history and articulated an idea of evolution, theorizing that all the planets had originally been thrown off from the Sun and were slowly cooling.

Within a century after Newton's *Principia* was published, John Ray and Carolus Linnaeus laid the foundations of systematic botany and zoology, Benjamin Franklin developed a comprehensive theory of electricity, and the steam engine was invented and perfected. In chemistry, the study of combustion gases revolutionized the old concepts of earth, air, fire, and water: Joseph Priestley in 1774–75 isolated oxygen, Joseph Black in 1775 isolated carbon dioxide, Henry Cavendish in 1781 separated water into hydrogen and oxygen, and Jan Ingenhousz in 1799 demonstrated the role of photosynthesis by plants in the carbon cycle. Finally, in 1789 Antoine Lavoisier published his *Elementary Treatise on Chemistry,* which established both the "principle of balance" — the thermodynamic law that matter and energy are neither created nor destroyed — and the systematic basis of chemical science.

By about the time the United States became a nation, in short, it had available to it most of the basic foundations of modern science, newly but solidly established and ready to be applied further. Time and motion were well understood, except for the concept of relativity; mechanical power was available through the use of basic engines, and enhanced by harnessing kinetic energy released by heat as steam. Understanding of electricity made possible both electromagnetics and electrochemistry; understanding of chemical oxidation permitted advances in metallurgy and industry; and selective breeding was being developed in agriculture. The analytical concepts and methods of empirical science provided an intellectual framework that could be applied to the untapped natural resources of the New World.

The Industrial Revolution

The rise of European commerce and the new practical scientific view of the world led to a transformation in material production processes, an "industrial revolution" (Toynbee 1956 [1884]). Within Europe, increasing population and monetary wealth expanded the markets for each nation's products (Hobsbawm 1968). Overseas trade and colonization created new markets for European manufactured products, both among the colonists themselves and among the native people with whom they traded: English woolen blankets, iron tools and pots, for instance, could be traded to American Indians for the furs Europeans wanted for their hats and coats. Commerce also created profits: investors accumulated large sums of capital through joint stock ventures, which could be used to finance even more profitable future ventures. The enclosure of land, which accelerated rapidly between 1750 and 1780, concentrated ownership in fewer hands for agriculture and especially wool production; it increased profits and simultaneously created a growing pool of cheap labor for industrial production.

New innovations in industrial organization and technology provided the means to exploit these opportunities. In the textile industry, entrepreneurs used their capital to buy raw material in bulk and "put it out" to non-guild artisans doing piecework in their houses, thus breaking the traditional output restrictions of the guild system. With the invention of large-scale power-driven machinery, such as Richard Arkwright's water-frame spinning machine (1769) and Edmund Cartwright's power loom (1785), workers were brought together in factories for larger-scale and more rapid production. In iron and steel production, Abraham Darby's conversion of coal to coke (1709) provided a cheap substitute for scarce charcoal, and Henry Cort's iron "puddling" process (1784) produced more malleable decarbonized iron. To transport bulk commodities, British entrepreneurs and engineers such as John MacAdam (1750) pioneered canal and hard-surface road construction, which dramatically reduced both the time and expense of transport, and thus the effective distance between raw materials, production processes, and markets.

Perhaps the most fateful single innovation of the Industrial Revolution was the steam engine, which permitted large-scale substitution of fossil fuel energy for animal and human labor. Invented by Denis Papin and perfected by Thomas Newcomen (1702) and James Watt (1763), the steam engine converted the heat energy of fire and fuel into mechanical energy. It could do work that human and animal energy could not, such as run effective mine pumps. It could also be used to increase human workers' speed and efficiency at jobs they could do, such as spinning and weaving. Finally, it could be used both for stationary power in industrial processes and to power steamboats and railroads. Probably no single invention more significantly reshaped natural resource use, material production processes, and even the patterns of human settlement in the industrialized world.

What consequences did this transformation of production processes have for world history, and particularly for the newly independent United States? First, it greatly increased human capacity to transform raw materials into manufactured products. This increased demands for natural resource extraction from the physical world, even as it made the comforts of these products available more cheaply to more people. It increased the level of human stress on the systems of the natural world as it measurably increased the welfare and comfort of human consumers.

Second, it achieved this goal at the cost of profound social and environmental change. A large and growing population was dislocated from the familiar and relatively stable life of agrarian production into the poverty, crime, and disease of overcrowded cities, and often into either unemployment or low-paying jobs where workers put in long hours under hazardous conditions. Power machinery increased the productivity per worker, but profit was only maximized if the workers kept up with it. Men and women, even boys and girls down to the age of four, worked from dawn to dusk in textile factories, machine shops, mines, and on construction projects. Weber (1971, 421) reports that at the height of the Industrial Revolution in England, in the first half of the nineteenth century, the real wages of textile workers and miners were actually decreasing by about 50 percent.

Third, the Industrial Revolution caused a major change in the scale of human organization. By sparking a shift from small factories to cities and urbanized areas, and later to industrial complexes and transnational corporations, industrial capitalism fundamentally restructured the relationships between people and their environments. As T. S. Ashton put it, "The industrial revolution is to be thought of as a movement, not as a period of time. . . . Everywhere it is associated with a growth in population, with application of science to industry, and with a more intensive and extensive use of capital. Everywhere there is a conversion of rural into urban communities and a rise of new social classes" (1964 [1948], 98). Industrial capitalism also became a driving force in nineteenth-century European colonialism, which provided new markets and new sources of raw materials; in twentieth-century economic imperialism by the industrialized nations; and in the emergence of today's integrated global economy.

At the time of the American Revolution, the eventual extent of this impact could not have been foreseen. The American economy remained largely agrarian for most of the following century, and did not industrialize on a major scale until after the Civil War. The emergence of this transformation in England and Europe, however, clearly influenced the patterns of environmental policy and development in America. Among the most significant effects, it provided growing markets for American raw materials, and sources of capital for investment in extracting and exploiting these resources. It led to the invention of labor-saving technologies for a country in which labor was scarce and natural resources plentiful, and it stimulated the invention and adoption of new technologies in American industries. Eventually, it forced American governments to choose between a predominantly agrarian and a predominantly commercial and industrial pattern for the United States' development.

The Enlightenment

The new world-view of science and technology produced a new naturalism and rationalism in the study of human society and institutions as well. "It would be very singular," as Voltaire expressed it, "that all nature, all the planets, should obey eternal laws, and that there should be a little animal, five feet high, who, in contempt of these laws could act as he pleased, solely according to his caprice" (quoted in Stavrianos 1971). It was not simply coincidental, therefore, that the English Civil War and "Glorious Revolution" were justified by ideas of the "natural" rights of individuals.

The century following Newton and the English revolution in the 1680s is frequently referred to as the Age of Enlightenment, so called because of the widespread confidence of its thinkers and writers that mankind was at last emerging from dark ignorance and superstition into the light of reason. Scientists were among the adherents and sources of Enlightenment ideas, but others were also important in extending these ideas to human nature and society.

John Locke wrote his *Treatise on Civil Government* in 1690, the year after William of Orange signed the English Bill of Rights. In it he justified the principle of government by social contract between sovereign and people, on the basis of the "natural rights" of individuals to agree on such a contract. Thomas Hobbes's *Leviathan* (1651) had characterized men as by nature self-serving, and human life in the "state of nature" as "solitary, poor, nasty, brutish, and short"; Hobbes therefore argued that absolute monarchy was necessary to save men from themselves. Locke, in contrast, argued that the natural man was decent, reasoning, and perfectible; capable of progress and self-restraint, and capable of living by informed consent and tolerance within a social contract with his fellows. Conversely, he was entitled to withdraw his support from the social contract if the sovereign violated it, a principle explicitly adopted in the American Declaration of Independence eighty-six years later. Locke's central ideas — belief in the basic goodness and perfectibility of man, in the existence of natural laws and rights underlying human society, in reason, and in government by social contract — amounted to an enlightened view of human nature. They also provided many of the arguments used to justify the American Revolution, American government and property rights, and American policies toward the use of natural resources. Building explicitly on Newton and Locke, the "philosophes" of the Enlightenment — men such as Voltaire and Montesquieu in Europe and Benjamin Franklin, Thomas Paine, and Thomas Jefferson in America — concluded that the way to human progress was simply to enlighten people, by education and logical reasoning, about their true nature and perfectibility and about the natural laws by which human society and history functioned.[2]

Many of the principles on which the Enlightenment's writers generally agreed are still among the most powerful foundations of American government and politics. One is the idea that all people are created equal and endowed with inalienable rights. Individuals are not predestined to particular roles, but are formed by their experiences and environments. Accordingly, social *progress* is possible, if people are provided with appropriate experiences and environments. This argument supported both universal education and universal suffrage, as John Stuart Mill suggested, as well as universal public participation in political decision-making. The ideas of egalitarianism, human perfectibility, and social progress were powerful motivating forces at the time — most obviously in the American and French Revolutions — and they remain strong in U.S. politics today.

Another powerful Enlightenment idea was utilitarianism. If the world were to be understood in terms of human reason and experience rather than divine intervention, how were good and bad to be determined, and progress and regress? What secular, humanistic principle could replace the normative role of the Church, not just in explaining how the world worked, but in prescribing the moral principles for what humans should *do* with it and with one another? The Enlightenment answer, stated most succinctly by Jeremy Bentham in 1776, was that the good society was one which maximized the happiness of its members: "the greatest good for the greatest number." Like Locke, Bentham implied in his approach a majoritarian form of government, and assumed that individuals would behave in accordance with principles of enlightened self-interest, seeking pleasure and avoiding pain. As Weber put it, "The *philosophe*'s ideal [was] liberty, property, and security. Liberty to pursue one's own happiness without injuring others. Property being the advantages that each man could gain by his own labor and talent; Security to enjoy these in peace, under laws which prevented others from depriving one of them by using force or privilege" (1971, 653).

The most persuasive statement of this theme at the time was Adam Smith's *The Wealth of Nations,* published in 1776. Smith argued that there was a natural order in the economic affairs of societies. Each individual was the best judge of his own interest, and would therefore seek to improve his condition as he best saw fit. Therefore, the best society was one in which each individual was left as free as possible to pursue his own self-interest, and which trusted to the "invisible hand" of this principle to achieve the greatest good for the greatest number of people. *Laissez-faire, laissez passer:* "let men act freely, let goods flow freely," and let the preferences of the majority define the good society through the natural economy of a free marketplace.

Smith's ideas challenged both the feudal idea of a moral economy ordered by principles of "just" prices and wages, and the mercantilist doctrines that commerce should be regulated in the interests of the state and that money or land was the proper measure of wealth. *Labor* was the proper measure of wealth and value, he argued: the value added to things by the infusion of human work. Smith applied the ideas of the Enlightenment to the domain of economics, and in the process articulated the principles of a free-market economy and the labor theory of value.

Summary

Early American environmental policies were shaped in a period which saw the development of some of the most powerful ideas and forces in human history. These included the rise of empirical science, the substitution of water and fossil fuels for animal energy and of machines for labor, a newfound belief in the potential for social progress and in the philosophy of utilitarianism, and the emergence of constitutional governance and the capitalist system of economics. It is no accident, therefore, that these ideas are deeply embedded in the framework of American society. The United States was the first society in history to pledge itself to "the pursuit of happiness" as a practical goal of government policy, and the very motto on its Great Seal—*Novus Ordo Seclorum,* a "new order of the ages"—expressed its recognition of its unique historical context.

By the same token, it should not surprise us that some of these ideas are less readily accepted by societies emerging in different conditions today. America did not invent most of these ideas, but its birth as a nation coincided with them. Its conjunction of favorable political and economic conditions with vast untapped stocks of natural resources gave it an extraordinary opportunity to apply these ideas to its own development.

3   Colonial Precedents: Environment as Property

> The shift from Indian to English dominance in New England saw the replacement of an earlier village system of shifting agriculture and hunter-gatherer activities by an agriculture which raised crops and domesticated animals in household production units that were contained within fixed property boundaries and linked with commercial markets. Ultimately, English property systems encouraged colonists to regard the products of the land — not to mention the land itself — as commodities, and so led them to orient a significant margin of their production toward commercial sale in the marketplace. — William Cronon, *Changes in the Land*

The colonial period is frequently overlooked in discussions of American environmental policy, but in fact it had great significance for much of what followed.[1] For more than a century and a half before the American War of Independence, British colonists in North America developed patterns of using its natural environment to support themselves and produce goods for export trade, and established both colonial and community policies for governing these patterns. These colonists set the precedents for some modern policies, such as the regulation of wildlife and common rights to navigable waters. More important than most of these specific actions, however, were the fundamental patterns that were established by policies of this period: patterns of settlement, of resource exploration and use, of property rights in the physical environment, and of governance and policy-making authority.

The attitudes of the United States' founders, and the principles which they incorporated into the Constitution and early statutory policies, were not invented overnight, but were deliberate adoptions or rejections of colonial concepts and precedents. When Americans declared themselves independent of the British they rejected policies that they considered vestiges of British paternalism, such as feudal land tenure and government control of forest resources, opening the way to largely unrestricted and unmanaged commercial exploitation of the American environment. These choices set the tone for many of the environmental policies of the following century.

The American Colonies

North America was a "new world" only to the Europeans: it was already populated by hundreds of indigenous peoples who had explored and settled throughout it for thousands of years (Sauer 1971). These were not merely nomadic hunters: many of them maintained highly developed societies, including agrarian and town-dwelling communities (Washburn 1959, 22–24). Wherever the explorers went they traveled by Native American ("Indian") trails, led by Native American guides, among settlements of Native Americans, eating food grown by Native Americans.

The Native Americans differed from the Europeans, however, in certain respects that left them at an immediate disadvantage. First, they did not have the Europeans' technological resources, most obviously ships, horses, and guns. Second, they had far more limited systems of trade. Third, they had a disastrous lack of resistance to European diseases such as smallpox and measles, to which they had never before been exposed: the total indigenous populations of the Americas may have been reduced by as much as 95 percent in a century due to disease (Dubos 1959; Stavrianos 1971). Finally, their concepts of property rights were generally based on village or tribal sovereignty over territory, with individual ownership only of specific use rights. Native Americans of many tribes held individual and often hereditary rights to the use of particular natural resources, such as garden plots, farmland, fruit and nut trees that required long-term care, and hunting and fishing territories (Anderson 1997, 47). This system was fundamentally different from European settlers' concept of land ownership, however, which also included individual rights to enclose, transform, and sell land for economic gain (Cronon 1983, 54–81).

The Spanish settled in the Americas a full century before the British, and the French not long after. Each empire settled in different places for different reasons, however, and thus had different impacts.

The Spanish came mainly to Central America and down the west coast of South America, seeking first a new route to Asia, then gold and silver and later sugar. They found these by subjugating native inhabitants such as the Aztecs and Incas, first looting their treasures and then putting them to work in silver mines and on plantations growing sugar, tobacco, cotton, and coffee. Spanish conquistadors built the first European colonial empire, first by military conquest and later by cultural domination. They transplanted Spanish culture, laws, language, and religion to Central and South America, establishing the basis for eighteen of today's Spanish-speaking nations; they built cathedrals and printing presses and two universities older than Harvard. By 1574, thirty-three years before the first English colony was established in Virginia, there were already about two hundred Spanish cities in the Americas.

The Spanish sent several expeditions into North America looking for new sources of treasure. Cortez explored the lower California coast in 1535, and Cabrillo ranged north of San Francisco in 1542, thirty-seven years before England's Sir Francis Drake reached the bay now named for him there. Coronado explored Arizona, New Mexico, the Grand Canyon, the Colorado River, and territory as far east as Kansas, and DeSoto traversed from Florida as far north as the Carolinas and Arkansas, but they turned back after failing to find the gold they sought. It was the Spanish who introduced horses to the Indians of the Great Plains in about 1680, allowing those tribes who possessed them to adopt far more widespread patterns of nomadic bison hunting and of raiding and warfare against the more agrarian tribes (Salisbury 1996). Spanish influence in North America was dominant until the 1600s, when the Spaniards were gradually eclipsed by British and Dutch competition in shipping and trade of manufactured goods.

The Dutch and French were interested in trade rather than conquest. The Dutch founded New Amsterdam (later New York) as a trading base, and established other trading settlements in the Caribbean and South America, but did not create many permanent colonies. The French built trading settlements throughout what is now eastern Canada and the upper Midwest, and in 1682 traveled down the Mississippi River to Louisiana — named for King Louis XIV of France — seeking mainly the fur trade.

The English, however, came to settle, and thus grew to dominate the development of North American culture and government. British cod fishermen had had contact with the North American coast long before settlers arrived, and Sir Frances Drake had explored the northern California and Oregon coasts in 1579. Once settlement began, however, the settlers came to stay rather than merely to trade. Some came to escape religious persecution, but many more came simply to improve their living conditions. In England labor was plentiful and wages therefore low, and land was scarce — largely as a result of the enclosure movement — while in America land was plentiful, labor scarce, and wages higher. By 1688 there were over three hundred thousand English settlers in America compared to twenty thousand French, and by 1776 there were over two million — a third of the total population of the English-speaking world.

Britain also needed the commodities that could be produced in America, and provided growing markets for them. These included fish, timber, and ship's stores from the Northeast, grain from the middle colonies, rice, cotton, tobacco, and indigo from the South. Primarily because of this difference in purpose and the wave of immigration that followed from it, American environmental policy grew mainly from its British roots rather than from those of the other European empires.

Britain had no overall environmental policy for the American colonies, but it did have clearly defined policies for trade and the development of natural resources. These grew out of its economic goals. To build its economic position, Britain wanted its colonies to produce cheap raw materials needed in Britain, especially those that would otherwise be bought from other empires. They should trade strategic materials only with Britain; they should ship their goods in British ships and pay taxes on both imports from and exports to other nations; and they should not export, or in some cases even produce, products which competed with those of Britain herself. In a much-quoted statement by a British writer in 1663, the purpose of the colonies was "to increase the wealth and trade of this nation, either in furnishing us, with what we are otherwise forced to purchase from strangers, or else by increasing such commodities, as are vendible abroad; which may both increase our shipping, and profitably employ our people" (Fortrey 1673, 34, 35, quoted in Beer 1893, 66). This statement captures the essence of the mercantilist perspective, which was to regulate colonial trade so as to maximize economic advantage to the mother country.

The American colonies became an integral element of the "triangle trade" systems between England, Africa, and the Americas. Ships carried American rum and British and European manufactured goods to Africa, then brought slaves from Africa to the sugar and gold industries in South and Central America, both of which needed cheap labor. They then carried back sugar, molasses, and gold, either directly to Europe or via the Atlantic colonies, where they picked up additional agricultural products and raw materials. In the opposite direction they carried American fish and other commodities to the West Indies, sugar and molasses to Europe, and manufactured goods and immigrants back to America.[2] This pattern had both economic and navigational advantages for sailing ships. Economically the exchange patterns balanced well, and since the prevailing winds blew from the west across the Atlantic ocean, it was almost as quick to sail down the African coast with the northeast trade winds, then angle across the Atlantic and up the American coast with the Gulf Stream and return to Europe with the west winds behind.

Colonists and Their Environment

Until Lewis and Clark and later explorers of the nineteenth century, settlers did not begin to know the richness and diversity of the continent: a land mass three thousand miles wide, used by the native population almost exclusively for subsistence on renewable resources. The eastern half of the continent was governed by a temperate climate all the way to about the one hundredth meridian of longitude — through what is now Kansas, Nebraska, and the Dakotas — with moderate temperatures and year-round rainfall. West from there to California was arid land, with little rainfall and shorter grasses holding the more fragile soils of the Great Plains and Great Basin. Fertile soils, sweeping grasslands, untouched concentrations of minerals, forests of giant pine, fir, redwood, and sequoia, an almost unimaginable abundance of wildlife — all these lay within the continent, environmental conditions formed by centuries of ecological dynamics, which would be discovered and labeled "resources" by later generations.

For the early colonists, their environment was the eastern coast and as far inland as was accessible to them. They found natural harbors and fisheries first — codfish off the coast and shad and shellfish further inshore — and forests and plentiful wildlife: deer and elk, moose and bear, beaver, waterfowl, and passenger pigeons. They found rivers to carry them inland — the Hudson, Connecticut, Delaware, and Susquehanna — then the barrier of the Appalachian and Allegheny mountains, which slowed their westward movement for a time.

The first need of the European settlers was subsistence, which required food, fiber for clothing and shelter, fuel for heat and light, minerals for tools, and the rights to land with which to produce these necessities. They found subsistence initially in hunting wildlife, fishing, gathering wild fruits, and growing crops introduced to them by the Native Americans: corn, pumpkins, sweet potatoes, beans, and squash. These indigenous peoples cleared land, both for agriculture and for easier hunting, by fire and by cutting or "girdling" trees to kill them, and they fertilized their crops with fish and seaweed. As crop yields declined, they would move inland, leaving the cleared land to regenerate. It was the

Native Americans who first tolerated European settlements, and taught the colonists their initial skills in American agriculture and forestry. Without them many of the settlements probably would not have survived.

The second need of the settlers, however, was economic survival in the manner to which their European backgrounds had accustomed them, and in this important respect they differed from the indigenous peoples they found. Economic survival for the settlers required the production of export commodities that could be exchanged with Britain and other empires for manufactured goods to meet their wants.

A most important influence on later American history was the fact that different regions presented the colonists with different ecological opportunities and constraints for economic production (Galenson 1996, 135–52; Meinig 1986, 231–39, 244–54). These differences led to profoundly different patterns of human use of the environment.

In the South, where English settlement began with the Virginia Company in 1609, the soils and climate were well adapted to large-scale production of staple export crops: first tobacco, an indigenous American and Caribbean crop which rapidly became popular in England; later rice, which was introduced (probably from Madagascar) in 1675; and finally indigo, used in the dying of cloth, which was domesticated in 1740 and whose harvesting periods complemented those of rice. Tobacco grew well in the coastal plains and rolling Piedmont uplands, and rice flourished in the wet lowlands along the South Carolina coast. The other main resource of the South was forest products: the live-oak forests near its coasts provided important sources of shipbuilding timber for the British navy, and its plentiful pines yielded other naval stores such as tar, pitch, resins, and turpentine.

From the perspective of the British merchants who were financing colonization, these conditions were ideal. Indigo previously had come only from Asia at higher cost, tobacco and rice were also profitable cash crops, and forest products were important strategic materials which otherwise would have had to be imported from Dutch traders in the Baltic. The only scarce resource was labor. This problem was mitigated first by the use of white indentured laborers — people willing to bind themselves to service for a given period of time in return for their expenses of travel and subsistence — and then by importation of black slaves from Africa.

In hindsight, the easy adoption of plantation agriculture was a fateful commitment. Tobacco rapidly exhausted soil nutrients, and thus required continuous movement to find new lands for it.[3] Slaves brought not only a labor resource but a human population, which would reproduce itself and eventually be granted the same rights and privileges as other Americans. Finally, the dominance of plantation agriculture caused a narrow specialization of the economy of the South, which left it far more reliant on the British for many of its needs, and for income from exports, than were other colonies, who early on were forced by less favorable trade circumstances to diversify. The South was not uniform in this pattern — North Carolina, for instance, had a substantial population of upland freehold farmers who got their start as "squatters" from Virginia — but it was the plantations' export crop production that dominated the region's economy.

In the Northeast, by contrast, environmental conditions were much less favorable for agriculture. The summers were hot, but the winters cold; the soil was rocky and inhospitable to large-scale agriculture; and the hinterlands were more dangerous than promising. From a mercantile point of view New England's only natural advantages were fish, furs, and forests. Fish were a key element of the triangular trade, providing a low-cost food high in protein and salt that could be traded as food for slaves in exchange for molasses — a waste product of Caribbean sugar production — to use in making rum. Furs were also profitable, especially after King Charles I ordered in 1638 that all English hats be made of beaver. Most furs were obtained by trade with the indigenous tribes in exchange for English manufactured goods: woolen blankets, iron implements, guns, and jewelry. New England's forests provided many naval stores, in particular large mast timbers, a scarce and important resource. In an age of sailing ships, England's sea power was its commercial lifeline, its defense against the Spanish empire, and its offense for capturing Spanish bullion. Without American sources it would have needed to obtain these supplies from the Baltic by trade with the Dutch, who were its competitors. In New England, therefore, Britain sought to increase and control the production of forest products and to promote stable fur-trading relations with the indigenous tribes.

The adaptation of the New England settlers was no less fateful than that of their Southern counterparts. Fishing, fur trapping, and logging were inherently more individualized occupations than plantation agriculture, and could not be organized on the same scale or along the same social hierarchy. Since no one crop was dominant, economic production was more diversified and thus more adaptable. The easy availability of forest products for shipbuilding led naturally to the development of industry and trade in the Northeast, and abundant waterfalls also provided a natural source of power for manufacturing. In these industries the New England colonies diverged most rapidly from the mercantile interests of England. Once New Englanders began to produce most of the materials for shipbuilding and Britain was preoccupied by its civil war, the colonists began to build and operate ships themselves, both to maintain their access to imported goods and export revenues and to expand their commerce. Nantucket thus became a whaling port, other New England fishing towns grew into centers of American shipping and shipbuilding, and a substantial portion of the New England colonies' income began to flow from trade with other colonies and other empires. Beginning in 1660, England inadvertently pushed New England further into manufacturing by enacting the "Corn Laws," steep import taxes on grains passed by the British aristocracy of the Restoration period to protect its own farmers at the expense of the farmers of the northern and middle colonies of America.

The "middle colonies" developed yet another pattern of adaptation. Their soils were more fertile than those of New England, leading them to be called the "bread colonies," and their rivers broader: the Hudson, Delaware, and Susquehanna all provided easy access inland, but had few waterfalls for manufacturing. Abundant forests benefited the development of shipbuilding, but the main export of these colonies was food grains. Other than grain and forest products, these colonies' main income came from commerce. New York and Philadelphia were key locations for the transshipment of commodities between Europe and the interior of the continent, which put their merchants, like those of New

England, into competition with the merchants of England. As long as the American merchants could find trade advantages with other ports to obtain money to remedy the colonies' chronic imbalances in trade with England, the system worked adequately; but when these relationships were disrupted in the 1760s by changes in British policy, the resulting economic impacts contributed strongly to the forces that led to revolution.

All the colonies, in short, survived economically by export trade in raw materials such as staple crops, forest products, furs and fish and whale oil, and food grains, and a few manufactured products such as rum. They subsisted largely on their own food crops, on animal skins and wool and flax for clothes, on timber for fuel and shelter, and on imports of salt, sugar, manufactured goods, and other commodities not available locally. Gradually they also built their own shipping, shipbuilding, ironworking, and other manufacturing industries that competed against those of England.

The consequences of English and European colonization for the indigenous American societies, meanwhile, were overwhelming and tragic. Most of those Native Americans who survived the exposure to new epidemic diseases were gradually uprooted from their own agrarian societies and forced into nomadic hunting and fishing, either to supply European consumers or simply for their own sustenance. Their only options were either to participate in the European trade system, usually in marginal roles, or to accept a far more primitive version of their own former culture outside that system's ever-expanding domain (Kupperman 1995, 14).

Colonial Land Policies

England had no overall policy for American land development. Its colonies were established piecemeal, in grants to various colonization companies and proprietors: to the Virginia Company, for instance, and to the Hudson's Bay Company for fur trading in northern Canada; to Lord Baltimore for establishing a haven for Catholics and a profit-making venture; and to William Penn as payment for royal debts owed to his father. Each colony's charter granted it jurisdiction over specified lands under various conditions, though the title remained with the king. As the American colonies grew, their immigrants brought with them both the legacy of feudal land institutions and their own varied attitudes toward the changes in those institutions that were then occurring in Europe.

To most immigrants land represented a primary form of wealth, and in the seemingly limitless land of North America they saw an opportunity for each individual to enjoy the property privileges reserved for the elite in England and Europe. Many saw land as a source of commercial wealth as well, particularly the entrepreneurs who first organized the colonies. The vast majority of people who went to the colonies to live were ordinary people willing to take the risks necessary to build materially better and more independent lives for themselves. They were people, in short, who almost inevitably viewed America's land not as a fragile ecosystem or a scarce resource but as a virtually free, abundant commodity and an opportunity for economic benefit.

The European nations claimed title to American lands and their resources on the grounds of discovery and settlement. The original English settlements were established on lands claimed by the king of England and granted by him to charter companies and colonial proprietors. They in turn consummated these claims by physical possession of them, in the persons of both settlers and soldiers. Those colonies that were surrounded by others, such as Delaware, Maryland, and Rhode Island, took on their approximate shapes at this time. The others, especially those whose borders were open to the west (such as Virginia, Georgia, and the Carolinas) claimed large western territories extending across the Appalachians "from sea to sea."

In principle all the colonies' lands were "the king's domain," to be administered for his benefit by the chartered proprietors and royal governors under feudal restrictions such as entail and quitrents (Nettels 1962, 138–40). These practices rapidly broke down, however, because of the sheer abundance of the land and the impossibility of policing it against "squatting" for agrarian use. Feudalism had prospered where land was scarce, but where land was abundant, and labor scarce and therefore expensive, people could not be kept within such a restrictive land-based system of social classes and controls. In New England land was owned individually from the outset (Jones 1996, 103; Nettels 1962, 139–40). The founders of most other colonies had envisioned a society of functionaries and peasants, but instead they rapidly became communities of yeomen and artisans (Handlin 1959, 5).

Within a few years, therefore, the companies and proprietors began to use land more liberally for economic purposes, by distributing it to individuals as incentives for immigration and agricultural productivity (McCusker and Menard 1985, 334). Colonial proprietors began to offer "headrights" to land, a guarantee of fifty acres to anyone who paid his own or someone else's passage to America, and advertised it with propaganda worthy of modern real estate hucksters (Jones 1965, 279–80). Essentially, they used the abundance of land as an incentive to overcome the scarcity of labor. Usually the only duty of the individual was to pay a nominal annual quitrent, a legacy of the feudal system of obligations which took the form of an acreage tax. Quitrents often proved uncollectable, and were gradually phased out in exchange for higher initial land prices. The headright system was an important antecedent of nineteenth-century American homesteading, similar in that it provided stated quantities of land per person without regard to race, creed, or color. It differed in that headrights were rewarded to the donor rather than directly to the settler, and could therefore be accumulated rather than distributed only one to a family. Because of the unlimited acreage that could thus be accumulated by payment of immigrants' passage, headrights became one of the principal methods by which the large plantations and estates of the southern colonies were assembled.

Land also was distributed by sale, though this practice was new and developed slowly. Pennsylvania was the first colony to sell lands: its charter holder, William Penn, began in 1681 to offer lands for sale in shares of five thousand acres for £100, subject to a quitrent of one shilling per hundred acres per year. These were large holdings, bought mainly by wealthy Englishmen and later for speculation by land companies who hoped to profit from their rising value at resale. Other colonies subsequently sold land in smaller quantities directly to settlers. Virginia, for instance, offered cheap land as an enticement for settlement in its backlands, despite an official veto of the practice by the king.

Finally, land was distributed by grants for special purposes, which provided important precedents for later land policies of the American republic. Land was granted to settlers as an inducement for frontier protection, as early as 1630 in Virginia. It was granted as a bounty for military service, especially after the French and Indian War and later the Revolution, a practice common in English history as far back as William the Conqueror. It was granted as an endowment for educational institutions, including both Harvard University and the College of William and Mary, foreshadowing the reservation of lands for education in the Northwest Ordinance of 1787 and the land grant college system of the nineteenth century. And it was granted as an inducement for the development of particular industries, an antecedent of the later federal grants of public domain lands to the railroad companies.

As early as the seventeenth century, therefore, the widespread availability of freehold land ownership was one of the most important differences between America and Europe, and the legacy of this difference is still evident in the legal and socioeconomic status of land in America. The abundance of land in America brought freehold ownership within the reach of a vast number of people, thereby offering a powerful incentive for immigration. The resulting diversification of land ownership in turn provided a principal foundation for the egalitarian institutions of American society. "If the multitude is possessed of real estate," wrote John Adams, "the multitude will take care of the liberty, virtue, and interest of the multitude in all acts of government" (quoted in Scott 1977, 41).

From the perspective of the colonists, the right of freehold land ownership was justified on three grounds. First, it was theirs by grant from companies (in the South), proprietors (in the middle colonies), or town corporations (in New England) chartered by the king, consistent with traditional European law. This basis sufficed where British authorities were concerned, but did not rationalize the appropriation of land from indigenous inhabitants. The Native Americans, after all, possessed the land by right of prior occupation and use, an argument usually respected among the European nations themselves.

The second argument for colonists' land rights, therefore, was that it was theirs by "natural right," justified by the "labor theory of value." In this view, argued by Governor John Winthrop of Massachusetts among others, the Bible directed man to "increase, multiply, replenish, and subdue the earth." All undeveloped and unworked land therefore remained the possession of no one, and could be claimed by anyone who invested it with his work.[4] Since these lands were typically used for subsistence hunting rather than for market agriculture, they were declared to be in an "unclaimed state of nature," available for English settlers seeking to appropriate as much land as they were able to productively cultivate.

To these arguments was added a third: that the colonists owned lands by virtue of payment for them. In many cases settlers paid indigenous tribes for land rights — however much or little the payments may have been — and then argued that these payments conferred title to their lands. In some cases, colonial settlers' property deeds reportedly documented purchases from Native Americans who held hereditary rights to exclusive use of particular tracts of land (Anderson 1997, 47). In other cases, native peoples may have thought that they were being paid simply for rights of shared use rather than for exclusive title, and this distinction was not necessarily made clear by the colonists; in many cases outright fraud and misrepresentation occurred. But whatever the justice of the specific transactions, the argument of land rights based on purchase was an important precedent for the emerging American system of property rights. It opened the door to the federal land disposal system of the nineteenth century, to speculation, and to many other practices that later became central to American environmental policy.

However, even freehold ownership never meant absolute right to do whatever one wished with one's land. It was, rather, a "bundle of rights" in which the individual normally controlled the preponderant number. The rights to tax, to condemn, and to police land were always reserved by the government. Colonial governments condemned private land by eminent domain when it was needed for public buildings, forts, ferries, waterwheels, towns, or other public purposes. By 1776 some species of wildlife, such as deer, were protected by closed seasons and wardens in all colonies but one, even when they crossed private lands. Gold and silver discoveries were subject to 20 percent royalties to the Crown. Timber was a strategic resource for shipbuilding and naval stores as well as fuel and construction, and forest resources were therefore regulated by both British and colonial authorities. Britain reserved the best trees for mast timbers for the Royal Navy, Massachusetts prohibited the destruction of young tar and pitch pines, and Pennsylvania required the preservation of one acre of forest for every five acres cleared. Water was owned only after it was appropriated by the user, though each owner was entitled to continuation of the natural flow of water over and along his land. Massachusetts levied a property tax as early as 1646; Pennsylvania levied a progressive land tax during the French and Indian War (1758–63). After the American Revolution, property taxes became additionally important as a source of revenue for state and local governments, since the Constitution transferred to the federal government the authority to tax imports and exports, which had been their other principal means of support.

Freehold ownership did not, then, imply absolute autonomy of individuals to decide the use of their land. Individuals were never free to use their property in such a way as to interfere with the rights of others ("nuisance"). They also had to pay taxes on it, and to abide by legal restrictions on the use of resources such as forests, wildlife, minerals, and water.

What freehold ownership did mean, however, was a presumption favoring the individual's autonomy within the constraints of the law. Individuals had the rights to possess land, to use it (except for nuisances), to receive its produce, to sell it, and to exclude others from it. Landowners were free to develop, sell, mine, or clear their land, unless prohibited by law, for whatever price the market would pay. The extent to which laws actually constrained the use of land has since varied greatly. The essential issues to the settlers were the principle of freehold ownership itself, the presumption in favor of the rights of the individual which it implied, and the republican form of government that followed from that presumption.

Land resources thus played a critical role in colonial America's agrarian economy, and its gradual conversion into an economic commodity that could be freely owned and sold played a pivotal role in the evolution of American environmental policy.

Agriculture

Britain pressured the colonies to produce crops and other raw materials that it wanted for its own use, especially those that would provide cheaper substitutes for materials that would otherwise have to be bought elsewhere. Some of these crops required no further incentives than those of the market: tobacco, for instance, could be sold in London for six times the price of wheat. For others, however, the government established production incentives, including bounties, planting requirements, market guarantees, and adjustment of tax rates. Bounties were offered to encourage the production of hemp (for rope making), indigo (for textile dyes), flax (also for the textile industry), wine grapes, and mulberry trees (to encourage silkworm culture). British import duties were lowered or eliminated on hemp, tobacco, molasses, indigo, and silk. Britain also provided market guarantees in the form of "enumeration lists," which prohibited the export of specified commodities to nations other than Britain but also guaranteed them a market in Britain (though at prices dictated by English merchants). Ginger, sugar, tobacco, cotton wool, and indigo, fustic, and other dyeing materials were enumerated in 1660; molasses, rice, and sugar were later added to the list, as were copper, iron, and various forest products.

Some of the colonial governments created their own production incentives. Virginia in 1669, for instance, offered fifty pounds of tobacco for every pound of wound silk made in the colony. Both Virginia and Connecticut passed laws requiring farmers to grow certain amounts of flax and hemp, because of their importance to textile manufacture and shipbuilding, and Virginia from 1658 to 1770 had a law requiring everyone to plant ten mulberry trees (for silkworm culture) per hundred acres of land cultivated. Virginia and Maryland restricted farmers' output of tobacco by assigning production quotas limiting the number of plants each farmer could grow and the number of leaves he could harvest — a precursor of modern tobacco quotas. They required also that each produce a minimum quantity of food crops. These laws were intended in part to control overproduction of tobacco and to lessen the region's dependence on imports, but also to keep the farmers from exhausting the soil by using it to grow only tobacco. In a sense these were America's first soil conservation laws, though they were neither effective nor intended wholly for that purpose.

With the exception of tobacco quotas, the colonies generally took no action to conserve soil fertility. Scotch-Irish and other immigrant farmers brought with them their practice of plowing up and down hillsides rather than across them, which promoted erosion (Jones 1996, 105), and colonial livestock management did not provide much manure for fertilizer (Nettels 1962, 173). Many farmers simply moved west to new land as old land became less fertile (Nettels 1962, 191). Even Thomas Jefferson once commented that "We can buy an acre of new land cheaper than we can manure an old acre" (quoted in McCusker and Menard 1985, 306). The economics of agriculture worked against conservation measures: labor was scarce and expensive, and the old eastern farms that needed conservation measures were competing at a constant disadvantage against cheap new lands in the West. By 1750 the earlier-settled portions of Virginia and Maryland contained large areas of abandoned lands, which reverted first to pastures and eventually to thickets and second-growth forests, and many communities were economically bankrupt. In the South, many planta-tions were operated by overseers who were paid a percentage of the annual crop, and who thus were motivated to squeeze from the land as much production as possible. Finally, independent farmers were a debtor class, generally poor and trying to make their way upward, running high risks from the weather and the market without reserves of capital or credit to put into conservation measures. For all these reasons and others, agricultural conservation policy did not become prominent in America until well into the twentieth century (cf. Scoville 1953).

Forests

Forest products were an essential strategic material during the colonial period. Timber was essential for ship construction, especially "great timbers" made of oak — valued for its strength and water resistance — including some with particular curvatures to make the sternposts, catheads, and "knees" for the hulls. Large, straight firs and pines and spruces were needed for masts and spars. A main mast on a large sailing ship required a straight tree forty yards long and forty inches in diameter, located close enough to water to be trans-ported to the shipyard: perhaps one tree in ten thousand. Before the colonization of Amer-ica most of these mast timbers were Riga firs from the Baltic region, traded by the Dutch.

England was chronically short of timber from the sixteenth century on: it exploited its own supplies heavily in the 1500s for the construction of naval and merchant ships, as trade increased and England became a sea power (Albion 1926). Englishmen recognized early the importance of the American colonies for forest products. Northern New En-gland and eastern Canada were rich in native white pines, ideal for mast timbers, and the hardwood forests of the central regions and the live oaks of the Southeast could relieve the pressure on English oaks. The southeastern longleaf pines, cedars, and cypresses provided additional timber plus other essential products for shipbuilding: tar, pitch, resins, and turpentine. The first cargo shipped back to Britain from the American colonies was a load of masts in 1609; clapboards were sent in 1623, and in the same year America's first sawmill was established in York, Maine.

Britain's desire for forest products initially complemented the needs of the colonies. The colonists had to clear land for settlement anyway, and New England in particular had little else to sell except furs and fish. Beginning with William and Mary in 1688, however, Britain began to apply more intense regulation, in part to remedy its Baltic trade balance and lessen its dependence on then-hostile Sweden, and in part to try to force the colonists to shift away from producing other products that competed with England, especially wool, ships, and fish.

As early as 1685, Britain appointed a Surveyor General of the Pines and Timbers of Maine, and this position was expanded in 1705 to include all of Her Majesty's Woods and Forests in America. In 1691 the new charter of the Massachusetts Colony reserved for the British navy all trees greater than twenty-four inches in diameter one foot above the ground which grew on lands not already granted to private individuals (that is, on the "king's domain"). This regulation became known as the "Broad Arrow" policy, because the trees were marked with an arrow-like configuration of three hatchet cuts as a sign of British navy ownership. Illegal cutting was subject to a penalty of £100 per tree.

The 1691 timber regulation was a precedent for later forest laws. A 1711 act of the British Parliament extended the policy to all lands from today's Maine to New Jersey. Meanwhile, a 1705 law prohibited cutting of tar and pitch pines less than twelve inches in diameter in order to allow them to mature, and a 1704 law established bounties of £4 per ton for tar and pitch, £3 per ton for resin and turpentine, and £1 per ton for spar timbers. A 1721 law prohibited all cutting of white pines without a royal license, and a 1729 act added many forest products to the "enumeration list" of commodities that could be exported only to England, cutting off the colonies' extensive timber trade with southern Europe and the West Indies.

Like its agricultural policies, Britain's colonial forest policies grew out of its broader mercantile trade objectives. Many of these policies were easily accepted by the colonies, since they often assured them of markets on preferential terms. The Broad Arrow timber reservations, however, were an important exception. Legally, the British forest policies were perfectly legitimate, but their effects differed greatly from those of its agricultural policies. American forest products benefited only from a 20 percent duty, not a market monopoly, and even the bounties did not compensate for the higher prices American exporters could otherwise get from the lumber markets of southern Europe. Moreover, more than half the bounties went to the southern colonies for ships' stores, while the prohibition on cutting white pines mainly affected the New England colonies. Finally, the latter prohibition posed a direct challenge not only to colonial trade, but to emerging popular principles of property rights.

For the colonists, the basic issue of the Broad Arrow controversy was whether or not Parliament had a right to restrict their use of timber on private lands. In this way it was not unlike twentieth-century controversies over government regulation of wetlands, flood-plains, and endangered species habitat. English kings had always claimed this prerogative for naval timber before Britain's civil war, but after the Restoration the Parliament—many of whose members owned oak groves—had refused to continue it in England. Yet now they were imposing on American colonies the same restrictions they had refused to accept at home. The American colonists from the outset had cut timber freely on lands to which they had title, yet Parliament was now asserting the right to control the resources of those lands and thereby to limit the economic livelihood of people who owned them.

As a result, the Broad Arrow policy not only failed, but became one of the irritants leading to revolution. Colonial legislatures ignored it, colonial courts refused to convict its violators, and colonists themselves flouted it, both by smuggling illicit timber and by cutting lumber into widths just under the twenty-four inches that would have provided evidence of illegal harvest.

An additional precedent of British colonial forest policy was a 1743 act which, instead of reserving all white pine, set aside specific reservation areas to which the king retained clear title. This measure was far less controversial, and provided a precedent for the forest reservations that were later established under U.S. policy. In 1783 Massachusetts became the first state to adopt a similar policy.

The colonial governments established forest policies beyond those of England. The Plymouth Bay Colony as early as 1626 restricted the cutting of trees greater than twenty-four inches in diameter on ungranted lands, seeking, like England, to preserve for ship-building trees that might otherwise be cut up more profitably into lumber. By about 1658 several New England colonies passed laws controlling forest fires — fires were often used to clear land for agriculture — and by the time of the Revolution all but four colonies had such laws. The first forest preservation law was enacted in Pennsylvania, where in 1681 William Penn ordered that for every five acres cleared one acre must be left as forest. By 1741 all the colonies from Maryland north had laws prohibiting unauthorized cutting of timber on public lands ("timber trespass"). The Massachusetts General Court in 1739 threatened fines of ten shillings for every bush, shrub, or tree less than six inches in diameter that was cut from beaches or marshes — perhaps America's first "coastal zone management" policy — because of concern over beach erosion and drifting sand.

In short, both British and American colonial forest policies showed a willingness to regulate the cutting and burning of forest resources, especially on public lands, and a recognition that the values of mature trees could be realized only if they were protected against earlier destruction. But the reactions to the British Broad Arrow policy also showed the early emergence of strong grass-roots attitudes concerning the rights of property owners to land-based resources, which would be a powerful driving force in environmental policy throughout American history.

Water

Unlike land and forests, water resources were early designated as common rather than private property. Navigable watercourses — rivers, lakes, and bays — were essential public transportation routes, especially for heavy or bulky cargoes such as timber, since overland transport of them was expensive or even impossible. Mainly because of this function, they came to be regarded legally as open to common use by the general public rather than as the property of riparian landowners.

In England, only tidal portions of rivers and estuaries were legally considered naviga-ble, a definition probably based on the history of manorial land rights and the small size of the rivers themselves. All non-navigable streams could be controlled by the adjoining landowners, who had the right to use the surface waters flowing across their property. In America, by contrast, large rivers were in fact navigable far inland, the land was unencumbered with prior rights, and the country was rich in timber that was only accessible by floating it downstream to mills and shipyards. Yet under British law any landowner could block the passage of these logs, appropriate those that stranded on his land, or even erect a milldam that would block all navigation.

The American colonies therefore broadened the definition of "navigability" to include all water that was in fact usable for navigation. A Connecticut law in 1752 defined rivers as common highways for the transport of logs and log rafts, and a New Jersey law in 1755 prohibited any obstruction of rivers, creeks, or streams used for navigation and transportation, except by act of the General Assembly. Pennsylvania laws in 1771 and 1785 declared portions of five rivers "public highways," mentioning specifically their importance for the development of inland timber resources. As this concept spread, any stream that would float a log or a boat came to be considered navigable.

Colonial water policy also included actions to protect public health and fisheries. Massachusetts in 1647 passed regulations prohibiting pollution of Boston Harbor, and South Carolina in 1726 passed a law prohibiting pollution harmful to fish. The most important water policies, however, were those establishing precedents of ownership, for these became the basis for American water resource policy. An important issue throughout the nineteenth and twentieth centuries, for instance, was the extent of federal jurisdiction over inland lakes and streams, not only for navigation but for other purposes including the production of hydroelectric power and the regulation of water pollution. A specific point on which that debate turned was the definition of "navigable" waters which the federal government was empowered to regulate.

Minerals

Britain's mineral policies were of two kinds: those dealing with precious metals (gold and silver) and those dealing with utilitarian materials such as iron and copper. Policies for precious metals were more important for the legal precedents they established than for their effects: each colonial charter except that of Georgia reserved to the Crown a percentage of any gold or silver that might be discovered, usually 20 percent. Since no significant deposits of these metals were discovered in the colonial period the policy had little effect, but it did set a precedent for reserving mineral rights in government ownership when public lands were sold or granted to individuals. Thus private ownership did not necessarily include rights to all the land's resources. Mineral reservations similar to these British policies became part of U.S. law as early as the Confederation period of 1781–89, and later versions of them produced conflict between ranchers holding surface rights for grazing on public lands and mining companies seeking to extract coal from them by strip mining.

Iron and copper, in contrast, were not reserved but were subjected to strict trade regulation. Like timber, iron was a strategic material, yet Britain was short of both the essential materials needed for iron making: ore for substance and wood for fuel. America has both in abundance. The iron industry began in Virginia as early as 1620 and in Massachusetts in the 1640s, and by 1700 the colonies were competing successfully against England in the production of iron, threatening Britain's own industrialization process.

With Abraham Darby's successful substitution of coke (made from coal) for charcoal in 1709, England overcame its fuel wood shortage and began forcing the export of colonial iron ore to supply its own needs. A 1750 law eliminated import duties on American pig iron, but also prohibited the construction of plating forges, steel furnaces, or rolling mills in any of the colonies, and condemned all existing ones as public nuisances. In 1764 iron was enumerated and thus barred from colonial export to nations other than Britain, thereby assuring the British of a supply monopoly at low prices. The goal was to reimpose a mercantile exchange pattern among American raw materials production, British manufacturing, and American markets for finished iron goods — such patterns included, of course, the Native Americans, for iron implements and woolen blankets were the two principal commodities that Britain traded to the Native Americans for furs.

The prohibition of iron manufacture, however, ranked close to the Broad Arrow policy as an ineffective restriction and a colonial grievance. The law was widely flouted, and by the time of the Revolution America was actually producing more iron than Britain.

Other sources of minerals were discovered during the colonial period, but most were not developed until after the Revolution. From the 1720s on, lead was mined in Missouri and shipped to the seaboard by way of the lower Mississippi River. Great Lakes copper was discovered in the seventeenth century, but was not used until 1845. Pittsburgh coal was not used until around 1800, though it was discovered by the 1750s: with wood still abundant, fossil fuels were neither necessary nor cost-effective. Even the salt deposits around Syracuse, New York were not worked for fifty years after they were discovered around 1725: only when imports were interrupted by the Revolution did they become a critical resource.

Fisheries

Fish were perhaps the earliest North American resource known to Europe: European fishermen worked the Newfoundland banks long before their governments established permanent North American settlements. British fishermen would set out from Bristol to Portugal, where they would take on a cargo of salt then fish the waters of Iceland — and after 1580 the waters of "new found land" — for cod, which, having no fat, had high nutritional content and could easily be preserved in salt. These they would exchange in Portugal for wine, oil, and more salt before returning home to Bristol.

Explorers as early as Cabot described the North American waters as "teeming with fish," but the English apparently did not discover the New England offshore fisheries until the early 1600s, about the time they colonized Virginia (1607). They planted fishing colonies in Maine in 1607 and 1611, and in 1614 Captain John Smith of Virginia discovered three major advantages of these fisheries: onshore as well as offshore fishing was possible, there was a double season (unlike in Newfoundland), and the cod arrived earlier via the Gulf Stream, allowing fishermen to get their catch to the London markets significantly ahead of those further north (Judah 1933).

These discoveries coincided with the rising dominance of entrepreneurial commercial interests in London. The Newfoundland banks had long been worked by the fishermen of west England, but it was the London-based capitalists who developed and controlled the New England fisheries, and in 1620 Sir Ferdinando Gorges's "Council for New England" was granted a monopoly charter to license and charge for fishing both offshore and onshore in New England. The charges amounted to 304 pence per ton, or about £20 per ship. Both the fishermen and the Virginia Company opposed this charter, and it probably retarded the growth of the New England fishing industry.

By 1628 the American fishing industry began to develop. Fishermen built their own boats ("shallops") first using equipment supplied by British companies, but gradually manufacturing more of their own gear. Massachusetts around 1640 exempted fishing

property from taxation for seven years to encourage the development of the fishing industry, much as today's towns offer tax breaks to industries to encourage them to locate there,
and it exempted fishermen from military service during the fishing season. England's Navigation Act of 1651 banned all imports of fish, oil, and whale products unless they were both
caught and carried by English ships, giving the English colonies' ships a guaranteed market
for their catch. The same law, however, also banned resale of these items to merchants of
other nations, and thus permitted London merchants to dictate prices to the fishermen.

Other than these few regulations Britain had no general policies for the New England
fisheries, and intervened only to resolve immediate conflicts. During its civil war Britain
ignored the New England fisheries almost entirely, and the colonies accordingly pursued
alternative markets and captured control of these fisheries, which they never again relin-
quished. By 1660, thirteen hundred New England boats were working the banks, marketing to Europe and the Americas, Malaga and the Canary Islands, Portugal and the islands
of the Caribbean.

New England's other major fishing industry was whaling, which supplied whalebone,
ivory, spermaceti for candle-making and oil, and ambergris for perfumes and cosmetics.
Since this activity took place on the high seas it generated little policy, but it was a major
colonial resource industry. By 1774, 360 ships collected forty-five thousand barrels of
sperm oil and seventy-five thousand pounds of whalebone per year.

Within the colonies, policies related to fishing emerged both to protect the resource
and to prevent private monopolization. Massachusetts in 1647 established free public
fishing and waterfowl hunting on all bays, rivers, and "great ponds" (an important corol-
lary of this law was the right of open passage across nonagricultural private lands to reach
these ponds, providing an early basis for hunters' trespass). In 1709–10 Massachusetts
passed further legislation to prohibit unauthorized blockage of fish passages in streams, a
measure probably aimed at the widespread construction of milldams. South Carolina in
1726 passed a law to prohibit pollution harmful to fish, aimed especially at the use of
poisoning as a harvesting method.

In summary, fisheries were not a major subject of colonial policy-making, but it is
significant that the colonies' early actions were to declare them a free and open resource.
This policy contrasted both with the British policy of granting monopoly control over
licensing of fishermen, and even with American policy regarding other resources such as
forests. Trees and other land resources were considered the private property of the owner
of the land, but water and its resources were considered the common property of the
society until captured by individual users. On these differences in legal status turned many
later issues of environmental policy, especially such issues as water pollution control,
interbasin diversion, and shoreline access.

Wildlife

An extensive body of wildlife laws and policies developed in Britain both before and
during the period of American colonization. Legal tradition as far back as the Roman
Empire held that wild animals (*ferae naturae*) were the property of no one — like air and

oceans — but could *become* someone's property by killing or capture. European kings gradually eroded these principles, however, by restricting hunting by the lower classes, ostensibly to limit the availability of weapons but perhaps also to limit the number of hunters. England, for instance, had "qualification laws" limiting the number of hunters on the basis of social class and property ownership: only those who owned land worth forty shillings per year (later raised to one hundred pounds) were allowed to hunt. Laws in the sixteenth to eighteenth centuries prohibited the hunting of animals during their vulnerable periods — for instance bird eggs and molting birds (1533, 1604), fish fry (1558), undersized lobsters (1699), and spawning salmon (1710). They also regulated the equipment that could be used, such as by restricting ownership of firearms (1389, 1531, 1548), limiting heron hunting to hawking and longbows (1503), setting minimum fishnet sizes (1558), restricting jacklighting (1581), and requiring coverage of eelpots to protect mature salmon (1705). Market restrictions were used to improve enforcement, such as the prohibition of the unlicensed sale of wildlife forage and cover plants, and of the sale or even possession of game by "unqualified" persons (1540, 1604, 1710) (Lund 1975).

After the Norman Conquest of 1066, successive British kings established a system of "royal forests," lands which were subject to royal jurisdiction over wildlife even though occupied by farmers and other users. This "Forest Jurisdiction" applied to both private farms and Crown lands, which were reserved for sport hunting by kings and their favorites (Lund 1975). It was administered under special royal laws and enforced by royal stewards, foresters, and other officials. Laws in these areas prohibited unauthorized purchase of hunting dogs, protected forage and shelter plants, limited livestock and prohibited sheep and goats except by license, required farmers to maintain adequate forage vegetation, and allowed foresters to cut winter browse for deer from private lands as necessary.

The Forest Jurisdiction established a royal policy that the king was the ultimate authority over wildlife on both private and public lands. Jurisdiction over wild animals was treated as a sole royal right: they were no longer subject to a common right of capture. Kings shared or delegated this right by franchises similar to the monopolies they granted to merchants and colonization companies. These franchise grants also were awarded for fisheries, and went by such names as park and chase, free warren, free fishery, several fishery, and common of piscary, each designating the specific resource and the degree of exclusivity of the privileges thus granted.

By the beginning of the thirteenth century, however, kings had granted so many fishery franchises that navigation was being impeded by the large number of private weirs erected on streams and estuaries. The significance of this problem was such that in 1215 the Magna Carta itself directed removal of such weirs. Later court decisions based on the language of the Magna Carta barred the king from granting private fisheries in tidal waters (Bean 1983 [1977], 11–12). These decisions in turn established precedents for American water and fisheries laws. With the exception of tidal fisheries, however, wildlife remained under the clear authority of the king and the Parliament. As Michael Bean put it, "Stripped of its many formalities, the essential core of English wildlife law on the eve of the American Revolution was the complete authority of the King and the Parliament to determine what rights others might have with respect to the taking of wildlife" (1983 [1977], 12).

These early British laws show that many principles of wildlife management have long been recognized. Eagles and other raptors were protected in England as early as 1494, as were other predators. The Forest Jurisdiction provided an early example of deliberate management of wildlife preserves, even to the point of managing some private lands consistent with wildlife habitat needs. These policies also demonstrate, however, the long-standing history of elitism and aristocratic privilege embedded in the goals of wildlife policy. Hunting was reserved for the upper classes by law, even to the extent that "unqualified" persons could not eat or even possess game species. These laws — which were widely resented and often flouted, as in the well-known story of Robin Hood — gave wildlife an "artificial preeminence" as a delicacy reserved for the tables of the rich rather than a source of nourishment for the general population.

With the exceptions of laws governing fisheries and furs, British wildlife policies for America were basically nonexistent, however, and what other policies did emerge originated in the colonies themselves and differed significantly from Britain's. America had no entrenched upper classes to lay claim to special privileges in sport hunting, and most wildlife was in fact hunted for sustenance, a practice to which colonists asserted their "natural rights." Deer and furbearers were widely hunted for commercial export as well as for domestic clothing (each deerskin brought a dollar, hence "one buck"). Finally, American immigrants in the eighteenth century included at least some individuals who could be counted explicitly in opposition to British wildlife policy, for laws of 1719 and 1737 had made seven years' exile in America the penalty for illegal taking of deer in England.

The initial concern of the colonies' own wildlife policies, therefore, was the protection of wildlife not for its own sake or for aristocratic sport or cuisine, but as a general source of food and commerce, especially as the skin trade began to threaten the supply of deer. Almost every colony enacted game laws, most of them aimed not so much at absolute protection as at limiting exports and saving wildlife for local use. Massachusetts established a closed season for fishing in 1652 and for deer hunting in 1694, New York did likewise for wild fowl in 1708, and by 1776 similar laws had spread to all colonies except Georgia. Other laws authorized the appointment of deer wardens (Massachusetts in 1739, New Hampshire in 1741), restricted the sale of deer skins, and prohibited night and Sunday hunting. These laws probably were not very effective, but they illustrate early concerns over the effects of market hunting, concerns that later prompted far more stringent and effective controls on commercial trade in wildlife.

Furs, Frontiers, and Taxes

Britain's principal wildlife interest in America was furbearing animals, and while it left the management even of these species to the individual colonies, it did establish policies both to control trade and to resolve frontier conflicts (Lawson 1943). For Europeans fur was a luxury good, used for fashionable winter clothing and especially, in the expanding British economy of the seventeenth and eighteenth centuries, for hats. Beaver underfur had a particular value for the manufacture of felt hats, since it had fine barbs that stuck to the felt, and demand increased rapidly once this was discovered. In 1638 Charles I issued a royal proclamation noting the popularity of beaver hats among the upper classes, and they remained the standard headwear for the well-dressed until they were replaced by silk in the early days of the Victorian era, around 1840.

The principal source of beaver was the northern tier of North America, and using the major rivers inland from New York and other seaports, the British were able to tap vast regions. Furs were light and valuable, and could easily be floated downstream to trading posts and shipped to England. In exchange, the British traded manufactured goods to Native American trappers, particularly woolen blankets and iron and steel implements such as knives, guns, traps, and cooking pots. Furs were the indigenous tribes' only exportable commodity at a time when the introduction of iron weapons and tools was fundamentally reshaping their economy of bone and wood, bark and skins; the British, conversely, needed the tribes' acquiescence for the survival and expansion of its colonies.

The result was a system of mercantile exchange that was relatively well balanced, except for two issues. First, the British colonies began to develop their own fur export and hatting industries in competition with Britain's. Parliament responded by enumerating beaver furs in 1721, and in 1732 further legislation prohibited all exports of hats from the colonies, and forbade even the manufacture of hats except by people who had apprenticed for at least seven years in England.

Second, the colonies' inland expansion brought them increasingly into conflict with both the indigenous tribes and the French settlers and traders of the trans-Appalachian region. Westward settlement was limited by the difficulty of transporting heavy supplies inland, such as salt and sugar and iron goods, but it spread steadily with the gradual extinction of furbearing animals in the East and the search for new supplies of them. Petulla (1988) reports that by 1750 some two million beaver had been killed in eastern North America; and first the eastern Native American tribes (such as the Iroquois) and then the whites began ranging further and further inland to trade and trap, causing increasing conflict with the French and indigenous tribes already there. Colonial traders further diminished the tribes' goodwill by promoting the use of alcohol (rum), swindling the tribes out of land, and opening the way for settlers to follow. Notwithstanding the French presence, many of the English colonies also claimed lands as far westward as the Mississippi River, and colonial land speculators encouraged the westward spread of trapping and settlement as a means of securing the frontier and consolidating their claims.

Britain, meanwhile, fought four major wars with France between 1680 and 1763, and all these conflicts affected the American colonies — the last one dramatically so (Sosin 1961). The French and Indian War began in America in conflicts between English and French trappers and settlers in the Ohio River valley. Running southwest from just east of the Great Lakes, the Ohio River was a strategic corridor both for westward movement of the English and for communication between French colonies in the North and South. It was also the central transportation corridor serving both the fertile lands and the fur trade of the upper Midwest. Beginning in 1754, therefore, a world war grew out of this conflict, which resulted in 1763 with the ending of all French rule in North America.

The consequences of this war included changes in policies that led directly to revolution. From the colonists' perspective, victory drove out the French obstacles to westward expansion, and colonial participation in that struggle gave them the right to the lands that were won. Land speculators such as the Ohio Company of Virginia, the Loyal Company, and the Greenbriar Company began gearing up for westward settlement based on prewar colonial land claims, including some that had guaranteed two hundred thousand acres of land bounties to Virginia militiamen for their war service. From the perspective of many midwestern Native Americans, the Anglo-Americans had driven out their French protectors and trading partners and left them vulnerable to encroachment by the British colonies, despite a 1758 treaty which reserved to them all trans-Allegheny lands as hunting grounds. From the British perspective, victory left a sorely depleted treasury, a vast expansion of territory to police and administer, and a dangerously ambiguous frontier between white settlers — who in British eyes had not carried their fair share of the burden of the war, either in money or manpower — and indigenous tribes. Britain moved promptly and firmly, therefore, first to try to stabilize the frontier, and second to raise more revenues from the colonies to support the British troops policing it (Higginbotham 1971, 29–34).

The Proclamation of 1763 was Britain's effort to stabilize the frontier for at least long enough to sort out and resolve these issues. Issued shortly after the Treaty of Paris which ended the war, it prohibited any further colonial settlement west of a line running roughly down the Alleghenies. From Britain's perspective it was an appropriate policy that not only protected its trading relationships with the Native Americans but also assured equitable treatment of Britain's new French and indigenous subjects. In fact, however, the Proclamation line did not accurately reflect many colonial land claims that already existed to the west. To colonial settlers, as well as to land speculators who held trans-Appalachian claims and even paid quitrents to Britain as late as 1766, the policy was a direct provocation. These land interests included many of the most prominent citizens, traders, and legislators in the colonies, among them George Washington and Benjamin Franklin. In their eyes the British troops were not protecting but blocking them, and British demands for more revenues from them to support this purpose merely added insult to their perceived injury.

Throughout the 1760s the British sought new methods of raising revenues to finance their garrisons on the western frontier, and with each attempt additional interest groups in the colonies became alienated. The colonies too had war debts to pay, and they had little means of paying them other than land bounties which were blocked by the Proclamation. Colonial revenues, which were already scarce due to wartime disruptions of trade with European and Caribbean ports, were now to be squeezed even further by new British trade restrictions and revenue measures. Britain gave the colonies a year to raise their own taxes, and when they did not, Parliament passed a series of revenue measures itself, including the Stamp Act of 1765 (taxing paperwork) and the Townshend Acts of 1767 (raising taxes on imports to the colonies). It also expanded the list of enumerated goods in 1764, to help rebuild its own economy, and began vigorously enforcing all its colonial export controls. By the late 1760s Britain's military priorities shifted from stabilizing the frontier to maintaining order in the eastern colonies, and it closed some twenty-two frontier forts, moving several regiments back into the colonies (Higginbotham 1971, 41).

Finally, in 1774, having failed either to raise significant revenues or to maintain the 1763 boundary, or even to reach any lasting agreement with the colonies over frontier bound-aries and defense revenues, Britain passed the Quebec Act. This law shifted administration of the entire upper Midwest to a military governor in Quebec, the only colony that got along peacefully with the Indians, and in the process it guaranteed freedom of religion and other civil rights to its new French Catholic subjects. Like the Proclamation of 1763 it was founded in good intentions, but it also ignored the claims of Virginia, Connecticut, and Massachusetts to those lands. Its effect was thus to enrage the colonial assemblies once again, and to further set the stage for revolution.

Summary

This brief overview of colonial environmental policies illustrates several points that remain important to American environmental policy today.

First, environmental policy is not a new invention of the late twentieth century, nor even of the U.S. republic. Environmental policies of many kinds existed in America from the earliest period of European colonization, both for land and natural resource use and for the protection of public health and other purposes. Land and water use, water pollu-tion, forest and mineral resources, fish and wildlife—all were the subjects of explicit government policies during the colonial period, created either by the British colonial authorities or by the colonial governments or both. These policies in turn were fundamen-tally interwoven with questions of property rights: who had what rights to use or trans-form the environment and its resources, what responsibilities went with those rights, and what restrictions might governments impose on the exercise of them.

Second, the initial British versions of many of these policies were fundamentally re-shaped when they conflicted with American environmental and economic conditions. Ownership of land in America came to represent a far broader "bundle of rights" than it did under either the feudal system of English land rights out of which it evolved or the Native American concept of "use rights" that it supplanted. This was especially true of the rights to exploit and transform the land's surface resources, and to subdivide and sell the land itself for profit. Traditional British restrictions on subdivision and sale of land, such as feudal quitrents and primogeniture, simply could not be sustained in an environ-ment where land seemed almost boundlessly available and where this easy availability was in fact a key incentive for attracting immigrants to increase the labor force.

Similarly, British water rights principles, which limited publicly shared use rights to navigable estuaries, could not be sustained in an environment where major rivers were navigable far inland, and where they served as essential highways of commerce through large regions. Nor could traditional British principles restricting hunting to the elite and fishing to monopoly concessions be sustained in the face of widespread use of these resources for subsistence and trade.

American environmental policies thus were powerfully shaped by the characteristics of the American environment itself, and by the different economic opportunities inherent in them. Far more generally, British regulatory policies aimed at maintaining Britain's own mercantile trade advantages could not be effectively enforced where they did not benefit the colonies as well, and such attempts left a legacy of hostility to regulation by central governments that has endured down to many modern U.S. controversies.

Third, policies for ownership and use of the environment varied from the outset among different environmental conditions. Ownership of land did not necessarily confer ownership of the minerals underneath it, the water that ran across it, or wildlife that might be present on it. Minerals were subject at least to government royalties, water was a shared public resource (and a regulated one, with respect to pollution), and fish and wildlife were subject to governmental regulation from very early in American colonial history. Contrary to American popular mythology, land ownership has always represented only a "bundle" of rights: the composition of the bundle has shifted over time, but has never been absolute.

Finally, the property principles and environmental policies of the European colonial governments fundamentally disrupted preexisting Native American resource-use regimes, and set in motion the large-scale conversion of the environment from a source of renewable resources for local sustenance to a source of commodities for global markets. Both the explicit environmental policies of the colonial governments and the underlying policies of the European empires — land ownership, colonization, open immigration, and mercantile trade — encouraged enclosure and commercialization of land. This transformation destroyed sustainable patterns of use rights that had been maintained by the Native American communities, substituting for them the abstract monetary value system of global economic markets. This in turn led to aggressive and wasteful exploitation of environmental resources for as long as they were more abundant and therefore cheaper than in Europe. As Cronon put it,

> Operating in an economy where labor was scarce and difficult to hire, where accumulated capital was smaller than it had been in Europe, colonists turned to the factor of production which could compensate for the ones they lacked: they turned to the land and all it contained. . . . The result was an economy which used natural resources in a way which often appeared to European visitors as terribly wasteful. . . . By integrating New England ecosystems into an ultimately global capitalist economy, colonists and Indians together began a dynamic and unstable process of ecological change which had in no way ended by 1800. . . . Ecological abundance and economic prodigality went hand in hand: the people of plenty were a people of waste. (1983, 159–70)

Similar patterns of economic and ecological imperialism occurred throughout the European colonial world, and accelerated dramatically in the late twentieth century with the liberalization of world trade and the concurrent substitution of global commercial and financial empires for political ones (The Ecologist 1993).

4 The Constitutional Framework

The Congress shall have power to lay and collect taxes . . . and provide for the common defense and general welfare of the United States; . . . To regulate commerce with foreign nations, and among the several States, and with the Indian tribes; . . . to dispose of and make all needful rules and regulations respecting the territory or other property belonging to the United States; . . . and To make all laws which shall be necessary and proper for carrying into execution the foregoing powers. . . . This Constitution, and the laws of the United States which shall be made in pursuance thereof; and all treaties made, or which shall be made, under the authority of the United States, shall be the supreme law of the land. . . .

No person shall . . . be deprived of life, liberty, or property, without due process of law; nor shall private property be taken for public use, without just compensation.
— United States Constitution

Between 1776 and 1790 the American colonies fought and won a revolutionary war, joined themselves into a loose confederation of independent states, and then strengthened that confederation into a federal government based on a constitution and a bill of rights. These events were shaped in part by the opportunities and constraints presented by the American environment. In turn, they shaped the policies that guided much of the use of the American environment for the following century. The basic legacy of this period and even many of its specific manifestations are still very much visible today.

Early environmental policies were not established in separate laws or by a separate agency, but were elements in a broader process of solving the political, social, and economic problems of the new nation. How could soldiers be paid, and a war be won? What balance should the new government strike between the rights of creditors and debtors, between personal rights and property rights, between the needs of sparsely and densely populated states? How could a new government support itself, establish its credit rating with other nations and investors, and rebuild its economy after cutting itself loose from its mother country? Should that economy emphasize capital-intensive commerce and manufacturing or agrarian democracy? These were among the central questions of the time. The answers that were chosen reflected choices both about the kind of society and government people wanted and about the role of natural resources and environmental conditions in that society.

Natural Resource Policies During the Revolution

From 1776 until the Treaty of Paris in 1783, the thirteen colonies, now declared independent but united states, were at war with Great Britain. They were the first colonies to break away from European rule — many others remained under European administration until as recently as World War II — and they did so under conditions of great hardship and scarcity. As is usual in wartime, environmental policies were shaped primarily by military demands.

Who made policy? The Declaration of Independence was signed in 1776, and the Articles of Confederation were drawn up in 1777 and ratified by 1781, but these articles provided for only a limited common government: a federal government representing the governments of the independent states, not a national government ruling the people directly. It had no president, and congressmen were appointed by each state government, not elected by citizens. The Continental Congress had no authority to conscript soldiers or to impose taxes, nor could it regulate commerce, either among the states or between them and other nations. The Congress could establish military manpower quotas for each state and call on each state to meet them, it could appoint military officers and negotiate with foreign nations, and it could print money, as could the states. Its only power over the states and their citizens, however, was the power to persuade.

This weakness was intentional. Supporters of the Revolution did not want to recreate strong national governance similar to British rule, and the state legislatures that sanctioned the Declaration had no interest in giving away their powers. The result was that most policy-making, environmental and otherwise, continued to be the responsibility of the individual states, except for treaties and several ordinances relating to public lands.

Shortages, Bounties, and Surveys

An immediate problem of the war was widespread economic disruption caused by the interruption of overseas trade. The American colonies had depended heavily on Britain for manufactured goods, and on export of their surpluses both to England and to other empires and colonies — as well as on profits from the carrying trade itself — for hard currency to pay for their imports. With the outbreak of revolution British suppliers and markets were closed off, including the economically important British West Indian colonies as well as England itself. British naval blockades battled American smugglers and privateers, with limited success, to cut off America's other trading partners (Matson 1996). New England's fishermen and whalers were seriously affected by loss of access both to their markets in southern Europe and the West Indies and to the resource itself (Nettels 1962, 18).

Excepting soldiers, Americans did not suffer from lack of food during the war (Carp 1984, 55–65). Many other commodities, however, were vastly inflated in price and in some cases physically scarce. Salt, for instance, a critical commodity for preserving meat, had to be obtained by imports from France and the West Indies. Woolen cloth for clothing — normally imported from England's textile mills — was scarce and required substitution of homespun (Nettels 1962, 41–42). Paper, which was necessary not only for newspapers and correspondence but for ammunition cartridges and for all the paperwork used to administer an army, had to be made not from wood pulp but from rags by skilled laborers, and both of these were in short supply. Recycling of rags was enforced by searches of attics, and even old sermons were converted into cartridge casings (Leonard 1950).

By far the greatest influence wartime policy had on the environment was the sheer magnitude of war production and consumption demands it generated. Key industries were permanently enlarged by this demand — among them the production of paper, pottery, shoes, gunpowder, certain textiles, and especially iron and steel — and spurred to adapt more advanced technologies and production techniques (McCusker and Menard 1985, 363–64; Nettels 1962, 42–44). For particularly scarce commodities the government exhorted frugality and recycling, as in the case of rags for paper and homespun for clothing, and for some essentials it offered premiums for increased production. Cash bounties were offered for increased production of textiles, and particularly of iron and steel products (Nettels 1962, 41). Many American manufacturers and merchants thus made handsome profits during the war years, encouraged by wartime production incentives and freed also from British colonial manufacturing and trade restrictions. The war also functioned as a protective tariff, freeing American manufacturers from the competition of British imports (Jensen 1962).

Overall, wartime economic conditions thus produced several new forces and perceptions that were important to subsequent environmental policy. The first was a major boost for domestic agriculture and manufacturing to meet military needs. The second was a widespread perception that domestic industries and markets were an important resource in wartime, and for that reason were to be preferred over dependence on imported goods. The third was a belief in the principle that government policy should therefore protect domestic manufacturers, yet at the same time seek free trade internationally, opening new export markets free of the British system of mercantile trade regulations (Matson 1996, 370–71).

Another wartime policy precedent was government support for natural-resource reconnaissance surveys. This policy grew out of wartime shortages of lead, which was essential for ammunition but scarce. Some lead was obtained from mines in what is now Missouri and shipped down the Mississippi, but by the end of the war pewter utensils, statues, and virtually every other available source of lead was recycled for the production of bullets. In 1775 and 1776, therefore, the Continental Congress requested that the states conduct surveys to search out new lead deposits. These surveys were probably the United States' first systematic attempt to gather information about a specific resource, and may have provided the basis for policies in the early federal land laws (1785, 1796) reserving one-third of all lead and salt deposits — as well as the traditional gold, silver, and copper royalties — to the government (Engelbert 1950). Such surveys were not extended to other resources until the state natural resource surveys of the 1820s and '30s.

A second sort of survey grew out of military needs for better knowledge of the terrain, both inland and along the coast. George Washington employed a geographer and a road surveyor to assist him in preparing for troop movements, and kept them on after the war.

They guided the land survey that was authorized by the Land Ordinance of 1785, and provided early impetus within government for geographic exploration (Engelbert 1950, 64). A corps of military engineers was also formed to construct roads, soldiers' quarters, and fortifications and to clear navigational obstructions from harbors. Much of their initial expertise was provided either by America's French allies or by trial and error, there being no school of engineering in America until West Point was founded in 1802. From these wartime roots grew, among other things, the U.S. Coast and Geodetic Survey, the leadership of the army in western exploration and topographical surveying, and the involvement of the Army Corps of Engineers in domestic water resource development. Finally, wartime troop movements and the logistics of supplying them necessitated the construction of roads and river transport routes — "internal improvements" — and of lodgings and supply depots, the seeds of many future towns, along these supply lines (Nettels 1962, 37–40).

Land Bounties and War Finance

Shortages of commodities caused some difficulties, but by far the most pervasive problem was the shortage of hard currency. The new government had no authority to levy taxes, and export earnings were cut off by the war; how was it to pay and provision an army? Its answer was to pay in the only coin it had to offer: the promise of winning. It printed paper money, it borrowed money with a promise of interest, and it promised land — which it did not then possess — to its soldiers (Harlow 1929; Gates 1968).

Borrowing to finance the war left the government with heavy debts. The money was owed in part to foreign lenders, but mainly to domestic merchants. The national war debt was an important source of class conflict, therefore, between the majority of American taxpayers — mostly poor farmers and artisans — and the wealthy merchant minority, who were both government's creditors and often their own. Debt policy would also shape the new government's credit rating with foreign holders of the hard currency it needed for investment. The need to pay off the national debt therefore became a central consideration in policy-making for public lands, the government's only tangible asset after the war.

At the outset of the war the federal government had no land. Half the states had land claims extending westward to the Mississippi, Virginia most prominently. These states used land bounties — warrants authorizing the bearer to take possession of a claim of specified size — to induce enlistment in their militias. Such bounties had been used frequently by colonial governments, not only as rewards for military service but also as fulfillment of headrights and inducements for frontier settlement. The other half of the states lacked this resource, however, and some had to offer cash bounties to achieve the same ends, which led to inequities and conflict among soldiers paid at different rates by different states. The Continental Congress likewise had no lands to offer, since it existed simply as a meeting of delegates of the various states — rather like the modern United Nations.

Despite its lack of any land to offer, however, George Washington persuaded the Continental Congress, beginning in 1776, to offer land bounties as bonuses to soldiers either for enlisting for the duration of the war (if they were Americans), or for deserting if they were British or Hessian (Engelbert 1950). Washington knew the strength of people's drive to own land, both to settle on and to speculate on like the large land companies — to "let the little guy speculate too" — and the Congress simply assumed that victory would make lands available to fulfill the promises made. By the end of the war, 16,683 land bounty warrants were given amounting to over 2.6 million acres, an area somewhat larger than the present state of Colorado (Berkhofer 1972). Each individual was entitled to between fifty and eight hundred acres, depending on his rank, with virtually no restrictions on its use.

In addition to committing a large amount of land by themselves, the Revolutionary land bounties had a many-fold greater effect as a precedent. Similar bounties were offered for service in the War of 1812 and the Mexican War of the 1840s, resulting in a giveaway of sixty-five million acres of public lands by 1860. They opened the way to widespread land speculation, and became one of the most notorious causes of unwise development in the westward settlement of the nation (Hibbard 1965 [1924]).

Public Lands and the Confederation

How did the federal government acquire the land to make good its promises? And how did the United States as a nation come to acquire such vast acreage of publicly held lands, an area which even today makes up fully one-third of the nation's land?

The lands were acquired first from the original thirteen states, and later from France, Spain, Britain, Mexico, and from the Native Americans. More recently, the federal government has acquired smaller areas by repurchase or by condemnation and compensation. It is a poignant irony of history, as lawyers today debate the authority of government to impose pollution control measures and ecological restrictions on the use of land, that from the Allegheny Mountains to the West Coast virtually all of America's lands were once under government ownership. Most of the areas that remain — especially national parks and forests, wildlife refuges, and the "public domain" administered by the Bureau of Land Management — are the residuals of far larger areas sold or given away by the federal government.

The original charters to seven of the colonies granted them lands from "sea to sea" in their specified parallels of latitude.[1] In 1763 these claims were cut off at the Mississippi River by England's recognition of Spanish claims west of that boundary. By 1776, however, those states that claimed lands west of the Alleghenies had already begun granting these lands for military service and selling them to raise revenues. Many were acquired by land speculation companies, whose principals often included state legislators and congressmen.

The other six states lacked extensive backland claims, and felt themselves both disadvantaged and threatened by the resulting imbalance (Rakove 1979, 156). Small but populous states like Maryland had high troop quotas but little land to offer as bounties. They also owed war debts to the Union for their share of defense costs, which they had little means to pay. Enclosed states such as Maryland, New Jersey, and Rhode Island foresaw a permanent and increasing imbalance of power between themselves and their expansive neighbors, in which they would eventually lose their equality in governance as settlers came to fill the vast lands of the larger states.

In 1776 the Continental Congress began drafting the Articles of Confederation, and the first draft explicitly provided that "no state shall be deprived of territory for the benefit of the United States." The enclosed states objected vigorously, however, and demanded that all land claims west of the Alleghenies be ceded to the new federal government. Since all the states were contributing to the war effort, they argued, all should share in the unallocated lands to be acquired by victory (Rakove 1979, 286).[2]

The Articles said nothing about western lands. They did not authorize the Confederation to receive lands, to manage or dispose of them, or even to make laws or institute governance for them. In 1780, however, during the darkest period of the war, the first states finally agreed to cede their claims, and Congress passed a resolution articulating how the ceded lands would be managed. First, they would be "disposed of for the common benefit of the United States." Second, they would be settled and formed into distinct republican states, which would become members of the federal union, and have the same rights of sovereignty, freedom, and independence as the other states. Third, they were to be "granted and settled at such times and under such regulations as shall hereafter be agreed to by the United States in Congress assembled" (U.S. Public Land Law Review Commission 1970, 51). Congress sweetened the terms by agreeing that ceded lands would be accepted by the Union in payment for war debts.

Maryland accepted the terms, ceding its own claims and ratifying the Articles in 1780. New York also ceded in 1780, and the other states did likewise within the following few years, with the exception of Georgia, which did not do so until 1803. In all, 237 million acres were thus ceded to the national government, or 12 percent of the total area of the United States today. Most importantly, the states ceded these lands completely, without reserving rights to water, minerals, or any other resources.

The acquisition of a national land domain had profound significance, not only for environmental policy but for United States history as a whole. First, it created the precedents of federal land ownership and of management of these lands for the common benefit — precedents which provided a basis for the later reservation of national forests and parks, hydroelectric dam sites, wildlife refuges, fuel mineral reserves, and many other public purposes. Even more important, it provided the initial basis for a *national* as opposed to a merely federal government: a government that was not just the sum of its thirteen states, but had assets of its own. These assets could be used to attract capital investment, to pay off war debts, to encourage immigration and settlement that would develop new resource supplies and markets, or for whatever other purposes the government chose.

Treaties: National Boundaries and State Jurisdictions

The Treaty of Paris in 1783 ended the American Revolution. By this treaty, England accepted the independence of the United States, and recognized its jurisdiction within boundaries roughly corresponding to the thirty-first parallel on the south (above Spanish-held Florida), the Mississippi River on the west, and the forty-fifth parallel and Great Lakes on the north. England retained its claims in Canada, which extended west to the Pacific and included what are now the states of Washington, Oregon, and Idaho.

Implied in this treaty was the transfer of all the king's rights to the governments of the individual states, subject to the limitations of the Articles of Confederation. In general, as the U.S. Supreme Court ruled in 1842, the states became successors to the Crown's authority over fish and wildlife, navigable waters, submerged lands, and other resources.[3] Undistributed Crown lands, for instance, became state lands, and to them were added the expropriated estates of Royalist sympathizers. Royal jurisdiction over wildlife became the states' jurisdiction. Virtually all the states immediately abolished feudal restrictions on land acquisition and transfer: entail, primogeniture, and quitrents. The result was to make land freely transferable, by sale or by grant, and divisible into separate pieces of whatever size and shape the owner saw fit. In short, land could now be freely bought and sold as a commodity. As John Adams put it, "The only possible way then of preserving the balance of power on the side of equal liberty and public virtue, is to make the acquisition of land easy to every member of society: to make a division of land into small quantities, so that the multitude may be possessed of landed estates" (quoted in Scott 1977, 41).

The states acted promptly to clarify their jurisdictions over watercourses that ran along their boundaries. New Jersey and Pennsylvania, for instance, declared the Delaware River a "common highway" and established a commission of six members to administer their concurrent jurisdiction over it; each state would continue to control its own shore fishery. Virginia and Maryland, similarly, declared the Potomac a free and common highway, and their harbors open to reciprocal free use; they would allow small craft to use all harbors freely, split the duties on larger ships, share the cost of navigational aids, and set up a joint company to develop the river for navigation (Jensen 1962, 342).

The Treaty of Paris settled America's jurisdictional claims with England, but additional treaties were necessary to negotiate its relationships with Native American tribes, especially those who occupied the vast trans-Allegheny region that had now been won. To most Americans these Indians were enemies: trading partners first of the French and then of the British, and still supplied and influenced by British trading posts on the Great Lakes. They blocked Americans' westward land speculation and settlement in the Ohio Valley, and were powerful enough to be a military threat. The Indians in turn were understandably apprehensive at the victory of the colonies over the British who had protected their interests. The United States negotiated several treaties in the 1780s by which various Indian nations ceded their claims in western New York and Ohio—the Treaty of Fort Stanwix in 1784 and the Treaty of Fort MacIntosh in 1785, for instance—but other tribes refused to accept these. As holders of military bounty warrants and other settlers, squatters, and speculators poured westward after the war, defying Indian occupancy, the treaties proved unenforceable against whites as well. The result was a decade of hostility and warfare in what is now Ohio, Michigan, and Indiana. The conflict was ended only by military force, when General "Mad Anthony" Wayne defeated the Indians in 1794 in the Battle of Fallen Timbers. By the Treaty of Greenville in 1795, the twelve Indian tribes of the "old Northwest" yielded their land rights to the federal government.

The Constitution

The Articles of Confederation deliberately created a weak central government: a federal congress of independent states rather than a national government preeminent over them. This suited many Americans, who preferred regional accountability and self-governance to a new central authority. It did not, however, suit the preferences of powerful groups whose interests extended across state lines: manufacturers competing against foreign imports, commercial and shipping firms, creditors of government receiving depreciated returns from a Congress strapped for tax revenues, and businesses facing debtor revolts. These groups, linked by shared economic interests, demanded a stronger *national* government to serve those interests: to protect their property rights, to enforce the stability of contracts, to provide credit for entrepreneurs, and in general, to protect the rights of the wealth minority against control of the democratic process by the debtor majority (Nettels 1962, 92). In 1787, against the background of economic depression and Shays's Rebellion, they succeeded in calling a constitutional convention to amend the Articles of Confederation. They then used this convention to substitute a far more nationalist constitution (Degler 1970, 87–88).

The Constitution is the essential foundation for all U.S. laws, regulations, and other policies, providing the source both for their authority and for its limits. That does not mean that it provides unambiguous solutions for every issue. Its meanings have been repeatedly stretched and reinterpreted over time, to fit new situations and to justify actions that the Supreme Court or a majority of Congress wished to take. When it was adopted, its immediate effect was to increase greatly the powers of the national government over the states, and reinterpretation since that time has generally increased this dominance.

Flexible or not, the Constitution is "the supreme law of the land," and the interpretation of its provisions has structured all subsequent debate over what environmental policies are appropriate to the U.S. government. If these interpretations have sometimes appeared strained, it has often been because they were the work of advocates who believed that an interdependent national economy and society require more national solutions than did the decentralized society of 1787, and that it is safer to stretch the Constitution than to risk the potential political mischief of a convention to revise it.

The central arguments of the constitutional debate were not over environmental issues, but over representation in governance and the balance between state and national power. What powers should a national government have? Should it have authority to tax and spend and to raise armies, which the Confederation did not? Should it be authorized to regulate commerce among the states, and with Indian and foreign nations? How should the representation of state governments be balanced against representation of populations, whose numbers varied widely from state to state? And how should abuses of centralized power be prevented and remedied?

The measures that resulted from these debates have influenced every U.S. public policy issue. The separation of government powers among three branches, for instance, provides different avenues for making and influencing policy than in other nations: citizen environmental lawsuits are a far more powerful weapon in the United States than in virtually any other country, due to the independent authority of its judicial branch. Several of the specific federal powers granted by the Constitution have particular significance for environmental policy, as do restrictions on government authority imposed by the Constitution's amendments. Among the most important sources of constitutional authority for environmental policies are the so-called commerce, property, and federal supremacy clauses, and the "general welfare" and "necessary and proper" clauses which amplify the others. Other occasional sources include tax clauses and the war, treaty, admiralty, and interstate compacts provisions. The most important limitation on environmental policy-making is the Fifth Amendment; others include the Fourteenth and Fourth Amendments.

The Commerce Clause

Article 1 of the Constitution vested all legislative powers in the Congress, and Section 8 of that article listed the specific powers that the Congress was to have. One of the most important of these was the power "to regulate commerce with foreign nations, and among the several States, and with the Indian Tribes." Some advocates of giving Congress this power had in mind such issues as competition from imported goods, against which they wished government protection. Others sought to end interstate trade wars and control by seaport states of commerce up the rivers — the "highways of commerce" to and from inland states. Still others sought national control over relations with Indian tribes, some to protect the Native Americans against actions of settler-dominated state legislatures and others to protect their own land interests against Native American claims. The result was a simple but broadly stated grant of authority that became the basis for a wide range of national policies and programs affecting the economy.

The authority to regulate interstate and foreign commerce was one of the most controversial and explicit powers by which the United States was transformed from a federal to a national government, and many central elements of U.S. environmental policy are derived from it.[4] Water resources, for instance, have often been valued for conflicting uses, such as commercial navigation and the operation of mills. Court decisions interpreting the commerce clause allowed the federal government a "navigation servitude" over all navigable waters to prevent the erection of barriers, such as milldams, that affected interstate commerce. This logic was extended to include the *promotion* of interstate commerce by federal investments in improving the navigability of waterways. Examples included federal subsidies for aids to navigation in coastal harbors, such as buoys and lighthouses, and for clearing snags and other impediments out of inland rivers. Later extensions of this policy included multibillion-dollar federal expenditures for water resource development projects built by such agencies as the Army Corps of Engineers, the Bureau of Reclamation, and the Soil Conservation Service, and wastewater treatment plants subsidized by the Environmental Protection Agency.

The commerce clause is also one basis for federal wildlife regulation. A federal role in such matters was first established by a 1900 law, the Lacey Act, which prohibited interstate commerce in illegally caught wildlife and thus effectively ended the market hunting industry.

In environmental protection, the commerce clause was further stretched to authorize federal regulation of air and water pollution. Effluents flow into navigable waterways and cross state lines in ambient water and air. They are also emitted by industries participating in interstate commerce, which might benefit from unfair commercial advantage over nonpolluters. In addition, polluting industries may affect other industries that are either involved in interstate commerce or are located across state lines, such as farms, beaches, and resorts. Vehicles that travel across state lines, including airplanes, trucks, and automobiles, are also covered, as are products that may affect neighboring states — pesticides and noisy machines, for instance (Soper 1974).

Finally, the commerce clause provided the basis for the federal government's authority over interstate flows of many natural resources, and its resulting jurisdiction over matters such as oil import quotas, oil and natural gas prices, hydroelectric power transmission, gasoline allocation, agricultural export deals, and marine fishery harvesting. In a nation pervaded by interstate mobility, the scope of the commerce clause has been extended to permit federal involvement in very nearly every significant issue of environmental policy.

The commerce clause had additional importance in that it prohibited actions by state or local governments that would interfere with interstate commerce. This was mainly aimed at prohibiting discriminatory prices or exclusionary laws that would protect local businesses from competition by interstate firms, but it has also had great significance for municipal waste management policies. State and local governments may not ban out-of-state wastes from their landfills, for instance, since these wastes are moving via interstate commerce, but this prohibition in turn has caused many communities to oppose even new "local" landfills since they could immediately become interstate dumping grounds. Local governments are also prohibited from enacting such policies as "flow control" ordinances, which would require that all local waste be delivered to designated local facilities — a provision that would help finance state-of-the-art facilities but would also disadvantage interstate haulers.

The Property Clause

Article 4, Section 3 of the Constitution gave Congress the power "to dispose of and make all needful Rules and Regulations respecting the Territory or other property belonging to the United States." This provision remedied the government's previous lack of legal authority to accept, manage, and dispose of the ceded public domain lands. It also provided the basis for most subsequent laws and regulations governing public lands, including those pertaining to national park and forest reservations, timber sales, mineral leases, offshore drilling permits, grazing fees, and wildlife refuges, to name a few. It permitted the government to protect its own property: for instance, by killing deer that overgraze it, by requiring adjacent stock owners to fence in their cattle, and conceivably even by setting other restrictions on adjoining landowners and resource users (Soper 1974).

The property clause was also significant to water resource policy. First, under the western "prior appropriation" principle of water rights, the federal government holds "reserved rights" to vast amounts of annual water flows in the arid West by virtue of being the earliest formal owner of the public lands. Some of these rights are associated with Indian reservations and thus derived from the treaty and commerce clauses, but others are associated simply with public lands. The federal government has never fully utilized these flows, but if it chose to do so — for instance, by selling them to mining companies — many present users such as farmers and ranchers, and even western cities, could face water shortages. Second, when the federal government builds a dam and thus *creates* a resource of impounded water — as by the Tennessee Valley Authority, or the Bureau of Reclamation — it owns that resource, and may manage it as it sees fit, deciding when and for what purposes flows will be released: for instance for power generation, flood control, irrigation, fish and wildlife habitat maintenance, or recreation.

Federal Supremacy

Article 6 declared that the U.S. Constitution, U.S. laws pursuant to it, and treaties are "the supreme Law of the Land . . . anything in the Constitution or Laws of any State to the contrary notwithstanding." In short, federal law was to prevail over state law if the two conflicted, so long as the federal law did not violate the Constitution. This is the principle of federal supremacy, intended by its authors to insure the authority of the national government over the states; without it each state could simply ignore the national laws and Constitution if it chose to.

Closely linked to federal supremacy was the doctrine of federal *preemption:* the principle that state lawmaking is preempted by federal law if the subject matter in question is constitutionally reserved to the federal government or if federal laws have been passed that supersede state laws. Some powers of government are exclusively assigned to the national government, such as the powers to administer federal lands, to negotiate treaties, and to regulate interstate commerce. In other cases federal and state authority overlap. Federal authority to regulate pollution under the commerce clause, for instance, overlaps the state's police power to regulate health and order. And the stretching of the commerce clause creates tension with the Tenth Amendment, which reserves to the states all powers not specifically assigned to the federal government. In short, federal law preempts state laws where they conflict, but frequently only case-by-case litigation — and in some instances Supreme Court rulings — can determine how much room federal statutes leave for additional state legislation.

Federal preemption is a two-edged sword in environmental policy, and has had profound effects on many substantive issues. Through the Migratory Bird Treaty Act (1918), for instance, it allowed federal conservation of waterfowl that might otherwise have been lost to conflicting and lax regulation in some states along their flyways. And federal air and water quality laws setting uniform minimum standards based on health criteria prevented a "race to the bottom" among states using weak regulations to lure industries away from stricter states. On the other hand, federal preemption has also been used to *weaken* state health and environmental standards in order to benefit manufacturers seeking uniform national standards for production and distribution of goods. Michigan, for instance, fought for years with the federal government to maintain tighter standards against hot dog adulteration, and soft drink manufacturers attempted to overturn state regulation of non-returnable bottles by arguing for federal preemption. Minnesota sought to impose tighter standards for nuclear power plants than those enforced by the federal Atomic Energy Commission, but the courts forbade it on the grounds that federal regulation preempted such an action — in effect forcing nuclear technology on Minnesota against its wishes.

In all such cases, the doctrine of preemption requires balancing of federal against state authority, an issue that has pervaded American law and policy since the Confederation. Over time the balance has tilted more and more toward centralized national policy-making, and the authority of the national government has increasingly been expanded into areas previously thought to have been reserved to the states. Whether this is thought good or bad often depends on the observer's attitude toward the substantive purpose thereby achieved. Manufacturers frequently applaud federal preemption that serves their purposes, and environmentalists likewise, but each objects when it serves the other at their expense.

In the 1990s a new version of this conflict was initiated by state and local governments arguing against "unfunded mandates": federal statutes that imposed responsibilities or restrictions on them without compensating them for the cost of implementation. Environmental regulations were among the leading examples of such laws. Examples included federal requirements for testing of public water supplies, for cleanup of sites contaminated with chemical wastes, for replacement of leaking underground storage tanks, for expensive safeguards in municipal landfills, and for removal of asbestos from schools and other public buildings. Even if each of these mandates was justified in itself, together they imposed significant new costs on many state and local governments. On the other hand, why should federal taxpayers subsidize environmental services that state and local beneficiaries should pay for themselves, or pay state and local governments to make their constituents stop polluting their neighbors? This question received little careful consideration in the rush to relieve municipalities from federally imposed burdens.

By the late 1990s, a conservative Supreme Court majority began to overturn preemptive federal laws in several other policy areas, such as gun control mandates, in rulings that might in the future become precedents for questioning federal environmental protection laws as well.

General Welfare: "Necessary and Proper"

In addition to many specific powers, such as the powers to tax, spend, and regulate commerce, Article 1, Section 8 provided Congress broad authority "to provide for the common defense and general welfare of the United States" and "to make all Laws which shall be necessary and proper for carrying into Execution the foregoing powers." The first of these phrases stimulated intense debate during the decades following ratification: if the Constitution was intended to grant specific powers to the national government and reserve all others to the states, didn't the "general welfare" clause risk justifying virtually any expansion of the national government's authority? Many early presidents vetoed such expansions out of concern that the clause would give Congress unlimited license if interpreted in this way. Yet if the Constitution's authors did not intend some additional grant of authority by this phrase, why was it included? Over time the latter reasoning prevailed, and the general welfare clause came to be used to justify some federal policies not already derived from more specific provisions. The main constraint was that the power had to be exercised for the common benefit, not merely for a local purpose.

The second phrase, the "necessary and proper" clause, acted as an amplifier of all the more specific powers. Its central purpose was to allow the federal government to adopt reasonable means for accomplishing its constitutional tasks. Inevitably, however, it also provided a means for extending the scope of the more explicit powers, against the wishes of supporters of a more narrowly limited federal government.

The War Power

Article 1, Section 8 authorized the Congress to provide for the common defense, to declare war, to raise and support armies and a navy, and to make rules for the government and regulation of these forces. Article 2, Section 2 provided that the president be commander-in-chief of the armed forces. These powers affected natural resources only occasionally, but significantly. Most exploration of the American West in the nineteenth century was carried out by army expeditions, led by such people as Lewis and Clark, Clarence King, and Major John Wesley Powell. Army engineers laid the foundations for American road and river transportation, actions justified in part by national defense arguments: even the modern interstate highway system was initially justified as a "national defense highway system." Army topographers surveyed the frontier before federal land sales, army troops enforced settlers' property claims against the Indian tribes, and wartime defense arguments were used to justify government rationing and control of natural resources. Army officers administered the Yellowstone Valley reservation for fifty years before the National Park Service was created in 1916, and they directed the Civilian Conservation Corps camps in natural resource restoration work in the 1930s. Even the Tennessee Valley Authority was connected to the army — it grew out of a surplus World War I army power plant and explosives factory on the Tennessee River, which were kept under government jurisdiction partly as a defense asset to assure abundant energy and munitions in any future war.

More recently, the federal government developed a new resource, atomic energy, primarily for national defense and secondarily for civilian power production. Military and defense procurement budgets for environmental cleanup in the 1990s dwarfed those of civilian agencies such as the Environmental Protection Agency, and army troops assist in coping with natural disasters such as floods. Therefore, both the constitutional powers to provide for the common defense and to make war, and the U.S. Army itself — the government's first supply of organized manpower — have played important roles in the evolution of U.S. environmental policy.

Treaty-Making

Article 2, Section 2 authorized the president to make treaties, subject to the approval of two-thirds of the Senate. These treaties become the "supreme law of the land" (Article 6), and therefore supersede any state laws with which they conflict. Treaties are a primary way to establish international environmental policies, and are sometimes used to regulate domestic resources as well. International treaties and conventions provide for the management of whales and marine fisheries, for instance, and for the protection of endangered species. They authorize management of the water resources of rivers and other bodies of water that span international borders, such as the Rio Grande, the Colorado River, and the Great Lakes. Broad multilateral treaties have also been negotiated to phase out the production of chemicals that damage the earth's stratospheric ozone layer, and for other environmental purposes.

Treaties passed for other purposes can also have important impacts on the environment. Recent amendments to the General Agreement on Tariffs and Trade (GATT), for instance, allow nations to regulate the environmental hazards of imported products but prohibit them from using trade sanctions against imports produced by environmentally damaging processes. This leaves no trade policy power to prevent industrial flight to "pollution havens" profiting from weak environmental controls. The amendments also require nations to use the "least trade restrictive" policies for environmental regulation, providing a basis for new legal challenges to state and federal regulations.

Finally, in at least one case Congress resorted to the treaty power when it was unable to enforce an environmental policy under the commerce clause. Early in the twentieth century the courts declared unconstitutional a federal law regulating migratory waterfowl, and Congress therefore negotiated a treaty calling for similar measures with England and Canada in 1916. This was implemented by an enabling law in 1918, which was held constitutional as a "necessary and proper" means of implementing the treaty.

Interstate Compacts

Article 1, Section 10 required congressional consent to any interstate compact or agreement, to guard against subnational alliances at the expense of the authority of the Union. In environmental policy, it had the effect of insuring a federal role in multistate resource management. Interstate compacts have been used for many years in the arid West, for instance, to apportion scarce water supplies among upstream and downstream states, such as in the Colorado River basin, and between states sharing a common border resource, such as Lake Tahoe and Pyramid Lake between California and Nevada. The U.S. government has acted not only as an additional party to these pacts, but also as spokesman for other stakeholders: for example, other nations holding treaty rights in the water flows (Canada and Mexico), and Indian tribes holding reserved water rights. More recently, the federal government has fostered multistate river basin commissions in other parts of the nation, for both multipurpose water resource development and water quality management, and it has been a party to compacts developed by the states to manage interstate rivers such as the Potomac, Susquehanna, and Delaware.

In the 1980s, federal legislation encouraged interstate compacts providing regional multistate management of some hazardous and radioactive wastes. These were different from water-resource management compacts in that they allowed groups of states to *exclude* wastes from nonmember states — in effect, to deliberately interfere with interstate commerce — as a reward for their willingness to build waste management facilities to serve member states. Such facilities were often difficult to site otherwise, due to political opposition from the states' own citizens.

Important questions about this practice have not yet been resolved. In effect, it amounts to using the interstate compacts clause to create an exception to the principles of the commerce clause, solely because hazardous and radioactive waste facilities are politically unpopular. But if a single state has no right to interfere with commerce in wastes, then why should a group of states be allowed to do so? Abuses are also possible: can a state such as California enter into a "paper compact" with, say, North Dakota to block California's neighbors from demanding access to its facilities? What happened is that a particular constitutional mechanism was used as an incentive to overcome political opposition to siting. The legitimacy of this approach remains debatable.

Tax Power

Article 1, Section 8 allowed the Congress "to lay and collect taxes, duties, imposts and excises." This is one of the most fundamental general powers of the U.S. government, and it has specific implications for environmental policy. Most fundamentally, in principle it permits the federal government to use economic incentives, rather than merely criminal penalties and prohibitions, to achieve environmental policy goals. Forested lands can be given special consideration in capital gains and estate taxes to encourage the long-term investments necessary for conservation. Pollution-control equipment can be depreciated rapidly to ease the cost of installing it, and tax credits can be provided for installation of solar or other energy-conserving equipment. Congress also has used tax policy to promote politically popular but environmentally damaging uses of resources, such as by establishing depletion allowances to encourage the rapid exploitation of minerals. Conversely, the government can selectively increase taxes — and thereby increase economic disincentives — on activities that Congress considers contrary to its policies, such as gasoline consumption, whiskey production, and the emission of pollutants.

Congress could, if it chose, charge a tax per unit of pollution emitted in order to discourage it, and some economists have urged a shift to this strategy from the current, predominantly regulatory approach. In practice, however, it has never done so, probably out of deference to the long-standing institutional separation between the taxing and spending agencies. The Internal Revenue Service has no mission or expertise to promote environmental protection, and the EPA and other programmatic agencies have never been given the authority to administer taxes.

The Fifth Amendment

The Constitution greatly broadened the powers of the national government relative to both state governments and individuals. It was ratified, therefore, only after assurances that limits on those powers would be spelled out in a Bill of Rights protecting states and individuals from abuse of centralized authority. This bill, the first ten amendments of the Constitution, was ratified in 1791. The rights therein were generally similar to those recognized in previous bills of rights in the state constitutions, and even to the British bill of 1688.

The fifth of these ten amendments has had particular significance for environmental policy. This amendment provided for protection against "double jeopardy" in criminal trials and for grand juries in all capital and infamous crimes. In addition, it included three momentous provisions: first, that no person shall be compelled in any criminal case to be a witness against himself; second, that no person shall be deprived of life, liberty, or property without due process of law; and third, that private property shall not be taken for public use without just compensation.

Self-incrimination. The first provision raises thorny issues in cases involving environmental record keeping, reporting requirements, and even firms' own environmental audits and monitoring data. Spills of toxic chemicals, for instance, are often accidental and must be contained and cleaned up as quickly as possible in order to minimize environmental damage. This speed frequently requires reporting by persons first on the scene — often the persons responsible for the spill — yet some toxic spills are also crimes. Also, many environmental laws require businesses to keep records on pollutant emissions and make reports to government agencies; do they too risk self-incrimination? Finally, pollution can only be reduced if businesses have clear incentives to identify and clean up their environmental problems, either themselves or with the help of "environmental audits" by consulting firms — yet if EPA lawyers can then use these reports as evidence of environmental crimes, companies may be tempted not to produce such information.

The courts generally have ruled that routine record keeping raises no constitutional problem, any more than does keeping income tax records. In cases involving the self-reporting of specific criminal events such as spills, however, opinions are divided, and the EPA has had to incorporate specific restrictions on the use of self-reported information in order to avoid problems (Soper 1974, 45–50). Proposals in the 1990s to affirm an "audit privilege," which would protect environmental audit information from public disclosure or regulatory use, have remained intensely controversial, as citizen environmental groups fear they could be used to weaken the enforceability of pollution control laws.[5]

Due process. The due process requirement established procedural rights for all citizens in their dealings with government authorities. Is government condemning land by eminent domain for a national park or a highway? Banning a pesticide? Deciding whether or not to license a nuclear power plant? Regulating air or water pollution, or protection of wetlands? Whatever the particular issue, the individual's right to do certain things — or even to enjoy existing environmental amenities — is considered property under the Fifth Amendment, and individuals cannot be deprived of it without due process of law.

The meaning of the due process provision was spelled out in far greater detail by the Administrative Procedures Act of 1946, which established specific citizen rights to government information, to participation in government decisions affecting them, and to legal accountability for the agencies' decisions (Kerwin 1994). Government agencies must provide advance notice and opportunity for comment, often including public hearings, to all citizens affected by a proposed decision, and they must document the justifications for their decisions in a "reviewable record." This record must demonstrate that their decisions are within their statutory authority that they have been made following proper procedures, that they are not "arbitrary and capricious" and that they are supported by "substantial evidence." Decisions that fail to meet these standards may be invalidated by the courts. Subsequent laws have added to these rights, including the Freedom of Information Act, National Environmental Policy Act, and provisions in other environmental statutes.

Arguments of due process have been used frequently in recent decades to block government actions, by both advocates and opponents of environmental protection. Environmentalist opponents of proposed government actions (the granting of nuclear power plant licenses, for instance) have argued for greater rights of public access to government information and decision processes. Industrial interests such as pesticide manufacturers in turn have argued for more and more detailed documentation of the justifications for proposed environmental regulations, including cost-benefit analyses, risk assessments, and other data. Both arguments serve to weaken the power of government agencies to make discretionary decisions. No one wants arbitrary decisions made without fair notice, hearings, and consideration of individuals' rights. In practice, however, the appropriate balance between insuring fairness of government procedures and preventing the stalemating of government decision-making is often difficult to determine.

Takings for public use. The most important provision of the Fifth Amendment for environmental policy purposes was the prohibition of "taking for public use without just compensation." If government occupies land to build a fort or a road, it clearly has taken it and must compensate the owner. If it needs partial use of some land, such as for a power line right-of-way, the government usually must compensate the owner for the value of that use. But suppose it merely regulates the use of the land, as in zoning, or prohibits development in floodplains or "critical environmental areas"? In some cases, of course, regulations *increase* property values by protecting amenities. In others, however, they may diminish the potential income that the owner could have generated from forbidden uses.

Some would argue that if regulations diminish a property's economic potential then they amount to taking the owner's development rights — "regulatory takings" — and should therefore require government compensation for the income loss. Others argue that such regulations are valid exercises of government's police power, and do not constitute takings so long as the owner retains some reasonable economic opportunities. Governments have always had the power to prevent and abate nuisances, and more generally to protect the public's health and safety and protect people's property rights. The Supreme Court as far back as 1837 held that the "interest of the public" justifies public regulation that might supersede private property interests, and that state governments' police power allows them to regulate on all matters necessary to their internal government except as prohibited by the Constitution (Futrell 1993, 13).[6]

This issue is central to land use policy, to pollution control regulation, to conservation and management of natural resources, and to every other environmental policy issue in which government asserts its authority to regulate. Does an industry have a right to keep on polluting, or does the community have a right (even if previously neglected) to a pollution-free river? Does a landowner have a right to fill a wetland and build a shopping center on it, or only the right to continue full use and enjoyment of it as a wetland? Does the government hold air, water, and other resources in trust for all Americans (Sax 1971), or do manufacturers have a right to discharge their wastes into it, or waterfront owners a right to build in a floodplain — a right that government can control only by purchase? Such questions are implicit in countless environmental controversies.

More than any other policy, the takings doctrine defines the boundary between government regulatory authority to protect resources and individual rights to exploit them for economic gain or other personal preferences. Clearly individuals must have some recourse against abuses of government regulation. On the other hand, extreme interpretations of the diminution-of-value principle could undermine legitimate and essential uses of such regulations.[7]

The courts have given many answers to the question of where such lines should be drawn, but since the 1970s they have generally leaned toward a case-by-case "balancing" of the public purpose against the extent of economic loss involved. Courts have ruled that government need not pay for every "diminution of value" if a legitimate public purpose is involved — landowners are not automatically entitled to the most profitable use of their property — but also that regulation may not go "too far": a regulation that destroys *all* economic value of a piece of property requires compensation. The practical effect is that most regulations have been upheld so long as a reasonable public purpose was involved (environmental protection, for instance) and some economic use remained available (a golf course rather than a shopping mall or housing development, for instance). Two Supreme Court decisions in the 1990s, however, signaled that conservative justices might look more critically at such regulations in the future, demanding both greater justification of the relationship between the public purpose and the regulatory action and "rough proportionality" between the severity of the regulatory restrictions and the impact that would otherwise occur (Kayden 1996).[8]

In 1995 a newly conservative House of Representatives proposed a radical shift in the takings doctrine, with several bills that would require compensation for any "diminution of value" greater than a specified percentage, which might be as little as 20 percent (or in some views, *any* diminution of value). None of these bills passed at the federal level, but as of 1996 five states had adopted such laws, and at least fourteen states had passed laws requiring a "takings impact assessment" before any proposed action, creating additional paperwork and also generating legal ammunition for challengers to use in litigation (Kayden 1996, 273). These proposals illustrate the continuing tension between private and public rights that underlies U.S. environmental policy-making authority.

The Fourteenth Amendment

The Fourteenth Amendment was ratified in 1868, soon after the Civil War, and was one of three intended to establish and protect the rights of black Americans. Among other provisions, it extended the requirement of due process to *state* government actions as well as national ones, and it forbade states to deny to any person the "equal protection" of the law. The logic of this provision was that no system of justice could be considered fair that did not give equal protection of its laws to all its citizens — a principle to which racial discrimination was a particularly visible affront.

In the field of environmental protection, however, the equal protection clause presents both opportunities and problems when applied to people in *unequal environmental* circumstances. On the one hand, one could argue that it demands equal provision of basic environmental services to all of a state's citizens, poor and wealthy alike, though the courts so far have rejected this argument (Soper 1974, 122–25). On the other hand, it has caused problems in the regulation of pollution by firms in different places. Consider two pulp and paper mills, for instance, identical except that one is located on a small stream and the other on a seacoast with strong tidal currents to flush its wastes. How much should each plant be required to reduce its organic wastes? One common answer is that both should have to install the same technology, so that the burden of the environmental protection laws falls on them equally — even though the cost of such action by the coastal plant may be far out of proportion to the social benefits gained. A less frequent answer is that unequal environmental circumstances may cause legitimate inequalities among firms, and that equal protection arguments, therefore, should not be used to impose burdens on firms whose locations provide natural environmental advantages.

The Fourth Amendment

The Fourth Amendment protected each person's right "to be secure in their persons, houses, papers, and effects, against unreasonable searches and seizure," and it required for each search by police or other government agents a warrant based on "probable cause" and describing the place to be searched and the persons or things to be seized. The purpose of this requirement was to protect innocent persons against harassment and abuse of police powers. It has been applied, however, to such matters as monitoring of compliance with environmental regulations or occupational health and safety standards, in which effective regulation and enforcement may require spot checks or other surprise inspections to insure against cheating. In one case, for example, an industry sued the EPA under the Fourth Amendment to block it from using aerial surveillance to detect pollution from its plant. In each such case the courts must balance the privacy protections of the Fourth Amendment against the equally legitimate responsibility of the government to protect public health, safety, and welfare as expressed in the anti-pollution laws (Soper 1974, 40–45).

Summary

The ratification of the Constitution marked the end of the Confederation period and the beginning of the U.S. government as we know it today. The underlying issues of the Confederation period, however, continued to be vigorously disputed. Who should benefit from the nation's abundant natural resources, the wealthy capitalist minority or the poor farmer majority? Should the nation pursue a primarily manufacturing or agrarian economy, and how deeply should the national government involve itself in the encouragement of one or the other? Some of these debates continue even today. Should government charge industries for the environmental and social damage caused by their pollution, or use the public's taxes to subsidize industrial cleanup? Should it give tax advantages to businesses for pollution-control investments, or increase taxes on them to pay for environmental services? Should it encourage agribusinesses or family farms, corporate forestry or small operators, large power plant systems or individual energy conservation and solar heaters?

The answers to these questions have varied widely over the course of American history, and in the contexts of different environmental circumstances and issues. The constitutional framework, however, defines a distinctively American set of principles and procedures for answering these questions. More perhaps than in any other country, it fragments the power to govern among separate branches, levels, and agencies of government, and restricts the government's power to regulate exploitation of the environment for private economic gain. More perhaps than in any other country, it requires government agencies to provide detailed scientific and economic justification for their actions, rather than to act on the discretionary authority of the state. Finally, more perhaps than in any other country, it allows both businesses and individual citizens to challenge the actions of government agencies through an independent judiciary, creating an adversarial context that increases accountability, but at severe costs to the efficiency and effectiveness of governance.

5 Land and Transport: Commercial Development as Environmental Policy

[I]n the formation of a plan for the disposition of the vacant lands of the United States, there appear to be two leading objects of consideration: one, the facility of advantageous sales, according to the probable course of purchases; the other the accommodation of individuals now inhabiting the Western country, or who may hereafter emigrate thither. The former, as an operation of finance, claims primary attention; the latter is important, as it relates to the satisfaction of the inhabitants of the Western country. It is desirable, and does not appear impracticable, to conciliate both. — Alexander Hamilton, *Report on Land Disposal Plan,* 1790

To what extent were the early acts the results of conscious policies? . . . [I]t cannot be said that a conscious policy worthy of the name existed. It was rather a series of expedient actions put into practice from time to time which must perforce be gathered together, classified as best they may be, and called the public policies, not forgetting that from 1784 to 1900 there was a strong popular belief that the land ought to be free to the settler. — Benjamin Hibbard, *A History of the Public Land Policies*

Land use in America has always been bound up in issues of public policy. Over 78 percent of the total 2.3 billion acres of the United States was once owned by the federal government, and more than a third of it was federal land as recently as the 1970s, including almost 45 percent of California, 52 percent of Oregon, 86 percent of Nevada, and 97 percent of Alaska (U.S. Department of the Interior 1973, 4, 10).[1] Most of the cities west of Pennsylvania were built on what had been public lands: Chicago, St. Louis, Denver, Seattle. The agricultural breadbasket of the Midwest was plowed out of public lands granted or sold to farmers. The transcontinental railroads were built with vast land grants given to railroad syndicates — for investment as well as for rights-of-way — and the steel and timber industries that supplied the syndicates also grew from these transfers of wealth. Without such government assistance, large-scale capital accumulation in the United States might have taken decades longer than it actually required (Peterson and Gray 1969, 240). During the nineteenth century, these "public domain" lands were the single most important tool of government environmental and economic development policy.

From the earliest land ordinances through the nineteenth century, U.S. government policy was to promote the rapid transfer of public lands into private hands, to generate both short-term revenues and long-term economic development. They were used to pay soldiers: land bounties totaling over sixty-one million acres were given to veterans of the Revolution and later wars. They were used to pay debts: land was sold wholesale to investment companies to raise revenues, then retailed by them to individual settlers at higher prices. They were used to develop educational institutions: public schools were subsidized and the "land grant universities" endowed in this way. More generally, they were used to attract generations of immigrants and speculators seeking better lives for themselves than they had found in Europe or in the eastern cities of the United States. Not until 1976, in fact — six years after the first Earth Day, and under the pressure of the modern environmental movement — did the Bureau of Land Management, overseer of some 474 million acres of federal public lands, finally obtain statutory authority to manage rather than dispose of these lands.

Public lands were also used to finance state and local governments and to bankroll public investments. The federal government's chief bargaining chip with the states was its power to offer federal lands in exchange for their support of development projects or other federal policies (Futrell 1993, 9). Privatized lands went onto the state and local property tax rolls, and over 328 million acres were granted directly to states to finance infrastructure development. These included almost 78 million acres for support of schools, 65 million acres for reclamation of swampland, 37 million for railroads, 6 million for canal and river development, 3 million for construction of wagon roads, and over 117 million for desert irrigation projects and construction of water reservoirs and other public facilities. Public lands were used to generate working capital for business as well: between 1850 and 1973 the federal government gave away over 94 million acres to private railroad syndicates, including 10 to 25 percent of the total lands of the states of Arizona, California, Montana, Nebraska, North Dakota, and Washington. The railroads could then sell off or mortgage prime locations and resource-rich lands to eastern and European investors, and thus raise the funds needed for construction (U.S. Department of the Interior 1973, 4, 9).

One scholar summarizes these policies by describing the public lands as a "balance wheel": a resource that could be used in place of tariffs as a source of revenue, as an incentive for national expansion, as a storehouse of natural resources, and as an outlet for western settlement by discontented groups from the more urban east (Hibbard 1965 [1924], 557). Another states flatly that prior to 1900, the questions of how to dispose of the public domain, and whether the federal government should finance "internal improvements" — a euphemism for roads, railroads, and water development projects — "ranked with the tariff as the foremost domestic political issues in the United States, other than slavery" (Smith 1971a, v). A leading environmental historian argues that U.S. economic wealth came not so much from the application of human labor to the environment, as conventional theory assumes, but rather from the ease with which *limited* labor could appropriate the vast abundance of natural value present in the landscape, which had been stored in the public lands by natural processes over millennia before the arrival of Europeans and their export trade economy (Cronon 1991, 148–51).

Even today, the two-century legacy of policies promoting the extraction and use of environmental resources for economic gain is a dominant force in American environmental policy. The logging and pulp and paper industries, the mining industry, and others still obtain much of their raw materials from the public lands. The aluminum industry obtains much of its energy, and California's huge farms their water, at cheap rates from federally financed dams. Ski resorts and other recreational businesses make their profits on inexpensively leased public lands, oil companies extract petroleum at low royalties from the public lands of Alaska and the outer continental shelf, and western cattle and sheep businesses graze their animals at costs far below those of their eastern competitors, who must pay for and maintain their own land. If this is the "rugged individualism" of free-market capitalism, it could just as accurately be described as individualism by government subsidy, socialism with a capitalist face. In reality the United States has always had an intricately mixed rather than a pure market economy, in which government policies promoting the extraction of marketable commodities from the environment have played a central role.

Many of the important issues of current American environmental policy arise from the continuing legacy of the public lands. In the Pacific Northwest, continued logging of public lands threatens to destroy the last 10 percent of the remaining old-growth forests, and with them fisheries, wildlife habitat, endangered species such as the northern spotted owl, and their ecosystems. Mining policies, largely unchanged since the 1870s, allow businesses to extract valuable minerals from public lands for a small fraction of their market values, and leave the resulting environmental damage for the taxpayers to clean up. Throughout the millions of acres of public lands, conflicts among uses and users dominate the agenda of American environmental policy: logging and mining companies versus tourists, ranchers versus wildlife lovers, motorcycle racers versus soil conservationists, resort developers and motorized visitors versus hikers and fishermen, and simply the congestion of *too many* users seeking to enjoy the most popular national parks and recreation areas (see e.g. Conniff 1994, 2–39).

The presence of the public lands therefore has been a central and distinctive element in the history of American environmental policy. Without them, the United States would not have had the vast stocks of natural resources that made possible today's widespread material affluence, nor the opportunities for prolonged open immigration and large-scale settlement that created a continental-scale society. The country would not have had today's national parks and forests, since no government could have afforded to purchase the quantities of such valuable lands that it was able simply to reserve and maintain in public ownership. Nor would so many distinctively American perceptions of the environment have developed, shaping both the country's policies and Americans' broader world view as a society: visions of superabundance of resources but also of desert wastelands, myths of pristine wilderness in the past and endless frontiers in the future, images of a "manifest destiny" to populate a continent and "develop" its resources, but also of a new Garden of Eden despoiled by human technology and pollution.[2]

Land Acquisition and Exploration

The federal government acquired the public lands first from the original thirteen states, and subsequently by treaties and purchases from other governments and from Native

Figure 2. Origins of the U.S. public lands. This map shows successive additions to the territory making up today's United States, with the dates of acquisition and the governments from which they were acquired. [U.S. Bureau of Land Management]

American tribes (fig. 2). Between 1780 and 1802, the original thirteen states ceded 541 million acres west of the Appalachian Mountains to the federal government as a condition of the original Articles of Confederation (Futrell 1993, 10). The Louisiana Purchase of 1803 added over 523 million acres, comprising the remainder of the Mississippi and Missouri River basins, an area nearly as large as all of Europe. A treaty with Spain in 1819 added Florida (43 million acres), and an 1846 treaty with England added 180 million acres of the Pacific Northwest, comprising the present states of Oregon, Washington, Idaho, and northwestern Montana. The vast area of California and most of today's Southwest, over 334 million acres, was captured from Mexico in 1848 in a treaty ending the Mexican War. Almost 79 million acres of today's New Mexico, Colorado, and adjacent states were purchased from Texas in 1850, after Texas declared itself independent from Mexico and was annexed to the United States; and the southern edge of Arizona, some 19 million acres permitting a railroad to be build around the southern end of the Rocky Mountains, was acquired from Mexico in the Gadsden Purchase of 1853. Finally, the 365 million acres of Alaska were purchased from Russia in 1867, as Russia retreated from its trans-Pacific colonial ambitions (Gates 1968, 75–86).

The government's motives for acquiring these lands varied with the times. The Louisiana Purchase, by far the largest land annexation, it had not even sought: U.S. envoys had been sent to France simply to buy the area around New Orleans as an ocean port for midwestern farmers, but found France willing to sell the entire claim. Later acquisitions, such as the Pacific Northwest and the Mexican lands, were more purposefully intended to benefit American settlers and fulfill America's "manifest destiny" to settle the continent from the Atlantic to the Pacific. Regardless of intent, the net effect was to bring under U.S. government ownership vast amounts of land and natural resources. These ranged from the humid wetlands of Florida and the lower Mississippi River to the woodlands and fertile prairies of the upper Midwest; from the arid plains and deserts of the intermountain basin and the gold and silver mines of California and Nevada to the coal fields of Montana and the oil deposits of Alaska; and from natural wonders such as Yellowstone's geysers and the Grand Canyon to unique ecosystems such as the old-growth forests of the Pacific Northwest and the Alaskan tundra.

The public lands were from the start a seedbed for scientific exploration and research as well as economic use. Government support for exploration began with the Lewis and Clark expedition through the Louisiana Purchase lands in 1803, and continued with over a hundred expeditions throughout the century. Early explorations were elements of a larger strategy to assert and document the expanding frontiers of the new nation, and to discover potential trade routes and resources (Ambrose 1996). Key figures included Dr. John Sibley (up the Red River, 1803), Zebulon Pike (southern Colorado, 1805–07), and Stephen Long (northern Colorado, 1819). Subsequent expeditions between 1845 and 1860 aimed more explicitly at the assessment of exploitable resources and engineering potential — the "Great Reconnaissance," in the words of one historian — opening the way for the "manifest destiny" policy of westward settlement. The expeditions of Captain John Fremont of the Corps of Topographical Engineers (1842–45) epitomized this era (Goetzmann 1993).

Finally, between the 1860s and the end of the nineteenth century the federal government sponsored a program of "Great Surveys," intensive scientific inventories of environmental conditions and assets by both military and civilian expeditions. Major explorations of this period included the army geological and geographical expeditions of Clarence King (1867–73) and Lt. George Wheeler (1869–78), the geological and land surveys conducted by the Interior Department under F. V. Hayden (1868–72), and the famous explorations of the Colorado River by Major John Wesley Powell between 1869 and 1873 (Goetzmann 1993).

President Thomas Jefferson and others expressed doubts about the constitutionality of federal support for purely scientific ventures, but justified these explorations in part by calling them incidental to military and diplomatic needs for knowledge of the newly acquired public lands, and to the federal government's responsibility for interstate commerce (Ambrose 1996). With repeated congressional budget allocations over time, constitutional doubts gradually became moot (Engelbert 1950, 157, 163). Many of these expeditions included civilian explorer-naturalists as well as engineers and military personnel: artist and ethnologist George Catlin, botanist John Torrey, paleontologist Othniel Marsh, and others. Over the course of the century they laid the foundations for much of U.S. scientific knowledge and public awareness: in geography, natural history, geology, botany, zoology, archaeology, paleontology, and the ethnography of American Indians in particular. The data and artifacts they brought back formed the basis for the collections of the Smithsonian Institution, and for later research by other federal agencies.

Despite occasional errors and misperceptions, the reports of these exploratory expeditions documented and thus promoted the economic opportunities presented by western environmental resources. They also promoted the growth of the applied sciences and technological invention developed for exploiting them, including scientific instrumentation; engineering, agricultural, mining, and transport technology; geology and metallurgy; and plant breeding.

No less important, they formed the basis for distinctive American beliefs about their country's environment: cornucopian beliefs about the superabundance of resource wealth, romantic images of the grandeur of the western landscape and the Edenesque nobility of its Indian peoples, and equally mythic images of the threats of the wilderness and of the barrenness and worthlessness of arid westward lands: a "Great American Desert" (Engelbert 1950, 163–73; Jones 1965, 366–74; Goetzmann 1993, 181–228; Krech 1994). Lewis and Clark, for instance, described an extraordinary number of species never before known to the American public, and brought back samples of some of them (Ambrose 1996). Explorers also saw wildlife in abundance never seen since: flocks of birds so numerous that they covered the sky and herds of bison that blackened the plains, said to be the largest herds of land mammals ever seen. The vision of such abundance was a powerful motivating force shaping American patterns of environmental development and use.

From the exploratory expeditions also arose the first government scientific agencies, charged with surveying and mapping the American environment, particularly those features that had potential military or economic value. A Coast Survey office was created in the Treasury Department in 1807, and made important contributions to understanding of U.S. geography and resources. Army engineers began conducting topographic surveys after the War of 1812, and feasibility surveys for river and harbor navigation improvements beginning in 1824. A separate U.S. Corps of Topographical Engineers from 1818 to 1863 produced much of the basic information about the country's geology, topography, and river basins (Engelbert 1950, 204–08, 214–19, 299). The General Land Office oversaw surveying to prepare public lands for sale, and later to identify routes for the transcontinental railroads. It also sponsored more specialized investigations to identify mineral deposits and other natural resources, and lands to be reserved for Indian tribes and other purposes.

Beginning in the 1830s many of the states also sponsored surveys of their own natural assets, focusing especially on agricultural and mineral resources but often including more systematic environmental assessments as well (Engelbert 1950, 296–311). However, these were often opportunistic and specialized ad hoc surveys, resulting in both errors and serious gaps in knowledge that hampered the development of systematic knowledge and well-informed environmental policies (Gates 1968, 420–22). In 1879, therefore, Congress established the U.S. Geological Survey (USGS) to unify, institutionalize, and professionalize government scientific surveying of the American West. The USGS in turn established the systematic scientific foundations — topographic mapping, resource inventories, hydrographic and irrigation potential surveys, and other procedures — for a far more active federal role in later environmental management.

Whose Environment? Native Americans Versus Settlers

Acquisitions from Mexico and European governments settled U.S. government owner-ship from those countries' perspectives, but they did not resolve the fact that these lands were already occupied and used by tribes of Native American peoples who had lived there for centuries. One of the most inglorious threads in the fabric of American history is the process by which waves of European settlers, backed by public policies favoring and legitimizing them — open immigration, military protection, treaties, incentives for west-ward settlement, and outright removal of indigenous tribes — relentlessly displaced the Native American peoples onto tiny plots of the least productive land, which became known as Indian reservations.

Conflicts between settlers and Indians arose as early as the colonial period, as westward settlers claimed and cleared land in the name of self-interest and "progress," encouraged by publicists trumpeting the spread of civilization and Christianity (Nash 1982 [1967], 35–43). Tensions intensified in the nineteenth century, as open immigration and railroad construction brought ever more settlers pushing westward, in disregard of Indians' tradi-tional occupancy and use rights and even of official policies and treaties with them. As settler populations and their military and economic dominance increased, treaties initially concluded as between equal sovereign nations were replaced by increasingly unfavorable terms, and ultimately, in 1871, by an end to treaty-making altogether.

Officially, public lands could only be settled after native claims to them had been resolved. In practice, however, such resolutions generally involved conflict between In-dians and settlers, misunderstandings or misrepresentations of the transactions, or out-right military duress. The U.S. treaty with Britain in 1783, for instance, required compen-sation of the Indians for their land rights, but subsequent treaties of 1784 and 1785 with the six Indian nations of the Great Lakes region included no such compensation. Later treaties also included a wide range of abuses, such as treaty provisions breaking up tribal lands into individual allotments — with portions often given as side payments to chiefs — which then passed rapidly into the hands of non-Indian speculators (Gates 1968, 452).

The reality was that settlement proceeded far ahead of official policies and agreements, and that public policies toward Indian rights therefore developed in reaction to conflicts between settlers and Indians. Politicians as early as Thomas Jefferson saw the vast lands of the Louisiana Purchase as a safety valve that could help defuse these conflicts, a territory so far from current settlement that Indians could safely be offered permanent ownership of lands there in exchange for those already under settlement pressure in the East (Meinig 1993, 78–79; Ambrose 1996, 124). Jefferson was hypocritical in this, however, inasmuch as he also promoted exploration and active development of non-Indian trade westward into these lands, trade that would inevitably be the forerunner of settlement pressures (Ambrose 1996, 336–37, 387, 398).[3] Some tribes reportedly agreed to such exchanges voluntarily, whatever that may have meant. In 1830, however, after an influx of gold

seekers overran the Cherokee lands in western Georgia and the federal government declined to defend the Indians against them, President Andrew Jackson and Congress imposed a forcible and unilateral solution. The Indian Removal Act allowed the president to
reserve public lands (hence "reservations") for Indian tribes in the West, to give them
permanent title to those lands, and to use military force to compel them to move from
Georgia and Tennessee to what is now Oklahoma—the infamous "Trail of Tears."[4]

Removal may have seemed to non-Indian politicians a pragmatic compromise between
the humanitarian instincts of those who imagined "civilizing" the Indians into agrarian
freeholders, and the more avaricious land hunger of others (Meinig 1993, 78–79). It
inflicted both injustice and suffering on the Indians, however, both those who were
moved and those already present on the lands to which others were displaced. Moreover,
its promise lasted less than twenty years before gold was discovered in California, and the
resulting pressures for transcontinental railroads rekindled pressures for white settlement
further westward. In the Kansas-Nebraska Act of 1854, the government abrogated its
agreement with the tribes, reopening to non-Indian settlement large areas of the territories that had been pledged to the Indians (Gates 1968, 369–70).

The railroad syndicates accordingly found themselves in constant conflict with the
Indians, as they sought to claim and sell lands previously guaranteed to the tribes but
subsequently granted to the railroads as a means of financing construction. The railroads
had an inherent economic incentive to increase traffic throughout their lines, which meant
vigorously promoting non-Indian settlement, tourism, and trade in timber, minerals,
cattle, and other commodities throughout the western lands. They also sponsored large-
scale slaughter of the plains bison herds, as a source of food for their workers, of sport for
tourists, of buffalo hides as a commercial product, and as a deliberate means of driving the
Indians away from their lines by destroying their subsistence. Well over four million bison
were destroyed in the southern plains alone within just four years of the coming of the
railroads and the emergence of a market in tannable hides (Cronon 1991, 213–18).

Treaty-making with the Native American tribes was ended in 1871, reportedly due to
increasingly abusive uses of it to arrange deals favorable to speculators outside the normal
framework of public land laws. Native Americans were not given American citizenship
and voting rights until 1924, however. In 1887, in another wishful compromise between
humanitarian reformers and land-hungry settlers and speculators, the Dawes Act broke up
many of the reservations into individual allotments—leaving the remainder of the tribes'
common lands too small to sustain the Indians' traditional common-use practices—and
opened much of the rest to non-Indian homesteading and preemption. Most of the Indian
allotments were eventually sold to non-Indians as well. In 1862 the Indian reservations
included 175 million acres, and in 1887 about 138 million; by 1935 the total had declined
to only 52 million acres (Gates 1968, 453–54).

The legacy of Indian displacement remains important in policies today. Native American water rights associated with the remaining reservations are an important factor in the
western water economy. Native American fishing rights in the Pacific Northwest and land
claims in Maine have both been subjects of recent litigation, and indigenous peoples'
claims to the vast resources of Alaska were the subject of major legislation as recently as

1979. Native American resources and policies are also important elements of American environmental policies more directly. Coal burned in power plants that are damaging the visibility of the Grand Canyon comes from mines on the Navajo reservation in Arizona, and native hunting with modern technologies in Alaska, if not effectively managed, may destroy endangered species just as effectively as poaching by others.

The displacement of localized tribal economies by a globally oriented market economy in nineteenth-century America has close parallels in many of the most important conflicts in global environmental policy today, in which central governments impose new property regimes on environments that have previously supported indigenous peoples using them at lower and more sustainable rates (Bromley 1992). An obvious example is the Amazon Basin, where the Brazilian government has promoted westward settlement into rain-forest lands occupied and used sustainably by indigenous peoples, as a safety valve against job-lessness and land-reform demands in more settled areas. Should one accept the claim that they are entitled to go through the same historical process that made the United States a world economic power? Or should one argue that they should pursue more restrained policies — and by implication, that Americans should likewise have done so? Similar cases can be identified throughout the world, from the tropics of Africa and southeast Asia to the autonomous regions and indigenous peoples of Siberia.

Economic Context

Five powerful economic and social forces shaped U.S. public land policies of the nine-teenth century, and were shaped in turn by public policies. One force was the new U.S. government's need to raise revenue to pay its Revolutionary War debts and assure its own future viability. A related political force was the new nation's imperative to secure its position in a world of powerful European empires, an imperative which drove broad policy visions such as "manifest destiny" — settling the continent westward to the Pacific Ocean — and the Monroe Doctrine, which called for ending the role of European empires in the Western Hemisphere.

A third force was European economic conditions. European hatmakers and weavers and their customers created a demand for American furs and cotton crops. Repeal of the English "Corn Laws" in the 1840s created incentives for large-scale American "bonanza farming" in the Midwest. Irish potato famines and European warfare drove generations of immigrants to seek new opportunities in America, and favorable interest rates and specula-tive opportunities lured European investment capital to commercial ventures in the Amer-ican West. A fourth force was the continuous westward extension of transportation net-works — roads, river channels and steamboats, and especially canals and railroads — which opened more and more of the continent to commodity production for urban and export markets. These networks were capitalized both by private investors and by vast public land subsidies.

Finally, a fifth force was the massive and continuous westward movement of a grow-ing settler population — a "mass-driven force of special character and power, a *demo-cratic imperialism*" (Meinig 1993, 193) — which appeared to be beyond the power of any government policy to guide or control. It was fueled and abetted by policies of unlimited immigration, which continued until the twentieth century, and by subsidized development of transportation infrastructure. Underneath these policies, however, lay the widespread popular desire for land ownership, and the equally widespread vision of economic opportunities in the West: trapping beaver for European hatmakers, growing food for eastern markets, growing cotton for export, and later, making quick fortunes in the gold and silver rushes and providing the materials and services demanded by the processes of settlement and railroad construction.

The result was a series of "frontiers" moving ever westward, each defined by a particular set of opportunities to convert environmental conditions into economic commodities. First came the trappers' frontier, from the colonial period through the early nineteenth century, involving the trading of manufactured goods to the Indians for furs to ship to England. Then came the loggers' and agrarian settlers' frontiers, the latter peaking with the settlement of the fertile Midwest and the agricultural boom of the 1840s, the former continuing to develop to supply the railroads and settlements across the treeless prairies, then booming again in the Pacific forests. Then came the miners' frontier, beginning with the 1848 California gold rush and moving back eastward into Nevada and the intermountain basin with successive mineral strikes. Finally came the grazing frontier, as the transcontinental rail lines of the 1860s opened opportunities to raise cattle on the western public lands yet still ship them to eastern markets, and the frontier of dry-land farming and irrigated agriculture in the arid West.

The boom periods of these frontiers were each followed by intensified conflicts among competing claimants, peaking in the late nineteenth century: settlers and railroads versus Indians, farmers versus ranchers, settlers versus speculators and railroads. These conflicts echo today in environmental policy conflicts between loggers and miners and environmentalists, between local communities and big corporations and distant governments, and between Native Americans and non-Indians still.

The Civil War marked a turning point in these processes. Southern secession from the Union, combined with the economic and political imperatives of the war and its aftermath, opened the way for policies explicitly favoring western homesteading, transcontinental railroad construction, and large-scale resource extraction and industrialization. The transcontinental railroads, driven by their economic imperative to increase traffic on their lines, were themselves perhaps the most powerful force luring settlement and resource extraction enterprises out across the arid Indian lands of the western territories.

During the "Age of Enterprise" or "Gilded Age" that followed, the United States shifted fundamentally from a predominantly agrarian to a predominantly urban and industrial society, a shift involving extraction of natural resources from the environment on an unprecedented scale. This process produced great economic wealth, but also severe environmental costs and intensified social conflict between small holders and large landowners and business corporations, among conflicting resource claimants and users, and between westerners and distant eastern governments and banks (Gates 1968, 440). These forces drove public policies, and were in turn further encouraged, legitimized, and amplified by them.

Land Disposal Policy

From its earliest land ordinances through the nineteenth century, American government policies promoted the rapid transfer of vast areas of public lands into private ownership, both to generate short-term revenues and to promote settlement and economic activity. There was intense debate about how this should be done, and for whose benefit, but the basic policy of privatization — land "disposal" — was clear. There was no expectation that the government itself would take responsibility for management of these lands. By the 1820s the government had already sold off over nineteen million acres, eleven new states had been added to the union, and the western settler population had more than tripled.

Implicit in this policy was a continuing tension among conflicting visions as to what pattern of economic development should be encouraged. In the aftermath of the War of American Independence, an increasingly widespread political philosophy was republicanism, which honored frugality and simplicity and advocated an agrarian economy and society in place of the aristocratic class structure of the British model (Jones 1965, 327; McCoy 1980, 62–63, 69). Nine out of ten Americans lived on farms at the time, and most influential writers — John Adams, for instance, and even Adam Smith in *The Wealth of Nations* — believed that America's apparent natural advantages lay in farming rather than manufacturing. Thomas Jefferson in the 1780s advocated an economy based on small family farms, arguing that even if these were less productive than large-scale agriculture or industry, they were more likely to produce a virtuous civic culture than would the "dependence, subservience and venality" which he associated with urban factories (Nettels 1962, 127).

Jefferson's ideal society was one of self-sufficient, land-owning farmers and communities, in harmony with the natural landscape in which they lived, whose desires were limited to their needs and who thus avoided dependence on the forces of markets, trade, and the factory production system (Gates 1968, 62; Marx 1964, 116–44, 147–48).[5] His constituency was primarily the debtor farmers and development advocates of the growing West (Nettels 1962, 127).

Treasury Secretary Alexander Hamilton and other nationalists, in contrast, advocated active government promotion of manufacturing. Led by President George Washington, the *nationalists* argued that the most fundamental necessity for the survival of the new nation was economic self-sufficiency, which in their view required government support for manufacturing, inland navigation, and development of domestic markets (Nettels 1962, 92, 104–05). Hamilton argued that the U.S. economy was too vulnerable to foreign restrictions on trade, and that a mixed economy would be both more stable and more prosperous than a purely agricultural one. He also advocated government subsidies for U.S. manufacturing enterprises, to help them compete against foreign businesses that were supported by their own governments. In his 1791 *Report on Manufactures,* the "charter of American industrialism," Hamilton advocated systematically exploiting the continent's abundant natural resources for economic use, and creating strong market ties and division of labor between farmers and manufacturers (Nettels 1962, 106–08; McCoy

1980, 148–50). Others also argued that mechanized manufacturing using water and steam power was separable from the evils of factory labor, and in fact was ideally suited to the abundance of resources and scarcity of labor that then characterized America. Machines rather than laborers would do most of the work, and the "clear air and powerful sun of America" would give its producers a natural environmental advantage over their European rivals (Marx 1964, 158).

These competing visions had direct implications for land policy. Jefferson advocated distributing public lands directly to settlers, in small parcels at nominal prices. Hamilton, in contrast, advocated selling public lands, primarily in large blocks, to "moneyed individuals and companies, who will buy to sell again, and associations of persons, who intend to make settlements themselves." His rationale was that rapid privatization and the greater resulting revenues were more attractive than the nation of farmers envisioned by Jefferson (Hamilton, *Report on Land Disposal Plan,* 1790, *Report on the Subject of Manufactures,* 1791, in Lowrie and Clarke 1832; Engelbert 1950, 115–16; Elkins and McKitrick 1993, 258–63; Marx 1964, 150–69). The tension between Jefferson's and Hamilton's views — and more generally, the tension between agrarian and urban/industrial aspirations for America's future — underlay many of the debates over land policy throughout the nineteenth century.

The Land Ordinance of 1785 and the Land Act of 1796 were the first laws to establish the terms on which public lands were to be sold. Key provisions established a uniform system of survey of public lands before they were sold; terms of minimum size, price, and method of sale; and reservation of some lands and resources for public purposes. These were the first of literally hundreds of federal land laws passed over the following century, and they exemplified many of the issues that were debated in public land policy over that period and beyond.

One issue was whether claimants should be able to obtain land wherever they liked, or whether government should control and shape the westward spread of development. In the southern states settlers had been allowed to choose their own lands, marking the boundaries of their claims by identifiable landmarks and natural features. This traditional system ("metes and bounds") was well suited to the realities of human behavior on the frontier, but it resulted in a patchwork ownership pattern in which boundaries were difficult to identify, and many conflicting claims resulted (Meinig 1986, 239–44). It also allowed speculators to quickly capture the most valuable lands, such as river crossings and lands with valuable resource endowments, leaving only poorer ones for later sale.

In New England, in contrast, lands were surveyed and laid out in rectangular plots as settlements, usually six to eight miles square (Harris 1953, 279). The New England system had the advantage of clear and systematic boundaries, compact and orderly development patterns, and easy record keeping to prevent claim disputes. Both northern and southern congressmen agreed, therefore, that the 1785 ordinance should incorporate this system (Onuf 1987, 21). Its legacy is visible in any aerial view of the Midwest: the entire region is laid out in townships six miles square, each divided into thirty-six sections of 640 acres each (fig. 3). Four of the sections in each township were reserved for government purposes, and one for public schools.

Once established, this system provided clear property boundaries and thus reduced conflict over them, but the process of establishing it was far slower than the actual pace of human settlement. A steady stream of settlers moved west far ahead of the survey and sale process, supporting themselves by the practical opportunities to extract or grow commodities for sale rather than by legal rights of ownership. The result was constant and growing conflict between "squatters" who claimed land by occupancy and labor, and later buyers who claimed it by legal right of purchase.

Another complication was that, not surprisingly, settlement grew most rapidly along rivers and other transport routes rather than homogeneously across a rectilinear landscape. The survey, however, imposed an arbitrary grid of ownership and jurisdiction cutting across streams and other features of the natural landscape. This effect was not recognized as a problem until a century later, when settlement spread to the arid plains where natural features such as scarce water supplies necessitated larger-scale and different land use patterns.

A second and more fundamental issue was, what should be the goal of land disposal policy? Should it be to maximize government revenues? The government owed millions of dollars in war debts, yet had no major sources of revenue with which to pay them other than to sell the public lands or to give them as payment for its obligations (to soldiers, for instance). Or should the goal be to capitalize economic development? The economy in 1785 was deeply depressed, and land sales to investors might attract needed currency from Europe to finance capital investments in economic development. Or should the goal be to increase the self-sufficiency of settlers? Farm exports paid the nation's bills, but individual farmers were chronically in debt; frontier settlement would provide new sources of raw materials and new home markets for the country's manufactured goods. And did the society not owe some reward to the settlers who endured the hardships of frontier life to produce the raw materials, defend and expand its borders, and break the way for others?

The answers to these questions were reflected in the terms of sale by which land was privatized. Low prices favored rapid settlement and benefited the individual settlers; higher prices increased revenues per acre, but slowed the pace and favored wealthier investors. Easy credit favored rapid sale (though not necessarily rapid settlement), but also encouraged land speculation; tighter credit kept development slower but reduced speculation. Auction sales in major cities speeded the sale process and increased government revenues from especially valuable lands, but favored large-scale investors and speculators over settlers. Preemption rights — the right of a prior settler to buy the land without auction competition at the minimum price — brought lower revenues and required greater administrative costs to government, but favored actual settlers (though fraudulent claims were a continuing problem). Finally, small minimum purchase sizes sold through field offices in the territory favored the actual settlers, while larger minimum sizes sold in the capital or other eastern cities favored the land companies, which would then subdivide and retail them to individuals.

The first land laws, in 1785 and 1796, were aimed mainly at using land to raise revenues to retire the public debt, and to that end creating a national market in western lands (Onuf 1987, 40–42). The 1785 ordinance mandated the clearing of Indian rights by purchase, the surveying of all public lands, and the reserving of some lands for government use, schools,

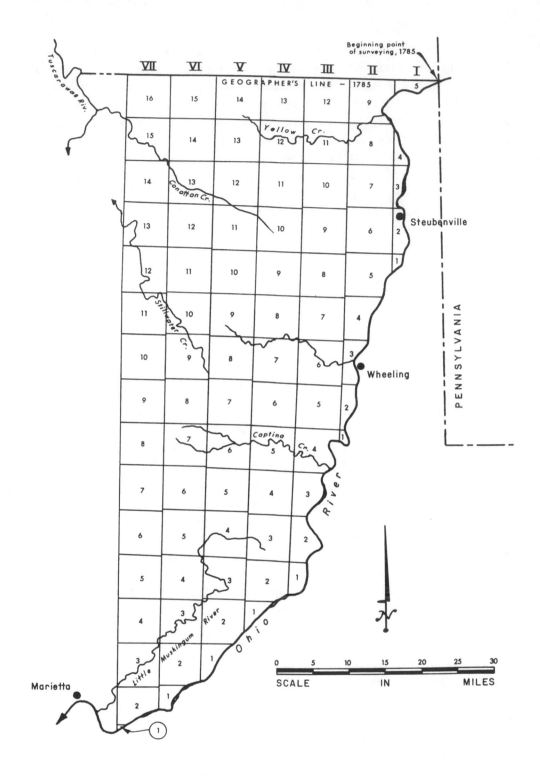

VII VI V IV III II I

Beginning point
of surveying, 1785

GEOGRAPHER'S LINE — 1785

Tuscarawas Riv.

Conotton Cr.

Stillwater Cr.

Yellow Cr.

Captina Cr.

Little Muskingum River

Ohio River

Steubenville

Wheeling

Marietta

PENNSYLVANIA

0   5   10   15   20   25   30
SCALE   IN   MILES

Figure 3a–c. These images show the rectilinear land survey system and its consequences. The map on the left illustrates the initial application of the rectilinear survey system for public land disposal, which was incorporated into the Land Ordinance of 1785 on the recommendation of Thomas Jefferson. The base point for the system is the place where the Ohio River crosses from Pennsylvania into Ohio. The diagram on the right shows each township composed of thirty-six mile-square sections, one of which was reserved for public schools. [U.S. Bureau of Land Management. The aerial photo below shows farmland in the Red River Valley, North Dakota, illustrating the translation of the Jeffersonian survey grid into agricultural reality. © Land Slides. Alex S. MacLean]

LAND ORDINANCE – 1785

36	30	24	18	12	6
35	29 Reserved to Religion	23	17	11 Reserved to U.S.	5
34	28	22	16 School Reserve	10	4
33	27	21	15	9	3
32	26 Reserved to U.S.	20	14	8 Reserved to U.S.	2
31	25	19	13	7	1

and military bounty claims. The remaining lands would then be sold at auction at a minimum price of one dollar per acre. Every other township would be sold in minimum lots of 640 acres (sections), the others as whole townships. No provision was made for terms of credit, nor for preemption rights of prior settlers, and the land was to be sold at offices in eastern cities rather than on the frontier in hopes of neutralizing the advantage of local squatters and speculators (Onuf 1987, 40–41).

The 1796 act reaffirmed the rectilinear survey system and the practice of selling land blocks in large units (quarter-townships of 5,120 acres, alternating with 640-acre sections). The land was to be sold at auction at a minimum price of two dollars per acre, with 5 percent cash required and credit for the remainder over one year. Few individual settlers could afford to purchase 640 acres, so this law favored land companies and investors. In addition, it set no maximum acreage that could be purchased, nor did it require actual settlement or improvements of the land as a condition of ownership (Gates 1968, 125). In reality neither of these laws led to any general rush to purchase land, but they did establish the precedents from which the later framework of public domain land sales developed.

The Northwest Ordinance of 1787 established principles of governance for the newly settled territories, and for dividing them eventually into coequal, self-governing states. It also established fundamental precedents of American land tenure policy. Individuals had full rights to own and transfer land as they saw fit, free of government intervention, and their property rights were guaranteed to descend to their families rather than revert to the state. No one would be deprived of property "except that public exigency made it necessary, and then only upon full compensation for the same" (Harris 1953, 392). Finally, state governments were forbidden to interfere with the privatization of federal lands or with any federal regulations established to secure clear title to their purchasers, nor were they permitted to tax lands that were the property of the United States. Federal lands thus did not automatically pass into state government ownership when states were created.

From these initial laws up through the General Land Law Revision Act of 1891, public land disposal policies became progressively more favorable to the interests of agrarian settlers. Cloaked in the rhetoric of Jeffersonian republican ideals, major land reform laws — the Harrison Frontier Land Act of 1800, the Preemption Acts (1830–41), the Homestead Act of 1862, and others — were aimed not at conservation or wise management of land and its environmental assets, but simply at promoting the interests of small-scale agrarian landowners over the interests of larger land companies and investors. The Harrison Frontier Land Act of 1800, for instance, extended credit to four years, and an 1804 law extended credit to six years, abolished interest payments on the balance not yet paid, reduced the minimum purchase size to a quarter-section (160 acres), and opened additional field offices in the areas being opened for sale. Land sales increased immediately, and surged with the economic boom after the War of 1812. In 1819, however, the boom collapsed in a financial panic, as overexpansion of agricultural production drove down prices and both speculators and banks collapsed under the accumulated debt created by credit-based western land purchases. The subsequent Land Act of 1820 reduced minimum land prices to $1.25 per acre, but required full cash payment rather than credit for all future land sales.

This cycle recurred in the 1830s, as an influx of eastern and foreign investors, attracted both by general prosperity and by the widespread extension of roads, canals, and railroads into the West, fueled another speculative boom in western lands, this time using paper money backed by state banks. Once again widespread speculative land purchases bid up the level of debt, until in 1836 President Jackson issued an order (the "Specie Circular") halting the process by requiring hard cash rather than paper currency as payment, and the resulting financial panics of 1837 and 1839 again collapsed inflated land markets (Gates 1968, 121–76).

A series of laws beginning in the 1830s promoted the privatization of land in other ways, on increasingly easy terms. Both settlers and speculators had developed collusive bidding practices such as "claims associations" to subvert the auction system, thereby avoiding higher payments for the true market values of resource-rich lands or for those that settlers had already developed. Speculators also used paid "entrymen" to pose as settlers, thereby evading sales restrictions intended to limit purchase sizes and thus favor actual settlers. The Preemption Acts, temporary in the 1830s but made permanent in 1841, essentially replaced the auction sale system by allowing settlers to purchase land at the minimum price without auction (to "preempt" it). The effect was to open up virtually the entire public domain to entry and staking of claims. The 1854 Graduation Act promoted even cheaper land sales by "graduating" the price downward for public lands left unsold (to a dollar per acre after ten years, and as little as twelve and one-half cents per acre after thirty years). The rationale was that these unsold lands had to be worth less than others, though in fact many valuable lands had merely been bypassed in the speed of the westward land rush and in the periodic speculative collapses that had punctuated it. The law's result was rapid and cheap privatization of the remaining public lands throughout the Midwest (Gates 1968, 182–96).

Finally, in 1862 the Homestead Act offered virtually free public land to actual settlers: 160 acres for $26 with a promise of five years' residency, or outright purchase at $1.25 per acre after six months, with a right to sell it to someone else so long as the government was paid its due. The real impact of the Homestead Act was actually far greater in the twentieth century than at the time: through the end of the nineteenth century only one to four million acres per year were homesteaded, while from 1908 through 1922 the total was seven to ten million acres per year. As a symbol, however, it represented the final victory of Jeffersonian land disposal policy. Agrarian settlers had finally triumphed, it seemed, over the land companies, the westward spread of slave-based cotton plantations, and other economic interests.

None of these laws, however, not even the Homestead Act, systematically reformed or replaced the land sales system itself, nor its speculative character. Each in turn claimed to promote the Jeffersonian vision of smallholding agrarian settlement. Each in fact, however, and others to follow in the 1870s, merely added one more legal mechanism to an incongruous patchwork of laws under which claimants could appropriate additional quantities of public lands at lower and lower cost. None took any significant account of differences in land characteristics—in forest and grass cover, mineral deposits, slopes and drainage, rainfall and fertility, even location and proximity to water or rail or road transport—that affected a property's environmental and economic values. Claiming to be an agrarian settler, for instance, one could make claims for each family member under each of these laws, cumulatively controlling far more land than the national policies of agrarian smallholding in principle allowed.[6] Or one could simply enter and claim forested lands, strip and sell the trees for more than the cost of the initial payment, and sell the remaining land or simply move on and repeat the process.

The reality was that rather than guiding settlement, each of these policies merely accommodated and legitimized the massive expansion of ad hoc settlement and land-grab practices that preceded it (Meinig 1993, 243–45). Ironically, by the time the Homestead Act was passed most of the best land for agrarian settlement — in the humid Midwest, east of the one hundredth meridian — had already been claimed anyway. Most of what remained was in the arid West, where the real resource values of land lay in timber, minerals, and cattle and sheep grazing rather than agrarian settlement. In the western plains, 160-acre plots simply were not viable for agriculture anyway, until irrigation projects — subsidized by federal investments — provided water to them.

Subsidies for Environmental "Improvements"

The public lands were only valuable for economic purposes to the extent that they were accessible, both for initial settlement and especially for moving crops and other commodities to eastern and European markets. Along with land sales, therefore, the U.S. government provided immense subsidies for construction of transportation infrastructure — "internal improvements," as they were called — including river and harbor clearing, roads, canals, and railroads. These subsidies were key determinants of both the patterns and extent of environmental transformation that occurred, and of the speed at which both internal markets and export trade developed. Seen in retrospect, they also set precedents for later subsidies for projects to transform the environment for other purposes, such as multipurpose dams and reservoirs, interstate highways, sewers, and wastewater treatment plants. Many of the defining environmental policy conflicts of the twentieth century centered on such subsidies: for the Hetch Hetchy Dam near Yosemite in 1913, the proposed Echo Park Dam in the 1950s, and many of the water resource and interstate highway construction projects planned in the 1960s and '70s.

The federal government financed transportation infrastructure in three ways. One was through public investments of general revenues allocated in the government budget. As early as 1789, for instance, the government financed construction of a lighthouse near the entrance to Chesapeake Bay, and in 1802 it spent $34,000 to construct public piers on the Delaware River (Smith 1966, 3). In 1806, when the treasury was running a substantial surplus, President Jefferson advocated spending this on "roads, rivers, canals, and other objects of public improvement" rather than reducing taxes (Nettels 1962, 340). In 1824 Congress passed the first of many Rivers and Harbors Acts, which allocated funds to the Army Corps of Engineers for construction projects to make rivers and harbors more navigable.

In 1808, Secretary of the Treasury Albert Gallatin wrote a report to the Senate suggesting the possibility of an extensive system of roads and canals to promote trade, both up and down the East Coast (via an intercoastal waterway) and between the East Coast rivers and those flowing into the Great Lakes (Meinig 1993, 311–16). The report argued that only the federal government had the means and the perspective to carry out such large interstate projects. Spurred by the logistic crises of the War of 1812, Secretary of War John Calhoun wrote a similar report in 1818, sketching a systematic national plan for roads, canals, and river navigation improvements to benefit both commerce and military security. Neither report was implemented, however, due to constitutional objections against such large-scale federal investments and the centralization of political and economic power that they implied (Meinig 1993, 349–52).

Meanwhile, between 1817 and 1825 the State of New York financed construction of the Erie Canal on its own, and the phenomenal commercial success of this project — it reduced freight costs between New York and the Great Lakes by 85 percent, and shipping time from thirty to eight days — spurred political pressures for federal support of similar ventures throughout the Great Lakes states. In 1820 Congress authorized the Army Corps of Engineers to begin conducting surveys of the feasibility of river navigation projects, dodging the constitutional issues by claiming that they were merely gathering essential information, like the exploratory expeditions that the government was already financing in the West. Constitutional objections were mooted in 1824 by the Supreme Court's landmark decision in *Gibbons v. Ogden,* which established federal authority over all navigable rivers as a matter of interstate commerce (Armstrong et al. 1976, 30). With a supportive president elected that year (John Quincy Adams), the federal government began funding river improvement projects for navigation.

Sadly, however, the Calhoun Report was the nearest approximation to a systematic plan of action that the Army Corps of Engineers ever had. From the 1824 Rivers and Harbors Act to the present, the Corps's appropriations have reflected not a comprehensive program but a patchwork of specific local projects advocated by particular congressional representatives. Since settlement and natural resource extraction activities tended to follow these lines of transport, moreover, they too developed in a similarly patchwork pattern.[7]

The second method for financing transportation infrastructure was to use revenues from the sales of public lands. Five percent of these revenues were earmarked to benefit the states in which the public lands were sold; 2 percent was specifically to be used by the federal government to build roads and other internal improvements in support of land sales and settlement. In 1802, for instance, Congress authorized construction of a "national road" from Cumberland, Maryland, to the Ohio River, and appropriated $30,000 for it from land revenues (Meinig 1993, 339). The national road was a special case, however, for while the states subsequently used these earmarked revenues extensively for road construction, the federal government did not provide further direct support for roads until it established the federal highway system in 1916.

The third strategy was to give actual grants of public lands, first for the rights-of-way for transportation routes, and eventually for investment and financing purposes as well. Over the course of the nineteenth century the federal government donated nearly 3.4

million acres to the states for roads, 13.9 million acres for canals and other improvements, and 37 million acres for railroads. Between 1858 and 1871 it also granted over 94 million acres directly to the railroad companies (Gates 1968, 384–85).

The federal government had donated rights-of-way to the states for road construction since as early as 1808, and from 1822 on it began doing the same for canals. Beginning in 1827 it took a major step further, granting additional lands to be sold to investors to finance construction as well. Most of these grants were made to the Great Lakes states, to connect their interior lands with the transportation route opened up by the Erie Canal. Advocates argued that since transportation access would greatly increase adjacent property values it would be a prudent public investment — and a way to bypass constitutional objections — to finance canals by giving sections of land to the construction companies to sell to investors at a profit. The federal government could then recapture the same total revenue by selling the remaining sections at twice the normal minimum price. This was what advocates today would call a "win-win strategy," by which everyone would benefit. State and local governments would gain increased revenues by getting these lands onto the tax rolls, and the whole economy would benefit from the resulting growth of production and trade.[8]

The grants therefore donated alternate 640-acre sections on either side within five miles of the route, throughout the length of the canal. Later grants, beginning in 1838, specified that the remaining lands be priced at double the usual minimum price. Since some of these lands might already be occupied by prior claimants, the canal companies were also given the right to claim additional lands six to fifteen miles further away (in lieu of those already claimed, or "lieu lands"). This policy allowed them to claim many of the best lands and to hold large areas off the market while they made their selections. In addition, claimants who had to be moved for construction were given scrip allowing them to claim lands elsewhere.

The canal grants became precedents for similar grants to states to finance railroad construction, which began with a grant to Illinois in 1850 for the Illinois Central Railroad. The California gold rush in 1848, and subsequent settlement of the West Coast, intensified pressures for transcontinental rail lines across territories where there were yet no states, and indeed which had previously been reserved in perpetuity to the Native American tribes. It was in response to these pressures that between 1862 and 1871 the federal government granted over ninety-four million acres directly to railroad companies (fig. 4). Initial grants typically gave the railroads a right-of-way plus ten alternate sections per mile, plus the right to take timber and stone from the public lands, as well as thirty-year government loans. Later grants gave them twenty sections per mile, and let the railroads select lieu lands virtually anywhere they wished. This concession allowed them, like the canal companies, to hold large areas of prime land off the market for years — blocking settlers' claims, and also delaying paying taxes on them — while they made their selections. Such practices allowed the railroads to gain control of large amounts of the most valuable lands. Along with monopolistic railroad pricing practices, they caused intense conflict between settlers and the railroads, ultimately producing the Grange movement of farmers demanding government regulation of railroad rates (Gates 1968, 356–81).[9]

The transportation grants were among the most powerful government policy incen-

FEDERAL LAND GRANTS FOR RAILROADS

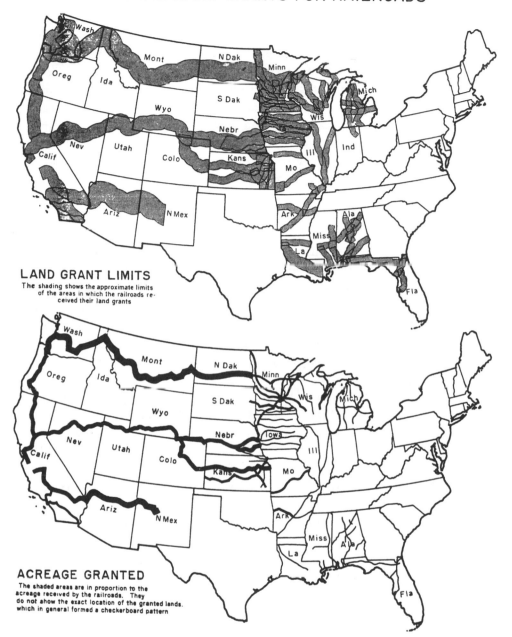

LAND GRANT LIMITS
The shading shows the approximate limits
of the areas in which the railroads received their land grants

ACREAGE GRANTED
The shaded areas are in proportion to the
acreage received by the railroads. They
do not show the exact location of the granted lands,
which in general formed a checkerboard pattern

Figure 4. Railroad land grants. These two maps show the vast areas within which private railroad syndicates were offered the opportunity to claim federal lands as incentives for the construction of rail lines, and
the approximate amounts they actually received. They were allowed to claim one-half the total area along
their routes (alternate sections), or the equivalent in a secondary area farther away in lieu of lands in the primary area that were already claimed by others. The gray shading indicates land grant limits; the black shading indicates the acreage granted. [U.S. Bureau of Land Management]

tives to promote immigration, settlement, and economic exploitation of the continent's environmental assets. The railroads had overwhelming incentives to attract both investors and users of their services, in order both to pay for construction and to generate traffic. They advertised vigorously for them both in the eastern United States and in Europe. The railroads thus became the most active and effective promoters of westward settlement, luring both settlers and investors far beyond the previous areas of settlement and promoting commodity use and tourism as well as further displacement of the indigenous peoples. Statesmen of the early nineteenth century had blithely predicted that settlement of the West would take centuries, yet by 1890 the superintendent of the census would declare that the unsettled frontier no longer existed.

Summary

The public lands were the central issue for national environmental policy in nineteenth-century America. The core of that policy was a strategic goal of asserting national authority over the entire North American continent except for Canada, of securing it by exploring and settling it, and of exploiting its abundant natural assets to build a national economy that could survive and thrive amid powerful European empires. It was implemented both by presidential exhortation and by specific government incentives such as land sales on increasingly easy terms, public expenditures, and outright grants of land for investment in transportation infrastructure and other facilities.

There was little or no concern for conservation or environmental protection in this policy. Indeed, land policy "reform" in this period meant making land virtually free for claiming by settlers, and most politicians were more concerned with the "waste" of land left undeveloped than with the widespread waste of its fertility and resources caused by the development process. It was nonetheless a deliberate national policy, driven by explicit goals and principles and promoted by government policy incentives. It did produce some remarkably effective policy innovations for its purpose, such as the sale of alternate sections along canals and railroad corridors to stimulate investment in them while simultaneously benefiting the treasury with rising land values. But its purpose was to privatize land for rapid economic development.

The thought that such a seemingly vast continent might anytime soon be fully settled or such abundant resources depleted, or that these possibilities would even matter to a public then concerned about making a living from commodity production, would have seemed inconceivable to most people. A few writers and artists articulated different visions — Henry David Thoreau the value of nature and simplicity in living for their own sakes, Ralph Waldo Emerson the infusion of nature with transcendent spiritual values, John James Audubon the beauty of its wildlife, and George Catlin the grandeur of its landscape and the nobility of its indigenous peoples — but their work had no impact on policy until a generation or more later.

The public lands had even greater impact in shaping Americans' beliefs about the uniqueness of their experience. The vast abundance of the public lands had no counterpart in Europe, nor did the freedom of opportunity these lands offered for individuals to make a living or even get rich by exploiting them. Such distinctively American ideas as "manifest destiny" and "the endless frontier" all derive from the perception of open-ended opportunity associated with the seemingly unlimited availability of western public lands and resources. Some commentators have even argued that Americans thus became distinctively a "people of plenty," and indeed that their continuing access to material abundance — first in natural resources, then in infrastructure, and eventually in technological capacity — has provided the essential foundation for America's egalitarian democracy itself (Potter 1954).

To note this larger impact, however, is also to acknowledge the extent to which the policies themselves were driven by larger forces and imperatives, rather than controlling or guiding these forces. Land disposal policies largely followed the settlers rather than leading them. They legitimized already-widespread land speculation and thus promoted it further, and served rather than restrained powerful economic and political interests. As Benjamin Hibbard noted, in the quotation that opened this chapter, these policies were more expedient than coherent. The national government simply had neither the administrative capacity nor the political support to restrain the all-out private appropriation and exploitation of the environment that economic opportunities and its own policies promoted.

These policies were spectacularly effective in promoting their intended goals. The American West was settled and developed for economic use far more rapidly than anyone in the early nineteenth century anticipated. The West was populated, canals and railroads linked it to markets, settlements grew into towns and cities, and the national economy grew rapidly — despite repeated cycles of speculation and depression — into a prosperous system of both internal markets and exports. Such policies had widespread public support, probably because they endorsed rather than controlled what most settlers and businesses wanted to do anyway. They were driven overwhelmingly by the self-interest and rising political power of the western settlers and development interests and of their representatives. In effect, these policies legalized and promoted all-out commercialization and exploitation of the environment for immediate, private economic gain: what was good for settlers and developers was presumed to be good for the country.

These policies, however, radically transformed the landscape and led to the waste and destruction of its resources. Loggers denuded the midwestern forests, sometimes for settlement but more often they simply felled the trees and moved on, leaving stumps and often continuing fires behind. Southern farmers exhausted the soil and moved west to new lands rather than put greater expense into fertilization. Hydraulic mining eroded entire hills and mountainsides, washing their soil downstream. Commercial hunting wiped out the passenger pigeon, nearly led to the extinction of the plains bison herds, and destroyed beaver and other species over large areas of their former ranges. The construction of flood control levees "reclaimed" large areas of riparian lowlands, but in the process exacerbated flooding and siltation downstream and encouraged development in low-lying areas at risk of catastrophic future floods. Overall, the United States developed into a prosperous, continental nation, but at a cost of enormous environmental transformation and in some cases permanent destruction.

6 Agencies and Experts: The Beginnings of Public Management

Comparatively short as is the period through which the colonization of foreign lands by European emigrants extends, great, and, it is to be feared, sometimes irreparable injury has been already done in the various processes by which man seeks to subjugate the virgin earth. . . . [W]e are, even now, breaking up the floor and wainscoting and doors and windows of our dwelling, for fuel to warm our bodies and seethe our pottage, and the world cannot afford to wait until the slow and sure progress of exact science has taught it a better economy. . . . The earth is fast becoming an unfit home for its noblest inhabitant, and another era of equal human crime and human improvidence . . . would reduce it to such a condition of impoverished productiveness, of shattered surface, of climatic excess, as to threaten the depravation, barbarism, and even extinction of the species. — George Perkins Marsh, *Man and Nature,* 1864

For all the vast government-supported transformation of the American environment that occurred over the course of the nineteenth century, the institutional capacity of government itself to manage or even monitor this process was appallingly limited. Initially the entire business of the government was carried out by just three departments. With respect to environmental functions, the State Department handled land acquisitions through treaties with foreign governments and Indian tribes; the War Department handled frontier security and exploration, and later surveying and construction of engineering improvements; and the Treasury Department handled surveying and disposal of public lands, and the resulting revenues. In 1812 Congress established a General Land Office (GLO) under the Treasury Department, to consolidate the public-land functions of the three departments under one commissioner. Thus was created the administrative unit that "was to manage close to a billion and a half acres spread over 30 states and to handle the transfer through sale, grants, and gifts of two-thirds of this acreage to individuals, companies, states, and railroads" (Gates 1968, 127). Significantly, this consolidation integrated only administrative functions, not laws and policies. For a full century and a half, until enactment of the Federal Lands Policy and Management Act of 1976, the GLO and its successor, the Bureau of Land Management, had no single overarching law to guide them, but were responsible merely for administering the hundreds of separate, conflicting, and often loosely drafted land disposal laws and resulting claims that emerged piecemeal over that period.

Historians have speculated as to how much more wisely the settlement process might have proceeded had the GLO been given more authority and resources to monitor the environmental conditions and resources of the public domain, and even to develop a more coherent and farsighted plan for the development of public lands. Its first commissioner did in fact propose collecting and disseminating data on the environmental conditions of the public lands, but he received no support from Congress. In practice, the agency's capabilities were simply overwhelmed by the demands of surveys and land claims, and by the associated political and economic pressures of claimants and their advocates (Engelbert 1950, 209–14). In 1849 the GLO was transferred to the new Department of the Interior, but internally it remained essentially unchanged until it was merged — with the later Grazing Service — into the Bureau of Land Management in 1946.

Another lingering anomaly in American environmental policy is the fact that a military agency, the Army Corps of Engineers, remains one of the principal agencies responsible for civilian water resource management. In reality its staff consists of some two hundred military officers directing a permanent staff of thirty-two thousand civilians, but it remains a branch of the army rather than of the Department of the Interior or of a Department of the Environment or of Public Works.

The Corps was created initially to construct military fortifications, but after the establishment of the U.S. Military Academy at West Point in 1802 it emerged as the main available source of engineering expertise more generally. It was asked therefore to conduct topographic surveys and, beginning in the 1820s, surveys of the feasibility of river and harbor improvements. With the 1824 Rivers and Harbors Act it became Congress's general contractor for *constructing* water resource development projects as well. This role was based initially on the rationale that navigation projects have dual value for military and commercial purposes. Such projects were claimed to be for the general benefit of interstate commerce and economic development, but in fact they provided particular benefits to the congressional districts in which they were constructed. Owing to the political popularity of such "pork-barrel" projects, they have remained an army activity ever since, despite the recommendations of several review commissions that they be consolidated with other natural resource and environmental functions in a civilian agency.[1]

Two other environmentally important agencies were created in the mid-nineteenth century, the Interior and Agriculture Departments. These agencies provide an interesting study in institutional contrasts. The Department of the Interior was created in 1849 in response to the internal needs of the federal government: the Treasury Department had become a catch-all for many time-consuming functions, of which one of the largest was land claims processing, and in the frenzy of the California gold rush Congress finally accepted the argument that a separate "home department" was needed to manage the country's internal affairs.[2] The department was formed merely by reorganization: the General Land Office, Patent Office, Indian Affairs and Census Bureaus, and several miscellaneous functions from the existing three departments were moved into a single new department. Significantly, the secretary of the new department was not given any statutory authority to integrate or coordinate these agencies toward common goals or priorities. In an ideal world the department might have become the foundation for integrative planning and management of the nation's environment, and ultimately for a Department of the Environment, but in fact it remained a loose collection of disparate and largely autonomous agencies.[3]

Equally important, the department became almost immediately a de facto "department of the West": the first federal agency to become consistently dominated by the economic and political constituencies of a particular region. This dominance emerged within the first two years of its existence, when its secretary in 1851 tried to strengthen enforcement of the timber trespass laws on the public lands, and faced a firestorm of political reaction from the western states. After the 1852 elections he was replaced, the timber agents were fired, and no further enforcement of the forest protection laws was attempted for another quarter-century.

This result served notice that the Interior Department would find it extremely difficult to implement policies that placed national interests over the immediate economic interests of its western political constituencies (Engelbert 1950, 371–81). The timber enforcement issue was strikingly similar to the "Sagebrush Rebellion" of the 1970s, in which western public land users—ranchers and mining companies in particular—mobilized following the enactment of the Federal Lands Policy and Management Act of 1976 to stop any more active federal land management by the Bureau of Land Management. As in the timber trespass case, this modern movement succeeded, under the Reagan administration, in getting key policies changed and partisans appointed to key positions in the Interior Department, although these victories were neither as total nor as enduring as those of the nineteenth century.[4]

The Department of Agriculture, in contrast, had a clear mission and client constituency from the start. Its antecedent was the Patent Office, whose commissioner in 1839, as agrarian settlement and grain production were on the rise, obtained congressional authority to gather and disseminate agricultural information and seeds. Farm interests had lobbied for a separate agency since early in the century, and with the election of Abraham Lincoln and the agrarian Republicans in 1860 they succeeded. The Department of Agriculture (USDA) was created, and unlike the Interior Department, given an explicit statutory mandate to "acquire and . . . diffuse among the people of the United States useful information on subjects connected with agriculture in the most general and comprehensive sense of the word." This mandate included conducting scientific experimentation as well, although at that time it did not include the power to impose regulations or to grant financial subsidies for agricultural investments. In the same year Congress passed the Morrill Act, providing land grants to the states to finance creation of a system of state agricultural colleges, the so-called "land grant" colleges and universities. For the department, these ultimately became an important network of grass-roots institutions for agricultural teaching, research, and technical assistance, as well as a means for forming political alliances. In 1876 a Forestry Division was established, making USDA the first federal agency to pay systematic attention to the nation's forest resources (Engelbert 1950, 381–89; Gates 1968, 438–39).

Thus, while the Interior Department inherited a patchwork legacy, a regionally defined constituency and a divisive set of political conflicts, the Agriculture Department from the start provided technical assistance to a single and popular nationwide constituency, farmers and agricultural businesses. The legacy of these differences later caused frequent interagency conflict and overlapping jurisdictions, such as between USDA's Forest Service and the Interior Department's Bureau of Land Management and National Park Service. It has remained an important element in environmental policy conflicts among agencies responsible for competing missions, such as promoting agribusiness versus protecting wildlife habitat or promoting commodity production versus preservation and recreation on the public lands.

Differentiation of Natural Resource Values

From the Revolution to the Civil War, public-land policy treated land by and large as a homogeneous commodity for agrarian settlement, disregarding its great variations in environmental conditions and assets. This policy had the advantages of simplicity of administration and speed of disposal, and was popular therefore with western politicians. It had serious limitations, however, particularly as settlement spread into regions that were not environmentally suited to family farming: the mineral-rich regions of California and the intermountain basin, the arid lands of the Great Plains, and the wooded mountains of the Rockies and the Pacific Northwest. In these areas, settlers sought commodity use rights to particular resources rather than agricultural land, yet the existing laws were not designed to accommodate and legitimize those uses.[5]

Beginning around mid-century, therefore, new policies began to emerge which differentiated among property and use rights to particular environmental assets.[6] These policies became a transitional step from undifferentiated privatization toward the reservation of resources in public management. Importantly, these laws were still land *disposal* policies, intended to privatize resources for their commodity values. By differentiating lands based on resource endowments, however, they began almost imperceptibly a process toward more formalized environmental characterization and classification, and toward reservation and public management of environmental resources.

One early form of resource differentiation was the recognition of poorly drained lands as less valuable than others (from an agrarian point of view, that is, since their importance as flood buffers, fishery spawning grounds, and waterfowl habitat was not yet well appreciated). Between 1849 and 1860, Congress passed three "swampland acts" donating wetlands that were "unfit for cultivation" to the states. The rationale was borrowed from earlier policies to finance canals and railroads. The plan was for the states to sell the lands to investors and use the proceeds to finance levees along the rivers to protect them from flooding, in the process enhancing the value of adjacent public lands. In this way, the swampland grants would provide a self-financing mechanism for transforming up to twenty million acres of unusable land into productive agricultural land. In practice, however, the law did not carefully define the "uncultivatability" of such lands, and thus invited opportunistic abuse. States and speculators ultimately used these laws to privatize almost sixty-five million acres of land, many of them far more valuable than had been envisioned, given away based on false claims of their worthlessness (Gates 1968, 321–34; U.S. Department of the Interior 1973, 6).

The mining boom triggered a far more widespread form of resource differentiation, with the California gold rush in 1848 followed successively by silver strikes in Nevada in 1858 (the Comstock Lode), gold strikes in Colorado in 1859, and other discoveries in Montana, Idaho, and neighboring states. Within months the large Spanish ranches that dominated California's landscape gave way to boomtowns of entrepreneurial prospectors and land speculators. The federal government, however, had no specific policies for lands that were chiefly valuable for their mineral resources. Early laws such as the land laws of 1785 and 1796 had provided that lead- and salt-bearing lands be reserved in public ownership and leased for the public benefit rather than sold or granted, and in the twentieth century mineral leasing would become an important form of federal policy for coal and oil deposits. In 1829, however, mining companies and land speculators had succeeded in abolishing the leasing system,[7] and by 1846 mineral lands were being offered for claim-staking and sale like any other public domain lands, with no special recognition of their mineral values (Mayer and Riley 1985, 20–39; Gates 1968, 707–08).[8]

Under the gold rush conditions of California, therefore, the federal government remained content to leave the gold mines as simply "a common field, open to the enterprise and industry of all our citizens," in the words of President Millard Fillmore (Gates 1968, 713). Without benefit of federal policies, miners simply staked claims and developed a rough system of property rights based on the concept of prior appropriation: the earliest claimants had the strongest claims. Not until 1866, more than sixteen years after the California gold rush and following subsequent mining booms, did Congress finally pass legislation legitimizing the system of mining claims that had developed.

Between 1866 and 1872 Congress passed a series of laws establishing policies for mining on public lands that have endured virtually unchanged to the present. The first, the landmark 1866 mining law, declared that "the mineral lands of the public domain . . . are hereby declared to be free and open to exploration and occupation" subject to the customs of the local mining districts. It authorized lode mining claims to lands containing valuable metal ores at a price of $5 per acre, with the single restriction that the claimant must have occupied the land and expended not less than $1,000 in labor and improvements. The Placer Act of 1870 extended these principles to placer mines — that is, hydraulic surface mining operations as opposed to deep mining of concentrated lode deposits — and in a remarkable and problematic policy change, allowed miners to preempt up to 160 acres that had virtually any kind of mineral deposits on them for a price of just $2.50 per acre. These included even lands that had been exhausted for mineral purposes but could now be claimed for agrarian settlement or other purposes, with no limit on the number of separate 160-acre tracts that could be claimed.

Finally, the 1872 General Mining Act restricted these principles to "valuable" mineral deposits (as opposed to all mineral lands), and required that claimants expend $100 per year in development work in order to retain such claims. At the same time, however, it extended these policies from the public domain per se to "all lands owned by the United

States government," that is, including later acquired lands. While nominally intended to benefit small-scale miners, in effect these laws extended the same opportunities to large companies, which were by far their greatest beneficiaries. They also made no provision either for royalties to the public from the enormous private wealth that might be extracted from these lands, nor even for repayment of the severe costs of environmental damage — soil erosion, acid drainage into streams, destruction of habitat and vegetation, and visual scarring of the landscape — that mining operations often cause.

In short, mining companies thenceforth could obtain valuable mineral assets for $2.50 per acre, wherever on the public lands they might find them — prices that are still in effect today, a century and a quarter later — and persons under the guise of mining could enter and claim public lands for virtually any purpose, fulfill the minimum occupancy and improvement requirements, purchase them for a modest price, and control their future use. This could be done whether that land was truly suited for mining or agricultural settlement, or whether its real value lay in controlling the trailheads of tourist attractions such as the Grand Canyon, or in speculating in lands under consideration for irrigation dams, or in other uses (Gates 1968, 708–23). Not until 1976, over a century later, were claimants even required to report their claims to the federal government: they needed only to file them with local land offices (Mayer and Riley 1985, 44). As of 1976 an estimated six million claims were outstanding, and a General Accounting Office study in 1974 found that 237 out of 240 randomly selected claims had never been mined, and that most were being used for other purposes. Many mining land claims continue today as privileged inholdings and conflicting uses on lands that are otherwise protected as national parks or for other purposes (Mayer and Riley 1985, 45–46, 78–82).

The anachronism of these laws was dramatized by several cases in the 1990s, when Secretary of the Interior Bruce Babbitt was ordered by the courts to approve mining claims worth billions of dollars, even by foreign firms, at a tiny fraction of their market value. Both environmental and fiscal reformers made repeated attempts to repeal or amend the old mining laws, but even in the face of such publicized abuses these proposals were always defeated by western senators supported by the mining companies (Wilkinson 1992).

An important exception to the mining laws, and yet another differentiation of resource values, was the different treatment of coal-bearing lands. The commercial value of coal had long been recognized: coal lands had been excluded from preemption claims as early as 1841, and an 1864 law offered them for sale at a minimum price of $25 per acre, ten to twenty times the price of other public lands. These prices were reduced in 1873 to $20 per acre, or $10 if the land lay more than fifteen miles from a rail line. Over six hundred thousand acres of coal lands were purchased under this system during the fifty years before the government changed its policy from sale to leasing of fuel mineral lands, in the Mineral Leasing Act of 1920 (Gates 1968, 724–25; Hibbard 1965 [1924], 519).

The mining claims system had important consequences for water resource policy. In the humid eastern United States, water law had been adapted from the English principle of *riparian* water rights, under which every owner along a watercourse shared an equal right to the flow of its water "undiminished in quantity and quality." These rights were ongoing elements of riparian land ownership, moreover, and continued whether they were actively used or not. In the West, by contrast, where water was scarce and essential — especially to the crude forms of hydraulic mining used to extract gold — the miners applied to water as well as minerals the principle of *prior appropriation*. This principle allowed users simply to appropriate the water they needed from what was available, for "beneficial uses," in the order in which they arrived: "first in time, first in right." This principle in effect treated water use rights as privately owned and salable commodities, separate from land ownership and conditional on use. The federal government ratified this system in the Placer Mining Act of 1870 and the Desert Land Act of 1877 (Getches 1990, 3–13, 79–80).[9]

The prior appropriations doctrine was better suited to regions where water was scarce than was riparian rights law. However, it left several important issues unresolved. First, it did not provide a clear system for allocating water among upstream and downstream states, whose water demands and water rights systems might conflict. This became a contentious issue between California and Nevada, and more generally among the states of the upper and lower basins of the Colorado River (and Mexico). Second, the hierarchy of water use rights was highly sensitive to changes in the use of the *reserved* water rights of the two earliest claimants of all, the Native American tribes and the federal government. These basic claims were not cancelable due to non-use, and increases in their use might therefore threaten lower-priority existing users. For instance, if the federal government were to sell or lease large quantities of water rights from public domain lands to energy mining companies, these could squeeze out many existing but lower-priority users.[10]

Finally, the traditional prior appropriations hierarchy was based only on specific "beneficial uses," which historically involved withdrawals of water for economic purposes. It therefore did not protect any in-stream flows for environmental purposes, such as sustaining fisheries and wildlife habitat. This issue increased in importance with the growth of western populations and of water-demanding activities, and the establishment of more recent statutory requirements to maintain "fishable and swimmable" water quality. Such requirements, often backed by court orders, forced some states to alter their water laws to provide increased protection for in-stream flows (Getches 1990, 116–19).

A third form of resource differentiation was the creation of a separate legal regime for disposal of "timber and stone" lands: that is, lands chiefly valuable for their forest resources and not suitable for ordinary agrarian settlement, such as the forested mountains of the western states. Timber trespass was a perennial problem on the public lands, ranging from the generally accepted practice of allowing individual settlers to cut timber for their own needs to the illegal but widespread practice of large-scale commercial logging: for settlement and railroad construction, for steamboat and railroad fuel, for mine-tunnel shoring, and for other profitable purposes (fig. 5). Efforts to control these practices only revealed the limits of the policies of an absentee central government when they conflicted with locally accepted practices — just as under the Broad Arrow policy of British colonial administration. Timber enforcement agents were either bribed or bullied, and ultimately driven from their posts by western political protests in the 1850s, after which timber trespass enforcement virtually ceased for a quarter-century. Local businesses argued in their own defense that there was no legal means by which they *could* purchase these lands

Figure 5. An example of "squatter" settlement on federal forestlands. This picture shows a squatter's claim in Idaho (on today's Selway National Forest), without any cultivated ground, located on an abandoned logging claim at the junction of the South and Little West Forks of the Bitterroot River. About 90 percent of the salable timber has been removed. [U.S. Forest Service photo, courtesy of the Forest History Society, Durham, N.C.]

for logging: the public land laws were designed only for agrarian settlement in 160-acre farms, a process that lagged far behind the westward spread of commercial timber harvesting.

As settlement spread into the western mountains in the 1870s, therefore, a new and more vigorous Secretary of the Interior, Carl Schurz, sought to revitalize timber enforcement and prosecution. Schurz was the United States' first great Secretary of the Interior, who brought competent scientist-administrators into the natural resource agencies and built alliances between these agencies and scientific and professional associations (Futrell 1993, 16).[11] Schurz advocated a more farsighted policy, that timberlands should be appraised and then sold at their market value rather than merely left open to private appropriation.

Instead, however, Congress in 1878 substituted legal privatization for enforcement, enacting the Timber and Stone Act, which allowed the purchase of forested lands in 160-acre tracts for $2.50 per acre: an estimated one-tenth of their actual value at the time. The law reaffirmed that it was illegal to cut or remove timber from the public lands, but it exempted miners, farmers, and ranchers from this restriction and even allowed those who were caught stealing timber to escape further penalties simply by paying the minimum land purchase price. Later in the same year, Congress also enacted the Free Timber Act, which allowed residents of the western states to cut timber freely on the public lands for agricultural, mining or "other domestic" purposes.

In effect, these laws blocked forest protection enforcement and created yet another policy tool by which commodity users of environmental resources could transfer them cheaply into private ownership. Nearly fourteen million acres were eventually privatized under the Timber and Stone Act (U.S. Department of the Interior 1973, 6). In the process, however, timber agents began to keep clearer records of the quantities and values of timber stolen from the public lands, and thus to provide documentary justification for policy changes that followed (Gates 1968, 531–55).

A final form of resource differentiation was the identification of desert lands as a distinct environment, requiring different legal treatment from the mainstream of agrarian settlement laws. Since the early explorations by Zebulon Pike and Stephen Long, the arid region westward of the one hundredth meridian had been characterized as a "Great American Desert," an expanse "wholly unfit for civilization, and of course uninhabitable by a people dependent upon agriculture for their subsistence" (Dick 1970, 298–99). By the 1870s it was evident that while settlement was in fact occurring there, the preemption and homestead laws were not well suited to its environmental conditions. The arid plains were better suited to grazing than to farming, yet areas far larger than 160 acres were required for cattle grazing. Much smaller areas would suffice for intensive agriculture, but only if they could be irrigated. Irrigation technology had already emerged as a natural technological extension of water diversion for placer mining, and the mining communities presented an economic opportunity since they required food. The total area to be irrigated, however, had to be far more than 160 acres, in order to pay the capital costs of irrigation systems.

In response to irrigation and livestock-raising interests, therefore, Congress passed the 1877 Desert Land Act, which allowed claimants to purchase single claims of 640 acres of unsurveyed desert land at $1.25 per acre, under the condition that they irrigate it within three years. In practice, this requirement proved unenforceable: to irrigate a full 640 acres in three years would have required major capital investment, and claimants' "irrigation works" were more often as nominal as a plow's furrow from a canal and a can of water. However, the opportunity to claim unsurveyed land at such cheap prices led to rapid capture of large areas of western land, especially 640-acre strips along watercourses which conferred de facto control of far larger areas of surrounding arid lands.

The effect of this policy thus was once again to permit transfer of large areas of public land into private ownership, chiefly by large-scale grazing businesses and land speculators. Over a quarter of a million acres were claimed under this law within its first four months, and in all nearly eleven million acres were privatized in the fourteen years before the law was repealed (Gates 1968, 638–41; U.S. Department of the Interior 1973, 6).

Resource Classification and Reservation

The gradual differentiation of legal regimes for lands endowed with different resources triggered a subtle but important institutional change: more detailed information on environmental conditions was required, and thus a larger and more technically trained government administrative staff was needed. Congress's appropriations act for the General Land Office in 1876, for example, directed the agency to focus on surveying lands that were arable, irrigable, timbered at commercial values, coal-bearing, or related to town boundaries or private land claims. The Desert Lands and Timber and Stone Acts added further requirements for resource classification, and accusations of widespread land fraud—increasingly common in the 1870s—created added pressure. Without accurate information on mineral deposits, for instance, valuable coal lands could simply be claimed as ordinary agrarian or even desert land at far lower prices (Hibbard 1965 [1924], 496–506).

Systematic geographic and geological surveys of the western territories began in 1867, therefore, and in the 1870s Major John Wesley Powell carried out a detailed scientific study of the Colorado River basin. Powell's seminal *Report on the Lands of the Arid Region,* presented to Congress in 1878, emphasized the special environmental constraints of a region whose values were defined by rainfall and resources rather than simply by arable farmlands and transportation. He recommended that these lands be systematically classified before disposal and priced according to their best uses: mineral, coal, irrigable, timber, or pasturage. Low-lying land near streams should be sold in plots no larger than eighty acres for intensive irrigated farming; pasture lands farther from water should be sold in units no smaller than four square miles (2,560 acres). Timber lands in the mountains should be sold explicitly for commercial logging, not under the pretext of agrarian settlement. Rangelands and irrigable areas should be managed cooperatively in special-use districts, to coordinate the use of these shared resources.

From a scientific perspective, Powell's recommendations were the first to propose a systematic set of policy and planning principles based explicitly on expert assessment of environmental conditions. Politically, however, they ignored important questions of governance. Western settlers opposed them, because legalizing such sales might allow timber, water, and large areas of pasture to be quickly captured by powerful economic interests at a time when such monopolization was a rising concern. The speculators themselves also opposed any advance classification process, since it might slow or limit their opportunities under the loose existing system and would at best lead to higher prices. Most of Powell's recommendations were not adopted, therefore, but they did lead to consolidation of federal surveying activities into a far more professional U.S. Geological Survey (USGS) in 1879. They also led to the creation of a commission to review the whole system of public land disposal laws, and to propose a public lands classification system based on environmental characteristics and use potentials (Hibbard 1965 [1924], 501–05; Gates 1968, 419–23). The USGS rapidly became one of the most stable and respected government scientific agencies, producing systematic topographic maps, geological maps and reports, and eventually a broad range of environmental information.[12]

Within ten years of its creation, however, the USGS was drawn into a far more politically charged form of analysis, which proved to be another key step toward government management of the environment. Land speculation under the Desert Land Act had become so widespread that it was actually hampering rather than advancing the settlement of irrigated lands, as speculators claimed key lands and held them for price increases. In 1888, therefore, Congress directed the USGS (under Major Powell, then its head) to conduct irrigation surveys to identify those public lands most suitable for irrigation as well as the sites necessary to store and transport water for them. Lest these surveys merely exacerbate the land speculation problem — by producing and publishing the very topographic and geologic information with which speculators could claim the most strategic lands — USGS was further authorized to reserve the irrigable lands from private claims until it could complete its task, echoing the recommendation of Powell's report for classification in advance of sale.

These reservations blocked speculative capture, but also suspended the process of land claims and settlement generally. In effect, this policy closed the entire public domain and made Powell the arbiter of the whole public land system, arousing the hostility of western congressmen. In 1890, therefore, Congress repealed the USGS's authority to reserve lands, except for reservoir sites it had already identified, and reopened the remainder to land claims (Gates 1968, 640–42; Hibbard 1965 [1924], 504–05; Miller 1973, 422–35). This change left an untenable policy vacuum, in which the federal government was essentially producing the information by which speculators could capture public lands and demand that those who needed these lands for irrigation projects purchase them back at inflated prices. The vacuum was filled in 1891 by one of the most momentous changes in the history of U.S. environmental policy, the General Revision Act of 1891.

Moment of Transition: The General Revision Act of 1891

The net effect of the nineteenth-century public land laws was to transfer vast acreages of public lands into private hands for economic commodity use, and by 1890 the Superintendent of the Census reported that there was no longer any identifiable frontier beyond the areas of continuous human settlement. The dominant ideology supporting these policies was the Jeffersonian ideal of a nation of small-scale agrarian landowners, but the primary consequence was the acquisition of far larger land areas and greater assets by large landowners and corporations: railroads, stock ranchers, timber and mining companies, and land speculators. In addition to the huge acreages given to the railroads, the Public Land Law Review Commission identified multiple examples of land acquisitions ranging from sixty-seven thousand to over a million acres, including some of the most valuable forest and mineral lands on the continent. And cattle enterprises in the plains used barbed wire to enclose and control far more public land than they actually owned (Gates 1968, 440–41, 467, 482–83).

The increasing monopolization of public resources by large businesses, in stark contrast to the public land laws' official spirit favoring small settlers, provoked rising public hostility in the West as well as the East. In response, Congress in 1891 passed a general revision of the public land laws. This General Revision Act repealed the Timber Culture and Preemption Acts, limited homestead claims to 160 acres, and limited all future claims other than mineral lands to a total of 320 acres per individual. It also tightened the requirements of the Desert Land Act, requiring more explicit evidence of irrigation plans and water access as well as annual investments in irrigation as conditions of sale. It did not

Figure 6. An example of the destructive effects of nineteenth-century forest exploitation. In the late 1800s and early 1900s, wildfires raged uncontrolled. These fires, combined with (and often originating from) excessive timber cutting, brought devastation to many areas throughout the country. [U.S. Forest Service]

repeal other laws that were equally problematic, such as the Timber and Stone Act,[13] but it did eliminate several of the most abused laws and thus simplified the land law system somewhat (Gates 1968, 484–88, 642).

In addition to these provisions, the General Revision Act included a momentous "rider" — an additional provision, and a pivotal change in policy, as later events would show — which authorized the president to "set apart and reserve" forested lands as public reservations. Political support for this amendment, the Forest Reserve Act, came from two sources: laymen and professional foresters concerned about commercial overcutting of timberlands, and western water companies seeking watershed protection for irrigation purposes (Hays 1969 [1958], 36).

There had been public and scientific concern since the 1870s over the systematic deforestation of the Great Lakes pine forests, and by the 1880s these concerns had grown into widespread fears of a "timber famine" that might leave the United States dependent on inferior trees or foreign suppliers. Large-scale logging in the West under the Timber and Stone Act increased these concerns (fig. 6). A concurrent issue was the apparent effect of deforestation on watersheds: concern over the gradual drying up of the Erie Canal, for instance, led in 1885 to permanent protection of New York's Adirondack Mountains as a state park. In 1889 the American Forestry Association, with the support of western irrigation interests, petitioned Congress to protect the most valuable remaining public domain forests by putting them under permanent public management (Gates 1968, 563–66).

The practice of reserving lands in government ownership was not unprecedented. Lands had been withheld throughout the history of public land sales for such purposes as schools, mineral leasing, fulfillment of military bounty obligations and treaty obligations to the Indian tribes, and, from 1888 to 1890, for irrigation reservoirs. Several sites (but only a few) had also been reserved as public parks. The Yosemite Valley was granted to California in 1864 as a permanent trust for public recreation, and in 1872 Congress reserved some two million acres of the Yellowstone Valley as a public park, with political support from railroad promoters who recognized its tourism potential (Nash 1982 [1967], 108–16).[14] Two million more acres were reserved as federal park and forest land around the Yosemite Valley in 1890, in response to lobbying by Sierra Club founder John Muir with quiet support from railroad interests (Wilkins 1995, 169–78). Notwithstanding these few exceptions, however, the fundamental policy for the public domain lands up to 1891 was to transfer them into private ownership for commodity use.

The General Revision Act, and the scale on which it was implemented by successive presidents, represented a fundamental departure from the nineteenth-century policy of land disposal. Within a month after signing the 1891 law, President Benjamin Harrison withdrew from the market over 1.2 million additional acres of forestlands around Yellowstone National Park, and by the end of his term he had withdrawn an estimated 13 million acres. Withdrawals by Presidents Grover Cleveland and Theodore Roosevelt increased the total to nearly 86 million acres by 1905 (Gates 1968, 567–68, 579).

Western economic interests were outraged, and sought congressional action to reverse these withdrawals, but the decisions held, backed by effective pressure from the Sierra Club, which John Muir and others formed in 1892 to preserve these lands (Wilkins 1995, 179–85, 196–98). In 1897 the Forest Management Act authorized the government to protect and manage the reserves on a permanent basis. These two statutes marked a pivotal transition from the policy of land privatization to a more mixed policy of privatization and public environmental management.

Summary

Overall, the laws that constituted the federal public lands policies of the nineteenth century amounted to an incongruous and cumulative patchwork. Nearly all of these laws promoted privatization rather than public management of public lands and their resources, but they served varied and often conflicting purposes and beneficiaries. There was a fundamental difference between the agrarian settlement policies of preemption and homesteading, for instance, and large-scale land grants to railroad investors, notwithstanding the ultimate economic interdependence of the settlers' need for railroads to get their crops to distant markets and the railroads' need for settlers as customers. These conflicts echoed the early clash between the agrarian and industrial visions of Jefferson and Hamilton, and are strongly evident in environmental and other public policy conflicts even today: between family farms and agribusinesses, between citizen environmentalists and multinational corporations, even between corporate and populist versions of environmentalism.

In their almost exclusive emphasis on privatization of the public lands and resources, these policies differed both from the British colonial policies that preceded them and from twentieth-century U.S. policies, which provided first for more active management of resources in public ownership, and more recently for radically increased regulation of the environmental effects of private businesses' activities.

Ernest Engelbert, whose 1950 study is in many respects the definitive assessment of American policy for natural resources up to 1862, comments that the years between 1828 and 1862 were a time when policies for conservation and protection of the environment should by right have emerged. The pace of resource exploitation had rapidly accelerated, and unmistakable signs of environmental damage had begun to be evident in soil, timber, and minerals. Thanks to government-sponsored exploration and surveys, information about this damage and about the limits of our environmental abundance was also becoming widely known. Instead, however, for more than a century American environmental policy simply promoted exploitation of the environment for its immediate market value, with little restraint or even assessment of its value as a natural system and its sustainability for future economic use. Individualism and private enterprise remained the dominant values, and were linked closely to the popular goals of democratic egalitarianism and of dismantling European and colonial policies that had previously restrained exploitation of environmental resources.

A particularly cautionary conclusion that can be drawn from Engelbert's work is that almost without exception, these policies were both consistent with and driven by public sentiment. Some public protests arose against land speculation, but others were at least as effective in blocking any meaningful restraint on resource exploitation. In Engelbert's view, the public tended to demand policies that were most politically and economically expedient in the short term, with consequences that were often environmentally disastrous.

The reality underlying this pattern was that the American West was settled not by heroic pioneers and yeoman farmers acting out the agrarian myth, but by waves of opportunistic businesses and individuals acting in their own immediate economic self-interests, backed by larger economic and political interests. The rhetoric of economic progress provided a powerful legitimizing force for these opportunists, obscuring both the violent imperialism by which they captured the land from the indigenous residents and often from one another, and the destructive and wasteful unconcern with which they extracted trees, minerals, beaver, bison, and other assets from the natural environment (Worster 1991). The real policy was using "free" natural resources to create concentrated capital wealth, using the western lands as a hinterland to exploit at will.

A primary consequence of this mindset for environmental policy was an almost total absence of anticipatory planning or prudence. Rather than forestalling problems, the government acted only after compelling problems had emerged, and even then its compromises were often inadequate, ineffectual, or even perverse. Only after the Civil War did there emerge the beginnings of a nationwide public concern about large-scale environmental destruction by big businesses — in essence, an alliance of environmentalism and populism — that galvanized a political movement for environmental protection and restraint (Engelbert 1950, 391–408).

For modern advocates of greater government accountability and citizen participation, this legacy is a two-edged sword. It is reassuring in that it suggests that American governance is in fact responsive to public concerns, but sobering in that for most of an entire century in which patterns of environmental use were being set and serious destruction was occurring, general public preferences were in fact causing rather than correcting the problem, and were just as subject to short-term and self-interested priorities as were those of many larger businesses and economic interests. Citizen participation in itself, in short, was not necessarily a reliable solution for the intrinsically problematic characteristics of environmental issues. Environmental policy involved inherent conflicts between incompatible uses and values, between individual wants and public rights and interests, and between the immediate economic benefits of commodity production and the long-term value of conserving sustainable ecosystems.

7   Public Health and Urban Sanitation

The condition of perfect *public health* requires such laws and regulations, as will secure to man associated in society, the same sanitary enjoyments that he would have as an isolated individual; and as will protect him from injury from any influences connected with his locality, his dwelling-house, his occupation, or those of his associates or neighbors, or from any other social causes. — Report of the Massachusetts Sanitary Commission, 1850

[B]y the end of the nineteenth century all major cities of the western world had done something to come up to the new level of sanitation and water management that had been pioneered in Great Britain, 1848–1854. Urban life became far safer from disease than ever before as a result. — William McNeill, *Plagues and Peoples*

American environmental policy developed in part from the natural resource conservation and preservation traditions, which demanded government action to restrain the destructive effects of market forces on natural landscapes. It emerged at least equally, however, out of the transformation of human settlements from decentralized towns and villages into large-scale urban and industrial regions, and from the resulting need for government actions to protect people from environmental causes of death and disease. In particular, it grew out of the nineteenth-century sanitation movement — an effort by doctors, engineers, and social reformers to provide reliable sources of clean water, control the disposal of sewage and noxious wastes, reduce smoke, and otherwise improve living conditions. This movement had only limited immediate effects on federal policies and institutions, and indeed only mixed success in remedying urban pollution problems. However, it laid the foundation for public management of urban water supplies, wastes, and wastewater, and for the establishment of public health agencies more generally.

These government interventions greatly improved the health of urban populations, yet they were initiated well before scientists had developed a clear understanding of the bacteriological causes and ecological transmission routes of disease (Ruckelshaus 1992, 146). The fact that the sanitation reformers thus did many of the right things for the "wrong" reasons contributed to both their immediate success and their ultimate decline as a political force. The sanitation movement fragmented in the early twentieth century, and while its several professional elements continued to develop and to make progress on some issues, no other broad-based movement to reduce urban and industrial pollution appeared until the modern environmental movement, more than half a century later and significantly different in form. Both the rise and the decline of the sanitation movement, therefore, provide important background for understanding environmental policy and politics today.[1]

The Urban Environment

Pollution problems are not unique to urban environments, but both their severity and the threats they pose to human health are magnified by high population densities and by the close commingling of human populations with other species and with industrial wastes. Urban settings offer new ecological opportunities to species that can adapt to them, such as some human disease organisms and their vectors. Also, transport and economic exchange, of which cities are the centers, create opportunities for long-range colonization in new locations, not only by humans but by any other organisms that can survive the trip: crops and domestic animals, and also weeds and diseases. In the words of one historian, "The problem of public health was inherent in the new industrial civilization. The same process that created the market economy, the factory, and the modern urban environment also brought into being the health problems that made necessary new means of disease prevention and health protection" (Rosen 1958, 201).

Even in the early colonial towns sanitation was an ubiquitous problem, and the environmental consequences of urban population densities and living conditions required government policy interventions (Bridenbaugh 1964, 18–19, 85–86, 93). Fire was a constant threat, and safe water supplies an ever-growing need (Bridenbaugh 1964, 55–63, 206–15, 372–74). Human wastes were discharged into backyard privies, or into neighborhood drainage ditches which became open sewers and receptacles for filth. Solid wastes were simply put out on the streets by householders and carried away by private "cartmen," a system which left the streets filthy and unsanitary. Pigs were turned loose in the streets to feed on what remained, while adding their own excreta (Bridenbaugh 1964, 19, 167). By the end of the eighteenth century most major towns had appointed official scavengers, who were responsible for supervising removal of garbage, rubbish, and dead animals from the streets and enforcing street-cleaning regulations against both cartmen and individuals. However, these measures were often ineffective (Bridenbaugh 1964, 165, 321–23).[2]

Food inspectors were also appointed beginning in the 1660s to police the adulteration of foods and unsanitary packing of meat barrels that were damaging to cities' trade reputations. These policies were unevenly enforced, however. Public and business support for regulatory measures blossomed with each crisis, but then faded as the crises subsided and the burden of regulation came to appear more onerous (Duffy 1990, 9–15).

Business and industrial activities compounded sanitation problems. Tanneries, slaughterhouses, fishmongers, and other businesses caused serious pollution and stench as their wastes putrefied, as well as food and water contamination and occupational hazards to their workers. Early municipal governments often sought to confine these noxious businesses to particular areas of the town — an example of rudimentary land-use zoning — but even in separate areas they were major sources of urban filth and pollution.

Rapid urban population growth magnified these problems. In 1790 the United States

had 24 cities, in 1840 131, and by 1920 over 2,700. In 1790 the urban population represented only 5 percent of the country's total, and only two cities had populations larger than
twenty-five thousand; by 1840 the urban population was about 1.8 million (11 percent),
and by 1920 it had reached 54 million (over 50 percent). This rapid increase, fueled both
by open immigration from Europe and by rural-to-urban migration within the United
States, caused serious crises in living conditions. By 1894, for instance, the population
density in one district of New York City was nearly 1,000 persons per acre (about 300,000
within five or six blocks), compared to about 760 per acre in Bombay and 485 per acre in
the worst slums of Europe (Melosi 1981, 13–16).

Fueling this urban population boom was the rapid growth of trade and industry.
Between 1820 and 1870 American cities grew into regional commercial and manufacturing
centers. The application of water and steam power permitted larger-scale factory manufacturing than was previously possible, and the development of canal and railroad networks
allowed larger-scale trade and more concentrated processing of materials from farms,
forests, and mines. All these enterprises added to the urban waste load, even though the
scale of most individual enterprises remained relatively small up through the Civil War
(Warner 1972, 60–62).

Between 1870 and 1920, with the introduction of coal and electricity and the completion of the rail network, American cities began to experience the full consequences of the
Industrial Revolution. The largest cities evolved into giant metropolitan areas and regional multicity manufacturing belts, dominated by far larger and more specialized corporate enterprises than had previously existed. As businesses grew in scale, their environmental impacts became more concentrated. Small slaughterhouses in many cities were replaced
by giant stockyards and meat-packing industries in a few. Small foundries were replaced by
giant steel mills. Water power was replaced by burning of wood and later coal, creating a
constant pall of smoke both from industries and from the railroads that served them. By
1895 coal had surpassed wood as the primary fuel for manufacturing and transportation,
particularly bituminous soft coal, which was burned at low efficiencies and emitted heavy
clouds of sulfurous smoke (Melosi 1980, 7; 1981, 17; Cronon 1991, 207–59).

Industrial employment grew rapidly as well, adding about a million or more industrial
workers to the work force each decade from 1870 to 1920. Jobs in basic iron and steel
making alone increased by 50,000 to 150,000 in every decade but one during this period
(U.S. Department of Commerce 1975, Series D, 152–81). With these changes in industrial
scale came greater differentiation of living conditions among different sectors of the population. Large corporations exacerbated previous differences in standards of living between
well-educated managers and skilled personnel on the one hand, and large pools of unskilled
workers who lived in poverty and poor sanitary conditions (Warner 1972, 98–100).

Substandard living conditions exposed urban dwellers to severe environmental health
hazards on a scale unknown in the United States today. Yellow fever epidemics — imported
from tropical countries via trade ships — swept through East Coast port cities repeatedly in
the 1790s, then returned to the southern port cities in the 1850s, killing hundreds and even
thousands of people in single cities in a single summer (Bridenbaugh 1964, 86–88, 240–
42, 398–463). Over 5,000 people died of yellow fever in Philadelphia in 1793, 1,500 to

2,000 in New York in 1798, and hundreds more in other cities from Boston to New Orleans. The 1853 epidemic killed 9,000 in New Orleans alone (Duffy 1990, 38–48, 100). Asiatic cholera spread to the United States in the 1830s and again in the 1860s, killing thousands more: 3,000 in New York City, 4,000 to 5,000 in New Orleans, over 2,000 in Cincinnati, and over 3,500 in St. Louis (Duffy 1990, 79–84, 121–23).

Outbreaks of typhoid, typhus, and other diseases were a constant threat and smallpox, diphtheria, and tuberculosis were widespread hazards as well (Duffy 1990, 194–201). In 1900, the average U.S. life expectancy was under fifty years, compared to over seventy today; the death rates for cancer was only 64 per hundred thousand (versus 163 in 1970), but the rate for tuberculosis was over 194 (versus less than 3); for influenza 202 (versus 31), for typhoid 31, for diphtheria 40, and for intestinal diseases 143 (versus negligible levels today) (U.S. Department of Commerce 1975, Series B, 149–66). Infant mortality rates in New York City were 65 percent *higher* by 1870 than they had been in 1810 (Melosi 1981, 19).

The causes of these diseases were unknown, but they were thought to arise either through contagion — that is, direct transmission by contact from infected victims to others — or perhaps from "miasmas": gases emanating from the ground or from the stench of environmental filth, especially in the heat of summer, when the disease epidemics typically occurred (Duffy 1990, 4).

Throughout the nineteenth century every American city had to deal not only with human and industrial wastes, but also with the impacts of horse-drawn transportation. Overall there were an estimated three million or more horses in American cities at the turn of the century. New York City and Brooklyn in 1900 were home to 150,000 to 175,000 horses, Chicago had over 83,000, Detroit 12,000 and even Columbus, Ohio, had 5,000. Milwaukee's 12,500 horses in 1907 produced an estimated 133 tons of manure per day, and officials in Rochester, New York, calculated in 1900 that the city's 15,000 horses produced enough manure each year to make a pile one acre in area and 175 feet high.

This manure harbored tetanus and other disease spores, and it provided a prime breeding ground for houseflies, which carried disease as well. It created severe stench in wet weather, it was ground into clouds of unsanitary dust when dry, and it required major municipal expenditures for street-cleaning equipment and personnel. Also, when each horse died, it left a thirteen-hundred-pound carcass to be removed and disposed. In 1880 the City of New York removed fifteen thousand dead horses from its streets, and as late as 1912 Chicago removed nearly ten thousand. From this perspective, motor vehicles appeared to offer a vast improvement in urban life: not only in convenience and speed, but also in reduction of the public health hazards — not to mention the smell and noise — that were attributable to the "horse-infected city" (Tarr 1971, 65–69, 106).

Public Health Regulation

Because of these disease hazards, protection of public health was an accepted justification for application of government police power as early as colonial times. Until the mid-nineteenth century this took the form of quarantine laws, which authorized involuntary confinement of persons carrying contagious diseases to prevent their contact with others. Quarantine laws were enacted under state rather than federal authority, and implemented by municipal governments as early as 1647 (Bridenbaugh 1964, 86). The Supreme Court confirmed these powers in 1824 in its famous *Gibbons v. Ogden* decision. That decision established the supremacy of federal authority over the states in interstate commerce, and specifically in navigation, but reaffirmed the states' authority in other areas such as public health regulation.[3] Typically, port cities authorized official physicians to inspect arriving ships for signs of disease, and to confine their personnel and cargoes either aboard ship or in local "pest houses" until they were free of symptoms — up to sixty days or more if necessary.

Given the medical theories of the time, quarantine seemed to be the only policy tool available to limit the spread of epidemics, but it was nonetheless controversial. It was attacked as a dictatorial and paternalistic form of government regulation: it caused unwelcome delays in business and commerce and even in the daily lives of doctors, who were themselves subject to quarantine when they treated disease victims. It was attacked as corruptible: the official port physician was a political appointee who supported himself by inspection fees charged to the ships, and might be tempted to bend his judgment in response to local political or economic pressures. Finally, critics attacked quarantine policies on the grounds of scientific uncertainty. Since many people who were exposed to disease victims did *not* become ill, and some persons fell sick with no obvious direct exposure to those who were sick, critics questioned the validity of the whole contagion theory of disease transmission, and ultimately advocated alternative solutions such as improvements in urban sanitation.[4]

The Sanitation Reform Movement

The idea of a broad government mission to protect public health was rooted in the eighteenth-century Enlightenment movement, championed by Voltaire, Jeremy Bentham, Adam Smith, John Locke, and others, which articulated powerful new beliefs in the power of science and human reason to improve human living conditions. The rise of these beliefs paralleled the influence of the same ideas on institutions of democratic governance, such as belief in the primacy of an informed and reasoning citizenry. Direct precursors of the public health movement included British initiatives for penal reform in the 1770s and for the protection of industrial workers and child workers in the 1780s. Particularly important for English and American policies was the work of Jeremy Bentham and his Philosophical Radicals, who advocated addressing all public problems on a rational scientific basis and called for fundamental reforms including free trade, birth control, legal and parliamentary reform, and educational reform. The legacy of these ideas remains an important current in American environmental policy today (Winslow 1923; Rosen 1958, 131–37, 192–201).

The sanitary reform movement began in England in the 1830s, prompted by reform of England's Poor Laws. Edwin Chadwick, secretary of the Poor Law Commission and an ardent Benthamite, commissioned a systematic survey of the sanitary conditions of the urban poor and of preventable causes of their sicknesses, arguing that the cost of disease prevention could be shown to be less than the costs of widespread disease. The resulting three-volume report, published in 1842 under the title *The Sanitary Condition of the Labouring Population of England,* offered a compelling case that high incidence of disease and mortality was related to the filthy environmental conditions to which the urban poor were subjected: lack of ventilation and drainage, lack of safe water supplies, and lack of means to remove refuse regularly from houses and streets (Rosen 1958, 192–216). It led eventually to passage in 1848 of Britain's Public Health Act, which charged the government with responsibility for safeguarding the health of its population (Okun 1996, 453).

The Chadwick Report is generally recognized as the most important document in the history of the public health movement (Winslow 1923; Barnes 1935, 451–53; Rosen 1958, 214). Its underlying theory of disease causation was later proven incorrect: Chadwick, like many in his day, believed that disease was caused not by contagion but by "miasmas," the foul gases arising from poor drainage and stagnant wastes. The report's *solutions,* however, were in fact an effective set of remedies for reducing human exposure to the environmental conditions in which the real causes flourished. It also redefined public health from a moral problem that could be blamed on the weak character and voluntary living habits of the poor, or a medical problem that could be treated by physicians one patient at a time, to an engineering and social problem that must be solved by municipal governments, by providing proper environmental services for water supply, wastewater drainage, and waste removal (Clark 1972 [1852], 29–30).

The Chadwick Report inspired similar investigations in many American cities. In 1845 Dr. John Griscom published a similarly titled report, *The Sanitary Condition of the Laboring Population of New York,* which painted an equally grim picture. It reported for instance that an estimated eighteen thousand people were living in cellars under filthy and dank conditions, many below the level of nearby privies and subject to seepage and contamination by them. Even some schools operated under equally dismal conditions (Winslow 1923, 8–11; Rosen 1958, 237–39). The 1850 *Report of the Massachusetts Sanitary Commission,* drafted by Lemuel Shattuck, documented similar conditions in Boston (Winslow 1923, 25–26).

Over the ensuing decades, almost all major American cities conducted sanitary surveys, usually prompted by cholera outbreaks. The surveys consistently recommended building municipal water and sewer systems, improving street cleaning and garbage collection programs, creating stronger local health departments, and passing more effective sanitary laws (Duffy 1990, 97–100). A New York Citizens' Association report in 1865, for instance, identified stark disparities in disease and death rates among the city's districts owing to environmental living conditions. In the worst districts, residents were subjected to overcrowding, lack of ventilation, nonremoval of putrefiable wastes, filthy cesspools and sharply higher incidence of malaria (fig. 7). The report recommended sanitary laws for tenant houses, and improved buildings that would provide fresh air and sunlight. It urged the creation of an effective system of medical and sanitary inspection, and of air sampling and chemical analysis of water supplies. Finally, it advocated a serious investment in sanitary engineering to increase urban cleanliness and remove public nuisances (Citizens' Association of New York 1970 [1865]).

Like the Chadwick Report, these reports did not produce immediate policy changes, but most of their recommendations eventually were adopted. In 1866, New York City

Figure 7. Urban living conditions at the turn of the century. Even as late as 1903, this photo of Elizabeth Street in New York City shows a neighborhood in which more than forty-four "water closets" (privies) are present in a single yard. New York at the time housed more than four thousand millionaires but also some of the most crowded slums in the world, where sanitary conditions were often appallingly poor. [The Jacob A. Riis Collection # ST-1, Museum of the City of New York]

passed a Metropolitan Health Law which became a model for other U.S. cities, and Massachusetts established the first state board of health in 1869. By 1880 at least 94 percent of America's cities had a board of health, a health commissioner, or at least a health officer. Public-health officers and sanitarians led in articulating American thinking about waste collection and disposal problems, as well as wastewater sanitation issues, up through the 1890s (Melosi 1981, 33).

Public Health and Public Works

The sanitation movement involved issues not only of public health but of public works: that is, the construction and operation of water supply, wastewater management, and solid waste disposal services. It was also a matter of governance, in that waste disposal responsibilities that had been left to individual households were gradually assumed by governments. Urban water supplies before the nineteenth century were drawn entirely from local wells, rainwater cisterns, and local ponds and streams, and wastewater was simply dumped into backyard cesspools or privy vaults or neighborhood drainage ditches. In a few larger cities storm-water sewers served to carry off rainfall, but these were not intended for removal of household or industrial wastes. Maintenance of these drains was an individual rather than a government responsibility, usually enforced only sporadically, when overflows created a nuisance.

With the rapid growth of cities in the early nineteenth century, local water supplies became both inadequate and contaminated. Larger populations and industries used more water and discharged far more wastes, and required more organized fire protection and street cleaning as well (Tarr et al. 1980, 59–60).[5] Between 1802 and 1860, 136 cities built waterworks to bring in water from distant sources, and by 1880, 598 had done so. The result was that far more water was piped into the cities, without any provision for its removal. Most people simply discharged wastewater into existing cesspools or storm-water gutters and ditches that had been designed for far smaller quantities. In effect, the land under the city became the "sink" for wastewater.

The greater availability of piped-in water promoted use of more water per person, particularly with the installation of flush toilets. In less than three decades, water use per capita increased from 33 to 144 gallons per day in Chicago, 8 to 55 in Cleveland, and 55 to 149 in Detroit. The result was a paradoxical mixture of environmental health improvement and deterioration. The greater availability of water improved personal health and hygiene for those who could afford it, but exacerbated sanitary hazards for those exposed to cesspool and privy vault overflows, leakage into wells and cisterns, and poor drainage (Tarr et al. 1980, 62; Tarr and McMichael 1977, 47–61; Okun 1996, 454).

The introduction of piped water thus created a major element of the sanitation crisis, and ultimately led to a need for additional investments in drainage and sewer systems. Between 1850 and 1911 every major American city constructed a sewer system to remove wastewater, and discharge it — usually untreated — into nearby watercourses. Eighty-eight percent of the water was discharged untreated in 1909, and probably far more in earlier decades. There were serious debates at the time over whether separate systems should be constructed to keep sanitary wastes apart from surface runoff, and in fact municipal laws had traditionally required this separation, banning disposal of human wastes into public drainage sewers in order to protect people from exposure to their miasmas (Armstrong et al. 1976, 400). Given the far higher cost of a dual system, however, most large cities opted for a single combined system. This reduced capital costs but created a costly problem for the future: combined systems indiscriminately mixed rainwater and other surface runoff with household and industrial wastewater, so that when wastewater treatment plants ultimately were built they operated at far lower efficiencies, and produced serious over-flows and pollution episodes during periods of heavy rainfall (Tarr et al. 1980, 68–69).

The construction of sewer systems without waste treatment caused serious health prob-lems for downstream cities, which drew their water from the same rivers into which wastes were being discharged. Ironically, many of these cities had built expensive sewer systems to discharge their own wastes farther downstream. A few chemists and engineers had questioned these decisions, but the dominant position at the time was that "running water purifies itself" and that therefore "the solution to pollution is dilution" (Tarr et al. 1980, 68–72; Tarr 1985b, 521–22). Only after severe outbreaks of typhoid in downstream cities did public officials recognize the inaccuracy of this conventional wisdom. Interdisciplinary research by bacteriologists, chemists, and sanitary engineers in the early 1890s demon-strated the transmission of typhoid by sewage contamination, and led to the rapid intro-duction of water supply treatment processes: slow sand filters, then coagulants added to mechanical filtration systems, and beginning in 1908 the addition of chlorine disinfectants to the water supply. In 1880 only thirty thousand people in U.S. cities had filtered water supplies; by 1920 the total had increased to over twenty million, and outbreaks of typhoid thereafter declined rapidly (Tarr 1985a 1059–60).

By the early twentieth century, then, both water supply and wastewater management had been transformed from individual responsibilities to public services, and from small-scale, labor-intensive technologies to the most capital-intensive municipal projects of the nineteenth century. Each city constructed major public works designed first to bring in large quantities of water, then to carry it away again after use, and finally to filter and treat its own drinking water as a defense against pollution from other cities upstream.

In effect, cities and industries simply displaced their wastewater disposal from land to water, and from their own jurisdictions onto their downstream neighbors. They also defined the water pollution issue almost exclusively in terms of the sanitary hazards of human and animal wastes, paying little or no attention to industrial chemical pollutants except those that caused distaste or odor or interfered with the water filtration process. These incomplete links in the "metabolism" of urban water resurfaced as key issues for federal environmental policy in the 1950s and '60s (Tarr and McMichael 1977, 58; Tarr 1985a, 1059–67; Tarr 1985b, 522–23).

Public Health and Public Services

Household garbage management, meanwhile, gradually was likewise transformed from an individual responsibility to a municipal service. Unlike water supply and sewerage, solid waste collection was not intrinsically a capital-intensive technology, but a simple service which could be provided either privately for those who could afford it or publicly—by municipal agencies directly, or by hired contractors—for everyone. Through much of the nineteenth century household waste disposal remained primarily an individual task. Those who could afford it hired "cartmen" to remove wastes and dump them on vacant land or in rivers outside the city. Others burned them, or simply dumped them into the streets to be scavenged by pigs and ultimately beaten into dust or muck by the traffic. Only street cleaning was a municipal responsibility, and even this was irregular and often haphazard (Melosi 1981, 43–46).

With the dramatic increase in the size and population density of urban areas, the accumulation of waste became a central issue for the sanitation movement. The Chadwick Report and the American sanitary surveys redefined wastes from a mere annoyance to a health hazard. The upper and middle classes might keep their own neighborhoods clean, but rich and poor alike had to live with the sight and smell of filthy streets in other areas, and the threat of disease associated with these conditions. Sanitary reformers also argued that a cleaner city would be an inducement to business and economic development, and would hardly cost more than the sums already spent on private cartmen and illness (Melosi 1980, 110–14).

As the sanitation movement spread and local health departments emerged, therefore, city governments began taking more active responsibility for street cleaning and refuse disposal services. This evolution was significant both as a shift in municipal environmental management, and as an element in the broader political movement for municipal autonomy from rural-dominated state legislatures ("home rule"). Contracting with private scavenging companies was cities' initial preference, because it required little or no capital outlay or supervision. Advocates of private enterprise also favored this approach, much as free-enterprise advocates argue for contracting out and privatizing municipal services today (cf. Savas 1982, vs. Salomon 1989).

In practice, however, the contracting system was criticized both for political corruption in the awarding of contracts and for poor service by unaccountable private monopolies. These abuses, as well as more general arguments that community health and sanitation were proper responsibilities of city governments themselves, led many cities to take direct responsibility for waste collection and disposal. By 1880, 70 percent of U.S. cities did their own street cleaning; by the turn of the century more than 65 percent had some form of municipal collection service; and by 1920 this had increased to 89 percent. Nearly all also had authority to abate nuisances caused by unsanitary disposal (Melosi 1980, 108–11; 1981, 153–55; Armstrong et al. 1976, 435).

The most fundamental reforms in urban solid waste management began in New York City in 1895 under the leadership of Colonel George Waring, a sanitary engineer and the newly appointed commissioner of street cleaning. Waring introduced the first comprehensive system of municipal waste management in the United States, pioneering both in its administrative reform measures and in its substantive innovations in waste separation and recycling. The core of his philosophy was that waste was a menace to health and to decent living conditions, and could be eradicated only by a combination of efficient municipal government services and civic action.

Administratively, Waring transformed the street cleaning department from an inefficient agency dominated by political patronage into a disciplined public service agency whose street cleaners dressed in white uniforms, were paid better, and developed a sense of pride in their work. He also promoted high-visibility civic involvement programs such as street-cleaners' parades, neighborhood improvement associations, and even a "junior street cleaning league" to promote sanitation among young people. Substantively, he introduced mandatory separation of wastes by householders (organic materials, rubbish, and ashes). With the revenues from the sale and other practical uses of these wastes (organic materials for fertilizer and pig feed, scavenging of reusable materials from rubbish, and use of ash as fill material), as well as the greater efficiency of his work force, he provided more comprehensive service at half the previous cost of collection. Death and disease rates declined as well, due to the whole range of sanitation measures then being introduced, but certainly in part to improved street cleaning and waste collection (fig. 8). Waring's department came to be considered a model of an efficient and professional government service agency, and his innovations were widely adopted (Melosi 1981, 51–78; Armstrong et al. 1976, 436–37).[6]

Even as waste disposal became a municipal service, however, its methods remained crude. Much of the waste was simply dumped onto open land with no sanitary precautions, and scavenging—gleaning from the waste barges and dumps—was a widespread though unhealthy occupation of the poor. Nearly 10 percent of the municipalities dumped their wastes into watercourses, including nearly a dozen of the largest cities. Coastal cities such as New York dumped their wastes in the ocean, often so close to the shore that it occasionally fouled harbors and beaches.[7] A large fraction of the waste stream was organic food materials, since the transition to canned and processed foods had not yet occurred; over 20 percent of wastes were therefore recycled to farms as pig feed and fertilizer.[8]

Beginning in the 1880s both incineration and garbage "reduction" (oil extraction) were introduced. Vendors of these technologies advocated them as "ultimate solutions" to the sanitary problems of garbage (Armstrong et al. 1976, 436–37, 447–49). Neither, of course, was such a solution. Using the technologies then available, incineration simply redirected pollution of the land or water into pollution of the air, and oil extraction was itself a noxious process (Melosi 1981, 103). Not until the 1950s were these practices generally replaced by "sanitary landfills": controlled dumps in which the wastes were compacted and covered daily to reduce their health and aesthetic impacts.

In short, over the course of several decades urban solid waste management was transformed from a private affair into a community-wide municipal service, a shift justified initially by public health concerns and later—as the scientific basis of the health argument came under attack—by broader goals of technical efficiency, aesthetic improvement, and civic pride.

Interestingly, concerns about resource conservation appear to have played almost no role in the urban solid waste debates. Also, unlike later environmental debates, these

Figure 8a–b. These two photos illustrate the effectiveness of the "Waring model" of urban waste management as an efficiently operated government service. They show the same street in New York City, before and after Waring's reforms. [The Jacob A. Riis Collection #337 and 336, Museum of the City of New York]

reforms involved no significant criticism of overall levels of material consumption, or even of wasteful production practices that produced the waste streams (Melosi 1981, 234–36). This seems surprising, since many of the key sanitation reforms occurred during the same period in which conservation, preservation, and fears of a "timber famine" were emerging as major issues in public land and natural resource policies. What *was* a common factor among these issues was a rising belief in the efficacy of government services: a call for *public* management of environmental conditions for the benefit of the general population in place of the previous laissez-faire ideology of private management for the benefit of those who could afford it. In this fundamental respect both the natural resource conservation and preservation movements and the urban sanitary reform movement were not simply about the environment per se but about its governance.

Professionalization of Environmental Health

The sanitation movement drew its political strength from a broad civic alliance that united physicians, engineers, and a wide range of social reformers. In its early stages, beginning in the 1850s, this movement formed the vanguard of the liberal reform movement against the

inadequate housing and appalling working conditions of a rapidly urbanizing and industrializing society (Rosen 1958, 289–90). The existence of preventable health hazards
provided a powerful justification for using stronger and more professional municipal
governance to improve citizens' living conditions.

The New York Metropolitan Health Act marked a turning point in the history of U.S.
public health, by creating the first clearly professional agency for local public health administration. Prior to 1866 public health had been advocated by loose coalitions of physicians and civic reformers, but local government agencies had limited health authority and
were staffed by patronage rather than competence. Under the new law, health administration was delegated to a board of health consisting mainly of physicians and police commissioners, which was given broad discretionary authority to investigate, regulate, promote,
and implement sanitation measures (Rosen 1958, 243–48). State boards of health also
proliferated, beginning in Massachusetts in 1869.

The professionalization of public health paralleled a similar differentiation of sanitary
engineering as a distinct expertise, specializing in the particular problems of urban water
supply and wastewater and solid waste removal. Sanitary engineers were both environmental generalists and technical specialists: they were technical specialists in the way they

approached the design and construction of complex water supply and sewer systems, but they were also the most knowledgeable experts about the general urban physical environment and its material and energy flows. Because of their commitment to urban service systems, their career opportunities lay in municipal government, and by the early twentieth century they had emerged as key policymakers for urban environmental services, even superseding public health officials as the latter shifted their attention to other health priorities (Melosi 1981, 79–104). The growth and professionalization of the public health movement also created increased demand for experts in related fields, including chemists, bacteriologists, and statisticians. In 1872 an interdisciplinary society for public health professionals, the American Public Health Association, was established to provide a common forum and identity among them (Duffy 1990, 95–97, 129; Rosen 1958, 243–48).

The professionalization of public health and sanitary engineering represented not only an important development in itself, but a leading edge of a more general trend toward professionalization in many fields, including medicine, engineering, forestry, geology, chemistry, bacteriology, and other natural sciences. Significantly, this trend also reflected a shift in attitudes about governance. The early Federalists had believed that government should be staffed by an intelligent aristocracy; President Andrew Jackson had substituted government by political patronage. Now came a third idea: that government should be staffed by technical professionals earning their positions based on merit. The creation of the U.S. Geological Survey in 1879 and the enactment of the Pendleton Civil Service Act of 1883 marked the ascension of this principle to the federal level, but it was foreshadowed by the professionalization of local and state governments, beginning with their newly created health departments in the 1870s.

The origins of this trend were more practical than ideological. Operation of water and sewer systems and other sanitation measures required the expertise of health and engineering professionals, a need that was further underscored by the bacteriological discoveries of Pasteur and others in the 1880s. Similarly, federal water resource projects had to be sited by trained geologists and designed and managed by competent engineers, and forests, it was argued, were best managed by professional foresters. Professionally staffed agencies were thus necessary to carry out the technically specialized responsibilities of environmental management, but their gradual specialization also led to schisms between experts' professional perspectives and the broader but less technical visions that motivated general public support. Where these agendas could be skillfully orchestrated by a charismatic administrator, as under Colonel Waring in New York City, significant improvements in environmental management could be accomplished. In the absence of such leadership, however, professionalized agencies and citizen reform groups often formed only uneasy partnerships, foreshadowing those among government agencies and environmental advocacy groups today.

Bacteriology and the "New Public Health"

The sanitation movement achieved major improvements in urban environmental conditions. Examples included the establishment of safe and sufficient water supplies, wastewater drainage and sewer systems, and refuse and excrement removal programs; cleaner streets and housing; significant reductions in death and disease; and the founding of professionally staffed municipal and state agencies for public health protection. But it had been justified to the public based on what proved to be an inaccurate theory — that diseases were caused by the breathing of miasmas (the odors of filth) rather than by contagion (transmission by direct contact with the sick) or some other cause.

In retrospect both contagionism and the anti-contagionist miasma or "filth" theory of disease causation had scientific flaws, and their advocates' recommendations based on claims of science were often colored by nonscientific factors such as judgments about their political, economic, and social consequences. Contagionism provided support for the quarantine laws, and for the authoritative regulatory role of government which they entailed. Anti-contagionism in turn was associated both with opposition to bureaucratic regulation and with advocacy of the liberal reform movement more generally (Rosen 1958, 287–90). Colonel Waring, for instance, the great "apostle of cleanliness" in New York City, advocated urban cleanliness as both a health-based attack on sewer gas and an aesthetic goal by which to measure a community's level of civilization (Melosi 1981, 60–61).[9]

The improvement of urban health following the introduction of sanitary measures provided apparent support for the anti-contagionist argument. However, the discoveries of bacteria as specific disease pathogens in the 1880s discredited miasma theory, and thereby undermined the scientific position of the sanitation advocates who had based their policy prescriptions on this rationale.[10] The scientific experiments of Pasteur, Lister, Koch, and others demonstrated that key diseases were caused not by gases or even filth in general but by specific microorganisms, and that artificial immunities to these could be developed. The work of Walter Reed and others on yellow fever in the 1890s took a further step, showing that traditional contagionism had also been overly simplistic: contagious diseases were not necessarily spread just by direct contact, but could also be transmitted ecologically, by intermediate host species (vectors) and healthy human carriers (Rosen 1958, 294–343).

These discoveries triggered a fundamental reorientation of public health policies and priorities. The new priority was on applying bacteriology to abate specific health risks, and immunology to prevent disease by vaccination, especially in children, the most frequent victims. A major effect was to shift the locus of public health professionals from environmental sanitation agencies to the laboratory. By the turn of the century, most major cities had not only health departments with professional staffs, usually headed by physicians, but also bacteriologists, engineers, chemists, statisticians, and laboratory facilities for bacteriological testing. Key policy changes included the introduction of bacteriologically-based initiatives to abate specific environmental health hazards, such as contaminated milk (combated by requiring "pasteurization" to destroy bacteria), unsafe drinking water (by filtration and disinfection), and exposure to insect vectors (by mosquito eradication). Also, typhoid outbreaks led to state health laws regulating stream pollution, and to federal research programs on stream pollution by the U.S. Public Health Service (Tarr and McMichael 1977, 55–57; Tarr 1985a, 1059–67).

The demise of the "filth theory" also led to a reappraisal of the role of environmental programs in health departments. Charles Chapin, health commissioner of the city of Providence, for instance, argued that the new science required public health officials to make distinctions between dirt that was dangerous and dirt that was not, rather than indiscriminately attacking general filth. He acknowledged that urban cleanliness was a legitimate goal in its own right, but to him it was no longer a high priority for health departments: "It will make no difference to a city's mortality whether its streets are clean or not, whether its garbage is removed promptly or allowed to accumulate, or whether it has a plumbing law. . . . [It is] more important to remove adenoids from the child than to remove ashes from the back yard." In his view, the health officer should be free to devote his energies to "what he alone can do. He should not waste his time arguing with the owners of pig-sties or compelling landlords to empty their cesspools." Improvement of personal hygiene could eliminate the need for costly capital expenditures: "The introduction, or even the purification, of a municipal water supply may cost millions. . . . To wash the hands before eating and after the toilet costs nothing" (quoted in Starr 1982, 190). By 1925 less than 20 percent of U.S. cities still had sanitary management functions in their health departments. Garbage collection, water supply, sewerage, and nuisance removal were now handled by sanitary engineers in separate departments, while health departments enforced only against public health nuisances (Melosi 1981, 81–84).

The clash between this philosophy and that of traditional sanitary reform advocates was perhaps most vividly illustrated by a major conflict between 1905 and 1914 over the question of whether sewage discharges should be allowed into waterways that served as sources of drinking water. Several leading physicians argued strongly against sewage dumping: the "new public health" to them meant not simply promoting personal hygiene, but vigorously controlling all direct routes of infection, particularly in this case typhoid fever. A 1908 report to the Conference of State and Provincial Boards of Health by its Committee on the Pollution of Streams endorsed this position, recommending that sewage disposal should not be allowed into streams used for water supply, and that it should be curtailed more generally because it was also hazardous to recreation. By 1909 a number of states had passed laws forbidding the discharge of raw sewage from new municipal systems (Tarr et al. 1980, 72–73; Tarr and McMichael 1977, 56–57).

More extreme advocates of the "new public health," however, flatly discounted any relationship between environmental service functions, such as garbage removal, and public health as unscientific and anachronistic, and advocated removal of these functions from health departments' responsibilities. The fact that poor sanitary conditions provided habitat for bacteriological pathogens and their vectors was swept aside in a fundamental shift of ideology among medical and public health professionals. The "old" public health — based on social reform impulses, sanitation projects and discredited science — was displaced by a "new public health" based on bacteriological science and modern medicine.

Sanitary engineers, meanwhile, argued that the dilution power of streams should be utilized to the fullest so long as doing so did not create a nuisance, endanger public health, or damage personal property: in the engineer's catchy sound bite, "the solution to pollution is dilution." Leading engineers argued that "a dollar spent in water purification goes much farther toward protecting a community from the dangers of sewage pollution in its potable water supply than a dollar laid out in sewage-treatment works" (quoted in Tarr and McMichael 1977, 57–58). This policy placed a heavy case-by-case burden of proof on opponents. Engineers also used the issue to assert their own professional authority, defending their judgment against oversight by the medical profession.[11] Sanitary engineering was strongly influenced during this period by the apparent effectiveness of the new technologies for drinking-water filtration and disinfection (chlorination), as well as by old beliefs that flowing water purifies itself and that cost-effectiveness should determine policy decisions (Okun 1996, 454–55).

The engineers' arguments were attractive to local governments, since in addition to being less expensive, drinking-water treatment protects a municipality's own citizens while sewage treatment protects only downstream communities. By the beginning of World War I engineers' policies had won out over the anti-discharge position of the "sentimentalists and health authorities," as one engineer described them. The result was a widespread increase in urban wastewater discharges to rivers and waterways, exacerbating ambient water pollution. This result would eventually lead municipalities to lobby for federal financial assistance to build sanitary sewer systems and wastewater treatment plants (Tarr et al. 1980, 73; Tarr and McMichael 1977, 56–57).

Historical accounts differ in their interpretation of this shift in environmental health policies and institutions. From one perspective, it was a major step forward, in which a broad but scattershot approach to sanitation was replaced with more effective targeting of public health measures: "A scientific understanding of the elements involved in the transmission of communicable diseases led health authorities to act with greater discrimination in quarantine and environmental sanitation" (Rosen 1958, 335). From a different perspective, however, it provided a rationale for public health officials to disengage themselves from commitments to moral or social reform and devote themselves to a narrower, more technical, and more politically comfortable agenda: "Whereas the sanitary movement had received a major impetus from civic groups and volunteer agencies, the public health movement was now firmly in the hands of physicians and other trained specialists. The proposals of the Progressive movement, with its emphasis on environmental reforms, required expensive social programs. Science, by providing new means for identifying, curing, and preventing contagious diseases, was thought to offer health departments a way to promote health without the cost of major social changes" (Duffy 1990, 206). Or more succinctly, "The dividing line between the old and new ideologies of public health was an explicit denial of responsibility for social reform" (Rosenkrantz, quoted in Starr 1982, 189, 196).

To the extent that health departments did continue to advocate a social reform agenda, the emphasis of the "new public health" was on personal hygiene, on universal medical examinations and health education, and on maternal and child health rather than on environmental sanitation. Primary activities now included distribution of safe milk supplies to the poor, outreach by public health nurses, vaccination campaigns, school health inspections, education of mothers aimed at reducing high infant mortality rates, and the establishment of neighborhood health centers for health education and social services for the poor (Duffy 1990, 209–15). Environmental sanitation problems had been demoted once again from health hazards to mere "annoyances."

Industrial Emissions: Pollution as Progress

For all the policy reform devoted to urban sanitation, there was virtually no comparable progress in controlling the massive increases in industrial pollution that occurred during the same period. In fact, the opposite occurred: traditional common-law principles that might have protected people from these impacts were systematically weakened in favor of industrial "progress."

Before the widespread construction of municipal sewer systems, industrial wastewater discharges were leading causes of stream pollution. Commercial fisheries commissions in several states, for instance, sought to prohibit discharge of the most noxious wastes — such as from distilleries, slaughterhouses, and textile and paper mills — as public nuisances in an effort to protect aquatic life (Colten and Skinner 1996, 23). Several of the nineteenth-century sanitary surveys identified these effluents as poisonous and as threats to health. However, they were not as obvious or widespread as urban filth and fecal wastes, and therefore did not attract the same attention from the sanitation movement. State agencies could point out these hazards, but few had effective powers to regulate or enforce against them.

Once sewers were built, downstream typhoid epidemics understandably reconfirmed the priority of bacteriological pathogens over industrial discharges as a public health issue.[12] Some public health experts at the time even considered toxic industrial effluents to be germicidal and thus beneficial or at least benign (Colten and Skinner 1996, 64). At worst they were assumed to affect health only indirectly, mainly by diminishing the natural capacity of flowing water to purify itself, and accordingly received little attention until after World War I (Tarr 1985a, 1059–65).[13] The only federal water pollution law prior to World War II was the 1924 Oil Pollution Control Act, which prohibited offshore oil discharges from oceangoing ships in order to prevent fouling of ships. Significantly, it did not apply to industries on shore or even to inland shipping (Colten and Skinner 1996, 75–76).

Industrial air pollution was a far more visible and ubiquitous problem, particularly the heavy, dark "smoke evil" of particulates and sulfur in the most industrialized cities. Smoke was recognized as a health hazard even then. It increased fatality rates from pneumonia, diphtheria, and other lung diseases, and also increased nasal, throat, and bronchial illnesses. The dark pall that it cast on surrounding areas was even attacked as a cause of mental health problems. It also damaged property, discoloring and corroding buildings and statuary, smudging goods and soiling clothing, necessitating costly maintenance and repainting, and destroying urban vegetation. It had a greater impact on the quality of life than perhaps any other urban ill, pervading daily experience with visible aesthetic blight and requiring constant housecleaning and rewashing of clothes (Grinder 1980, 83–87).[14]

One might ask, why did the courts not provide protection against air and water pollution? The traditional riparian law of water rights entitled each user to water "undiminished in quantity and unimpaired in quality" from that of upstream users, and the common law of nuisance had long required that each individual use his property only in such ways as not to harm others (Futrell 1993, 23–24). These were basic principles of the common law of torts, which allowed individuals to go to court to protect their rights and obtain compensation for damages caused by others. Also, municipalities' police power allowed them to regulate public health hazards, and some even created special zones for noxious industries and garbage dumps that might otherwise be public nuisances. Often the only salient effect of such policies, however, was the gradual migration of industries to the periphery of cities, where they were less subject to lawsuits and regulations (Colten and Skinner 1996, 70–73, 93).

The courts did provide relief in some cases. In some water pollution suits against municipalities, for instance, they distinguished a right to discharge surface runoff from a right to discharge wastes hazardous to health. However, they were often unwilling to take strong environmental protection positions in cases involving scientific claims that were difficult to prove, leaving downstream victims with a formidable burden of proof in pursuing actions against upstream polluters. Courts were willing to hold upstream polluters responsible for downstream property damages whose causes were clearly demonstrable, but not for less provable disease outbreaks.

In considering industrial pollution, the courts faced a conflict between fundamentally opposed principles of property rights: did industries have a legitimate right to discharge pollutants as an unfortunate but unavoidable byproduct of the material benefits they provided, or did those who suffered the consequences have a right to pure air and water undefiled by industry? Traditional common law in principle supported the victims, but these principles arose from British precedents favoring recreational enjoyment of land by the landed aristocracy: wealthy landowners could block development on grounds that it interfered with their "quiet enjoyment" of the "natural use" of their estates. The common law in America, in contrast, had gradually evolved to favor the rights of those who first put natural resources to productive use, as in the prior appropriation doctrine for western mining and water rights and the preemption claims of western settlers (Horwitz 1988, 51–52).

The courts thus began with common-law principles protecting pollution victims, and even with criteria for "reasonable use" that limited dischargers' right to impose pollution risks on others, but gradually shifted to a doctrine that industrialization represented progress, and that its pollution damage was therefore simply the unavoidable side effect of a desired social goal. In an age of booming industrialization, the courts were reluctant to interfere with this "release of productive energy," and therefore treated pollution as a mere annoyance rather than a legal nuisance or an actionable health hazard. In essence, they adopted a rudimentary "cost-benefit balancing" approach. Rather than protecting individuals from harm, they weighed the damage to the injured party against the economic burden to the industry of abating its pollution — or even worse, the imagined economic damage to society as a whole that might result from slowing down industrial growth — and generally sided with industry (Grinder 1980, 90–93). The 1939 Restatement of Torts confirmed this utilitarian approach, and redefined the "reasonability" of a nuisance from a matter of clear victims' rights to a process of "balancing" the utility of the actor's conduct against the gravity of the harm (Colten and Skinner 1996, 75–78).

In effect, these decisions replaced the principles of common-law rights with doctrines of economic balancing, which in practice permitted municipal and industrial pollution to continue.[15] These precedents were similar in concept to more recent legal arguments for balancing of the economic interests of polluters against those of their victims rather than upholding clearly the rights of the victims (Rosen 1993, 303–81). During the subsequent Progressive reform era they were overturned in some states, though not in all.

With the erosion of common-law protections, the only remaining recourse for environmental protection was to expand state and municipal regulation of pollution as a public health hazard. By 1912, twenty-three of the twenty-eight largest cities had passed smoke abatement ordinances, and nearly every major city had a smoke inspector, although they often had little power and many judges refused to levy more than token fines for violations. Smoke inspectors themselves were torn between adversarial and cooperative approaches: some argued for aggressive prosecution of polluters while others were content to try to educate them, urging them to adopt more fuel-efficient technologies in their own self-interests. Some cities also passed water pollution ordinances, but local governments by themselves had no jurisdiction over many upstream sources, and most states gave only advisory and investigative powers to state health authorities. Many large cities were located on *interstate* rivers, and legal controls for these began to develop only in the 1920s — and even then the controls pertained only to a few watersheds, such as the Delaware and Ohio Rivers and the Great Lakes (Grinder 1980, 91–95; Tarr et al. 1980, 70–72; Tarr 1985b, 524). Ironically, while these statutes began to lay a basis for government monitoring and protection of air and water, they often further undermined common-law rights against polluters as well. Statutes superseded common-law principles, but often with weak or unenforceable provisions. Some were riddled with exemptions for favored industries, and many even explicitly authorized use of some streams for waste disposal rather than protecting them. State laws also had no leverage against upstream sources that lay across state lines (Colten and Skinner 1996, 75–77).

In short, control of industrial water pollution did not become a significant policy focus until the 1920s, and industrial air pollution policy, despite active political pressure during the Progressive era, was limited to relatively ineffectual local smoke abatement ordinances. The onset of World War I crippled even limited reforms, justifying all-out production regardless of pollution in the name of the war effort;[16] and in the postwar laissez-faire spirit of the 1920s, the most that could be expected of environmental policy was pro-business efforts at education and friendly persuasion. Many of the hazards of pollution were known to experts at the time, but the industries retained control over their own waste management decisions. They exercised that control with some concern for public safety, but also substantial deference to convenience and expediency. Overall, the net impact of legislation and enforcement on industrial pollution prior to 1960 was negligible (Colten and Skinner 1996, 46, 94, 162–63).

From a governance perspective, a key reason for the failure to address industrial pollution was not that its effects were less serious than other environmental hazards, but that pollution control required regulation of private behavior rather than merely provision of water supply and sanitation services. More particularly, it required regulation not just of individuals, but of powerful economic interests, the industrial firms that provided the community's jobs, taxes, political contributions, and philanthropy. Even the earlier sanitary reform movement had drawn some of its support from business and medical opponents of quarantine regulation. By the late nineteenth century the concentrated economic and political power of the major industrial corporations, as well as their promise of general wealth and prosperity, made them formidable opponents of regulation.

Environmental Policy as Civic Reform

By the beginning of the twentieth century, urban environmental quality had evolved from a sanitation or public health agenda to a far broader public movement for urban livability and civic reform. Its advocates were now a new and vigorous array of voluntary citizen groups. Many of these groups were involved in the broader Progressive movement for civic reform. These groups sought an overarching goal of reform of elective politics, improvement of education and working conditions, and protection of the welfare of women and children. Environmental improvement to them meant promoting cleanliness and efficiency in both waste management and urban governance. Other groups lobbied more narrowly for particular causes — noise abatement, sanitation, urban beautification, clean air — and never coalesced into any overall environmental movement comparable to that of the 1970s and '80s. Women's organizations played major roles in these movements. Many women were "social feminists," committed to civic improvement, urban cleanliness, and improving the living conditions of children and the poor as well as to seeking voting rights and greater social justice for their gender. By the early years of the twentieth century the involvement of women's organizations in civic causes had become so widespread that the term "municipal housecleaning" became synonymous with sanitation reform (Melosi 1985, 494–515; Grinder 1980, 88–90; Hoy 1995).

What these groups shared was a commitment to broad civic reform and to improved urban livability. This commitment meant not rejecting city life in favor of romanticized nature, nor even rejecting industrial production per se, but advocating urban livability as a legitimate goal in its own right. The "City Beautiful" movement epitomized this new focus. Beginning with the visionary urban exhibits of the 1893 Columbian Exposition in Chicago — the five hundredth anniversary of the European discovery of America — urban reformers sprang up in many cities, spreading the idea that an attractive urban environment need not be a matter merely of efficiency or even of health, but was an expression of a common aspiration to be a civilized community.

The urban reformers brought with them a dual commitment both to lobbying for government action and to mobilizing direct citizen participation through city clean-up days, youth sanitation activities, and other projects. These tactics were quite different from the narrower professional agenda of institutionalizing environmental management responsibilities in efficient and competent administrative agencies. Then as now, these approaches complemented each other but often coexisted in uneasy partnerships. Public participants lacked the professionals' technical expertise and sought broader goals, and professionals in turn disdained both the more superficial understanding and sometimes the broader goals themselves that were inherent in public voluntary organizations.

In a sense, therefore, the broader civic improvement movement strengthened the movement for urban environmental reform, broadening its political constituencies and appeal at just the time when its older health justification was being undermined. The environmental reform movement's actual accomplishments, however, were limited to relatively ineffectual smoke and noise abatement laws. Significant reductions in industrial pollution did not occur until the 1930s and '40s, and then they were mainly due to techno-logical changes such as natural-gas pipelines that made pollution abatement cheaper and more efficient rather than the result of regulations.[17]

The Progressive urban environmental movement has therefore been dismissed by some later commentators as futile and naive, particularly for its advocates' belief that fundamen-tal economic and industrial processes could be changed by legislation rather than by technological progress. As a policy goal, urban beautification was more vulnerable to political pressures than was public health, and was no match for the preoccupation with patriotism and national security that took over the American policy agenda with the onset of World War I. Nonetheless, the urban environmental movement created key founda-tions for later and more aggressive policies: government responsibility for a broader range of environmental conditions, smoke inspection programs, government studies document-ing air and water quality hazards, and other measures.

National Policies for Environmental Health

Environmental health was an important urban issue from early on, but the federal govern-ment played virtually no role in environmental health policy, nor indeed even in public health policy more generally, until the twentieth century.

The predecessor of the U.S. Public Health Service was a system of federally sponsored hospitals for seamen, which was authorized in 1798 and expanded with the steamboat trade up the Mississippi River valley during the early nineteenth century. This system was formalized as the Marine Hospital Service in 1870, and its mission was soon broadened to include helping state and local governments apply quarantine laws to interstate and for-eign shipping. Beginning in 1878 it was authorized to impose federal quarantine regula-tions, which might if necessary be more stringent than those of state and local govern-ments (Mullan 1989, 14–20).[18]

The study of occupational health hazards was also an important foundation for later public health and environmental regulatory policies, but such hazards attracted little pol-icy attention until the twentieth century. Early observers such as Benjamin Franklin and Cotton Mather were aware of some workplace hazards, such as the dangers of lead poison-ing among typesetters, but occupational causes of disease generally received little attention before the 1830s. Increased awareness spread to the United States in the 1830s from England, but a report by the American doctor Benjamin McCready in 1837 (*On the*

Influence of Trades, Professions and Occupations in the United States in the Production of Disease) was virtually the only systematic study on the subject in the United States before the twentieth century.

Initial public policies dealing with American occupational issues were concerned not with environmental health hazards but with general working conditions for women and children. Most northern industrial states passed child labor laws between 1848 and 1860, and laws limiting the length of the work day followed, but federal laws even for these protections were not enacted until the Progressive era of the early twentieth century. There were few laws requiring industrial health and safety practices, and little inspection and enforcement even of these. A modest body of medical literature on occupational health effects accumulated during the latter half of the nineteenth century, particularly on the health hazards of mining, but these studies led to no public policies until the twentieth century (Duffy 1990, 95; Rosen 1958, 271–75).

Environmental causes of disease assumed increased national prominence in 1898 as an occupational hazard for American soldiers. During the Spanish-American War, American troops were sent overseas for the first time to an environment where yellow fever was endemic (Cuba), and many suffered the consequences. In a major breakthrough for environmental health, army surgeon Walter Reed and his colleagues identified mosquitoes as the disease's vector, and the Marine Hospital Service in 1901 was given funds for a new Hygienic Laboratory to continue and expand these studies. The agency was renamed the Public Health and Marine Hospital Service in 1902, and in 1912 it was finally renamed the U.S. Public Health Service, by a statute which extended the agency's mission beyond epidemic diseases to include sanitation, sewage, water pollution, and occupational health hazards. With these changes the Public Health Service became in effect both the first national agency for public health and the first federal *environmental* health protection agency (Tobey 1926, 75–102; Duffy 1990, 239–42).

The Progressive era produced a gradual increase in government attention to health hazards in the workplace environment. A key figure in this change was Dr. Alice Hamilton, whose studies of the health of men and women working with phosphorus, lead, radium, and other dangerous substances were landmarks in occupational health. Company doctors tended to side with employers in blaming occupational injuries and diseases on individual workers, but a series of workplace crises gradually demonstrated that conditions beyond the workers' control were often to blame, and some policy reforms followed. Mining disasters, for instance, led to the creation of a Bureau of Mines in the Department of the Interior in 1910 to investigate safety and health in the mines. Its activities were later expanded to include studies of other health hazards, such as lead poisoning in mines and from motor vehicles, in cooperation with the Public Health Service (Tobey 1926, 296–99).

By 1910 the Departments of Commerce and Labor had published a list of hazardous trades and occupational illnesses, and in 1915 the Public Health Service created a Division of Industrial Hygiene and Sanitation. By 1940 researchers began to codify maximum allowable concentrations (MACs) for toxins in the workplace. These were not legally enforceable regulations, but served as benchmarks of voluntary safe practice (Colten and Skinner 1996, 16–18).

A Children's Bureau was created in 1911 to improve children's working conditions, followed by a Department of Labor in 1913 and an Office of Industrial Hygiene and Sanitation in the Public Health Service in 1914. Fires and other identifiable health crises sparked ad hoc reforms: examples included phosphorus poisoning among match factory workers, the Triangle Shirtwaist Factory fire, and radium poisoning in watch-dial painters. Like the Environmental Protection Agency, however, the federal Occupational Safety and Health Administration and its regulatory authorities were not created until 1970 (Duffy 1990, 286–87).

Two other important precursors of modern federal environmental regulations were the Pure Food and Drugs and Meat Inspection Acts of 1906. These laws were inspired in part by government experts in food hygiene who campaigned for higher standards of purity in food canning. The issue was projected vividly into public awareness by the "muckraking" writer Upton Sinclair, whose exposé *The Jungle* documented grossly unsanitary conditions in the meat packing industry. Perhaps counterintuitively, however, the reformers succeeded in part because they had strong backing from influential businesses. The major food and drug companies, which were then consolidating their positions in national and export markets, actually welcomed government regulation as an asset that would drive out cheaper competitors and simultaneously back their products with the reassurance of government certification (Keller 1994, 190–94; Bosso 1987). This was friendly regulation of producers, in addition to protection of consumers (Horwitz 1988, 76).[19]

The Food and Drug Act established federal authority for regulation of food and drug contaminants, which soon came to include pesticide residues (Tobey 1926, 187–97). Not until years later was this mission moved from the U.S. Department of Agriculture to an independent Food and Drug Administration (FDA), and until 1970 food and drug regulation remained one of the few precedents for a federal environmental health regulatory program.[20]

The only other important nineteenth-century predecessors for modern federal environmental health agencies were several bureaus of the Department of Agriculture. USDA's Bureau of Chemistry was responsible both for the promotion of agricultural production through chemical research, and for studies related to adulteration of foods. In practice the bureau had little real effectiveness, since while it cited thousands of firms for violations, the penalties were so light as to be meaningless (Keller 1994, 193). USDA's Bureau of Entomology, established in 1904 from programs dating to 1877, was responsible for studies of insects both as agricultural pests and as environmental vectors threatening to human health, such as mosquitoes, fleas, flies, lice, and ticks. These studies laid the basis for many of the large-scale pesticide application programs of the twentieth century (Tobey 1926, 221–24).[21] Finally, USDA's Bureau of Biological Survey (prior to 1896 the Division of Ornithology and Mammalogy) began as a research unit concerned with native wildlife and its relationship to agriculture, but grew in the twentieth century into a major operational program for the eradication of species viewed as agricultural pests or environmental disease vectors. This program began with rodents such as rats and ground squirrels, but later included larger predators including wolves and coyotes. The effectiveness of this program contributed to driving some of these species close to extinction.

Summary

Both the nineteenth-century sanitation movement and the urban environmental reform initiatives that followed achieved important gains in environmental living conditions and public health. They contributed to significant improvements in urban housing conditions, in drainage and sanitation, and in purity of water and food. Beginning as early as 1870, public health statistics began to show steady declines in mortality, due at least in part to these measures. Among the chief beneficiaries were children. Infant mortality rates in New York City, for instance, dropped from 273 per thousand in 1885 to 94 in 1915 (Rosen 1958, 338–43). Vaccination programs and other public health measures contributed to these outcomes, but environmental sanitation measures clearly remained important and effective methods for reducing public health hazards, as well as for improving urban living conditions more generally.

The sanitation and urban improvement movements also produced enduring changes in American environmental governance. Urban water supply, sanitation, waste management, and smoke abatement became government responsibilities, as did public health functions more generally. The scientific and technical aspects of these issues helped to force professionalization of government service, and this professionalization in turn opened new political cleavages between technical elites and citizen advocacy groups that recur in environmental policy controversies today.

In the classic definition by C. E. A. Winslow in 1923, public health is "the science and the art of preventing disease, prolonging life, and promoting physical health and efficiency through organized community efforts for the sanitation of the environment, the control of community infections, the education of the individual in principles of personal hygiene, the organization of medical and nursing service for the early diagnosis and preventive treatment of disease, and the development of the social machinery which will ensure to every individual in the community a standard of living adequate for the maintenance of health" (1923, 1).

Public health in this view is not a single intellectual discipline, but a field of social activity. It includes applications of chemistry and bacteriology, of engineering and statistics, of physiology and pathology and epidemiology, and in some measure of sociology, and it builds from these basis sciences a comprehensive program of community service. This diversity has led to substantial tensions among professions and priorities, and among public health aims, environmental quality for its own sake, and other civic goals. These tensions were evident when widespread public health policies were first introduced, and they have remained persistent challenges for American environmental policy.

Today as then, environmental policy both is and is not a public health issue. Most of the Environmental Protection Agency's programs were created primarily to protect public health: from air and water pollution, from toxic chemicals and pesticides, from hazardous wastes, and from other exposures. Many scientists and health professionals, however, remain deeply ambivalent about the priority of these hazards compared to other causes of death and disease. To some, the industrial carcinogens feared by the public are the miasmas of the twentieth century: a source of unsubstantiated fears that burden the economy with high costs and divert attention from more obvious causes of death and disease (see e.g. Doll and Peto 1981; Ames et al. 1987; Mossman et al. 1990). Today as then, such voices call for more elaborate scientific study and evaluation of relative risks and priorities before government action, and for more narrowly targeted measures to abate the worst problems, rather than for broader and more politically controversial social reforms (e.g. Graham et al. 1988; Abelson 1994).

Others, however, argue that prudence calls for preventive action based on more preliminary evidence, rather than allowing "paralysis by analysis" until statistically significant numbers of people have died (e.g. Bailar et al. 1988). They argue too that history has vindicated this more cautious approach (e.g. Tesh 1981, 1988; Shy 1990), and that new evidence suggests both additional hidden risks that have not yet been carefully studied (e.g. Colborn et al. 1993) and the reemergence of old scourges in forms resistant to purely medical solutions (e.g. Garrett 1994). The most famous act in public health history, after all, was Dr. John Snow's legendary removal of the handle of London's Broad Street pump after he had observed that many of his cholera patients had drunk from it—thirty years before Pasteur and others identified the actual microbiological agent responsible for the disease (Rosen 1958, 314; Okun 1996, 453). Public health decisions inevitably are matters of political debate over proof versus prudence: since knowledge will always be imperfect, when does one know *enough* to justify government action, given the risks and the costs of either acting or not acting?

To the general public, meanwhile, the environmental quality issue in the 1990s, as in the Progressive era, represents a broad complex of civic concerns. Health risks clearly remain a central focus, despite confusion over the arguments among experts. Of equal importance, however, are the preservation of natural landscapes and amenities, the attractiveness of human communities, and the restraining of big businesses. Faced with growing economic insecurity and anti-government political rhetoric, ordinary citizens in the 1990s are more and more cynical about the ability of government to address any of these problems. This attitude is markedly different from that of the nineteenth-century reformers and itself serves the goals of those who oppose strong environmental governance.

An important lesson from the sanitation and urban environmental quality movements is that creating and sustaining political legitimacy for government action in the name of common public goals is a constant challenge. In American politics, health hazards have long been a justification for government action, from the quarantine laws to sanitation programs to modern risk regulations. They also have achieved great improvements in human living conditions, despite causing some new problems as well. Even actions such as these, however, remain vulnerable to attacks based on scientific uncertainty, on the economic burdens they create, and on general ideological hostility to "big government." Broader visions of a desirable environment are even more difficult to implement: they are constantly at risk of counterattack by self-interested constituencies painting them as matters of mere amenities and individual taste, which if imposed by governments could be tarred as elitist paternalism. The cross-cutting tensions between health and other goals of environmental policy, between official experts and interested citizens, and among claims of individual and common public interests remain fundamental and problematic characteristics of American environmental policy issues.

8 Progressivism: Conservation in the Public Interest

> The principles which govern the conservation movement, like all great and effective things, are simple and easily understood. . . . The first principle of conservation is development, the use of the natural resources now existing on this continent for the benefit of the people who live here now. . . . In the second place conservation stands for the prevention of waste. . . . [T]here is a third principle. It is this: The natural resources must be developed and preserved for the benefit of the many, and not merely the profit of a few. . . . Conservation means the greatest good for the greatest number for the longest time. — Gifford Pinchot, *The Fight for Conservation*

American environmental policy today involves many federal agencies. Each has specific statutory missions — such as pollution control and protection of endangered species — and specific limitations, as well as a more general mandate to promote harmony between human activities and the natural environment.[1]

At the end of the nineteenth century, however, neither these policies nor most of the agencies now responsible for them yet existed. The General Land Office was responsible for disposal of public lands. The Army Corps of Engineers was responsible for clearing streams for navigation and building levees along their banks for flood protection. A few relatively new agencies — the U.S. Geological Survey in the Interior Department and the Bureau of Forestry in the Department of Agriculture, for instance — were responsible for environmental data collection and applied research. Yellowstone National Park and a few other areas had been reserved in federal ownership, but they were merely policed by the army: there was no National Park Service. Nor were any federal agencies responsible for multipurpose water resource or forest management, for soil conservation, for wildlife protection, for air or water pollution control, for protecting public health, or for the many other government functions that represent environmental policy today. The dominant environmental policies were to encourage the conversion of the continent's environmental assets into economic commodities, and to provide government-owned environmental resources to private entrepreneurs as subsidies to promote this goal.

In the half-century between the 1890s and 1946, these policies were overlaid by a new and radically different principle: that both water resources and large areas of the public lands should remain in government ownership, and that federal agencies staffed by professional experts should manage them. The primary goal of this policy was still commodity production for national economic growth, but by a different set of governance principles and policy tools. The origins of this fundamental change lay not just in Franklin Roosevelt's New Deal of the 1930s, as is often supposed, but in the Progressive administration of his Republican cousin Theodore, a quarter century earlier. Theodore Roosevelt became president by chance with the assassination of President McKinley in 1902, after moving rapidly from New York City police commissioner to governor to vice president. Aided by a brain trust of thoughtful and purposeful reformers — Gifford Pinchot, WJ McGee, and others — he introduced a radically new "Progressive" philosophy of national governance, and a philosophy of planned and managed conservation of the resources of the natural environment (Lacey 1979).

In Roosevelt's view, government should be an active force to achieve the public interest, a *counterweight* to the concentrated economic power of big business, not simply a "night watchman" or laissez-faire protector of property. The "public interest" meant utilitarian efficiency — "the greatest good for the greatest number of people over the longest time" — and the broadening of the middle class, not simply the enrichment of powerful special interests. The president should use his powers to their fullest to direct this program, and should run government like an efficient business enterprise. Government should be staffed not through political patronage, but by competent professionals — scientists and engineers — with broad discretionary authority to manage resources for the overall public good, rather than for partisan advantage or personal gain. Natural resources should be developed for economic use, but efficiently and for the general public benefit, not simply given away. Efficient planning by government engineers and scientists should replace the economically wasteful speculation and inequitable monopolization of resources that had resulted from wholesale privatization. The problems of an increasingly urban and industrial society could and should be corrected by public policy (Hays 1969 [1958]; Keller 1994, 194).

The Progressive program and its New Deal successor greatly enlarged the role of the federal government, from merely administering a privatization process to actively managing the environment for multiple and often conflicting uses. Most of the major federal environmental management agencies were created during this period, including the Bureau of Reclamation, Forest Service, Public Health Service, National Park Service, Fish and Wildlife Service, Soil Conservation Service, Tennessee Valley Authority and other hydropower agencies, and the Bureau of Land Management. The period also saw a major expansion of the mission of the Army Corps of Engineers.[2]

American governance itself was thus transformed as well. From a system largely limited to congressional lawmaking it became an elaborate structure which relied heavily on administrative agencies with discretionary authority to translate broad strategy mandates into the technical details of day-to-day implementation. An administrative system largely staffed through political patronage was transformed into one staffed by scientific and technical professionals, and advocating "efficiency" as an overarching goal of government action. The creation of these agencies established the institutional context for most of the issues and conflicts of American environmental policy today, with the exception of pollution control.

A vital question for the new Progressive paradigm was: for what purposes and for whose benefit should federal agencies manage environmental resources? What *was* "the public interest" in any specific situation? For the Progressives it was economic efficiency: preventing waste and using resources efficiently for middle-class economic progress. For most congressmen, however, the public interest still meant simply satisfying the immediate economic self-interests of their constituents, both individuals and businesses. For the new environmental movement of the time, exemplified by John Muir and the Sierra Club, the public interest lay in protecting the natural landscape from excesses of economic use, and preserving the most beautiful and awe-inspiring places for human enjoyment and renewal.

The character of environmental politics thus shifted profoundly. By the late nineteenth century, public-lands politics had already evolved from the simple regional interest coalitions of the early nineteenth century into a more complex array of conflicts among competing user interests. These pitted farmers and cattlemen against railroad monopolies, settlers and water companies against grazing interests and mining firms, cattlemen against sheepmen, local users against distant governments, small-scale entrepreneurs against giant corporations, Progressive "conservationists" against landscape "preservationists," and so forth. The Progressive administrative agencies themselves, which began as idealistic champions of the public interest, evolved into brokers among conflicting claimants of private use rights to the resources they administered. Governance by technical experts also produced new political conflicts among the environmental ideologies of particular professions, and between their values and those of user constituencies, of politicians, and of the general public.

Economic and Political Transformation

The 1890s marked the beginning of a major transformation of the American economy and governance structure. The period from the Civil War to the 1890s was an "Age of Enterprise" dominated by industrial expansion and political conservatism (McCloskey 1964 [1951]), and by 1900 the United States was well on its way to becoming the world's largest and most powerful economy. Politically it was beginning to express international ambitions, colonizing Cuba, Puerto Rico, Hawaii, and the Philippines, and asserting new ambitions as a global power. The steamship, the telegraph, and the railroad connected American raw materials producers with urban and global markets on a far broader scale than before, and created opportunities for enormous profits from converting the landscape into marketable commodities. By the same token, these linkages exposed American farmers, workers, and small businesses to far more powerful and impersonal international market forces than they could control or even comprehend.

As industrial production expanded, its production processes were also rapidly transformed by a widespread movement among industrial engineers to make them even more rational and efficient in their use of materials, energy, and labor to create profitable goods. Known as "scientific management" or "Taylorism," this movement was led most prominently by Frederick Winslow Taylor, whose work in the steel industry and others laid many of the foundations both for assembly-line mass production and for an enduring American ideology of efficiency as the goal of both business and government.

A wave of business consolidations integrated much of the relatively decentralized and competitive economy into one with a far smaller number of holding companies dominated by finance capitalists. The concentrated power of these "trusts" dominated both their markets and even governments. The census of 1900 reported the existence of 73 industrial conglomerates with capital of more than $10 million each, many of which controlled more than 50 percent of the production in their fields. Only twenty of these had existed before 1898; by 1909, however, just 1 percent of the country's industrial firms produced 44 percent of the nation's total manufactured goods. Some of these firms, particularly the railroad, mining, grazing, and logging firms, and electric power companies, were among the most active speculators in western lands, seeking control over assets for future development. Then as now, advocates of corporate consolidation promised that these new configurations would be more "efficient," reduce "wasteful" competition and duplication of resources, stabilize the economy, and permit more effective competition against foreign firms. However, consolidation also left farmers and small businesses at the mercy of monopolistic suppliers and purchasers, and concentrated economic power in business elites far removed from the lives, jobs, and communities affected by their decisions (Mowry 1962, 4–10).

As a result, the United States by 1900 had become a highly stratified society, with a few immensely rich industrialists and financiers at the top, a moderate number of small businessmen, professionals, and others in the middle, and a large and growing population of immigrants and native blacks living in appalling conditions at the bottom. Supporters of these trends justified the results by appeals to science. Herbert Spencer's and William Graham Sumner's "social Darwinism" argued that industrialization represented "progress," and successful capitalists represented the social equivalent of Darwin's natural selection by "survival of the fittest," and that they should therefore be left free to continue succeeding without government interference. This laissez-faire philosophy conveniently overlooked the important role of favorable government policies, among other factors, in their success in the first place.[3] The great depression of 1893 exacerbated economic disparities: a collapse of global agricultural markets wiped out both farm product prices and the speculative western land values on which farmers also depended for credit, causing widespread unemployment, bankruptcies, farm foreclosures, and both urban and rural impoverishment (Hofstadter 1955, 50–54, 56–59).

The resulting social conflicts transformed the Age of Enterprise into an "Age of Reform," lasting from the agrarian Populist movement of the 1890s, through the more urban and middle-class Progressive movement of the early 1900s, to Franklin Roosevelt's New Deal of the 1930s.

This reform era began perhaps most dramatically in environmental policy, as successive presidents in the 1890s used the forest reserves provision of the 1891 General Revision Act to set aside millions of acres of federal lands in public management. The Forest Management Act of 1897 added explicit authority to manage these lands, rather than simply "lock them up." The result was to transform the federal government within a decade from passive donor or seller to active owner and manager of the environment. This new role was most clearly evident in the emergence of federal authority for multiple-purpose management of water resources, for multiple-use management of vast acreages of national forests, and for leasing of fuel mineral lands. It was also evident in new agencies to manage national parks, monuments, and wildlife habitat.

Multiple-Purpose Water Resource Management

Federal responsibility for water resource management evolved almost unintentionally from a convergence of nineteenth-century public-land and internal-improvements policies. Since the Land Ordinance of 1785 the federal government had promoted agrarian land settlement, and with the Desert Lands Act of 1877 it began promoting the settlement of irrigable lands in the arid West as well. The Army Corps of Engineers, meanwhile, had received budget appropriations since the 1820s to subsidize clearing of rivers and harbors, and later for construction of levees for flood protection, but it had argued relentlessly that the federal government's only proper role in water management was to improve navigation for interstate commerce.[4] Before the 1880s, therefore, no federal agency had asserted any broad federal authority for water resource management.

The development of irrigable lands presented a new situation, however, due to the large-scale projects necessary for viable irrigation. Land claimants were required to prove irrigation on large acreages within three years. To achieve this required construction of dams at technically suitable locations, and of canals to carry water from them to irrigable lands. It also required that claimants obtain property rights both in irrigable lands and in the water needed to irrigate them, and that enough landowners along the canals participate to cover their costs; this in turn required financing of credit over long enough time periods to amortize the investments. Such ventures required well-managed projects, not simply individual land claims. They were frequently stymied by the widespread practice of land speculation, by which profit-seekers could simply claim key sites, not to participate in an irrigation venture but simply to sell them back at inflated prices. During the 1880s many private irrigation ventures failed, due both to land speculation and to drought.

The U.S. Geological Survey therefore began to conceive a more far-reaching federal role in water resource management. USGS was initially created simply to integrate and professionalize federal surveying activities for western lands and resources. In response to the mounting frustration of irrigation advocates, however, Congress in 1888 directed it also to conduct hydrographic surveys to identify those public lands most suitable for irrigation, as well as the sites necessary to store and transport water for them. What Congress apparently intended was that USGS simply perform a "quick and dirty" survey to assist private developers in identifying and developing the most promising sites. USGS, however — then directed by Major John Wesley Powell, whose 1878 report had first articulated the need for scientifically based classification and development of the western lands — took this legislation as a mandate to systematically assess the irrigation potential of the western lands, and by implication, to suspend the land claims process for the several years necessary for this process. A fierce political backlash from land speculation interests led Congress in 1890 to halve the USGS budget and to reopen most of these lands to settlement claims.

The boom and bust of private irrigation development in the 1880s and the abortive USGS initiative convinced irrigation advocates that larger-scale federal financing was necessary. Only the federal government had the necessary financial resources, the constitutional jurisdiction to override interstate conflicts over water allocations, and the statutory authority to prevent speculation in crucial sites from blocking development. The forest reserves provision in the 1891 General Revision Act allowed presidents to set aside critical land for reservoirs, thus blocking further land capture by speculators; and in 1894 irrigation advocates succeeded in passing a new land grant policy, the Carey Act, which offered one million acres to each of the western states to be used to finance irrigation projects. This act had little effect, however, because most states lacked the financial capital to finance irrigation projects and the most promising sites had already fallen into private ownership (Hays 1959, 6–11; Gates 1968, 648, 650–51).

In 1902, therefore, irrigation advocates led by Rep. Francis Newlands of Nevada passed the Newlands Reclamation Act with the support of newly inaugurated president Theodore Roosevelt. This law created a federal Reclamation Fund to pay for irrigation projects from the proceeds of western land sales, and provided discretionary authority for the Secretary of the Interior to select projects and allocate funds to them. Roosevelt created a new branch of the Geological Survey, the Reclamation Service, to administer the program, and in 1907 it became a separate agency within the Department of the Interior (Gates 1968, 640–42; Hays 1959, 6–19).

The Reclamation Fund was superficially similar to previous internal improvement policies, but in four key respects it represented a new and far-reaching innovation in environmental governance. First, it created a large earmarked fund to be used for a particular purpose. Previous internal-improvement policies had either given public land revenues to the states to use or kept them within the annual congressional appropriations process. The Reclamation Fund was conceived instead as a "revolving fund" which would finance the capital costs of construction and then be replenished by water use payments from irrigators over the next ten years. In practice, however, as the time of repayment approached, farmers mobilized to lobby successfully for more lenient terms, retroactively converting much of the program from loans to outright subsidies (Hays 1959, 246–48).[5]

Second, the Reclamation Act delegated broad discretion over the use of this fund to an administrative agency. The Secretary of the Interior was empowered to make key decisions about projects and expenditures without project-by-project congressional approval. The rationale for this innovation was to avoid both the land-speculation opportunities and the pork-barrel politics of the annual congressional appropriations process, which had become a staple of the Corps of Engineers' river and harbor projects.[6] In so doing, the Newlands Act marked the first statutory affirmation of the Progressive idea that environmental assets should be managed not by elected representatives, but by technical professionals and politically neutral administrators working toward the efficient realization of an overall public interest.[7] It thus placed federal administrative officials in a position of direct power over both private and state development plans throughout the West, and of brokering conflicts among all the western water-dependent user constituencies.

Federal financing of irrigation projects may have seemed superficially similar to financing of navigation or of flood control levees, but in practice it created a fundamentally new set of conditions, both environmentally and institutionally. Environmentally, the construction of dams created a new resource: stored bodies of water, each both ecosystem and commodity, available for multiple uses which were technologically interdependent. Stored water could be released in rainy periods to make room to store anticipated floodwaters, or it could be saved from rainy to dry periods ("conserved") to maintain downstream navigation or water quality by augmenting low flows. It could be released through turbines to generate hydroelectric power, or through pipes and canals to provide either irrigation or urban water supply. Or it could be used in place, both by fish and wildlife and by humans for recreation. Institutionally, each of these pools of water was controlled by a human operator who allocated it among these uses, and thereby exercised monopoly power over those who depended on it.

Third, the Newlands Act authorized the federal government not only to finance but also to own and operate the major irrigation dams and canals. Most western politicians wanted the federal government simply to subsidize three reservoirs in each state, then turn them over to private businesses. Newlands and Roosevelt held out successfully for government ownership, however, to protect both the government's investment and the farmers whose livelihoods would remain dependent on the resulting water monopoly. In effect, the Newlands Act thus nationalized the management of western water resources, which were to be operated by a technically competent federal agency in the name of a statutory mission rather than by private monopolies pursuing their own economic interests.

Fourth, the Reclamation Act established a second federal agency for water resource engineering and management, separate from and inevitably competing with the Army Corps of Engineers. Contrary to some political caricatures, such bureaucratic duplication was not necessarily wasteful, since as in markets it could provide instructive comparisons among the services of similar agencies. However, the resulting bureaucratic competition also fragmented the management of water resources within the federal government, and led to several decades of interagency infighting.

Concurrent with the irrigation era, even stronger economic forces were promoting hydroelectric power projects. By the turn of the twentieth century, demand for power production was growing rapidly as the nation electrified, and hydroelectric generation offered a source that was both cheap and clean compared to coal-fired boilers. Private companies and speculators moved rapidly to preempt the best dam sites, using mineral land claims as a subterfuge, yet their projects were often too small or too narrowly conceived, capturing the best sites for small power dams and thereby blocking more broadly conceived projects that might have also provided urban water supply and irrigation. The proliferation of private hydropower dams also blocked navigable streams, thus interfering with water-borne commerce.[8] In an era in which the economic power of large business monopolies was already a political issue, private control over hydropower production threatened to create new monopolies dominating entire populations dependent on electricity.

In the East and Midwest, meanwhile, regional economic interests had long sought larger federal subsidies for interstate waterway development projects. Beginning around 1895 they began to mobilize widespread political support. Major floods in the lower Mississippi River valley increased pressures for federal flood protection subsidies, and increases in railroad freight rates mobilized shippers to lobby for more canals and waterways to compete with the railroads. Eastern states pushed for construction of an intra-coastal waterway system and a cross-Florida barge canal, for instance, and midwestern states sought a waterway that would accommodate oceangoing vessels from the Great Lakes to the Gulf of Mexico. Many of these proposals were inherently multiple-purpose: the Bureau of Reclamation's first project had included hydroelectric power production as well as irrigation, and the Deep Waterway proposal was to be financed in part by sales of hydroelectric power from its dams (Hays 1959, 91–100).

President Roosevelt and his advisors therefore argued for *multiple-purpose* federal water resource development projects, and *multiple-use* river basin planning on a nationwide scale. By capturing and storing otherwise "wasted" and destructive flood waters, multiple-purpose projects could tame the forces of nature and "conserve" them for productive human uses. Multiple-use plans in turn would allocate them to their most efficient uses, and minimize wasteful conflicts among human users. The necessary premise of this approach was that technical experts in government would be managing the water and deciding on a day-to-day basis which uses were most productive.

In 1907 Roosevelt appointed an Inland Waterways Commission, and charged it with developing comprehensive multiple-use plans for the most efficient use of each river system. Based on its recommendations, a second Newlands Act was proposed, which would have created an Inland Waterway Fund to finance water projects of all kinds. In effect, this proposal would have extended the Reclamation Act idea into a nationwide program for multiple-purpose water resource development, in place of the pork-barrel politics of project-by-project annual appropriations. This proposal failed, however, due to congressional opposition to such sweeping changes in political power and administrative discretion (Hays 1959, 100–14).

A fundamental issue to Progressives was whether private hydropower companies should gain windfall benefits from the use of public water resources, or should pay user fees for them. Privately owned hydroelectric dams used the public resource of navigable streams, often in ways that impeded other public uses (navigation, for instance), to enrich their investors, often at monopolistic profit levels. Roosevelt argued that users of the public's natural resources should pay fair market value for them, and in 1907 he reinterpreted existing statutes to require user fees and rate regulation for private hydropower dams on navigable streams. His successor, President William Taft, initially reversed this policy, but ultimately endorsed the principle in 1911, and the Water Power Act of 1920 established a statutory policy of federal regulation of hydroelectric power production.[9] This act marked the end of the Progressive legislative agenda, since it compromised away the principle of multiple-use federal water management even as it confirmed the principle of federal control over hydropower production.

In short, Theodore Roosevelt and the Progressives laid the foundations for federal development and multipurpose management of water resources. Many observers have since come to view the Bureau of Reclamation as an anachronism, but at the time it was a pioneering reform in environmental management. Multipurpose water management was ultimately adopted as a general federal policy during the New Deal administration of Franklin Roosevelt, but it was Theodore Roosevelt and the Progressives who were its first promoters.

Multiple-Use Forest Management

Theodore Roosevelt and his advisors articulated an equally strong policy of multiple-use federal management for the national forest reserves. Since the 1860s there had been growing public and scientific concern that deforestation resulting from uncontrolled commercial logging was both diminishing water supplies from forested watersheds and creating the risk of a future "timber famine." These concerns led cities, scientists, and irrigation advocates to support the 1891 forest reserves provision (Hays 1959, 36; Gates 1968, 575). Presidents Harrison and Cleveland each reserved millions of acres under this authority in the 1890s, but had no authority for active federal management of them. This limitation left their reservations open to political attacks from western interests calling them merely a "lock-up" of valuable resources, as well as a disruption of the land claims process.

In 1897, therefore, on the recommendation of the National Forestry Committee of the National Academy of Sciences, a new Forest Management Act authorized the Secretary of the Interior to *manage* the reserved forest lands. The Geological Survey was to survey the reserves, and the Secretary of the Interior was authorized to protect them against fire and trespass, and to sell "dead, mature, or large growth trees" at not less than their appraised value. Most important, the act confirmed that the reserves would remain in federal ownership and management.[10]

The significance of this law for federal forest lands was similar to that of the Reclamation Act for water. It gave discretionary authority to a federal administrator to make technical decisions that had broad socioeconomic and environmental consequences. Like a reservoir of stored water, a forest was both ecosystem and commodity, a single resource available for technically interdependent and competing uses: logging, grazing, mining, watershed protection, wildlife habitat, recreation, and others. Effective management of such a resource required technical expertise on a day-to-day basis, at a level of detail impossible for a legislature. Yet the cumulative results of these technical decisions in fact comprised the real policy, and allocated resources to some uses and users rather than others. Such a system thus turned federal administrators into brokers among all the constituencies who sought to use or preserve these lands.

The Interior Department, however, did not have the technical expertise necessary for this role: its Geological Survey was expert in water, but its General Land Office (GLO) was staffed only by law clerks processing land disposal transactions.[11] Federal forestry expertise was located in the Agriculture Department's Bureau of Forestry, headed by Gifford Pinchot, who was one of Roosevelt's closest personal advisors on natural resource policy. Pinchot campaigned for transfer of the forest reserves to the Department of Agriculture and in 1905 Congress approved the shift, creating in the department the U.S. Forest Service.

Like the Reclamation Act, the creation of the Forest Service established a second agency separate from and ultimately competing with an existing but more limited resource administration agency. Today both the Forest Service and the Bureau of Land Management — successor to the GLO — manage western forest lands for many of the same combinations of uses, and in some regions these agencies' lands are even checkerboarded amongst each other where integrated management would be more logical. As in the case of water resources, the resulting organizational competition has sometimes produced intense and wasteful interagency conflicts.

The 1905 Forest Transfer Act established an enduring institutional framework under which the national forests have been managed ever since. Pinchot recruited eastern support for the transfer by arguing that it would substitute expert professional management, efficient enforcement, and user fees for the land frauds, political conflicts, and disposal mentality of the General Land Office, thus protecting the public's environmental assets from environmentally wasteful destruction.[12] At the same time, however, he recruited western support by promising to open the reserves to more active commercial exploitation than under the Interior Department, thus preventing economically wasteful *preservation*.

It was Pinchot who defined natural resource "conservation" as "wise use," and perpetuated the definition with the slogan "wilderness is waste" (Wilkins 1995, 218).[13] Serving the overall public interest in his view meant efficient management for commodity production under federal administration. He cultivated forest industry support with promises to treat the national forests strictly as supplements rather than competitors to private holdings, and to make national forest timber available only to meet local needs (Steen 1976, 93, 257, 280).[14] Finally, he built additional support from the livestock industry by reopening the forest reserves to grazing as well as logging and other marketable uses rather than preserving them — as hunting, recreation, and wilderness advocates sought — for their beauty or ecological integrity or as hunting or wildlife reserves. Symbolically, the 1905 legislation renamed the forest reserves "national forests," reflecting the idea of management for use rather than simply reservation. The overall institutional mission of the Agriculture Department also favored the idea of "farming" trees for commodity use, as well as using forest lands for cattle and sheep grazing, rather than preserving forests as undisturbed ecosystems (Hays 1959, 38–46).

These policy principles were clearly articulated in the Secretary of Agriculture's charge to Pinchot as the first head of the Forest Service.[15] He was to manage the forests for "the most productive use for the permanent good of the whole people, not the temporary benefit of individuals or companies." However, the reserves were to be managed for use, including wood, water, and forage, not simply locked up. They were to be managed "for the first benefit of the home builder," and thereafter for agriculture, mining, lumber, and cattle, "considering the locally dominant industry first." Pinchot did introduce user fees for forest commodities — stumpage fees for timber and "animal unit month" grazing fees — but the rates generally remained far below market values. He also created a strongly decentralized administrative system within the Forest Service, under which local and regional forest managers lived in the regions for which they were responsible and exercised strong local autonomy. This approach made them knowledgeable about local conditions, but also far more sensitive to pressure from local resource-production businesses than from broader national constituencies (Wilkinson 1992, 127–35).

Environmental policy for the U.S. national forests was thus shaped from its foundations by a primary mission of commodity use and specifically timber production. Even "multiple-use/sustained-yield management," which later became the official and in 1960 the statutory policy of the Forest Service, did not connote a truly ecological vision of sustainable, biocentric management of the forest as an ecosystem. To the Forest Service the policy implied a continued primary commitment to production of economic commodities from the forest. Even today, the Forest Service's planning and management decisions remain strongly influenced by centrally determined targets for annual timber cuts based on political demands for commodities from the public forests, rather than by ecologically based determinations of sustainable yield from each forest.[16]

Roosevelt and Pinchot did, however, vastly enlarge the total amount of lands reserved in federal management. At the beginning of Roosevelt's administration these comprised 46.4 million acres, but by his departure in 1908 he had added 148 million acres more, of which 26 million were in Alaska and the remainder in the lower forty-eight states (Gates 1968, 580). The purpose of these reservations was not merely timber production, but also to assert federal control over other valuable lands, especially coal and oil deposits and dam sites.[17]

Not surprisingly, Roosevelt's aggressive assertion of executive powers eventually precipitated a showdown with Congress. In 1907 Congress attached a rider to the Forest Service annual appropriation bill which required congressional approval for all future forest reservations in the western states, effectively repealing the president's discretionary authority to reserve forest lands.[18] Additional forest reservations were later created, but primarily by purchase under the 1911 Weeks Act, which authorized federal repurchase of cut-over eastern forest lands for watershed protection.[19]

In short, Theodore Roosevelt's forest policy was to maintain the forested public lands in federal ownership for active commodity production. He did set aside some exceptional areas for preservation, tourism, and appreciative use as national parks, national monuments, and wildlife refuges, but even on most of these his policy was to allow multiple uses rather than strict preservation. At the same time, he advocated charging market-based fees for the extraction of commodity resources from federal lands, selling timber, minerals, and grazing rights at appraised prices rather than simply giving them away. He also supported vigorous enforcement of the laws in place of the informal systems of private appropriation of public resources that had developed over the nineteenth century (Futrell 1993, 25).

Leasing of Use Rights: Mineral and Grazing Lands

Two further applications of the Progressive conservation philosophy were Roosevelt's proposals for leasing of coal and oil extraction rights and for fee-based grazing permits. Coal-bearing lands had long been recognized as having high economic value, and had therefore been excluded from preemption claims as early as 1841. An 1864 law offered them for sale at a minimum price of $25 per acre, ten to twenty times the price of other public lands.[20] In practice, however, claims under the General Mining Act and other land laws were widely used to capture coal lands in the absence of government information on their true values.

Lacking congressional support for correcting these abuses, Roosevelt and his advisors unilaterally withdrew all coal-bearing federal lands from land claims, and directed USGS to conduct a systematic geological survey of all such lands. He also raised their prices from the traditional minimum price per acre to levels more consistent with their true value. Finally, he proposed that these lands thenceforth be retained in federal ownership, and leased rather than sold for coal extraction. Mining interests themselves ultimately advocated such leasing systems, as a means of establishing long-term legal rights to these resources and restricting or even excluding competitors (Mayer and Riley 1985, 127–45). Leasing was not approved during Roosevelt's administration, but it was ultimately adopted for Alaska in 1914 and nationwide in the Mineral Leasing Act of 1920. The 1920 law established the basis on which coal, oil, phosphates, and other minerals — including today's Alaskan and outer continental shelf oil deposits — would be managed (Hays 1959, 82–90; Mayer and Riley 1985, 123–54).[21]

The federal rangelands, meanwhile, had been left essentially open and unmanaged since the destruction of the bison herds, available to as many cattle and sheep as users wished to turn loose on them. They could not legally be claimed in sufficient acreages for profitable grazing operations, since the laws were written to promote only small-scale agrarian settlement, but the use of them was not controlled. In a classic example of the "tragedy of the commons," they were severely overgrazed and denuded as a result. Protection of the range required some management regime for controlling the total numbers of livestock and for maintaining the range. Cattle interests themselves advocated more controlled allocation of use rights, particularly since it would tend to favor established local ranchers. Under such a system, existing users would obtain long-term use rights to the range, and be able to exclude new cattle operations, seasonal sheep herds, potential settlers, and other competing users.

The Interior Department began controlling grazing on the public lands through a permit system in 1898, and in 1906 Pinchot instituted user fees per animal unit month for these permits on the national forest lands (Hays 1959, 49–65). These policies benefited environmental protection of rangelands, but they also placed Roosevelt on the side of cattle interests against western farmers. Politically, this position contributed directly to Congress's ultimate rejection of his overall conservation policies in 1907–08.

A fundamental tension in both the mineral leasing and rangeland use permit systems was that while they established federal management control over important environmental assets, they did so on terms that were highly favorable to the very commodity user interests that were ostensibly to be restrained by federal management. Once leases or permits were granted they conferred in effect a kind of property right that was actually far cheaper than outright land purchase, yet almost as durable. It was and is extremely difficult for the federal government to cancel or transfer such privileges, even in the face of violations of lease or permit requirements. Compared to the unrestrained competitive exploitation that preceded them, these policies did provide for more prudent environmental management. However, they also provided government-sponsored advantages as well as serious loopholes to the remaining users, some of whom were symbols of excessive economic power and "special interests" to populists, Progressives, and landscape preservation advocates. This ambiguous relationship between environmental and populist values remained a continuing contradiction in modern American environmental politics.

Roosevelt's idea of conservation, in short, was not politically neutral, nor did it necessarily favor the sort of populist advocacy for the "little guys" against powerful businesses that is sometimes imagined for it. Rather, it favored protecting the rangelands as an economic asset by converting them from an open-access to a common-property management regime, in which economically powerful interests in fact had greater opportunities to benefit than did smaller, less organized interests. Roosevelt's policy of legitimizing grazing as a long-term use was fundamentally at odds both with agrarian views of grazing as a transient activity to be gradually replaced by agrarian settlement, and with preservationists' opposition to grazing due to its environmental impacts. User fees for grazing were an important innovation in market-oriented environmental management, but while they were authorized in 1906 in the national forests, a broader federal policy of leasing use rights for grazing was not enacted until almost thirty years later, with the Taylor Grazing Act of 1934.

"Conservation" Versus "Preservation"

A common theme underlying the water, forest, and other environmental policies of the Progressive era was their explicit commitment to utilitarian efficiency as a philosophy of governance. Roosevelt populated his administration with experts in hydrology, forestry, agricultural sciences, geology, and anthropology; professional technicians linked by the goal of efficiency in resource utilization (fig. 9). His program received its primary support from other organizations that were attempting to promote efficiency, such as the professional engineering societies.[22] In historian Samuel Hays's words, "The broader significance of the conservation movement [under Roosevelt] stemmed from the role it played in the transformation of a decentralized, nontechnical, loosely organized society, where waste and inefficiency ran rampant, into a highly organized, technical, and centrally planned and directed social organization which could meet a complex world with efficiency and purpose" (1969, 2).

An unresolved issue, however, was whether the goal of government should *always* be commodity production, or whether some natural landscapes and species should simply be preserved for their ecological, aesthetic, or religious values. Commodity-use advocates

Figure 9. Leaders of the initiative for federal management of the environment. This picture shows President Theodore Roosevelt (third from left), Gifford Pinchot (back), and John Muir (fourth from right) on a field trip in California in the early years of the twentieth century. [U.S. Forest Service]

might point to the biblical injunction to "multiply and subdue the earth," but others — John Muir and earlier writers such as Emerson and Thoreau, for instance — voiced equally ancient religious injunctions. The earth, they argued, is an expression of the perfection of the Creator; it is useful to humans not only for material sustenance, but also for religious inspiration, and humans have a religious duty to use it for the common good, not simply for personal gain.[23] Nineteenth-century naturalists and scientists added secular and practical concerns.[24] In a widely read book published in 1864, the farmer and U.S. ambassador George Perkins Marsh used his observations of the eroded and denuded civilizations of the Mediterranean to argue for greater restraint in American exploitation of the natural environment. His *Man and Nature, or, Physical Geography as Modified by Human Action* was the first book to document systematically the destructive effects of human activities on Earth's natural systems and landscapes, to argue that these human impacts went far beyond those of other species, and to urge actions to minimize and mitigate these impacts.

John Muir and others echoed these beliefs: they were skeptical of the Progressive view of an urban and industrial economy based on "efficient" natural resource exploitation, and advocated more principled restraint in human exploitation of the landscape. For his own political reasons, however, Gifford Pinchot reduced all these concerns to an oversimplified choice of "conservation versus preservation." The implication was that to oppose his philosophy of conservation for commodity production was to advocate simply "locking up" America's environmental assets and thus "wasting" them (Turner 1985, 320–24). In practice Roosevelt was an avid outdoorsman and an accomplished amateur naturalist who recognized the value of maintaining the special character of some unique landscapes as national treasures. Pinchot's dominant policy, however, was that environmental management should be for economic use, and that even preservation should be left open to future reconsideration if the preserved lands should be wanted for more active economic use.

By 1900 Congress had approved the creation of six national parks: Hot Springs (1832), Yellowstone (1872), Mackinac Island (1875), Sequoia and General Grant (1890), and Mt. Rainier (1899). During the Roosevelt and Taft administrations, and with their support, Congress established five more—Crater Lake (1902), Wind Cave (1903), Platt/ Sulfur Springs (1906), Mesa Verde (1906), and Glacier (1910)—and accepted Yosemite back from California into federal protection and management. Roosevelt also created the first national wildlife refuge (at Pelican Island, Florida, in 1903), and a National Bison Range in Montana in 1908.

A key constraint on the creation of national parks, however, was that unlike the forest reserves, they could be created only by specific congressional legislation rather than by presidential proclamations. By the time Congress could act, however, speculators would have months or years in which to claim and capture the key lands. Around the rim of the Grand Canyon, for instance, speculators used "mining claims" to capture control of the canyon's viewpoints and trailheads, and thus of the lucrative tourism business that might follow.

Roosevelt and several previous presidents therefore used forest-reserve designations to protect not only watersheds but also potential parks and other valuable sites from capture by speculators, for long enough to obtain legislative action. With the 1907 amendment ending the president's authority to proclaim forest reservations, Roosevelt lost that policy tool.

But a substitute tool had unexpectedly appeared in 1906, in the language of the American Antiquities Act. This law was passed in reaction to looting of Mesa Verde and other American Indian archaeological sites, and allowed the president to act quickly to protect what were envisioned as limited and specific sites: "historic landmarks, historic and prehistoric structures, and other objects of historical or scientific interest situated on government lands." Such sites could be set aside by presidential proclamation as "national monuments," limited to the smallest area compatible with their proper care and management. In practice, however, the Antiquities Act created a new tool for unilateral presidential action to preserve larger areas as well. Between 1906 and 1910 Presidents Roosevelt and Taft proclaimed twenty-three areas as national monuments, including several that later were redesignated as national parks: Grand Canyon, Death Valley, Katmai, and Glacier Bay. In the late 1970s, faced with obstructionist tactics by Alaskan senators over Alaskan lands legislation, Interior Secretary Cecil Andrus used the law to declare millions of acres "national monuments" and thus force congressional action (Wilkinson 1992, 55).

The designation of national parks as reserved lands did not resolve the question of how they should be managed, however. The Yosemite Valley, for instance, had been granted to California as a park in 1863, but was then logged, burned, and overgrazed for decades under California's permissive multiple-use concept of a park (Richardson 1962, 120; Udall

1963, 128). John Muir created and led the Sierra Club in a campaign first to have a trained forester appointed to administer the park, and later, beginning in 1893, to have the park returned from state to federal management. He convinced President Roosevelt to support a return to federal management in 1903, and in 1905 succeeded in getting the necessary bills through both the state assembly and Congress.

Conflict immediately resurfaced, however, over a proposal to dam the Hetch Hetchy Valley—adjacent to Yosemite and a part of the same land reservation—to provide water and hydroelectric power for the growing city of San Francisco. Reservoir advocates defined the issue in Progressive economic-efficiency terms, arguing that while there were several other possible sources of water for San Francisco, Hetch Hetchy would be the cheapest and would generate the most electric power.[25] Muir and his allies responded that the valley was even more beautiful and pristine than the Yosemite Valley itself, and should be preserved inviolate (Udall 1963, 133; Hays 1959, 193–95). Roosevelt temporized, but Pinchot sided clearly with the reservoir advocates, supporting both the political agenda of urban Progressivism in San Francisco and the more general utilitarian principle of multiple-purpose water resource development over Muir's aesthetic and religious arguments for preservation.[26] Amid the political demands for better fire protection after the 1906 San Francisco earthquake, the Secretary of the Interior issued a reservoir permit to the city in 1908 (Turner 1985, 228).

The Hetch Hetchy project was not finally approved and constructed until 1914, years after Roosevelt and Pinchot left office, but the issue produced a national environmental cause célèbre and a permanent schism between the conservation forces—Pinchot and the commodity-oriented natural resource management professionals in the federal agencies, and other advocates of multiple-use management—and the preservationists, led by Muir and the Sierra Club, who came to totally distrust the multiple-use management philosophy of the forest and water management agencies. The immediate practical result was a successful preservationist campaign in 1916 to create a separate National Park Service in the Interior Department, to manage the national parks explicitly for their preservation and secondarily for public enjoyment and education. Creation of the Park Service was a direct rebuff to Pinchot's philosophy of commodity-oriented multiple-use management. Since many of the most pristine natural landscapes had already been set aside through the national forest system, it also set the stage for long-term bureaucratic rivalry, as national park advocates sought to redesignate and preserve lands that were already held by the Forest Service for multiple-use management (Hays 1959, 189–98).[27]

Not surprisingly, Roosevelt's ambitious policies also attracted increasing hostility both from powerful economic and bureaucratic interests and from their supporters in Congress. In the face of this growing opposition, Roosevelt and Pinchot appealed to the public: "[Faced with this opposition,] those in the vanguard of the Roosevelt resource movement turned more and more to the general public for support, and unleashed a veritable crusade of enthusiasm for conservation. In this fashion a movement peculiar to federal scientists and planners became deeply rooted in the minds of the public at large" (Hays 1969, 122). In distinct contrast to the modern environmental movement, that is, the conservation movement of the early twentieth century was orchestrated from the top down, as a presidential initiative to mobilize support for policies stalemated by legislative opposition.

To make this appeal, Pinchot sought to broaden the administration's constituency beyond Washington-level technical professionals, and to mobilize others under a broader umbrella of "conservation": engineers and other professionals, inland waterways advocates, moral crusaders against private resource exploiters, public power lobbyists, and Progressives in general. The strategy achieved results: a White House Governors Conference in 1908 issued a "Declaration for Conservation of Natural Resources" supporting Roosevelt's policies. Roosevelt himself appointed a National Conservation Commission, which completed the first broad inventory of the nation's natural resources, and whose report was also endorsed by the governors. The popular support that was built up provided the impetus for Gifford Pinchot's National Conservation Association, which was founded in 1909.

However, the creation of a broader popular movement also required alliances with constituencies with far more diverse and conflicting views of environmental policy than Pinchot's "gospel of efficiency." Like "environment," "conservation" served as a broad conceptual umbrella for groups that differed significantly in their specific values and priorities (in President Taft's words, conservation was "a good thing, whatever it means").[28] In Samuel Hays's words,

> This bid for popular support brought into the conservation movement a new and disturbing influence. Heretofore, specific interest groups . . . had comprised the major political backing for the administration's resource policies. Concerned primarily with economic growth, they aided Pinchot and his friends because of a common interest in rational development. Those who came to the support of conservation in 1908 and 1909, however, were prone to look upon all commercial development as mere materialism, and upon conservation as an attempt to save resources from use rather than to use them wisely. The problem, to them, was moral rather than economic. . . . The common denominator which drew all these groups together and attracted them to the conservation movement was a feeling that a desire for material gain had become too prominent in America, and that other values should be stressed. . . . A wide difference in attitude separated Roosevelt, Pinchot and [Secretary of the Interior] Garfield from the new enthusiasts. (1969 [1958], 141–42 and 145–46)

The result of Roosevelt's co-optive strategy, therefore, was a heightened level of conflict among factions within the conservation movement, and eventually — after Roosevelt left office — a fragmentation of that movement into subgroups arguing over the utilization of particular resources.

Summary

Theodore Roosevelt and his Progressive advisors fundamentally reshaped the character of American environmental policy. They established environmental management as a major and explicit responsibility of the federal government, and they nailed to the door of government, figuratively speaking, the credo of utilitarian values, economic progress, efficient management of natural resources, and administration by technical experts in the public interest. Roosevelt set aside vast areas for public management of resource commodity production as well as some key sites for permanent preservation, both for human enjoyment and wildlife protection. He made the problem of natural resource scarcity a national issue, a real and important concept in the consciousness of the general public, and he provided active national leadership against the waste and destruction of natural resources for private profit. Most important, he asserted the need for stewardship of resources at the highest level of government, invigorated conservation law enforcement, and brought the functions of natural resource planning and management into the federal government in order to fulfill that responsibility.

On the other hand, Roosevelt's and especially Pinchot's adoption of economic efficiency as the fundamental objective of that management discounted other environmental values and goals, such as those that had been articulated by Marsh half a century earlier and by Muir in their own era, values that far more Americans would come to consider representations of the "public interest" in later years. They thus unwittingly laid some of the foundations for later public cynicism and conflict involving the federal environmental management agencies. From the perspective of the present, the commodity-oriented values and practices of Progressive conservation were not and could not be politically neutral, and they gradually came to appear as simply a new version of the old problem of environmental overuse and destruction for short-term economic self-interest.

9 Administering the Environment: Subgovernments and Stakeholders

> Nature has given recurrent and poignant warnings through dust storms, floods, and droughts that we must act while there is yet time if we would preserve for ourselves and our posterity the natural sources of a virile national life. . . . Prudent management requires not merely works which will guard against these calamities, but carefully formulated plans to prevent their occurrence. . . . A comprehensive program of flood control must embrace not only downstream levees and reservoirs on major tributaries, but also smaller dams and reservoirs on the lesser tributaries, and measures of applied conservation throughout an entire drainage area, such as restoration of forests and grasses on inferior lands, and encouragement of farm practices which diminish runoff and prevent erosion on arable lands. — Franklin D. Roosevelt, Message to Congress, 1937

War, as historian Richard Hofstadter once noted, has always been the nemesis of the liberal tradition in America (1955, 241–42). The onset of World War I significantly reduced American environmental policy. It redoubled the activist management role of government, but subordinated all other policy goals to the single priority of winning the war. Timber from the northwestern spruce forests, and even from the national parks, was logged for aircraft construction. National parks were used for troop quarters, and domestic environmental programs were put on hold.[1] Wartime propaganda urged frugality in household consumption: "Hooverizing" was a popular term for conserving food and fuel, and home "victory gardens" were encouraged to augment food supplies.[2] These policies were intended solely to free up more resources for the war effort, not to protect the environment, and both industrial pollution control and occupational health protection programs were sidetracked in the name of all-out war production.

More fundamentally, World War I was the first global-scale war fought with modern industrial technology: tanks, trucks, aircraft, toxic chemicals, and other weaponry. Its policy consequences therefore included massive government incentives for expansion of those sectors of the economy. These incentives had permanent environmental consequences. Once scaled up for wartime needs, these sectors would not simply disappear, but would seek both continued government support and new civilian markets, and would therefore continue to look to the natural environment as a source of raw materials and a sink for their wastes.[3] World War I was also the first global-scale war fought with petroleum-fueled technology, which dramatically increased the use of oil but also increased policy concern for its conservation: unlike wood, oil was extracted from finite and nonrenewable deposits.[4]

Finally, the totality of war mobilization both galvanized and exhausted public support for activist government management. It left in its wake a postwar period of popular disinterest in civic reform, business pressures to "get the private economy going again," and over a decade of stand-pat, laissez-faire governance by Presidents Harding, Coolidge, and Hoover.[5] Conservative judges reemphasized the primacy of private property rights, affirming the validity of land-use zoning — and thus protecting property owners against economically damaging actions by their neighbors — but also upholding mining companies' claims against governmental regulation of their impacts, holding that such regulations were a "taking" of the company's property rights under the Fifth Amendment (Futrell 1993, 30).[6]

In this vacuum of presidential leadership, interest groups seeking particular uses of the nation's environmental assets renewed and strengthened their political influence: stock grazers, water power speculators, irrigation developers and other commodity user groups, and now sportsmen, park lovers, wildlife enthusiasts, and others as well. These pressures reopened intense domestic political debate over how the nation's environmental assets should be used, but now in the context of administrative decision-making by federal management agencies.

The stock market crash of 1929 and the Great Depression that followed fundamentally altered the policy context once again, as the United States confronted simultaneously the most devastating economic and ecological disasters in its history. Franklin Roosevelt's New Deal responded with a forceful reaffirmation of government leadership in managing both the economy and the environment, and in integrating the two to maintain the well-being of its citizens. The environmental results were unprecedented in their scope, and overall extraordinarily beneficial. At the same time, the government agencies assigned to carry out these measures were both more limited in their idealism and more vulnerable over time to political influence than either Franklin or Theodore Roosevelt had envisioned. The result was a gradual but steady retreat from the ideals of integrated environmental management for the common good to management by fragmented "subgovernments" brokering the interests of powerful client constituencies.

Environmental Agencies as "Subgovernments"

In a time of diminished presidential leadership and intensified stakeholder pressures, the environmental agencies that had emerged during the Progressive era came to operate more and more as specialized *subgovernments*. Each had considerable discretionary authority to manage and allocate natural resources within the broad limits of its jurisdiction and multiple-use mission. Each was responsible by law for administrative decisions in "the public interest" among competing resource claimants, but in reality each found that it must develop political alliances with its clients and beneficiaries in order to maintain support for its budgets and decisions. These constituencies thus came to have as much influence over the agencies as the agencies had over them: the agencies controlled resource use rights, but the resource user groups could mobilize either congressional support or opposition to the agencies themselves. Each needed the other, and the resulting pattern of "iron triangles" — agency, client group, and congressional subcommittee — came to dominate American environmental policy and indeed national policy-making more generally.[7]

An important change in the character of these client-constituency relationships was the emergence of landscape and wildlife protection groups as political forces in their own right. These groups were no longer as marginalized as they had been under the ideology of commodity production that had dominated nineteenth-century privatization policies, nor under Pinchot's utilitarian policies of multiple-purpose resource development. Key stakeholder groups now had their own experts within the executive branch: the National Park Service for landscape preservation and the Biological Survey and Bureau of Fisheries (forerunners of the Fish and Wildlife Service) for wildlife protection. These agencies functioned in practice not just as disinterested managers, but as bureaucratic advocates for competing public purposes. The threat of competition from the National Park Service, for instance, forced the Forest Service to address non-commodity values such as wildlife protection and recreation, lest it lose key lands to the national park or wildlife refuge system. These adaptations in turn increased the tensions among conflicting interests *within* each agency, setting the stage for many of the pivotal policy conflicts of the modern environmental era.

The Reclamation Service was the first and classic example of an administrative subgovernment, since its water users depended on it from the outset. By the 1920s, however, its program was in disarray, wracked by slow settlement and participation rates, by higher than expected costs, by user complaints, and by congressional relief acts that reduced the revenues it had expected from loan repayments. Beginning in 1925, the renamed Bureau of Reclamation instituted reforms to decrease its constituents' complaints and to stabilize its financing, particularly by redefining repayment schedules in proportion to land productivity, completing existing projects rather than starting new ones, and placing completed projects under the control of local user organizations.

The Forest Service similarly adapted to the laissez-faire Republicanism of the 1920s by emphasizing cooperative programs with state forestry agencies and private forest owners rather than activist federal regulatory initiatives.[8] Exemplified by the 1924 Clarke-McNary Act, these cooperative programs emphasized forest fire protection, reforestation, and technical assistance.[9] The Forest Service also expanded its research programs, both to increase its service to forest user constituencies (imitating the successful USDA agricultural research programs) and to justify its programs with "better science."[10]

At the same time, however, the agency found itself increasingly on the defensive against proposals by wildlife, recreation, and wilderness advocates, and their advocates within the new rival National Park Service, to set aside areas of the national forests for permanent preservation rather than commodity production. To avoid outright loss of these areas, the Forest Service sought to accommodate these new non-commodity constituencies by adding wildlife protection and wilderness preservation programs while maintaining its own discretionary authority for future use changes. The result was to increase internal conflicts between its commodity user clients (timber, mining, and grazing users) and its wildlife, recreation, and wilderness constituencies (Swain 1963, 9–29). Pinchot's vision of a single overall public interest best known to government scientists was difficult to sustain against the constant brokering of interest groups that was the Forest Service's day-to-day reality.

The National Park Service, meanwhile, set out under the exceptional leadership of Stephen Mather to solidify and expand its role through constituency development. Administratively, Mather consolidated the parks into a unified system under three clear policy priorities: unimpaired preservation, active public use consistent with preservation, and business enterprises in the parks (such as commercial services) only to the extent consistent with preservation and public use. Politically, Mather aggressively mobilized and broadened the parks' constituencies. He publicized the parks with enormous amounts of pictorial propaganda, promoting park tourism both directly and through tourism interests such as the railroads and the hotel, food, and adventure concessionaires. He organized "park safaris" for congressmen and prominent journalists, and even obtained a resolution from the American Association for the Advancement of Science urging permanent protection of the parks against commercial use.[11] Unlike his Forest Service counterparts, Mather successfully resisted the political pressures of most conflicting user constituencies, fending off proposals to open the parks for hydropower production, grazing, and other commodity uses. The Park Service still had to broker conflicts between wilderness purists and advocates of more intensive recreational uses, including the concessionaires whose economic interests lay in more developed uses, but this was a far less complex task than that facing the Forest Service.

At the same time, Mather and his successor, Horace Albright, effectively used their growing base of political support to expand the national park system, often at the expense of the Forest Service. Mather even proposed to establish Park Service jurisdiction over recreational programs on the national forest lands, arguing (correctly) that the Forest Service considered these uses merely incidental and subordinate to commodity production goals. This pressure left the Forest Service constantly on the defensive, and forced it to incorporate recreation and preservation more explicitly into its management.[12]

Yet another politically charged subgovernment was the wildlife management program of the Agriculture Department's Bureau of Biological Survey. State wildlife protection laws had existed since colonial days, prompted by overhunting of deer and furbearers, and by 1900 both state and federal laws sought to protect and promote some valuable species of mammals, birds, and fish. A federal Bureau of Fisheries was created in the Agriculture Department in the 1870s, and an economic ornithology office in 1885; the latter was renamed the Biological Survey in 1896 and given bureau status in 1906. The Lacey Act of 1900 established federal regulatory authority over interstate and international commerce in wild game, and thus effectively ended the commercial hunting practices that had driven the passenger pigeon and other species to extinction. The 1918 Migratory Bird Treaty Act established federal authority over migratory waterfowl, and by 1920 Congress had established a series of seventy federal wildlife refuges.[13]

By the 1920s the Biological Survey faced constant conflicting pressures from two powerful and fundamentally opposed constituencies: wildlife protection advocates on the one hand, and sportsmen, arms manufacturers, and eventually farmers on the other. Both animal protection advocates and scientists urged far stricter regulation of hunting seasons and bag limits to reduce destructive overhunting, against the determined opposition of hunters and gun manufacturers. Despite intense lobbying by animal protectionists led by the distinguished zoologist William Hornaday, the pro-hunting faction maintained control of this issue until the late 1920s, when a systematic waterfowl survey proved Hornaday's concerns correct. Animal protectionists argued that wildlife refuges should be managed as sanctuaries, while hunters argued that they should be managed as hunting preserves. The animal protection forces won this battle,[14] but their own absolute position against hunting was undermined by the disastrous starvation of deer on Arizona's Kaibab Plateau, caused by their own overpopulation in the absence of predators or hunting pressures (Swain 1963, 30–43).[15]

A third major constituency became a powerful and divisive influence on the Biological Survey Bureau after 1915, when stockmen and farmers persuaded Congress to support large-scale programs to exterminate predatory species. Between 1921 and 1924 alone the Biological Survey was responsible for killing by indiscriminate poisoning almost four hundred thousand predators: wolves, bobcats, mountain lions, bears, coyotes, and many others. In later years this program was continued and expanded, despite perennial criticism by wildlife conservationists and many scientists, to include ferrets, prairie dogs, and other species that farmers and ranchers considered "pests." In effect, the Biological Survey's mission was reoriented from scientific research to wildlife extermination services for farmers and ranchers. Wracked by constant conflicts among its constituencies, and failing to stop the decline of American wildlife species, the Bureau of Biological Survey ultimately alienated much of its support and fell increasingly into disrepute. In 1939 it was finally consolidated with the far less controversial Bureau of Fisheries into the U.S. Fish and Wildlife Service. However, this consolidation did not end its responsibility for predator and pest control programs (Swain 1963, 43–52).

Managing Environmental "Commons": Fisheries, Oil, and Agricultural Markets

In a famous article published in 1968, Garrett Hardin described the "tragedy of the commons" that occurs when multiple users share uncontrolled access to a common resource. Each user has an individual incentive to use it more and more intensively, and the aggregate effect of these individually rational decisions is to overuse and destroy it, unless there is some legally binding management regime — "mutual coercion, mutually agreed upon" — to limit the overall effect and ration it among its users (Hardin 1968).

Hardin's example was historically flawed,[16] but the problem he described was well illustrated by several environmental policy issues as early as the 1920s. One was hunting: without adequate controls on hunting seasons and bag limits, as well as habitat protection, the cumulative effect of individual hunters' successes and individual farmers' land conver-

Figure 10. This 1928 photo of Texas's Wortham oil field illustrates the "tragedy of the commons" resulting from multiple firms each competing to pump oil as rapidly as possible from the same pool. The original caption notes "This field rapidly declining in oil production." [U.S. Bureau of Mines]

sions was to reduce or even destroy wildlife populations, as had already happened to the passenger pigeon, beaver, bison, and some other species.

Another example was fisheries. The valuable Alaskan salmon fisheries were steadily declining by the 1920s, so much so that even the otherwise laissez-faire President Harding in 1922 signed an executive order creating a fisheries reservation under the regulatory control of the federal Bureau of Fisheries. Congress confirmed this regime in the Alaskan Fisheries Act of 1924, which authorized federal regulatory control over both fishing seasons and methods and equipment, and created programs to improve spawning waters. The result was a clear reversal of the fisheries decline by 1926, and a persuasive example of the value of a competent governance regime for such resources (Swain 1963, 47).

A third environmental commons problem of the 1920s was the over-exploitation of American oil fields. World War I had demonstrated both the strategic importance of petroleum and the associated national interest in using it efficiently and in maintaining domestic reserves. In the postwar era civilian fuel demand soared, driven by the availability of cheap mass-produced cars and by the creation of a federally subsidized highway system initiated in 1916 during the war years.

Unlike solid minerals such as coal, oil was usually found in large underground pools that could rarely be controlled by a single producer. Since multiple producers were pumping oil from the same deposits, each had a practical incentive to pump as fast as possible so as to capture more than the other producers. The result was severe overproduction, which drove down prices and thus reduced the profits to each producer (fig. 10). This in turn drove each to produce even more rapidly to try to cover their fixed costs, and simultaneously promoted wasteful consumption of energy by businesses and consumers.

The incentive to overproduce oil was exacerbated by the federal policy of allowing virtually unlimited prospecting for oil on the public lands under the 1920 Mineral Leasing Act. Every oil prospector's incentive was to find oil deposits as fast as possible, and to claim them by developing and pumping them out before a competitor did so. Many energy-using businesses and consumers supported these policies, since their immediate benefits were cheap fuel prices and erosion of the economic power of the large oil companies. However, their long-term effect was to waste a nonrenewable and strategically important resource.[17]

The unsustainably low prices of domestic oil during this period, and the resulting business and consumer dependence on them, created a fundamental and problematic dogma in American policy, namely the doctrine that national economic growth *depended* on cheap energy and thus that U.S. policy should be to keep it cheap. In the long run, the availability of cheap energy promoted *reliance* on cheap energy, by encouraging capital investments in energy-wasteful buildings, technologies, and urban settlement patterns.

This doctrine was not new, reflecting as it did the nineteenth-century legacy of exploiting environmental assets for economic gain. But neither was it economically sound. Keeping a scarce resource artificially cheap destroyed market signals to conserve it, to adapt to its scarcity, and to develop alternatives to it, and thus allowed serious crises to build up.[18] The doctrine's basic premise, that cheap energy was vital to economic progress, was also incorrect: in response to rising energy prices in the 1970s, many countries in fact continued to grow economically even while greatly reducing their industrial energy use (UNIDO 1989; Jänicke and Weidner 1996).

The policy was nonetheless fateful, in that it shaped the modern U.S. economy in a pattern deeply and structurally dependent on cheap fossil fuels. This pattern produced many material benefits, including technological innovation, widespread availability of air conditioning and labor-saving appliances, mobility, and low-density suburban residence patterns. However, it also produced serious costs and risks, including air pollution and oil spills, declining domestic supplies, economic and political dependence on foreign fuel sources, and consequent military costs and risks to maintain access to them.[19]

From a public policy perspective, overproduction could only be corrected by reducing the incentive for competitive pumping. Two solutions were possible: either allow the oil companies themselves to collude in restricting production and thus controlling prices, or ration output under government regulations, and operate each oil field as a single unit with an overall production quota prorated among its producers. President Hoover demonstrated the latter approach at the government's Kettleman Hills oil field in California, providing a model both for other federal oil fields and for state programs by most of the oil-producing states.[20]

Just as the Great Depression was having its own devastating effects on oil demand and prices, however, the discovery of the huge new Joiner oil field in east Texas threatened to add vast new quantities of surplus oil to the market, driving prices still lower. The resulting crisis led to enactment of the Connally Hot Oil Act of 1935, which prohibited interstate shipment of oil produced in violation of state laws, and thus promoted stricter state oil conservation laws (Owen 1983, 118). The Connally Act stabilized oil production against the worst excesses of competitive overproduction, but it did not create a framework for integrated, efficient management of each oil pool. It thus fell clearly short of a long-term, sustainable fuel resource conservation policy, and left the United States still with far lower oil prices than most other industrial nations. Policy and production continued to follow the interests of the major producers rather than of any long-term policy goals for resource conservation (Lowitt 1984, 100–12; Owen 1983, 118).

A final commons problem worth noting concerned the competitive conditions in agricultural markets. High prices for agricultural products in one year encouraged each producer to plant more the following year, creating aggregate surpluses which reduced prices to levels often below the farmers' production costs, and drove many into bankruptcy. This happened repeatedly throughout the nineteenth and early twentieth centuries. Years before the Great Depression, farm organizations and journals began advising farmers to reduce production voluntarily from the boom levels of the war years in response to shrinking markets and declining prices. They met with little success, however. Voluntary programs were not a sufficient response to the individual incentives that drove agricultural production decisions, especially in impersonal national and international markets in which farmers could not trust others not to gain advantages by planting more.

An alternative solution was to promote cooperative marketing organizations, voluntary associations of producers which would manage output and stabilize prices. This idea fit President Hoover's vision of governance by coordination among producers, and was incorporated into the Agricultural Marketing Act of 1929. This too failed, however, leading the Federal Farm Board which oversaw it to recommend explicit regulation of either acreage planted or quantities sold or both. The inadequacy of these voluntary measures for dealing with the agricultural production "commons" led directly to the agricultural stabilization policies of the New Deal era (Rasmussen et al. 1976, 1–2).

In sum, the natural resource problems of the 1920s provided some of the clearest and most persuasive examples of tragedies of the commons, as well as a few models for federal responses to them.

New Deal Conservation

The economic crash of 1929 and Great Depression that followed created a radically new context for federal environmental management. When Franklin Roosevelt took office in 1933, the entire economic system was essentially in collapse. Total national income had declined by more than 50 percent in just four years, an estimated 25 percent of the work force was unemployed, and people were starving in the richest country in the world. Hundreds of thousands of farm families faced foreclosure, and on the very day of Roosevelt's inauguration the entire U.S. banking system locked its doors.

Economic collapse was compounded by environmental disaster, as years of drought followed by giant dust storms and floods devastated the country's agricultural heartland. The magnitudes of these disasters are almost incomprehensible in retrospect: one of these dust storms removed an estimated three hundred million tons of topsoil from the Great Plains in a single day. Commentators described the era's drought as arguably the worst ecological disaster in American history (Lowitt 1984, 35, 37). Under these circumstances, Congress and the public were prepared to support almost any decisive presidential leadership that might provide solutions. From an environmental as well as a social reform point of view, both Congress and the president were for the first time simultaneously supportive of strong federal initiatives (Futrell 1993, 31).

Franklin Roosevelt brought to office both a willingness to use government initiatives to remedy social and environmental problems and a lifelong personal commitment to environmental conservation.[21] FDR's New Deal therefore offered the most sweepingly interventionist approach to federal governance in American history, with programs ranging from short-term emergency relief measures to more far-reaching reform of banking and stock markets, agriculture and business, labor and social security, and natural resource development and management, as well as a newly explicit federal role in stabilization of the overall economy (Schlesinger 1965, 1–23, 68–70).

Environmental policy initiatives were explicit elements of this agenda. Major examples included the creation of the Civilian Conservation Corps, the Soil Conservation Service, and the Tennessee Valley Authority, multiple-purpose water resource development and river basin planning, other public works projects (such as federal subsidies for construction of wastewater treatment plants), public purchases of key lands, reforms in grazing and wildlife policies, and serious attempts at interagency coordination of federal conservation programs. Agricultural stabilization policies and other New Deal initiatives also had far-reaching environmental consequences.

FDR's New Dealers shared with the Progressives a willingness to make active use of government intervention for the general public welfare. Some of their initiatives, such as multiple-purpose water resource development, in fact represented long-delayed victories for Theodore Roosevelt's Progressive agenda: progressive Republicanism finally implemented in alliance with liberal Democrats. This should be no surprise, as FDR himself had been a conservation leader in New York during the days of the earlier Progressive movement. In effect, the New Dealers rebuilt and greatly increased public faith in government as a steward of natural resources and of its own people's well-being (Futrell 1993, 31).

The New Dealers differed from the Progressives, however, in important respects. Theodore Roosevelt and Pinchot used government as a counterweight to centralized business power. To them, government's role was to make an expanding economy more efficient, to correct the destructive side effects of unrestrained environmental exploitation — such as speculation, monopolization, and destructive stripping of environmental assets for immediate profit — and to replace growing economic disparities with middle-class economic progress.

FDR and the New Dealers, in contrast, used the powers of government to *rebuild* the economy, and its environmental conditions, from a state of collapse. They used government to provide jobs, used those jobs in turn to achieve conservation goals — reforestation, erosion control, water resource development, and others — and used federal spending on these jobs to rebuild purchasing power (to "reprime the economic pump"). At the same time, they redesigned key elements of the underlying institutional structure — agricultural production, banking and investment, and labor laws and social security in particular — to increase their long-term stability (cf. Hofstadter 1955, 302–16).[22]

The Civilian Conservation Corps

One of Roosevelt's first emergency measures was creation of a Civilian Conservation Corps (CCC), to provide earnings and a work ethic for millions of young men who found themselves jobless during the Depression era. From 1933 to 1941, unemployed men aged eighteen to twenty-five were recruited by the Labor Department and put to work on conservation projects directed by the Agriculture and Interior Departments in camps run by the army. In the national forests, CCC projects ranged from planting trees and controlling insect and tree disease infestations to building trails, bridges, lookout towers, and firebreaks (fig. 11). CCC workers also helped the Forest Service to plant over two hundred million trees in windbreaks across the Great Plains ("shelterbelts") to forestall recurrence of the great dust storms. In the national parks, projects included building trails as well as clearing beaches and campgrounds, restoring historical sites, installing water and sewer lines to recreation areas, and many other improvements. Overall, CCC workers planted close to three billion trees, stocked nearly a billion fish, built a million miles of roads and trails, and worked nationwide in soil erosion control, rangeland and habitat restoration,

Figure 11. The Civilian Conservation Corps at work. A crew of enrollees planting ponderosa pine transplants on a fire-scarred area of the Harney National Forest near Custer, South Dakota. [U.S. Forest Service]

wildlife habitat improvement, drainage projects, and other activities (Schlesinger 1965, 337–40; Owen 1983, 128–45; Leuchtenburg 1995, 268–69).

In all, more than 2.5 million young men worked in the CCC, most for six months to a year. The program was finally terminated and replaced with the military draft in 1941, when the United States entered World War II. It was arguably the most successful of the New Deal relief programs, and left as its legacy the most effective eight-year record of conservation work in U.S. history. It advanced the nation's forest and conservation programs immeasurably and increased the value of the nation's environmental assets by hundreds of millions of dollars. Perhaps equally significant, it introduced hundreds of thousands of young men to the knowledge and appreciation of nature, the principles of conservation, and the pleasures of outdoor life. One may suspect that many of these young men of the 1930s became the parents who fueled the outdoor recreation boom of the 1950s, taking their children to camp where they had camped, to walk the trails they had built, and to see the places they had seen and the trees they had planted.

Water Resource Projects

A second major relief program was the Public Works Administration (PWA), which provided government jobs and funding for large-scale infrastructure construction projects intended to revive heavy industry. Chief among these were water resource development projects, but others included highways and bridges, docks and airports, schools, court-houses, and other public buildings, municipal water supply systems, and over five hundred wastewater treatment facilities. Examples included the major dams of the Tennessee Valley Authority, Boulder (Hoover), Grand Coulee, and Bonneville Dams, California's massive Central Valley Project, Denver's water supply system, Chicago's subway and sewage systems, New York's Triborough Bridge and LaGuardia Airport, the port of Browns-ville, Texas, and hundreds of other structures and facilities (Schlesinger 1965, 287–88; Owen 1983, 84–85; Armstrong et al. 1976, 418; Leuchtenburg 1995, 256–60).[23] Taken together, these projects represented a massive government investment in environmental transformation, intended to promote industrial revitalization but also profoundly reshaping the landscape for human use.

Water resource development projects epitomized this process. In the mid-1920s, severe flooding in California's Imperial Valley had catalyzed support for the first truly large-scale multiple-purpose water project, the Boulder Canyon Dam (Hoover Dam) on the Colorado River, to provide flood control and irrigation plus hydroelectric power production to finance its cost.[24] This project set the precedent for the large federal water projects of the New Deal and post-World War II periods: the Grand Coulee Dam, the Columbia Basin project, the Upper Colorado and Missouri River basin proposals, and others (Swain 1963, 73–95).[25] Congress in the same year directed the Army Corps of Engineers to systemati-cally study the navigation, hydropower, flood control, and irrigation potential of some two hundred rivers. The resulting "308 reports" laid the foundation for a nationwide water resource development program that was implemented during the Depression and postwar years (Swain 1963, 96–122).

In 1936, devastating spring floods in the eastern states led to powerful pressures for federal subsidies for flood protection, with proponents arguing that the upstream causes of such disasters were beyond the reach of the victim states. Since its earliest flood-control mandates the Army Corps of Engineers had provided flood protection solely through building levees along the riverbanks: the option most clearly consistent with its strict constitutional mission of improving navigation. Levees, however, simply worsened the flood risk: they cut rivers off from their natural overflow areas, and forced more water through narrower channels, increasing flooding downstream. The "protected" areas behind the levees meanwhile became prime sites for economic development, increasing the damage from flooding when the levees were overtopped. By the 1930s a century of navigation improvements and levees had laid the foundation for such disasters.

The Flood Control Act of 1936 in response established permanent federal authority for flood control projects. Dams and reservoirs, not just levees, would finally tame destructive floods, and store their water instead for controlled release to other economically useful purposes. The federal government would pay 100 percent of the costs of flood control projects, thereby attracting political support for the act from flood-prone regions such as the Mississippi Valley.

The New Deal water development program thus represented the triumph of both the New Deal and the Progressive ideal: a demonstration that government could not merely preserve but effectively control, manage, and improve the workings of natural processes for human benefit. Irrigation channels would protect against drought, locks and water level controls would expand commercial navigation, cheap and clean energy would be provided by hydroelectric power facilities, and revenues from electric power sales would defray much of the cost of the projects (cf. Nixon 1957a, 438–40). Theodore Roosevelt and the Progressives had proposed multipurpose water control structures as early as 1907, and the Federal Power Act of 1920 had supported the idea of coordinated development of hydropower and other related uses. The immediate objectives of work relief and economic pump-priming were subsumed into a far broader program of federal water resource engineering for economic development.

However, the advent of federally financed flood control also created a powerful new opportunity for congressmen to seek pork-barrel projects merely to benefit their own districts. The New Deal water development policies thus set in motion one of the most massive environmental transformation processes in history, a forty-year program of large-scale federal subsidies for water control projects interrupted only by the war years of the 1940s. Between 1936 and 1976 the Corps of Engineers built over 400 multipurpose dams in 42 states. The Bureau of Reclamation built 300 more, the Tennessee Valley Authority 23, and the Soil Conservation Service nearly 1,100 smaller projects; scores of others were considered (Armstrong et al. 1976, 251, 333, 272, 288). These projects dammed virtually all the nation's major rivers, at almost every location that was technically feasible and politically attractive: the Tennessee, Columbia and lower Colorado Rivers in the 1930s, the Missouri and upper Colorado in the 1950s and '60s, and many others. Federal water projects provided massive subsidies to the localities where they were built, and thus galvanized local economic and political interests into forming alliances with the water development agencies to compete for them.[26] Between 1936 and 1956 the Soil Conservation Service expanded its agricultural erosion-control programs into a "small watersheds program" of multipurpose water projects to build headwater dams and reengineer stream channels. Many of these projects were indistinguishable from those of the Corps and Bureau of Reclamation except in size and in the way they were funded. This expansion thus added yet another bureaucratic competitor to vie for federal water-project funds (Armstrong et al. 1976, 249–80).[27]

Ironically, the political success of this policy converted it by the 1960s into one of the chief targets of the rising environmental movement. Water projects were inherently damaging to some values even while they advanced others, and as early as the 1930s this led fish and wildlife advocates to demand "fish ladders" to protect spawning runs for Pacific salmon and other anadromous fish. The Fish and Wildlife Coordination Act of 1934, passed at their instigation and strengthened in 1946 and 1958, required the water agencies to consult with the fish and wildlife agencies to minimize and mitigate these impacts in their project designs. By the 1960s, publicity campaigns by the Sierra Club and fish and wildlife protection groups against water projects had redefined the water resource agencies from Progressive heroes to environmental villains, mindlessly destroying the landscape for short-term economic, political, and bureaucratic purposes.

In an effort to contain congressional pork-barrel pressures, the 1936 Flood Control Act directed that projects should only be approved if "the benefits, to whomsoever they accrue, exceed the estimated costs." It thus established economic benefit-cost analysis as a formal analytical requirement and decision criterion for water resource projects. This was a logical and prudent constraint: Congress's tendencies were well known, and since the explicit justification for federal funding of water projects was to promote national economic development, it was legitimate to require that their measurable benefits to that goal should exceed their costs. Ironically, this requirement later became a target of environmentalist attack, for its exclusion of many kinds of environmental benefits and costs. To restrict pork-barreling, benefit-cost analysis was defined as strictly as possible in order to justify only projects that clearly benefited national economic development. This very narrowness ruled out consideration of environmental benefits and costs, however, lest noneconomic environmental "benefits" be inflated in order to escape the restraining influence of the analytical requirement. In practice such inflation is precisely what happened: to justify politically popular projects, the water agencies gradually stretched the analytical methods so as to include ever more speculative economic surrogates for environmental "benefits" of the projects to be built, while continuing to count as costs only the out-of-pocket outlays for construction, operation, and maintenance rather than the full social and environmental costs of the projects.[28]

River Basin Management: The Tennessee Valley Authority

Perhaps the most radical innovation of the New Deal environmental programs was the Tennessee Valley Authority, the first and only working example of large-scale, multiple-use river basin management in the United States. The seven-state watershed of the Tennessee

Valley was one of the regions most severely impacted both by poverty and by deforestation, soil erosion, and flooding. It was also the site of a federal dam and war-surplus munitions plant at Muscle Shoals, Alabama, which private businesses had lobbied for years to
take over at a bargain price for power production and fertilizer manufacturing. In opposition, the remaining Progressives in Congress argued to retain it as a public hydropower
"yardstick" against which to compare the electric rates charged by private monopolies.[29]

Roosevelt converted this public-power proposal into a far larger experiment: a federally
sponsored river basin authority, managed as a public corporation, to oversee comprehensive economic development of the valley.[30] A series of multiple-purpose dams would
control flooding, open navigation throughout the river, and produce cheap and clean
electric power. As a public corporation rather than a normal government department, the
TVA would collect the revenues from electric power sales and keep them to finance both
its generating facilities and broader conservation and development programs. Immediate
construction jobs would alleviate poverty, and long-term employment would be created in
industries that would be drawn to the valley by waterways and cheap power. Erosion
control, reforestation, fertilizer production, and better waterway transport would promote agricultural revitalization as well (Schlesinger 1965, 319–34).

The TVA became a worldwide model for integrated river basin management, and
achieved major results in improving both economic and environmental conditions in a
severely impoverished region (fig. 12). It is far more widely known and more highly
regarded by water resource development experts around the world than by most Americans. Its early success led to proposals for similar management institutions for seven other
major river basins: a Columbia Valley Authority, a Missouri Valley Authority, and others.
These visions were ultimately blocked, however, by bureaucratic rivalries among the federal agencies that would have been affected (Leuchtenburg 1995, 188–95). Major multipurpose dams were built, transforming river after river into a controlled system of storage
reservoirs for economic use, but the idea of a comprehensive river-basin governance
institution was never repeated.

In practice, the TVA evolved into an institution both more limited and more controversial than was initially envisioned. Its stated purpose was comprehensive regional
development, but most of its budget was tied to specific construction projects rather
than broader regional planning.[31] Its directors' philosophies also diverged immediately,
with the majority favoring "grass-roots democracy" — which in practice meant forming
constituency-building alliances with powerful local economic interests, like other federal
conservation agencies — over the more ambitious planning favored by its first chairman
(Selznick 1949).[32]

By the late 1960s the TVA had completed the most economically attractive water
projects, and was advocating far more marginal and controversial proposals. Examples
included the Tellico Dam, which would destroy a legendary fishing stream, ancient Cherokee burial grounds, prime farmland, and an endangered species (the snail darter) to
create a dubiously justified industrial site, and the Upper French Broad project, a series of
fourteen headwater dams ("toilet tanks," as environmentalists labeled them) designed to
subsidize downstream paper mills by flushing their pollution.[33]

BENEFITS OF TVA

The once uncontrolled Tennessee River, harnessed by dams under the Tennessee Valley Authority, produces 12 million kilowatts of electricity for municipal, home, farm, and factory use. (Above: A TVA-lighted city.) The project also has halted erosion in the 41,000 square miles of the Tennessee's watershed and reduced flood levels on the Mississippi, into which the Tennessee drains.

Kentucky Dam can store the Tennessee's flow for several days. The TVA system is capable of reducing a Mississippi flood by 3½ feet.

Contrast: Eroded field (right) and field reclaimed under TVA supervision (left).

Cheap TVA electricity has brought modern conveniences to farm homes.

TVA electricity heats and lights this home near Norris, Tenn., and runs the radio.

Repairing a plow with an electric bit on an electrified Tennessee Valley farm.

Cheap electricity lightens farm chores. A corn shucker at work.

Electrically heated chicken houses improve fowl and increase the egg yield.

Figure 12. This photo montage depicts the benefits of multipurpose water resource development projects, which converted the devastating destructive power of floods into a managed resource for human benefits, while creating a wealth of federal construction jobs and infusing investment dollars into depressed local economies. It was prepared for a U.S. Information Agency exposition in 1947 to illustrate the multiple benefits of the Tennessee Valley Authority, all flowing from its management of the river system. [U.S. State Department]

Even more controversial, the TVA gradually became dominated by the electric power program that generated its revenues and in which it had its greatest autonomy. By the 1960s it branched out from clean hydropower to huge coal-fired plants, and became the nation's largest consumer of strip-mined coal and emitter of sulfur dioxide air pollution. It opposed occupational health and safety laws for miners, and fought alongside private power companies against pollution-control legislation (Leuchtenburg 1995, 160). Ultimately it also evolved into one of the nation's largest nuclear power utilities, operating some of the nation's largest reactors (including Browns Ferry, whose control room was destroyed by a major fire in the 1970s) and in turn providing cheap electricity to subsidize the federal nuclear fuel refinement plant in Oak Ridge, Tennessee.[34] Both its coal and nuclear operations represented significant departures from the TVA's Progressive origins as a proponent of hydropower and conservation.

The Soil Conservation Service

Yet another major New Deal environmental incentive was the conservation of agricultural lands. The economic boom years of agriculture's "golden age," between 1909 and 1914, had created pervasive incentives for agricultural expansion. Far more homesteads were claimed under the Homestead Act during this period than during the nineteenth century, as settlers plowed up more and more of the western prairies for new crop production, and grazed more and more cattle and sheep on the remainder at levels far above those at which the vegetation could regenerate itself.[35]

Beginning in the early 1930s, just as economic depression was undermining the socioeconomic system of American farming, half a decade of droughts and windstorms created a simultaneous environmental disaster. Giant dust storms swept across the plains and the Midwest, carrying away vast amounts of unprotected topsoil and depositing it in huge drifts against houses and fences and sometimes as far away as Washington and New York. An estimated nine million acres of land were ruined, and another fifty million severely damaged (Lowitt 1984, 57). Floods then eroded the underlying landforms into gullies and muddy rivers. These "natural disasters" of the 1930s — or more correctly, these natural consequences of imprudent human land use — dramatized to the public and politicians alike the destructive effects of unrestrained sodbusting and unrestricted grazing on the arid western lands.

The New Deal response was to create a Soil Conservation Service, one of the most important permanent environmental agencies established during the New Deal era. Throughout the 1920s an Agriculture Department soil expert, Hugh Hammond Bennett, had conducted almost a single-handed campaign in the Agriculture Department for more serious attention to soil erosion. When the dust storms of the 1930s proved him right, he was put in charge of a new agency to address the problem. First created as a Soil Erosion Service in the Department of the Interior in 1933, it was transferred to USDA and renamed the Soil Conservation Service in 1935. In the 1990s it was renamed the Natural Resource Conservation Service.

The SCS operated from its inception through a network of some three thousand local "conservancy districts," ultimately covering 98 percent of America's farm acreage. Each district was administered by supervisors elected by its client farmers and other "land occupiers," and thus was clearly controlled by its local constituencies (Morgan 1965, 37–40). SCS achieved significant gains in land and soil conservation by providing technical assistance in soil classification and analysis, and by promoting conservation farming: terracing, strip-cropping, crop rotation, planting and utilization of woodlots, and other measures (Rasmussen and Baker 1986, 209–16).

To conserve soil, however, was to manage water, by assuring not only that there was enough to prevent wind erosion but also that it flowed slowly enough off the land not to erode the soil itself. The Flood Control Act of 1936 therefore authorized SCS to study watersheds above flood control projects, to determine the effect of watershed treatment methods in reducing erosion and retarding runoff. The Flood Control Act of 1944 expanded this mandate into an authorization to plan and carry out basinwide watershed protection and flood prevention programs in eleven designated river basins.[36] Finally, in 1954 the Watershed Protection and Flood Prevention Act authorized federal financial assistance to "local sponsoring organizations"—usually soil conservation districts, or local governments directly—to prevent erosion, flooding, and sediment damage and to promote the conservation, utilization, and disposal of water.

Like the larger water projects of the Corps and the Bureau of Reclamation, SCS projects included federal subsidies for 100 percent of the costs related to flood control and for 50 percent of those related to recreation and fish and wildlife development. These federal subsidies led SCS projects to evolve from primarily farm conservation programs to broader multipurpose water resource engineering projects. Amendments in 1956 broadened their scope to include additional water uses, at the behest of congressmen from nonagricultural constituencies seeking shares of the program's benefits. Except for being generally smaller in scale, many of its projects thus became virtually indistinguishable from those of the Corps and the Bureau of Reclamation.

In only two respects did SCS water projects remain different from the others. First, SCS projects were funded as federal *assistance to local sponsors* rather than as federal projects per se. This led SCS to restrict their designs to purposes supported by specific local user interest groups, such as agricultural flood control and irrigation, rather than including other features, such as recreation or fish and wildlife improvement, that would benefit broader but unrepresented constituencies. Second, the SCS law required that as a condition of federal funding at lest 50 percent of the lands in a given watershed be farmed according to conservation farming practices. In both these respects SCS was even more explicitly dependent on its client constituencies than were the other water resource development agencies.

Agricultural Stabilization

A related but far broader New Deal farm initiative, which had mixed consequences for the environment, was the agricultural "adjustment" program. The primary goal of this program was to stabilize the devastating economic impacts of agricultural price downturns; it was also designed to promote soil conservation. Agricultural adjustment policies set target prices for six "basic commodity crops" based on "parity" with the agricultural golden era of 1909–14, and sought to maintain these prices through reductions of acreage planted ("allotments"), marketing agreements ("quotas"), processing taxes, and government purchases of surplus crops.[37] Additionally, the Soil Conservation and Domestic Allotment Act of 1936 provided payment incentives for farmers to shift acreage from soil-depleting to soil-conserving crops, and to retire marginal lands from production altogether.[38] As FDR advisor Rexford Tugwell put it, "Under this plan, it will pay farmers, for the first time, to be social-minded, to do something for all instead of for himself alone" (quoted in Schlesinger 1965, 72).

The New Deal agriculture programs initially represented creative policy innovations to try to correct the devastating economic and environmental effects of agricultural collapse. Rationing of acreage planted would share the available market demand among the farmers and take the most erodible acres out of production. Government purchases of surplus crops would stabilize prices, assure farmers of livable incomes, and thus motivate them to trust and comply with the system.

In practice, however, this system had serious flaws, both economically and environmentally (Paarlberg 1989). Economically, it benefited only growers of the designated "basic" crops and not all farmers, and it raised prices for their consumers, who were often even poorer. It kept these price supports in place for more than fifty years, until long after the end of the Great Depression. Finally, it created implicit incentives for the best-capitalized farmers and agribusinesses to intensify production on the allotted acres by applying heavier treatments of fertilizer and pesticides and improvements in plant genetics (Schopsmeier 1986, 230–31). These technological changes created surpluses yet again, which the federal government then purchased at the expense of the taxpayers. In reality, agricultural overproduction even in the 1930s was reduced far more significantly by droughts than by these policy incentives. And environmentally, they dramatically increased the problems of water pollution from agricultural runoff due to the increase in fertilizer and pesticide use.

The agricultural stabilization programs became one of the most powerful influences on agricultural land conservation, both positive and negative. On the positive side, they promoted increased conservation when subsidies for acreage retirement increased, and when over time additional soil-conservation mandates were added as conditions of receiving continued price supports. On the other hand, they also promoted increased destruction of marginal lands, wetlands, shelterbelts and other lands during periods when the incentives encouraged increased planting.

From the war years on, federal price supports served far more to stimulate than to curtail overproduction, since farmers now were guaranteed a minimum price for their output. Increased production was a policy goal during the war, and was politically difficult to reduce again thereafter.[39] The resulting surpluses were diverted in part to welfare relief and school lunch programs, and after 1954 to poor countries under the "Food for Peace" program (Schopsmeier 1986, 227). Ironically, the United States thus weakened farm prices and undermined the farm economy in those countries for the benefit of urban consumers, and thus encouraged more rapid urbanization. What seemed to most Americans a humanitarian gift to other countries in fact served a narrower economic and political interest of their own country: getting rid of politically embarrassing domestic surpluses that were stimulated by government subsidies (Schlesinger 1965, 35–84; Rasmussen et al. 1976).

In short, New Deal farm policies provided some environmental benefits from land retirement in the short term, but over the long term they failed to control the steady environmental impacts of intensification of agricultural production on fewer acres by fewer and larger agribusinesses. They also exacerbated the environmental impacts of these trends through policies that encouraged heavier and heavier applications of fertilizers and pesticides.

Grazing Management

Overgrazing on federal lands presented a special version of the agricultural problem, a classic tragedy of the commons in which too many cattle were destroying the drought-parched public rangelands. To address this problem, Roosevelt's Secretary of the Interior, Harold Ickes, joined forces with western congressmen to pass the Taylor Grazing Act of 1934. Under the Taylor Act, eighty million acres of federal public lands were formally redesignated as rangelands, to be administered in "grazing districts" under the overall management of a new Grazing Service in the Department of the Interior. Each user had to obtain a permit and pay a fee for each "animal unit month" of use. Like the grazing laws of Theodore Roosevelt's administration, the Taylor Act thus confirmed formal federal management authority over the rangelands. Grazing was now recognized as an official use of the public lands, subject to use rights which would preempt claims by new settlers or other would-be users. In effect, the public domain lands were now finally closed to most future settlement claims, and their entire acreage was now under formal governmental management authority.

The terms of the Taylor Act, however, also confirmed and strengthened the established ranchers' control over actual use rights and practices.[40] Its provisions in effect forbade any significant reduction of total grazing levels. Grazing fees were authorized, but were set at levels the Forest Service had charged in 1906, rather than at comparable levels in 1934, which at market prices would have been nearly three times higher. Amendments to the law in 1936 created formal national and local advisory boards, dominated by the ranchers themselves, to recommend the agency's management policies for each district. Such user-dominated groups in principle represented institutional solutions to the commons problem of overgrazing: what Garrett Hardin would later call "mutual coercion, mutually agreed upon" (Hardin 1968). In practice, however, the policy created privileged, government-sponsored oligopolies of existing users who effectively ignored values other than domestic livestock production, such as wildlife protection and particularly the protection of species that stockmen regarded as enemies or pests.[41]

The Grazing Service was merged with the General Land Office in 1946 to create the present Bureau of Land Management (BLM). Not until the Federal Lands Policy and Management Act of 1976, however, was BLM given statutory authority for multiple-use management of these lands. Until then its policies were essentially controlled by rancher interests and their congressional advocates, and to a significant extent they still are. Any hint of management initiative on the part of BLM led to immediate threats by western congressmen, who controlled its oversight and appropriations committees, to slash its budget or simply hand over the rangelands to the western states.[42] Grazing fees remained far below market levels, and more importantly, cattle and rangeland management remained lax. The result was that by the 1990s only 15 percent of the range was improving, an equal amount was in outright decline, and nearly 70 percent of the rangelands remained in only fair or poor condition (Wilkinson 1992, 93–101, 110–11).

Wildlife Management

A less widely noted but more successful arena of New Deal environmental policy innovation was wildlife policy. Federal wildlife responsibility prior to FDR had been divided between the competent but limited Bureau of Fisheries in the Commerce Department and the politically torn Biological Survey in the Agriculture Department, each of which had only limited authority and resources for their missions. FDR appointed a highly respected wildlife conservationist, Jay N. "Ding" Darling, to head the Biological Survey, and in 1939 he consolidated the two agencies in the Interior Department as the U.S. Fish and Wildlife Service.

To solve the funding problem, Darling obtained legislation extending to the wildlife agency the Progressive idea of earmarked funding based on user fees. The Duck Stamp Act of 1934 established a licensing fee on hunters, and the Pittman-Robertson Act of 1937 broadened this to a tax on sporting goods and ammunition. The proceeds were specifically earmarked for wildlife refuge acquisition, federal wildlife research and management programs, and tax-sharing with state wildlife agencies by a formula based on their area and numbers of hunters. A similar levy on fishing equipment, the Dingell-Johnson Act, was added in 1950.

The effect of these laws was to create not only a dedicated revenue source outside the annual budget struggle, but also a powerful set of client constituencies to support the agency: hunters, fishermen, and state fish and wildlife agencies. The National Wildlife Federation was formed in 1935, a powerful umbrella organization of state hunting and fishing groups that by the 1970s was ten times the size of any other environmental group. Many other such funding mechanisms have created enduring political problems, such as the Forest Service's dependence on revenues from logging companies, TVA's evolution into a self-serving electric power production company, and the road-building juggernaut of the Transportation Department fueled by earmarked fuel taxes. In the case of fish and wildlife, earmarked taxes similarly promoted domination of policy-making by hunting and fishing interests, but it also provided a critical new source of stable revenues for an otherwise weak sector of environmental policy, and these interests ultimately realized that ecosystem protection was vital to game as well as nongame species.

With the New Deal boom in both agricultural assistance and water resource development, however, fish and wildlife advocates found themselves increasingly on the defensive against federally financed projects for agricultural wetland drainage, dam building, and the conversion of trout streams and salmon runs into flat-water reservoirs. In 1934, therefore, they successfully lobbied for a Fish and Wildlife Coordination Act, which required the water development agencies to formally consult with the wildlife agencies in planning their projects. Such consultation allowed the Fish and Wildlife Service to act as a bureaucratic champion for fish and wildlife, and to negotiate for both minimization and mitigation of damage. Examples of measures that resulted include the addition of "fish ladders" for salmon around dams. Amendments in 1946 required the water agencies not only to consult with wildlife agencies but also to prevent such damage, and further amendments in 1958 directed them to include *enhancement* of wildlife habitat in their projects. The Fish and Wildlife Coordination Act thus served as a direct forerunner and precedent for the National Environmental Policy Act of 1969, which required a comprehensive interagency review and comment process — "environmental impact statements" — for major federal actions that might affect the environment.

National Parks and Forests

Another little-remembered environmental contribution of the New Deal was its sponsorship of large-scale land acquisition for expansion of the national forest and park systems, this time by repurchase rather than reservation. Using the authority of the Weeks Act, Roosevelt's National Resources Board identified an estimated seventy-five million acres of submarginal, deforested, and eroded agricultural and forest lands, and arranged for federal purchase of over eleven million acres for restoration, adding them to the national forests, national parks, and other land management systems. More than a million acres were transferred to the states, and the Fulmer Act of 1935 helped states to acquire some nineteen million acres of state forest lands while economic conditions allowed them to be purchased cheaply. The Roosevelt administration also bought additional large acreages to round out the national park system, particularly those that had special value for recreation. Important examples included the Blue Ridge, George Washington, and Natchez Trace Parkways, as well as the Florida Everglades, Great Smoky Mountains, and Olympia National Parks, and Cape Hatteras National Seashore (Graham 1976, 37–39; Owen 1983, 106–07, 120–21; Leuchtenburg 1995, 267). The Park Service also expanded its jurisdiction to include national recreation areas — especially around the lakes being created by multiple-purpose water projects — and national historical sites, responsibility for which had previously been scattered among the military services, the Interior Department, and other agencies.

Policy Coordination and Integrated Management

The New Deal environmental policy agenda of the 1930s was not merely a collection of isolated issues that could be solved by individual agencies and programs, but a complex of interrelated economic and environmental problems which required integrated solutions. The reality of the emerging federal governance, however, was a proliferation of frag-

mented, mission-oriented administrative subgovernments whose bureaucratic fragmentation and rivalries thwarted the very efficiency of management that the Progressives had
created them to provide. FDR and his administration therefore advocated two more
fundamental changes in environmental policy-making institutions to achieve greater policy integration. One was a proposal to reconfigure the Department of the Interior as a
Department of Conservation, and the other was to create a more effective policy planning
capacity at the level of the president.

The idea of a Department of Conservation was a major initiative of Roosevelt's ambitious Secretary of the Interior, Harold Ickes, who sought to unite in one department all
the major federal soil, water, and forest conservation programs. In the West many Forest
Service and Interior Department lands were literally checkerboarded amongst one another, demanding coordinated management, and Ickes argued that the Interior Department was more open to the full range of uses and constituencies of these lands than was the
Agriculture Department, with its timber-production ethos. In opposition, however, were
the long Progressive history of removing the forests from the politics and underfunded
management of the Interior Department, and the powerful farm and forest-products
industry lobbies allied with the Agriculture Department. In 1936 a President's Committee
on Administrative Management, chaired by the distinguished public administration expert Louis Brownlow, endorsed the change as part of a sweeping set of proposals to
consolidate ninety-seven administrative agencies into twelve departments.[43] The Forest
Service and agriculture and forestry interests successfully blocked these proposals, however, as they did similar initiatives by later presidents.[44] The result was an enduring,
politically determined fragmentation of the federal agencies that most directly shared
responsibility for land management and conservation (Gates 1968, 616–17).[45]

More generally, the federal government lacked any institutional capacity for coordinated policy planning or management across the fragmented array of federal agencies that
had been created. By the time of the New Deal, the federal government comprised far
more agencies and responsibilities than it had a generation before, yet there was no
Executive Office of the President, and no ongoing technical staff except the Budget Bureau
to provide institutional memory to each new president. Nor was there any ongoing
mechanism for presidential oversight or purposeful management of the executive branch
other than ad hoc meetings.

Throughout his presidency Roosevelt sought repeatedly to create a high-level staff
agency for policy planning and presidential coordination of the federal bureaucracy. He
first established a rudimentary National Planning Board in the Public Works Administration in 1933, to produce a congressionally mandated comprehensive plan for development
of the nation's rivers. He then broadened it into a more broadly interagency National
Resources Board in 1934, then a National Resources Committee in 1935, and finally a
National Resources Planning Board (NRPB) from 1939 to 1943, with modest changes in
membership each time but continuity of staff.

The NRPB and its predecessors produced a large body of information and assessments
on both natural and socioeconomic conditions, and their reports provided valuable foundations for policy analysis and improvement. However, they faced constant and effective

resistance from the mission-oriented agencies and their entrenched beneficiary interests, as well as from conservatives in Congress who were hostile to any increase in presidential power or "national planning." From 1936 until the early 1940s, Roosevelt repeatedly proposed legislation to create a permanent National Resources Board, but Congress with equal regularity refused to act on it. Finally in 1943 Congress destroyed the NRPB outright, by striking its entire appropriation from the budget and forbidding use of any other funds for its continued support. As with Theodore Roosevelt's earlier Inland Waterways Commission and National Conservation Commission, proposals for more effective presidential management were no match for the myriad interests with established positions of influence that benefited from the status quo, and these forces had only been strengthened by their close alliances with the administrative subgovernments within the executive branch (Graham 1976, 49–68).

FDR's efforts did lead to creation of an Executive Office of the President, to unify presidential advisory and oversight staffs. The more general pattern of U.S. governance established by the 1940s, however, was not the efficiently planned and managed state envisioned by the Progressives, nor even the coordinated programs and initiatives promoted by the New Dealers. Rather, it was a "broker state" in which fragmented administrative subgovernments intervened on an ad hoc and piecemeal basis to help particular client constituencies that were organized and powerful enough to get government attention (Graham 1976, 50–66; Schlesinger 1965, 352). Each agency was directed in principle to serve the overall public interest, but in practice each tended to define that interest through the narrower and conflicting visions of its own professional staff and its client constituencies.

The history of the water resource development agencies, for instance, reflects a cumulative broadening of the range of purposes that the agencies were directed to consider in planning the development and management of water resources: navigation and flood control, irrigation and hydropower, drainage, beach erosion control, water quality improvement. To these were gradually added fish and wildlife protection, recreation development, and in 1970 the enhancement of environmental quality in general. Despite this broadening of statutory authority, however, the agencies remained focused on specific and limited sets of missions, explicitly or implicitly disregarding other important public values — even the missions of other agencies — that were impacted by their actions. As noted in testimony by the Corps of Engineers' director of civil works in 1971, for instance, "In practice . . . only demonstrable economic benefits and costs based on market values were considered. . . . It wasn't until the passage of the National Environmental Policy Act that we really had in our hands the authority to spend money, time, and effort in this field over and above what were the precedent-setting studies in which economic development and the benefit-cost ratio were the be-all-and-end-all" (Maj. Gen. Frank P. Koisch, in U.S. Congress 1971, 557, 580).

In the face of congressional refusal to support integrated presidential policy planning, the main substitute that emerged was statutory requirements for increasingly comprehensive *coordination* of planning. This trend dated to the Fish and Wildlife Coordination Acts of 1934 and 1946, and culminated with the National Environmental Policy Act of 1969, which in effect required each agency proposing an action to consult with every conceivably affected agency and interest group. As one scholar noted:

> Agencies with limited rather than general interests in river basin development . . . have promoted administrative procedures and in one case [the Fish and Wildlife Coordination Act] legislation that require the principal planning agencies . . . to refer to them for review all proposed plans, so that the limited-purpose agencies can determine whether their interest has received proper attention. . . . In the case of water resource planning this stratagem got off to a good start in the late 1930s and early 1940s because the principal planning agencies were themselves more interested in developing certain purposes than others — the Corps of Engineers in navigation and the Bureau of Reclamation in irrigation and electric energy; and because the technique of benefit-cost analysis was developed in those years in a way that restricted the types of benefits and costs that could be counted, so that most of the benefits and costs of some special purposes were of necessity excluded from the important planning calculation. (Maass 1970, 213–16)

Summary

The New Deal era left an unprecedented legacy of conservation achievements to American environmental policy. No other era in American history produced such an extraordinary record both of restoring and enhancing the environment, and of creating an improved sense of harmony between human communities and their environmental surroundings. Multipurpose water projects represented triumphs of human technology that could literally convert destructive floods into productive economic assets. Unemployed people could regain their pride and sense of self-worth by replanting the soil, reforesting the landscape, and building trails, campgrounds, and community facilities so that future generations could enjoy their environment rather than merely extract commodities from it.

The New Deal thus marked the historic peak of a powerful and distinctive vision of environmental policy: that the natural environment could be developed and managed in an integrated fashion for human benefit, that this could be done in ways that restored and conserved nature itself rather than merely exploited its commodities for profit, and that government leadership, rather than just the invisible hand of the market, was a necessary and effective instrument to accomplish this.

Like Progressivism, the New Deal was led and implemented from the top down, by what might be called enlightened and pragmatic paternalism rather than by citizen activism. It was conceived and administered by a "brain trust" of professors and intellectuals, idealistic aides to Roosevelt who adopted and exemplified the belief that government could be active, effective, and humane rather than merely regulatory or tyrannical (McElvaine 1993 [1984], 327). It worked through large-scale mobilization of willing citizens, and it worked only because the public was willing to accept such a vast government-led initiative to rebuild from disaster — but it *did* work.

For all its conservation successes, however, the New Deal also left a legacy of imperfectly fulfilled and eroded ideals. FDR achieved only temporarily the integrated resource planning agency he sought, and the TVA swiftly abandoned its visionary ideals for political accommodation of key stakeholder interests. More generally, the environmental management agencies as a group rapidly adopted this pattern, evolving from expert organizations serving a common public interest to fragmented subgovernments closely allied with their primary political constituencies. In the aftermath of the New Deal, the efficient state of the Progressives and the benevolent state of the New Dealers became instead a "broker state" of bureaucratic politics.

In practice, the "iron triangle" alliances among agencies, clients, and congressional committees became profoundly resistant both to other legitimate interests and to changing public values and priorities. As Mancur Olson and others would later point out, the most persistently well-organized and effective client constituencies were usually those with well defined economic self-interests in the outcome of a particular issue, rather than broader and more representative voices for a general public interest (Olson 1965). The result was domination or even outright capture of many of the agencies by some of the very interests they were supposed to restrain or regulate.

By the end of the New Deal era, national environmental policy still did not include many environmental issues that became key concerns in the 1970s. Notably absent, for instance, were any significant federal policies for addressing air or water pollution, waste disposal, toxic chemicals other than food and drug contaminants, or land use other than on federal lands. Many policies that did exist were far more limited than those of the 1970s, and far more fragmented among separate mission-oriented agencies allied with different and often competing interests. It was in response to both these concerns — environmental problems not yet addressed by the federal government, and, at least equally, the environmental impacts of the actions of the federal agencies themselves, in alliance with powerful economic beneficiary interests — that the modern environmental movement arose.

10 Superpower and Supermarket

The question, "Has the United States the material means to sustain its civilization?" would never have occurred to the men who brought this Nation into greatness as the twentieth century dawned. But . . . [b]y the midpoint of the century we had entered an era of new relationships between our needs and our resources. . . . We had completed our slow transition from a raw materials surplus nation to a raw materials deficit Nation. . . . After successive years of thinking about unemployment, re-employment, full employment, about factory production, inflation and deflation, and hundreds of other matters in the structure of economic life, the United States must now give new and deep consideration to the fundamental upon which all employment, all daily activity, eventually rests: the contents of the earth and its physical environment.
— President's Commission on Materials Policy, *Resources for Freedom,* 1952

World War II plunged the country once again into war mobilization, with pervasive and permanent environmental consequences. All-out industrialization, arguably the most massive industrial buildup in the history of the world, dramatically increased resource extraction and pollution pressures. A continuing postwar boom in material and energy production, fueled both by Cold War military spending and by mass consumption, generated ever-increasing pressure for exploitation of environmental assets at home and worldwide. The "baby boom," rising middle-class affluence, and the resulting proliferation of car ownership and suburban settlement patterns magnified the demand for materials and energy, but also produced a citizenry that was increasingly concerned about outdoor recreation and preservation of the beauty of the natural landscape.

In this postwar boom era, therefore, public consensus on the appropriate role and goals of government fragmented once again. The military agencies maintained their power and budgets for another two decades, supported by the continuing public consensus over containing Communism. The civilian agencies, however, came to be perceived no longer as the neutral, expert voices of a general public interest, but as a patchwork of powerful and self-interested subgovernments, each acting as a mouthpiece for powerful client constituencies and as a vehicle for its own staff's ideologies and ambitions. In short, federal resource management agencies came to be perceived as part of the problem rather than the solution. In reality what had happened was not only that the agencies had formed supportive alliances with powerful constituencies, but also that public consensus on their policy goals had itself unraveled, opening a new era of rising conflict between extractive and protective uses of the environment. Both the increases in landscape transformation and pollution, and the complicity of federal agencies in exacerbating these impacts, triggered the mobilization of the modern environmental movement.

World War and the Environment

The United States' entry into World War II in 1941 triggered an all-out war mobilization, which finally brought the entire national work force back to full employment and thus ended the Great Depression. World War II was above all a war of industrial production, which revitalized the economy with government spending on a far more massive scale than the programs of the 1930s. Government purchases increased from $10 billion in 1940 to $95 billion in 1945, nearly all defense-related. The gross national product more than doubled in five years, from $100 billion in 1940 to $213 billion in 1945, 40 percent of the increase related to the war. Despite wartime rationing of most commodities, civilian standards of living increased over the depressed levels of the preceding decade, and inflation was even limited to 35 percent over the course of the war (Graham 1976, 72).[1]

New Deal programs that were consonant with the war effort were continued and even expanded, while relief programs and others were closed out. The Civilian Conservation Corps was disbanded and replaced by the military draft. Staffing of the National Park Service, Forest Service, and other civilian conservation agencies was severely reduced. Construction of multipurpose water projects continued, however, providing cheap hydroelectric power for the expansion of defense production in the Pacific Northwest, Tennessee Valley, and elsewhere.[2] Agricultural adjustment subsidies were increased, offering farmers 110 percent of parity prices to promote increased food production for the United States and its European allies. At the local level, severe pollution and occupational hazards were once again accepted as necessary side effects of war production (Colten and Skinner 1996, 139–40).

A long-term consequence of war mobilization was a permanent enlargement of the resource extraction and manufacturing industries. War mobilization demanded huge quantities of transport vehicles — aircraft, ships, trucks, tanks, jeeps, and others — and thus required major expansion of the auto, aircraft, and shipping industries. It required massive production of armaments and munitions, and thus similar expansion of the chemicals and weapons industries. It required vast quantities of housing and other durable goods, and of food and other supplies necessary to equip and sustain armies. The manufacturing industries in turn demanded increased extraction of raw materials and primary production — mining and smelting of iron, steel, aluminum, and other metals, extraction of coal, oil, uranium, timber, and other forest products — all of which intensified both commodity-extraction and pollution pressures on the environment.[3] Manufacturing of durable goods nearly doubled between 1939 and 1947, as did energy consumption; electric generation alone increased by more than 50 percent.[4]

Wartime priorities were also used as an excuse for proposals to open the national forests and parks to more intensive commodity extraction, such as logging of Sitka spruce in Olympic National Park for aircraft construction (Steen 1973, 250; Richardson 1973, 11–

13).[5] Most such overt challenges to national parks and forests were rebuffed, but the overall rate of logging in the national forests doubled during this period, from two to four billion board feet (BBF) per year, and resource extraction on private lands increased even more rapidly (U.S. Department of Commerce 1975, 534, L15–17).

No less significant was the sharp increase in federal support for scientific and technological research. During the 1930s the federal government paid for an estimated 20 percent of total U.S. research expenditures; during World War II this increased to 65 percent, and it remained at over 50 percent after the war (U.S. President's Commission on Materials Policy 1952, 16).[6] Military research and development (R&D) spending promoted the rapid development of new organic chemicals, first for munitions but ultimately also for civilian products such as rayon and nylon fabrics, pesticides and solvents, and plastics. It played equally important roles in health and agriculture, through the development of such products as modern antibiotics and DDT and other insecticides for control of disease vectors.

Military R&D spending thus laid much of the groundwork for the new technologies and new patterns of environmental impacts, both beneficial and problematic, of the postwar era. On the one hand, for instance, new weapons permitted not just more effective destruction of military facilities and personnel, but deliberate ecological warfare on a devastating scale, such as the widespread use of napalm firebombs and herbicides in Vietnam. At the same time, remote sensing research funded for military intelligence made possible both systematic global reconnaissance of the earth's environmental conditions and resources and also the first photos of the earth from space, which radically refocused public awareness on the smallness rather than the vastness of the planet, and on the finitude and apparent fragility of the earth as a unique environment for living organisms.

For the general public, the war years produced full employment but also new hardships. Wartime produced a half decade of regimentation, of rationing even of such basic commodities as food and fuel, of postponed families and careers, and for many, death or disability. For the longer term, the war caused widespread changes in patterns of living that had important environmental consequences of their own. Thousands of young men went into combat units, but many more went into support units, starting their working lives in the technical and administrative jobs of bureaucratic employment. At home, thousands migrated from impoverished rural areas to defense industries in urban regions, and shifted from farming or independent employment to jobs in industry or government. The United States became more than ever a nation of employees. All built up hopes for peace, prosperity, and family life, as well as savings to be used, after the war.

Finally, war mobilization reshaped institutions for governance, and attitudes toward them as well. Congress abolished the National Resources Planning Board in 1943, but it approved far more autocratic temporary powers for wartime agencies — the War Production Board, Office of Price Administration, and others — to regulate the economy. These agencies controlled the allocation of food and fuel, of labor and transport, and virtually all other aspects of the economy. The United States became in effect a centrally planned and controlled economy for five years, on a scale far beyond anything attempted by the New Deal. The staffs of the wartime agencies were largely made up of volunteer businessmen, many of whom ironically became convinced of the value of government planning for large-scale industrial production. Government could play valuable roles, they discovered, in co-ordinating production and transportation and in restraining labor demands in the name of inflation control. These benefits to big business, as well as rationing and paperwork, in turn aroused greater hostility to government planning among workers, small businesses, and others. In practice, farmers got 110 percent of parity and business profits were left essentially uncontrolled, while workers' incomes were controlled in the name of inflation, and small businesses faced rationing and increased paperwork as well as more effective competition from larger firms. Consequences included frequent strikes and an increased general sense of inequity and resentment toward government planning (Graham 1976, 74–77).

"Resources for Freedom"

As the war ended it was widely feared that demobilization would trigger a recurrence of prewar economic depression and unemployment. What followed, however, was arguably the longest sustained economic boom in world history. It was fueled by a combination of continued federal expenditures for military production and civilian public works projects, expanding export markets, and dramatically increased consumer purchasing power resulting from war savings, veterans' benefits, and well-paid jobs (Graham 1976, 88–89). Industries expanded for war production did not simply scale back or close down, but sought new civilian and export markets as well as continued government support. Auto and aircraft industries sought new markets for cars, airplanes, and rockets. The chemicals industry sought new markets for fuels, fertilizers, pesticides, synthetic fabrics, and plastics. The nuclear industry sought civilian applications of nuclear energy, both to create markets and to allay public fear of its destructiveness. The timber industry sought new access to the public forest lands, to replace private supplies overcut during the war.

The Cold War provided continuing markets for military production, as well as a military rationale for federal policies to keep these industries' productive capacities high. During World War II enemy attacks had severely reduced imports of critical raw materials: aluminum ore shipping, for instance, declined 22 percent during the first seven months of the war, and oil and gasoline imports dropped by 3.5 percent per month (U.S. President's Commission on Materials Policy 1952, 156). Postwar military reviews, as well as Cold War and Korean War fears, led to new studies of natural resources as national security issues and geopolitical assets. The result was a new policy concern about the adequacy of U.S. and "free world" supplies of strategic materials, and a new internationalism in U.S. foreign policy aimed at maintaining access to foreign supplies of these materials.[7]

In 1951 President Truman appointed a U.S. President's Commission on Materials Policy (PCMP), chaired by William Paley, to examine the role of strategic materials in military preparedness. The commission's five-volume report, published in 1952 under the title *Resources for Freedom,* provided both an articulate documentation of this concern and a detailed snapshot of U.S. commodity use at that time. The Paley Commission reported that the United States was using up its own known reserves of strategic materials far more rapidly than other countries, and had shifted from a raw-materials exporting economy to one far more dependent on raw materials imports. In 1900 the United States produced 15 percent more materials than it consumed, while in 1950 it consumed 9 percent more than it produced, and it was expected to consume as much as 20 percent more by 1975.[8] Perhaps most significantly for the future, in the mid-1940s the United States had become for the first time a net importer of petroleum (PCMP 1952, 12). The commission did not recommend that the United States attempt to regain self-sufficiency in raw materials except under wartime necessity, but it urged deliberate expansion of trade with the resource-rich but economically undeveloped countries of South America, Africa, Asia, and the Middle East, both for economic advantage and to form political and strategic alliances with other free-world countries (PCMP 1952, 12).

As war-preparedness measures, the commission also recommended policies to *accelerate* the growth of materials production, processing, and transportation capacity within the United States, particularly in steel, oil, aluminum, and electricity (PCMP 1952, 156).[9] Such policies would prevent a repetition of the World War II crash programs to scale up industrial production to wartime levels, and would also maintain peacetime economic growth and industrial employment. The result was that military spending continued at high levels: first for maintenance of Cold War force levels and for the Korean War (and later Vietnam), then for the arms race and the space race, and more generally simply to keep defense industries operating at a high productive capacity for any future war. All these policies served to continue and even increase the already high levels of extractive and pollution pressures on the environment.

A key difference from the 1920s, in short, was that after World War II there was no attempt to dismantle the government's enlarged wartime role in the economy. As after World War I, there was a general conservative yearning for peace, prosperity, and freedom from wartime regimentation, but after World War II this was coupled with deliberate policies to maintain wartime levels of materials extraction and manufacturing and to promote overall economic prosperity. Political parties competed to do the most to increase the gross national product, using government as both a gigantic investor and consumer and as a friendly regulator of markets (Graham 1976, 91–93). Significantly, major forces within the business community now supported a strong government role in regulating the economy. Businessmen who had managed the economy during the war had come to believe in the value of government planning with a "conservative face," using fiscal and monetary tools along with "sensible" regulation to damp down economic fluctuations, to control labor unrest, and to provide government subsidies and markets for their own industries (Graham 1976, 80–81, 100).

Nuclear Weapons and Civilian Power

No technology more vividly exemplified the federal policy of promoting civilian industries for military purposes than that of the nuclear industry. Created by the federal government in wartime to produce nuclear weapons, it was both continued for that purpose and deliberately expanded as a civilian industry after the war, with federal policy support and economic subsidies.

The Atomic Energy Act of 1946 established a five-member Atomic Energy Commission (AEC) and a Congressional Joint Committee on Atomic Energy, to assert continuing federal supervision over nuclear technology. Their initial policy focus was to assure both security and civilian control over nuclear weapons, which were rapidly increasing in both numbers and destructive capacity as a central element of the "arms race" with the Soviet Union. Under AEC management the United States created an entirely new and largely secret industry, operated in government laboratories and contractor facilities, to produce and continually improve nuclear weapons and propulsion technologies. These facilities also produced vast amounts of toxic and radioactive wastes and pollutant discharges, though the magnitude and toxicity of these wastes were discounted and kept secret for decades and only systematically documented and made public in the 1980s. At sites throughout the country—Hanford, Washington; Fernald, Ohio; Oak Ridge, Tennessee; Savannah River, South Carolina; Rocky Flats, Colorado; and many others—the nuclear weapons industry created a legacy of toxic and radioactive pollution, a "Cold War mortgage" as cleanup costs were billed to the next generation (Gerber 1992, 1–10; U.S. Department of Energy 1995). Cold War ideology and fears of the Soviet Union served to justify continuation of the wartime mentality of rapid production regardless of environmental costs, to justify keeping secret for decades the records of these pollution discharges, and even to justify outright deception of the public concerning the risks being imposed on them.

By 1950 the nuclear industry had developed an additional interest in the adaptation of nuclear energy for electric power production. The heat of controlled nuclear reactions could be used to drive steam turbines, producing "clean" nuclear energy that could replace coal and oil combustion, easing urban air pollution and reducing the country's rising dependence on foreign oil.[10] In 1953 the Atomic Energy Commission declared the development of civilian nuclear power a "national objective," and President Dwight Eisenhower, in a major speech to the United Nations ("Atoms for Peace"), promoted the expansion of civilian uses of nuclear technology. The Civilian Nuclear Power Act of 1954 chartered the AEC to develop peacetime applications, in part to sustain the industry's strategic capacity for military purposes and to serve the industry's own aspirations, but also for propaganda purposes, to allay public fears of nuclear power by demonstrating its civilian benefits. The act authorized federal licensing of commercial applications of nuclear power, and encouraged the building of "demonstration" and "experimental" reactors for civilian nuclear power.

The federal government thus both promoted and subsidized the development of nuclear power production, with glowing propaganda visions of electricity that would be "too cheap to meter," and it encouraged electric utilities to construct nuclear-powered generating stations as a "clean" alternative to coal and other fuels.[11] In this policy it was rapidly successful. In 1957 there were only 3 civilian nuclear power reactors in operation, by 1962 there were 7, by 1970 there were 13, and by 1975 there were 55 in operation with 158 more under construction or on order (Armstrong et al. 1976, 393). The size and capacity of these facilities grew as well: installed nuclear power production capacity increased from 112,100 kilowatts in 1957 to 5.6 million in 1970. Their actual power output increased from 10 million kilowatt-hours in 1957 to 1.7 billion in 1961, 12.5 billion in 1968, and 21.8 billion in 1970. This still represented only a small fraction of total U.S. electricity production, but it was a remarkably rapid growth rate for a new industry.

The superficial success of the civilian nuclear power program, however, masked important unexamined aspects of its environmental and even economic risks. Environmentally, nuclear power plants were clean in the sense that they produced none of the choking levels of air pollution generated by coal- and oil-fired power plants. However, nuclear power brought its own environmental hazards. Uranium mining caused serious pollution and health risks to the miners, and refinement of it into nuclear fuels required intensive use of energy itself. Nuclear power generation produced large quantities of heated wastewater, which killed fish and damaged water quality downstream. Spent fuels represented a growing quantity of intensely radioactive waste materials, which had to be either reprocessed (risking diversion into weapons production) or stored safely for centuries. Reactors themselves eventually had to be decommissioned, and either added to these wastes or permanently entombed. Finally, all these steps, and particularly the operation of the reactors themselves, involved small but real risks of potentially catastrophic accidents, as nearly happened at the United States' Browns Ferry and Three Mile Island reactors and did occur in 1986 at the USSR's Chernobyl plant.

In economic as well as environmental terms, the United States' policy of subsidies and other incentives for rapid scaling-up of nuclear reactors promoted a risky and ultimately unstable pattern of development in the U.S. nuclear industry. A simplistic but widespread belief in increasing economies of scale, combined with the licensing of reactors as "research" facilities, led U.S. companies to build reactors rapidly and idiosyncratically, every facility different and larger than the last, rather than standardizing designs at a known scale for careful study and refinement over their lifetimes. These practices increased costs, delays, and unanticipated errors and failures, as well as public fears and opposition.

Also, from the point of view of skeptical citizens and some scientists, the governmental framework for nuclear policy-making represented a troubling conflict of interest. Nuclear power plants were to be built and operated by private utilities, but the Atomic Energy Commission was charged both to regulate and to *develop* nuclear energy. The creation of a single Congressional Joint Committee on Atomic Energy also meant that congressional oversight would be conducted only by a small group of insiders operating largely in secrecy.[12] These arrangements may have seemed warranted by security concerns, particularly in the context of the nuclear espionage scandals of the time, but they also created dangerous bureaucratic incentives for the AEC to concentrate narrowly on commercializing the technology, and to underestimate potential risks.[13] The agency's unwillingness to deal openly with these risks — both environmental and economic — exposed it to increasing public attacks, leading to the virtual demise of the U.S. nuclear power program in the 1970s. It also kindled a broader public loss of trust in scientists' and engineers' authority as public officials, a distrust that came to pervade U.S. environmental policy debates.[14] Ultimately, this distrust was an important factor in the rise of public cynicism toward the Progressive ideal of governance as a whole.

The Economy of Mass Consumption

The postwar industrial boom reshaped the economy of work and consumption as well as production. Businesses' search for new markets found a powerful match in American households' pent-up yearnings for peace, prosperity, and family. It also tapped substantial savings — from war bonds bought with incomes that could not be spent due to rationing, from G.I. veterans' benefits, and from wages available in well-paid postwar jobs — that could now be spent on consumer goods. Military service and defense-industry jobs trained a generation of young workers for manufacturing, technical, clerical, and administrative employment, and relocated many from rural areas to cities where the defense industries were expanding. G.I. benefits opened the door to higher education for returning service-men, further distancing them from prewar occupational patterns. Agricultural employ-ment dropped by 72 percent from 1940 to 1970, while manual and service employment increased by almost 50 percent and white-collar jobs increased by nearly 250 percent (U.S. Department of Commerce 1975, 139). Gross personal savings — which had totaled only $4 billion per year between 1929 and 1940, then temporarily swelled to an artificially high $27–$37 billion per year during the war — grew steadily from $7 billion in 1946, to $15 billion in 1950, $22 billion in 1963, and $56 billion per year in 1970 (U.S. Department of Commerce 1975, F553).

In short, a decade and a half of depression and war were suddenly succeeded by an era of unprecedented general affluence. In this new postwar era, not just the wealthy but most households now lived in urban rather than rural areas, and could afford a house, a car, major durable goods and conveniences, recreational trips, and other amenities. From 1934 to 1972 the percentage of American families owning their own homes increased from 44 percent to 63 percent, and car owners increased from 56 percent to 82 percent of the population. Coupled with the extraordinary new access to education made possible by veterans' benefits, the war and its aftermath transformed the United States for the first time into an overwhelmingly urban, middle-class nation.

At the same time, wartime disruptions in family patterns produced the postwar "baby boom," as thousands of young couples delayed by military service now started families, and women displaced from defense jobs by returning servicemen found new vocations in raising families. Between 1946 and 1957 U.S. birth rates increased by almost 25 percent, to about twenty-five per thousand, before gradually receding to about eighteen per thousand in 1970 (U.S. Department of Commerce 1975, B5).[15] This surge in the number of young children produced with each succeeding decade a new set of demands and impacts. The larger-than-normal cohort of infants of the 1940s became the young families demanding single-family houses, schools, and recreation in the 1950s, the teenagers seeking college education in the 1960s, the young workers seeking jobs in the 1970s, the families raising their own children in the 1990s, and the disproportionately large cohort of retirees antici-pated in the coming century.

These socioeconomic shifts caused dramatic increases in overall and per-capita con-sumption of environmental commodities, and in associated environmental impacts (fig. 13). The Paley Commission reported in 1952 that the United States had become the

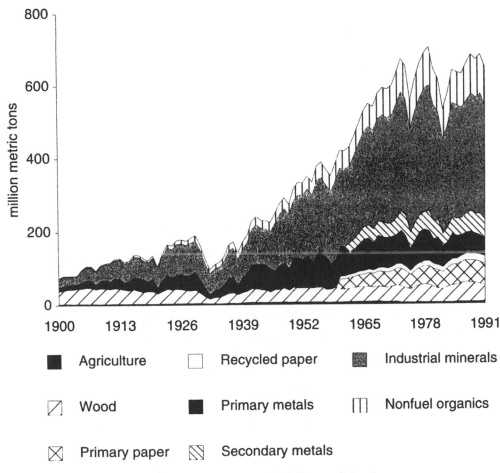

Figure 13. U.S. consumption of raw materials, 1900–91. [U.S. Bureau of Mines]

biggest materials consumer of the non-Communist free world, with only 10 percent of the population and 8 percent of the land area yet consuming close to half the total annual volume of materials, and its demand continued to rise. Per-capita consumption had tripled between 1900 and 1952 with yearly use of coal increasing by two and one-half times, copper by three times, iron ore by three and one-half times, zinc by four times, natural gas by twenty-six times, and crude oil by thirty times (U.S. President's Commission on Materials Policy 1952, 1–6). Similar increases occurred in consumption of lumber, pulp and paper, and other commodities. At the consumer level this meant unexpected growth in the purchasing of single-family homes, cars, electrical appliances (especially washing machines, dryers, air conditioners, and even garbage disposals and "all-electric" homes), and disposable "convenience" products: soaps and detergents, household bug sprays, paper diapers, packaged foods, and others. Packaging itself became a major growth industry, by appealing both to consumers' desire for convenience and to producers' mass-marketing interests as "supermarkets" replaced neighborhood stores. Its sales increased by 63 percent between 1958 and 1976. Simultaneously, it increased both per-capita waste disposal and roadside litter (Hoy 1995, 174). These trends continued and even accelerated over the following two decades, fueled by steady rises in the population, the gross national product, and Americans' disposable incomes. The United States became the world model of a "throwaway society."

Pollution Pays: Environmental Impacts of Technological Change

A profoundly important consequence of these shifts in the economy was a major change in the mix of products and production technologies themselves. This shift included both increased production of pollution-intensive commodities and displacement of less-polluting substitutes, causing pollution to increase by an estimated ten times faster than the gross national product. Between 1946 and 1970, for instance, the production of materials for basic human needs, such as food, clothing, shelter, and basic metals, increased more or less in proportion to population, and overall production of nondurable goods tripled. Chemicals production, however, increased sixfold, aluminum production four times over, and rubber and plastics nearly five times (U.S. Department of Commerce 1975, M83, P18–39). Whole new categories of environmentally significant materials were introduced into widespread use for the first time, including organic chemical pesticides, detergents, plastics, and man-made radioactive materials.

Pollution-intensive consumption increased as well. Annual automobile sales doubled, and owners of second cars increased from 3 percent to 28 percent of the population (U.S. Department of Commerce 1975, Q148, Q175). Small automobile engines were replaced by far larger and less fuel-efficient ones, which required more heavily leaded fuels. Intercity highway travel in private cars more than doubled, and fuel use more than tripled (U.S. Department of Commerce 1975, Q1–11, Q156). Air conditioning came into widespread use, and annual energy consumption rose from 219 million British thermal units (BTUs) per capita in 1950 to over 327 million BTUs per capita in 1970, nearly a 50 percent increase (U.S. Council on Environmental Quality 1997, 506). Phosphate detergents began rapidly displacing soap products in 1948, with production increasing tenfold to over five billion pounds in 1970, while soaps declined by 60 percent. In agriculture, total production increased about 45 percent between 1949 and 1968, while harvested acreage declined by 16 percent, but use of pesticides increased 168 percent during the same period, and use of fertilizer nitrogen by about 648 percent *per year*. These changes evidenced a dramatic intensification of the use of chemical inputs on farmland and crops (Commoner 1971, 149–50).

Pollution of many kinds increased accordingly, at rates far above either population growth or increases in general affluence and consumption. Annual phosphate discharges in municipal sewage increased sevenfold from 1940 to 1970, while discharges of nitrogen oxides and tetraethyl lead from automobiles increased sixfold and fourfold, respectively. During the same period, agricultural discharges of synthetic pesticides increased nearly threefold, and of inorganic nitrogen fertilizers nearly eightfold. One of the few beneficial trends was the gradual replacement of coal by natural gas for urban heating as new pipelines made gas more widely available, reducing the most severe forms of smoke and sulfur pollution in cities (Tarr 1985, 527–28). Overall, increased pollution per unit of production accounted for an estimated 95 percent of the increase of pollution levels other than those associated with auto travel (Commoner 1971, 176–77).

Interestingly, some of these trends were in fact identified and criticized at the time, almost two decades before the emergence of the modern environmental movement. The 1952 report of the President's Commission on Materials Policy, for instance, explicitly identified both pollution and inefficient production methods as forms of waste that should be reduced. Fifty percent of most coal and oil deposits were simply left in the ground by mining operations, 10 percent of copper was discarded as slag during smelting, 35 percent of the average tree was thrown away, more sulfur was emitted as air pollution than was used in products, and enough natural gas was wasted annually to supply the needs of eleven million homes. Much of this waste was due to outmoded and wasteful production technologies by firms that "had not explored carefully enough the potential profit in waste reduction." The report also noted the wastefulness of poorly made products that had to be replaced frequently, of corrosion caused by pollution, of the costs of frequent repainting and protective coatings to prevent it, and of failure to recycle and re-use materials. It further criticized the overdesign of products: heavier cars than needed, adorned with wasteful and unnecessary chromium decoration and burning heavily leaded high-octane gasoline, all wasting materials on trivial and transient tastes.

Almost twenty years before the modern "environmental era," in short, farsighted public reports had identified many of the environmental problems of industrial pollution and recommended increased attention to correcting them (PCMP 1952, 8–11, 160–61). These recommendations had little immediate impact on the "affluent society" of postwar America, however. The self-interests of wartime-scale manufacturing industries, of newly affluent customers, and of government all coincided in continued and increasingly intensive exploitation of the environment for material consumption (Gottlieb 1993, 75–80).

The Heyday of Federal Water Control Projects

One of the most visible direct roles of the federal government in the environment during the postwar era was its continued financing of major construction projects—particularly dams and other water projects, and after 1956 highways as well—even in a time of economic prosperity. The period from World War II through the 1960s was the heyday of federal multipurpose dam construction. No longer needed for Depression-era jobs, such projects were now urged instead to control flood damage, to provide cheap public electric power, and to promote regional economic development. Water projects were promoted as public *investments:* projects too big or too multifaceted to leave to commercial syndicates (and involving the allocation of a historically public resource, flowing water), and which, like the nineteenth-century canal grants for navigation, would harness the "free" public water resource to return greater benefits to the economy than their costs.

Overall, the federal budget for water resource projects increased from $323 million in 1940 to $1.1 billion in 1950, and remained high throughout the following decades.

Between 1936 and the 1970s the Corps of Engineers alone completed some thirty-four hundred flood control projects, including over four hundred dams in forty-two states, and the TVA completed thirty-three on the Tennessee River and its tributaries (Armstrong et al. 1976, 251, 272). The Bureau of Reclamation and the Bonneville Power Administration built thirty-one multipurpose dams for power production on the Columbia River and its tributaries, and others throughout the West (Armstrong et al. 1976, 366). In 1954, the Small Watersheds Act gave the Soil Conservation Service its own program to build dams and reengineer watercourses for local business interests.

As the most cost-effective projects were built, however, and more and more reaches of the rivers were dammed, the remaining projects became increasingly controversial.[16] Many were transparent and even hypocritical monuments to regional self-interest, as even politicians who publicly deplored federal spending lined up for their own shares to subsidize speculative local economic development schemes. Some projects also reignited old conflicts over preservation of natural areas and fisheries, as dams were proposed that would back water up into national parks and national monuments, or destroy fish spawning runs or the last remaining whitewater reaches, such as Hells Canyon on the Snake River. Public demand for outdoor recreation was rising dramatically, and with it the popularity of sports that required free-flowing rivers, such as trout fishing and wild-river running (Richardson 1973, 47–48).

These forces collided directly when the Upper Colorado Storage Project was proposed in the 1950s. In 1948 the five states of the upper Colorado River basin proposed a set of high dams backing water up into a series of deep, spectacular canyons of the Rockies to draw population and industry into the region. This plan would impinge on over a dozen units of the national park system, particularly the Dinosaur National Monument, an especially beautiful network of canyons that had been set aside in 1915 and enlarged in 1938. President Truman's administration approved one of these dams, the Echo Park Dam, in 1950, siding with local chambers of commerce over strong opposition from preservation advocates, and President Eisenhower did likewise in 1954. These actions galvanized a massive publicity campaign by preservation groups to stop the dam.

The campaign against Echo Park Dam united the Sierra Club, the Izaak Walton League, the Wilderness Society, and others into a new and effective coalition, the Council of Conservationists, which used the mass media to produce nationwide publicity and to generate intense and sustained public protest against the dam (Richardson 1973, 134–52).[17] Their rallying cry was "No more Hetch Hetchys!" recalling the legendary conflict in which Gifford Pinchot and his utilitarian allies had approved damming rather than preservation of the second valley of the Yosemite. They publicized photographs showing the natural beauty of the canyon, and increased visitation to the site six times over by organizing raft trips through it. They forced the Bureau of Reclamation to acknowledge errors in both its technical analyses and its speculative assumptions about the need for the project, and they hammered at the high cost involved, noting that the project would cost sixteen times more than the total assessed value of farm lands and buildings in the four surrounding states, and thus represented a massive subsidy from taxpayers elsewhere.[18] Project supporters responded by vilifying the opposition, portraying them as a conspiracy of a few long-haired fanatics and wealthy, idle elitists from the East and West Coasts. This served only to broaden the conflict, however, alienating other constituencies and opening debate on the whole policy of federal water development subsidies.[19] In a surprise victory, the preservationist coalition won the Echo Park battle, and the proposed dam was removed from the Upper Colorado Basin Project authorization in 1956 (Richardson 1973, 139).

The Echo Park victory was only a single battle, and ironically it stopped only one dam while the rest of the Upper Colorado Basin Project went ahead—including other projects that were just as damaging, such as Glen Canyon Dam. It also failed to slow the broader momentum of federal subsidies for water projects, though in retrospect it marked the beginning of the rapid decline of the Bureau of Reclamation.[20] Nonetheless, as a precursor and training ground for the modern environmental movement it was a key turning point in American environmental politics, both symbolically and practically. The Echo Park controversy marked the postwar rebirth of the ecological preservation groups as an effective political force, and taught them new tactics for using the mass media to mobilize broad-based political opposition. From this experience they began to generate organizational momentum for more far-reaching campaigns: for wilderness protection and pollution control, and against the huge federal subsidy programs for water projects, highways, nuclear power plants, and other forms of landscape transformation. They also shifted their tactics from ad hoc publicity campaigns on behalf of particular places into more organized and ongoing political lobbying in state capitols and Washington, which no conservation group had previously done.[21]

Outdoor Recreation

With the postwar emergence of a largely middle-class, suburban American society, the boom in young families, and the widespread increases in both automobile ownership and leisure time, outdoor recreation emerged in the 1950s as both a major activity and a rapidly expanding sector of the economy (Armstrong et al. 1976, 565–67). Wartime military service had exposed a growing number of Americans to organized outdoor recreation activities, though it also had limited tourism: national park use shrank during the war years to less than half its 1941 visitation. After the war, however, outdoor recreation and tourism surged to unprecedented levels. By 1956 visitor levels at national parks had increased to almost two and one-half times their prewar levels (Foresta 1984, 50).

The rising demand generated increased pressure for funding and redirection of the National Park Service, not so much to acquire or preserve parks but to accommodate more outdoor recreation and tourism. In 1956 the National Park Service embarked on "Mission 66," a decade-long program of construction and improvements to existing parks. Its goals were to restore the parks to high quality by 1966, the fiftieth anniversary of the Park Service's creation, and to upgrade public outdoor recreation facilities at federal reservoirs. The national parks were to be marketed as "Parks for People," rather than just preserved undisturbed as natural wonders. The Park Service astutely cultivated political support from President Eisenhower and in Congress, and from the major park-related interest groups, and obtained large and steady increases in appropriations as a result. Mission 66 was aimed especially at building recreational user constituencies at those parks that were most vulnerable to resource exploitation schemes. One strategy, for instance, was to build two thousand miles of scenic roads to counter proposals for logging roads, and thus to attract the support of the driving public and the American Automobile Association (and more generally to reassert its leadership after the Echo Park battle, in which its own lack of effective leadership had left the lead to citizen preservation groups).

Mission 66 was aimed not just at accommodating but at *increasing* public use of the national parks. It included a public relations campaign oriented to auto-based and overnight accommodations, construction of ostentatious visitor centers, and development of large-scale tourism in the parks. All these initiatives broadened the parks' political support, but also aroused serious concern among the parks' traditional preservation constituencies that the parks could be overrun with "honky-tonk" development rather than preserved for their intrinsic natural values. Mission 66 also enlarged the Park Service's responsibilities to include management of the flat-water recreation areas around federal dams, such as those built as part of the water resource development program in the West. This expanded the agency's jurisdiction and influence, but also blurred the distinction between the "crown jewels" of the parks — the truly unique parks which had been set aside as natural wonders and distinctive ecosystems — and a far larger collection of sites and facilities that were valuable primarily for tourism and mass outdoor recreation.

The tensions between proponents of preservation and recreational development intensified as both outdoor recreation demand and other economic pressures continued to mount. These pressures focused on the parks and on other natural lands of all kinds, particularly on the remaining seashores, lakeshores, and other open-space lands near urban areas. A National Park Service report in 1956, *Vanishing Shoreline,* calculated that out of 3,700 miles of U.S. coastline, only 640 miles were still available for public acquisition, and recommended that government agencies purchase half of that total. The Eisenhower administration opposed public land acquisition, but President John Kennedy reversed this policy. Under the Kennedy administration Cape Cod National Seashore was created in 1961, a series of other national seashores, lakeshores, and recreation areas were proposed,[22] and funds were added to the 1961 Housing Act for local acquisition of park and open-space lands.

In 1958, meanwhile, the prestigious Outdoor Recreation Resources Review Commission was created to review the overall status and trends in the supply and demand for outdoor recreation opportunities. Its report, completed in 1962, made a powerful case for more aggressive policy initiatives. It predicted a tripling of outdoor recreation demand by the year 2000, and recommended that provisions for outdoor recreation therefore be made an integral part of future metropolitan growth. It urged that additional public recreational lands be acquired, especially near urban areas, and that a federal Bureau of Outdoor Recreation be created in the Interior Department to coordinate these efforts.

In 1965 Congress went further, creating one of the most successful but little-remembered policy innovations for landscape preservation since the original national forest reserves: a Land and Water Conservation Fund, to finance acquisition of public recreational lands by all levels of government. Revenues for the fund — $200 million per year initially, increasing to $2 billion per year by 1975 — came primarily from federal royalties on offshore oil and gas leases, as well as from park entrance fees, motorboat fuel taxes, and sales of federal real estate. Sixty percent of the revenues were designated for grants to the states for land acquisition, park development, and recreation planning. In its first few years, the fund paid for public acquisition of nine new national parks and recreation areas, several protected wild rivers, and innumerable additions of land to "round out" existing parks, and it created an important new source of federal financial assistance for state and local parks as well.[23]

Logging the National Forests

The postwar decades also produced rising public opposition to logging of the national forests. Like the water-project conflicts, these controversies revealed the changing environmental perspectives of an increasingly suburban, middle-class population with rising preferences for outdoor recreation and for nature as an amenity rather than for commodity production. They were also legitimate reactions to a sharp change in Forest Service policy, from relatively modest logging for local and regional needs to large-scale commercial timber production. The reality was not just that a more middle-class public perceived logging less favorably: logging on the national forests was itself expanding rapidly, at larger scales and using more destructive methods than ever before.

Forest Service policy since the time of Gifford Pinchot had been to give highest priority to timber production for home building, but also to manage the national forests only as local supplemental sources rather than as competitors to timber companies on private lands (Steen 1976, 90). National forest timber was made available, therefore, only to keep local mills running at steady and comfortable levels rather than for national or international commercial markets. As a practical matter the private forests were generally more accessible anyway, since the commercial logging companies during the nineteenth century had claimed the more accessible commercial-quality lands. As a result, the amounts of timber cut from the national forests remained relatively low until World War II, amounting to less than two billion board feet (BBF) per year before 1939.

During and after World War II, however, the national forests came under increasingly heavy pressures for higher rates of logging. The wartime annual cut was doubled, from 2 to 4 BBF, although even then most of the total national timber demand was met from private commercial forest lands. By the end of the war, however, private commercial forestlands had been heavily cut over and were rapidly declining in productivity. The President's Commission on Materials Policy in 1952 estimated that 90 percent of the virgin timber in U.S. commercial forests had been cut, that reforestation had not kept pace, and that the current rate of annual use was 40 percent greater than the growth rate of replacement timber (PCMP 1952, 1–6). The immediate reason for this decline was wartime demand, but the more fundamental cause was a long history of poor logging and inadequate reforestation practices. The private growers had been practicing "one-shot forestry" rather than long-term management, often simply taking the best trees or even clear-cutting entire stands without systematic reforestation and management: in effect, mining the forests rather than managing them (Wilkinson 1992, 136–39).

In the postwar years demand continued to be high, fueled by continued military and industrial uses, by the boom in suburban housing construction, and by the growth of export markets. Domestic pulpwood production increased by three and one-half times between 1950 and 1970, and per-capita consumption of both plywood and newsprint more than tripled. Exports also increased dramatically, including a tripling of softwood exports and a quadrupling of Douglas fir log exports from the Pacific Northwest between 1963 and 1970 alone.

The timber industry therefore turned to the public lands, and advocated opening the national forests — particularly the profitable old-growth forests of the Pacific Northwest — to intensive commercial logging (Steen 1976, 257). Because the national forests were generally less accessible than private commercial lands, such a policy also required a major forest road-building program to open them for commercial use. President Eisenhower supported this policy change, steadily increased the annual cut, and included in his first budget request a doubling of the appropriation for building forest access roads (Richardson 1973, 101; Hirt 1994). As a result, both road building and logging on the national forests increased dramatically. Forest road mileage doubled between 1940 and 1960, from 80,000 to 160,000 miles, and the annual cut more than doubled from its already-doubled wartime levels, to 9 BBF by 1962, and tripled to over 12 BBF by 1970. Overall, between 1950 and 1966 twice as much timber was cut from the national forests as had been cut in the entire previous forty-five years since creation of the national forest system (Steen 1976, 284, 314; U.S. Department of Commerce 1975, L15–17, L138–39, L146, L155, L166; Wilkinson 1992, 136–39).

A kind of technical double-speak initially blurred the implications of these policy changes, which the Forest Service described as "sustained yield" forestry. The Sustained Yield Forest Management Act of 1944 formalized the principle of sustained yield for management of public forest lands, and authorized a system of "cooperative sustained yield management units," some comprising only national forest lands and others combining public and private lands. The public image of sustained yield forestry was that a tree was planted for each one logged, thus in principle assuring a continuous supply into the indefinite future. To the Forest Service and the timber industry, however, sustained yield management meant not just replanting, but also harvesting the *maximum* biological potential of each acre. Since relatively little logging had yet occurred on the national forests, this meant dramatically increasing logging on those lands, particularly of the mature old-growth trees that could be replaced with younger, faster growing ones. It also meant applying to the public lands the industrial practice of clear-cut logging, or harvesting the entire biomass of an area rather than merely the dead or mature trees.[24]

The creation of "cooperative units" for sustained yield management allowed the Forest Service and the timber industry to combine the unlogged national forests with cut-over private lands for purposes of sustained yield calculations, averaging the "sustainable" yield across both. The practical result was to clear-cut the entire remaining stands on the public lands while the cutover private lands were supposedly regrowing to harvestable dimensions (Hirt 1994, 34–41).[25] To the public, these practices looked like the very ones which the Forest Service had long held up as examples of bad land management by private firms (Steen 1976, 285, 302).[26]

This increased logging occurred precisely during the period, moreover, in which the national forests as well as the parks were experiencing rapidly growing demands for outdoor recreation, both for intensive activities such as skiing and for more individual activities such as hiking, camping, hunting, and fishing. With the growth of mobility and increases in the number of young families, the public was now out in the forests — whether for recreation, to appreciate the beauty of unspoiled mountains and forests, or to view with pride the trails, facilities, and conservation projects built by fathers who had once been young men of the Civilian Conservation Corps — and seeing the effects of large-scale commercial logging. These visitors rapidly became a large new constituency opposed to such logging, and particularly to industrial-scale clear-cutting.

Even westerners and some Forest Service professionals felt the pressures of conflicting priorities. Though they benefited from the commodity-extraction economy, many were also hunters and fishermen whose own values were rooted in the conservation ethic, and whose own special places were now targets of the new cross-pressures for increased logging, increased tourism, and permanent protection (Wilkinson 1992, 136–39). Aldo Leopold, for instance, whose earlier work in the Forest Service had defined the field of wildlife management as "harvesting the surplus" of wildlife populations for human hunting and fishing demand (Leopold 1933), now spoke in a very different voice, arguing in his famous *Sand County Almanac* for a biocentric "land ethic" in which humans would be viewed as "plain members and citizens of the land-community rather than conquerors of it." In his words, "people should quit thinking about decent land-use as solely an economic problem. Examine each question in terms of what is ethically and esthetically right, as well as what is economically expedient. A thing is right when it tends to preserve the integrity, stability, and beauty of the biotic community. It is wrong when it tends otherwise" (Leopold 1966 [1949], 238–40, 262; see also Flader 1974).

The result was a frontal collision between commercial pressures for commodity production and public demand for preservation and appreciative uses of the forests. The Forest Service had long accepted the principle of "multiple use" of the forests, but had always defined it as a mix of uses compatible with a primary goal of timber production (the "dominant" use), rather than a varying mixture of all uses on an equal footing. It also had adamantly opposed proposals to set lands aside from commodity production uses, such as the national parks. This they viewed contemptuously, in the language of Pinchot and his successors, as "locking them up" rather than as "wise use" of them. As recreation and preservation advocates saw the massive expansion of commercial clear-cutting that was taking place on the national forests, however, and heard the Forest Service describe this practice as "multiple use" and "sustained yield," they fundamentally lost faith in the agency's commitment to genuine conservation of the forests (Hirt 1994, 162–70). Preservation groups therefore began to lobby for designation of the most pristine national forest lands as legally protected "wilderness areas," off-limits for commercial timber and mining exploitation and even for intensive recreation development. In particular, this designation would protect them from the forest road-building program that would open the way for more intensive uses.[27]

By the end of the 1950s, the forest industry's biggest worry therefore was the loss of commercial-quality national forest lands to recreational uses — or worse yet, to restrictive designation as wilderness areas (Steen 1976, 295). The political campaign for wilderness areas began in 1955, on the heels of the movement to stop Echo Park Dam; legislation was proposed by the Wilderness Society in 1956, but drew sustained opposition from the commodity production industries, from western states, from the Forest Service and Interior Department, and even from outdoor recreation groups seeking development of more intensive recreational access and use. The Forest Service therefore proposed a new Multiple Use-Sustained Yield Act, as an alternative to preservationists' proposals for wilderness legislation.

The Multiple Use-Sustained Yield Act of 1960 reaffirmed the principle of multiple-use management of the forests, and specifically recognized recreation as a new official use to be incorporated into forest management. It stated in law that "the National Forests are established and shall be administered for outdoor recreation, range, timber, watershed, and wildlife and fish purposes." Forest resources were to be utilized in combination to meet these needs, in principle on an equal footing, and economic return was not in all cases to be the determining factor (Steen 1976, 298–307). Since the act set no specific priorities among these uses it did not explicitly challenge the traditional priority of logging, but left this judgment to the discretion of the forest manager. The timber industry was unhappy with this result, since with all uses having equal priority, the forest manager would probably have to act case by case on the basis of public pressure. The Sierra Club, however, was equally unhappy, since the forest managers were the very people whose judgments had always favored commodity production (Hirt 1994, 188–89).[28]

Forest preservation advocates therefore continued to campaign for wilderness legislation, and finally succeeded with the enactment of the Wilderness Act in 1964. The Wilderness Act authorized setting aside up to nine million acres of national forest lands as permanent pristine wilderness areas outside of the multiple-use management system (Wilkinson 1992, 136–39). It directed the Forest Service both to designate currently identified wilderness areas immediately, and within ten years to review all other primitive and roadless areas for potential wilderness designation. However, at the insistence of western legislators it left the existing mining-entry laws in force in these areas through 1983, as well as the opportunity to permanently patent claims developed during that period. This exception virtually invited accelerated prospecting during this two-decade window of opportunity on the very lands that were designated for preservation. Timber advocates also used the ten-year review period to propose roads through some key areas, thereby disqualifying them for designation (Sundquist 1968, 336–40, 358–61).

Suburbanization and Its Consequences

Changes in U.S. industrial production were accompanied by sweeping changes in residence patterns and population densities. Between 1950 and 1970 the populations of central cities increased by 25 percent, while the populations of their surrounding suburbs doubled (U.S. Department of Commerce 1975, A264–75, A82; Jackson 1985, 283–84). The roots of this suburban growth lay not only in wartime rural-to-urban migration, but in earlier New Deal programs to revitalize the construction industry by providing easier credit for home buyers.[29] The National Housing Act of 1934 created the Federal Housing Administration (FHA) to reinsure mortgage loans up to 93 percent of property value, and thus made home ownership affordable to far more households and home-construction lending attractive to far more investors. A similar program specifically for veterans was added in 1944.[30] New housing starts increased dramatically as a result, and since FHA underwriting standards heavily favored particular kinds of housing over others—new single-family residential developments for economically stable and homogeneous white communities, rather than multifamily units or buildings in core cities—much of the construction occurred in suburban areas on the urban fringe (Jackson 1985).[31]

The net effect was a powerful federal policy incentive for the construction of low-density, automobile-dependent suburbs for affluent white families on the urban fringe—"Levit-towns" and other large-scale developments of mass-constructed tract housing—which simultaneously, if inadvertently, undermined the economic vitality and socioeconomic integrity of the core cities themselves (fig. 14). Between 1950 and 1970 the suburban population doubled from thirty-six to seventy-four million, and 83 percent of the nation's total growth took place in these areas. Eighteen of the nation's twenty-five largest cities suffered net losses of population over the three decades following 1950, and by 1980 suburban populations exceeded those of their cities in fourteen of the nation's fifteen largest cities (Jackson 1985, 283–84). Federal mortgage insurance subsidized suburban housing while state and federal gasoline taxes subsidized the roads that provided access to it, and federal income tax deductions for mortgage interest payments subsidized its owners.

The remarkable achievement of these policies should not be underestimated. They opened up to a large fraction of the population the opportunity to live in an environment that had previously been available only to the wealthy: to realize the American Dream. However, their achievements cannot be separated from their other consequences, which included economic decline and even abandonment of large areas of existing cities, increasing segregation by race and economic class, geographic separation of homes from work and shopping and recreation, and a pervasive transformation of the landscape from relatively coherent urban communities and rural hinterlands into low-density, automobile-dependent sprawl (Jackson 1985, 216–17). Within the cities, meanwhile, federally subsidized "urban renewal" projects demolished large areas that had been hollowed out by the changing economy and demographics, and replaced many with parking lots for commuters: by 1960, one-third of many cities was given over to parking (Futrell 1993, 35).

The suburbanization of America greatly increased demand for construction materials, for appliances and the environmental raw materials necessary to manufacture them, and for municipal infrastructures and services—roads, water supplies, wastewater treatment plants, solid waste disposal services, schools, electric and gas utilities, and others—to serve the new communities. Between 1946 and 1955 more than twice as many houses were constructed as in the previous fifteen years, and in the peak year (1950) over one million

Figure 14a–b. These two aerial photos show Lakewood Park, a "new community" housing development of some 17,500 homes in southern California, begun in 1950 and considered at the time the largest community housing development ever built. One of its marketing pitches was that each home had its own garbage pulverizer. The above photo shows the overall magnitude of the project (the open area in the middle was reserved for a shopping center); at right is a group of the units in the early framing stage, illustrating both the mass-production construction methods and the heavy demand for lumber that was implicit in such large-scale suburbanization. [Photos taken by William Garnett, reprinted by permission]

single-family homes were begun (Melosi 1980, 25). These pressures resulted in major new federal spending programs for urban and transportation infrastructures in the 1950s. A massive new program of federal expenditures for road building, for instance, was authorized in 1956, to construct a 42,500-mile system of interstate highways with 90 percent of the cost to be paid for by earmarked federal motor fuel taxes through a Highway Trust Fund. Nominally justified as a "national defense highway system,"[32] its real backing came from the American Road Builders Association, a powerful coalition of industries that would benefit from increased road construction and highway use.[33] Between 1945 and 1970 the number of miles of federally subsidized highways more than doubled, from 309,000 to 895,000, and more than 20,000 miles of new highways were completed each year from 1952 to 1962 (U.S. Department of Commerce 1975, Q64–68).

Other new programs of federal "categorical grants" to states and municipalities were also created: for roads, for housing and "urban renewal," for health and other human services, and ultimately for water and wastewater treatment facilities and other purposes as well. Paradoxically, however, such projects often exacerbated the very problems they were intended to solve. For instance, expressways designed to relieve existing congestion increased traffic by up to 60 percent, as well as increasing pressures for economic develop-

ment of newly accessible areas, such as the building of shopping centers at highway interchanges.[34] Similarly, installation of sewers in suburban areas increased real estate values, encouraged land speculation, and promoted additional low-density development rather than more compact urbanization.

Summary

The unprecedented postwar expansion of industrial production, mass consumption, and suburbanization, and the rise of general affluence produced powerful and conflicting political pressures, as demand rose both for material goods and for the environmental amenities threatened by their production. On the one hand, both military and consumer demand reinforced the economic power and political influence of the resource extraction, manufacturing, and construction industries. On the other hand, their expansionary success galvanized opposition from a public that now sought to enjoy environmental amenities as well as consume products.

This conflict intensified with the concurrent rise of several separate sets of political forces which ultimately converged — albeit with some continuing differences of interests —

into the broader alliance of the modern environmental movement. One force was the revitalization and political mobilization of the landscape preservation groups, most notably the Sierra Club but also the National Audubon Society, Izaak Walton League, and others. A second force was the emergence of a far broader mass demand for outdoor recreation and tourism, and of specific economic interest groups — the American Automobile Association, recreational vehicle equipment manufacturers and outfitters, park concessionaires, and others — that lived off the business generated by this activity. A third force was the increasing influence of the booming suburban governments, which sought federal financial assistance to pay the rapidly rising costs of infrastructure to serve urban revitalization and suburban growth, including roads, schools, housing, water and sewer services, public transportation, and other needs. To these forces were soon added others, particularly a new public outrage at industrial pollution and toxic and radioactive contamination. All of these forces came together in 1970, when an unprecedented nationwide mass movement coalesced demanding federal leadership to protect the environment.

11   The Rise of Modern Environmentalism

Through all these new, imaginative, and creative approaches to the problem of sharing our earth with other creatures there runs a constant theme, the awareness that we are dealing with life — with living populations and all their pressures and counter-pressures, their surges and recessions. Only by taking account of such life forces and by cautiously seeking to guide them into channels favorable to ourselves can we hope to achieve a reasonable accommodation between the insect hordes and ourselves.

The current vogue for poisons has failed utterly to take into account these most fundamental considerations. As crude a weapon as the cave man's club, the chemical barrage has been hurled against the fabric of life — a fabric on the one hand delicate and destructible, on the other miraculously tough and resilient, and capable of striking back in unexpected ways. . . . It is our alarming misfortune that so primitive a science has armed itself with the most modern and terrible weapons, and that in turning them against the insects it has also turned them against the earth. — Rachel Carson, *Silent Spring*

Even as postwar economic prosperity and general affluence surged, powerful new political conflicts began to develop between advocates of commodity production and technological transformation of the environment on the one hand, and of environmental conservation and protection on the other. Some of these conflicts were new versions of familiar bat-tles — dams versus natural parks, and logging versus forest preservation — only now aug-mented by far broader and growing public support for landscape preservation and out-door recreation. The Sierra Club and the nature protection constituency more generally were rapidly becoming far more than an upper-class California hiking club, and the histor-ical dominance of commodity producer interests in shaping federal environmental policy was for the first time exposed to serious challenge.

Other conflicts reflected the rising power and environmental concerns of a suburban, middle-class polity. Air and water pollution, long imposed on the public by powerful industries as the unavoidable side effects of economic progress and wartime production, were no longer automatically acceptable to a public that aspired to better health, more attractive communities, and swimming and boating for recreation. Fast-growing suburbs needed to build water supply and wastewater treatment facilities, and sought their "fair share" of the federal taxes that already subsidized rural water projects.

Perhaps most genuinely new among these conflicts was the sudden eruption of outrage against involuntary exposure to nuclear radiation, pesticides, and other man-made toxins in the environment. This outrage was triggered by dramatic events — the discovery of radioactive fallout in human milk, the "cranberry scare" of 1959, when a suspected carcinogen was found in cranberries, and publication of Rachel Carson's best-selling *Silent Spring,* which chronicled the devastating effects of indiscriminate pesticide spraying on wildlife — but it represented a profound and enduring change in public consciousness and concerns. Television reporting amplified these concerns and mobilized opposition, creating a mass constituency for environmental protection.

The most revolutionary element of this new public consciousness was a powerful new awareness of the environment as a living system — a "web of life," or *ecosystem* — rather than just a storehouse of commodities to be extracted or a physical or chemical machine to be manipulated. Unlike physical or chemical materials, biological organisms actively grow, reproduce, evolve, use and transform the materials and energy in their environments, and interact with one another. Human actions such as nuclear testing and insect-spraying campaigns thus had far more complex ecological consequences than expected, many of them disastrous for valued species or for humans themselves. It was this new awareness of the potential for severe ecological consequences that gave the new environmental movement its coherence and enduring power across many more immediate issues.

The science of ecology was not itself new: its intellectual roots went back to nineteenth-century natural historians, and perhaps most powerfully to Charles Darwin's work on evolution and natural selection. In public awareness and policy-making, however, it had long been dominated by the more mechanistic approach of physical scientists, by the commodity-production perspective of agronomists, foresters, and even wildlife managers, and by the utilitarian efficiency goals of engineers. Pasteur and the microbiologists had made great studies in understanding disease organisms and their vectors, but even this knowledge had been subsumed into relatively simplistic management responses such as vaccinating children, using drugs to cure disease, and spraying insecticide to kill disease-bearing insects. Concern about human exposure to toxic chemicals was limited to occupational exposures, and residues of lead and arsenic insecticides on foodstuffs.

The simultaneous revolutions in atomic energy and organic chemicals technologies in the 1940s, however, ignited first a blaze of glib advertising propaganda touting the benefits of these "modern" technologies, and then an unprecedented backlash of public outrage against their risks to ecological processes, living species, and human health. Public concerns about these ecological effects fused with those of organized nature-preservation groups and with more general public demand for outdoor recreation to form a mass movement of unprecedented strength and political diversity. Symbolizing these common concerns was the compelling new photographic image of the planet Earth seen for the first time from outside itself, a beautiful but finite blue ball whose thin surface of air and water was all that made possible the proliferation of living species and communities and the achievements of human knowledge and technology.

By the end of the 1960s, a diverse range of constituencies representing previously separate aspects of environmental protection — such as pollution abatement, radiation and pesticide control, nature preservation, and protection of national parks and other areas of natural beauty—coalesced into a broad movement demanding changes in both the substance and the process of environmental policy. In substance, those who spoke for this movement sought stronger federal policies to protect the environment from the impacts of urban and industrial growth. They also sought more direct access to government policy-making for those who held these values. In effect, they demanded equal access to the "broker state" for *all* interest groups, rather than just for the commodity producers and other economic users of the environment who had previously dominated environmental policy-making. The environmental result was an unprecedented outpouring of national regulatory policies to preserve and protect nature and reduce pollution. The result for environmental governance was an equally dramatic repudiation of the Progressive model of administration, and of the belief in politically neutral expertise that underlay it. What replaced them was a far more openly politicized process of administrative and judicial policy-making. Thus began the "environmental era" of American public policy.

Nationalizing Pollution Control

As recently as 1960, the president of the United States vetoed federal funding for municipal waste treatment plants, arguing that water pollution was a "uniquely local" problem that should be solved by state and local authorities rather than the federal government (Sundquist 1968, 323). The reality, however, was that water and air pollutants flowed constantly across municipal and state boundaries, and that polluting industries could usually block local or even state controls by threatening to relocate. Local investments in wastewater treatment facilities, moreover, had almost never kept pace with their growth rates: wastewater treatment, after all, benefits downstream communities rather than the city that builds it. Within a year after President Eisenhower's veto, President Kennedy signed legislation creating a $100 million-per-year subsidy program for wastewater treatment, and by the following decade the federal government had expanded this program sevenfold and assumed nationwide responsibility for air and water quality regulation. Two central elements of the modern environmental policy agenda were thus put in place: the nationalization of pollution control, and the adoption of large-scale federal subsidies and regulation as its primary policy instruments.

The nineteenth-century sanitary reform movement established government responsibility for municipal water supply and wastewater and waste management, but until the postwar era these authorities were left almost entirely to state and local governments. State policies for water quality management developed slowly, focusing primarily on drinking water purity and municipal sewage disposal rather than industrial discharges. Only a few broader interstate initiatives were begun, on rivers in several heavily urbanized and industrialized regions.[1] State sanitary engineers formed a professional association in 1920 (the Conference of State Sanitary Engineers), which provided a forum for development of uniform state laws and practices, but by 1935 only eight states had effective water pollution control laws. Twenty-six had partial or ineffective controls, and fourteen had none at all. By 1946 the number of states with effective control laws had increased only to twenty-one, and many state statutes simply exempted major industries and municipalities and even entire rivers. Depression-era federal wastewater treatment subsidies more than doubled the volume of wastes receiving treatment, but even so, as of 1940 only 25 percent of urban sewage received secondary treatment, another 25 percent primary treatment, and the rest was simply discharged raw (Dworsky 1971, 15, 108–12, 116).

Construction of municipal sewers and wastewater treatment plants was perennially underfunded, meanwhile, due to competing local priorities and resistance to urban needs by rural-dominated state legislatures. Only during the 1930s did construction of municipal wastewater plants keep pace with urban growth, aided by Depression-era federal public-works programs which financed over five hundred wastewater treatment plants, twenty-three hundred miles of sewer lines, millions of sanitary privies in rural and suburban areas, and other water and sewer facilities in some eight thousand communities. These programs were discontinued during the war years, but provided precedents for later federal aid programs (Sundquist 1968, 323; Dworsky 1971, 20, 23–25; Armstrong et al. 1976, 418).[2]

Only three federal regulatory powers over water quality existed before 1948. The earliest was the so-called 1899 Refuse Act, which required a permit from the Army Corps of Engineers for discharge of any "refuse" into navigable rivers and harbors, but this applied at the time only to solid matter that might be hazardous to navigation, and specifically exempted liquid wastes such as sewage. It was later reinterpreted, by a court decision in the 1960s, to cover municipal and industrial chemical pollution as well. The second was Public Health Service standards for drinking water on interstate carriers such as ships and trains, which were established in 1914 and revised in 1925 and 1946. The third was the Oil Pollution Control Act of 1924, which authorized the Secretary of the Army to regulate oil discharges from ships to protect public health and shipping; but this was difficult to enforce, regulated only ships rather than factories or cities, and applied only to coastal waters (Armstrong et al. 1976, 417–18; Dworsky 1971, 11–21, 27, 83, 88–90, 143–51).

The U.S. Public Health Service was authorized to conduct research on water pollution as early as 1912, and it produced important studies of the Great Lakes watershed and several industrialized rivers, of water quality biochemistry and measurements, of wastewater treatment technologies, and of shellfish sanitation. It developed cooperative programs with state and local agencies in the 1920s to improve drinking water purification and sewage disposal, and during World War II it analyzed the toxicity of effluents from munitions plants and advised that dumping of toxic wastes into public waters could have fatal consequences (Colten and Skinner 1996, 21). After World War II the agency intensified its research into industrial pollutants to determine lethal doses to marine life as well as humans. Not until 1948, however, did its authority extend beyond surveys and research investigations, except with respect to health standards for drinking water on interstate transport.

Public Health Service studies in the early 1950s documented more than twenty-two thousand sources of water pollution nationwide, over 50 percent of them municipal but almost half industrial, reflecting the vast expansion of industrial production during and after the war. Municipal officials in 1956 estimated a backlog of almost $2 billion in funding needs for wastewater facilities, plus over $3.4 billion more needed for renovations and service to new populations over the following decade.

With the postwar suburban development boom, local governments mobilized through the American Municipal Association to seek federal funds for infrastructure facilities, including sewer systems and wastewater treatment plants as well as housing, roads, schools, and other needs.

The Water Pollution Control Act of 1948 authorized expansion of federal water pollution research as well as planning grants and low-interest loans to local governments, although no funds were ever appropriated for the grants and loans. Key provisions of this law had actually been proposed as early as 1936, but never enacted. Amendments in 1956 authorized $3 million per year for federal support of state water pollution control agencies, and $50 million per year for local construction grants, under which the federal government would pay 30 percent of the costs of constructing municipal wastewater treatment facilities. The Eisenhower administration resisted these pressures for federal spending on urban needs, and twice attempted to return the program to the states along with some federal revenue sources, but failed due to congressional and state opposition.[3]

Presidents Kennedy and Johnson, however, came to office with stronger political commitments to the cities and their growing suburbs. The result was a steady expansion of federal financial assistance for municipal wastewater treatment facilities, beginning with a 1961 statute that increased funding to $100 million per year. Congress also added water quality control to the multiple-purpose objectives of federal water projects (the goal being to dilute pollution by releasing greater quantities of water during dry periods). Advocates for federal funding of "internal improvements" had justified federal expenditures in previous eras for river and harbor clearing, canals, railroads, irrigation and hydropower dams, then multipurpose facilities; now the definition was extended once again to help provide wastewater treatment for cities and growing suburbs.

In 1963 federal pollution control policy gained an important new congressional champion when Senator Edmund Muskie (D-Maine) was appointed chairman of the new Subcommittee on Water and Air Pollution of the Public Works Committee.[4] His Water Quality Act of 1965 again expanded the construction grants program, to $150 million per year, and increased the maximum federal subsidy per project from $600 thousand to $1.6 million. Amendments in 1966 increased total funding to $3.5 billion over five years, and increased the maximum federal contribution to 50 percent of the total project cost. The 1965 act also offered federal funding for state planning efforts to promote regionwide water quality management (Sundquist 1968, 324–27; Dworsky 1971, 26–31, 275, 364–66).[5]

Along with federal subsidies, these laws began a gradual nationalization of the authority to set and enforce water quality standards. Prior to 1948, federal water quality standards were limited to drinking water standards for interstate transportation carriers. These standards in turn were adopted by some judicial decisions as reasonable norms for water purity, and thus became de facto national standards for public water supplies. The 1948 water pollution law for the first time authorized the federal government to initiate legal proceedings against pollution on interstate rivers: to notify the states and dischargers, convene hearings to recommend solutions, and with the consent of the affected states, bring federal lawsuits for abatement. The 1956 amendments removed the requirement for state consent, and authorized the federal government to initiate interstate "conferences" to encourage cooperative abatement programs. The 1961 amendments extended federal jurisdiction from interstate to all navigable waters, and even to intrastate waters at the request of the governor. These procedures remained cumbersome, however, and the federal government still sought to leave the states in charge, with the threat of federal intervention as merely an incentive. This gradualism reflected significant debate as to whether the federal government had constitutional authority to impose air and water pollution control mandates. Fundamental change in this gradualism occurred first not in environmental policy, but in the landmark Civil Rights Act of 1964, whose motivation — racial justice — was so compelling that it warranted national enforcement, thus opening the door to other federal regulatory initiatives (Futrell 1993, 38).

Nationalization moved a major step further in the Water Quality Act of 1965. This law for the first time stated an explicit "national policy for the prevention, control and abatement of water pollution." It required the states to establish ambient water quality standards within two years or face loss of eligibility for federal grants, and it authorized the federal government to set standards for states that failed to set adequate standards of their own. The federal government thus had the power to approve or disapprove the states' standards, and to impose its own standards if it did not consider the states' adequate.

This marked a fundamental shift in environmental governance. In effect, the act established federal authority to set criteria for minimum water quality standards nationwide. It did not yet authorize federal discharge standards for particular sources, and it still functioned only through enforcement conferences and threats of federal lawsuits, but it marked a major departure in authorizing a federal agency to compel and approve state environmental regulatory programs. It thus set the stage for the fundamental revision of federal water pollution policy that subsequently occurred in 1972. President Johnson also issued an executive order requiring secondary wastewater treatment at all federal facilities, and directing that pollution be minimized by all federal grantees and contractors (Dworsky 1971, 30–32, 413–24).

Finally, the 1965 Water Quality Act directed a major reorganization of federal water pollution activities, removing water pollution control from the Public Health Service and creating a new agency, the Federal Water Pollution Control Administration, which reported directly to the Secretary of Health, Education, and Welfare (HEW). President Johnson almost immediately moved the agency again, from HEW to the Interior Department, and renamed it the Federal Water Quality Administration.

These organizational changes reflected several demands for water pollution control that were not being met within the Public Health Service.[6] Water quality was important for many reasons in addition to health, including agricultural irrigation, industrial process-water needs, fisheries, and recreation. Most of these needs were peripheral to the health mission of the Public Health Service, however, and were therefore undervalued there. Moreover, the Public Health Service had developed as a scientific research and technical assistance agency, in a cooperative and supporting relationship with state health agencies: it had little inclination or expertise with which to take an adversarial regulatory position toward them, nor to administer a burgeoning construction grants program for municipalities (Sundquist 1968, 332–33, 352).[7]

From the Interior Department's perspective, water quality management was inherently interdependent with other aspects of water resource management, especially on the growing number of rivers whose flows were managed by federal multipurpose dams. Interior Secretary Stewart Udall also had strong ambitions to revitalize his department into a broader Department of Conservation, as Franklin Roosevelt's Interior Secretary had attempted before him (Sundquist 1968, 364–67; Dworsky 1971, 30–32, 320–28).[8]

These organizational changes imposed important costs, however. One was a loss of expertise: an estimated 50 percent of the professional staff opted either to remain in Public Health Service career tracks or to take early retirement. Another was fragmentation of health-related functions: the change linked water management functions but split apart the Public Health Service's environmental health programs, separating water quality organizationally from air quality, waste management, and other sanitation programs (Dworsky 1971, 551; Eisenbud 1978, 351–53).[9] No organizational structure can coordinate all functions equally well, and in this case the intended benefits of moving the water quality agency into the "conservation" structure involved a simultaneous loss in the potential effectiveness of the "environmental health" structure.

A similar evolution occurred in air pollution policy. Urban air pollution was protested as both a health hazard and a nuisance as early as the late nineteenth century, and its most serious forms were well understood scientifically.[10] However, urban air pollution could not be solved by public sanitation services, and industries and railroads successfully resisted any effective regulation for decades. Real progress occurred only as diesel-electric engines gradually replaced coal-fired locomotives, and more generally as cheap natural gas became available as a substitute for coal heating via new pipelines in the 1940s.

Even after World War II, however, serious improvement was evident only in a few leading cities (Tarr 1985, 525–28; Dworsky 1971, 560–62, 629–30). Air pollution control simply was not a well developed function in most cities prior to federal policy initiatives in the 1960s (fig. 15). Pittsburgh and several others passed smoke-control ordinances in the early 1940s, but did not begin serious implementation and enforcement until after the war. Los Angeles established a county-level air pollution control office in 1945, and a special Air Pollution Control District with enforcement powers in 1947. The first statewide air pollution control law was not passed until 1947 (by California); a few other states followed in the 1950s, but most merely passed enabling acts that left enforcement to local agencies.[11] Even with these laws, moreover, state governments could not control sources in upwind states, and they risked industrial flight if they tightened their own regulations unilaterally. By 1963 only fourteen states had enacted statewide air pollution laws (Dworsky 1971, 560–62, 629–33, 666). The role of the federal government, meanwhile, was limited to Public Health Service research, mainly on occupational lung diseases.[12]

Severe air pollution episodes beginning in the late 1940s, however, provoked nationwide public concern. In Donora, Pennsylvania, a dense smog over several days in 1948 sickened over 40 percent of the population and killed twenty people, triggering a national investigation. Similar events killed at least four thousand people during five days in

Figure 15. Smoke belching from the open-hearth steelmaking process of the Bethlehem Steel Company's Johnstown plant, November 15, 1963. [Photo courtesy of the *Johnstown Tribune-Democrat*]

London in 1952, and at least two hundred in New York City in 1953. Los Angeles experienced a severe episode in 1954, and similar crises recurred in Los Angeles, New York, and elsewhere during the 1960s (Dworsky 1971, 548–49, 570–82).

The mid-century smog disasters forced air pollution onto the federal policy agenda. The first federal air pollution law was passed in 1955 and extended in 1959; it reaffirmed that the primary responsibility for air pollution control lay with state and local governments, but authorized $5 million for federal research and technical assistance. Additional laws in 1960 and 1962 authorized federal studies on motor vehicle emissions.

Beginning in 1963, a series of five federal laws in seven years shifted federal policy from modest support of state and local initiatives to a fully nationalized framework for air pollution regulation. The Clean Air Act of 1963 provided federal grants for two-thirds of the costs of starting up state air pollution programs, and in addition authorized federal regulation of motor vehicle pollution and federal enforcement against health and welfare hazards. In 1965 the Motor Vehicle Air Pollution Control Act authorized federal emissions standards for mobile sources, and amendments in 1966 provided 60 percent federal operating subsidies for state and local air pollution control programs (previous grants had been limited to program initiation funds).[13]

The Air Quality Act of 1967 established an explicit national policy goal for air pollution control: "to protect and enhance the quality of the Nation's air resources so as to promote the public health and welfare and the productive capacity of its population." It spelled out this policy in a dramatic expansion of the federal regulatory role. Among its specific provisions, it authorized the Secretary of HEW to regulate stationary as well as mobile sources; to seek immediate court-ordered abatement for air pollution that presented an "imminent and substantial danger"; to establish both inter- and intrastate air pollution control regions; to require state air pollution control standards for selected regions, and to impose federal standards if states failed to act; to develop and publish "criteria documents" for control of specific pollutants; and to study the possibilities for developing national emissions standards for major industries (Dworsky 1971, 555–59, 652, 665–66).[14] A presidential executive order in 1966 also mandated air pollution control by federal facilities. Finally, the Clean Air Act of 1970 established primary federal regulatory authority for national ambient air quality standards, industrial emissions permits, and severe restrictions on motor vehicle emissions.

This series of statutes laid the foundations for a primary federal role in nationwide regulation of air pollution. Unlike the water pollution laws, moreover, federal air quality mandates and grants actually created and subsidized many of the state air pollution control programs as well. Only fourteen states had statewide air pollution statutes in 1963, yet within the following four years thirty-one additional states had passed such laws, and federal grants subsidized the creation of eighty new state and local air pollution control programs and the upgrading of forty existing ones (Dworsky 1971, 638–39, 646, 666–67).

Such a sudden and unprecedented expansion of federal regulatory authority deserves close attention. It would be tempting to attribute it to the rising influence of environmental advocacy groups, or of mass public concern for the environment, but in fact all these statutes except the 1970 Clean Air Act were enacted *before* those forces had coalesced at the national level.

A more persuasive explanation, therefore, is that as a few leading states and cities began to toughen their air pollution control regulations — though only a few, such as California, Pennsylvania, New York City, and Los Angeles — key industries themselves acquired a powerful new interest in obtaining moderate and uniform federal standards that would preempt more stringent and inconsistent state and local standards. The automobile industry, for instance, wanted assurance that they could manufacture their cars for nationwide sale under uniform standards no stricter than California's. The soft-coal industry, similarly, wanted to obtain federal standards requiring emission-control technology — binding on all power plants — and thus to preempt municipal regulations that might instead have required switching from high- to low-sulfur coal (Elliott et al. 1985; Sundquist 1968, 370–71; Bryner 1993). Significantly, much of the law that created these standards was written by Sen. Jennings Randolph of West Virginia, a major soft-coal-producing state.

Much of the nationalization of air pollution control law, in short, was built on the influence and interests of key industries themselves, who might ultimately have preferred no regulation but clearly preemptive federal control at a "moderate" level to the likelihood of diverse and sometimes tougher state and local laws. Even Senator Muskie, the "policy entrepreneur" who built a national reputation and a presidential candidacy on his authorship of the federal air and water quality laws, was writing basically this sort of moderate, industry-supported legislation until he was publicly challenged on it in 1970 by citizen advocate Ralph Nader, precipitating a "bidding war" for public credibility as an environmental leader between Muskie and President Richard Nixon.

Civic and conservation groups were nonetheless vitally important as well, in that they pushed for the pioneering municipal and state laws that precipitated this sequence of events. In fact the League of Women Voters and the national organizations of municipal governments also played key roles in lobbying for stronger federal legislation (Sundquist 1968, 332–33, 351–55). Many state governments were more ambivalent toward federal intrusion in their prerogatives, and even the Public Health Service preferred to maintain its less adversarial role in research and technical assistance. Even some states, however, found it politically convenient to have uniform national standards. National standards forced upwind states to comply, and prevented states' own industries from moving to ones with looser standards. They allowed the states to blame the federal government for compliance costs, rather than confront powerful industries by themselves. And unlike many other situations where federal mandates were imposed, the federal government supported state air pollution control programs with continuing subsidies.

Environmental Perceptions and Preferences

A nation of middle-class suburban families had radically different perceptions and preferences about the environment than a nation of rural settlers and entrepreneurs, or a nation of finance capitalists and urban masses, or a nation in economic depression or at war. Middle-class families wanted the security of their own homes, the mobility of an automobile, and the material comforts and conveniences of a consumer economy. They also wanted the amenities of natural beauty, outdoor recreation, travel and tourism, and enjoyment of nature. To farmers, loggers, and miners, and to mining and manufacturing businesses, nature was at best the ordinary raw material of economic commodities and livelihoods, and at worst a resistant or even threatening adversary, though as individuals they might also enjoy hunting and fishing. To a suburban family, in contrast, nature was an idyllic landscape to be experienced: a destination for an outing or vacation trip, be it a day at the beach, a weekend in the mountains, or a once-in-a-lifetime visit to the Grand Canyon. It was an unspoiled retreat, a respite from the crowds and noise and traffic of cities, and from the regimentation of work, the steady bulldozing of the natural landscape for suburban housing developments and shopping centers, and the pollution and ugliness and stress of urban life.

Widespread education and the growth of the mass media, particularly the introduction of television in the 1950s, amplified these perceptions and mobilized environmental activism. On the one hand, television promoted ever more wasteful uses of materials and energy: financed by advertising, its true business was to spur continuous growth in mass consumption, by incessantly urging consumer spending. Paradoxically, however, it also created national constituencies for nature. People in eastern suburbs could now see the beauty of the Grand Canyon and the redwood forests as well as the smog of Los Angeles and the oil spills of the Santa Barbara Channel. People on the West Coast could be aroused by threats to the Everglades in Florida or salt marshes in Connecticut — or for that matter, by starvation in Africa. Previously localized issues could now arouse far larger constituencies and symbolize national or global threats, sometimes to the extent that public sentiment outweighed the traditional power of businesses and political elites. Even advertising itself—for washing machines, garbage disposers, "whiter than white" detergents and other cleaning products—promoted a distinctively American preoccupation with cleanliness that no longer accepted the presence of human and animal wastes, odors, and other pollutants that had been considered normal just a decade or two before (Hoy 1995, 151–78). Mass markets for commercial advertising were also mass constituencies for political mobilization.

The emergence of nationwide mass-media constituencies thus propelled several new kinds of environmental issues onto the national agenda. One was a resurgence and expansion of support for nature preservation: groups such as the Sierra Club, the Izaak Walton League and the Wilderness Society found new opportunities to dramatize their concerns to a broader public, to mobilize public opinion, and to build far larger national memberships. A second was a growing market and constituency for outdoor recreation, including both the expanding commercial travel and tourism industries and growing user interest groups: hunters, fishermen, cyclists, wilderness backpackers, motorcyclists, off-road vehicle owners, and others. A third was civic demands for solutions to urban environmental problems, including air and water pollution and traffic congestion, as well as for federal financing of highways, urban renewal, and wastewater treatment facilities. Finally, a fourth was public fear and outrage over toxic hazards in the environment, particularly fallout from nuclear radiation, overuse of pesticides, and other contaminants.

Radiation, Toxic Chemicals, and Public Science

As recently as the mid-1950s, one could walk into an American shoe store and put a coin in a vending machine to see the bones of one's feet under a radiation-emitting fluoroscope. One could see children at public swimming pools hosed down with DDT solutions in the hope of preventing malaria, polio, and other diseases. Yet during the same period, powerful public fears of the hazards of humanly introduced chemicals and radiation were also beginning to emerge. Conventional wisdom dates this shift to Rachel Carson's best-selling book *Silent Spring,* which was serialized in *The New Yorker* and published in 1962. In fact, however, the issue had already been building for a decade or more.

The earliest postwar example of such fears was local opposition to the addition of fluoride to public water supplies, which public health authorities promoted to prevent tooth decay.[15] Research in the 1930s had identified the benefits of this treatment, and Public Health Service experiments in several cities in the mid-1940s confirmed it; Madison, Wisconsin, fluoridated its water supply in 1947, and other cities followed. Organized opposition appeared, however, and fluoridation proposals were repeatedly defeated in public referenda. Some scientists and physicians argued that it was unnecessary and might be hazardous, despite the fact that many communities had equal or greater natural levels of fluoride in their water (it can in fact have adverse side effects in some individuals, such as kidney-disease victims). Libertarians, health-food store owners, Christian Scientists, and advocates of natural medicine argued that it was "compulsory medication," an unconstitutional infringement on their personal rights and preferences, and an example of "socialized medicine." The Daughters of the American Revolution and the Liberty Lobby even attacked it as a "Communist plot" to poison the American water supply. By the 1990s, after half a century of evidence of its effectiveness, only about half of the U.S. population was receiving fluoridated water, and referenda on it still were frequently defeated (Duffy 1990, 288–90).

Ironically, the anti-fluoridation battles pitted citizen opponents not against self-interested businesses, but against public health authorities, doctors, dentists, and other scientists of the Progressive tradition who viewed themselves as apolitical experts acting in the broad public interest (indeed, in the case of dentists, acting *against* their own economic self-interests). One result may have been to increase public health professionals' disdain for laymen's concerns more generally, heightening mutual distrust. In almost every year of the 1950s, the leading public health journal carried editorials reiterating the scientific evidence and benefits of fluoridation, and attacking the opposition movements as reflecting an alliance of vested interests and fanatics promoting "an exaggerated fear of change. . . . [of] any departure from the supposedly beneficent processes of nature."[16]

A far more serious issue arose in the mid-1950s, however, with the discovery that radioactive fallout from above-ground testing of nuclear weapons was dispersed worldwide, and that some of this fallout—particularly the isotope strontium 90—was not simply dispersed harmlessly, as government nuclear scientists had assumed, but was taken up with calcium into grass, eaten and reconcentrated into milk by cows, and thus consumed in potentially dangerous quantities by humans (fig. 16).[17] Suddenly the authoritative reassurances of government scientists were proven false: because of environmental connections such as stratospheric air currents and ecological food chains, radiation could be released at the farthest point on the globe, carried around the world, reconcentrated through ecological food chains, and end up in human bone tissue and in the milk of mothers nursing infants.

The nuclear fallout issue produced a 1958 moratorium and 1963 treaty banning above-ground testing of nuclear weapons, but it also drove a wedge within the scientific community as well as the general public, between those who continued to support such experiments and to advocate uncritical faith in "progress" through modern technology, and those who were increasingly apprehensive of its hidden hazards. Atomic Energy Commission officials, for instance, continued to promote above-ground applications of nuclear explosions, creating a whole new program in 1957—"Plowshare"—to develop proposals such as blasting canals and clearing navigational obstructions. A growing number of biologists and other scientists, however, were now convinced that decisions involving such hazards were matters of social and moral judgment, which must be made by the full public rather than by closed groups of experts.[18] The Federation of American Scientists (FAS) was formed to lobby for civilian control and nonproliferation of nuclear weapons, and in 1958 biologist Barry Commoner and others created the Scientists' Institute for Public Information (SIPI) to promote wider public awareness of technological hazards. FAS and SIPI in turn built alliances between citizen activists and concerned scientists

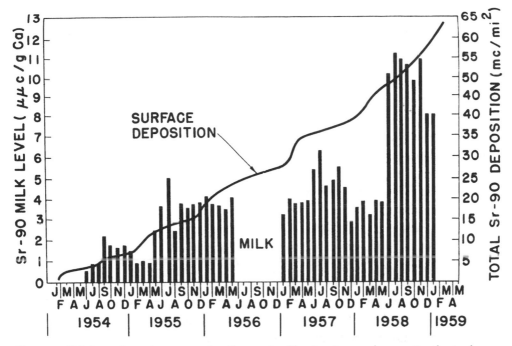

Figure 16. This figure shows data presented to Congressional hearings in 1959, documenting the steady accumulation of strontium 90 in New York City's soil and milk products resulting from atmospheric nuclear weapons testing thousands of miles away. Strontium 90 had the capacity to bond to calcium, and thus to be taken up with it into grass, then cows, their milk, and ultimately the human infants who drank it. Data for late 1956 are missing in original. [U.S. Congress, Joint Committee on Atomic Energy]

against government actions that appeared to threaten both human health and ecological processes (Whelan 1985, 62–63).[19] The emergence of activist groups of scientists seeking to educate the public on the hazards of technologies was a remarkable phenomenon, as was their gradual success in forcing increased research and critical attention within the science and technology community on the hazards as well as the benefits of technological progress.

A third public issue broke in November 1959, seventeen days before Thanksgiving, when Arthur Flemming, Secretary of the Department of Health, Education, and Welfare, announced that traces of an herbicide that might cause cancer—aminotriazole (3-AT)— had been found on cranberries in Oregon and Washington. Aminotriazole had been approved in 1956 for use in cranberry bogs after harvesting, but some growers also applied it during the growing season, in defiance of Food and Drug Administration restrictions, because it suppressed weeds and thus increased yields and profits (Bosso 1987, 96). Positive evidence of any health hazard was weak, and even detection of 3-AT residues at the levels found—less than one part per million—was only possible with a newly developed analytical method.[20] Scientific and congressional concern about pesticide residues on foods was rising, however—just the previous year, Rep. James Delaney had finally succeeded in passing a new amendment to the Food and Drug Act banning any food additive that had been found to induce cancer in humans or other animals — and Secretary Flemming therefore chose to "get out in front" of the issue with a strong posture favoring health protection. Acting on data from scientists in the Food and Drug Administration and the National Cancer Institute, he ordered impoundment of more than three million pounds of cranberries for testing, and urged consumers not to buy cranberry products unless they could determine where they had been grown. Supermarkets and restaurants removed them from their shelves and menus and several states banned cranberry sales. Ultimately the government seized only 1 percent of the cranberries tested, radio and television reduced the issue to jokes, and presidential candidates John Kennedy and Richard Nixon both ate cranberries publicly during their campaigns. Public fears subsided, but cranberry sales for 1959 fell by two-thirds and cost growers an estimated $15 to $20 million in losses (Bosso 1987, 99).[21]

Political scientist Aaron Wildavsky characterized the "cranberry scare" in retrospect as "the first shot . . . for the nascent environmental movement . . . in a campaign to raise public fears about cancer from synthetic chemicals in food and water" (Wildavsky 1995, 19, 15–16). In fact, however, in this case the "first shot" came not from the public or from environmental advocacy groups but from a cabinet official in a conservative Republican administration. Public health should be government's top priority, Secretary Flemming argued, and a substance that had been proven to produce cancers in animals should be considered dangerous at any dose until proven safe. Flemming's initiative also reflected his sensitivity to the recent Delaney Amendment, and to rising public concerns about pesticide residues, nuclear fallout, and ecological food chains. It may also have reflected an impulse to reassert the leadership and trustworthiness of HEW's public health agencies amid the rising distrust of government scientists over these issues.

The cranberry scare foreshadowed a far larger and more enduring controversy which became public in 1962, over explosive growth in the use of synthetic organic pesticides. These included especially DDT, aldrin, dieldrin, and related organochlorine compounds.

A century of sanitation and public health measures had dramatically reduced water-borne disease epidemics in the United States, and vaccinations and pasteurization had solved others, but insect-borne diseases remained the great public health scourges, killing millions more people even than the great world wars — particularly young children — not to mention posing hazards to military troops. The insecticidal properties of DDT were first identified in 1939, and it was quickly hailed as a virtual wonder chemical, a magic bullet against insect vectors of disease — malaria, yellow fever, and typhus in particular — as well as insect pests in agriculture (Wargo 1996). It was relatively cheap to make, highly effective (at least initially), had low acute toxicity to humans, replaced less effective and more acutely toxic pesticides such as nicotine and copper and lead arsenates, and retained its effectiveness for long periods of time (Eisenbud 1978, 229–30). The Public Health Service therefore promoted DDT as a new technological wonder and enthusiastically promoted its use, both directly on people and sprayed in quantity for vector control wherever insects might breed (fig. 17).

In agriculture, meanwhile, farmers welcomed the synthetic organic pesticides as an almost miraculous alternative to the costly, less effective and far more toxic prewar insec-

Figure 17. An example of the indiscriminate aerial spraying of insecticides common in the postwar era. Here a town has hired a helicopter to spray the nearby river, stagnant pools, and backyards from treetop level with an aerosol fog of DDT. [National Archives]

ticides. They were also a vital element of the postwar technological revolution in agriculture. Wartime demand, postwar export markets, selective breeding, rural to urban migration, and federal subsidies all encouraged the intensification and mechanization of agricultural production, allowing larger crop yields with less land and labor. The result was a massive increase in the use of chemical fertilizers, insecticides, and herbicides (Bosso 1987, 27–33).

The Department of Agriculture itself embarked on a series of ambitious, heavily publicized campaigns to eradicate several nuisance insect species, in particular gypsy moths, which were denuding New England's forests, and fire ants, stinging ants that built nuisance mounds across the agricultural South (including Mississippi, home state of the Agriculture Department's congressional appropriations chairman and de facto director, Rep. Jamie Whitten). To exterminate the gypsy moth, the USDA in spring 1957 sponsored indiscriminate aerial spraying of pesticides on some three million acres of forests, towns, and watercourses across New England and New York, causing massive fish kills as well as damage to crops, gardens, local wildlife, and valuable insects such as bees as well as to the moths. To eradicate the fire ant, the USDA with Whitten's support began a program to apply two and one-half pounds per acre of dieldrin, a chemical related to DDT but far more potent, to the affected areas of the South. Simultaneously, it orchestrated a propaganda campaign aimed at creating exaggerated fears about the dangers of being bitten by this minor nuisance species. To Whitten and southern agriculture commissioners, the wonder chemicals of agricultural technology would modernize the backwardness and poverty of southern agriculture. The result was a spraying campaign that continued inconclusively for decades, indiscriminately destroying many of the ant's natural predators and other southern wildlife. Ironically, the ant is itself a natural predator of another insect pest, the cotton boll weevil (Bosso 1987, 79–94).

The 1950s have thus been described as the "golden age" of pesticides (Bosso 1987, 63–65). Between 1947 and 1960 the use of synthetic organic pesticides increased more than fivefold, from 124 million to over 637 million pounds per year (Carson 1962, 25). Nationwide they became the insecticides of choice for general use as well as use against agricultural forest pests and disease vectors. To farmers still recovering from the disastrous erosion and dust storms of the 1930s, chemical herbicides offered an alternative to heavy tillage for weed control, conveying an image of better land stewardship by minimizing soil disturbance (Wargo 1996). The 1948 Federal Insecticide, Fungicide, and Rodenticide Act required that all pesticides shipped in interstate commerce be registered with the federal Department of Agriculture, labeled for specific crops and conditions of use, and supported by evidence that they were both effective and nonhazardous to public health or wildlife. In reality, however, it was the federal agency rather than the manufacturer that had to bear the burden of proof for any decision to prohibit or de-register a pesticide (U.S. Department of Health, Education and Welfare 1969, 7). The Agriculture Department in practice was concerned only with acute toxicity, and had neither the resources nor the knowledge of ecology to investigate pesticides more critically.

Some wildlife scientists raised concerns as early as the mid-1940s about the ecological hazards of synthetic organic pesticides, particularly since they were highly persistent in the environment and could accumulate in fatty tissues. These warnings were dismissed and even ridiculed by public health and agriculture advocates, however, who dwelt overwhelmingly on their benefits. A 1946 editorial in the leading public health journal, for instance, hailed DDT as "with penicillin, one of the two greatest contributions to public health science . . . in the last decade." The writer noted that indiscriminate use of it might pose dangers, but concluded that its "use in general will not be such as to threaten the wide disturbances of the balance of nature which have been anticipated by some timid souls."[22] A 1948 editorial took an even stronger position, quoting approvingly a statement that "DDT when used as an insecticide, with reasonable intelligence and the precautions normal to the use of modern insecticides, is harmless to man and animals."[23] Public health authorities in fact became strong allies of the agricultural chemical producers throughout the two postwar decades in advocating continued use of these chemicals, downplaying their risks, and opposing stricter regulation of them (Wargo 1996). By the late 1950s, however, studies of fish and wildlife were steadily increasing ecologists' concerns, and other scientists were suggesting the possibility of human cancer effects, calling into question the claims of public health scientists who had confidently asserted the pesticides' safety to both humans and wildlife. The National Audubon Society by the mid-1950s began to document alarming drops in some bird populations from field surveys by its members. The gypsy moth campaign in 1957 triggered numerous complaints from farmers and at least one lawsuit, by a distinguished Long Island ornithologist and other residents, protesting damage to wildlife and property from indiscriminate spraying. As the Echo Park Dam proposal had politicized the Sierra Club, the insect eradication campaign of the late 1950s mobilized and politicized the National Audubon Society (Bosso 1987, 81–85).

In 1962, biologist Rachel Carson published a potent critique of the hazards of persistent pesticides, *Silent Spring*. A gifted science writer with long experience in the Fish and Wildlife Service, Carson combined what scientific evidence existed with powerful anecdotes and emotionally compelling arguments to make a case for more stringent restrictions of indiscriminate insecticide use. More systematic research subsequently confirmed that in just twenty years, the residues of these chemicals had become virtually ubiquitous in wildlife and their habitats worldwide, especially in aquatic and wetland species, which transferred them to one another through ecological food chains, magnifying their effects. It also showed that in some species, such as pelicans, eagles, hawks, ospreys, and even robins, they reached concentrations that were disastrous to reproduction even though not toxic to the individuals affected (Eisenbud 1978, 232; American Chemical Society 1969, 224–30). A 1963 report of the President's Science Advisory Committee supported many of Carson's arguments, as did a more detailed subsequent study in 1969 (the Mrak Report) by the Department of Health, Education, and Welfare. Massive fish kills in the lower Mississippi River, traced in 1963 to a Memphis pesticide manufacturing plant, also underscored her concerns (Graham 1970, 76–80, 94–108; Bosso 1987, 129).

Silent Spring became an immediate best-seller. More than any other work, it catalyzed public awareness of the world as an ecosystem, of the risk that damage to the ecosystem could be as threatening to both humans and nature as acute poisoning, and of the fact that ecological processes also could quickly thwart the intended purposes of "pest eradication" programs.[24] With an equally revolutionary effect, it documented the excessively cozy relationships throughout the pest-control "subgovernment" among government agencies and powerful pesticide manufactures, user constituencies, and even scientists beholden to them for research funding (Bosso 1987, 116–17). In effect it challenged not only the propaganda of the chemical industry but also the Progressive myth of scientific neutrality. Coming as it did on the heels of the nuclear fallout issue as well as the cranberry scare and the revelation that a drug widely prescribed to women in Europe caused birth defects, it sparked an outpouring of both public concern and political response.[25]

The reactions of both industrial and government scientists, however, reconfirmed the widening rift not only between these public concerns and the agencies, but also between the scientific and professional communities who defined their missions as food production and public health and those who were concerned with the consequences for wildlife and ecosystems. Many of the former responded to Carson's arguments not as a legitimate issue for scientific concern and remedy but as a personal attack on their reputations and a dangerous political threat to their programmatic missions. Denigrators labeled it "science fiction," and accused her of advocating a ban on all pesticide uses and thus of endangering food production and health protection — a position which Carson in fact had not advocated. A report by the National Academy of Sciences-National Research Council, a group dominated by agricultural advocates, heavily emphasized the benefits of pesticides and downplayed their ecological hazards (Graham 1970, 36–47; Bosso 1987, 116–18).[26] The Public Health Service in 1964 even began an expensive and ineffective new program to eradicate *Aedes aegypti* mosquitoes nationwide through widespread DDT spraying campaigns rather than localized sanitation measures (Graham 1970, 76–80, 211–21). During the Vietnam War the U.S. Army and Air Force practiced chemical destruction of ecosystems on a massive scale by defoliating the forests of Southeast Asia to deny cover to Communist troops.

In short, the radiation and pesticides controversies demonstrated that public agencies and even their scientific professionals often developed narrow and dogmatic commitments to particular views of their missions, which led them to discount the evidence of broader ecological consequences of their actions. This revelation seriously eroded public belief in the unity and objectivity of scientists, and in the Progressive ideal of public administration by politically neutral experts. To many government scientists in agriculture and public health, the public outcries over radiation and pesticides may have looked simply like new versions of the fluoridation issue, pitting knowledgeable and public-spirited experts against emotional, fearful know-nothings and fanatics. To concerned citizens, however — and importantly, to scientists from other fields, such as ecology and wildlife biology — the claims of such experts looked increasingly like arrogant assertions of personal judgments in the name of science but in the service of particular missions and ideologies.

The Discrediting of Progressivism

The cumulative result of these controversies was a gradual discrediting not merely of individual scientists or agencies, but of the Progressive philosophy of governance itself, a shift which was amplified immeasurably by larger events such as the Vietnam War.

Beginning in the late 1940s and '50s, many political scientists and economists as well as political activists had begun to attack the disparity between the Progressive ideal and the political reality of U.S. agencies' behavior.[27] With each controversy the belief that scientific or technical expertise conferred a special knowledge of the "broad public interest," let alone a dispassionate commitment to act on it, came to appear a myth. Agencies and their administrators in practice appeared to act on behalf of particular personal and political views of the public interest, which were neither scientific or consensual. Other critics attacked the ideal itself, arguing that administrative agencies tended to be "captured" by self-interested clients and congressional subcommittee members whose gains from their decisions were symbiotic to the agencies' needs for their political support. Therefore, they argued, political decisions in reality reflected not the interests of broad majorities but those of organized minorities with economic interests at stake (Olson 1965). Still other critics argued that agencies tended to become advocates for their own organizational interests and for the individual and shared interests of their employees (Wildavsky 1964). By the late 1960s political theorists had developed a new consensus that the actions of government agencies did not demonstrably represents an overall "public interest" discovered and implemented by apolitical expert administrators, as the Progressive philosophy had argued, but rather that they were merely the political results of competing pressures and influences by organized interests — "interest-group pluralism" — both within and outside government (Lowi 1969).[28]

In the pluralist view, therefore, the overall public interest lay not in delegating discretionary authority to administrative elites, but in making them more politically accountable. The essential question was how best to do this.

One option was to reassert congressional authority, creating policy through detailed statutory mandates rather than delegating broad grants of discretionary authority to administrative agencies. During the 1950s and '60s Congress wrote increasingly prescriptive requirements into many statutes and appropriations bills, especially for "categorical grant programs," which offered federal grants for housing, highways, urban renewal, wastewater treatment facilities, and other purposes but in exchange required compliance with a growing number of federal requirements. Congressional earmarking of funds for particular projects and locations also became increasingly common. In the 1970s and '80s similarly detailed mandates were added to some regulatory laws as well, such as statutory standards for motor vehicle emissions.

Congressional control was an attractive alternative for critics of the administrative agencies. It appealed simultaneously to a broad public that distrusted bureaucrats and liked the idea of political accountability, to congressmen themselves, and to many interests that had greater influence with legislators and congressional subcommittees than with administrators and technical professionals in the agencies. These included traditional industrial and resource extraction interests, but also, interestingly, environmental protection activists who believed that only statutory mandates were strong enough to force agencies to stand up to powerful industries. However, congressional micromanagement by statute introduced rigidities that sometimes lagged behind changing scientific knowledge, did not fit varied circumstances, favored particular privileged interests, and imposed on Congress itself a burden of ongoing technical details and adjustments that the institution could not sustain (Andrews 1993b).

A second option was to continue delegating responsibility to administrators, but to compel them to justify their decisions more explicitly. The Administrative Procedures Act of 1946 required agencies to produce a written "reviewable record" justifying every admin-istrative decision and showing "substantial evidence" to support it, and it authorized the courts to halt administrative actions that did not fulfill these requirements. Administrative requirements within the executive branch also forced more detailed documentation: guidelines beginning in 1950, for instance, mandated economic cost-benefit analyses for all federal water development projects, based on language in the 1936 Flood Control Act that the aggregate benefits of every federal water project must exceed its costs.[29] Such paperwork mandates had only modest effects through the 1950s and '60s, but became far more influential in the 1970s and thereafter in the form of requirements for "environ-mental impact statements," "regulatory impact analyses," "risk assessments," and other written justifications.

A third option was to make administrative decision processes more transparently polit-ical, subject to formal coordination requirements as well as judicially enforceable pro-cedures, and thus open not just to potential economic beneficiaries but to any affected interests that might organize themselves to participate. The Administrative Procedures Act of 1946, for instance, spelled out specific procedural as well as documentation stan-dards for fulfilling the Fifth Amendment's "due process" guarantee. The advocates of government regulations had to bear the burden of proof to justify them, and every govern-ment action had to be preceded by formal public notice, opportunities for public com-ment and often hearings, a reviewable record, and documentation of substantial evidence justifying it. The courts were empowered to reverse administrative actions that were judged arbitrary and capricious or beyond the agency's statutory authority, or that had not satisfied these requirements (Administrative Conference of the United States 1991, Ker-win 1994). The Fish and Wildlife Coordination Act required the water resource develop-ment agencies to consult formally with the fish and wildlife conservation agencies, and the 1965 Federal Water Project Recreation Act required full consideration of recreation and fish and wildlife enhancement in all future federal water resource projects (Armstrong et al. 1976, 312). The Freedom of Information Act required public disclosure of most gov-ernment documents and decision rationales. All these requirements had the effect of making administrative decisions more visible and accessible to their potential opponents and victims, rather than merely to their beneficiaries.

Finally, a fourth response was to widen public access through the courts, allowing legal challenges to the agencies by a far wider range of interests. Civil rights challenges to the licenses of segregationist radio stations in the 1960s led to dramatic liberalization of judicial "standing to sue": where plaintiffs had previously had to prove that they had suffered personal economic injury, federal courts now allowed suits to remedy "injury in fact" to any "legally protected interest."[30] Environmental plaintiffs first used this oppor-tunity in 1967 in a challenge to a hydropower license (*Storm King v. Federal Power Commis-sion*), and their success in this case led to a revolution in the use of litigation to challenge administrative decisions on environmental grounds. Shortly thereafter the Environmental Defense Fund was created, out of an alliance of concerned scientists and lawyers who had first brought suit in 1966 to stop indiscriminate DDT spraying by local governments on Long Island, and subsequently in Michigan and Wisconsin. While they lost some suits on legal grounds, the publicity they generated and the evidence they thus placed in the public record doomed many of the spray programs politically (Graham 1970, 251–59; Bosso 1987, 135).

A whole new spectrum of environmental advocacy organizations emerged from this process: "public interest environmental law" groups, whose goal was to change federal policies through strategic legal challenges rather than merely to organize lobbying campaigns and represent the interests of national memberships. Examples included the Environmental Defense Fund, the Natural Resources Defense Council, and the Sierra Club Legal Defense Fund. What was important to these groups was not only to win cases on their merits, but to force the agencies to defend themselves in court—in sworn testimony and in the glare of publicity—where the differences between scientific evidence and unsupported or self-interested ideologies could be publicly exposed. Later environmental statutes included provisions specifically permitting citizen suits to compel or challenge agencies' actions.

These tactics were a radical departure from the previous strategies of conservation and preservation advocacy groups, which had relied on publicity campaigns and ad hoc lobbying rather than lawsuits to influence public policy. They represented an equally radical shift in American doctrines of governance, from ostensibly apolitical administrative discretion to openly political administrative decision processes. Taken together, these changes amounted to a radical "reformation of American administrative law," whose consequences were central to both the strengths and limitations of environmental policy in the quarter-century that followed (Stewart 1975).

Political Representation of Environmental Preferences

The transformation of administrative accountability was paralleled by equally fundamental changes in Congress, as its districts were redrawn in the 1960s to reflect the great rural-to-urban demographic shifts of the postwar decade. Throughout the 1950s, representation in Congress predominantly reflected the less urbanized demographic patterns of the preceding decades, and its seniority rules gave disproportionate power to representatives of agricultural and resource-extraction interests from rural districts over representatives of urban areas, where political turnover was more common. Rural representatives exercised these preferences to control committees of general power (such as Appropriations and Rules) as well as those dealing with their own district and state interests, such as Agriculture, Interior and Public Works. These were the committees to which environmental legislation was most often referred, and they used this power to block, weaken, or delay environmental protection legislation.[31]

Rural representatives typically viewed pro-environment legislation either as a costly new tax burden to serve other constituencies (as with urban sewers, for instance), or as an imposition of urban recreational or aesthetic preferences in conflict with traditional resource-extraction livelihoods. In either case it represented unwelcome increases in federal power and spending. In a very few cases the system produced committee chairmen with different values, such as Senator Edmund Muskie of Maine, who succeeded Senator Robert Kerr of Oklahoma in 1963 on the Senate Public Works Committee. Muskie was from a rural state, but one whose lobster industry had a strong interest in clean water, and he saw air and water pollution legislation as a pathway to higher national office. Muskie was a rare exception, however.

In the early 1960s the courts mandated congressional redistricting to reflect the greatly changed residence patterns of the postwar population, and with this redistricting the balance of power shifted dramatically from rural to urban areas. The power of entrenched resource user interests was significantly reduced, first by turnover and eventually, in the 1970s, by changes in rules and a proliferation of subcommittees which distributed power more widely among the members.[32] Representatives who voted most consistently in favor of "environmentalist" positions in the 1960s came disproportionately from urban districts and their surrounding suburbs: the Boston-Washington corridor alone produced one-third of such votes, and the rest came predominantly from urban areas throughout the country.[33] In part, this reflected the environmental issues affecting their constituencies: pollution, congestion, and an interest in outdoor recreation. However, it also reflected a more positive attitude among urban constituencies toward federal intervention more generally. Cities had many special needs, not just environmental, which rural-dominated state legislatures had been unwilling to support, and urban congressmen therefore sought federal intervention and assistance to meet them. This different attitude was evident irrespective of region, party, or ideology, although a higher proportion of Democratic than Republican and of "liberal" than "conservative" representatives favored pro-environmentalist positions (Martis 1976, 299–302).

Changes in presidential leadership also reflected this political shift, with the changes of policy from the Eisenhower administration to those of Presidents Kennedy and Johnson. President Eisenhower sought to dismantle the New Deal agencies, to devolve additional federal powers to the states (control of offshore "tidelands" for oil extraction, for instance), and to avoid new federal spending for environmental purposes such as wastewater treatment plants and parklands acquisition.[34] Kennedy's and Johnson's political constituencies, in contrast, were the Democratic activists of the growing urban and suburban areas, and their different priorities were constantly evident: they favored federal leadership and funding for air and water pollution control, for outdoor recreation initiatives and wilderness preservation, for preservation of natural beauty and billboard control, and for other environmental initiatives. President Kennedy appointed an active environmentalist from the West, Steward Udall, as his Secretary of the Interior, and convened a White House Conference on Conservation in 1961 to echo and redirect Theodore Roosevelt's utilitarian conservation agenda of 1908 (the "new conservation," in Kennedy's term). President Johnson in 1965 sponsored a White House Conference on Natural Beauty for America, defining natural beauty and pollution cleanup as essential elements of his "Great Society" vision for America (Sundquist 1968, 361–63). Both presidents initiated important environmental legislative initiatives, and made the protection of public health and nature visible priorities of the federal government.

Convergence of Agendas: Environment as the Focus

In 1963 an article appeared in the leading journal of public administration, *Public Administration Review,* under the title "Environment: A New Focus for Public Policy?" The article, by Professor Lynton Caldwell of Indiana University, focused not on pollution or natural resource conservation or landscape preservation per se, but on the *governance* problem that pervaded all of these issues: the radical segmentation of U.S. actions and policies affecting natural resources and the human environment among separate agencies with conflicting missions. Throughout U.S. history, Americans had invoked the powers of government to "develop" selected aspects of their environment, to reduce environmental hazards to public health, and for other purposes. Despite all these particular uses and policies, however, no overall public responsibility had ever been assigned for the environment as a whole. This "practical" approach to problems had again and again created new problems even as it attempted to solve old ones. Each agency pursued its own mission without regard to those of the others, equating the overall "public interest" merely with benefits to its own client constituencies.

Caldwell proposed instead that the "environment" be adopted as a central integrating focus for public policy. The environmental problems of the late twentieth century, he argued, would require a more comprehensively ecological approach, focusing in an integrated fashion on the interrelated problems of particular environments. Such an approach was no panacea: it would require constant effort to reconcile the interests and values affected. But it would at least focus attention on the central questions: what is a "good" environment, to what kind of environment should we aspire, and what indicators could be used to measure and monitor it? Two things would be needed to achieve this focus: first, public demand for it, and second, more effective coordination among the agencies that shared environmental responsibilities.

Caldwell's idea was not adopted as public policy for another seven years, but his article focused attention on the environmental governance problem: conflicting agencies with conflicting missions, conflicting public values, and powerful, self-interested client constituencies.[35] The water resource development agencies were building dams on every reach of every river that Congress would approve, gradually converting every fishing stream and rafting rapids into flat-water reservoirs and even flooding portions of national parks. The Forest Service and Bureau of Land Management were approving ever more extensive logging, grazing, and mining on the public lands, at the expense of their ecological functions as well as aesthetic and recreational values. The interstate highway program was paving over thousands of miles of natural lands across the country, even bulldozing through parks where that was the cheapest or most direct route, and in the process promoting both urban traffic congestion and residential and commercial development of the countryside. The Atomic Energy Commission was promoting commercial nuclear power reactors with little concern for their hot water discharges into watercourses, or for the long-term costs and risks of their radiation hazards. The Soil Conservation Service was "channelizing" streams to benefit towns and farmers with little concern for either downstream flooding or the natural habitats it was destroying.

To the general public, these events and others presented an increasingly visible and powerful image of both big business and big government run amok. The postwar era had produced a quarter-century of unprecedented peacetime levels of material and energy production, technological change, mass consumption, and middle-class affluence and amenities. By the late 1960s, however, the environmental consequences of these patterns were increasingly visible. In 1969 and 1970, accidents at offshore oil drilling rigs spilled thousands of tons of oil along the Santa Barbara Channel in California and off the Louisiana coast. The Cuyahoga River in Ohio burned for eight days due to the concentrations of pollutants on its surface (Whelan 1985, 225), and dangerous levels of mercury were found in some Great Lakes fish. Lake Erie was even declared "dead" due to excessive pollution.[36] A few states, cities, and industries had begun to abate some of the worst problems, but these remained exceptions. Throughout the country, major cities discharged raw sewage into rivers and estuaries, industries discharged toxic wastes into rivers or dumped them into unprotected lagoons or municipal landfills, and factories and power plants as well as cars and trucks caused worsening air pollution in cities.

New proposals threatened additional hazards as well. A proposed trans-Alaska pipeline would carry millions of gallons of oil across environmentally fragile tundra and undisturbed wildlife habitat; it would then be shipped through valuable marine fisheries. Nuclear power plants proposed to discharge hot water into lakes and estuaries, disrupting their ecosystems (such as Biscayne Bay, Florida, which was later designated a national monument to protect the unusual diversity of its tropical biota). A petrochemical plant was proposed in an area of valuable fisheries and natural beauty near the South Carolina coast; a jetport planned for Miami would threaten the Everglades National Park; a fleet of "supersonic transport" planes (SSTs) would emit jet exhaust into the stratosphere with unknown consequences (Quarles 1976, 8–12). Paul and Anne Ehrlich's *The Population Bomb,* published in 1968, raised these concerns to the scale of a global crisis: population, resource use, and pollution were increasing not just locally but on a global scale, and not merely steadily but geometrically, by compound interest, adding yet more urgency to the need to correct them (Ehrlich 1968).

News reports of these threats were broadcast in stark visual detail into American living rooms by the newly ubiquitous medium of television. They also were juxtaposed with reports of the greatest American technological achievement of the same era, manned space flight. Astronauts' photographs from space captured dramatically the unique and finite beauty of Earth, the only life-supporting "blue planet." Conventional wisdom produced the obvious challenge: "If we can send men to the moon, why can't we clean up pollution before we foul our own nest?" Gradually these reports fused into one compelling story: the story of a unique, beautiful, life-supporting, but finite planet becoming overrun with people, stripped of its resources, ravaged by bulldozers, and polluted by human excreta and industrial wastes.[37]

The effect of these reports was to galvanize a national outpouring of public demand for government action, on a scale that had few precedents in American history. Interest groups and ad hoc protest coalitions — traditional nature-preservation and hunting and fishing groups, civic and scientific organizations, consumer advocates such as Ralph

Nader,[38] and newly founded public-interest environmental law groups[39] — were already active on particular controversies, but by themselves they had only marginal political influence. The civil rights and anti-Vietnam War movements had begun to show, however, the power of mass public concern to influence government policy; and with these movements as models, the environmental groups suddenly coalesced into a loosely unified but far broader social movement for environmental protection. The first "Earth Day," April 22, 1970, was initiated by a handful of volunteers led by Senator Gaylord Nelson of Wisconsin, but it grew spontaneously into what *Time* magazine described as "the biggest street festival since the Japanese surrender in 1945." It included mass rallies of up to twenty-five thousand people in major cities, as well as "teach-ins" involving an estimated ten million young people at over ten thousand schools and some two thousand colleges and universities (Quarles 1976, 12–13). Opinion polls and media coverage confirmed the result: environmental quality had become a broad-based, high-priority and active concern for the American public.[40]

In short, in the late 1960s a number of previously separate environmental issues suddenly converged, creating an image of environmental destruction powerful enough to mobilize mass public concern, and to unify previously disparate advocacy groups into a far broader alliance. Traditional nature preservation groups such as the Sierra Club, Wilderness Society, and National Audubon Society; sportsmen's groups such as the Izaak Walton League, Ducks Unlimited and National Wildlife Federation; civic groups such as local garden clubs and especially the League of Women Voters; city governments seeking federal funding for wastewater treatment; neighborhoods in the path of highways or dams; more diffuse constituencies such as college students; and even many conservatives and commercial interests (water utilities and recreation and tourism businesses, for instance) — all these groups could find common cause in their demands for federal action to protect the environment.

Protecting the environment offered a powerful new opportunity for broad-based civic action toward a positive common purpose. Previous sources of common national purpose had lost much of their urgency or consensus, or both. The economy was thriving, and the goal of protecting the world from tyranny had become far more divisive with the Vietnam War; the civil rights issue was also divisive, even if profoundly important. Perhaps equally significant, both the goals and the villains of the environmental movement were traditional ones. The beauty of America had long been a powerful common value, reflected in the words of "America the Beautiful," in the pages of *National Geographic,* and in the longstanding patriotic pride in national parks as an American equivalent to the "crown jewels" of Europe. The villains, in turn, were the traditional villains of American popular folklore: the greedy magnates of big business and the bureaucrats of big government. In reality, pollution and environmental damage came also from small businesses, from land development and farms, from local governments' sewage outfalls and landfills, and from millions of individuals' consumption decisions. At least initially, however, the most obvious polluters were few, easy to identify, and big enough as symbolic targets to be called to account by public opinion.

In 1970, these forces coalesced in a series of defining events which set the political framework for the quarter-century "environmental era" that followed. The first event was enactment of the National Environmental Policy Act, signed by President Nixon on national television on New Year's Day of what he declared the "decade of the environment." Nixon declared that the time was "now or never" to clean up pollution and correct environmental destruction by federal agencies. The second was Earth Day, an extraordinary nationwide mass demonstration of environmental concern that vividly demonstrated public support for strong government action. The third was enactment of the 1970 Clean Air Act, the first in an unprecedented series of federal environmental regulatory laws which established nationwide minimum standards, permit requirements, and implementation mandates for reducing and cleaning up pollution. Finally, the fourth was the creation of the federal Environmental Protection Agency, a single agency to integrate the diverse and growing federal regulatory programs for pollution control.

12   Nationalizing Pollution Control

The great question of the seventies is, shall we surrender to our surroundings, or shall we make peace with nature and begin to make reparations for the damage we have done to our air, our land and our water? Restoring nature to its natural state is a cause beyond party and beyond factions. It has become a common cause of all the people of America. — President Richard M. Nixon, State of the Union Message, 1970

U.S. environmental policy prior to 1970 included over seven decades' experience in managing the environment as a natural resource base, but almost none in the regulation of environmental quality. Federal management of public lands and waters was well established, as was the federal role in funding major public infrastructures (highways, dams, military technologies, and research and development more generally). Federal economic regulation was also well established: the Interstate Commerce Commission had existed since the 1880s, and the Federal Trade Commission, Securities and Exchange Commission, and others since the 1930s. All reflected a combination of producer interests and public beliefs that free markets required a "level playing field," protecting both buyers and sellers against abusive practices and competitive excesses.

In contrast, federal authority to protect public health, safety, and environmental quality was limited almost exclusively to ingestible products. The Food and Drug Administration regulated food additives, drugs, and cosmetics, and the Department of Agriculture administered food inspection programs as well as a weak pesticide control statute. The Public Health Service had long-standing research and technical assistance programs for air and water quality, sanitation and solid waste management, and occupational health and safety, but with few exceptions it left regulation and enforcement to the states.

Beginning in 1970, U.S. environmental policy entered a fundamentally new era, defined by a greatly enlarged federal role in environmental protection, by federal minimum standards and regulations as primary policy tools, and by greatly expanded access for citizen environmental advocates both to administrative procedures and to the courts as a recourse. Over a dozen federal regulatory statutes were enacted to protect public health and the environment from pollution, and enforcement of most of these mandates was delegated to the new Environmental Protection Agency (EPA). No longer would air and water pollution be considered "uniquely local problems," as President Eisenhower once characterized them: the federal government would establish national minimum standards for environmental protection which state and local governments would be required to implement, thus protecting all Americans from environmental hazards and protecting progressive states and industries from recalcitrant neighbors and competitors.

Significantly, many of these were to be *funded* mandates: the federal government would pay a substantial fraction of state and local governments' implementation costs. In most cases, state and local governments remained free to set additional or more stringent requirements as well. The federal government, however, would establish the minimum standards and the overall framework; and it would do so primarily by federal regulation and enforcement, rather than merely by grants, subsidies, services, technical assistance programs, moral suasion, or other previous policy tools.

It would be difficult to overstate the magnitude of these changes in American environmental policy and governance. Policy functions that previously had been almost exclusively state and local prerogatives were suddenly subjected to national minimum standards and program requirements. State governments were mandated both to comply themselves and to implement and enforce these requirements as delegated agents of the federal government. The principal policy tools were federal environmental standards and permits, which had no close precedents in previous policy, and which placed the federal government in a new and adversarial relationship with industries as well as with state and local governments. Finally, the leadership for implementing these policies was no longer entrusted to government alone, as under Progressive technical professionals or New Deal entrepreneurial administrators: citizen environmental advocacy organizations were armed with expanded rights to disclosure of government documents, with access to administrative proceedings, and with new rights to challenge government agencies in the courts. These changes had far-reaching implications both for the environment and for American governance.

After twenty-five years of this "environmental era," one outcome was a substantially cleaner environment, even though the economic activities that cause pollution continued to expand. A second result, however, was a sizable gap between the statutory mandates and their implementation and enforcement, and a continuing legacy of pollution problems and sources that resisted regulatory solutions. A third was a complex and fragmented patchwork of regulatory programs, which were increasingly recognized as having serious limitations and imposing costly burdens. Finally, a fourth result was a greatly altered relationship between the federal government and the states, which continued to shift with changes in federal mandates, subsidies, and political pressures. These results coexisted in shifting tensions for a quarter-century, but with the election of a radically antigovernment congressional majority in 1994, an increasingly conservative Supreme Court, and growing tension between EPA and state and local governments, important elements of federal environmental regulatory policies were suddenly reopened to fundamental debate.

The "Environmental Decade"

The sudden and dramatic coalescence of the American environmental movement, most compellingly in the Earth Day demonstrations of 1970, had immediate effects on national policy. Both Democrats and Republicans responded with an outpouring of federal legislation to protect the environment. Senator Edmund Muskie, a leading Democratic presidential candidate, sponsored amendments to the federal air and water quality laws which shifted their emphasis from state to federal primacy. Senator Henry Jackson (D-Wash.), another presidential aspirant, sponsored a National Environmental Policy Act, which ordered all federal agencies to make environmental quality an explicit goal of their actions.

By the end of 1980, bipartisan majorities had passed an unprecedented body of federal environmental protection legislation. Over a dozen major new statutes set ambitious goals for clean air and water and safe drinking water, and established far-reaching new regulations for pesticides, toxic substances, and solid and hazardous waste management. Others addressed coastal management, endangered species and marine mammals, ocean dumping of wastes, protection of the national forests and public lands, energy conservation, alternative energy sources, and other environmental issues. Both Republican and Democratic legislators supported these laws, and presidents of both parties added their own initiatives.

President Nixon had no personal history of commitment to environmental protection, and his inclination was to admire leading industrialists and to disdain young environmental activists (U.S. EPA 1993a, 10–11). Nixon saw in the environmental issue, however, both a political opportunity to lead on a consensual issue and the political necessity to lead on an issue of such widespread public concern, and importance to his Democratic presidential rivals. He signed the National Environmental Policy Act on live television on New Year's Day 1970, with a speech in which he declared the 1970s the "decade of the environment" in which it was "literally now or never" to abate human damage to the environment. In February he issued an executive order directing all federal facilities to reduce their own pollution, and delivered a Presidential Environmental Message to Congress presenting a thirty-seven-point program for environmental protection. In July he sent Congress a reorganization plan calling for the creation of a federal Environmental Protection Agency, integrating in one agency most of the existing federal programs that dealt directly with pollution and toxic hazards to the environment. The reorganization became effective in September, and EPA went into operation in December.[1] The environmental decade had begun.

EPA: The "Gorilla in the Closet"

The Environmental Protection Agency was created to integrate in one agency the widely scattered federal research and regulatory programs dealing with environmental pollution. The National Air Pollution Control Administration, formerly a bureau of the Public Health Service, was moved from the Department of Health, Education, and Welfare, along with the Public Health Service's bureaus for solid waste, water hygiene, radiological hygiene, and pesticide research. The Federal Water Quality Administration was transferred from the Interior Department, where President Johnson had moved it from HEW in 1965. Pesticide regulation was brought in from the Department of Agriculture, pesticide research programs from Interior, and radiation regulation from the Atomic Energy Commission. EPA became an instant agency of some five to six thousand people (U.S. EPA 1993a, 3).

Most people therefore think of the Environmental Protection Agency as the agency with overall responsibility for protecting America's environment, and for preventing or cleaning up the most serious risks to it. In fact, however, the EPA reorganization plan simply transferred into one agency a set of existing programs and their associated statutory authorities.[2] It established no overall mission or framework for the agency, since that would have required legislative action rather than merely a reorganization plan. Congress, constrained by the entrenched and decentralized power of its committees — each more interested in its own jurisdictional piece than in a broader whole — never corrected this omission.[3] EPA's powers therefore remained fragmented across a complex patchwork of legally separate programs. Each was created by different statutes, defined by different mandates, criteria, priorities, and budgets, and overseen by different congressional subcommittees. EPA's administrator had only limited discretion to integrate or set priorities among these separate statutory programs. The agency did, however, have one single, clear political goal: unlike the complex departments from which its programs came, it was created as an independent agency whose sole reason for existence was to protect the environment.

From EPA's earliest days, a key policy decision was to emphasize aggressive standard-setting and enforcement rather than negotiation and assistance. The agency's first administrator, William Ruckelshaus, was a prosecutor who had worked aggressively to abate air and water pollution in Indiana, and his state experience convinced him that strong federal enforcement was essential to make the most intransigent polluters act. In his first week at EPA he issued water pollution abatement orders against three major cities (Atlanta, Detroit, and Cleveland), and within a year EPA had referred 152 industrial pollution cases to the Justice Department for prosecution.[4]

The core of Ruckelshaus's strategy was to use high-visibility enforcement lawsuits to establish the agency's power and credibility, and thus to generate mass public support as a counterweight to the entrenched power of industrial and municipal polluters (Quarles 1976, 35, 39–48). EPA's first major test case set the tone. In 1971 it won a court order against Armco Steel, a chronic industrial polluter, for polluting the Houston Ship Channel. Armco sought White House intervention to rein in the EPA, but newspaper reports exposed Armco's campaign contributions to President Nixon, and the resulting outcry forced the White House to retreat and Armco to accept EPA's terms. Congressional leaders in turn used the opportunity to reinforce EPA's accountability to its statutes and to congressional oversight committees, rather than to the political agenda of the president (U.S. EPA 1993a, 13–14; Quarles 1976, 58–76). Ruckelshaus continued with a sustained campaign of enforcement actions for water pollution abatement and standard-setting and permit-writing for air pollution.

Aggressive federal enforcement threats thus replaced the ineffectual compliance schedules that many industrial polluters had negotiated with state agencies, and galvanized support for EPA among the press and the general public. In effect, they established the agency as an advocate for environmental protection and public health, that would err in that direction if necessary rather than on the side of making concessions for economic reasons. They also defined the distinctively adversarial character of the U.S. environmental regulatory process — in contrast for instance to those of England, Canada, and most of the European industrial democracies — and they put far more visible pressure on the states and municipalities as well as industrial polluters.[5]

The independent, adversarial position of EPA as a national environmental protection regulator agency was a phenomenon which had no parallel in other industrial democracies and almost none in American history.[6] It also represented a sudden and extraordinary reversal of the long-standing primacy of business interests in American governance, a loss of leverage from which it took these interests some years to recover (David Vogel, quoted in Bosso 1987, 147).

EPA's aggressive enforcement stance never extended, however, to agricultural pollution. It was an independent agency within the executive branch but its budget still came each year from Congress, where it was controlled until 1975 by Rep. Jamie Whitten (D-Miss.) and the old rural-agricultural power structure (Bosso 1987, 187–90). This reality severely limited EPA's effectiveness in dealing with agricultural water pollution and pesticide use. Ruckelshaus did cancel the registration of DDT in 1971 for all domestic uses except public health and agricultural pest quarantine, but only under court order, as a result of lawsuits filed by the Environmental Defense Fund (Bean 1983 [1977], 243–45).[7]

EPA's aggressive regulatory policy has sometimes been characterized as an intrusion on state prerogatives. In the main, however, EPA's policies served not to replace the states' environmental leadership but to strengthen it. They reinforced the states' power to deal with industrial polluters, and forced them as well as paid them to clean up pollution from their own local governments — and in many cases, subsidized the creation of state environmental agencies that did not previously exist. Some states complained about EPA requirements, therefore, but many privately welcomed them: EPA was their "gorilla in the closet": the scapegoat they could blame when they imposed new controls on powerful industries (Portney 1990, 263; the phrase was Ruckelshaus's). State governments could set tighter environmental standards if they wished to, and some did: California's air quality standards, for example, and later New Jersey's Community Right-To-Know Act and Massachusetts's Toxic Use Reduction Act. However, they now had to at least implement the federal regulatory mandates, or face direct EPA regulation of their industries.

EPA Structure: Central or Regional, Media or Functions?

Ruckelshaus's aggressive strategy required a change of roles for most of EPA's staff, whose previous organizational cultures, especially at the Department of Agriculture and the Public Health Service, had emphasized cooperation with businesses and assistance to state agencies rather than enforcement (Wellford 1972, 150–51). EPA's initial staff units represented separate environmental media and pollutants: air, water, land, pesticides, and radiation. These units brought to their tasks distinctive differences of discipline — air and water treatment engineers, toxicologists and health scientists, radiation experts, lawyers, economists — as well as different organizational cultures and ideologies.[8] Influential advisors recommended reorganizing the agency by functions, such as criteria setting, enforcement, planning and management, research and monitoring. The urgency of standard-setting and enforcement took precedence, however, and new statutes reinforced the existing program structures and loyalties.

The agency therefore settled quickly into a hybrid mix of "media" programs (air and water), "categorical" programs (pesticides, radiation, and solid wastes), and functional units (enforcement, research, policy analysis, administration), which continued with only minor changes until the 1990s (U.S. EPA 1993a, 5–9).[9] This pattern provided a tolerable compromise for the scientists, engineers, and lawyers who worked within the agency and for the congressional committees that oversaw its pieces, but it also created a structure that was both burdensome to industries and inimical to integrated solutions. Air, water, wastes, and chemicals from the same factories were regulated by separate bureaucracies, under separate laws and criteria, with no mechanism for making tradeoffs or integrating the results.

The Nixon administration meanwhile directed that EPA serve as a model of decentralized regional structure, a showpiece for its policy of "new federalism." Half its staff members were assigned to ten regional offices around the country, and still others to geographically scattered laboratories, making it one of the most decentralized of federal agencies.[10] The regional offices were given substantial autonomy in permitting, enforcement, and program development, and this strategy turned out to be far more effective than if all decisions had had to be approved in Washington. It also gave the agency broader political support in the states and congressional districts that benefited from its jobs and expenditures, and allowed greater sensitivity to regional environmental and political differences, with both the benefits and the risks that that involved. Regional autonomy allowed accommodations to environmental differences such as between the arid West and the humid East, but it also left the regional offices in a poorly defined middle ground between federal and state governments, with unclear accountability and consequent risks of bureaucratic self-interest and capture by state and regional interests (Quarles 1976, 34; National Academy of Public Administration 1995).

Regulating Air and Water Pollution: Technology or Risk?

The first major new statutory tasks assigned to EPA were to create national minimum standards for ambient air quality and technology-based standards for approving permits for air pollution emissions and water pollution discharges. Prior to 1970, pollution control had been left almost exclusively to state and local governments. Most of these governments, however, had developed little institutional capacity to control pollution. Water and air pollutants flowed constantly across municipal and state boundaries, polluting industries could usually intimidate state and local governments by threatening to relocate, and cities chronically underinvested in wastewater treatment facilities: wastewater treatment, after all, benefited downstream communities rather than the one that built it. Few states had effective environmental statutes or agencies, and fewer yet were willing to challenge powerful industries, confront their own municipalities, or raise taxes to pay for cleanup. Businesses retained almost total autonomy in emissions and waste disposal, and effectively resisted proposals for regulation. Such was the power of the most influential business interests that they were able to keep issues such as air pollution off many governments' agendas entirely (Crenson 1971).

By the 1960s most states had shown themselves unwilling or unable to correct these problems by themselves. Neither industrial compliance schedules nor interstate enforcement conferences had produced adequate results, and by 1970 no state had put in place a complete set of standards for any pollutant (Bryner 1993, 81). Beginning in 1970, therefore, Congress enacted almost a dozen major federal pollution control statutes: the Clean Air Act, Clean Water Act, Federal Environmental Pesticides Control Act, Safe Drinking Water Act, Toxic Substances Control Act, Resource Conservation and Recovery Act (solid and hazardous waste regulation), CERCLA (the "Superfund" Act), and reauthorizations of these laws and numerous others.[11] Taken together, these statutes authorized an unprecedented federal campaign to regulate and clean up pollution, and to compel state and local governments to participate in implementing the new policies.

A central question faced by the designers of these laws was whether they should be based on an "air or water quality management" approach or on a "best-practice" approach. In 1990s terms, this is similar to choosing between a "risk-based" or "risk-balancing" approach and a "technology-based" approach. In principle, air and water are public resources, and an agency could have been designed to manage their quality the way the Forest Service managed forests, or the way the Army Corps of Engineers managed rivers: as a multipurpose public resource to be conserved and allocated among competing uses. As a practical matter, however, this approach appeared administratively complex and vulnerable to endless argument. No one seriously envisioned giving EPA the degree of control over manufacturers' production decisions that the Forest Service had over timber cuts or the Corps had over the release of water from dams. And to approach the problem this way meant relying on standards that would always be based on disputable data, placing a large burden of proof and discretion on the agency without clear decision criteria, and leaving it open to endless litigation. There was simply no clear legal standard by which the agency could allocate pollution-reduction mandates among industries and other polluters without endless lawsuits over how much was "fair" to impose on each.

A best-practice approach, in contrast, merely required each firm to use the best available control technology, as defined by engineers familiar with what the best firms in each industry were doing, or to demonstrate equivalent pollution-control performance. It was a familiar approach to the engineers who had to implement it, and straightforward to implement and enforce. It also appeared to have the potential to minimize the constant lobbying and litigation that would be likely to continue under the air- or water-quality management approach.

The first of the new statutes, the Clean Air Act of 1970, authorized EPA to set national ambient air quality standards (NAAQS), based solely on human health risk without regard to cost, for the six most common air pollutants: sulfur and nitrogen oxides, carbon monoxide, particulates, lead, and ozone. It required the states to develop [state] implementation plans, subject to EPA approval, to achieve these standards.[12] Second, however, it required every new "point source" of air pollution to obtain a federal permit, and these permits were based not on risk but on technology: "new source performance standards" requiring the "best available technology" for controlling pollution. Third, it required automobile manufacturers to achieve 90 percent reduction in air pollution from new vehicles beginning in 1975: a technology-*forcing* requirement, obligating the industry to develop whatever new technology was needed to achieve the required result.[13] Fourth, it authorized EPA to develop risk-based standards for control of "hazardous air pollutants": those that were less common than the primary six but might cause serious hazards in local areas where they were emitted. Finally, the act increased federal operating subsidies to state air pollution control programs. Amendments in 1977 authorized EPA standards for "prevention of significant deterioration" in areas of good air quality, in order to prevent dirty industries from simply moving from polluted regions to cleaner ones. They also eased some compliance deadlines, but allowed the EPA to set tighter technological .requirements — the "lowest achievable emissions rate" — on new sources locating in non-attainment areas (Bryner 1993, 81–86; Portney 1990, 38).

The 1970 Clean Air Act thus represented a dramatic policy shift, from ad hoc state negotiation of industrial air pollution control to uniform federal minimum standards and technology-based permits. Its philosophy was that protecting public health was paramount, and that the polluters themselves should pay whatever it cost to achieve this. Air quality standards should therefore be set based on medical science alone, rather than on balancing of health against compliance costs. The law was implemented primarily by forcing big industries and automakers to adopt the best existing technologies for controlling pollution at the "end of the pipe," not by encouraging them to rethink their production processes and material and energy inputs in any fundamental way.

The Clean Air Act contributed to dramatic reductions in air pollution from large industries as well as motor vehicles. Between 1970 and the 1990s, smoke pollution (particulates) decreased by nearly 80 percent, lead emissions by 98 percent, and most other air pollutants by at least one-fifth to one-third, even as economic production and growth continued to increase; only nitrogen oxide emissions continued unabated (U.S. Council on Environmental Quality 1997, 179, 182). From 1980 to 1991 the pollution standards index (PSI) for major U.S. urban areas improved by 50 percent (Portney 1990, 44). Violations continued in some urban areas, particularly of ozone standards, but it was unlikely that the U.S. would ever again experience the severe air pollution emergencies that had occurred in earlier decades (fig. 18).

These reductions were not caused solely by the Clean Air Act. EPA data showed that ambient levels of particulates had already decreased by 22 percent in the 1960s, and of sulfur dioxide by 50 percent, primarily due to state and local controls on burning of garbage, coal, and high-sulfur fuel oil. Some analyses suggested that other factors — weather, industrial activity, and fuel choices, for instance — also played important roles. However, the extraordinary degree of improvement across nearly all pollutants during this period provided persuasive evidence of the Clean Air Act's importance, both in improving U.S. air quality and in preventing further degradation (Portney 1990, 50–52).

The law had serious limitations, however. In principle it required only that each facility achieve a specified emission-control performance goal, but in practice these goals were derived from particular technologies and were imposed on each individual pollution

Figure 18a–b. Air pollution, before and after federal regulation was implemented in the 1970s. The smoke-stack on the left shows dramatic evidence of the effectiveness of "end-of-pipe control technology" — in this case, an electrostatic precipitator removing over ninety percent of particulate emissions from an electric power plant. The photo on the right shows smoke pouring out of the stack before the precipitator was installed. [Photo courtesy of Con Ed, Chicago]

source, leaving firms with few real options for control methods. Second, it authorized rigorous control of new sources of air pollution but "grandfathered" existing ones. This eased its economic impact and political resistance to it, but created perverse incentives for firms to operate old, polluting factories longer. Third, its emphasis on "best current practice" control technologies accelerated the adoption of the best existing equipment, but also created a disincentive for developing more innovative technologies and more efficient production processes. Fourth, the control-technology approach removed substantial quantities of pollutants from the air, but in effect shifted them to water or land rather than reducing them: "end of pipe" technologies kept pollutants from being expelled into the air which then had to be put somewhere else. Finally, since the law's standards were intended to prevent direct harm to human health, compliance monitoring points were located immediately around the point sources themselves. However, this practice created an incentive simply to build higher stacks, dispersing air pollution over greater distances downwind. The result was to increase the long-range transport of air pollutants, which advocates assumed would be harmlessly dispersed but which instead increased downwind deposition of acid rain (de Nevers et al. 1977, 25–27, 33–35; Portney 1990, 38–39).

Perhaps the most fundamental deficiency was what the law did not do. It set ambient air quality standards, but did not set any overall limit or "cap" on emissions that would achieve these standards. Instead, it settled for mandating controls on new sources, augmented by state planning mandates to impose additional controls in polluted areas. Only a decade or more later would serious reductions in total emissions of some pollutants be mandated, first for lead (a near-total phaseout from auto emissions), and then, in the 1990 Clean Air Act, for sulfur (a cap significantly reducing emissions from coal-fired power plants).

Water quality, meanwhile, was already subject to state ambient standards based on the intended use of the water, though some of these standards were quite lax. The Federal Water Pollution Control Act Amendments of 1972 did not set national ambient standards for water quality, therefore, but instead declared sweeping national goals that all surface waters be "fishable and swimmable" by 1983 and receive "zero pollution discharge" by 1985.[14] In a major step beyond the Clean Air Act, it also required permits for *every* major discharger, not just new sources.[15] These permits in turn were to be based on technology-based performance standards, equivalent to the "best practicable" technology by 1977 and the "best available" control technology by 1983. The rationale, as in the case of air pollution, was that without clear technology-based requirements for pollution control, industry had too many opportunities to evade serious reduction of discharges (Quarles 1976, 149–52). The act also authorized EPA to set standards for "toxic water pollutants," similar to those for hazardous air pollutants under the Clean Air Act, and specifically allowed citizens to bring lawsuits to compel implementation.[16]

Unlike air pollution, significant amounts of wastewater discharges came from publicly owned municipal wastewater treatment plants. As a practical matter EPA could neither close these plants nor require local voters to approve bond issues to upgrade them, and local voters could not be counted on to support improvements since cleanup benefited downstream communities rather than themselves. The 1972 act therefore included a massive program of federal subsidies, $6 billion per year for three years, to provide 75 percent of the cost of constructing publicly owned wastewater treatment plants.

The construction grants program provided a leading example of a federally funded mandate, in which a federal regulatory mandate was accompanied by substantial federal subsidies to pay for its costs. By the 1990s this program had provided billions of dollars for municipal facilities, making it the largest federal public works program in history. Under legislation passed during the Reagan administration, however, the federal share was reduced to 55 percent, then ultimately converted to a state revolving loan fund beginning in 1987 and phased out in 1994. The rationale for this phaseout was that the federal government should not be paying costs of infrastructure investments that local governments and their taxpayers should pay themselves. In effect, a major federal mandate was gradually *de*funded, as one conservative principle was trumped by another (National Academy of Public Administration 1995, 106–07).

Like the Clean Air Act, the 1972 water pollution law produced major reductions in pollution from urban and industrial discharges. By 1982 an estimated 96 percent of industrial sources had installed the required control technology, reducing industrial water pollution from oxygen-demanding organic materials by an estimated 65 percent, from suspended solids by 80 percent, from dissolved solids by 52 percent, and from oil and grease discharges by 21 percent. Municipalities' compliance rates were substantially lower, but still greatly improved. A significant number of both cities and industries, however, reported substantial continuing noncompliance with the requirements of their operating permits. Sixteen percent of industries and almost one-third of cities reported "significant noncompliance," meaning periods during which their average discharges exceeded their permit restrictions by at least 50 percent for four months in a row (Portney 1990, 113). Actual changes in water quality included substantial improvements in some heavily polluted areas, but no significant progress in many others. Some streams were even getting measurably worse, mainly because "nonpoint sources"—farms, construction sites, and urban stormwater runoff—remained exempt from regulation. For these sources EPA was authorized only to develop nonenforceable voluntary guidelines for "best management practices" (Portney 1990, 120).[17]

Environmental Politics: the "Issue-Attention Cycle"

The environmental movement derived its initial power from the nationwide outpouring of grass-roots, bipartisan popular support, amplified and sustained by television and other mass-media publicity. It was similar in this respect to the civil rights and antiwar movements of the 1960s, as well as to nineteenth-century Populism, and distinctly different from the top-down leadership of Progressive and New Deal conservation. Such mass movements were powerful while they lasted, but were intrinsically harder to sustain than the efforts of smaller constituencies with direct economic interests at stake (Olson 1965). As early as 1971, political scientist Murray Edelman noted politicians' tendency to use symbolic actions to mollify mass public constituencies while continuing to allocate more tangible benefits to powerful economic interests (Edelman 1971).

Environmental policies were particularly vulnerable to this strategy. Political scientist Anthony Downs predicted that the environmental issue would not endure, but would follow a natural "issue-attention cycle" common to other public concerns: early attention by a few groups, then rising public awareness producing demands for action, then a cooling of support as boredom and the costs of solutions took their toll, and ultimately a shift of public attention to other issues, leaving the issue more institutionalized than it had been initially but far below its peak (Downs 1972).

The environmental protection issue had distinctive elements that strengthened it against this cycle. It touched deep American emotional values about natural beauty and distrust of big businesses, and it was easy to convey visually in the mass media. It also provided a common theme or "news peg" for many loosely related issues. Despite these advantages, however, it remained vulnerable due to its two core characteristics: at root, it sought protection for long-term, nonmarket values that were inevitably in conflict with short-term self-interests, and it required sustained support for collective action, rather than just individual choice, to achieve its goals. The public supported this agenda most strongly when its targets were wealthy corporations rather than individuals, and when they themselves felt economically comfortable rather than insecure.

Not surprisingly, business interests immediately and constantly sought opportunities to neutralize the momentum of environmental politics, to redirect the force of mass public opinion and regain their accustomed influence by relabeling the agenda in ways that served their purposes (Hays 1987, 422–26). News stories about environmental protection faced corporate press releases attacking "overregulation"; campaigns against big business were deflected into images of "big government"; proposals for public investments in environmental protection were vilified as "taxing and spending." Even within the literature of environmental economics, the initial emphasis on charging polluters the full environmental costs of their pollution — "internalizing the externalities" — subtly but steadily shifted to attacks on the business costs imposed by government regulations and the imperfections of government regulatory programs themselves. Such counterpressures surfaced repeatedly: during the energy crisis following the Arab oil embargo of 1973–74, the western Sagebrush Rebellion of the late 1970s, the antiregulatory campaign of the Reagan administration, the antigovernment diatribes of radio talk shows in the 1990s, and the "Contract with America" of conservative Republican congressional candidates in 1994.

The politics of environmental protection shifted rapidly and necessarily, therefore, from mass mobilization and demonstrations to interest-group representation and lobbying for tougher environmental laws, regulations, and enforcement. By 1971 almost seventy environmental advocacy organizations had established offices in Washington, creating both a political presence and continuing leadership for citizens concerned about environmental protection. The membership of these organizations also grew dramatically: the Sierra Club from 48,000 in the 1960s to over 130,000 in 1971, the National Audubon Society from under 80,000 to 148,000, and others by similar proportions (Bosso 1987, 146). Overall, membership in environmental groups grew from an estimated 500,000 to 2.5 million over the fifteen-year period beginning around 1970 (Futrell 1993, 43).

The intense but short-term influence of mass public protest, in short, was channeled into longer-term representation by environmental interest groups, which in turn hired permanent staffs to research and publicize issues, lobby for tougher legislation, monitor and challenge the administrative agencies, and mobilize new public protests against proposals that posed egregious threats to the environment. Environmental protection interests became for the first time an ongoing and influential interest-group presence and lobbying alliance in national policy-making.

EPA staff, meanwhile, spent most of their first half-decade in a crash effort to finalize national ambient air quality standards, write technology-based requirements for pollution control in each major industry, and approve the permit applications they required. This was a monumental administrative task, eased only by the agency's decentralized regional structure.

Even as EPA's air and water pollution programs began to take effect, however, two developments in 1973–74 revealed the political vulnerability of its dependence on general public support and the mass media. One was the 1974 oil embargo by the Organization of Arab Petroleum Exporting Countries, which suddenly interrupted U.S. fuel supplies and aroused widespread public fears of shortages, inflation, and economic instability. This crisis quickly supplanted environmental headlines in the mass media, and some industries immediately exploited it to seek waivers of environmental regulations and shift policy priorities back toward natural resource extraction and industrial production.[18]

The second issue was a political backlash against EPA air pollution control proposals aimed at automobile use. Urban commuting was a major source of air pollution, and EPA therefore proposed both regulations and economic incentives to reduce commuting and parking in polluted urban areas. Requiring big auto companies to produce low-pollution vehicles had widespread support, but restricting the use of motor vehicles challenged the everyday choices of ordinary people, whom the automotive and highway-construction lobbies skillfully mobilized in a campaign to defend the "freedom to drive."[19] The House Appropriations Committee responded by eliminating EPA funds for urban transportation planning. Both these events eroded EPA's political support, and created the risk of a political climate in which the momentum of the agency's initiatives could be slowed down, deadlines stretched out, and regulations bogged down in endless negotiation (U.S. EPA 1993a, 20–24).

Accountability by Lawsuit

If constant mass public support and media attention could not be counted on, how could environmental protection avoid the fate of other public policy issues, in which the agencies charged with implementing them were inexorably co-opted by powerful economic interests? EPA's statutes were written in a period not of Progressive idealism about expert administrative agencies, but of deepening public distrust toward agencies' use of their administrative discretion (Lazarus 1991). Some advocates for environmental protection feared policy capture by the regulated industries; others, by the self-interests of the agency's own staff members, who might ultimately bargain away environmental values in comfortable compromises rather than sustain thankless confrontation against powerful adversaries. Many feared, with justification, that Congress's own commitment to environmental statutes was merely symbolic: many members were simply "voting with the chorus" for images such as safe drinking water, but were not committed to the restrictive regulation or public expenditures that were authorized by the laws and necessary to their achievement. Industries, meanwhile, feared that the agency would be captured by the opposite forces, becoming a "runaway bureaucracy" of environmental zealots.

One answer was to limit EPA's discretion by statute. From the 1970 Clean Air Act on, Congress set specific tasks for the agency, directing it to write detailed standards by specific deadlines, and in a few cases (automotive emission reductions, for instance) even specifying the standards themselves. By 1989, environmental statutes and court decisions had imposed over eight hundred specific regulatory deadlines, 86 percent of them aimed at EPA itself rather than at regulated industries. One-third of these required action in six months or less, and 60 percent in one year or less. These demands and deadlines, however, proved impossible for the agency to fulfill: by 1991 it had met only 14 percent of its deadlines. This failure triggered a self-reinforcing cycle of distrust. Rigid deadlines combined with underfunding of the agency produced unachievable demands. EPA therefore failed to fulfill them, environmental groups attacked these failures and demanded stricter deadlines and more funding, Congress attacked EPA to deflect attention from its own underfunding and wrote stricter deadlines, and further cycles of distrust and even more rigid mandates followed (Lazarus 1991).

A second answer was a profound change in administrative procedure: the opening of regulatory processes to broader public participation and legal challenges. Traditionally, such processes were limited primarily to the regulated parties: the agency itself was presumed to represent the "public interest" of the citizenry. Several effective environmental lawsuits in the late 1960s, however — the *Storm King* case against the Federal Power Commission and the Environmental Defense Fund lawsuits against DDT spraying — had undermined this Progressive idea, and revealed the inherent tendency toward agency capture by the interests with which they interacted most closely. A series of environmental law groups rapidly emerged — chief among them EDF, the Natural Resources Defense Council (1970), and legal defense fund arms of other groups such as the Sierra Club — which were distinctive in that their primary strategy was to use test-case litigation, rather than traditional legislative lobbying or participation in public hearings, to force administrative implementation of the environmental laws.[20] Most were funded not by mass memberships but by philanthropies such as the Ford Foundation, which remain among the most important yet under-recognized forces behind the modern American environmental movement.[21]

In an influential book in 1971, law professor Joseph Sax argued for a more fundamental innovation. First, he argued, the citizens' right to a clean environment is a "public trust," equally important as private property rights. Second, since administrative agencies often failed to represent the broad public interest, and negotiated compromises instead with the interests with which they interacted, citizen groups should therefore be able to represent their own views of the public trust, both in administrative proceedings and before the court. They should be able to act, that is, as "private attorneys-general," to demand that the agencies implement the public interest as expressed in the environmental protection laws. Third, for the same reason, the courts should drop their traditional deference to administrative agencies and ask hard questions as to whether the agencies' decisions have a well-justified relationship to the broad public interest. If they disagree, they should halt the agency's action and *remand* it either to the agency or to Congress for reconsideration. In short, the courts should serve as an open forum for citizen participation in democratic processes, and as an independent check on whether agencies' decisions really are in the broad public interest.

Other environmental advocates quickly endorsed Sax's proposals, and influential congressmen adopted them, adding citizen-suit provisions to the 1972 Clean Water Act amendments and many of EPA's subsequent statutes.[22] Under citizen-suit provisions of the four major environmental regulatory laws, if the agency did not diligently prosecute a violator, any person could bring a private citizen enforcement lawsuit.[23] Citizens also could sue the EPA regulatory officials themselves, to compel them to carry out "nondiscretionary duties" such as setting standards, issuing regulations, determining compliance, and making findings concerning violations. The key innovation in these provisions was that citizens could now sue on behalf of the community at large, as "private attorneys-general," not merely as individuals to recover for economic damage to themselves (Gauna 1995, 40–45, 69–77).[24]

By the mid-1970s, environmental advocacy groups had developed a substantial professional capacity to use these tools effectively. A 1971 lawsuit by EDF, for instance, forced EPA to hold public hearings on whether or not to ban DDT. A series of lawsuits by the Natural Resources Defense Council in 1973 and 1974 attacked EPA for failing to write standards for control of toxic water pollutants; it was settled in the 1976 "Flannery decree," in which EPA consented to a court-ordered deadline for writing standards for some sixty-five pollutants. EPA then used this commitment as a justification for requesting additional appropriations from Congress to fulfill it.

The professionalization of these environmental law groups, along with other national environmental lobby groups, thus created the more enduring organized constituencies that EPA needed to sustain it through diminished mass public or media support. Their access to the courts, moreover, provided an effective new counterweight to the economic power of the polluters as well as the agency's own tendencies toward self-protective inertia (Berry 1984). In a very real sense, the courts thus provided the "gorilla in the closet" that EPA itself needed—just as the states needed EPA—as a scapegoat responsible for its efforts to regulate powerful polluters.

One of the most distinctive features of modern U.S. environmental protection policy, accordingly, is the unprecedentedly broad right of access to the regulatory process, which extends not only to affected businesses but to citizens advocating environmental protection. The granting of this access represented a sharp break with the Progressive philosophy that had guided U.S. governance through most of the first half of the twentieth century, which had accorded strong deference to expert public administrators acting in the name of the overall public interest. It was an equally clear departure from traditional court doctrines that had limited challengers to plaintiffs demonstrating clear individual economic injury from government actions. Taken together, these changes amounted to a profound shift in the process of U.S. governance, democratizing the administrative and regulatory processes as a counterweight to economic vested interests but at the same time politicizing them.

The result was a far more intensely politicized and adversarial process for environmental decision-making, in which the ultimate arbiter was the courts. Many of EPA's major regulations were ultimately challenged in the courts, some in lengthy and repeated proceedings, and EPA's perception of what the courts would approve thus became a primary influence on its regulatory programs (Lazarus 1991, Andrews 1993b).[25] Contrary to industry propaganda that environmentalists were "clogging the courts" with lawsuits, the proportion of these challenges that were initiated by environmental groups was actually relatively small: the majority by far were brought by the regulated industries themselves, resisting proposed new regulations (Hays 1987, 480–81). For all its limitations, however, this new approach did achieve precisely what its advocates had hoped for, something no previous policy had produced: a continuing and legally protected voice in environmental policy-making for advocates of environmental protection rather than merely self-interested environmental use.

Regulating Toxic Chemicals: Public Health or Chemophobia?

Events of the mid-1970s, meanwhile, galvanized general public concern about environmental quality once again, but redirected its focus from air and water pollution to the insidious and seemingly pervasive hazards of toxic chemicals. Fear of chemical hazards was not new — it had been increasing since the pesticide-spraying controversies of the 1950s — but it grew into a major public concern as it was linked to the fear of cancer. President Nixon declared a "war on cancer" as a policy initiative in 1971 (Rushefsky 1986, 71–72), and a 1971 report by the president's Council on Environmental Quality identified toxic industrial chemicals as a possible cause of it (U.S. Council on Environmental Quality 1971; Gottlieb 1995, 59). The Environmental Defense Fund in 1971 won a court decision ordering EPA to ban DDT and other persistent pesticides, and beginning in 1973 the Natural Resources Defense Council sued EPA repeatedly to force it to set standards for toxic water pollutants. Meanwhile, polychlorinated biphenyls (PCBs), which were widely used as lubricants in electrical transformers, were discovered in fish as a result of past dumping into harbors, mercury residues were detected in swordfish, and a steady diet of similar news stories stirred public concern about unwitting exposures to toxic contaminants. In July 1976 a disastrous industrial contamination accident occurred in Seveso, Italy, contaminating an entire town with the highest concentrations of dioxin to which humans had ever been exposed.

These stories converged into a potent new version of the environmental issue: industrial pollution and pesticides threatened not just the beauty and "birds and bunnies" of nature, but human health directly.[26] This new health-driven round of environmental politics produced three statutes in the mid-1970s, broadening EPA's responsibility from emissions of air and water pollutants to man-made chemical hazards as a whole: the Federal Environmental Pesticide Control Act (1972), Safe Drinking Water Act (1974), and Toxic Substances Control Act (1976).

Pesticides had been regulated in the United States since the 1906 Pure Food and Drug Act and the 1910 Federal Insecticide Act, but these laws regulated only food adulteration: their goal was simply "truth in labeling," to protect the reputations of farmers and drug producers from adulteration or misbranding of products. Pesticide residues on food were a long-recognized concern, but one that was effectively suppressed from public view until the 1950s by the Agriculture Department and its congressional patrons lest it reduce public confidence in the safety of their food (Bosso 1987, 47–53).[27] The Federal Insecticide, Fungicide, and Rodenticide Act of 1947 added a requirement that manufacturers register all new pesticide products — the country was then in the midst of the postwar proliferation of new synthetic organic pesticides — but it remained simply a labeling law, which provided no mechanism to control pesticide use and no authority to remove dangerous pesticides from the market. It was administered by the Department of Agriculture, which before 1967 initiated criminal proceedings only twice in two decades, investigated less than sixty out of an estimated fifty thousand pesticide accidents per year, and until 1969 never even set up procedures which the 1947 act had authorized to recall unsafe pesticides (Bosso 1987, 53–59; Wellford 1972, 159, 149; Benbrook 1996, 91). The Food and Drug Administration began setting explicit tolerance levels for pesticide residues on food in 1954, and the 1958 Delaney Amendment, the "cranberry scare," and *Silent Spring* focused increased public attention on pesticide risks, but no significant new regulation of them resulted until 1972.

The Federal Environmental Pesticides Control Act of 1972 (FEPCA) substantially rewrote U.S. pesticide law, but with far more limited powers than the Clean Air and Water Act. Pesticides were now regulated by the EPA, not the Agriculture Department, and they could be used only for specifically approved uses. These approved uses could be canceled if they proved to have "unreasonable adverse effects" on the environment. However, FEPCA was fundamentally a *risk-balancing* statute, unlike the Clean Air Act, which set ambient air standards on the basis of health protection alone. EPA had to weigh the environmental and health risks against the economic benefits of agricultural production, and even repay the manufacturers and users for any stocks left unsold if a product was deregistered.[28] Only "affected parties" could bring challenges in the courts: citizen public-interest lawsuits were not allowed. Perhaps most problematic of all, FEPCA granted registered status at the outset to all pesticides sold commercially before 1970, "grand-fathering" them until EPA reviewed them. Industry thus bore the burden of proof for justifying new pesticides, even if they might be far safer than existing ones, while EPA bore the burden for banning existing ones: new pesticides were guilty until proven innocent, while old ones were innocent until proven guilty (Benbrook 1996, 93).

The Safe Drinking Water Act directed EPA to set health-based standards for minimum contaminant levels in public water supplies, and to require local water utilities both to monitor for them and to install EPA-approved technology to control them. Finally, the Toxic Substances Control Act (TSCA) was intended to forestall new hazards before a firm had invested heavily in their production. It required testing and premanufacturing notification to EPA of all new chemical substances, and allowed EPA to restrict use of any chemical that posed "unreasonable risks" (risk balancing). It also allowed emergency action against "imminent hazards," and required a phaseout of PCB use. The act thus appeared at face value to be a potent new policy tool, but in practice it was one of the least effective EPA programs.[29]

Even as EPA was still struggling to finish permitting air emissions and wastewater discharges, these new mandates forced it to develop the extensive information and methodologies necessary to regulate thousands of individual pesticides and toxic chemicals, substance by substance and use by use (Wargo 1996). For pesticides, for instance, EPA faced a 1974 deadline to produce uniform, comprehensive, guidelines for registration and classification, and a 1976 deadline to retroactively reregister some fifty thousand existing products and uses under its new guidelines for "unreasonable risk."

For most of these, however, systematic and up-to-date test data did not even exist. Of necessity EPA took on faith whatever industry data existed, only to discover several years later that a firm which had tested some two hundred of these products for registration had criminally falsified its data. In 1975 EPA set up an informal "rebuttable presumption against registration" procedure to negotiate problem chemicals with their producers, but this produced unmanageable quantities of data to evaluate for only some forty-five chemicals, and angered environmentalists who were excluded from these informal proceedings. In effect, these "science wars" inherently favored the producers of existing chemicals, who could tie up EPA's analytical process for years, both for canceling old compounds and for registering new ones, while continuing to market and profit from their existing products (Benbrook 1996, 94).

To maintain the agency's image of credibility, meanwhile, EPA Administrator Russell Train began cancellation proceedings against several high-visibility compounds, including persistent organochlorines such as aldrin and chlordane, and later Mirex (the fire-ant poison) and the herbicide 2,4,5-T ("Agent Orange"). These decisions in turn inflamed farm-state congressmen, causing exhausting and virtually continuous political battles as Congress refused to reauthorize the Pesticides Control Act for more than a year at a time (Bosso 1987, 184–206). By the mid- to late 1970s, both pesticide regulation and the other substance-by-substance regulatory programs were mired in unwinnable battles, over both individual compounds and support for the overall programs themselves.

Sadly, none of these battles even addressed the more fundamental issue of the actual use, misuse, and overuse of pesticides in day-to-day farming, golf course maintenance, lawn care, and other applications where changes in actual practices might have made far more difference for environmental and health consequences (Hornstein 1993). The Safe Drinking Water and Toxic Substances Control Acts were no better: both imposed similar burdens of generating and sifting huge quantities of scientific data and inferences, based on varying and uncertain evidence, for thousands of compounds and an almost unlimited range of possible effects.

To try to break these stalemates, EPA administrators took the first steps toward a generic approach to chemical regulation, based on quantitative health risk assessments. Douglas Costle, EPA administrator in the Carter Administration, went further. In frequent statements he argued that the Toxic Substances Control Act made EPA explicitly a public-health agency as well as an environmental agency (Walsh 1978, 598). Costle saw public health as a more compelling political argument than ecology: he urged leaving ecological issues to the Interior Department and focusing EPA more explicitly on health. He succeeded with this strategy in obtaining a 25 percent budget increase in 1979 to implement the drinking water, toxic substances, and hazardous waste acts (Landy et al. 1994, 41). In the process, however, he gambled the agency's future on the importance of toxic chemicals as public health hazards, a presumption for which the evidence was not yet well developed.

In short, substance-by-substance regulatory statutes placed EPA in a no-win situation, in which its agenda was dictated by ad hoc external challenges rather than by systematic priorities. They appeared to allow EPA to regulate virtually any chemical that might cause unreasonable risks to human health, but in practice they were unworkable. Instead of dealing with mere hundreds of firms applying for air and water permits and using known technologies, EPA now was responsible for decisions involving tens of thousands of potentially hazardous substances, all of them commercially valuable rather than mere wastes. It had to bear the burden of proof for regulating them, which required scientific evidence that often did not exist, and for balancing their risks against their economic values. It therefore lived in constant threat of public embarrassment—from "chemical of the week" horror stories in the mass media, such as the 1975 Kepone spill into Virginia's James River, which poisoned workers and caused massive fish kills (Bosso 1987, 198–99)—and of costly and time-consuming litigation, either from chemical producers and users with large economic interests at stake or from environmental groups which could invoke public fear of health hazards. The agency also lived with constant congressional battles over whether the statutes would even be continued, let alone funded, and if so whether Congress would enact a "legislative veto" clause allowing itself to overrule any EPA decision that was unpopular with influential legislators.

Successive EPA administrators responded by introducing quantitative risk assessment procedures as a basis for justifying regulations and setting priorities, but in practice these programs were among the agency's least effective, requiring heavy investments in research and analysis but producing regulations for only a handful of substances. The *appearance* of such extensive regulatory powers, meanwhile, provided a new opportunity for opponents to shift public attention from "big business" polluters to "big government" regulators, and to redefine the political agenda from environmental protection to "overregulation."

Waste Management: Disposal Versus Reduction

The Clean Air and Clean Water Acts regulated two of the three forms of waste disposal, but solid waste management had always seemed the most distinctively local of responsibilities. Since the turn of the century, most municipalities had managed the disposal of household garbage as a sanitation responsibility, either directly or through private contractors. Major businesses, industries, and rural residents had handled their own disposal, either themselves or through commercial haulers. The resulting practices were cheap and casual. Many coastal cities simply dumped their garbage in the ocean; most others hauled it to open-burning, unlined dumps on the cheapest and most convenient land available,

Figure 19. An open municipal dump burning in West Redding, California, December 1965; note the disposal of automobile tires along with other municipal wastes. This was a common practice to reduce the volume of municipal wastes until U.S. EPA regulations in the 1970s banned open dump burning, required segregation of industrial and other special wastes such as tires in special facilities, and mandated far safer sanitary landfills or incinerators for municipal waste disposal. [Courtesy of the *Redding Record-Searchlight*]

which often included wetlands (fig. 19). The most conscientious built "sanitary landfills," where they reduced air pollution and sanitation hazards by covering the wastes daily, but these still lacked any barriers against seepage into groundwater. Industrial wastes, including barrels of toxic liquids as well as ordinary trash, were commonly dumped into these same sites. Otherwise they were simply discarded on private lands, usually into unlined pits, lagoons, or open dumps, without any public oversight or regulation. Ironically, these practices were exacerbated by the new air and water pollution regulations: end-of-pipe control technologies extracted pollutants that would otherwise have been discharged into the air or water, creating larger quantities of noxious wastes — wastewater sludges, combustion ash, and their contaminants — to be discarded on land (Tarr 1985a, 1985b).

The Resource Recovery Act of 1970 authorized increased federal funding for waste recovery and recycling programs, but otherwise left waste management practices undisturbed. In June 1971, however, EPA Administrator Ruckelshaus initiated one of the most sweeping but least noted environmental success stories of the 1970s, a "Mission 5000" to close five thousand of the estimated fourteen thousand open dumps within one year. The 1972 deadline was not met (Schaeffer 1972, 241–56), but by the late 1970s virtually all open dumps had been closed and consolidated into sanitary landfills, which were subjected to far more stringent construction and operating standards.

In 1976 Congress proposed a law to provide economic incentives for recycling and recovery of waste materials: the Resource Conservation and Recovery Act of 1976 (RCRA). This purpose was overshadowed, however, by reports of accidental spills and deliberate "midnight dumping" of industrial wastes in rivers and rural areas. In 1975, dangerously high levels of PCBs were discovered in the Hudson River and other waterways, and the Kepone pesticide waste spill in Virginia amplified these concerns (Nader et al. 1981, 172–73; Regenstein 1982, 231–33). Congress therefore added a new section to the RCRA bill to regulate hazardous industrial wastes: that is, those that were either highly flammable, reactive, corrosive, or toxic, or were specifically listed by EPA for other reasons. Henceforth industries had to treat, store, or dispose of these wastes only in EPA-approved facilities, and EPA would issue technology-based standards for construction and operation of these facilities.[30] All firms that generated large quantities of these wastes had to keep records of them, including "cradle-to-grave manifests" documenting all off-site shipments. A final section of the bill directed EPA to set standards for municipal landfills as well, less stringent than those for hazardous wastes but far more rigorous than past practices.

RCRA required safer practices in current waste disposal, but did not deal with the effects of past dumping, though leachate from such dumping might continue for decades to seep slowly through the soil into downstream wells and water supplies. In the late 1970s public fears and outrage ignited yet another round of environmental policies, as discoveries of severely contaminated waste sites — the Velsicol Company's wastes in the Hardeman County Landfill in Tennessee, the Love Canal dump in Niagara Falls, New York, the "Valley of the Drums" in Kentucky, California's Stringfellow Pits, and others — revealed a widespread toxic legacy of past disposal practices (Nader et al. 1981; Epstein et al. 1982; Regenstein 1982). These events catalyzed a new network of grass-roots environmental advocacy groups, far more blue-collar and often more racially diverse than the national environmental groups, whose goals were to remove hazards in specific communities and resist the siting of new ones. Critics sneered at the groups as mere parochial protectors of their own self-interests ("NIMBY," or "not in my back yard"); they themselves, however, claimed to speak for a more general public interest, that toxic-waste landfills and other hazardous facilities should not be sited in *anyone*'s backyard. From these groups also came, in the 1980s, a new demand for environmental *justice:* an end to the disproportionate burden of environmental impacts on racial and ethnic minorities and poor communities.

In response, Congress in 1980 enacted the Comprehensive Environmental Response, Compensation, and Liability Act (CERCLA) to provide for cleanup of past dump sites. CERCLA authorized EPA to identify all contaminated sites, assess their risks, develop a "National Priority List" of the most dangerous of them, and take emergency action to control immediate hazards. It also asserted that everyone who had used these sites was jointly and individually liable for the costs of cleanup and damage: that is, that any one of them could be held responsible for the entire cleanup cost without regard to their degree of fault. Finally, CERCLA established a multibillion-dollar federal trust fund — a "Superfund" — to pay for emergency measures as well as cleanup of sites for which responsible parties could not be identified. The fund was financed by special taxes on the chemical industry as well as general revenues.

The Resource Conservation and Recovery Act transformed U.S. waste management practices. Within half a decade, it virtually ended the practice of ocean dumping and open burning of wastes. It ended the commingling of industrial chemicals in municipal landfills and the uncontrolled dumping of industrial chemicals in general, and it led to the closing of thousands of substandard disposal sites. As safer sites and practices replaced them, waste management became rapidly and dramatically safer. The increased cost of safe landfilling and incineration in turn fueled dramatic growth in recycling and waste reduction, adding new incentives for more efficient use of materials and stabilizing markets for capital investment in recycling facilities.

CERCLA too had powerful effects. Within a decade, EPA had used its authority for emergency actions to contain the risks at thousands of sites, leaving none that posed immediate threats to public health (de Saillan 1993). Its threat of joint and several liability created a powerful incentive for safe management of future wastes, or even substitution of nonhazardous materials, which stimulated industrial initiatives for hazardous waste minimization. It revolutionized real estate law with its new principle of environmental liability, and effectively stopped any future proliferation of new contaminated sites.

CERCLA's positive effects, however, were overshadowed by arguments over its longer-term cleanup program: how much cleanup was ultimately required ("how clean is clean?"), who should pay for it, and whether the program was worth its cost. Its liability provisions created a legal tangle of counterclaims among the many parties who had used contaminated sites: industries and cities, hauling companies, their banks and insurers, and even innocent later owners of the sites. Potentially responsible parties sued each other to force wider sharing of the costs and sued EPA to reduce their liability, claiming it was using costlier cleanup measures than necessary. Neighborhood and environmental groups in turn sued EPA for not cleaning up thoroughly enough. Critics attacked the program for spending too much money on studies rather than cleanup, for running up high legal costs to determine liability, for cleaning up few sites, and for demanding years of costly measures to clean sites up to pristine standards rather than to levels safe for industrial redevelopment.[31] By the 1990s, many cities were demanding more flexible cleanup standards to permit "brownfields" redevelopment: that is, industrial redevelopment of contaminated urban sites in preference to "greenfield" locations in suburbs and rural areas.

All in all, however, the transformation of waste management practices was one of the most impressive yet least noted successes of American environmental policy in the 1970s.

Environmental Federalism: EPA and the States

The core common element of nearly all the federal environmental policies of the 1970s was the assertion of national minimum standards and program requirements for environmental protection. At face value this represented a radical expansion of federal authority to regulate both the behavior of businesses and individuals within the states and the behavior of the states themselves. State governments were the delegated implementers and enforcers of federal environmental regulations, as well as in some cases the targets of them: they had to clean up their own pollution as well.

Despite primary federal regulatory authority for pollution control, however, the realities of implementation required close cooperation between EPA and the states. EPA never had the staff, budget, or state-by-state expertise it would have needed to implement the statutes by itself. In air pollution, EPA set the national ambient and emission standards, but the states then had to develop implementation plans to achieve them, subject to EPA approval. Once approved, the states were delegated authority for implementation, permitting, and enforcement, but EPA would subsidize operation of these programs. Similar interactions occurred in water, waste management, and other programs, with some variations such as major federal construction grants for wastewater treatment plants and Superfund subsidies for cleanup of hazardous waste sites. In short, much of federal environmental regulation was in fact a matter of intergovernmental relations, not direct federal regulation, and it functioned only to the extent that there was an effective social contract and cooperative relationship between EPA and the states.

Prompted by federal mandates and subsidies, therefore, and in varying degrees by their own political constituencies, the states and some local governments developed environmental regulatory agencies, programs, and technical expertise of their own, both to carry out the federal mandates and in some cases to go further with initiatives of their own. On many environmental issues, especially those involving land-use controls, local governments remained strongly influenced by development interests, though these did often include image-conscious "boosters" sensitive to their city's environmental attractiveness. Also, many remained resistant to regulations requiring enforcement at their expense or costly cleanup of their own municipal facilities (such as sewage treatment plants and landfills). Many state governments were similarly influenced by powerful businesses and industries, which used state legislation to preempt stronger local environmental protection laws. By 1980, however, most states had developed far greater environmental expertise and regulatory capacity than they had had before 1970, and some even created environmental "superagencies" consolidating environmental management and regulatory programs (Hays 1987, 432–35).

With this capacity, however, a new degree of ambivalence emerged in their relationships with EPA. Still dependent on EPA for subsidies and specialized research to support standards, and as a "gorilla in the closet" to blame in confronting influential polluters, they nonetheless chafed at the rigidity of EPA's requirements and began to press for greater autonomy. The best of them created environmental policy innovations that went beyond federal reforms: early examples included California's air standards and emission-trading programs. Others, however, sought flexibility to ease the burden on influential industries, and still others passed laws explicitly limiting their environmental regulations to the federal minimum. All served as the primary environmental policymakers in the many areas of environmental policy not covered by federal laws, and as their capacity increased, more and more began to assert that they understood their state's environmental conditions and priorities better than EPA did (Ringquist 1993, Rabe 1996).

Regulatory Reform Initiatives

The proliferation of federal regulation in the 1970s signaled a new willingness to use federal authority to achieve social purposes, an extraordinary shift from traditional American hostility toward "big government" and "bureaucrats." From the perspective of the regulated industries, however, the rapid growth of regulation not only imposed costs to remedy past practices, but created new problems as well. Some regulations set what industries regarded as unrealistic goals and compliance deadlines, and costly margins of safety. Others were frustratingly rigid, preventing businesses from using cheaper means even to achieve accepted ends. All added to the cost of administrative paperwork. Even from an environmental perspective, the lack of coordination among environmental mandates created a kind of "shell game," in which pollutants controlled in one medium simply transferred by default to another.

Perhaps most important, the burden of regulation was increasingly unpredictable. Statutes were enacted at different times, and imposed different standards and criteria, yet each required compliance by many of the same major industrial facilities and processes, so that new regulations might easily negate expensive investments to comply with previous ones. The result was a patchwork of complex but separate regulations, lacking any single framework for setting priorities or developing integrated solutions. As former EPA Deputy Administrator John Quarles testified in 1982, "Despite success, essential soundness, and continuing political support, the federal environmental regulatory programs are beset with serious problems. . . . The chief weaknesses of EPA's regulatory programs are that they are (a) unmanageably and unnecessarily complicated, (b) unrealistically idealistic and overly ambitious, (c) in some instances, not cost-effective, and (d) in their cumulative administrative impact, totally beyond the institutional capacity of the federal, state, and local regulatory agencies responsible for their implementation" (quoted in Andrews 1984a, note 4).

Each of the presidents in the 1970s recognized these problems early on, and tried with varying motives to address them administratively. Some sought to increase White House political control over EPA regulatory proposals: President Nixon established a National Industrial Pollution Control Council under the Commerce Department, through which industrial members could review EPA's regulations before they were publicly proposed ("quality of life reviews").[32] President Ford required "inflation impact statements" for all major regulatory proposals, to be reviewed by his Council on Wage and Price Stability. President Carter broadened these to "regulatory impact analyses," and created a White House-level Regulatory Analysis Review Group to critique both the quality of the analyses and the economic effectiveness of the regulatory proposals themselves.

Each of these oversight initiatives at best created a process for reviewing and debating regulatory justifications, but provided no mechanism to change the priorities or to reform the rigidities of the statutes themselves. More troubling, they created a problematic form of executive oversight, aimed at micromanaging particular regulatory decisions rather than guiding overall policies and priorities. Such oversight risked corrupting the regulatory process with covert political influence on particular decisions, and thus undermining its legitimacy (Percival 1991). Some of these mechanisms were in fact transparently intended to accommodate powerful political constituencies and to rein in the independence of EPA administrators.

A more substantive series of reforms came from within EPA, in experimental initiatives to ease rigid pollution control requirements. The Clean Air Act, for instance, at face value required expensive control technology on every vent and stack at facilities in nonattainment areas, and could have prohibited any new industry from locating in such areas until pollution was reduced to within the standards. Clearly, however, EPA could not shut down the economy of the Los Angeles basin and other urban areas, so it developed policy innovations to accommodate economic realities. Through a creative interpretation of the Clean Air Act, for instance, it allowed new industries to locate in nonattainment areas if they acquired "offsets," purchasing emissions rights from companies whose emissions were greater than those the new plant would create, thereby reducing existing levels. This policy permitted trading of emissions rights among firms in regional airsheds, including even "banking" of pollution rights from overcontrol to sell to later users. Amendments to the Clean Air Act in 1977 endorsed this policy, and an elaboration in 1979 — the "bubble" policy — encouraged businesses to produce excess "emission reduction credits" which could be traded and averaged with other sources that needed such credits, as though they were all enclosed under one "bubble" with the same net reduction of pollution (Liroff 1986).

Finally, a third set of reforms sought to coordinate regulatory requirements and streamline their burdens. During the Carter administration, the administrators of the four major regulatory agencies (EPA, the Food and Drug Administration, Occupational Safety and Health Administration, and Consumer Product Safety Commission) formed an

Interagency Regulatory Liaison Group to coordinate regulatory requirements affecting common industries and substances. President Carter subsequently created a broader U.S. Regulatory Council, chaired by the EPA administrator, to coordinate regulatory programs and eliminate duplication and gaps. The Regulatory Council also produced a semiannual calendar of regulations in progress, and developed common policies for cross-cutting issues such as regulation of chemical carcinogens (Landy et al. 1994, 172–203). The 1980 Paperwork Reduction Act also increased the power of the Office of Management and Budget to limit paperwork requirements generated by agency regulations.

Despite these initiatives, however, the cumulative total of regulations kept growing. As it did so, business interests mobilized to redefine the political agenda from protection of health and environment to relief from the burden of regulation itself. By 1980 a decade had passed since the passing of the Clean Air Act, and the time was ripe for such reassessments. Some were already scheduled, such as reauthorization of the Clean Air and Water Acts, and Congress also was debating general regulatory reform legislation. Regardless of who won the 1980 election, therefore, reform of regulatory policy was ripe for serious consideration.[33]

Summary

The creation of a national regulatory framework for pollution control was an extraordinary new element in American environmental policy, as was the empowerment of citizen groups to intervene as its advocates in administrative proceedings and litigation. Together, these new policies produced an unprecedented outpouring of federal environmental regulations to protect air, water, and drinking water quality, to control pollution and toxic chemicals, and to ensure safe waste management.

Most of these policies were remarkably successful in achieving what they were designed to achieve. Later commentators often spoke contemptuously of technology-based regulations as "command and control" and "one size fits all" measures, but in fact they were understandable, enforceable, and did in fact force laggard firms to install best-practice control technologies. Industrial and municipal emissions to both air and water dropped significantly, as did wastewater discharges, and air quality became measurably cleaner for most pollutants. Automobile emissions dropped dramatically, and airborne lead emissions most dramatically of all. Waste dumps were closed and replaced by far safer disposal facilities, and both waste management and recycling were transformed into professional and profitable business.

These policies were not as fully successful, however, in achieving systematic or lasting solutions to the problems they addressed. Auto emissions per vehicle dropped, but the number of vehicles and of miles traveled continued to increase, offsetting the benefits of improved design: controlling vehicle use was far less accepted than improving their design. Industrial air pollution dropped, but the cumulative contributions of innumerable smaller sources continued to rise. Municipal and industrial wastes were reduced, but stream waste quality did not improve proportionally: much of this pollution was from agriculture and other nonpoint sources, which the statutes were designed by Congress not to control. Some of the control strategies, moreover, simply displaced problems: tall stacks reduced local smoke but transported pollutants further downwind as acid rain, and end-of-pipe control technologies created ash and sludge wastes that then had to be managed on land rather than in air or water.

With few exceptions — leaded gasoline, PCBs, and a very few pesticides — none of these policies were designed to systematically reduce the actual production and use of serious pollutants. Nor were they designed to manage more pervasive causal factors in human behavior patterns and economic activity, such as the continuing urbanization of the landscape and its ecosystems and the increasing use of energy and materials per capita. Not surprisingly, therefore, by and large they failed to do so. They also imposed substantial administrative costs both on industries and on governments themselves, and their emphasis on uniform adoption of enforceable existing technologies created inadvertent barriers to more innovative and efficient solutions that might have reduced pollutants from production processes entirely.

The least effective regulatory programs, ironically, were not the technology-based air and water permitting programs, but the risk-based, substance-by-substance statutes regulating pesticides and toxic chemicals. These statutes placed an unworkable burden of analysis and proof on the EPA, and subjected it to unceasing wars of attrition in both Congress and the courts, with the result that only a handful of substances — out of tens of thousands of candidate compounds — were even fully evaluated, let alone regulated. Arguably, some of these laws were even misdirected to begin with. *Silent Spring* had warned of the impacts of indiscriminate and excessive pesticide use, yet these regulatory programs did not even address use rates, let alone create incentives to reduce them. Pesticide use actually increased by 170 percent from 1964 to 1982 (Hornstein 1993, 392–93). Substance-by-substance regulations were gradually marginalized into endless arguments over what was "good science," rather than what actions would reduce the use of hazardous substances and consequent environmental and health impacts: Under the Toxic Substances Control Act, for instance, by 1994 EPA had issued regulations to control only nine chemicals out of an estimated seventy thousand in general use (U.S. General Accounting Office 1994, 3).

National pollution-control regulation under the new U.S. model was in effect a far-reaching policy experiment, whose first decade left several major governance issues unresolved and in continuing flux. One was the effectiveness and side effects of the regulatory programs themselves, as discussed above. A second was the efficacy of politicized administrative proceedings and citizen litigation as safeguards against business intransigence and bureaucratic inertia. The politics of regulation arguably required such safeguards for effectiveness, and the record shows overwhelming evidence of the roles such citizen pressures played in forcing far more extensive implementation and compliance than would otherwise have occurred. It was nonetheless a blunt and limited weapon, which imposed high costs and delays on all parties. It was far more effective in stopping bad decisions than in rewarding or encouraging good ones. Its fundamentally adversarial approach, moreover, was immensely successful in leveling the playing field — giving environmental advocates, finally, a legitimate voice in policy decisions along with business interests and government agencies — but far more uneven in producing consensus on decisions. As business interests regained influence and leverage in the White House and in Congress, symbolic posturing and adversarial gridlock often supplanted good faith negotiation of workable solutions.

Finally, a third unresolved governance issue was the long-term implications of national environmental regulation for American federalism. The national regulatory statutes were reactions to real deficiencies in state policies. Most states had shown neither the will nor the expertise and administrative capacity to address pervasive and growing pollution problems. They faced implicit risks of competition from one another if they imposed stricter regulations on their businesses, and they inherently lacked authority to control transboundary air and water pollution. Even many industries were better off with one national regulatory framework than with fifty different ones.

Nonetheless, federal environmental regulation raised potentially problematic constitutional issues that might someday be challenged. By what authority could a federal government of ostensibly limited powers impose not only national minimum environmental standards but also detailed national implementation requirements and program models on state and local governments? Which environmental problems were sufficiently national that federal regulation could be justified, and which (if any) were properly reserved to the states under the Tenth Amendment? To what extent could the federal government legitimately mandate that state and local governments implement federal programs as its delegate, and must it provide funds for the implementation costs if it did so? Conversely, to what extent could state and local governments enact more stringent environmental policies of their own, even if they might in effect create barriers to interstate commerce — or to international trade?

None of these issues became a major obstacle to the sweeping introduction of federal environmental regulatory programs during the 1970s, nor to their initial successes in implementation. All remained implicit, however, as governance issues that could resurface in future challenges as political opportunities and popular concerns shifted.

13 Reform or Reaction? The Politics of the Pendulum

The anti-environmental push of the nineties is prompted by the pro-environmental excesses of the late eighties, which was prompted by the anti-environmental excesses of the early eighties, which was prompted by the pro-environmental excesses of the seventies. . . . [T]hese violent swings of the pendulum have had . . . a uniquely devastating effect on the executive agency entrusted to carry out whatever environmental policy the nation says it wants. . . .

EPA was launched on a huge wave of public enthusiasm. Its programs have had an enormous and beneficial effect on all our lives. The gross pollution we were all worried about twenty-five years ago is either a memory or under reasonable social control. Why is EPA now the agency everyone loves to hate? — William Ruckelshaus, "Stopping the Pendulum"

The wholesale nationalization of pollution-control regulation in the 1970s was unprecedented in American history, and reflected an extraordinarily widespread popular demand for the federal government to control the environmental damage of postwar manufacturing and urbanization. This demand was amplified and sustained by newly mobilized environmental lobbying groups and strategic lawsuits.

In effect, the pollution-control laws added a regulatory counterpart to the many federal financial aid programs — "categorical grant programs" — which since the 1950s had provided financial support for highways, housing, wastewater management, urban renewal, and other municipal infrastructure and human services costs. These funding policies had been accepted, albeit in varying degrees, by both Democratic and Republican presidents since the New Deal, who supported using the vast and progressive federal income tax system to help finance the needs of an increasingly mobile and national society. In environmental protection policy, federal regulations in effect fused with federal financial assistance: federal financial grants for state and local environmental programs made federal regulation palatable, and federal minimum standards put all states on an equal footing with their upwind neighbors and their competitors in industrial recruitment.

The 1980s opened on a diametrically opposite note, with the election of a president who was fundamentally opposed to federal regulation and domestic spending, and who was both supported and surrounded by advocates of all-out reversal of these policies. Environmental policy was just one element of Ronald Reagan's sweeping "neo-conservative" agenda, but inasmuch as it combined both regulation and spending, it was an especially vulnerable target.

Many of the major manufacturers, those who had accepted environmental mandates and invested in control equipment, backed environmental regulatory reforms with the goal simply of stabilization. The aim was to rationalize the patchwork that had emerged, streamline paperwork, fix unworkable and inconsistent requirements, and slow down the pace of new mandates, but to keep enforcing the existing rules so that their competitors must also comply. Others, however, preferred *deregulation*: not just to reform, but to *reverse* the growth of business regulation. These advocates included intransigent polluters, such as many mining and primary processing firms, as well as some trade associations. They also included some firms that had complied with the initial environmental statutes, but now faced yet more regulatory demands. These forces allied themselves with other constituencies — traditional western opponents of public-lands regulation,[1] "cowboy cap-italists" seeking unregulated opportunities for profit, and pro-business and antigovern-ment ideologues more generally — in a massive lobbying and advertising campaign against government "overregulation" (Weidenbaum 1980). They also actively supported Ronald Reagan's presidential campaign, and when Reagan was elected in 1980, he made a fateful decision to attempt radical dismantling of federal environmental regulation rather than implement the more moderately conservative agenda of the reform advocates.

Reagan's campaign against environmental regulation is widely remembered, as are its direct effects on EPA and other federal environmental programs. Far less clearly noted were its broader consequences, however, particularly those resulting from the public backlash his policies produced. On the one hand, this backlash produced a decade of reaffirmed legitimacy for the implementation and expansion of federal environmental regulation, from the 1984 to the 1994 congressional elections. Congress passed a major new round of highly specific environmental laws and amendments, and EPA as well as environmental litigants targeted industries for increasingly vigorous enforcement, now including criminal sentences as well as civil penalties.

An extraordinary range of new experiments in environmental policy and management blossomed during this period of clear public commitment to environmental regulation, a period of "innovation in the shadow of regulation." Examples included economic incen-tives and emissions trading, corporate environmental auditing and management reform ("pollution prevention pays"), strict liability for hazardous-waste dumping and disclosure requirements for toxic releases, and new analytical procedures within EPA, such as risk-based decision-making.

At the same time, however, the cumulative effect of the tough new statutes that Con-gress enacted in response to Reagan's abuses was to impose heavy and nondiscretionary burdens on new groups of regulatees: small business, local governments, and individuals. These groups were often just as much causes of the pollution problem as were large manufacturers and utilities. Politically, however, they could not be forced to accept costly new regulations without federal financial assistance. Yet if Reagan failed in his attempt to deregulate, he nonetheless succeeded in starving down the federal domestic budget, through tax cuts, military spending, and unprecedented deficits. These mandates thus set in motion an increasingly extreme cycle of reactions and counterreactions — "pendulum politics" — that has characterized environmental regulatory politics ever since.

Reform Derailed: Reagan's Deregulation Initiative

Ronald Reagan entered the presidency with a long-standing ideological commitment to shrinking the role of the federal government. Three weeks after the election his designated budget director, David Stockman, issued a public "manifesto" predicting a "Republican economic Dunkirk" unless Reagan took swift action to curtail federal regulation. Stockman pointed to "over a dozen sweeping 1970s environmental, energy, and safety statutes devoid of policy standards and criteria," leading to a "mind-boggling outpouring of rule-makings, interpretive guidelines, and major litigation" which would "sweep through the industrial economy with gale force." As examples, Stockman listed EPA's proposed regulations for carbon monoxide, bus and truck noise, hazardous wastes, toxic chemicals, and industrial boiler emissions, and he warned that "unless swift, comprehensive, and far-reaching regulatory policy corrections are undertaken immediately, an unprecedented, quantum scale-up of the much-discussed 'regulatory burden' will occur during the next 18–40 months" (Andrews 1984a, note 7).

With Reagan's approval, Stockman implemented an aggressive three-pronged policy for reducing the role of the federal government in environmental protection: deregulation, defunding, and devolution. *Deregulation* meant not simply regulatory reform or consolidation, but halting outright the growth of federal regulations, and relaxing existing ones that were targeted as especially burdensome by the regulated industries. *Defunding* meant drastic cuts in the regulatory agencies' budgets, along with large tax cuts to prevent future spending. *Devolution* meant turning over as many functions as possible to state and local governments, or to voluntary action if state and local governments were unwilling to accept them. Deregulation was thus to be achieved not only by changes in the regulations themselves but by reducing the budget and staff available to implement and enforce them, and by leaving them to the states or abandoning them outright.

Stockman implemented this agenda not by seeking congressional approval or public support, but by "an orchestrated series of unilateral administrative actions to deter, revise, or rescind existing and pending regulations where clear legal authority exists" (Andrews 1984a, note 8). On Stockman's advice, Reagan declared an immediate moratorium on new regulations, and appointed a Regulatory Relief Task Force — chaired by Vice President George Bush, and staffed by personnel from the Office of Management and Budget — to review and potentially reverse or rescind existing regulations. This task force compiled a "hit list" of regulations nominated by regulated industries and their trade associations for reconsideration, and singled out 110 of them for immediate reconsideration. Among those targeted were all regulations affecting the auto industry, especially various air quality standards and gasoline lead limits, and EPA's regulations for hazardous wastes, industrial pretreatment of wastewater discharges to public sewers, premanufacture notification and testing of new toxic chemicals, and pesticide registration. By August 1982 fifty-one rules had been revised or rescinded, thirty-five more were under review, and twenty-five were still pending (Andrews 1984a, note 9).

Meanwhile, President Reagan issued an executive order requiring that the agencies conduct economic cost-benefit analyses for all proposed regulations, and that unless the laws specifically mandated other criteria, they must select the least-cost option. These analyses were to be reviewed and approved by the Office of Management and Budget (OMB), to which the agencies must also submit their work plans for developing new regulations — their "regulatory calendars" — for approval months in advance.

OMB could thus delay proposed regulations almost indefinitely, unless they were subject to statutory or court-ordered deadlines, simply by claiming dissatisfaction with EPA's economic analyses; it could even block the development of new regulations at their earliest stages by disapproving the agency's proposed regulatory calendar. Because OMB was an advisory agency to the president, moreover, it could not be required to keep a reviewable record of its comments or the agency's response to them, nor to document its recommendations in the public record (Percival 1991). This was a sharp departure from the accepted principles of regulatory procedure, which required that all comments affecting proposed regulations be made in public and incorporated into a formal, reviewable record so that they could be debated openly.

Stockman also used budget reductions as both pretext and weapon to reduce the influence of the regulatory agencies. These agencies' allocations represented a minuscule fraction of the federal budget compared to defense or human-services entitlements, but proportionally they were cut far more deeply. Before Reagan's EPA administrator was even sworn in, Stockman had already cut EPA's staff by 11 percent, and other regulatory agencies by equal or greater amounts: the Occupational Safety and Health Administration by 11 percent, the Consumer Product Safety Commission by 20 percent, and Interior's Office of Surface Mining by 40 percent. Reagan requested initial budget cuts of about one-third in EPA's four primary regulatory programs, and further cuts in each of the next several years (Bartlett 1984, 127–131). These cuts severely reduced EPA's capacity to do its job, and devastated its internal organization and morale.

Finally, Reagan made aggressive use of political appointments to control the regulatory agencies by putting ideological loyalists in key positions. Anne Gorsuch (later Burford), Reagan's first EPA administrator, was a lawyer for a telephone company with brief experience as a state legislator; she had no experience in managing a large organization of any kind, let alone a federal regulatory agency with complex scientific and technical responsibilities. Her primary qualifications for the job were simply ideological loyalty and powerful friends. Rita Lavelle, appointed head of the multibillion-dollar Superfund program, was a public relations officer for a major industrial polluter; other appointees were similarly lacking in experience or expertise.

These appointments reflected not just the familiar practice of spoils-system appointments of political supporters — "to the victor belong the spoils" — but a far more Machiavellian policy of *not* appointing experienced leadership to the regulatory agencies, even experienced Republicans. White House strategists deliberately appointed regulatory administrators who were not recognized experts or experienced administrators in their fields. Such people would carry out Reagan's deregulation agenda on automatic pilot, with allegiances and even personal ties only to other Reaganites. They would have no previous relationships of their own with their agencies' constituencies, since they would be deliberately drawn from outside the "issue networks" of people who shared common understandings of what the regulatory statutes meant and what their central issues were (Heclo 1978). They would thus be less likely to become sympathetic to the ideas of their agencies' career staffs, or to develop independent ideas about how to manage their agencies and make regulatory decisions.

The one exception to this stratagem, one which had Stockman as its architect, was Reagan's appointment of James Watt as both Secretary of the Interior and the cabinet-level environmental coordinator to whom all the other environmental agencies would report. Watt had previous experience as head of Interior's Bureau of Outdoor Recreation in the early 1970s, and had thereafter moved back to the West to create a conservative counterpart to the new pro-environmental public interest law firms such as EDF and NRDC—a "public interest law firm" for resource industries and property owners. He returned to government under Reagan with a strong ideological agenda as well as close ties to those interests, and with his administrative experience he was far more effective in undermining environmental protection policies, at least for the several years he lasted, than Reagan's less experienced appointees. Watt was eventually dismissed in 1984, after his opinions and actions became a lightning rod for overwhelming public outrage over Reagan's anti-environmental-protection policies.

In both its substance and its tactics, Reagan's deregulatory initiative caused deep and lasting damage to EPA, and to the evolution of U.S. environmental policy more generally. It seriously destabilized the agency's effective functioning, and devastated its staff's professional morale. It eroded the agency's expertise, and tainted it for the first time with corruption and scandal. More broadly, it fractured the public consensus that had been emerging in support of regulatory reform, and triggered instead a more bitter and far more partisan period of distrust and ideological trench warfare over environmental protection policy.

At the request of Reagan supporters in the gasoline blending industry, for instance, administration officials pressured EPA to relax its regulations limiting lead additives in gasoline, despite the well-documented evidence of automotive lead's serious effects on urban children. The result was a sharp backlash from the public-health and environmental communities, as well as from some major refiners who had already been required to phase out their production of leaded fuel. Ultimately the standard was tightened rather than relaxed—one of very few such decisions in the first Reagan administration—but the initial attempt to loosen it fueled public distrust of the administration's agenda.

In its hazardous-waste regulations, EPA abruptly lifted its ban on disposing liquids into chemical waste landfills—at least in part, apparently, to benefit a particular firm in Gorsuch's home state of Colorado—then reinstated it just a few weeks later, under fire from state governments and environmental groups and even from the waste disposal trade association. In its toxic-substance regulations, EPA adopted unenforceable voluntary testing and self-certification by chemical manufacturers as a substitute for regulation, and developed proposals to exempt 60 percent of all new chemicals from the premanufacture notification requirements of the Toxic Substances Control Act.

These anecdotes represent just a few examples of a broad and systematic attempt to deregulate by administrative fiat. Many of these regulatory relief attempts were eventually overturned by the courts (Lash 1984; Andrews 1984a, notes 20–22).

Equally important was EPA's *in*action under Gorsuch. The implementation of its regulatory mandates slowed to a trickle: by July 1982 EPA had adopted only three of twelve new source performance standards for air quality that had been proposed when Gorsuch took office, and had proposed only one of eleven others that were technically ready for issuance. Gorsuch proposed to delay indefinitely EPA's regulations for toxic water pollutants discharged to public treatment plants; this action was reversed by court order as an illegal form of deregulation. Regulations that were issued were weakened: Gorsuch eliminated reporting and insurance requirements for hazardous waste facilities, and substituted voluntary testing of toxic chemicals instead of EPA rules. Acid rain, formaldehyde, and other hazards were deliberately left unregulated on the grounds that evidence was not yet sufficient, and EPA's one expert on indoor air pollution hazards was reassigned to other duties. EPA's enforcement budget was cut by 26 percent from 1981 to 1983; its enforcement staff was reorganized every eleven weeks during Gorsuch's first year, and the number of civil cases it filed and administrative orders it issued dropped by over 50 percent. Gorsuch herself, meanwhile, reassured at least one company that it need not worry about enforcement against its violations of gasoline lead regulations (Andrews 1984a, notes 23, 26).

By the midpoint of his first term, Reagan's environmental deregulation strategy had produced a powerful public backlash, and had become his worst policy failure and most glaring political embarrassment. Environmental crises continued to surface—the entire town of Times Beach, Missouri, was evacuated in December 1982 due to PCB contamination—and as EPA implemented the Superfund statute, investigators unearthed a lengthening list of thousands of old chemical waste dumps and contaminated areas. Surveys documented rising public criticism of Reagan's environmental policies, and even the National Wildlife Federation—the largest and most conservative of the nation's conservation groups, nearly 70 percent of whose members had voted for Reagan—broke its traditional neutrality to condemn the administration's policies (Shabecoff 1993, 209–10). Membership in environmental groups increased dramatically, as did financial donations to them, and in the 1984 elections environmental candidates scored major victories. Reagan's policies had seemingly damaged both the regulatory process itself and EPA's public credibility.

Even many business leaders became increasingly apprehensive, in part because they needed an EPA whose actions were predictable and whose officials were competent, and partly because they recognized that as the traditional public villains of environmental politics, they would be the ultimate victims of political recriminations if the public believed that EPA was being corrupted. In Congress, EPA Administrator Gorsuch became the highest ranking official ever cited for contempt, and both Republican and Democratic leaders of the environmental committees rejected her policies. In the courts, many of the administration's major deregulatory decisions were reversed. Within the administration itself, the demoralization of EPA prompted heavy criticism of the president without even achieving the major regulatory changes he sought, and relationships both within EPA and between EPA and the White House reached a point of breakdown.

In 1983 Reagan finally dismissed Gorsuch and over thirty other senior EPA appointees, and replaced them with new appointees headed by William Ruckelshaus, EPA's founding administrator and a symbol of its public rectitude and vigorous commitment to enforcement. These changes clearly signaled the administration's admission that its attempt at environmental deregulation had failed.

The Pendulum and Its Consequences

Ruckelshaus took over EPA again in May 1983 with a mandate to restore public trust in the agency. His appointment offered a second chance for the moderate-conservative reform agenda that had been developing before Reagan's election, and that had even been advocated by Reagan's own environmental transition team.[2] Among his priorities were to vigorously enforce the laws, improve management of the Superfund program, develop a strategy to deal with acid rain, and clarify the proper relationship between federal, state, and local governments. Significantly, he reaffirmed that effective environmental regulation and enforcement were necessary even for free enterprise itself: Gorsuch's "voluntary compliance" left responsible firms at the mercy of scofflaw competitors. "The only voluntarism at EPA," he told the *Washington Post* in 1983, "is if the EPA voluntarily decides not to enforce the law."

Even with effective leadership back at EPA, however, the damage caused by Reagan and Stockman's deregulation initiatives could not be fully reversed. EPA's budget was never fully restored, even though its responsibilities continued to increase. Key staff experts had left, and others were permanently jaded by the experience. The levels of morale, trust, and organizational effectiveness within EPA have never returned to their earlier levels.

The consequences for EPA's relationships with Congress were more far-reaching still. Reagan had taken office at a time of widespread support for moderately conservative reform of environmental regulation. Two of the agency's most basic statutes were up for reauthorization — the Clean Air and Clean Water Acts — and both provided rare windows of opportunity for reforms. With his own popularity, combined with Republican capture of the Senate and the normal deference accorded to a new president, Reagan had an extraordinary resource that he could have used to adopt and implement this agenda. Instead, however, his quest for deregulation derailed the campaign for more moderate regulatory reforms, and poisoned for years ahead the atmosphere of trust and cooperation that would be needed to rebuild it.

An unexpectedly fateful consequence was a dramatic "swing of the pendulum" from presidential to Congressional micromanagement of EPA policies. The 1984 election did not turn out Reagan himself, but it swept into Congress a far more Democratic and far more aggressively pro-environment group of legislators, who were determined both to strengthen the environmental laws and to preclude any recurrence of Reagan's administrative undermining of them. They sharply increased both the scope and detail of the environmental statutes, extending them to cover yet more environmental hazards and imposing ever more prescriptive statutory mandates. To many statutes they added rigid implementation deadlines, enforced by "hammer clauses" that imposed severe automatic consequences if the deadlines were missed.

Amendments to the Resource Conservation and Recovery Act in 1984, for instance, extended hazardous waste reporting requirements to "small quantity generators," and required replacement of the thousands of underground storage tanks that had been corroding and leaking underneath old gas stations, businesses, and motor pools since the 1950s. Amendments to the Superfund Act (1986) expanded EPA's authority for cleaning up contaminated sites, and sharply limited its discretion to set priorities among them.

Amendments to the Safe Drinking Water Act (1986), meanwhile, ordered EPA to set standards for an additional twenty-five drinking water contaminants every three years, imposing a steady increase in burdens on local water utilities.[3] The Asbestos Hazardous Emergency Response Act (1986) ordered that every local school develop plans for asbestos inspection and management, and for parent notification. Amendments to the Clean Water Act (1987) ordered the states to identify "hot spots" where toxic water pollutants were not fully controlled by existing technologies, and to implement individualized plans for meeting the standards within three years. Amendments to the pesticides law (1988) required EPA to reregister or cancel some fifty thousand old products that had been allowed to continue under pre-1972 safety and testing requirements.

Taken together, these new statutes did force EPA to write far more regulations, and more rapidly as well. In the process, however, they created a vast range of new regulatory mandates and allowed EPA less and less discretion to set priorities among them. These statutes were widely popular at the time: Congress was reaffirming the public's commitment to cleaning up the environment, and putting a stop to the corporate influence and administrative abuses of the first Reagan administration. Little noticed at the time, however, was a problematic side effect of this larger political morality play. The new statutes imposed costly new burdens not just on the big manufacturers and electric utilities that had previously been regulated, but on new targets who were far less affluent and far less accepted as environmental villains: small businesses, local governments, and water utilities. They thus sowed the seeds for another backlash against EPA, against unfunded mandates and against federal environmental regulation more generally.

"Pollution Prevention Pays"

For the major regulated industries, meanwhile, the collapse of Reagan's deregulation initiative confirmed the continuation of the environmental regulatory system, and the reappointment of Ruckelshaus — architect of EPA's confrontational enforcement policy — sent a clear message of commitment to it. In 1982 EPA began referring environmental cases to the Justice Department for criminal rather than merely civil enforcement, and through 1985 these cases resulted in about forty indictments and half a million dollars per year in fines. By 1989 these numbers had increased to over one hundred indictments and convictions and over $12 million in fines annually (U.S. Council on Environmental Quality 1990, 156, 174). Also, several of the major environmental law firms opened new litigation programs aimed not just at EPA—their primary target in the 1970s—but at major polluters themselves, particularly under the Clean Water Act, which imposed costly penalties for serious water-quality violations.[4]

Most large firms therefore resigned themselves to implementing and adapting to the environmental regulations. As they did, some discovered an unexpected insight: pollution was not just a public nuisance, but a cost to themselves as well. Reducing it, therefore, might also reduce costs, spur innovation, and open new market opportunities.

Throughout the 1970s, most businesses viewed environmental protection from the perspective of pollution-control engineers: as a mandate for "end-of-pipe" control technology, calling for the addition of devices to extract air and water pollutants before discharge and the engineering of disposal facilities to provide adequate containment. The federal air and water pollution statutes ratified this perspective—in preference to ambient air and water management, but without any serious consideration of more fundamental production changes—and EPA's aggressive enforcement preoccupied most firms simply with obtaining technology-based permits and installing compliance equipment (de Nevers et al. 1977, 25–27). Pollution control was left therefore to engineers and corporate lawyers, rather than integrated into business decisions more generally.

Standard textbooks, meanwhile, taught a conventional wisdom that the greater the degree of pollution control, the higher the control costs. These would reach exorbitant levels for improving, say, from 95 percent to 99 percent reduction of wastes (e.g. Stern et al. 1973, 401–02).[5] Implicit in this calculation was the crucial assumption that the only way to achieve greater pollution reduction was to install costlier versions of the same end-of-pipe technologies, which did nothing except extract pollutants from waste streams. Control costs thus seemed to rise exponentially with every increase in regulation, with no apparent benefits to the firm.

In fact, however, pollution was a signal of business inefficiency. Every pollutant was also a raw material that had been paid for but then discarded, inflicting additional disposal costs and environmental damage in the process. Sometimes, perhaps, there really was no economic use for these "residuals," but most firms simply had not paid much attention to them. Material costs had declined steadily compared to labor, and had come to seem so unimportant that most firms did not monitor their materials and energy closely: they monitored cost data, but rarely the physical quantities themselves. Since waste disposal was cheap, many treated waste management costs simply as a general overhead expense rather than charging them back to the units that produced them.

In 1978, business consultant Michael Royston proposed a bold new argument: *pollution prevention pays* (Royston 1979, 1980). It pays, he argued, not only for society but for businesses themselves. It reduces disposal costs, as well as the costs of raw materials to replace those discarded. It reduces the unproductive administration costs of regulatory compliance, and it sometimes generates new revenues from byproduct sales. It also reduces the costs of health and injury to workers, and related labor productivity losses; and it reduces more general liability for damage to public health and the environment.[6]

Case studies quickly confirmed his claim. A comparison of major chemical refineries,

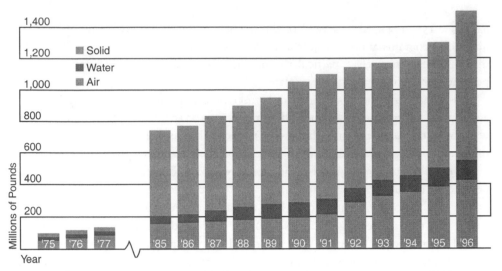

Figure 20. The 3M Corporation was one of the first of many companies to inaugurate a major "Pollution Prevention Pays" campaign during the 1980s, offering incentives to all its employees to identify opportunities to reduce pollution and at the same time reduce costs for the company. This figure shows the results. Note particularly that the results were not simply a one-time correction of previously overlooked waste, but continued to improve each year. [Courtesy of 3M Corporation]

for instance, showed that some even lacked storage-tank covers that would have paid for themselves in a matter of months, reducing air pollution while saving product (Sarokin et al. 1985). Far from operating at their peak of efficiency, many businesses were operating by habit, well below their "production possibility frontiers," so that they could actually *save* money by reducing pollution. In rapid succession, several leading firms issued corporate environmental policy statements and began aggressive waste-reduction campaigns: 3M's "Pollution Prevention Pays" (fig. 20), Dow's "Waste Reduction Always Pays" (WRAP), Chevron's "Save Money and Reduce Toxics" (SMART), and others (Gottlieb 1995, 80).

EPA echoed and endorsed these ideas, but its actual policies remained ambivalent. Its policy statements endorsed a normative "waste management hierarchy": first reduce wastes as much as possible, then re-use what cannot be reduced, recycle what cannot be re-used, recover energy value from what cannot be recycled, and as a last resort only, treat and landfill the residues. Its regulations, however, continued to reflect its statutory requirements for a control-technology approach. Amendments to the hazardous waste law in 1984 endorsed the hierarchy, but addressed only hazardous wastes, and did not change the control-technology emphasis of EPA's air and water regulations. Influenced by its own engineering culture, EPA also allied itself in the early 1980s with the commercial waste disposal industry, one of its few natural allies in the business community, in campaigning for new landfills — rather than waste reduction and recycling — to replace the thousands of substandard dumps that were being closed, and in demanding that all states produce "capacity assurance plans" documenting adequate waste disposal capacity for the future (Gottlieb 1995, 75–78).

Many voices in industry resisted the waste management hierarchy as unduly rigid and simplistic.[7] The Pollution Prevention Act of 1990, passed in the closing hours of the One Hundredth Congress, directed EPA to review its regulatory requirements with an eye to coordinating them more explicitly with the goal of pollution prevention. However, it did not change or ease these requirements, and it left the actual implementation of pollution prevention to voluntary industry initiatives (Gottlieb 1995, 74–75).

In reality, EPA's strongest policy incentive for waste reduction was not so much its advocacy of the hierarchy as the cost of its regulations themselves. Corporate slogans notwithstanding, pollution prevention did *not* always pay. Some pollution prevention measures did reduce business costs by correcting wasteful practices, but others paid only less tangible benefits to the company's public image. Still others paid only because of the rising costs imposed by the regulations. Air and water pollution standards demanded costly control technologies, as did landfill standards. EPA's regulations closing substandard facilities drove up prices at those that remained, and recycling markets thus expanded as the costs of disposal went up. EPA bans on some disposal practices, such as landfilling of industrial liquids, forced more fundamental reassessment of waste streams and of the processes that generated them, and the threat of catastrophic economic liability under the Superfund Act created a powerful new incentive to eliminate hazardous wastes.[8] The sheer paperwork burden of compliance also created costs that could be avoided by eliminating regulated wastes, and lengthy delays for permit modifications created costly problems for firms that had to change their product mix rapidly to compete in shifting markets.

In short, EPA's regulations continued to emphasize control technology rather than prevention, but by the costs that they imposed they also created some real economic incentives—even if unintended—for waste reduction (Gottlieb 1995, 2). To the extent that some of these costs represented reasonable approximations for the real environmental damage of the pollution itself, they were even arguably good policies, forcing the polluters to reduce their pollution or pay its "external" costs in this surrogate form. Other costs, however, were simply deadweight economic losses that could not be reduced by "doing the right thing."

The cumulative impact of environmental costs, liabilities, and market opportunities produced a widespread maturation in corporate environmental management. Leading firms issued corporate environmental policy statements, created integrated offices for environment, health, and safety, offered employee incentives for waste-reduction suggestions, and introduced more systematic environmental compliance-auditing procedures. Some companies took their audits a step further, to identify opportunities for cost-effective waste reduction and pollution prevention. Banks and insurers, meanwhile, discovered themselves unexpectedly liable for their companies' risks and became reluctant but influential sources of additional pressure for environmental risk reduction. To protect themselves, they demanded audits and site assessments to identify any potential liabilities for environmental or occupational hazards, and began to scrutinize business practices more closely.

By the 1990s, some businesses began to introduce environmental considerations far more pervasively into their decision processes: in product design ("green engineering," "design for environment"), process operations ("industrial ecology"), marketing, accounting, strategic planning, and other areas.[9] In the wake of a disastrous 1989 oil spill by the *Exxon Valdez* in the Gulf of Alaska, a few leading corporations also endorsed a set of "Valdez Principles" for corporate environmental responsibility.[10] By the early 1990s, an international business group, the International Organization for Standardization even began developing voluntary standards for corporate environmental management systems ("ISO 14000" standards) that might ultimately become certification requirements for many international trade transactions.

In effect, these voices urged a fundamental shift in the way businesses thought about their environmental responsibilities, from reliance on end-of-pipe technology toward pollution prevention and greater efficiency throughout the entire "life cycles" of human use of materials and energy. The driving force behind this shift was enlightened self-interest, taking into account the regulatory costs both of safe waste disposal itself and of permitting and compliance requirements.

Risk-Based Decision-Making

Within EPA, meanwhile, the task that faced Ruckelshaus in 1983 was not only to rebuild the agency's credibility and effectiveness, but also to wrest control over its agenda from the many external forces which vied to capture it — the White House, Congress, environmental and business constituencies — and from the sheer inertia of its disparate programs. Ruckelshaus was an outspoken advocate of balancing the social benefits of environmental rules against their economic costs, and of creating a government-wide process for assessing and managing risks. Beginning in 1984, he proposed the concepts of "risk assessment" and "risk management" as a common language for justifying regulatory proposals across the agency. In 1987 a major agency report stated flatly that "the fundamental mission of the Environmental Protection Agency is to reduce risks," and another in 1990 recommended that EPA "target its environmental protection efforts on . . . opportunities for the greatest risk reduction" (U.S. Environmental Protection Agency 1987, 1990). By the end of the 1980s, the rhetoric of risk became the agency's primary language for justifying its decisions (Russell and Gruber 1987).

EPA had begun developing quantitative risk assessment techniques as early as the mid-1970s, to set priorities among pesticides, drinking-water contaminants, and other toxic chemicals and to justify regulations for them. These techniques gradually evolved into a highly technical four-step procedure — hazard identification, dose-response assessment, exposure assessment, and risk characterization — for estimating the health risks, and particularly cancer risks, of specific chemicals (cf. Covello and Menckes 1985). Typically these assessments combined data and assumptions from pharmacological, toxicological and epidemiological studies as available, using mathematical models to extrapolate from high experimental doses on laboratory animals to lower expected doses on humans, and then to predict the actual exposures that might occur in human populations. Significantly, EPA defined this procedure as a purely *scientific* activity, separate from risk *management* decisions in which the risk assessment would be weighed among other considerations: statutory requirements, costs, public values, and politics.

In practice, however, risk assessment was not a purely scientific activity. Like cost-benefit analyses, its procedures were unavoidably permeated by nonscientific human assumptions and value judgments: choices of what substances to select for risk assessment in the first place, what health effects ("end points") and indicators to consider, what data and previous studies to trust, and what assumptions to use in drawing inferences. Judgments were compounded when a characterization of overall risk was constructed out of the diverse, uncertain, and sometimes conflicting estimates derived from the previous three steps.

Beyond these judgments about individual substances lay the multiplicity of risks involved in real EPA decisions: risks of multiple kinds of health effects to different groups of people, risks to different species and ecosystems, and risks of economic and aesthetic damage and other effects. The image of scientific method and precision in risk assessments thus obscured the many human assumptions and judgments that were implicit in their results.

From the perspective of the EPA administrator, however, formal risk assessment offered an important new management tool. EPA's two most intractable problems were the growing burden of proof necessary to defend its regulatory proposals in the courts and the proliferation of uncoordinated statutes, programs, and regulatory mandates, each advocated by powerful constituencies and reinforced by innumerable ad hoc requirements — including statutory deadlines and "hammer clauses," court orders and consent decrees — by which these constituencies sought to force EPA's agenda toward their own priorities. To Ruckelshaus, "risk" offered a scientific language by which to rationalize the regulatory decisions he ultimately had to defend to the Office of Management and Budget — under its expanded authority to review the costs and benefits of regulations — external constituencies and the courts (Andrews 1996). Whatever its imperfections, risk assessment also allowed EPA to wrap its decisions in the apparent objectivity of science, and in the language of health effects rather than merely of OMB's cost-benefit analyses (Andrews 1984b).

Risk assessment thus strengthened EPA's hand in dealing with OMB, but it also increased tensions between EPA and its public constituencies. Quantitative risk assessment seemed to tip environmental decisions in favor of business, by implicitly accepting business demands for detailed scientific proof to justify every regulation and thus miring the regulatory programs in endless litigation over the imperfections of science: "paralysis by analysis." EPA's risk-based laws were its least effective, yet their approach was now to be imposed on all EPA programs (Hornstein 1993; Gottlieb 1995, 59–67). In addition, most risk experts were employed either by businesses or by the regulatory agencies themselves; greater emphasis on risk assessment thus strengthened the ties between experts in the agencies and in the regulated industries, and redefined the issues as matters of expert reason versus the lay public's irrationality. Not surprisingly, the public in turn came to distrust both the jargon and the value judgments of risk experts (Krimsky and Plough 1989).

Risk assessment thus became an increasingly central rationale for EPA decisions, but an arguable one and increasingly politicized. In 1990 Congress delivered a major rebuff to the risk-based approach: frustrated by the snail's pace of risk assessment in the hazardous air pollutant program, it ordered EPA instead to set technology-based standards for some 189 substances listed as high-priority pollutants, and then to reconsider any remaining risks eight years later. By the mid-1990s, however, conservative legislators seized on risk assessment as a tool to slow down the regulatory process, and proposed legislation that would require it for all major regulatory proposals and that even detailed what assumptions and analytical approaches were to be used.

Comparative Risk Assessment

Quantitative risk assessment was developed to estimate health risks of specific substances, not to set priorities among more diverse kinds of environmental problems, such as between a chemical threatening health and water pollution degrading an ecosystem. EPA administrators from Douglas Costle on had cast EPA primarily as a public health agency, with correspondingly less emphasis on protecting ecosystems. By the mid-1980s, however, ecological threats once again claimed public attention. Acid rain, exacerbated by tall stacks built to meet air-quality standards, threatened both fish populations and forests. Chlorofluorocarbons, or CFCs, once hailed as "wonder chemicals" for aerosol propellants, solvents, coolants, and plastic foam products, appeared to be gradually destroying the earth's protective stratospheric ozone layer. Worldwide carbon dioxide emissions appeared to be affecting Earth's basic temperature balance, threatening a potentially unprecedented warming of the global climate. Meanwhile, urbanization and agriculture continued to destroy wetlands and other natural habitats.

Ruckelshaus's successor, Lee Thomas, therefore launched an ambitious initiative: to conduct an agency-wide *comparative* risk assessment, as a framework for setting priorities across all its programs. Lacking a statutory framework for agency-wide decision-making, he used the concept of risk to create one by administrative action, justified by the common-sense need for reasonableness, consistency, and the appearance of scientific objectivity.

In a pioneering EPA study sponsored by the administrator's office in 1987, some seventy-five EPA senior managers compared the "relative risks" of thirty-one environmental problems spanning the full range of EPA's responsibilities. The study, entitled *Unfinished Business,* considered four different kinds of risk: cancer, non-cancer health risks, ecological effects, and other effects on human welfare, such as pollution damage to historic structures. It found that the information available to assess most risks was surprisingly poor. It also found that the agency's actual risk-management priorities were more consistent with public opinion than with the problems EPA managers thought most serious: EPA was devoting far more effort to waste disposal issues, for instance, than to indoor air pollution and radon, whose statistical risks to health appeared far more serious. Third, it found that in all programs except water quality, EPA had been far more concerned with public health than with the protection of natural habitats and ecosystems. Finally, it found that localized hazards appeared to cause much higher risks to individuals than nationwide averages revealed (U.S. Environmental Protection Agency 1987).

A 1990 sequel by outside scientists and policy experts endorsed the report, and recommended a series of shifts in EPA's policies and priorities. It recommended increased emphasis, for instance, on reducing human destruction of natural habitats and species, and on slowing stratospheric ozone depletion and global warming, and correspondingly less emphasis on more localized concerns such as oil spills and groundwater contamination. Among health risks, it recommended greater emphasis on air pollution, drinking-water contaminants, and occupational and indoor exposures, and less on hazardous waste sites (U.S. Environmental Protection Agency 1990).

To open such a public debate about priorities was a bold overture by EPA's administrators. In effect, they asserted that many of EPA's current priorities were driven by arbitrary statutory mandates and public fears rather than by "real" risks, calling into question many of the public concerns about toxic chemicals and hazardous waste sites that had mobilized the agency's political support since the 1970s.[11] They also advocated a fundamental change in EPA itself: that the agency should pursue an overall mission based on risk priorities, not simply implement the patchwork of separate laws Congress had delegated to it. In effect, they proposed a neo-Progressive vision of EPA: that it should plan and manage toward an overall goal of environmental protection, based primarily on the risk judgments of scientific experts, rather than serve merely as a "transmission belt" uncritically implementing congressional mandates or popular preferences (cf. Hays 1969 [1958], Andrews 1993b).

EPA Administrator William Reilly used these studies to introduce more systematic risk-based decision processes at EPA (Reilly 1991). He ordered EPA's programs and regional offices to submit risk-based budget proposals, and directed EPA's enforcement staff to use risk as a basis for their priorities as well, focusing on important hazards rather than more trivial violations. Finally, he provided EPA funding for state-level comparative risk studies, and offered to let states shift some EPA funding to higher-risk priorities as an incentive.

The fact remained, however, that without congressional action, risk-based priorities — or indeed *any* kind of priorities — remained largely beyond the administrator's power to implement. EPA's regulatory mandates and programs, fragmented by statute and driven by statutory and court-ordered deadlines, remained untouched, and without changing these, the administrator had only minimal discretion to alter priorities.

The core idea of risk-based decision-making remained controversial as well. How could "risk" alone guide decisions? It was not obvious, for instance, that one should always put highest priority on reducing the most serious risk if the available solutions are highly costly and uncertain themselves, or if one can reduce a risk almost as serious at far lower cost. Such procedures in effect used scientific language to mask fundamentally political decisions, and to allow policy to be controlled by an EPA subgovernment rather than by a broader political process (Hornstein 1992).[12]

Arguments about the assumptions and inferences in risk assessment in turn served as surrogates for arguments about the real issues. How important were health risks and environmental impacts? Should particular substances or business practices be more tightly regulated? Were there less costly ways of achieving the same benefits? Who should bear the risks and the costs, and should such decisions be made by experts or by public debate? EPA *did* need authority to set priorities, and comparative risk assessment offered one innovative justification. Modeling EPA policy on an expert technical procedure rather than an open political process, however, was not a viable solution, and by the mid-1990s this approach appeared to have faded from the administrator's agenda.

"Command-and-Control" Versus Market-Based Incentives

Comparative risk assessment addressed the need to set priorities, but it did not answer the inseparable question of what EPA should do to implement them. Most of EPA's statutory authorities dictated "command-and-control" solutions: they directed EPA to *regulate* environmental problems, by setting national standards, issuing permits, inspecting and enforcing compliance, ordering corrective action, and fining violators. These solutions worked well for some problems, but for others they had two serious flaws. For polluters that had options for pollution reduction other than the ones dictated by EPA, they were inefficient: their uniform requirements sometimes imposed costlier burdens than necessary to achieve the desired results. For problems caused by many small sources, meanwhile, they were ineffective: it was neither practical nor politically feasible to impose uniform national regulations on small businesses, local governments, households, and politically powerful sources such as farms that had been exempted by statute from some regulations.

For both these reasons, regulatory reform advocates proposed using what they described as "market-based incentives" to augment or even replace EPA's "command-and-control" regulations. Economists and some legal scholars had advocated economic incentives since before EPA was created (Kneese and Bower 1968). Their usual prescription was to levy a charge per pound of pollutants emitted, to "internalize" environmental costs and thus influence polluters to manage waste materials more efficiently (Ackerman and Stewart 1985, 1988). Congress, however, had rejected such an approach as being unreliable and unrealistic (as well as unwelcome to key industries, such as West Virginia's soft coal producers—see Ackerman and Hassler 1981, Elliott et al. 1985). Polluters might simply pay and continue to pollute, and inflation would erode financial incentives. Taxes tended to raise revenue rather than to change behavior, and were politically difficult to adjust upward if the initial rates proved to be too low to reduce emissions (Latin 1985).

A few economists advocated an alternative approach: set an overall emissions cap equivalent to the ambient standard, and then issue an equivalent quantity of marketable permits that could be bought and sold among the polluters—or for that matter, bought by environmentalists and retired from use (Dales 1968). This system too was rejected, however, as being hard to monitor and to some, immoral, in that it in effect granted a "license to pollute," though ordinary emissions permits also granted such rights (Liroff 1986).

For practical reasons, however, EPA soon introduced several experiments with emissions trading. In 1976, it used a creative interpretation of the Clean Air Act to allow new pollution sources to locate in nonattainment areas if they obtained "offsets" from existing facilities that reduced their emissions. This interpretation was validated in the 1977 amendments to that law. In 1979 EPA announced a "bubble" policy, which encouraged firms to create excess "emission reduction credits" that could be traded to other sources to meet their emission reduction requirements.[13] By the 1980s the agency had introduced several further variants: emission trading among mobile sources, and tradable allowances to let producers share more efficiently the costs of phasing down leaded gasoline and chlorofluorocarbon (CFC) production. Trading also let some regulated polluters reduce pollution by buying up and closing down unregulated sources, when that would be cheaper than controlling one's own emissions. One refinery, for instance, was allowed to buy up and destroy old high-emission cars ("cash for clunkers") and some municipal water utilities subsidized water pollution reduction by farmers rather than install costly new technology themselves ("point-nonpoint" trading).

In a major statutory breakthrough, the 1990 Clean Air Act amendments created a national market for sulfur oxide emissions, capping the total permitted emissions at ten million tons-per-year less than in 1980, and allowing polluters to buy and sell pollution permits nationwide. Initially this program applied only to the 110 dirtiest coal-fired facilities, but by the year 2000 it was to be extended to all major power plants.

By 1997 this approach had produced exceptionally promising results. In 1996 all 445 utility boilers and combustion turbines that were subject to these regulations met their required standards. Utilities had reduced their emissions 30 percent below what the cap required, at about half the expected cost, and acid rain in the Northeast had declined by an estimated 10 to 25 percent. It achieved this primarily by a provision allowing the utilities to burn more western low-sulfur coal, which laws shaped by eastern coal-state senators had previously discouraged (Swift 1997, Ackerman and Hassler 1981, Elliott et al. 1985). Its focus on controlling total emissions rather than on installing mandated control devices created economic incentives to reduce use of the dirtiest facilities, which previous laws had "grandfathered," and to develop more efficient emissions-control technologies. Future reductions might eventually require more costly technologies, such as emissions scrubbers, and other emissions remained uncorrected, but in the meantime economic incentives were producing far more rapid and cheaper reduction of sulfur emissions and acid rain than technology-based regulations had achieved.

With the exception of the Clean Air Act's national sulfur market, however, by the mid-1990s emissions trading had produced only limited results. In practice, many of these initial trading experiments were still closely tied to the preexisting point-by-point, technology-driven control requirements, leaving only slim opportunities for additional benefits—often less than the additional monitoring and transaction costs. From an environmental perspective, trading did not produce any better environmental results than regulation, since emissions-trading markets in principle required as many undercomplying permit buyers as overcomplying sellers. At worst they provided new opportunities for firms to "game the system," trading paper reductions for real emissions. Interregional trading also raised questions of fairness and risk: reductions of sulfur pollution in the Great Lakes might be traded to continue it in the Great Smokies, with possibly greater impacts (Liroff 1986, Hahn and Hester 1989).

The promise of the emissions trading approach for the future, however, lay not so much in trading per se, but in two additional benefits not yet widely recognized. First, it allowed capping and gradually decreasing the total quantities of pollution emitted: the sulfur-trading program, for instance, was designed to reduce overall sulfur emissions from electric utilities by 50 percent. This was a significant new element in pollution control policy, and potentially a major step forward. Second, it allowed market forces to reduce pollution from unregulated as well as regulated sources, by allowing regulated polluters to pay unregulated sources to reduce their emissions, thus drawing these additional and sometimes substantial sources of the problem into the overall solutions.

Both William Reilly, EPA administrator under the Bush administration, and Carol Browner under President Clinton sought to introduce other forms of flexibility and market-oriented incentives. Reilly promoted several voluntary programs to promote energy conservation and reduction of toxic emissions: a "green lights" program to promote use of low-energy lighting, and a "33/50 program" to recognize industries that reduced their use of certain toxic chemicals, first by a third, and then by half. Browner continued these programs and added a "Common Sense Initiative," a partnership with industries to identify the most cost-effective ways to reduce pollution in six high-priority sectors.[14]

Wider use of market-based incentives required not simply a more market-oriented EPA, however, but statutory change. EPA simply did not have the statutory authority to choose the best solutions from a policy "toolbox" of regulatory and economic options. By law, it operated as a regulatory agency implementing specific statutory mandates: mandates that remained inefficient for some problems, ineffective for others, and hamstrung by the burden of proof and procedures required for federal regulation (Andrews 1993).

Information Disclosure as a Policy Tool: The "Right to Know"

An unexpectedly potent new incentive for environmental protection, however, resulted from new requirements for public disclosure of pollutant releases. By merely requiring disclosure rather than imposing regulatory restrictions, this approach bypassed many of the administrative constraints of the regulatory process, and relied on the influence of information itself to create pressure for pollution prevention.

The pollution-control statutes of the 1970s in principle regulated all the major forms of industrial waste disposal, but except for pesticides and newly created toxic compounds they said nothing about the use of hazardous chemicals before they became wastes. Companies were required to report on compliance with the regulations, but not on the actual quantities of chemicals they released to the environment, much less the quantities they used. Decisions about chemical use remained at the core of corporate autonomy, guarded by claims of trade secrets.

Chemical use decisions were also at the core, however, of occupational hazards to workers who lacked information about the risks of chemicals to which they were exposed, and of emergency hazards to communities around factories and transport routes. At least half a dozen chemical-car derailments between 1979 and 1983, for instance, required evacuations of thousands of people, yet often not even local emergency personnel had adequate information to handle such crises. Public reactions led to state-level "right-to-know" campaigns, in cooperation with unions and worker support groups, and by 1985 twenty-nine states had passed some form of worker or community right-to-know law (Gottlieb 1995, 133).

In December 1984, the worst industrial disaster in history took place when a poorly maintained Union Carbide chemical plant in Bhopal, India, released some forty tons of toxic fumes, killing at least twenty-five hundred people and seriously injuring at least ten thousand. The Bhopal catastrophe discredited industry arguments against chemical disclosure requirements and led to a nationwide right-to-know statute, the Emergency Planning and Community Right-To-Know Act (EPCRA), which was enacted as part of the Superfund Act Reauthorization Amendments (SARA) of 1986.[15]

EPCRA required state and local governments to create committees to plan for emergency response to chemical releases, and required industries to report publicly their use and releases of several hundred toxic chemicals. They had to report significant chemical releases immediately, and inform local and state emergency planning committees on an ongoing basis of all significant quantities of these chemicals that they stored or used. They also had to report annually to EPA on the total quantities of their releases of these chemicals, and both their local reports and those to EPA — the "Toxics Release Inventory," or TRI — were designated public documents.[16]

The Toxics Release Inventory provided an unexpectedly powerful new incentive for pollution reduction. Manufacturers who had long reassured the public that they were in compliance with all regulations and had reduced emissions by 90 or 95 percent, for instance, now had to publicly disclose that the remaining 5 to 10 percent still amounted to millions of pounds per year. Newspaper and television reporters compiled "dirty dozen" lists of the worst polluters, heightening public pressure, and tracked their progress or regress each year (fig. 21). State officials compared plants in their jurisdictions with similar facilities elsewhere, and asked pointed questions about why theirs were not being operated as cleanly as others. Even many corporate executives for the first time confronted quantitative estimates of the materials they were discarding into the environment, and the evidence of economic waste as well as environmental damage that these represented.

EPCRA had important limitations. Its lists of reportable chemicals were cobbled together somewhat arbitrarily; some with relatively low risk were included while more dangerous ones were omitted. Reports were not subject to independent verification, and some important sectors were exempted outright: utilities, mining, oil and gas production, agribusiness, municipal waste management facilities, and all federal facilities (Gottlieb 1995, 135–37).[17]

The TRI was nonetheless an extraordinarily influential new policy tool. Reporting mandates did not require the endless procedures and burden of proof necessary for EPA standard-setting, yet the very production and disclosure of information on quantities of emissions created new pressures for their reduction. On the eve of the first TRI reporting deadline, the Monsanto Corporation volunteered to cut its emissions by 90 percent within five years. A number of firms created advisory panels of neighbors and employees, and the Chemical Manufacturers Association developed a "Responsible Care" program to promote community outreach, emissions reduction, and assistance to other firms by their members.[18]

The Nation's Polluters – Who Emits What, and Where

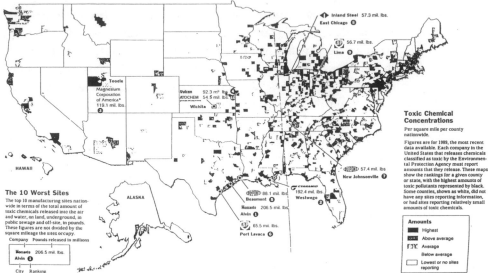

Figure 21. The Toxics Release Inventory (TRI), mandated by amendments to the Superfund Act in 1986, for the first time required public reporting of each firm's total annual amounts of toxic emissions and discharges, rather than merely compliance with regulatory standards and permit requirements. The result was a dramatic increase in negative publicity to the firms that released the most pollutants, as illustrated by this map published in the *New York Times* in 1991. Perhaps equally important, collection and reporting of the TRI data created information that the businesses themselves did not previously consider, documenting the huge amounts of materials they were wasting and thus creating incentives for them to reduce waste and pollution for their own benefit. [Barton Silverman/NYT Permissions]

EPA in 1991 created a voluntary program to encourage such initiatives, challenging businesses to commit to reduce emissions of seventeen high-use toxic chemicals by 33 percent by 1992 and 50 percent by 1995 (the Industrial Toxics or "33/50" Program). Over eight hundred firms responded, and by 1994 EPA could report that emissions of these chemicals had been reduced by over 50 percent. Much of this success was due to the TRI disclosure incentive alone — a major portion of the reduction occurred after 1986 but before 33/50, and large reductions came from non-33/50 firms — but the combined result was nonetheless an important success (Gottlieb 1995, 79–83; Davies and Mazurek 1997, 9–18).

TRI was not the only EPA use of information as a policy incentive. Radon contamination in homes posed a high risk compared to many others the agency regulated, yet it had no direct human cause and EPA had no authority to regulate it. EPA responded therefore by promoting inexpensive radon testing by homeowners, and recommending a nonbinding "action level" (4 pc/l) above which owners were urged to take corrective action. Individuals could act voluntarily on this recommendation, and realtors and home buyers could use it to demand testing and corrective actions as conditions of sale.

The radon information campaign was less influential than TRI, since market forces reached only houses offered for sale and homeowners faced conflicting interests between their desire to reduce hazards and the potential costs and moral obligations that could result from documenting them. As with transportation controls, many people were more inclined to support restrictions on corporations than on themselves. EPA pursued an information strategy on "passive smoking" as well, for which it also lacked regulatory authority, using the influence of its research findings to encourage control measures by state and local governments and by employers.

In short, information disclosure requirements offered an important though limited new policy tool for promoting pollution prevention and risk reduction beyond what EPA could achieve with formal regulation.

New Tools or New Targets? Small-Business Burdens and Unfunded Mandates

For many of the large firms that had been targeted by the environmental regulations of the 1970s, the decade following Ruckelshaus's return in 1983 was a period of resignation to the necessity of compliance, and for some, of innovation and cost savings. For many other businesses, however, the same period brought a daunting barrage of new regulatory burdens. Small businesses had faced few of the regulatory demands that were imposed on large factories and electric utilities in the 1970s. The environmental mandates of the 1980s, however, not only were more prescriptive and inflexible, but also imposed far greater costs on small businesses. The 1984 amendments to the hazardous-waste laws required cleanup of active sites as well as old ones, burdening thousands of businesses with new costs for hazardous-waste disposal. Thousands of "small quantity generators" such as dry cleaners now had to report their hazardous wastes, and pay high costs for disposal. Thousands of gas stations had to dig out and replace their underground storage tanks, and pay for costly cleanup if the tanks had leaked. Many small manufacturers faced the prospect of "maximum achievable control technology" standards to reduce toxic air emissions under the 1990 Clean Air Act, and others faced lawsuits from larger firms to share the costs of Superfund cleanups. The banking and insurance industries found themselves unexpectedly sharing huge financial liabilities for Superfund sites with their clients, and thus unexpectedly becoming participants in environmental regulatory proceedings.

For state and local governments the burden of new regulations was even greater. The states had always been ambivalent toward EPA: it imposed new mandates on them, but it also protected them from upstream and competitor states, and provided them a necessary "gorilla in the closet" to blame for effective regulations of their own. Most of EPA's mandates were delegated to states that wished to accept them rather than imposed unilaterally, but they did place the states in an unaccustomed new role of implementing federal regulatory mandates subject to EPA approval.

The cities, in contrast, had been important supporters of federal action since at least the 1950s, particularly of wastewater treatment financing, along with the many other "categorical grant programs" to finance urban needs that rural-dominated state legislatures had ignored. The federal pollution control statutes in effect represented an implicit social contract or "quid pro quo," under which the federal government assumed authority to set minimum national standards but provided technical assistance and paid a substantial fraction of the costs of implementing them.[19]

Reagan's defunding and devolution policies deliberately broke this social contract. State and local government organizations had given Reagan little support in his presidential campaign, and were among the most outspoken critics of his domestic policies. Reagan's budgets cut federal funding to these groups dramatically, tearing apart the fabric of intergovernmental cooperation both between federal and lower levels of government and among state and local governments themselves. It thus pushed them into more competitive relationships with one another and more adversarial relationships with the federal government (Levine and Thurber 1986, 202–20).[20]

Reagan did streamline some requirements that were burdensome to the states, but also dramatically reduced federal subsidies to implement these mandates. Gorsuch eliminated EPA backlogs in approving state air and water programs, and shifted EPA's underlying policy toward the states from a presumption of close oversight to one of deference. The number of states authorized to administer its program for preventing air quality deterioration (the "prevention of significant deterioration" program) increased from sixteen to twenty-six, and hazardous wastes from eighteen to thirty-four; three more states took over water quality permitting, and twenty-six took over underground injection control.

At the same time, however, EPA's budget reductions cut federal assistance to state environmental programs by 47 percent, and Gorsuch announced that her ultimate objective was to reduce all state grants to zero. According to a survey by the National Governors Association, most states could not make up even a 20 percent reduction in federal support, and many asserted that they would seriously consider eliminating or proportionally reducing environmental programs if federal funds were cut (Andrews 1984a, note 29).

For local governments, meanwhile, the burden was even greater. Local governments were environmental regulators in their own right, but were also delegated responsibilities to implement many federal mandates; and simultaneously, they were the *targets* of many federal regulations. The Clean Water Act required cleanup of municipal wastewater discharges, but throughout the 1970s the federal government had provided substantial subsidies for this task. By the late 1980s, however, these federal wastewater treatment construction grants were being phased out and replaced by loans. The Land and Water Conservation Fund had financed state and local as well as national parkland acquisition with federal oil and gas royalties; Reagan diverted it to other uses. EPA's new landfill standards increased the cost of municipal solid waste management by as much as ten times, and its drinking water standards required more expensive monitoring and purification measures. Local governments and school-bus depots had to replace their underground fuel tanks as well, and every school had to inspect for asbestos and report to parents, a process which almost triggered political pressures for expensive removal procedures. For cities not yet meeting Clean Air Act standards, the 1990 amendments added costly automatic penalties if they did not achieve new compliance timetables, and some of the measures necessary to do this — reformulated fuels and automobile inspection and maintenance requirements, for instance — were politically unpopular.[21]

CERCLA's Superfund liability, meanwhile, burdened cities in several ways at once. Many old municipal landfills were contaminated sites, for which the cities faced partial cleanup liability. Cities also became owners by default of many abandoned sites, and many of these "brownfield" sites were unusable and untaxable until cleanup was completed, a process mired in litigation over cleanup standards and cost-sharing. As EPA began suing industries more aggressively for cleanup costs, they in turn sued the cities for larger contributions, as a political tactic to force federal concessions (Barnett 1994, 263–64).

For all Reagan's rhetoric about giving more autonomy to states and local governments, in short, his legacy ultimately was not fewer federal mandates but less federal funding to implement them, and the congressional backlash to his deregulation policy led to far more burdensome mandates still. The net result was that state and local governments were required to implement more and more federal rules, but federal financial support was diminished, converting the states and cities gradually from supporters or at least acceptors of federal environmental mandates to adversaries.

Faced with more and more federal mandates, with no discretion to set priorities among them and fewer federal subsidies to sweeten them, by the 1990s many cities joined small businesses and other antiregulatory forces to demand an end to unfunded federal mandates. The alienation of such an important and historically supportive constituency, particularly at a time when federal budget politics offered no realistic chance of increased funding, posed a serious threat to EPA.

The Political Debate over Environmental Risks

By the 1990s the issue of environmental risk became a focal point for a broad national political battle about tradeoffs between environmental protection and public health on the one hand, and the burdens and costs of regulation on the other. Throughout the 1980s, even as EPA was committing itself to risk-based decision-making, skeptics questioned whether many environmental risks were in fact significant. Some of these voices could be viewed as merely self-serving industrial interests or antiregulatory publicists (e.g. Efron 1984, Whelan 1985). Others, however, included respected academic scientists and commentators. British epidemiologists Richard Doll and Richard Peto argued that there was no clear epidemiological evidence that general public exposure to industrial chemicals led to increases in most cancers (1981). Biochemist Bruce Ames, inventor of the Ames toxicity test, argued that people routinely ingest natural carcinogens far more potent than most manmade chemicals to which they are exposed, without evident ill effects (Ames et al. 1987). Philip Abelson, editor of *Science,* repeatedly questioned the assumptions and extrapolations used in EPA's risk assessments, arguing that they raised needless public fears and wasted money on costly and unnecessary protective measures (e.g. Abelson 1994).

These arguments attacked federal health-risk regulation of a number of chemicals, such as asbestos, formaldehyde, ethylene dibromide (EDB, a grain fumigant), and some drinking-water contaminants, but the most public clash occurred in 1989 over Alar (daminozide), a chemical used to regulate the growth rate of apples (Benbrook 1996, 100–03). EPA had proposed twice during the 1980s to end the use of Alar for this purpose, due to a carcinogenic breakdown product that formed when Alar-treated apples were heated to make juice or applesauce — two products that young children consume in disproportionate quantities. The agency had been blocked, however, by determined resistance from the chemical's manufacturer, the Uniroyal Company, and by demands by the agency's scientific advisory panel for additional studies.

In 1989, a two-part report on CBS's *60 Minutes* featured a hard-hitting study by the Natural Resources Defense Council which attacked EPA's inaction on Alar as a prime example of its inability to remove unsafe agricultural chemicals from the market, endangering the health of children. The report vividly illustrated the double standard of the pesticide law: if Alar had been proposed for registration as a new product EPA would have disapproved it, but to remove it from the market the agency had to bear a far heavier burden of proof, and could be blocked by a determined manufacturer.

The *60 Minutes* report triggered widespread public outrage and immediately depressed sales of apples and apple products, just as in the cranberry scare of thirty years before. Parents stopped putting apples in their children's lunches, and some local school boards even removed apples from their school-lunch menus, despite official reminders that it was only processed products that posed the risk. The EPA, FDA, and Agriculture Department tried to calm public fears by claiming authoritatively that no more than 5 percent of apples had been sprayed with the chemical, but independent tests quickly established that 30 to 40 percent of the apples then on sale had been treated with it and some two-thirds of apple juices contained at least some residues. In the storm of public criticism that followed, government scientists' reassurances were once again discredited, and the apple growers themselves finally petitioned EPA, successfully, to cancel all food uses of Alar.

The direct effects of the Alar controversy were to remove from the market a substance that EPA had been attempting to remove anyway, to promote increased diversification and pesticide consciousness in the apple-growing industry, and to stimulate far greater attention to an important but previously overlooked aspect of pesticide and food-safety risks, namely their potentially greater risks to children than to healthy adults. The National Academy of Sciences, for instance, in 1993 published an influential study on pesticides in the diets of infants and children, and by 1997 EPA had made environmental health risks to children a primary priority for its research and standard-setting programs. The Food Quality Protection Act of 1996, passed in the heat of the 1996 election campaign, finally and fundamentally reformed the pesticide laws to require consideration of risks to children, rather than simply carcinogenicity, as a basis for pesticide registration decisions.

Politically, however, conservative opponents of EPA chemical regulations seized on the Alar controversy as an example of public hysteria driven by deliberate environmentalist "scare campaigns," of overregulation of trivial risks, and of "junk science." They used it to redirect political attention from the risks of the chemicals themselves — and the industry's own complicity in the ineffectiveness of the regulatory process — to images of environmental extremism and regulatory zealotry.

By the 1990s influential critiques were challenging the risks of several costly environmental regulations — some with arguably greater justification, such as those regulating asbestos — and other prominent academics and journalists had joined the skeptics (see e.g.

Graham et al. 1988; Mossman et al. 1990; Breyer 1993; Schneider 1993; Wildavsky 1995). Even some federal officials, such as one who had played a major role in a decision to evacuate the town of Times Beach, Missouri, in the early 1980s due to dioxin contamination, questioned in retrospect whether their judgments had been correct. Defenders of EPA's regulations countered these criticisms with new evidence suggesting additional environmental risks that had not yet been carefully studied, such as hormonal hazards to wildlife and potentially to humans due to the estrogen-mimicking properties of dioxin (Colborn et al. 1993). A review by the National Academy of Sciences also reaffirmed the reasonableness of EPA's risk-assessment methods and assumptions (National Research Council 1994). Despite these counterarguments, however, skeptics gained increasing influence in challenging EPA's use of scientific risk claims to justify its regulatory decisions (Finkel and Golding 1995).

In 1993 and 1994, risk assessment suddenly emerged as a focal point for congressional debate over federal environmental regulation, though one fraught with misunderstandings and hidden agendas. As one knowledgeable observer noted, "no other issue is marked more by confusion and misinformation than the current debate over risk assessment" (Davies 1995, 7). Some members, such as Senator Patrick Moynihan (D-N.Y.), proposed bills to make risk assessment a more explicit and visible basis for setting EPA priorities, essentially supporting EPA's comparative risk initiatives. Others, however, proposed legislation to prescribe changes in risk-assessment methodology by statute, such as requiring EPA to use "best estimates" of risk rather than "upper bounds," so that fewer regulations could be justified. Still others sought to make risk assessment a procedural weapon to block environmental regulation, by proposals that would add industry representatives to scientific "peer reviews" and open EPA risk assessments to additional litigation and judicial review.

These proposals were all presented as seemingly reasonable demands for analysis of the risks and costs of regulatory proposals, and could easily have been confused with one another. Most were unacceptable to EPA supporters, however, due to concern that their real effect would be to bog down the regulatory process in paperwork and litigation. A coalition of congressional conservatives discovered that they could thus block environmental legislation by attaching risk-assessment requirements to proposed bills. They derailed a 1993 bill to upgrade EPA to the status of a cabinet department by attaching such an amendment, and similar threats ultimately blocked nearly all environmental legislation in the 103rd Congress. For regulatory opponents, statutory risk assessment requirements became one of three tactical devices — along with unfunded mandates and "takings" bills, collectively labeled the "unholy trinity" by environmental groups — for blocking new environmental laws (Davies 1995, 5–8).[22]

In the Republican-dominated Congress of 1995, even stronger versions of these anti-regulatory proposals passed the House as elements of Speaker Newt Gingrich's "Contract With America" legislation. They remained controversial, however, both in the Senate and even among moderate Republicans in the House. In fall 1995 Congress enacted a limited restriction on unfunded mandates, but a bipartisan coalition of moderates had stalled both risk-assessment and takings legislation in the Senate. Opponents of EPA regulation, meanwhile, shifted their tactical emphasis to the appropriations process, seeking radical budget reductions and specific spending restrictions — as well as risk assessment requirements attached to budget bills — to block regulations they opposed.

EPA at a Turning Point

EPA in the mid-1990s thus stood at a crucial turning point. Its administrative leaders for two decades had fostered the development of systematic procedures for risk-based decision-making, initiated comparative-risk processes for setting priorities, and advocated "market-oriented" policy incentives to reduce these risks. Yet EPA's statutes remained a fragmented patchwork of disparate mandates, most of them dictating specific regulatory programs with rigid timetables and little discretion among either priorities or solutions. Most promoted risk reduction more by their regulatory burdens than by purposeful incentives. Some pollutants that appeared to pose only remote risks continued to be regulated, while many other important environmental risks remained largely unaddressed: nonpoint sources of water pollution, losses of natural habitat, global climate change, and archaic sectoral subsidies promoting excessive mining, agriculture, logging, grazing, water use, energy use, and motor vehicle transportation, among others.

The 1994 elections produced a radical insurgence of conservative Republican candidates, who seized control of Congress and removed from power many of the architects and protectors of EPA's statutes. This shift made serious statutory reform conceivable, but placed it in the hands of radical ideological opponents of federal regulations and spending. EPA's programs retained broad public support, but politically they were under more critical fire than ever before. In effect, EPA was now repeating the political battles of the early Reagan years, only this time with its opponents in Congress and its defenders in the White House.

Summary

For all the criticism and political conflict that were directed toward EPA's regulations, in reality they were extraordinarily successful in reducing pollution, at least from major industries and municipal sources. For example, they achieved major reductions in most air pollutants, substantial reductions in urban and industrial water pollution, and dramatic improvements in the management of wastes (U.S. Council on Environmental Quality, 1997).

Emissions of particulate matter (smoke) dropped by nearly 80 percent from 1970 to 1994, for instance, and of lead by 98 percent, even as the U.S. population increased by 27 percent, its gross domestic product by 90 percent, and its vehicle use by 111 percent. Emissions of carbon monoxide and volatile organic compounds each dropped by over 20 percent, and sulfur by one-third; only nitrogen oxides increased (U.S. CEQ 1997, 179, 182). The pollution standards index (PSI) for major U.S. urban areas, perhaps the best integrated indicator of air pollution exposure, improved by 72 percent from 1985 to 1994, with the exception of Southern California, where it improved by 27–35 percent. Airborne releases of reportable toxic chemical pollutants decreased by over 40 percent from 1988 to 1994. For water quality, most of the most conspicuous water pollution from point sources was eliminated. Biochemical oxygen demand and total suspended solids from municipal sewage plants decreased by 36 percent even as loads to them were increasing by 30 percent, and direct industrial discharges were also reduced dramatically (U.S. CEQ 1997, 12–13).

The United States ended the disposal of hazardous industrial wastes into urban solid waste landfills, and it reduced their quantities substantially. It required far more secure measures for treating the remainder, and it substantially increased the proportion of wastes recycled. Over a period of less than a decade, it also ended the practice of open burning of wastes at municipal dumps, closed down hundreds of leaking municipal landfills, replacing them with far safer facilities, and increased municipal recycling from an insignificant level to an estimated 25 percent of the nation's wastes.

The United States also significantly reduced rates of energy consumption per unit of economic production. U.S. industrial energy consumption per constant dollar of gross domestic product declined by almost 45 percent from 1970 to the 1990s. Overall energy consumption declined dramatically between 1973 and 1983, but then increased steadily once more as real fuel prices declined again; by the late 1990s it appeared to have stabilized, at least for the short term. The use of agricultural chemicals also leveled off from 1980 to 1995, after continuous prior annual increases since the 1940s, though it still continued at relatively high levels.

Despite unprecedented policy initiatives and notable successes, however, other environmental problems resisted solution. Airborne emissions of nitrogen oxides, for instance, remained stubbornly constant, offsetting air pollution reductions by industry and per vehicle. The number of vehicle-miles traveled also continued to increase rapidly, offsetting gains in fuel efficiency and threatening new increases in urban pollution. As for water quality, by 1997 more than half of American rivers, lakes, and estuaries were reported in good condition for their intended uses, but over one-third were still only in fair or poor condition (U.S. CEQ 1997, 12–13). A 1996 study found that as many as one-third of the major facilities regulated under the Clean Water Act had committed "significant violations" of their discharge permit limits in 1994 (U.S. General Accounting Office 1996).

An estimated 40 percent of water pollution in U.S. rivers came from agriculture, yet it remained unregulated. Shellfish bed closures increased dramatically in some regions, and many fisheries declined to their lowest levels ever, due to both overfishing and pollution (Safina 1994). Solid-waste discards also continued to increase far more rapidly than recycling, both absolutely (by over 40 percent from 1970 to 1994) and per capita (from 3.29 pounds per day in 1970 to 4.4 in 1994), even though recycling increased from 7 percent in 1970 to over 17 percent in 1990 and a reported 25 percent in 1994 (U.S. CEQ 1997, 483).[23]

Policies for pesticides and toxic chemicals, meanwhile, remained largely ineffectual. From the 1960s to the 1990s, both the percentages of major crops treated with pesticides and the number of treatments per crop continued to increase significantly. The types of risks shifted somewhat, but the overall public health hazards from pesticide use in agriculture remained largely the same as in the 1970s (Benbrook 1996, 42–49).

EPA's policies produced impressive results for some environmental problems, in short, but left others relatively untouched and continuing to worsen. They were dramatically successful in improving waste management practices, but far less so in controlling toxic chemicals. They were relatively successful in controlling point sources of air and water pollution, but far less so in reducing nonpoint sources, so that their overall environmental results often fell far short of their intended goals. They reduced pollution per vehicle dramatically, but did not stop the constant increase in vehicle miles traveled and related transport and land use patterns, which continued to erode the benefits of the technical measures. Finally, most policies remained focused on pollution-control requirements, despite rhetoric promoting pollution prevention, and some even created disincentives to prevention alternatives.

Many of the measures that had been reasonably successful in reducing pollution from large point sources, moreover, were not easily transferable to pollution by other sources that were major contributors to the remaining problems. EPA attempts to strengthen emissions inspection and maintenance programs for motor vehicles, for instance, aroused immediate and effective political opposition. There was simply far less political will to impose serious restrictions on farms, land development, small businesses, local governments, households, and individual behavior such as motor vehicle use, than on large manufacturing industries.

For all the successes of national environmental regulation, therefore, serious environmental problems remained uncorrected, and the regulatory programs themselves had become increasingly gridlocked by political conflict. Other industrial nations had begun to move ahead of the United States in some policy innovations rather than following its lead: Japan in imposing economic charges on emissions, Germany in waste recycling and product stewardship requirements, others in setting quantitative national targets and timetables for pollution reduction. In the United States, however, the pendulum politics of reaction and counterreaction had so repeatedly poisoned the well of trust, first under Reagan and again in the 1994 Republican congressional insurgency, that environmental groups were more determined than ever to maintain the existing system of regulations and litigation rights, and to resist any proposals for reform that might prove to be simply new covert tactics for weakening the regulatory system.

The tragedy of this gridlock was not just the stalemating of new regulations or the costly burdens imposed on businesses and governments, but the breakdown of effective governance, and even of the political support for effective governance, that was necessary to solve environmental problems. The support for effective governance that created the New Deal, or even that produced EPA itself in the 1970s, had been replaced by a pervasive distrust toward governance, which was all too easily justified by politicians who cynically manipulated public distrust to further weaken and undermine effective federal environmental governance.

Thoughtful observers of the environmental regulatory system shared a strong consensus that fundamental reforms were needed, and about the basic principle that should guide them. The National Academy of Public Administration in 1995 recommended that Congress give EPA an explicit and integrated statutory mission, and the flexibility to set priorities and carry them out. It should authorize "accountable devolution": EPA should continue to set and enforce national standards, but should be authorized to delegate far more flexibility to state and local governments as to how to achieve them. It should authorize the EPA to make far more flexible use of market-based incentives as means to achieve better as well as cheaper environmental results. Finally, EPA's fragmented statutes should gradually be integrated into a single coherent framework (National Academy of Public Administration 1995).

Terry Davies and Jan Mazurek (1997b) offered similar recommendations. EPA's pollution-control programs should be redesigned to focus on results rather than prescribed methods, its historically fragmented programs and functions should be integrated, and they should be economically efficient, participatory, and continuously improved by far richer use of information. The National Environmental Policy Institute, a group headed by a former congressman, made similar recommendations, as did the Enterprise for the Environment, chaired by former EPA Administrator William Ruckelshaus, in 1997.

For all this reasoned consensus on desirable policy reforms, however, by the late 1990s there appeared no political coalition strong enough to champion them, and mutual distrust remained too widespread to build an effective alliance between environmentalists seeking better results and businesses seeking cheaper ones. EPA was the agency politicians and businesses loved to hate, stalled at a turning point between reform and reaction. Powerful and conflicting constituencies — innovative and recalcitrant businesses, progressive and reactionary states, environmental advocacy groups, and supporters of each of these interests in Congress — each had the power to veto the others' proposals. With a few rare exceptions, however — notably the enactment of two statutes reforming the pesticide and drinking-water laws just before the 1996 elections — none of these groups had sufficient power or trust to build winning coalitions for reforms. Further improvements in environmental policy appeared to require either some major new precipitating event or a redefinition of the issues to insert environmental policy provisions into legislation reforming agriculture, defense, energy, trade, transportation, and other sectors. After a quarter-century of impressive though imperfect results, and of considerable experimentation and innovation at its margins, national environmental regulation in the United States was largely stalemated, carrying on with some progress and regress at the margin but with little political room for significant reform.

14 The Unfinished Business of National Environmental Policy

> The Congress, recognizing the profound impact of man's activity on the interrelations of all components of the natural environment, and particularly the profound influences of population growth, high-density urbanization, industrial expansion, resource exploitation, and new and expanding technological advances . . . declares that it is the continuing policy of the Federal Government . . . to use all practicable means and measures . . . in a manner calculated to foster and promote the general welfare, to create and maintain conditions under which man and nature can exist in productive harmony, and fulfill the social, economic, and other requirements of present and future generations of Americans. — National Environmental Policy Act of 1969

The nationalization of pollution control was one historic sea change of the "environmental era" that began in 1970. The larger story of that era, however, was the attempt to forge a more coherent overall environmental policy across the many agencies whose actions affected the environment. As in previous periods, policies shaping other major sectors of the economy that used materials and energy and transformed the landscape for other purposes often had far greater impacts than EPA's limited regulatory tools.

The National Environmental Policy Act of 1969 was one such attempt, as were statutes protecting natural lands, ecosystems, and species. Others included changes in the laws and policies governing agriculture, energy, transportation, public land management, and other sectors. At least as important were policy changes that were not made, leaving some environmentally damaging activities virtually unchecked. Attempts to create effective institutional mechanisms for overall environmental policy integration, moreover, were effectively blocked.

By the mid-1990s, a resurgent alliance of resource-extraction interests and antigovernment conservatives in the Congress was threatening to roll back many of the environmental provisions that had gradually been added to many statutes. This was particularly true for provisions that directly protected natural lands and species: the Endangered Species Act and wetland protection requirements. Several policy changes undertaken for other purposes — deregulation of agriculture and electric utilities, for instance — also threatened to undercut environmental safeguards that had been embedded in the previous system, though they promised also to remove perverse incentives for overuse of resources that were likewise embedded in the old system.

U.S. environmental policy remained therefore a ragged and uneven patchwork. At the outset of the environmental era, the United States was without question the world leader in this effort, and its policy innovations were widely emulated worldwide. By the mid-1990s, however, other countries had moved ahead — the Netherlands, for instance, with its national environmental policy plan, Germany with product-stewardship legislation, and others with "sustainable development" programs formulated in response to the United Nations' 1992 Conference on Environment and Development (the "Earth Summit," discussed in Chapter 15). Many U.S. initiatives meanwhile stalled in a cycle of pendulum politics, alternating between largely symbolic environmental victories and changes favoring resurgent resource-extraction and property-rights interests.

The National Environmental Policy Act

The late 1960s produced a clear public consensus that the federal government should take the lead in controlling pollution and correcting environmental destruction. In its impacts on the landscape and ecosystems, however, the federal government was as much the cause of problems as were big businesses. It was federal land management policies that were allowing clear-cut logging of the national forests, and it was federal agencies that were damming and channelizing rivers and bulldozing the interstate highway system across the landscape. It was federal policies too that were promoting large-scale nuclear power plants, strip mining of coal on the public lands, oil extraction from vulnerable coastal waters and Alaskan tundra, supersonic transport aircraft (SSTs) that might pollute the stratosphere, and many other activities that adversely impacted the natural environment.

Correcting these problems therefore required change in the government's own policies and actions. It required a government-wide policy balancing resource extraction and landscape transformation benefits against their impacts on other environmental values. Equally, it required integration of this policy at an operational level across the patchwork of conflicting agencies, missions, and public values that were actors in each environmental context. In the words of a 1968 congressional report, "There are conflicts when environmental quality is managed by different policies, originating in conservation, agriculture, esthetics, recreation, economic development, human health, and so on. . . . The operational engineering programs which may affect the quality of the environment are not coordinated through a single group, but are handled through individual inter-agency liaisons (if they are coordinated at all)" (U.S. Congress 1968).

The National Environmental Policy Act of 1969 (NEPA) was designed to provide such a policy. Developed by Senator Henry Jackson (D-Wash.), with the assistance of public administration expert Professor Lynton Caldwell, it passed both houses of Congress by overwhelming majorities and was signed by President Nixon on national television on New Year's Day 1970. Four months before Earth Day, and nearly a year before EPA was created, the enactment of NEPA marked the beginning of the environmental era in U.S. governance. Twenty-eight years later its brief text remained unchanged by any significant amendment, and it had been emulated by over half the U.S. state governments, by over eighty other national governments, by regional economic institutions such as the

European Union, and by international lending institutions such as the World Bank and Asian Development Bank.[1]

NEPA was designed as a government-wide policy framework—in effect, a "super-mandate"—to ensure that all federal agencies would incorporate environmental concerns into their actions. Its text comprised three mutually reinforcing elements: a declaration of policy, a series of implementing mechanisms, and an oversight organization (the President's Council on Environmental Quality, or CEQ).

NEPA's first element was a substantive statement of national environmental policy, applicable to all agencies of the federal government. NEPA declared a national policy to maintain "productive harmony" between man and nature while fulfilling the social, economic, and other requirements of present and future generations of Americans. It went on to identify six specific principles: government agencies should strive

1. to fulfill the responsibilities of each generation as trustee of the environment for succeeding generations;
2. to assure for all Americans safe, healthful, productive, and aesthetically and culturally pleasing surroundings;
3. to attain the widest range of beneficial uses of the environment without degradation, risk to health or safety, or other undesirable and unintended consequences;
4. to preserve important historic, cultural, and natural aspects of our national heritage, and maintain where possible an environment which supports diversity and variety of individual choice;
5. to achieve a balance between population and resource use which will permit high standards of living and a wide sharing of life's amenities; and
6. to enhance the quality of renewable resources and approach the maximum attainable recycling of depletable resources.

The significance of this policy statement was widely overlooked. Conventional wisdom dismissed it as a merely philosophical or rhetorical preamble, not enforceable by the courts and therefore unimportant. Whether or not it could be enforced by litigation, however, it provided a sweeping statutory grant of authority to the president and executive agencies to take action to protect the environment. The law "authorized and directed" the agencies to administer their responsibilities in accord with NEPA's policy principles, as well as to take specific procedural actions. Agencies that had been constrained from considering environmental factors by narrower statutory missions or criteria—such as the water-resource and highway construction agencies, which operated under narrowly defined economic cost-benefit criteria—now had authority to consider them.[2] This mandate was largely ignored, but remained available if a president or agency were to seek authority to justify stronger environmental leadership (McElfish and Parker 1995).

To assure that these principles were implemented, NEPA included a second element, a series of "action-forcing mechanisms": specific tasks and procedural requirements to assure that the agencies must actually consider and implement the policy statement in their day-to-day actions. The most specific of these was a requirement that before taking any "major federal action significantly affecting the quality of the human environment," the responsible agency must prepare a detailed statement of its environmental impacts and alternatives: an "environmental impact statement" (EIS), as it came to be called. Significantly, it required that the statement discuss not only the environmental impacts of a proposed action, but also alternatives to it that might lessen its adverse impacts. Before taking action, the agency must then circulate a draft of this statement for review and comment to all other affected agencies and to the general public. This requirement opened all federal actions to input and challenge by anyone who had environmental concerns about their potential impact or proposals for better alternatives to achieve their purposes, from major corporation or national environmental advocacy group to state agency or local neighbor.

In NEPA's first nine years, agencies prepared more than eleven thousand impact statements. Over a thousand of these were litigated, and about 20 percent of those agencies sued were enjoined by the courts, normally to halt the action pending changes in the proposal or at least in the statement. By the late 1980s, the number of EISs had stabilized at four to five hundred statements per year plus some fifty thousand "assessments" (preliminary reports to determine whether or not to prepare a formal EIS).

The EIS was a distinctive innovation in administrative reform.[3] Before NEPA, federal agencies had essentially no responsibility to consider alternatives to or consequences of their actions; their sole criteria were cost and the implementation of their own mission. They were also free to define that mission in ways that suited powerful beneficiaries rather than the full range of people who would be affected by their actions, and even other government agencies often had no advance input to decisions that might affect their responsibilities. NEPA's review and disclosure requirements called for documentation not just to inform and justify administrative decisions, as in the past, but to open them to public scrutiny. The EIS thus became not just an administrative document but a political instrument: it forced coordination with all other agencies whose missions might be impacted, and it opened access to all stakeholders. In the EIS procedure, NEPA fundamentally altered the procedures and politics of administrative decision-making.

The EIS procedure was most actively used to challenge federal highway and water-resource construction projects, license applications for nuclear power plants, and logging and grazing on the public lands. Many of these activities were debatable on economic as well as environmental grounds, but previous reform attempts — requiring cost-benefit analyses, for instance — were not enforceable by the courts.[4] The EIS provided a new vehicle for legal challenges to such projects, and also for publicizing their negative impacts and thus undermining their political benefits. In one sector after another, citizen groups used the EIS to challenge federal actions that promoted environmental damage (fig. 22). NEPA did not explicitly change the agencies' authority to approve such actions, but it clearly altered their political context in ways that stopped some major proposals, required modifications of others, and prevented still others that might otherwise have been initiated (cf. Andrews 1976; Mazmanian and Nienaber 1979; Taylor 1984; Smythe 1994).[5]

In a larger sense, the NEPA challenges to federal water projects, nuclear power licenses and public-land management marked the end of the era of large-scale federal public

Figure 22. An early target of the National Environmental Policy Act's environmental impact statement requirement. Construction of a major new jet airport in 1969 in the heart of the Everglades National Park aroused vehement protests from ecologists and nature conservationists, who feared that air and water pollution from aircraft exhaust and jet fuel, as well as constant noise, would destroy the ecological functions of the Everglades and adjacent Big Cypress Swamp as wildlife refuges and sources of clean water. In the face of these protests the airport was eventually abandoned, even though construction had been completed, and the Big Cypress National Preserve was established instead. [U.S. National Park Service]

investment projects and domestic development subsidies, and rang in a new period of far greater public skepticism and argument—from both the left and the right—over the merits of government-led initiatives of any kind. They opened up the cozy subgovernments of agencies and their primary beneficiaries to far broader scrutiny and debate, particularly by their opponents and victims, and they substantially raised the political costs of many economically wasteful and environmentally damaging proposals. Many of these actions well deserved to be stopped, and it is a credit both to the EIS procedure and to the citizen groups who used it that they accelerated this outcome.

Lost in this change of eras, however, was a larger value as well: the belief that government should or even could be an instrument of larger shared purposes than markets alone could provide, such as integrated conservation of entire watersheds or river basins. The era of large-scale national development programs was ending.

In practice the EIS requirement had important limitations. First, most EISs were produced by just a handful of agencies — the Forest Service, Bureau of Land Management, Department of Housing and Urban Development, Army Corps of Engineers, and Federal Highway Administration — and the overwhelming majority were simply rubber-stamped without serious debate.[6] Second, producing impact statements did not always produce better decisions: the same agencies still made the decisions, the same congressional committees oversaw and funded them, and the same beneficiaries still lobbied them for federal support. Third, the primary influence of the EIS was therefore on *controversial* actions. Not all controversial actions caused the most serious environmental damage, however — some simply had the best-organized opponents — and the most serious environmental threats did not always attract effective opponents.

A more serious limitation was the rarity of EISs on truly fundamental policy decisions. The EIS requirement was mainly applied to specific projects and management plans, not to the broader policies, legislative initiatives, or appropriations bills that underlay them. Project Independence, for example, a presidential policy initiative in response to the Arab oil embargo of the early 1970s, called for widespread actions to accelerate exploitation of U.S. fossil fuel resources, yet it was never subjected to an environmental impact statement. Other examples included agricultural, logging, and mining subsidies, U.S. positions in trade negotiations, and the entire field of tax policy (see e.g. Faeth et al. 1991; Repetto and Gilles 1988; McKenzie et al. 1992).

Finally, NEPA's EIS requirement was limited to proposed actions of the federal government. It did not require federal agencies to propose *additional* actions to protect the environment, nor did it force reconsideration of policies that were already in effect.[7] It had little effect, therefore, on the impacts of broad patterns of economic activity that were promoted by entrenched public policy incentives or that did not require new federal action. Examples included combustion and energy use, agricultural production and land conversion, urbanization of coasts and estuaries, and habitat destruction from construction and development.[8]

The EIS approach to administrative reform — the use of documentation requirements as an action-forcing mechanism — was thus both important and problematic. On the one hand, it greatly increased public accountability of administrative decision-making, by providing widely available documentation of impacts and an opportunity for challenge at the point of practical action. On the other hand, it served more to politicize individual decisions than to change broad patterns of policy, and it greatly increased the political and procedural costs of government action, sometimes to the point of stalemate or gridlock. The courts ultimately proved willing to enforce the EIS requirement only as a procedural requirement, not as a procedural tool to force implementation of NEPA's substantive policy statement. Agencies and presidents alike therefore absorbed and marginalized the EIS mandate as a paperwork requirement, while largely ignoring the mandate and grant of authority in NEPA's policy statement for active, environment-centered policy-making. By itself, therefore, the EIS did not assure implementation of a national environmental policy, though it did provide an important procedural weapon against specific proposals that were arguably at odds with such a policy. NEPA's policy statement prefigured the substance of a national environmental policy, but it was never elaborated into operational form and implemented.

The third of NEPA's three elements was the establishment of an organizational champion, the President's Council on Environmental Quality (CEQ). CEQ was to oversee the policy's implementation, advise the president on environmental issues, and issue public reports annually on the state of the nation's environment (e.g. U.S. Council on Environmental Quality 1990, 1996). The Council was to consist of three distinguished experts, appointed by the president and confirmed by the Senate, supported by a staff in the Executive Office of the President. Throughout the 1970s, CEQ also sponsored special studies of emerging problems, adding them to the national agenda. Examples included studies of toxic chemicals in the environment (paving the way for the Toxic Substances Control Act), off-road vehicle impacts, environmental research needs, agricultural lands, and wildlife law, and, perhaps most widely publicized, the 1980 *Global 2000* study of worldwide environmental trends and problems (U.S. Council on Environmental Quality 1971, 1977, 1978, 1980a, 1980b). Several of these studies were hotly debated, but as a group they illustrated the value of an effective high-level advisory body in framing the national environmental agenda.

The weakness of the CEQ model, however, was its inherent dependence on the personal support of the president. Through the 1970s CEQ's professional staff grew to about fifty, including members with expertise in the ecological and environmental sciences as well as economics, policy, and law. Under both Republican and Democratic presidents it had modest but real influence with the agencies and in presidential policy debates. President Reagan, however, decided that he had no interest in an executive-level environmental policy integration staff, and through OMB director David Stockman he deliberately destroyed the Council in all but name, firing its entire staff, drastically reducing its budget, and staffing it only with a handful of political loyalists and temporary consultants (Bartlett 1984; Vig 1984). President Bush appointed an experienced professional to head CEQ, but did not restore its critical mass of budget, staff expertise, or influence.

President Clinton, despite the strong environmental commitment of his vice president, Al Gore, initially showed no greater understanding than Reagan of the need for the ongoing policy integration that CEQ was created to provide: he proposed to abolish CEQ in favor of a White House Office of Environmental Policy and a cabinet-level EPA.[9] White House staff come and go with each president, however, while Executive Office agencies serve as career staff to the presidency. The Office of Management and Budget was created to provide this ongoing integrative capability for budget policy, and CEQ was created to provide a similar capacity for environmental policy (Caldwell 1997). In 1994, under pressure from environmental supporters in both parties, President Clinton withdrew his proposal to abolish CEQ and instead nominated the White House environmental policy staff director, Katie McGinty, to head it. In 1996, supporters beat back an attempt by the Republican 104th Congress to halve its budget and specify that the remainder be used to terminate it.

Overall, NEPA thus provided a farsighted vision of the need for an integrated national environmental policy, and an innovative series of steps toward the creation of such a framework. It had only limited and largely ad hoc effects on the policies and programs of most federal agencies, however, and it faced steady resistance from political forces that had always thwarted executive-level policy integration and effective presidential management of environmental programs. For all its foresight and innovation, NEPA remained only a first step toward a national environmental policy.

Preserving Nature

One logical step beyond NEPA was to create stronger substantive national laws to protect natural lands, ecosystems, and species. U.S. policies since the late nineteenth century had protected some lands for designated purposes, but even many public lands were subject to mining, logging, and grazing, and landscape protection outside the public lands was left almost exclusively to the discretion of landowners and developers. The result was widespread and often careless landscape transformation: conversion of wildlife habitat into urban and industrial development, paving over of streams and watersheds, draining and filling of wetlands, and other changes, carried out with little attention to their ecological impacts. Even fish and wildlife policies were largely limited to species of interest to hunters and fishermen. If natural species and ecosystems were to be protected and managed, therefore, stronger and more substantive legislation than NEPA was required.

In 1971 Senator Henry Jackson, the author of NEPA, proposed a National Land Use Policy Act (NLUP) as a sequel. Versions of this bill contained provisions for comprehensive river-basin planning, grants to state and local governments for environmentally protective land-use plans, and a ban on federal aid for environmentally damaging or poorly planned projects. President Nixon also proposed planning grants for local governments, especially in coastal areas, as well as centralized approval of power plant sites and transmission corridors, tax incentives for historic preservation, and regulation of the environmental impacts of mining. Despite the bipartisan support of both Senator Jackson and President Nixon, however, the NLUP was blocked by land-development interests and never enacted.[10]

In its place, Congress in 1972 passed the more limited Coastal Zone Management Act, which provided similar incentives for environmental planning and management in coastal areas, where both ecological values and development pressures were greatest. The act offered federal incentives for states to create planning commissions to develop plans for managing and protecting the environmental resources of coastal areas. In return, the law provided financial assistance and specified that federal actions must also conform to the plans, a power over federal actions which the states did not otherwise have.[11] The result was at least a microcosm of more active environmental planning in particularly sensitive and high-priority environments, but little more.

A second initiative was federal regulation to protect wetlands. Wetlands were vital for fisheries and waterfowl habitat, and valuable for filtering human pollutants and other natural functions as well. However, they were always in danger of being drained by farmers, dredged for boating, or filled for waterfront development projects. Historical data documented steady and increasing losses of these ecosystems to more intensive uses.[12] Some wetlands were protected by public-trust sovereignty over surface waters, but others were on otherwise private lands, ranging from low-lying areas along rivers and streams to seasonally wet drainages and "prairie potholes" that provided vital habitat for migratory waterfowl.

Section 404 of the 1972 Federal Water Pollution Control Act amendments therefore required landowners to obtain permits from the Army Corps of Engineers for dredging or filling of wetlands linked to navigable waters. This law did not control agricultural and logging activities, nor wetlands unconnected to navigable waters, but it did limit some threats, such as marinas and waterfront development. It therefore became a major grievance of land developers and property owners, who claimed that such controls amounted to a "taking" of their property. Under the Fifth Amendment, takings of property must be compensated at the market value of the land, which at the developable value of waterfront property could be unaffordable. At stake was a fundamental issue: was wetland dredging and filling a public harm or nuisance that could legitimately be controlled by the government's police power, or was wetland protection merely a public use or amenity for which the public should pay the owner?

Throughout the 1970s and 1980s, the courts generally upheld such regulations so long as some reasonable public purpose could be documented and some economic use for the property remained. However, decisions in the early 1990s reopened the issue of regulatory takings, and property-rights advocates introduced both federal and state bills that would define such takings not just by a total loss of economic use, but by some lesser percentage of "diminution of value" (Kayden 1996).[13] If successful, such arguments had the potential to undermine not only wetlands regulations, but even the principle that government may legitimately regulate to prevent one individual's actions from harming others, leaving governments open to blackmail by rent-seeking individuals demanding to be paid not to take harmful actions. Even many property-rights conservatives found this idea less attractive in reality than in rhetoric, and as of 1998 it had not passed Congress.[14] Wetland regulations thus remained in place, but vulnerable to future attacks by property-rights advocates.

A third nature-protection initiative was federal regulation to protect endangered wildlife species. Like pollution control, wildlife management prior to the 1960s was primarily a state matter: federal policy was limited to controlling interstate commerce in wildlife, managing national wildlife refuges and fisheries affected by federal water resource projects, and occasionally intervening to manage certain species on federal lands.[15] With the exception of migratory waterfowl, there was no comprehensive or coordinated federal program for wildlife protection (Bean 1983 [1977], 281).

The rising environmental awareness of the 1960s, however, included increased public concern for natural species. A 1966 law authorized the Interior Department to conserve native species threatened with extinction, and to list them publicly. Amendments in 1969 extended this authority to species threatened with worldwide extinction, and banned commercial imports and exports of them. The 1969 law thus became a precursor of the 1973 Convention on International Trade in Endangered Species (CITES), which in turn provided a new justification for federal endangered-species policy in its constitutional power to make law through treaties.[16] Several subsequent laws expanded federal programs for protecting particular species, such as wild horses and burros, eagles, and marine mammals.[17]

In 1973, Congress asserted for the first time a general federal responsibility to protect endangered plant and animal species. The Endangered Species Act of 1973 (ESA) authorized the U.S. Fish and Wildlife Service to list species that were either endangered or threatened, and prohibited federal agencies from taking actions that would destroy the "critical habitat" essential to their survival. It also prohibited not just federal agencies but anyone from "taking" endangered or threatened species; and the Fish and Wildlife Service defined such taking to include not only harming or harassing them directly, but also harming their habitat and thus disrupting their breeding, feeding, and sheltering needs.

The Endangered Species Act thus became the most clear-cut and absolute federal policy mandate for the protection of nature. Its prohibition of federal actions that harmed critical habitat made it a weapon of last resort against environmentally damaging federal actions. Examples included the Tennessee Valley Authority's Tellico Dam, which threatened the habitat of the snail darter (a species of minnow), and the Forest Service's old-growth logging practices, which threatened the habitat of the northern spotted owl in the Pacific Northwest. Many of these actions were economically dubious as well, but had powerful beneficiaries.[18] To opponents of such actions, the endangered species were important not only for themselves but as "canaries in the mine" — indicators of fundamental damage to whole ecosystems, of which the endangered species were the most sensitive members. Project advocates in turn portrayed the ESA as the epitome of environmental extremism, destroying jobs and stopping economic activities to protect seemingly trivial species.

Importantly, however, a growing body of research revealed that a large majority of endangered species and their habitat were located in the South and Hawaii, predominantly on privately owned lands (Dobson 1997). The definition of habitat modification as a "taking" of endangered species thus raised an even more volatile issue: the prospect of federal regulations and environmentalist lawsuits against uses of private lands, such as land development in the California desert and logging of pines in the South. Destroying critical habitat would clearly destroy the resident wildlife, but to prohibit modifying the habitat of any such population raised the specter of open-ended challenges to virtually any land use that some environmental group or government agency opposed. In an important 1995 decision, however, the Supreme Court upheld the Fish and Wildlife Service definition, leaving further debate to Congress.[19] In the wake of this decision, leading states and the Clinton administration promoted a boom in "habitat conservation plans," negotiated agreements that approved some habitat destruction or private lands in exchange for commitments to leave other areas untouched. Whether these remaining areas will be sufficient to sustain the species, or whether such agreements will in retrospect prove to have been merely politically expedient deals on the way to further development pressures, remains unknown. The comparable history of nineteenth-century Indian reservations is not reassuring.

At its root the Endangered Species Act raised unresolved questions of both science and public values. Species evolution and extinction are natural processes that are exacerbated by human impacts, and any location might easily be populated by thousands of species of animals, plants, and microflora, at least some of which are localized variants or are trying to survive near the natural limits of their ranges. It seemed plausible therefore that enterprising scientists could discover such populations virtually anywhere they might look hard enough, especially if they were motivated not by systematic priorities of scientific or public importance but by the tactical impulse to stop a particular project. Was it really vital to preserve all localized variants of a species? And was it really worthwhile or realistic, given nature's own processes, to try to prevent *all* extinctions? Which ones really mattered? Politically, it is far easier to marshal public support for protection of a few species that are well known and widely loved — whales and eagles, for instance — than for the nearly infinite range of plants and smaller animals.

On the other hand, many less-familiar species clearly *are* important in maintaining vital ecological processes, often far more so than most large mammals and raptors, and the loss of some "sentinel species" clearly *does* signal potential danger to the ecosystems that support them. More fundamentally, the aggregate pressures of human population growth, urbanization and industrialization clearly *have* created unprecedented pressures on ecological systems worldwide, and radically diminished their natural diversity of species. But how could the "important" species losses be distinguished from those that were not, both by scientists and by politicians and the public? Lacking clear answers to these questions, in the mid-1990s the Endangered Species Act became a primary focus for conflict over the proper boundary between nature-protection policies and property rights.[20] The law officially expired in 1992, and while Congress continued to extend it on a year-to-year basis, repeated efforts to formally reauthorize it failed due to opposition by property-rights advocates.

Resource Conservation: Managing Commercial Fisheries

Another possible step beyond NEPA was to strengthen the conservation laws for managing renewable resources such as fisheries, and thus to protect them from the tragedies of the commons that otherwise threatened to overexploit and destroy them. During the postwar era commercial fishing technology evolved rapidly to the scale of huge factory ships, with increasingly precise navigational tools and gear so efficient that it could systematically mine entire fisheries, often destroying their habitat and other species in the process.[21] By the mid-1970s, as Russian factory ships were poised to wipe out some of the most productive fisheries off the U.S. coasts, Senator Warren Magnuson (D-Wash.) sponsored legislation to declare U.S. economic sovereignty over a two-hundred-mile offshore "exclusive economic zone," and to ban foreign fishing fleets from these waters.[22]

The 1976 Fisheries Management and Conservation Act ("Magnuson Act") was a landmark of fishery conservation law. It saved the fisheries from destructively efficient harvest by foreign factory ships, and it set up eight regional fishery management councils to administer each of the major commercial fisheries. Its presumption was that councils made up of the fishermen themselves, with access to scientific expertise from the National Marine Fisheries Service, would manage the fisheries sustainably.[23]

Tragically, however, the Magnuson Act also created a federal investment-incentive program to "modernize" the U.S. fishing fleet, providing financial subsidies for construction of new American commercial fishing vessels. These incentives triggered rapid overexpansion of the fleet to unsustainable levels. With more and more fishermen using increasingly efficient gear, each trapped between fish stocks that were once again declining and the mortgage payments on their boats, few fishermen had the perspective or the will to restrict harvests. By the 1990s U.S. fishermen had thus reached the verge of destroying many of the major offshore fisheries by themselves. Only lawsuits by environmental groups, such as the Conservation Law Foundation, eventually forced more effective restrictions. A 1996 reauthorization of the Magnuson Act included promising new provisions to tighten loopholes in allowable catch limits, to reduce the number of boats through government buy-backs, and to authorize study of "individual transferable quotas" as an economic incentive for capping and allocating the maximum sustainable catch — much as tradable emissions permits allowed capping and efficient trading of air pollution emissions. There remained no guarantee however that these innovations would save the fisheries from more efficient harvest by the remaining boats. Every policy option seemed to contain some loophole by which self-interested fishermen might continue to overfish the dwindling stocks.[24]

Commercial fisheries remained therefore a classic example of the tragedy of the commons, and of both the market and institutional failures that made sustainable management of such resources enduringly problematic.

Energy

Given the limitations both of NEPA and of the explicit nature-protection statutes, a broader strategy for national environmental policy was to try to insert environmental considerations into the statutes governing major economic sectors. Those in which the most important policy changes resulted, though not always for the better, included energy, transportation, agriculture, and the national forests and other public lands.

No sector of human activity impacts the environment more pervasively than the production and use of energy. Examples include the effects of coal, oil, and uranium mining, of hydroelectric dams and electric power plants, of air pollution from energy combustion, of oil spills, of global warming, and of nuclear waste management. From the nineteenth century on, U.S. energy production and use were shaped by government policies promoting development of each major fuel: coal, oil, natural gas, electricity (including hydroelectric power production), and nuclear energy. These policies shared two underlying principles, which were considered so fundamental as to be virtually beyond debate. One was that cheap energy was essential to economic progress, and the other was that government policies should therefore be used to assure abundant supplies at low prices. Implicit in these principles was the assumption that energy resources would themselves continue to be abundant, due either to new discoveries or to technological breakthroughs. That is, these principles were designed to assure and manage energy *surplus* rather than scarcity.

These principles were generally successful, at least until 1973. They produced constant energy surpluses except under wartime pressures, and U.S. energy prices actually declined continuously throughout this period even as people used more and more of it. Absent, however, was any serious consideration of the associated environmental impacts, of the vulnerability of an economy structured around the assumption of cheap energy, or of other hidden costs of policies that subsidized low energy prices even as the cheapest sources were steadily depleted.

These principles took varied forms in the largely separate policies and subgovernments for each fuel (Davis 1993, 6). Coal policy included little more than policies for mine safety and for leasing of federal lands for mining, plus three sets of environmental controls added in the 1970s: air quality regulations on coal combustion, water quality regulations on acid mine drainage, and in 1977 the Surface Mining Control and Reclamation Act, which required restoration of strip-mined sites. Oil policy, designed to assure both abundant supplies and stable profits for producers, was more complicated. Production controls were instituted in the 1930s to limit competitive overpumping (see Chapter 9). These were gradually replaced in the 1950s and '60s by incentives to promote continued production at low prices as cheap domestic supplies were exhausted. These included tax benefits ("depletion allowances") to promote exploration for new supplies, cheap leasing of federal lands and of the outer continental shelf, and import quotas to protect domestic producers against cheaper foreign sources.[25] Major oil spills in the late 1960s — the *Torrey Canyon* shipwreck and the offshore oil platform blowout off Santa Barbara, California, in 1969 — ignited public pressure to regulate offshore drilling and shipping of oil more closely, to stop leasing of wild lands and of offshore tracts for oil extraction, and particularly to stop the proposed Trans-Alaska Pipeline System, which would open the unspoiled wilderness of northern Alaska to oil extraction. These pressures led to stricter environmental regulation and to moratoria on offshore leasing, but they did not stop the trans-Alaska pipeline, nor did they produce any fundamental shift in policies promoting continued production of oil at artificially low prices.

For electricity, unlimited cheap access was promoted as a public right by state regulatory commissions.[26] Consumer prices were kept regulated at inexpensive levels, to prevent profiteering by regional electric monopolies, but the utilities were also held responsible for providing adequate electricity to meet whatever growth in demand occurred at those prices. Federal policies promoting cheap electricity included subsidies for hydroelectric power production in federal water resource projects, favorable regulation of interstate electric transmission by the Federal Power Commission, and the rural electrification program begun in the 1930s. Federal support also subsidized the development and use of nuclear electric generation: research and development programs, cheap rates for nuclear fuel production in federal facilities, liability limits for nuclear accidents, and gross undercharging for the future costs of nuclear waste management and decommissioning of obsolete facilities.[27]

By the 1970s, environmental regulations had addressed some of the most obvious impacts of energy production, and public challenges to proposed new power plants had proliferated.[28] However, energy markets still did not reflect the full environmental costs of energy production and use, nor did they reflect even the true economic costs of energy production itself. Nor, finally, did they reflect accurate information about the relative costs of energy consumption and conservation.[29]

The result was that postwar U.S. energy use increased rapidly and continuously, growing by 3.5 percent per year from 1950 on and by 4.5 percent per year after 1965, and electricity use grew at twice those rates (Kash and Rycroft 1984, 9). As a long-term consequence, the basic structure of the U.S. economy — defined by capital-intensive buildings, equipment, and appliances, and spatial patterns of low-density, transportation-dependent settlement which locked in energy-use commitments over many years — developed in patterns that were dangerously vulnerable to any shift from energy surplus to scarcity. As far back as the early 1950s energy experts raised concerns about potential future shortages and overdependence on unreliable foreign supplies, but only after 1973 did the United States even begin to confront the interrelated realities of energy resource scarcities and environmental impacts of energy production and use.

The vulnerability created by these policies was suddenly revealed in October 1973, when the Organization of Arab Oil Producing and Exporting Countries (OPEC), which by then controlled 60 percent of world oil production, embargoed oil exports to the United States for 5 months in retaliation for the Arab-Israeli War. The resulting shortages produced a public crisis, symbolized by long lines at gasoline pumps, schools without heat, urban "brownouts," and a dramatic leap in fuel prices. The long era of cheap energy seemed abruptly ended. Coal, oil, and gas producers immediately sought policy concessions, warning that their supplies would quickly be depleted and urging that both environmental and price controls be relaxed and more public lands opened to energy extraction. Consumers and environmentalists in turn accused the energy industry of exploiting the crisis to raise profits and recapture control over environmental policy.

This crisis produced three major changes in U.S. energy policies, which had important environmental impacts. First, from President Nixon's Project Independence on, every president promoted expansion of domestic energy production, particularly large-scale surface mining of coal on western public and Native American lands, where it was abundant. The EPA, which had been encouraging utilities to convert from coal to oil and gas as cleaner fuels, now was compelled to urge them to switch back to coal. As a result U.S. coal production increased by 40 percent during the 1970s, with all the attendant environmental impacts of its mining, combustion, and wastes. Presidents Nixon and Ford sought to open up far more of the public lands and outer continental shelf to oil wells, and President Carter, even while trying to protect more natural lands and maintain environmental controls on energy production, promoted subsidies for the development of synthetic fuels from coal and oil shale. President Reagan attempted simply to sweep aside many of the environmental regulations and public-land restrictions of the 1970s, and to open vast new areas of the public lands and outer continental shelf to fuel mining.

Domestic fossil-fuel production alone, however, could not begin to sustain the continued abundance and low prices of the past. Coal was abundant but required costlier environmental controls than in the past, and the cheapest domestic oil and gas fields had already been tapped. Also, the nuclear electricity industry declined steadily throughout the 1970s because of continued public opposition, widely publicized accidents (Browns Ferry in 1974, Three Mile Island in 1979), and, perhaps most seriously, its own rising costs, as the hidden liabilities of waste management, accidents, and premature shutdowns became more visible. By the end of the 1970s no nuclear power plants were on order, and many previous orders had been canceled.[30]

The second policy change, therefore, was a new recognition that energy conservation was an essential element of any solution. Consumers' responses to the sudden price increases showed that higher prices in fact led to more efficient use, and that more efficient use in turn allowed savings of both energy and cost as well as reduction of environmental impacts. To the extent that this was true, cheap energy was not essential to economic prosperity after all: gross domestic product continued to increase while energy use leveled off. In a seminal article in 1976, "The Road Not Taken," conservation advocate Amory Lovins contrasted the "hard path" of expensive, large-scale, capital-intensive, subsidized electric power generation with a "soft path" relying far more on energy conservation and on dispersed, smaller-scale sources of renewable energy. Lovins argued that the latter was superior not only for environmental reasons, and because it allowed for more democratic local control over energy production, but on economic grounds as well. Some conservation gains required only market forces as incentives, such as the dramatic increases in fuel prices in 1973–74 and again in 1979–80, and these were furthered by President Reagan's decontrol of energy prices in 1981. Electric utilities found themselves caught between regulated rates and the rising costs of building new power plants, creating an incentive for them to promote energy efficiency as an alternative to new construction. Many utilities by around 1990 had undertaken "demand-side management" programs, which included incentives particularly to reduce peak-load demands, including time-of-day price differentials and rebates for interruptible service to water heaters and air conditioners during peak hours. Some utilities also offered incentives to reduce total energy use, such as lower rates for increasing insulation and using low-energy appliances, and at least one even gave away low-energy light bulbs to its customers. A few regulatory commissions amended their policies to encourage this shift as well, by allowing the utilities to recapture conservation costs in their rate base.

Other conservation gains required policy incentives, however, to create stable market expectations of future energy costs. Mandatory energy-consumption labeling of consumer appliances, for instance, made energy efficiency a competitive factor in major consumer purchases, and corporate average fuel efficiency (CAFE) standards required auto manufacturers to produce more energy-efficient vehicles.[31] President Carter declared that reducing dependence on foreign oil should be considered the "moral equivalent of war," and promoted a series of initiatives to that end: conservation standards for heating and cooling of buildings (sixty-five degrees maximum in winter, seventy-eight degrees minimum in summer), elimination of bulk-rate electric discounts, tax credits for insulating houses more efficiently and installing renewable-energy equipment, and solar and renewable energy research. Not all these incentives were popular: a 55 mph national speed limit annoyed the large western states,[32] auto manufacturers continually resisted CAFE standards, and a broad-based tax on energy consumption was debated but never passed.[33] Overall, however, energy conservation policies strengthened public awareness that future energy prices would more likely reflect increasing scarcity rather than continued abundance.

Lovins's forecasts of dramatic gains in energy conservation were considered beyond the pale by other energy experts in the 1970s, but in fact he was far closer to the mark than they. By the 1980s all major demand estimates had been repeatedly corrected to levels lower than his original predictions, and in 1986 overall U.S. energy consumption was virtually identical to 1973 even while the gross domestic product had increased by 45 percent (Blair 1993, 14). The decline in energy demand also undermined the economics of building large new power plants, particularly high-cost nuclear facilities, further reinforcing the incentives for conservation.

Energy use rose steadily and steeply again after 1986, however, increasing by 22 percent from 1986 to 1995 (U.S. Council on Environmental Quality 1997, 505). A particularly disturbing element of this trend was the nation's continued increase in oil consumption and reliance on foreign oil (fig. 23). Price increases resulting from the 1973 OPEC embargo sparked a worldwide competitive boom in oil production, from the North Sea to the river delta of Nigeria, the jungles of the Ecuadorian Amazon, and elsewhere. The environmental result was a vast global expansion of the impacts of oil extraction and refining, whose real costs to the environment—and to many indigenous cultures in previously remote areas—were often severe, virtually unregulated, and uncounted in the market price of the oil.[34] The economic result was to drive down world oil prices, so much so that by the 1990s U.S. consumers were actually paying *less* for oil, after adjustment for inflation, than at any time in decades—even in the face of continuously rising oil demand, both domestically and worldwide. U.S. oil imports peaked in 1977, then fell off to almost half that level in 1982–85 (due partly to increased Alaskan production); then rose steadily again to late-1970s levels by 1993, as U.S. oil production declined to its lowest level in thirty-five years (U.S. Council on Environmental Quality 1993, 247–48). At that rate, it was predicted that imports would increase to over 70 percent of all U.S. oil consumption by the year 2015.

In short, for all the talk about "energy independence" in the 1970s, by the 1990s U.S. energy consumption rates had risen steadily to record highs, its car sales had shifted from energy-efficient small cars toward gas-guzzling sport utility vehicles, and its dependence on foreign supplies had actually increased to more than 50 percent of its oil consumption and was forecast to rise to over 65 percent by 2010 (Blair 1993, 16). This trend left the U.S. increasingly vulnerable to any political disruptions in world oil markets as well as to rising demand pressures from other countries, notwithstanding the concurrent diversification of sources. Economically, fuel imports represented a huge continued drain on its balance of trade, as well as high hidden costs to maintain military forces capable of assuring continued access. Environmentally, the impacts of oil production had simply been externalized to an unregulated global scale, even as they were more effectively controlled domestically; and even domestically they could still produce severe impacts, such as the 1989 *Exxon Valdez* shipwreck in the Gulf of Alaska.

The risk of rising import reliance, dramatized again in 1991 by the Iraqi invasion of Kuwait, produced a new energy policy statute to promote efficiency and alternative fuels. Passed amid scientific and public concern that fossil fuel combustion was causing an unnatural warming of Earth's climate, the Energy Policy Act of 1992 directed the Department of Energy to develop a least-cost national energy strategy to promote energy efficiency and reduce greenhouse gases, and specifically to achieve a 30 percent increase in energy efficiency by 2010 and a 75 percent increase in the use of renewable energy by 2005. It mandated that owners of large auto fleets phase in vehicles running on alternative fuels, that tax incentives be restructured to promote conservation and renewable fuels as well as

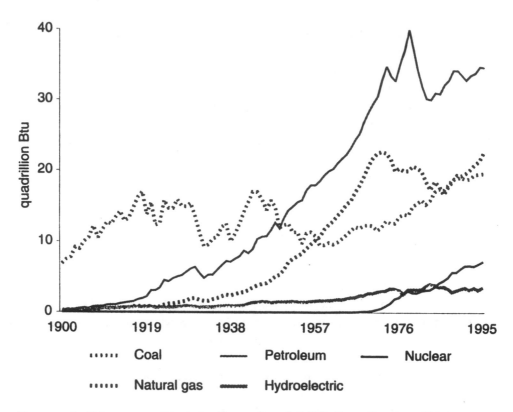

Figure 23a–b. U.S. energy consumption and import dependence. The figure above shows U.S. energy consumption by source, 1900–95. Note the dramatic increase in petroleum consumption from the late 1930s on, the precipitous falloff following the OPEC oil embargo in 1973 and price increases of 1979, and the relatively steady increase since the mid-1980s. The figure at right shows net U.S. imports of energy sources, 1950–95: note the overwhelming dominance of petroleum imports, and again the dramatic and continuing rise in import dependence except for the brief interruption from 1978 to 1985. [U.S. Council on Environmental Quality]

mass transit and carpooling, and that energy efficiency standards be developed for commercial and government buildings, manufactured housing, electric motors, lights, and other energy uses.[35] It also expanded alternative energy research programs, and demonstration programs for electric vehicles, renewable energy technologies, and advanced nuclear reactor technologies. It did not mandate increased energy efficiency for cars and trucks, however, as environmentalists had urged, but neither did it open the Arctic National Wildlife Refuge to oil production, as the energy industry wanted. Most of its initiatives ultimately remained unfunded amid the tax-cutting and budget-reduction politics of the 104th Congress.

The third important energy policy change brought on by the OPEC embargo was a major shift toward open competition in electric power production. Electric utilities had long been thought of as "natural monopolies," both producing and distributing power within exclusive regional service areas. By the late 1970s, however, they had in fact developed widespread interconnections through regional and national transmission grids, to

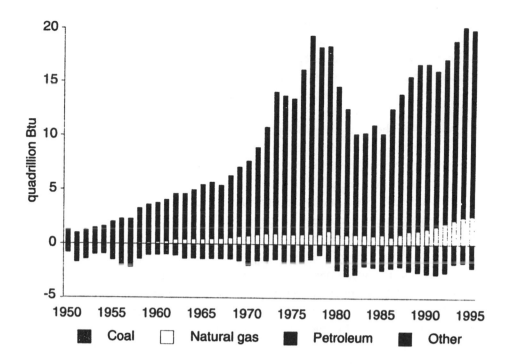

meet interregional differences in demand by buying and selling power among themselves. The Public Utilities Regulatory Policy Act of 1978 opened these grids to other producers: it required the electric utilities to accept and pay fair wholesale rates for power transmitted on the grid by independent producers, thus creating markets for other entrepreneurs to compete in energy production. Some of these new producers used renewable fuels, such as small dams rebuilt for hydroelectric production and solar- and wind-power experiments. Others were merely large industries producing their own energy and selling surplus on the grid ("co-generation"), while still others were investors in small gas-turbine plants that were more efficient than the utilities' own big coal- and nuclear-fired stations.

The Energy Policy Act of 1992 carried this shift further, allowing both the utilities and other producers to operate wholesale generating plants outside the utility's distribution region. In effect it thus severed power generation from the "natural monopoly" of electric transmission and distribution. Many environmental advocates supported this policy change, to encourage a shift from large fossil-fuel and nuclear plants to renewable energy sources. A serious risk, however, was that it would merely shift power production to the cheapest generating stations wherever they might be located, based on immediate market prices (Begley 1997). These cheapest plants might well include not new renewable-energy plants but old high-pollution, coal-fired plants in states with lax regulatory policies. This would shift much of the pollution to these places, creating more air pollution in the South to provide cheaper power for the Northeast.

By restructuring the utilities to make power production independent of distribution, this policy change also removed incentives that had led the utilities to promote demand-side energy conservation. Why should a utility that was making profits solely from either producing or distributing energy, rather than trying to use a fixed investment in its own power plants most efficiently, care about continuing to reduce energy demand? The result might be to leave conservation incentives to the vagaries of short-term market prices, and perhaps even to undermine them by making short-term energy prices cheaper. Ironically, therefore, the energy policies of the early to mid-1990s contained the potential for significant *regress* in environmental protection and sustainability, unless they were accompanied by significant restructuring of other laws and policies (Burtraw et al. 1996).

In short, U.S. energy policies in the mid-1990s remained deeply ambiguous toward the interdependent goals of environmental protection and energy conservation. Substantial gains in energy efficiency had occurred, and air-pollution regulations had significantly reduced some of the worst pollutants from energy combustion, but oil imports and overall fossil-fuel use continued to rise along with their attendant environmental impacts.

Transportation

The transportation sector is another pervasive source of environmental impacts in the U.S. economy. From rivers and harbors to roads, canals, railroads, and modern superhighways and jet airports, transportation provides ever-increasing access, mobility, trade opportunities, and convenience, but also massive transformation of the landscape, obliteration of smaller communities and ecosystems, pollution, and congestion. Three-quarters of annual U.S. petroleum use is for transportation, primarily cars. From the 1950s on, U.S. passenger transportation has been increasingly dominated by automobiles, light trucks, and airplanes, with buses a distant fourth and rail travel in steady decline. By the 1990s 60 percent of freight still moved by rail and ship, but truck transport began increasing rapidly after its deregulation in 1980.

As in other sectors, the United States had no overall environmental policy for transportation: environmental impacts were treated merely as side effects of mission-focused policies to promote the expansion of transportation infrastructure, particularly highways. Much of the direct cost of highway construction was financed by user charges (taxes on gasoline, heavy trucks, and tires), which were earmarked for that purpose in a Highway Trust Fund. If one includes the uncharged costs of associated environmental and social impacts, however, all the major forms of transportation were substantially subsidized (McKenzie 1992).

Environmental policies beginning in 1970 attacked some of the most obvious direct impacts of transportation, but ultimately achieved only partial and piecemeal results. NEPA's EIS requirement forced mitigation of the environmental impacts of many transport infrastructure projects, as did the wetland-protection provisions of the Clean Water Act. The Clean Air Act forced dramatic improvements in auto emission control and fuel efficiency, as well as aircraft emissions and noise, and the phaseout of lead from gasoline reduced ambient exposures to lead by over 90 percent — a major victory for public health. A nationwide speed limit of 55 mph (passed after the 1973 energy crisis) moderated fuel use and reduced related air pollution, but it was repealed by the antiregulation congressional majority in 1995. The 1992 Energy Policy Act mandated development of alternative fuels and electric vehicles, but these remained underfunded experiments.

None of these policies reversed the relentless increase in vehicle miles traveled each year, nor the accompanying urban pall of nitrogen oxides and volatile organic compounds, nor the continuing cycle of congestion, new highway construction, and sprawling low-density strip development that resulted. In addition, until the 1990s, Highway Trust Fund revenues were limited strictly to highway construction, and were fiercely protected by the highway construction lobby and related interests.

One of the few significant changes in transportation policy during the "environmental era" was the Intermodal Surface Transportation Efficiency Act of 1991 (ISTEA, or "ice tea"). Promoted by an unusual coalition of nontraditional transportation interests and farsighted members of Congress in the aftermath of the 1990 Clean Air Act, this act for the first time incorporated environmental considerations specifically into transportation planning, and allowed more flexible use of funding for high-speed rail and other modes in addition to highways. ISTEA provided funds to integrate transportation planning with the air quality planning required by the 1990 Clean Air Act amendments, and 80 percent federal funding for projects to reduce transportation-related air pollution in cities that exceeded air pollution standards.[36] It also allowed wetland "mitigation banking," or replacing of wetlands destroyed for highways with others bought for permanent preservation.[37]

ISTEA was thus an important breakthrough in environmental policy for the transportation sector, but in practice it remained severely underfunded. Authorized funds were repeatedly held back as a federal budget-balancing measure, and under amendments enacted in 1995 Congress limited the congestion-management portion of these funds, targeted the intermodal funding for reduction, and revoked EPA's authority to mandate state inspection and maintenance programs.[38] ISTEA required reauthorization in 1997, and supporters proposed to increase spending for its innovative environmental incentives programs and remove federal policy barriers that limited use of economic incentives to reduce environmental effects of traffic congestion ("NEXTEA"). Highway construction interests, however, sought to eliminate even the 5 percent designation of transportation funds for congestion reduction and air quality management, and to sharply reduce ISTEA's permission to shift funds from highway construction to mass transit.

In May 1998, Congress overwhelmingly approved and President Clinton signed a new transportation bill that replaced the ISTEA program with a $200 billion authorization for new transportation projects. This new legislation amounted to the largest public-works program in the nation's history, and represented a 44 percent increase in federal funds for transportation projects. While the new statute continued the ISTEA principle of including some support for mass transit and safety programs, more than 80 percent of the funds were earmarked for highway and bridge construction. The effect therefore was to begin a massive new round of large-scale construction projects impacting the landscape and to further expand an overwhelmingly highway-based transportation system.

The reality was that U.S. transportation policy continued to be dominated by a powerful coalition of concentrated and well-organized economic interests that shared a primary goal of highway construction rather than balanced transportation options. These included the construction industry itself plus automobile manufacturers and dealers, trucking companies, the outdoor advertising and gasoline industries, real estate interests, and others. No other transport interests were as organized or influential. Public sentiment supported technical standards for auto emission control and fuel content, and greater flexibility in federal subsidies to support integrated transportation planning, but the public showed little political will to challenge the persistent increases in automotive travel and urban sprawl — nor to change individual behavior patterns such as low vehicle occupancy and lax maintenance — that were at the heart of the environmental impacts of transportation.

Many more effective policy incentives were proposed and in some cases introduced, ranging from urban parking restrictions and preferential lanes for mass-transit and high-occupancy vehicles to alternative fuels and vehicles, congestion charges based on the time of day and even tax systems to impose "full-cost pricing" on automobile users. Both in the 1970s and again in the 1990s, however, EPA initiatives to require more intensive vehicle inspection and maintenance, promote increased vehicle occupancy, or discourage urban commuting aroused sharp political backlash. Fuel taxes were targeted for reduction as a hostage of election-year politics, and land-use controls, the other major policy tool that could address these problems, remained a limited and local prerogative. Only the 1990 Clean Air Act amendments, which imposed increasingly severe automatic penalties on nonattainment areas, and the glimmer of new funding flexibility offered by ISTEA, seemed to provide serious incentives for more effective policy interventions by the cities themselves.

Agriculture

Like energy and transportation, the agriculture sector also has pervasive impacts on the environment: runoff of sediment and chemicals into waterways, human and ecological effects of pesticides, destruction of wetlands and wildlife habitat, groundwater depletion and contamination, even air pollution. Because of its political influence and its hold on the popular imagination, however, these impacts have remained far less regulated than similar ones from manufacturing, energy production, or even urban wastewater discharges. Once the major industries reduced their wastewater discharges in the 1970s, "nonpoint discharges" from agriculture represented a primary source of the remaining water pollution, yet the Clean Water Act allowed only nonbinding guidelines for "best management practices" rather than mandatory pollution controls or performance requirements for farms. For many rivers these exceptions nullified the benefits of the costly control measures required of cities and industries. Pesticides for many years could only be banned if EPA paid to buy back unsold stocks. Wetland protection rules exempted agriculture, though agricultural operations were a leading cause of wetland losses nationwide.

In reality, agriculture was increasingly conducted in large, concentrated operations like other major industries, often vertically integrated by powerful corporations all the way from feed and fertilizer to processing and marketing of the products, rather than on the small family farms of American history and mythology. Yet these exemptions allowed such corporations to continue to impose far greater environmental damage on society than comparable businesses in other sectors.[39]

Despite its large and widespread environmental impacts, the United States has never had an explicit or systematic environmental policy for agriculture. Rather, it has had a commodity production policy with a few environmental issues tacked on. Ironically, agriculture has been controlled and promoted by more detailed *economic* regulation than almost any other sector, in the form of production controls and market stabilization price supports dating from the 1930s. Yet many of these incentives actually promoted the intensification of agriculture that exacerbated its environmental impacts, and the industry's congressional patrons successfully protected it from most environmental regulations (Faeth et al. 1991, Faeth 1995).

Some long-standing environmental protection incentives did exist within federal agricultural policies (Opie 1994 [1987], 152 ff.). The Soil Conservation Service (now the Natural Resources Conservation Service) beginning in the 1930s encouraged voluntary adoption of agricultural soil conservation practices, and from the 1950s on offered federal financial subsidies for small water-control projects as an incentive. The Great Plains Conservation Program promoted planting of "shelterbelts" to reduce wind erosion in arid regions, and a "conservation reserves" program beginning in 1956 (with the passage of the Soil Bank Act) paid farmers to take erosion-prone lands out of production for three to ten years at a time.

Over time, however, as the great droughts and dust storms of the Depression era faded from memory, these practices were displaced by more powerful incentives for large-scale commercial production. First wartime food demands, then continuing federal price supports and growing world markets created overwhelming enticements to adopt new high-yield crop varieties that depended on large quantities of chemical fertilizers and pesticides, to consolidate farms into fewer but far larger integrated agribusinesses, to replace small-farm conservation technologies with large-scale machinery and irrigation systems, and to plant every possible acre, right to the fences and stream banks. Conservation reserves programs did nothing to discourage more intensive production on lands not put into reserve, and many of the Soil Conservation Service watershed projects had damaging rather than beneficial environmental impacts. This was especially true for "stream channelization," a common practice until 1976, which often destroyed wetlands and increased downstream flooding in order to drain more land for planting or urban development.

To what extent then could federal agriculture policies themselves be made to promote environmental protection more effectively? Increases in fuel prices after 1973 and again in 1979–80 caused a cost crisis for farmers worldwide, and rekindled some interest in "alternative agriculture": in essence, contemporary versions of traditional conservation practices. Many of these, however, were available only to farmers who were still farming on small scales and were not already heavily mortgaged for large-scale equipment. In 1977 a Soil and Water Resource Conservation Act (RCA) authorized nationwide inventories of soil and water conservation conditions and needs, implying a more active future federal role in soil and water resource protection. Like the geological surveys of the 1880s, the inventories resulting from the RCA produced powerful documentation of the extent and location of highly erodible lands and other sensitive environmental areas, thereby laying the foundation for more effective programs to conserve them.

By the mid-1980s, public concerns about the environmental impacts of large-scale agriculture converged with a growing crisis in farm-subsidy policy, as rising competition in world grain markets produced huge surpluses of higher-priced U.S. crops. The 1985 Farm Security Act (FSA) therefore made significant policy changes aimed at making farming more responsive to markets. For the first time, it also added to the federal "farm bills" important new incentives to reduce production, especially on the most environmentally sensitive lands.[40] The FSA created a program for "low-impact sustainable agriculture" (LISA), a small but significant acknowledgment of the merits of conservation farming. It also created a new Conservation Reserve Program, aimed specifically at retiring wetlands and "highly erodible lands" from production, by offering federal rental payments on these lands for up to ten years. And in perhaps the most significant departure from historical policies, the FSA included "sodbuster" and "swampbuster" penalties that denied federal program benefits to any farmer who initiated new production on highly erodible lands or wetlands.

The 1990 Food, Agriculture, and Conservation and Trade Act (FACTA) expanded several of these initiatives and added others. The LISA program grew into a Sustainable Agriculture Research and Education Program, the sodbuster and swampbuster programs were extended, and the Conservation Reserve Program was expanded into an Environmental Conservation Acreage Reduction Program with particular attention to protecting stream-bank buffers. Perhaps most significantly, FACTA also offered financial incentives: 50 percent cost-sharing to farmers who would plant permanent vegetation along waterway buffer zones, up to 100 percent of the costs of conservation measures on environmentally sensitive lands, and additional payments for restoring and protecting wetlands, though the definition of wetlands was narrowed to cover fewer lands. In all, FACTA included over two hundred pages of conservation provisions aimed at promoting environmentally beneficial practices in agriculture, ranging from integrated conservation farm plans to agricultural water quality protection and safe pesticide use.

With the Conservation Reserve Program and the sodbuster and swampbuster provisions, which made conservation of sensitive lands a requirement of eligibility for federal program benefits, the 1985 and 1990 farm laws for the first time incorporated farmland soil conservation into the system of federal production incentives that had shaped American agriculture since the 1930s (Opie 1994, 206). This was a major policy victory for environmental protection, and its results were quickly evident. Estimated benefits of these programs between 1989 and 1995 included increases in the use of conservation tillage from 25 percent to 35 percent of field crop acres, and an estimated 25 percent reduction in cropland erosion from 1982 to 1992 (U.S. Council on Environmental Quality 1997, 468).

Left unresolved, however, were four key issues. First, even as FACTA endorsed "sustainable agriculture," it defined it in such a way as to continue primary emphasis on large-scale industrial agriculture for competitive production in a global export economy. Second CRP land retirements were only for ten years, after which they might simply be plowed under again, as had happened to Soil Bank lands in the 1970s; and in the meantime, CRP land retirements might simply be compensated for by more intensive and damaging production practices on other lands.[41] Third, these programs showed great benefits but required significant federal expenditures, leaving them vulnerable to the politics of federal budget reduction. Finally, all these programs depended on the incentive value of eligibility for traditional federal farm subsidy programs, which left them vulnerable to any elimination of those programs. Such a change might have seemed totally improbable in 1985 or 1990, but with the arrival of the 104th Congress in 1995 just such a policy change was enacted.

The 1996 Federal Agriculture Improvement and Reform Act (FAIR), a compromise between Senate moderates and antigovernment conservatives in the House of Representatives, set in motion a seven-year process for phasing out much of the price-support system for field crops, leaving farmers free to plant in response to market conditions rather than government incentives. This change promised to solve the problem of surplus production, and also to remove the system's perverse incentives for intensive monoculture production to maximize federal price-support benefits. If it does in fact phase out as stated, it will stand as the most fundamental change in agricultural policy since the New Deal, and should dramatically reduce the previous subsidy-driven incentives for intensive overproduction and related environmental impacts.

At the same time, however, it left market forces free to encourage farming of every available acre as world demand tightened, and in eliminating government subsidies it also destroyed the program-eligibility incentives for conservation of highly erodible lands and wetlands. The conservation and wetland reserve programs were extended, for instance, as were cost-share programs for conservation of wetlands and wildlife habitat, retirement of flood-prone lands, and easements to protect farmland subject to urban encroachment, but all these programs were subject to annual budget appropriations which were concurrently being reduced. FAIR also greatly weakened the laws' most potent conservation incentives. Sodbusters and swampbusters would now be denied federal program benefits only for the sensitive lands themselves, not for their entire farms. The benefits denied would no longer include federal crop insurance, one of the strongest and most ubiquitous incentives, and ineligibility would start only when they began producing on wetlands, not when they first drained or filled them. "Minor" wetland changes were categorically exempted, and a larger fraction of the wetlands reserves were designated for temporary rather than permanent protection. The Agriculture Department was given far greater discretionary flexibility in enforcement, and was no longer required to consult with the Fish and Wildlife Service on wetland decisions. Finally, there remained the possibility that at some time during the seven-year phaseout period, some crisis in agricultural costs or prices would provide a pretext for continuing or reinstating the subsidies, with or without conservation incentives.

In short, the 1996 farm bill marked a dramatic change in U.S. farm policy, which promised to reduce both the environmental and economic costs of the outdated price-support system, a result welcomed by many environmental protection advocates. The great remaining risk, however, was that market forces alone would continue to exacerbate agriculture's environmental impacts. Major new consumers such as China were poised to enter world grain markets, and without effective environmental regulations or strong government incentives for conservation, farmers might well simply shift toward all-out production to profit from world market demand.

Left totally untouched by the 1996 farm bill, as by its predecessors, moreover, were the many forms of increasingly intensive agriculture that had never been subject to the price-support system in the first place, yet had substantial environmental impacts of their own. A prime example was livestock production. During the 1980s and 1990s, first poultry and then hog farming were dramatically restructured into highly concentrated, vertically integrated business operations controlled by a few large firms. Most individual farmers now worked as contract suppliers for these firms rather than as independent producers. These new enterprises were immensely more efficient and profitable than the many small farms they replaced, but the intensive scale of their contract operations also produced far more concentrated environmental impacts—hog wastes equivalent to the wastes of a large city, for instance, often with no waste management other than lagoons and landspreading. Yet these firms remained largely exempt from federal water-quality and waste-management regulations.

National Forests

The federal public lands represented yet another important sectoral context for environmental policy. Chapter 10 described the rising tensions of the postwar years among advocates of resource production (logging, mining, and grazing), intensive outdoor recreation and related commercial development (such as off-road vehicle use and tourist-service concessions), and preservation of the natural character of the lands, wildlife, and ecosystems. New laws during the environmental era raised these tensions to a level of institutionalized political conflict, by requiring formalized planning and decision procedures that gave environmental protection and preservation advocates more explicit rights to participate in public-lands decision-making.

For the national forests, the dominant issues involved wilderness designations and the environmental impacts of logging.[42] The Forest Service was responsible for 191 million acres of national forest lands, and under the Multiple Use and Sustained Yield Act of 1960 it was to manage these lands for a mixture of uses. In practice, however, the agency continued to emphasize timber production, and the 1964 Wilderness Act therefore mandated separate and protective management of lands relatively untouched by human activities. The National Historic Preservation Act (1966), Wild and Scenic Rivers Act

(1968), and National Trails System Act (1968) also affirmed the importance of preserving values other than marketable commodities.

The Wilderness Act ordered a review of all public lands that might qualify for wilderness designation, although as a compromise it allowed continued mineral exploration for twenty years before closing them to extractive uses. The Forest Service's first Roadless Area Review and Evaluation (RARE, eventually RARE I) report, issued in 1971, recommended that six million acres be designated for wilderness protection, but the Sierra Club sued because the review had excluded many other valuable areas from consideration. The resulting second-round evaluation (RARE II), completed in 1977, recommended fifteen million acres for wilderness designation and ten million more for further study, not counting Alaskan lands (Mayer and Riley 1985, 258–60).[43] During the decade-long review process, the Forest Service was required to suspend resource extraction on all lands under review, effectively holding off mining or logging on the entire sixty-two million acres of these lands until the review was completed.

The environmental era also galvanized opposition to clear-cut logging on the public lands. Clear-cutting involved cutting not just mature trees but entire stands at one time, which allowed the logging company to use heavy machinery more efficiently and to replant the entire area for more intensive "even-aged management" of commercial species. The Forest Service itself had opposed clear-cutting until the 1950s, but then yielded to its advocates, citing scientific arguments that some species actually appeared to require it for their propagation. In effect, the Forest Service allowed logging companies to cut entire stands of old-growth trees and replace them with young, faster-growing ones, then use optimistic claims of their future yield to justify even larger harvests. Forest propagation did not require clear-cutting on a large scale, however, nor on steep slopes — common in many western old-growth forests — where regeneration was problematic and where the resulting erosion could severely damage salmon runs and trout fisheries.

In 1964 the Forest Service announced a huge proposed sale of 8.75 billion board feet of timber to be clear-cut on the Tongass National Forest in Alaska's coastal panhandle. It also proposed to clear-cut the Monongahela National Forest in West Virginia, a second-growth forest that had been restored in the 1930s and had become a favorite of hunters and fishermen. Environmental groups strenuously opposed both proposals, and by the early 1970s reports even by professional foresters harshly criticized Forest Service clear-cut practices (fig. 24). Especially influential was a 1970 evaluation of the Bitterroot National Forest in Montana, which accused the agency of nonrenewable "timber mining" by clear-cutting and terracing on mountainsides. It recommended an end to logging on steep, marginally productive sites — which included most of the national forest lands in Montana.[44] The report blamed these practices on priorities that originated in the postwar housing boom but continued, due to congressional and presidential mandates and the political power of the timber and housing-construction industries, despite profound changes in the condition of the federal lands and in their public value for preservation and recreation (Hirt 1994, 244–48).

The continuing influence of the commodity industries was reflected in the 1971 report of the Public Land Law Review Commission, chaired by Rep. Wayne Aspinall of

Figure 24. An example of the destructive effects of forest clear-cutting. This photograph, taken at the mouth of Gold Creek on the St. Joe River in Idaho, shows how improper cutting in large clear-cut blocks can damage an area. This land was burned over after it was logged, destroying second-growth trees and causing erosion from the rapid runoff of water from the nearby treeless hills. [U.S. Forest Service photo, courtesy of the Forest History Society, Durham, N.C.]

Colorado. Environmental concerns notwithstanding, this report sought to reaffirm a national policy priority for commodity extraction on the public lands, and to declare logging the "dominant use" (rather than just one among other "multiple uses") of the national forests. President Nixon's Advisory Panel on Timber and Environment took a similar position in its 1973 report, recommending that logging of old-growth western forests be increased by 50 to 100 percent, and the Forest Service's own *Environmental Program for the Future* proposed that ninety-seven million acres be dedicated to intensive commercial production to produce a 70 percent increase in allowable cut, from 13.6 to 21 billion board feet per year.

A centerpiece of the timber industry's policy agenda was the 1974 Forest and Range Renewable Resources Planning Act (RPA), which required five- and ten-year plans for timber harvest from the national forests, accompanied by budget estimates. For the timber industry, such plans would lock in long-term logging decisions from the top, before they reached particular forests where environmental groups could mobilize to block them: RPA had no provision for citizen input. For the Forest Service, RPA would provide support for professional forest-planning and also lock in long-term budget commitments, since the act required special justification for any deviation from the planned budget estimates (Hirt 1994, 243–45).[45]

Faced with this continuing dominance of timber-industry priorities in the Forest Service, and similar influence of mining, grazing, and other interests on BLM lands, environmental groups turned to the courts to protect non-commodity values (Hirt 1994, 248). In a series of cases brought by the Sierra Club, Environmental Defense Fund, Natural Resources Defense Council, and others, the courts granted environmental groups standing to represent environmental values affected by public land management decisions, and held in their favor repeatedly on particular decisions. One of the most important of these held that the practice of clear-cutting on the Monongahela National Forest violated the specific language of the 1897 Forest Management Act, the basic statutory authority for national forest management, which authorized logging only of "mature trees, marked and designated, cut and removed."[46]

The Monongahela decision forced congressional review of the whole practice of forest management. The resulting National Forest Management Act of 1976 (NFMA) authorized clear-cutting as a legitimate forest management practice, but also established restrictive guidelines for its use, and reaffirmed "non-declining even flow" of timber—the most protective definition of sustained yield—as the basic principle for national forest management. It also required management plans for each individual forest unit, with mandatory public input, which had not been required under RPA and previous Forest Service practices.[47]

On its face, the NFMA thus represented a major victory for environmental groups, and it led to significant changes in management of some national forests. However, it also included loopholes for "salvage" logging, as well as for "earned" harvest excesses: that is, optimistic projections based on predicted yields from intensive management of reforested areas. The result was a continuation of unsustainable cutting of old-growth forests, exacerbated by the Reagan administration's attempts to sweep away environmental protection restrictions and reaffirm commodity production as the dominant policy. A series of reports beginning in the 1980s attacked timber sales on economic as well as environmental grounds, showing that on some western national forests as many as 60 to 90 percent of timber sales actually cost more than the revenues they produced. Also, technical experts working with environmental groups discovered hidden assumptions built into forest planning computer models to protect the status quo, such as gross overestimates of future yields and constraints that prevented the models from presenting any significant reductions in timber cuts (Hirt 1994, 263–65, 272–83).[48]

Faced with the continuing entrenched influence of the timber and construction industries, environmental groups turned again to the courts, using several environmental protection laws but particularly the Endangered Species Act as tactical weapons to reduce unsustainable harvest levels. By the late 1980s they began winning major lawsuits, showing that the Forest Service was continuing to systematically violate environmental laws in order to keep producing politically mandated excessive cuts. The courts therefore began to issue orders to stop excessive logging on the national forests, to demand scientifically credible forest plans, and to stop violations of water quality, fish and wildlife protection, and endangered species mandates (Hirt 1994, 288). The most celebrated of these decisions involved the habitat of the northern spotted owl in the old-growth forests of the Pacific Northwest, but others involved the grizzly bear, salmon runs, the red-cockaded woodpecker in southeastern pine forests, and others.

The reality was that most of the old-growth timber of the Pacific Northwest had already been cut, except on a few forests in Alaska, and that the timber industry was therefore being forced to contract and change in ways that threatened jobs and communities. Many of the national forests, meanwhile, had been heavily damaged by past practices and inadequate rehabilitation, and it became more and more obvious that the remnants of the old forests were the last habitat not only of spotted owls but of hundreds of species that depended on these ecosystems. It was this underlying conflict between declining national forests and a declining timber industry, not simply the decision of one court, that produced the "train wreck" of political conflict over national-forest management in the 1990s.

Legal battles over the northwestern old-growth forests produced widely publicized media propaganda over "jobs versus the environment," but no real policy reforms until early 1990s, when monitoring showed dramatic declines in harvest yields on the national forests that appeared to confirm environmentalists' arguments. The Forest Service in 1990 publicized a "new perspectives" initiative for environmental sensitivity, and in 1992 an "ecosystem management" approach, but these amounted to only vague and nonbinding statements, implemented on some forests but contradicted on others by operational forest plans and cut decisions. In 1992 a report by the Congressional Office of Technology Assessment concluded that forest plans continued to emphasize timber and grazing, gave little attention to sustaining ecosystems, and did not adequately monitor the results. It also confirmed that planning decisions were dominated by budget influences, and that national timber output targets often nullified local management plans that were based on good multiple-use forest practices (Hirt 1994, 271, 278). Intensive reforestation appeared to have been less successful than predicted, the monetary costs of "earned harvests" were proving to be greater than their benefits, and the environmental impacts were violating statutory mandates such as the Clean Water Act and Endangered Species Act.

As in other sectors, in short, forest policy even on the public lands remained primarily driven by the economic self-interest of the industry that was most effectively organized to influence national statutes, budgets, and sector-specific mandates such as allowable cut targets. This dominance was constrained somewhat by citizen legal challenges, and by mixed support from Forest Service professionals themselves, but it remained the primary force influencing Forest Service policy.

With the Clinton administration in 1992 came a new attempt to hammer out an acceptable policy for managing the national forests. President Clinton appointed the first Forest Service chief who was neither a forester nor an engineer (wildlife biologist Jack Ward Thomas, who had chaired the interagency committee on management of spotted-owl habitat), and convened a Northwest Forest Conference in 1993 to negotiate a management plan. However, the rhetoric of cooperation confronted serious conflicts that had no easy solutions, both among stakeholder constituencies in the region and even among the six major federal agencies involved (Hirt 1994, 288 ff.). The reality was that only three broad options were available: either reduce old-growth logging for years until second growth came in, or relax environmental laws to allow continued or increased cuts, or compromise with environmental groups to settle their successful lawsuits.

In 1994, the election of the 104th Congress shifted legislative power to the Republican party, placing control of the natural resource committees not just in a different party but in the hands of aggressively pro-timber and anti-environmentalist representatives from Alaska and elsewhere in the West. These congressmen and their allies sought systematically to nullify federal environmental protection mandates and reopen the national forests to large-scale commodity extraction. A "Forest Health Act" mandated a rapid increase in "salvage logging," ostensibly aimed at speeding up emergency removal of dead trees to reduce fire and insect hazards, but it also required the Forest Service to reopen logging on many healthy forests that had been withdrawn from logging for environmental protection reasons, and summarily waived compliance with environmental laws that restricted logging practices on these cuts. President Clinton signed it, reportedly on the assumption that he could limit its effects administratively, but a federal court eventually ruled that he was required to carry out its provisions as stated in the law.

The result was a dramatic increase in cutting: nearly 600 million board feet of Olympia National Forest were projected to be logged under this rider, for instance, more than triple the cut in any of the previous five years (*New York Times,* March 1, 1996). Congress also considered proposals to mandate a 75 percent increase in logging on the Tongass National Forest in southeastern Alaska (*Washington Post,* July 27, 1995). Forest policy remained driven not by the scientific management and rational planning that its statutes proclaimed, but by the economic and political self-interests of commodity producers and their political representatives, constrained by lobbying and litigation on the part of organized forest and wildlife preservation groups.

For the future, the Forest Service faces the prospect of intensified pressures and unresolved conflicts between the commodity and nonconsumptive values of its lands. By the year 2040 demand for hardwood is expected to increase by 57 percent, and for softwood by 28 percent, while demand for forest-based recreation is expected to more than double. In 1996 the leading timber-industry trade association itself undertook a "sustainable forestry initiative," which required all its member companies to reforest every acre they harvested; but the conflicts between commodity harvest and environmental protection on the national forest lands remains intense and unresolved.

Public Lands and the Wise Use Movement

Similar conflicts intensified on the public lands managed by the Bureau of Land Management. The BLM was responsible for four times the land area managed by the Forest Service—not even counting the outer continental shelf and mining leasing under all public lands—but had only one-third the budget and one-seventh the staff. Until 1976 it lacked even a basic statute authorizing it to manage these lands: created in 1946 by a merger of the Grazing Service and General Land Office, it inherited a legacy of over thirty-five hundred public-land laws, all premised on the nineteenth-century policy that these lands were being held temporarily for eventual privatization. While the Forest Service operated with clear statutory authority and through decentralized expertise in individual forest units, therefore, the BLM's far thinner staff could only hope to work cooperatively with state and local governments and with local ranchers, mining companies, and other public-land users.[49]

The Federal Lands Policy and Management Act of 1976 (FLPMA) finally confirmed the BLM's permanent management authority over the public lands, and eliminated hundreds of archaic land laws.[50] FLPMA authorized multiple-use management of BLM lands, but did not set specific statutory goals or priorities for resolving the inevitable conflicts among these uses. It also required written filing of all public land claims (for the first time!), but did not reform the 1872 General Mining Act, which continued to allow mining companies to claim lands worth billions of dollars for prices of $2.50 to $5.00 per acre with no royalties or environmental cleanup guarantees.[51] As an environmental policy, FLPMA finally gave the BLM statutory authority and responsibility to actively manage the public lands toward overall national goals.

The prospect of the BLM's increased authority triggered a backlash among western public-land users, however, who organized a lobbying campaign — the "Sagebrush Rebellion" — to intimidate the agency out of any intervention in their traditional local control. In principle these users had no greater right to the public lands than anyone else, but in reality many had long operated ranches that depended on public-land access as an extension of their operations, and market forces had in effect capitalized these privileges into the valuation of their businesses. Many also felt that they understood range management better than the sometimes young and usually distant BLM staff, and resented too the steady incursion of vacation-home "ranchettes" and "eastern" attitudes into their resource-production economy.

Similar opposition came from "inholders," holders of land claims in and around the national parks. With the new funding provided since 1964 by the Land and Water Conservation Fund, the National Park Service sought to acquire many of these lands to complete the parks, stirring hostile reactions from those who benefited from them.[52] Larger interests encouraged this opposition, particularly mining companies and western state governments which for their own self-interest sought devolution or even privatization of the BLM lands.

President Reagan adopted these groups' agenda, placing its leaders in key appointments. James Watt, his Secretary of the Interior, was a conservative activist lawyer; Robert Burford, his BLM director, was a Colorado rancher and state legislator; and the head of the National Inholders Association was appointed a senior official of the National Park Service. Reagan also created an Asset Management Program and Presidential Property Review Board to recommend public lands, even some national parks, to be sold or given away. This land disposal initiative fizzled after just six months, as the western states realized how much more it would cost to manage these lands themselves and the ranchers realized that the mining and energy companies would outbid them if the lands were put up for sale. In reality they all gained more from privileged access to federally subsidized lands, so long as the BLM was kept subservient to their wishes (Klyza 1996, 94 ff.).

However, Secretary Watt also radically reduced parkland acquisition, diverted Land and Water Conservation Fund revenues to maintenance and deficit reduction, and promoted a vast expansion of mineral leasing on the public lands and outer continental shelf (Mayer and Riley 1985, 264). Watt was ultimately forced to resign, and the most extreme of his initiatives were derailed by the resurgent environmental movement and its congressional allies. For much of a decade, however, the Interior Department was preoccupied with recovering from his radical reversals of policy: few new public-lands initiatives emerged until the 1990s.

In 1992 President Clinton once again appointed strong environmental protection supporters to the Interior Department, and in 1993 proposed an ambitious new round of policy initiatives for the public lands. These initiatives combined environmental protection with arguments for greater economic and administrative efficiency, and a strong new emphasis on negotiating consensus among ranchers, mining companies, environmental groups, state and local governments, and other stakeholders. Interior Secretary Bruce Babbitt, a former governor of Arizona, introduced a series of new range-protection policies, including shifting grazing seasons, ending some pesticide uses, controlling water rights, and breaking some leases for mismanagement. He also proposed to charge more of the costs of maintaining BLM rangelands to the ranchers who benefited from them, by raising grazing fees closer to their market value (from $1.86 to $5.00 per "animal unit month"). He also lobbied vigorously for mining law reform, publicizing the economic as well as environmental illogic of laws that required him to give away vast economic assets for a pittance, even to non-U.S. firms. To strengthen the department's biological-science expertise, he created a National Biological Service (initially a National Biological Survey) to pull together experts who had been scattered among the National Park Service, Fish and Wildlife Service, and other agencies.

As the federal agencies had slowly rebuilt their effectiveness and environmental groups had begun winning strategic policy lawsuits, however, western foes of federal land management had also begun building a new and more sophisticated opposition movement. Calling themselves the "wise use" movement—an echo of Gifford Pinchot's definition of conservation—organizers mobilized a coalition of corporate and grass-roots interests bound together by antigovernment ideology, property-rights rhetoric, and hostility to federal environmental protection policies.[53] Unlike the earlier Sagebrush Rebellion, the political goal of the wise use movement was not simply to win piecemeal policy concessions but to fundamentally destroy the environmental movement and the federal environmental management programs they associated with it.

They brought to this cause both an intensely antigovernment, property-rights rhetoric and sophisticated organizational techniques: direct-mail fund-raising; using right-wing talk radio shows to share anecdotal grievances; creating front groups whose names sounded like citizen environmental groups;[54] establishing conservative "think tanks" to produce revisionist publications questioning environmental science and policy; orchestrating "fax attacks" to lobby legislators; networking on the Internet and others (Brick 1995; Lewis 1992). Some also used the older and cruder tactics of threats and physical violence against environmental advocates, Forest Service and BLM staff, and even elected officials and judges. By the early 1990s these tactics proved increasingly influential in reframing the political agenda once again from environmental concerns to government overregulation — even in the midst of widely publicized global environmental concerns, including the "ozone hole," global warming, the loss of biodiversity, and the United Nations' "Earth Summit" in Rio de Janeiro.

The wise use movement was too divided between George Bush and Ross Perot to be effective in the 1992 elections, but won widespread victories with the election of the 104th Congress in 1994. This election gave control of Congress to the Republican Party, and control of key environmental and natural resource committees to a group of aggressively anti-environmental Republican legislators — particularly several from Alaska, Texas, and other western states — who set out to reassert commodity production and extraction as the primary uses of the public lands, and to do away with all federal environmental protection restrictions that impeded that goal.

The sobering lesson was that on the public lands and other issues as well as in pollution control, U.S. environmental policy remained a battleground of pendulum politics between advocates of environmental exploitation and protection, and more fundamentally between supporters and opponents of a government role in protecting the environment. What was most lacking and most needed was some political impetus to shift the process of environmental policy-making from political and legal warfare to problem-solving, with environmental results rather than merely ideological or economic advantage as the test of success.

The Unfinished Business of National Environmental Policy

The National Environmental Policy Act marked the beginning of the "environmental era" in U.S. governance and policy, and was intended as a foundation for systematic integration of environmental considerations into all the agencies and sectors that have important environmental impacts. In practice, however, it provided only a symbolic starting point. Here and there promising environmental initiatives did emerge in the policies of some major sectors, such as energy conservation and agricultural conservation incentives, but most were relatively limited in their effect, and all remained deeply vulnerable to changes in the sectoral policies to which they were attached. They also remained vulnerable to the influential economic and political forces — world markets, corporate restructurings, anti-government resentments, and others — that drove each of these sectors. In reality, powerful economic and political forces remained serious and in some cases increasing threats to whatever progress the environmental era had achieved.

Perhaps most revealing is to note not just the policies that *were* enacted, but environmental policies that the United States did *not* have by the 1990s. It had no systematic environmental policy for agriculture, aside from modest land-reserve incentives. It had none for energy or transportation, even as both vehicular pollution and dependence on foreign oil continued to increase. Nor did it have any overall policy strategy for reducing combustion, even as worldwide concern increased over evidence suggesting excessive global warming. Its environmental policies for industry and mining were a fragmentary and burdensome patchwork of disparate regulations, rather than an integrated system of incentives for pollution prevention, even as its per-capita waste generation continued to rise. It had no policy except the Endangered Species Act for protecting natural lands and ecosystems, except on some government-owned lands: land use decisions were left almost exclusively to private owners and local governments, and thus based on economic rather than environmental criteria. One of the great classics of the early environmental era was Ian McHarg's *Design With Nature* (1969), which laid out systematic principles for fitting urban development into the landscape in ways that preserved the best of both. A quarter century later, however, U.S. public policies remained virtually silent on this issue, even as more and more of its natural landscape was paved over in incremental sprawl.

Missing from all the reforms of the environmental era, in short, were two essential elements of a true national environmental policy. One was a systematic, operational statement of the environmental performance targets that Americans as a nation sought to achieve and sustain, and setting specific timetables for their achievement. The second was an integrated institutional framework for implementing such a statement: for coordinating the multiple agencies and levels of governments involved, for negotiating targets and timetables with each sector and its constituent units, and for monitoring and correcting the results as needed.

Models for such policies existed. The Dutch National Environmental Policy Plan, for instance, enacted in 1989, established a twenty-year strategic plan which stated not only fundamental policy principles but also measurable objectives and benchmarks for reducing emissions, using materials and energy more efficiently, and achieving high quality in both production processes and products. It covered six basic sectors: agriculture, transportation, industry, energy, building trades, and waste processing. The plan was to be implemented jointly by the four primary environment-related ministries, with additional steps by research institutes, societal organizations, and consumers, to achieve the essential elements of sustainable development (Netherlands Ministry of Housing 1990; Bennett 1991). In the United States, the state of Oregon in 1991 defined a set of specific state "benchmarks"—operational objectives, with special criteria and deadlines for their achievement—for environmental as well as other state policy goals (Oregon Progress Board 1991). Other countries began similar initiatives (Jänicke and Jörgens 1996), and the Swedish government in 1997 began a process of integrating all its environmental laws into a single comprehensive framework based on the principles of sustainable development.

The fundamental differences between these national environmental policies and NEPA were that they set measurable goals to achieve specific environmental results, and that they charged all the key sectoral agencies to take specific actions by explicit deadlines to achieve them. These approaches were not perfect solutions themselves: they often relied on unenforceable voluntary agreements between governments and trade associations, without participation or rights of challenge by citizen environmental groups, and may thus simply have delayed stricter controls (Beardsley et al. 1997, 34). These nations would undoubtedly face continuing economic pressures and political challenges as the implementation deadlines approached, but they had at least set explicit goals and directed all their ministries and industries, not simply environmental regulatory agencies, to implement them.

This was a major step beyond NEPA, and defined the unfinished business that the United States must address in order to build a true national environmental policy on the foundation NEPA laid.

The key unfinished business of U.S. national environmental policy, in short, was to spell out at least the most fundamental substantive criteria for NEPA's "conditions under which man and nature can exist in productive harmony," and to operationalize these in specific targets for environmental results and benchmarks for their achievement, mandated to all the agencies whose policies directly affect them. As of this writing, the United States has not done this, and it shows no sign of doing so. It thus remains unclear whether the United States will continue to make serious progress toward a substantive and effective national environmental policy, and reaffirm its early world leadership in this commitment, or whether it will settle instead for a continuing pendulum politics of rhetorical battles among political ideologues. Real environmental problems, meanwhile — produced by powerful forces of economic self-interest, and unchecked by a diminished and discredited public sector — continue to fester and reemerge in more problematic forms.

15 Environmental Policy in a Global Economy

> Our world today is dominated by a complex and tragic division. One part of mankind has undergone the revolutions of modernization and has emerged on the other side to a pattern of great and increasing wealth. But most of the rest of mankind has yet to achieve any of the revolutions. . . . The gap between the rich and the poor has become inevitably the most tragic and urgent problem of our day. — Barbara Ward, *The Rich Nations and the Poor Nations*

Until quite recently a book on American environmental policy would probably have ended at this point. It was simply taken for granted in the United States that environmental policy was a matter of domestic policy, and that the United States had the political, geographical, and economic independence to act autonomously in such matters. If international environmental issues were discussed at all, they were considered merely a few exceptions to the rule — trafficking in endangered species, transboundary issues such as Great Lakes water quality and acid rain, protection of whales and ocean fisheries — and peripheral to the mainstream of U.S. foreign policy, which was dominated by Cold War national security issues and, more recently, economic issues such as trade-balance deficits and manufacturing competitiveness.

The reality today, however, is that international trends have become integral forces in American environmental policy, and that they will rapidly grow more dominant. Most of the important environmental threats are now global issues: thinning of the stratospheric ozone layer, global warming, depletion of fisheries, mass urbanization of human populations, and the increasing environmental impacts of worldwide fuel and mineral extraction and crop production. Transboundary issues are also more important: acid rain across the Canadian border, water pollution along the Mexican border, and others. U.S. policies have had a direct impact on most of these issues: even as the United States has strengthened its domestic environmental protection policies, it has simultaneously promoted foreign trade, aid, and economic policies that have exacerbated environmental problems elsewhere.

At the same time, national governments, even the United States', simply are no longer ultimate and autonomous. They are limited by law in such forms as the General Agreement on Tariffs and Trade (GATT), which prohibits national or subnational regulations that create "technical barriers to trade." They are far more limited in practice by the unprecedented new mobility of global finance and trade, which allows businesses and investors to move rapidly to countries anywhere in the world whose policies allow them the highest and quickest profits.

American environmental policy thus operates today in a world of increasingly dominant global economic forces. Created by postwar international policies promoting worldwide free trade and export-oriented patterns of economic "development," in which the United States has played a central role, these forces are now more powerful and more autonomous than national governments themselves. Once created, these forces operate with such pervasive and anonymous power that they may systematically undermine all values other than their own narrow criteria. They operate not through the "faceless bureaucrats" of a formal world government such as a strengthened United Nations, but through the equally faceless bureaucrats of transnational corporations and financial markets, of the World Bank and International Monetary Fund, and of the newly created World Trade Organization.

These forces sometimes promote environmental protection. To the extent that pollution represents uncompetitive waste that reduces immediate economic returns, they should effectively correct it, producing some environmental improvements. When free-trade policies force elimination of governmental subsidies to environmentally damaging activities, such as mining, logging, and intensive agriculture, they benefit the environment as well as global trade. And when companies go global, they sometimes — but not always — take with them environmentally superior technologies and operating practices, thus disseminating better practices worldwide.

However, free trade also creates powerful new competitive pressures *against* any measures that go beyond business self-interest to protect the environment, workers, or local communities. Each national government and community remains formally free to regulate its own industries, but in reality free to bid them good-bye if these measures disadvantage them compared to competitors elsewhere. Externalities and tragedies of the commons — the classic forms of environmental problems, and of some fundamental social problems as well — remain *by definition* unsolved and unsolvable by self-interest alone.

The reality, therefore, is that national environmental policy by itself is no longer sufficient to govern the externalities and tragedies of the commons that persist in humans' relationships with their environment. New institutional mechanisms must be created to manage these effects in a global context. Formal institutions of world government — a United Nations EPA, for instance — seem unlikely, given both political resistance and the serious imperfections of the models that exist. A second option might be to reassert national sovereignty over international trade conditions, reaffirming the nineteenth-century doctrine of promoting internal markets and reducing dependence on foreign trade; but this too seems unlikely, except as a reaction to global war or economic collapse. Both producers and consumers are now inextricably linked with and dependent on the global economy.

The only viable strategy may therefore be to build effective environmental protection into the world trade system itself. For both good and ill, this system now exists, and is driven by pervasive forces that can either advance or seriously undermine environmental protection. This system itself requires governance functions: most obviously to maintain its own stability, but also to regulate what kinds of trade practices are allowable, and to adjudicate disputes, such as what kinds of national regulations amount to illegitimate "technical barriers to trade." Ultimately, the trade system's own long-term survival will require governance mechanisms to prevent unsustainable levels of environmental destruction and human impoverishment. If such mechanisms can no longer be exercised effectively by national governments alone, they must be built into the world trade system itself. To do this, however, requires a revolution in global environmental politics as well as policies. Whether this can and will occur is not yet clear.

Historical Context

During the four centuries in which American environmental policies have developed, the world's larger environmental history has been dominated by a series of powerful transformative forces. The Great Transformation marked the emergence of European societies with agricultural surpluses sufficient to support large-scale cities and armies. The development of Renaissance science and technology permitted further advances in agriculture, manufacturing, and long-distance exploration and trade. With these changes, and with the concurrent social transformation of feudal societies into political nation-states, the European nations expanded into competing global empires, colonizing distant cultures to extract their resources and create new markets for their own manufactured goods. The colonization of North America represented one manifestation of these policies, which consisted primarily in using colonized societies as raw-materials suppliers, markets, and outlets for surplus labor, while keeping for the colonizing empire the high-profit functions of manufacturing finished products, all on terms of trade managed by the empire.[1]

The Industrial Revolution vastly expanded the capabilities of these societies to transform materials and energy into products, and to dominate societies that lacked them. Environmentally this period might be labeled the Carbon Age, since its central feature has been the development of the capacity to extract huge quantities of carbon deposits from ancient vegetation stored over millennia as coal and oil, convert them into products for human use, and burn them to produce energy for industrial production, transport, and consumer comfort, while discharging their combustion products into the earth's atmosphere.

The result of these successive developments was some four centuries of unprecedented economic dominance for the European empires, based initially on global-scale extraction and trade of natural resources and then rapidly and steadily augmented by advances in industrial technology.

The United States' policies, in contrast, were until the mid-twentieth century overwhelmingly domestic rather than global in their emphasis, with little aspiration for international power or influence beyond the consolidation of its own continental domain. Throughout the nineteenth century its guiding principles were to develop *internal* markets, by building infrastructure for trade among the differing regions within the domestic United States, and thus to avoid entanglements with the politics of the European empires.

The United States did use deliberate policy incentives to attract European immigrants and capital investments — open-immigration policies and railroad land grants, for instance — and it produced significant exports. But it was basically self-sufficient in energy and other essential materials, and relatively uninvolved with global issues other than tariff policies.

In the 1890s the United States first began to project international military and economic power, following the emergence of American financial and industrial empires in the late nineteenth century. Examples included the Spanish-American War in the Caribbean and the Philippines, and subsequent military interventions in Latin America and elsewhere on behalf of American overseas businesses such as the United Fruit Company. Up to its entry into World War II, however, the U.S. took an overwhelmingly domestic view of its role in the world.

This domestic emphasis was especially true of its environmental policies. U.S. policies on international environmental issues included a few bilateral negotiations with Canada and Mexico, such as over transboundary air pollution from the Trail Smelter in Canada, management of the St. Lawrence Seaway and Great Lakes basin, and allocation of the Rio Grande and the Colorado River between the United States and Mexico. They also included a few negotiations for protection of migratory fish and wildlife: the Fur Seal Treaty of 1911, the Migratory Waterfowl Treaty of 1918, the Whaling Conventions of 1931 and 1938, and creation of the International Whaling Commission in 1946. Occasional U.S. interventions on behalf of American businesses in other countries were arguably environmental policies as well, since they forcibly promoted those countries' transitions from domestic self-sufficiency to reliance on export agriculture as European colonizers had done before them. Despite these exceptions, however, environmental policy remained overwhelmingly domestic.[2]

U.S. Policies and the Postwar World

With its entry into World War II, and its strong influence in creating the international arrangements that followed it, the United States' role in world affairs changed radically from one of isolation to global dominance. The European empires disintegrated during the two world wars, and were replaced by eighty to one hundred newly independent but economically and politically fragile nation-states. The political functions of empires were replaced in part by negotiative institutions such as the United Nations, but more pervasively by Cold War military and economic competition between the two remaining "superpowers" — the United States and the Soviet Union — and by global economic institutions: transnational corporations, "development banks" such as the World Bank, and more recently, interconnected financial markets.

These shifts had major consequences. First, the Cold War arms race placed unprecedented military power in the hands of the United States and the USSR, but the very unthinkability of global nuclear warfare in effect stalemated that power, forcing them to compete instead for economic and political influence — and thus to concede greater autonomy to the new nation-states. Second, this economic competition brought many of the new nation-states rapidly into the world economy, on terms brokered by the transnational corporations and financial institutions and promoted by subsidies from the industrial countries. Export trade and foreign aid in turn increased the wealth and power of indigenous national elites, often at the expense of more localized, less intensive indigenous environmental management practices. Finally, increasing world trade produced worldwide dissemination of military and industrial technologies, medicine, consumer products, and televised advertising, all of which promoted modern ("western") consumption patterns among those who could afford them.

For the United States this was a period of "fortuitous affluence" (Miles 1976). Its economy emerged from the war uniquely intact and robust, its military power was rivaled only by that of the Soviet Union, and its socioeconomic conditions provided widespread middle-class material comfort and economic security. The collapse of the European empires opened new resources and markets to U.S. firms worldwide.[3] Their replacement by new U.S.-sponsored institutions for economic recovery, trade, and multinational negotiation — the Marshall Plan, the International Bank for Reconstruction and Development ("World Bank"), the International Monetary Fund (IMF), the General Agreement on Tariffs and Trade (GATT), and the United Nations and its specialized agencies — created an era of unprecedented U.S. involvement and dominance in world affairs.

Development Aid

The United States was a leading force in the creation of the new postwar international institutions. Beginning with the Marshall Plan and the World Bank, these institutions were originally designed to rebuild the war-torn economies of Europe and Japan, and thus to avoid a repeat of the economic grievances that followed the First World War and led to the rise of Hitler. They evolved, however, into a more ambitious program for promoting economic development of poor countries more generally, augmented by many bilateral aid programs with specifically nationalistic objectives. To President Truman, economic development aid was essential to give the world's poor an alternative to the Communist dream (Athanasiou 1996, 287). Poor countries with strategic locations or resources thus received competing offers of economic aid from free-world and Communist countries, and others also received assistance in exchange for their economic cooperation and political support. To U.S. business interests, aid was also a tool to open cheap new sources of raw materials and energy, to develop suppliers and export markets for American producers, and to dispose of subsidy-driven surpluses of American crops.

Many of these foreign-aid programs financed construction of large-scale infrastructure projects, such as highways and multipurpose dams. The rationale behind this was that the availability of such infrastructure would create favorable conditions for private investment and economic growth. The model for these programs was the United States: notwithstanding its free-market rhetoric, the United States was perhaps the most successful model of "state-led development": using massive public investments and land-grant subsidies to build canals, railroads, multipurpose water projects, highways, and other major public infrastructure facilities, and thus to promote new private economic opportunities.

Other programs promoted a "Green Revolution" in food production in poorer countries, by using western science and technology to develop high-yield crop varieties for increased production. These programs too followed the example of the U.S., whose land-grant universities had produced repeated technological improvements in commercial farming. Many of these programs were highly successful, especially, for instance, in increasing rice and wheat production in Asia. However, they typically required far heavier application of chemical fertilizers and pesticides than previous practices, and promoted the conversion of small-scale farms that used diverse, indigenous seed stocks into larger-scale monocultures operated by fewer and larger farm businesses.

One policy initiative that had multiple environmental consequences was the Food for Peace program, created by Public Law 480 in 1954. Under this program U.S. surplus crops were donated to less-developed countries, some for short-term famine relief but far more on a longer-term basis. By 1989 the program had distributed over three hundred million tons and $35 billion worth of food aid, representing 60 percent of total world food aid (U.S. Congress 1990, 24).

To most Americans this program sounded like a model of humanitarian generosity, but in reality it served mainly to open export markets for U.S. farmers and to promote U.S. foreign policy interests (Sorenson 1979). Only 20 percent of the food aid was distributed directly to hungry people: the remainder was given to friendly governments to sell to their consumers (U.S. Congress 1990, 27–28). Disproportionate amounts were distributed not to the hungriest countries but to militarily strategic governments, to countries where the Agriculture Department wanted to promote American farm exports, and to countries where U.S. administrations sought to promote U.S. political interests, such as in Central America under President Reagan.[4]

The Food for Peace program had several environmental consequences. Domestically, dumping surpluses in other countries defused political pressures to reduce federally subsidized overproduction, and thus continued to promote intensification of agriculture.[5] Overseas, the influx of U.S. food grains made food cheaper for urban populations and thus undermined prices for the countries' own farmers, destabilizing their rural economies and encouraging increased rural-to-urban migration. They thus promoted the emergence of the sprawling "megacities" that are now characteristic of many poorer countries.[6]

The foreign aid programs reflected a basic presumption that all the newly independent countries both could and should move through a series of "stages of economic growth" toward the models of the United States and other industrialized capitalist countries (cf. Rostow 1960). Their instrument was to promote large-scale public investments in transforming the world's landscapes for export production and for industrial, urban, and more intensive agricultural uses, with both the benefits and the costs and environmental impacts that accompanied such uses. When such project were financed by foreign loans, moreover, they risked heavy debts if the costs turned out to be higher than estimated or if for any reason the anticipated benefits failed to materialize. In some countries, the benefits of economic development went primarily into the pockets of powerful elites rather than into widely shared economic gains. In many, the sharp increases in world oil prices during the 1970s fundamentally undermined the balance between export earnings and import costs, plunging them into devastating levels of foreign debt which then had to be refinanced by a relentless treadmill of domestic cutbacks.[7]

To its credit, the United States also led in creating worldwide programs for family planning, both directly and through the work of private philanthropies such as the Ford and Rockefeller Foundations. One of the most powerful new environmental threats, rapid global population growth, had been inadvertently created by the worldwide spread of western medicine, which sharply reduced worldwide death rates without at the same time reducing birth rates. Providing education and products by which people could limit their reproduction was thus an essential complement to economic development programs. The United States led the initiative to create the United Nations Fund for Population Activities in 1969, and became by far its largest contributor; and both Democratic and Republican political leaders, such as President Nixon and future president George Bush, supported international family-planning programs so long as they relied on voluntary measures (Teitelbaum 1992/93).

The Rise of Environmental Diplomacy

By the late 1960s the environmental impacts of population growth and economic development programs were becoming more widely recognized. Paul and Anne Ehrlich's *The Population Bomb* (1968) created mass public awareness of the threat of accelerated global population growth to both human welfare and the environment. M. Taghi Farvar's *The Careless Technology* (1972) documented many cases in which dams and other infrastructure projects had had serious unintended environmental consequences, such as the spread of disease and loss of fisheries in the Nile delta after construction of Egypt's Aswan High Dam. Other authors popularized more extravagant claims, such as predictions of massive famines by 1975 as food production failed to keep up with population growth (Paddock 1967). Finally, Donella and Dennis Meadows's *Limits to Growth* (1972) used computer models to illustrate the interdependencies among population, natural resource extraction, and pollution rates, and to argue that if existing trends and policies in *all* these dimensions were not corrected, they would lead to crisis in one form or another.[8]

A more general critique of economic-development theory, meanwhile, argued that it was not achieving even its own goal: the economic gap between rich and poor countries was widening rather than narrowing. The result appeared to be a permanently impoverished "Third World"—in contrast to the industrialized, capitalist "first" and state-controlled, Communist "second" worlds—composed of countries that were becoming increasingly impoverished for the benefit of indigenous elites, transnational corporations, and consumers in the affluent countries (Ward 1962). Their plight was catastrophically exacerbated, except for those few which produced petroleum, by the dramatic rises in world oil prices in 1973–74 and again in 1979–80, which left many of them hopelessly burdened with debt.

The rising criticism of aid-financed projects paralleled the rise of the modern U.S. environmental movement, and the awakening of international environmental concerns more generally. As early as 1949 the United Nations had sponsored a Scientific Conference on the Conservation and Utilization of Resources, an idea conceived by President Franklin Roosevelt and implemented after his death by President Truman.[9] Worldwide public reaction to the discovery of nuclear fallout in the 1950s produced probably the single most important international environmental agreement prior to the 1970s, the 1963 treaty banning atmospheric nuclear testing, but other agreements were limited to a few negotiations on fishery conservation and maritime oil pollution (Caldwell 1990, 349–50).

An important transitional issue to more explicit international environmental diplomacy was the "law of the sea" negotiations, which combined resource-use conflicts over ocean fisheries and undersea mining with military and commercial issues such as navigation rights for freighters and warships. Under the traditional "customary law" of the seas, each country could claim sovereignty out to only twelve miles from its shores, based on long-standing principles as to how far out it could reasonably defend. With the development of offshore oil-drilling technology by U.S. firms in the 1940s, however, President Truman unilaterally declared economic sovereignty over the outer continental shelf (OCS) out to the limits of this technology, which in some areas — the Gulf of Mexico and Atlantic coast — was as far as two hundred miles. U.S. laws in 1954 further declared that undersea lands for the first three miles offshore ("tidelands") were the property of the abutting U.S. state, and that the remainder of the OCS was U.S. federal property, thus dividing with the states the future royalties from OCS oil and gas production.

Peru, lacking a similar continental shelf but having a major offshore anchovy fishery, in response declared sovereignty over fisheries in a similar "exclusive economic zone" out to two hundred miles from its coast, and other nations promptly followed suit. There followed two decades of intermittent conflict between offshore and onshore fishing fleets and their respective governments, which President Nixon in 1971 sought to resolve by starting worldwide negotiations toward a comprehensive new international treaty on the law of the sea. The United States took active leadership in this process throughout the 1970s, seeking confirmation of key principles such as rights of commercial and military passage through straits and of economic exploitation of fisheries and seabed minerals.

In 1968 the United Nations Educational, Scientific and Cultural Organization (UNESCO) convened a Conference of Experts on the Biosphere, which for the first time affirmed the importance of viewing the world's environment as an organic, interrelated whole — a *biosphere* — rather than merely a collection of individual, economically-useful resources. It also identified the role of human activity as a pervasive altering agent, and the possibility that such activity might cause irreversible damage. Based on these concerns the conference's experts called for the first full-scale United Nations Conference on the Human Environment, which was held in Stockholm in 1972 (Caldwell 1990, 44–54).

The 1972 Stockholm conference was a landmark event in raising worldwide awareness of environmental issues. Its debates were marked by intense conflict between speakers concerned about human impacts on the biosphere, and speakers from poorer countries who retorted that these issues were merely the narrow concerns of the affluent nations, and that the real issues should be socioeconomic development and the correction of economic injustice. As India's prime minister Indira Gandhi argued, "*Poverty* is the greatest polluter." The result was a compromise document, which declared that nations had an obligation to ensure that their actions did not cause environmental damage to others, but also that they had a sovereign right to exploit their own resources in any way they chose. These debates foreshadowed the acrimonious debates between the nations of the affluent "North" and the poor "South" during the 1970s over proposals for a "new international economic order."

Despite these conflicts, the Stockholm conference produced several valuable results. It legitimized the biosphere as a subject for national and international policy-making, and delineated over one hundred sets of issues and recommendations (Caldwell 1990, 55–93). It also led directly to creation of the United Nations Environment Program, and to the emergence of an active network of international nongovernment citizen environmental organizations (NGOs). A continuing series of conferences followed, on more specific environment-related topics: population (1974, 1984, 1994), food (1974), human settlements (1976, 1996), water (1977), desertification (1977), climate (1979, 1990), and renewable energy (1981).

By 1973 major international agreements were signed on protection of the world's cultural and natural heritage, prevention of marine pollution by waste dumping, restricting trade in endangered species, and reducing pollution from ships.[10] A convention on long-range transboundary air pollution was signed in 1979, and further protocols dealing with sulfur and nitrogen oxides in 1985 and 1988. The Law of the Sea Treaty was also concluded in 1982, though it was not ratified by enough countries to take effect until the 1990s.

A series of international environmental disasters in the 1980s mobilized far more widespread environmental concern among the world's governments. In 1983, dioxin wastes from a notorious chemical-factory disaster in Seveso, Italy, were discovered to have been secretly moved into storage in France. In December 1984, toxic chemicals from a leaking pesticide production plant in Bhopal, India, caused a fatal mass poisoning of nearby residents; the worst industrial accident in history. The plant was jointly owned by a U.S. firm (Union Carbide) and the Indian government. In November 1986, an industrial fire and chemical spill in Switzerland caused massive fish kills in the Rhine River. Meanwhile, long-range transport of air pollutants from power plants caused acid damage to forests throughout Europe — including "Waldsterben" ("forest death") endangering parts of Germany's famous and beloved Black Forest — as well as in the United States and Canada.

The discovery in 1985 of a progressively deepening "ozone hole" over the Antarctic provided a strikingly vivid image of a new scale of environmental threat: human actions were now causing truly *global* impacts on the biosphere. A scientific conference in Villach, Austria, in the same year concluded that fossil-fuel combustion and other human activities might be causing unprecedented warming of the global climate, and a series of unusually hot drought years amplified this concern in the minds of the public. The explosion of the Chernobyl nuclear power reactor in the Ukraine in 1986 caused serious international exposure to radionuclides throughout Europe, underscoring and amplifying fears of growing environmental hazards. Also, new aggregate data on tropical deforestation kindled scientists' concerns of a worldwide loss of biodiversity: tropical forests were being rapidly cut to produce timber for Japan, to open more land for beef production for U.S. tables, to explore and exploit oil deposits, and for other purposes.

These issues produced new international agreements on protection of the ozone layer, on notification and assistance after nuclear accidents, and on transboundary movements and disposal of hazardous wastes. They also led to further negotiations on conservation of biological diversity, on global climate change, and on sustainable economic development policies more generally.

A particular success story was the Montreal Protocol on Protection of the Ozone Layer, in which the United States among others played a key leadership role. Chlorofluorocarbons (CFCs) such as Freon™ had been produced in increasing quantities since the 1960s, primarily by about a dozen firms in the United States, Europe, and Japan. CFCs seemed to be wonder chemicals for several uses: as a propellant for aerosol sprays, a blowing agent for producing insulation and other foam products, a degreasing solvent in the manufacture of computer chips, and a cooling agent in refrigerators and air conditioners. They were cheap to produce, and so inert that they posed virtually no health risks, unlike several products they replaced. Scientists in the 1970s, however, proposed that CFCs' very inertness might cause a more serious problem: they would remain in the air long enough to rise to the stratosphere, where sunlight would trigger a chemical chain reaction destroying the ozone layer that protects the earth from excessive solar radiation. The results could include increased worldwide risks of skin cancer, eye damage, threats to marine organisms, and excessive global warming.[11]

The United States in 1978 banned "nonessential" uses of CFCs as aerosol propellants, but by the mid-1980s these reductions were more than offset by growth in other uses. In 1985, most of the industrial nations and some others signed an initial international agreement to continue studying the issue (the Vienna Convention), but almost immediately thereafter, British scientists unexpectedly discovered a deepening seasonal "ozone hole" over the South Pole, which provided empirical evidence for this concern. Continuing negotiations produced the Montreal Protocol in 1987, whose signers agreed to phase out the production and use of CFCs. As the science continued to grow more persuasive, the phaseout timetable was tightened in London in 1990 and again in 1997, and additional countries, including several of the largest and fastest-growing less-developed countries, agreed to join the agreement.

The Montreal Protocol offered a hopeful example for other international environmental issues. Figure 25 shows the dramatic reductions that resulted in U.S. production of CFCs, and similar success occurred in the other producer countries: by 1996 most developed countries had met their commitments to phase out production of CFCs, though black-market production remained a problem in some countries and production of halons — similar to CFCs, but even more damaging — was increasing, especially in China (World Resources Institute 1998, 178). Unusual among international treaties, the Montreal Protocol incorporated a procedure for continuing review and for refinement if scientific knowledge changed, and it required that a strong majority of the producer nations sign on as a condition of its going into effect. The United States played a leader-

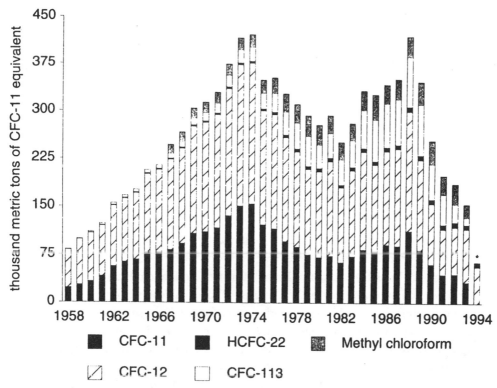

Figure 25. Success of a treaty: U.S. production of selected ozone-depleting chemicals, 1958–94. Note the rapid rise in production from 1958 to 1972, the temporary decline and eventual resurgence following publication of the CFC-ozone depletion hypothesis in the early 1970s, and finally the rapid and near-total phaseout of production following adoption of the Montreal Protocol in 1987. [U.S. Council on Environmental Quality]

ship role, as did some of its leading producer firms, which followed the judgments of their own scientists and positioned themselves to produce substitute chemicals instead.

However, the ozone layer issue was easier in several key respects than many others. It was a threat to everyone: there were no potential winners from ozone-layer damage. The producers of the problem were few, and were concentrated in just a few industrial countries: it was feasible to control production and monitor compliance. Perhaps especially helpful, the scientific evidence steadily grew more consensual and compelling.

More generally, however, environmental treaties were only as strong as their weakest links. Not all countries signed them, some signed but failed to ratify them, and even those that ratified them varied widely in their commitment to implementation and enforcement.[12] The United States, for instance, never ratified some major environmental accords, such as the Basel Convention on hazardous waste transport and the Law of the Sea Treaty. It was not clear therefore how easily the success of the Montreal Protocol could be transferred to more complex and controversial issues, such as biodiversity conservation or global warming.

"Sustainable Development"

In 1980 the United Nations Environmental Program began a broad series of initiatives to move international discussions beyond the divisive rhetoric of "North versus South" and "environment versus economic development." In 1980 it collaborated with the non-governmental International Union for the Conservation of Nature in publication of a "world conservation strategy," which stressed the fundamental interconnections between environmental protection and economic development (Caldwell 1990, 322–23).[13] In 1982 the U.N. General Assembly, led by Zaire and a coalition of Third World nations, overwhelmingly endorsed a "World Charter for Nature," which asserted principles for ethical conduct toward the biosphere.[14] Far more governments were willing to profess such a commitment than to live up to it in practice, but it was nonetheless an important symbolic action: many of the Third World governments that endorsed the World Charter would not have agreed to such a statement even symbolically at Stockholm ten years before.

In 1983 the General Assembly appointed a World Commission on Environment and Development (WCED), chaired by Prime Minister Gro Harlem Brundtland of Norway, to propose long-term strategies for achieving "sustainable development": combining global economic and social progress with respect for natural systems and environmental quality. The report of this commission, *Our Common Future,* became the primary document framing issues of the world environment. *Sustainable* development, it argued, meant development that would meet the basic needs of the present generation of humans without compromising the needs of future generations (WCED 1987). Unlike many environmental protection advocates, the commission focused attention on the dire economic plight of the poorer countries, and on the reality that they had become even worse off during the 1980s than before. It therefore urged a renewed commitment to promoting economic growth in the poorer countries, particularly in impoverished Africa and debt-laden Latin America. However, it urged that the core elements of this growth be radically redirected from past policies and priorities, to emphasize less energy-intensive technologies, stabilization of human population levels, intensified conservation of natural systems and of energy, and reorientation of technologies toward reduced risks.

The Brundtland Commission report was remarkably successful in redefining the international environmental policy agenda. Sustainable development became and remained the central concept of that agenda, and both environmental and economic interests as well as governments adopted its rhetoric. Almost entirely marginalized or ignored in this redefined agenda, however, were several fundamental and problematic issues. First, sustainable development was an attractive but empty aspiration: real development decisions represented real tradeoffs among the interests of present and future generations in the use of the finite resources of the world's ecosystems. Second, it virtually ignored the vast environmental impacts of wastefully affluent consumption levels, focusing instead on the environmental impacts of the poor, and calling for renewed commitment to more universal economic growth. In effect, it reaffirmed the "economic development" paradigm but in greener language, without dealing with the hard but real issues of the ecological impacts of the global mass-consumption economy, the ownership and allocation of finite ecological resources (*whose* common future?), or the possibility that economic growth policies, even reinstituted in somewhat "greener" forms, might be inherently unsustainable (Chaterjee and Finger 1994).

The Brundtland Commission report became the foundation for the 1992 United Nations Conference on Environment and Development in Rio de Janeiro (UNCED), the so-called Earth Summit, which marked the twentieth anniversary of the Stockholm conference. The organizers of the conference sought painstakingly to move beyond the divisions of the Stockholm conference and to orchestrate a common international commitment to sustainable development: an "Agenda 21" for the twenty-first century. Action items included a Framework Convention on Climate Change, a Biodiversity Convention to protect endangered species, a draft agreement on forest conservation, and a "Rio Declaration" restating the core principles of international environmental law.[15]

The Earth Summit was the largest single gathering of world heads of state in human history, and raised widespread expectations of new international cooperation to address global environmental problems. It generated large amounts of publicity, but its actual results were disappointing. It focused on worldwide attention on global environmental issues, and on their inherent interactions with economic choices. It also marked a high point for organized civic input into international negotiations, from some twenty-five hundred nongovernment organizations that met concurrently in Rio. But it produced few new agreements, and even these had only indifferent support from the United States and other key countries. At the insistence of the poorer countries, it also explicitly affirmed the national sovereignty of every country to exploit its environment in any way its national government chose. This was hardly significant progress. A follow-up working conference in 1997, five years later, regressed into disputes between the rich and poor countries, and failed to produce agreement even on a final statement of implementation commitments (*Washington Post,* June 28, 1997).

The United States' Role

The United States has been an important participant in international environmental policy-making, sometimes in a leadership role and often as a model for other countries' initiatives, but often also as a serious obstacle to progress on issues that conflicted with U.S. political and economic interests.

Many U.S. environmental policies became influential models for other countries and for international approaches. Examples included both technology- and health-based pollution standards, and the extensive U.S. scientific basis for them; NEPA's environmental impact assessment procedure; endangered species legislation; and provisions formalizing the rights of citizen groups to obtain government documents and participate in policy-making. Others included market-oriented innovations such as tradable permits, disclosure requirements such as the Toxics Release Inventory, and a substantial body of economics literature (though little actual implementation) advocating pollution taxes and charges.

Unlike many other countries, however, the United States showed little reciprocal influence in its own environmental policies. International environmental policy documents asserted broad principles that should guide decisions — the "polluter pays principle," the "precautionary principle," and the "subsidiarity principle," for instance — but this language rarely trickled down into U.S. environmental laws or policy debates. The 1992 UNCED conference produced a systematic framework for country-level environmental action programs to achieve sustainable development goals, and many countries used this framework to develop systematic national environmental action programs, even if they often were very vague and general ones (Jänicke and Jörgens 1996). In the United States, however, it attracted virtually no public attention or discussion. The sustainable development concept attracted somewhat greater attention — President Clinton appointed a Presidential Commission on Sustainable Development, and some state and local governments adopted its rhetoric in a smattering of initiatives — but it remained a focus of largely cosmetic and piecemeal projects rather than a core principle driving significant decisions. With only a few exceptions, such as the ozone layer and global warming, U.S. environmental policies continued to be framed almost entirely as domestic issues, driven by ad hoc political pressures rather than by international priorities or policy debates.

The reality was that even as environmental policy became a major new subject of domestic regulatory legislation, in foreign policy it remained almost entirely marginal to the core issues that defined and dominated U.S. assertions of its national interest: national security, as defined by Cold War anti-Communism, and from the mid-1970s on, international trade and economic competition. The one major policy challenge to this orthodoxy was a report by the Carter administration in 1980, *Global 2000*, which systematically documented global environmental problems and asserted a serious U.S. national interest in addressing them. However, President Carter did not remain in office long enough to act on this report.[16]

With the election of President Reagan in 1980, the United States systematically retreated from international leadership both on environmental issues and in multilateral policy-making more generally. The Reagan administration immediately dropped the *Global 2000* study, and in particular its assertion of a U.S. national interest in international environmental governance efforts. In contrast even to previous Republican presidents, Reagan rejected the idea that the United States would benefit from any kind of "world order," and he repudiated agreements such as the proposed Law of the Sea Treaty — which had actually been initiated by President Nixon, and offered substantial benefits to U.S. interests such as shipping and commercial fishing — as manifestations of a "collectivist ideology" (Morell 1992, 202–03).[17] At the 1984 United Nations Population Conference in Mexico City, Reagan ended U.S. support of international family planning programs as well, converting them instead into a domestic political "wedge" issue to mobilize alliances among political, economic, and religious conservatives.[18] Under Reagan the United States also was the only nation to vote against the innocuous World Charter for Nature in 1982, and against a 1983 General Assembly resolution to protect people from imported products harmful to health and environment (Caldwell 1990, 91).

These changes reflected reassertion of a fundamentally unilateral approach to world affairs, returning primary emphasis to national self-interest as the end of foreign policy and U.S. military and economic pressure as the means (Morell 1992, 205–06). Reagan had always opposed world-level governance institutions, and had little use for the United Nations or for development aid except as instruments of U.S. self-interest. By the end of his term the United States had left a substantial fraction of its dues to the United Nations unpaid, nominally to force increased efficiency in U.N. agencies but also out of a deeper opposition to the U.N.'s role and programs.[19] By 1996 the United States' overall international development aid budget had been reduced to a lower fraction of its gross national product than that of any of the other twenty leading industrial nations (*International Herald Tribune*, July 6–7, 1996).[20]

President Bush softened the Reagan administration's policies somewhat. Bush campaigned in 1988 on a desire to be the "environmental president," thus distancing himself from Reagan's unpopularity on this issue and successfully obscuring his own earlier role as chairman of Reagan's regulatory relief initiative (Bryner 1993, 94).[21] Once elected, he initially acceded to pressure from Republicans in Congress to demonstrate that Republicans too could lead on environmental protection issues, and he backed EPA Administrator William Reilly in a number of initiatives during his first two years in office. Examples included advancing the 1990 London amendments to the Montreal Protocol on the Ozone Layer, negotiating a major new Clean Air Act statute, negotiating acid-rain concerns with Canada (and incorporating them into the 1990 Clean Air Act amendments), calling for international regulations on greenhouse-gas reduction, and after 1989 contributing EPA aid to environmental management agencies in Eastern Europe.[22] Bush also allowed the EPA and other agencies to promote international research and technical cooperation on global warming, and to participate actively in the preparations for the 1992 United Nations Earth Summit in Rio de Janeiro.

By 1991, however, Bush began to distance himself both from environmental issues generally and from international environmental issues in particular. He allowed Reilly and EPA to move them ahead, but personally equivocated rather than leading, lest he jeopardize his support among Reaganite conservatives and business interests.[23] Nowhere was this more evident than in his lengthy vacillation as to whether he would even attend the Rio Earth Summit. After belatedly agreeing to attend, he then studiously avoided leading or even supporting most of the central issues under consideration. Alone among the developed countries, the United States under President Bush refused to sign the Biodiversity Convention, and the U.S. also led opposition to binding targets or deadlines for reducing greenhouse-gas emissions.[24] Bush also refused to commit funding to the Global Environmental Facility, a new $1.2 billion multilateral funding agency for global projects on global warming, ozone depletion, biodiversity, and international waters; ultimately he pledged a token $50 million (Congress eventually appropriated $30 million) plus $150 million in bilateral "parallel funding." The one issue on which Bush did take any leadership was forest conservation, an issue on which he chose to lecture the developing countries rather than share in responsibility for solutions (Soroos 1996, 293).

Like Reagan at the Mexico City Population Conference, Bush's evident priority was to position himself for domestic conservatives as a defender of U.S. sovereignty, a promoter of economic growth (as if this were inevitably in conflict with environmental protection), and a tough advocate for their positions, rather than to position himself for Americans more generally as a leader and consensus builder among the other nations. In the end he thus alienated all sides, left the United States isolated, and substantially weakened the overall results of the conference. Due in no small part to the United States' nonsupport, the conference's ultimate result was largely empty rhetoric without concrete policy advances. It was a sorry performance, unworthy of the nation that had led almost all global-scale international environmental initiatives up to that time.

President Clinton appeared initially to reverse the decline of U.S. international environmental leadership that had occurred under Presidents Reagan and Bush. He aligned himself with knowledgeable advocates of environmental protection and sustainable development, choosing Al Gore as vice president (author of his own popular book on global environmental problems, *Earth in the Balance*) and appointing as Assistant Secretary of State for Environment former senator Tim Wirth, who had cosponsored bipartisan congressional initiatives toward market-based policy tools for environmental protection. He also immediately reversed the Reagan and Bush positions on several major issues. He reaffirmed U.S. support for the United Nations Population Fund, signed the Biodiversity Convention and the Law of the Sea Treaty, and endorsed the goal of stabilizing U.S. greenhouse-gas emissions at 1990 levels by the year 2000. All these actions required Senate ratification, however (or in the case of population, funding), which by 1998 had not occurred under the Republican-controlled Congress (Soroos 1996, 294–95).

Clinton's most basic foreign-policy priorities, however, were to reduce the U.S. budget and trade deficits, and to that end to expand U.S. foreign trade and export markets. Initially he sought to incorporate environmental goals into this agenda by promoting U.S. exports of environmental technologies and services, but he was soon blocked by conservative congressional opposition to government "technology policy": that is, to subsidies for new and different technologies rather than for those from which U.S. businesses already benefited.

Clinton's clearest and most effective commitment of his personal influence was to secure congressional approval of two key free-trade agreements, the North American Free Trade Agreement (NAFTA) and amendments to the General Agreement on Tariffs and Trade (GATT). The Biodiversity Convention that he signed was a weak compromise, including key elements written by U.S. biotechnology firms to promote their own interests.[25] After the 1994 elections his priorities were severely limited by the conservative Republican Congress, which sought to radically reduce the budgets of all the international programs as well as those of EPA and other domestic environmental programs.[26]

One more major international environmental agreement was negotiated in December 1997, at the Kyoto conference on a proposed United Nations Framework Convention on Climate Change. The goal of this meeting was to define binding commitments for reducing emissions of carbon dioxide and other "greenhouse gases" from human sources, in order to slow the excessive buildup of those gases in the atmosphere and the increased global warming that many streets believed might already have begun to result from them.[27] The Clinton administration initially endorsed binding timetables for emission reductions, but later equivocated in response to intense opposition from businesses and Congress (Soroos 1996, 294). The resulting agreement called for 5 percent reductions in emissions by all industrial nations from 1990 to 2012, including 7 percent by the United States, 8 percent by Europe, and 6 percent by Japan. Even that commitment might not be ratified by the U.S. Senate, however, in the face of fierce lobbying and propaganda campaigns by the energy and automobile industries, labor unions fearful of job losses, and other opponents.

Meeting a commitment of 5 percent reduction below 1990 emissions by 2012 would require significant policy and economic changes by the United States, since its emissions were otherwise projected to increase by 34 percent over the same time period (World Resources Institute 1998, 176). Advocates argued that the cost savings from increased energy efficiency would defray much of the costs or even produce net gains, except of course for the fossil–fuel extraction industries themselves. Optimists also hoped that the basic principles of the agreement—a "cap and trade" framework, like the sulfur emissions trading program created by the 1990 Clean Air Act—would create effective incentives both for cost–effective emission reductions and for other desirable results, such as electric utilities paying for reforestation programs in poorer countries to convert atmospheric carbon dioxide into oxygen through photosynthesis. Skeptics, however, saw such trades as loopholes by which U.S. utilities could cheaply continue to pollute at their own power plants, and U.S. energy producers adamantly resisted any effective curbs on their continued extraction of fossil fuels. In February 1998, President Clinton announced a $6.3 billion budget proposal for tax incentives and research to reduce greenhouse gas emissions through increased energy efficiency, but opponents in Congress attacked these proposals as well.

The Collapse of Soviet Communism: Pyrrhic Victory for the Environment?

In 1989 the Soviet empire collapsed, and with it the Cold War political and economic order that had shaped four decades of postwar history. The Berlin Wall and the Iron Curtain were dismantled, the countries of Central and Eastern Europe reclaimed their autonomy, and the Soviet Union itself fractured into some half-dozen fragile, independent countries. The threat of strategic nuclear warfare eased, and the Soviet military threat was suddenly transformed into a crisis of economic deprivation in a political vacuum.

As the authority of these regimes eroded in the years before Communism's collapse, environmental issues became important mobilizing points for civic opposition movements, particularly after the 1986 explosion of the Chernobyl nuclear power plant and the widespread radiation exposures that followed. Communist governments for decades had denounced pollution as a uniquely capitalist problem, a result of free-market greed that simply would not occur in a socialist country where government managed the economy for the good of everyone. They set environmental-protection standards that were more stringent on paper than those of the western democracies, but in practice did not enforce them, and suppressed evidence of environmental problems in their own countries. The Chernobyl disaster dramatically unmasked the falsity of Communist environmental policies, and opened the way for far more widespread public opposition.

Once the regimes fell, environmental damage provided dramatic visual images for mass-media reports about the destructive impacts of Communist governments on their own countries, and about the hypocrisy of their previous denials. Scientists made public the previously secret records of pollution, and new governments published reports documenting the devastating impacts of their predecessors' policies. Story after story in the international press showed the world the "black triangle" of air pollution in North Bohemia and Silesia, the soot-covered children of Romania, the dirty steel mills of Poland, the poisonous smelters of Bulgaria, and the chemical and nuclear legacies of Russia's arms-production regions and military bases. The United States and other western governments promoted these stories, offering foreign aid for environmental cleanup and at the same time using these news accounts to drive the final nails into the coffin of Communist governance. Communist governments, the message was, had used their authoritarian power and secrecy to devastate the health and environment of their own people; now free-market capitalism and democracy would save them.[28]

The reality of the transition to market economies imposed severe hardships itself, however. The immediate result was not environmental cleanup but economic collapse. Export trade shriveled, production shrank, prices soared, jobs disappeared, government budgets plummeted. The emerging environmental movements withered as economic insecurity replaced the euphoria of political freedom. Environmental conditions improved initially simply due to the loss of production, but some of the worst pollution sources — mines, power plants, smelters, and steel mills — were kept operating as essential sources of energy and jobs. Budget cuts undermined environmental ministries: the best staff members were lured away by higher pay in the growing private sector, while the rest were left with little money or authority. In the former Soviet Union the collapse of government authority brought widespread looting of environmental resources for personal survival and for enrichment of the departing Communist managers. Countries that made successful transitions to reasonably prosperous market economies, such as the Czech Republic, began to see significant reduction in pollution as a byproduct of economic modernization (Andrews 1993a, Andrews et al. 1994, Schnoor et al. 1997). Countries whose economies remained depressed, however, such as the former Soviet Union itself, continued to experience severe pollution and unmanaged natural resource exploitation (Kotov and Nikitina 1993). Overall, both economic and environmental improvement were far slower, more painful, and more uneven than western propaganda had led people to expect.

The most far-reaching consequence of the Soviet collapse was the end of the Cold War competition for global dominance between the capitalist United States and the communist Soviet Union, and with it the political and economic order that had framed world history since the end of World War II. This change brought great benefits, in particular a dramatically diminished risk of global nuclear warfare. However, it also brought severe economic deprivation to the countries of the former Soviet bloc, and great economic uncertainty to Third World countries worldwide. Cold War competition had allowed poorer countries to gain increased influence and aid, as the two superpowers bid for their resources, markets, and support. With the end of the Cold War, capitalism had won, and the "great powers" no longer had national security interests in assisting them: they were now at the mercy of world market forces. With the defining issues of international politics suddenly gone, the central international issues were no longer political but economic, and international initiative shifted from the actions of governments to those of transnational corporations and financial empires.

From Political to Business Empires

Beginning with the end of World War II, worldwide political stabilization supported by U.S. military commitments and Cold War economic competition permitted American and other businesses to become truly transnational corporations. Such firms first traded and eventually manufactured on a global basis, wherever they found the most profitable combinations of low taxes and cheap labor, energy, and materials. Transnational corporations rapidly became so effective that they could often control the terms of trade among suppliers and even among entire countries.[29] By the 1990s the Fortune 500 companies controlled 25 percent of the world's output and 70 percent of world trade; five companies or fewer controlled more than 50 percent of the global market in each of seven major sectors, and more than 40 percent of the market in three others (*The Economist,* quoted in Korten 1996, 18).[30]

These trends accelerated dramatically with the more recent globalization of finance. The postwar era produced unprecedented concentrations of economic assets: in transnational corporations, in "petrodollars" controlled by oil-rich governments, in mutual investment funds, in banking conglomerates deregulated by the Reagan administration, and in corporate empires built on a wave of business consolidations and "leveraged buyouts."[31] By the 1980s, computer technology and permissive government policies allowed instantaneous transfers of these assets among international financial markets. These changes combined to produce huge pools of capital in the hands of money managers using computers to seek the most instantaneously profitable investments anywhere in the world, irrespective of nonmarket costs such as environmental impacts or the welfare of workers.

The net effect of these policies was to place enormous new emphasis on short-term calculations of financial return, and to relentlessly subordinate other values to that criterion. Worldwide, computer-driven financial trading operated so impersonally, and with such singular attention to short-term financial returns, that it seemed to leave little room for environmental concerns, worker welfare, community stability, or other values beyond those that contributed directly to short-term profitability.

The rapid spread of computerized automation also fundamentally changed the relationships between corporations and their workers. Computerization allowed machines and robots to replace humans in many dangerous jobs, but also in many jobs more generally. The result was a vast increase in productivity per worker, and in some cases worker safety, but also far fewer workers and far less job security. Skilled workers in particular lost economic leverage to machines capable of doing their work. Many new jobs were created, but many of these jobs provided fewer prospects of long-term economic security than those they replaced. Increasing economic insecurity in turn eroded public support for environmental protection, as people had less time to volunteer for nonpaying activities and greater fears about its possible economic consequences. Environmentalists and environmental regulators made convenient scapegoats for job losses, diverting attention from the business decisions and larger, impersonal economic forces that really caused them.

The fundamental development of the postwar period, in short, was the creation of a truly global economy, from whose influence virtually no country could remain isolated. This economy was strongly abetted by the policies of the United States and other nations: policies promoting free trade, deregulating banks, allowing leveraged buyouts, easing antitrust restrictions, and others. Once created, it operated across national boundaries by such impersonal and autonomous forces of short-term self-interest that it was increasingly beyond the control of national or local government policies, even those of a country as large and influential as the United States.

Global Urbanization and Industrialization

The global economy produced several profound changes in human living conditions. One was an increasing gap between the affluence of elites and the poverty of the majority of the world's people. By the 1990s the combined income of the top 20 percent of the world's population was nearly sixty times larger than that of the bottom 20 percent — double what this gap had been in 1960. The combined net worth of some 350 billionaires alone exceeded the combined annual income of 45 percent of the world's population, and that gap was growing as well (UNDP *Human Development Report 1992,* quoted in Korten 1996, 16).

A second change was a massive shift from predominantly rural to overwhelmingly urban living conditions (Linden 1996; World Resources Institute 1998, 39). Within just four decades, most of the world's growing population came to live not in relatively self-sufficient rural communities but in urban areas and particularly in vast "megacities," pulled by the hopes of better opportunities built up by world trade and aid, and pushed by the corresponding decline of the rural economy (fig. 26). Most had no choice but to live in sprawling unofficial squatter settlements, which often lacked even the most basic housing, water, and sanitation services. By the end of the twentieth century, therefore, a large and growing fraction of the world's people were again living in the sorts of unhealthy urban environmental conditions that the nineteenth-century sanitation movement in the United States and European nations took pride in having eradicated. Some of the old disease scourges of that period, such as cholera and tuberculosis, threatened to reemerge in new and drug-resistant forms.

Finally, the global economy brought intensive industrialization to many of the poorer countries, benefiting their economies (sometimes) and those who controlled them, but also importing new environmental and health risks. In many "developing" countries, rapid industrialization increased people's exposures to industrial pollution and toxic chemicals, even as they were still exposed to the environmental risks of poverty: food and water contamination, smoke from unventilated cooking stoves, and unsanitary living conditions. Between 1980 and 1985, industrial energy use in the poorer countries increased almost 5 percent while output increased by only three-hundredths of one percent.[32] The five most material-, energy-, and pollution-intensive sectors — iron and steel,

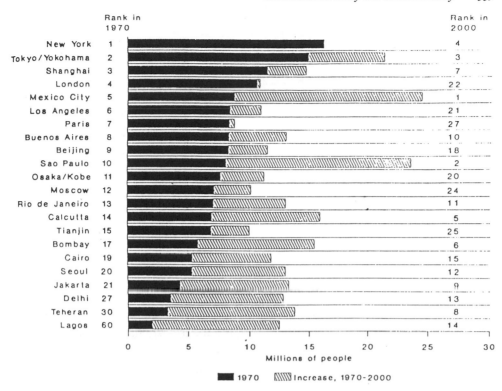

Figure 26. Global urbanization: population of the world's fifteen largest cities, 1970 (actual) and 2000 (projected). Note the overwhelming increases both in the populations of specific cities of the developing world (such as Mexico City and Sao Paulo), and in the aggregate of them: most of the cities on the list are in less-developed countries, and together they dwarf the populations of New York, London, and other developed-world cities. [U.N. Department of International Economic and Social Affairs. *Prospects of World Urbanization, 1988,* Population Studies No. 112, ST/ESA/SER. A/112 (New York, 1989).]

nonferrous metals, nonmetallic minerals, chemicals, and pulp and paper — grew twice as fast in the less-developed countries as in the developed ones during the 1980s (United Nations Industrial Development Organization 1989, 1991).

The United States and other industrialized countries played active roles in this process, and therefore shared responsibility for its impacts as well as its benefits. U.S. environmental protection laws rarely extended to the actions of American corporations operating overseas. Hazardous wastes from industrial countries turned up more and more frequently in poorer countries, sometimes through black-market transfers but often legally as well, with far fewer safeguards than were required in the developed countries. Pesticides restricted in the United States were still regularly exported to poorer countries, where they were used with far less understanding of their risks, and far fewer safety precautions.[33] Ironically, they were often used on crops that were then exported to U.S. consumers, in a "circle of poison" (Vogel 1995, 202–06). The worldwide race to exploit petroleum deposits brought severe pollution and destruction to previously stable ecosystems and communities.

Most of these poorer countries had little or no institutional capacity for environmental management and protection. Many lacked even basic environmental laws, and those that had nominal policies often lacked either the financial, technical, or political support to implement and enforce them (cf. World Bank 1992).[34] Nationalistic governments and self-interested economic elites — often the same individuals — resisted as "paternalistic" any proposals that the developed countries impose environmental-protection requirements on their businesses operating in other countries, or on other businesses exporting to them, and asserted their national sovereignty to pollute or destroy their environments for economic gain if they wished to. Transnational business interests echoed and encouraged these arguments, disingenuously overlooking the enormous inequalities in global market forces, especially those driven by the huge U.S. consumer market, that drove this global industrialization and its impacts.

Economic Restructuring

In the 1980s, economic crises further undermined what little environmental-protection authority most poor countries had. Steep increases in OPEC oil prices devastated their budgets, except for those few that produced oil, and the concurrent worldwide economic recession undermined the economic revenues they had counted on to repay international loans they had accepted for development projects in the 1960s and '70s. Many of these development projects had failed, plunging the countries into acute debt crises which compelled them to beg the International Monetary Fund (IMF) to refinance their loans. The price of refinancing these debts was that they accept IMF demands for "structural adjustment": that is, that they adopt policies to systematically shift their economies toward world-market exports rather than internal self-sufficiency, expand private enterprise, reduce government services and regulation, remove barriers to international capital flows, and restructure domestic labor markets to favor market-driven production (Reed 1996).

To critics, the IMF's structural adjustment requirements amounted to a global economic policy on behalf of its sponsors: the United States, other investor nations, and their banks and corporations. The policy was to extract repayment of their loans by forcing debtor countries more and more fully into the global market economy, as producers for export markets subject to world-market competition. The requirements often included severe cuts in public services, such as health, education, housing, and environmental protection, combined with economic policies to promote export revenues from raw-materials extraction and low-wage agriculture and manufacturing.

To structural-adjustment advocates, such requirements were essential steps toward the creation of viable economies in the debtor countries. Some of these countries, they argued, had relied too heavily on public-sector employment and programs, often run more for elite enrichment and political patronage than to provide efficient or even effective public services. Most, they argued, needed the discipline of developing more competitive private-sector economies to wean themselves from the vanishing foreign-aid aftermath of colonial administration and to function successfully in the modern world of global capitalism. Some emerged through this process from the "Third World" into a new category labeled "newly industrializing countries," with economic growth rising and population growth stabilizing. Others, however, remained trapped among the forces of debt, poverty, lack of economic assets, and other political and social barriers to the changes demanded.

From an environmental perspective, structural-adjustment policies were beneficial in some respects but disastrous in others (Pearce et al. 1995, 54–55). Reducing government subsidies for intensive agriculture and other environmentally damaging sectors was clearly beneficial. Some commercial farmers increased their efficiency, with some resulting environmental benefits, but most subsistence farmers were left far worse off, forcing them to expand onto marginal lands and causing increased environmental damage. Countries with mineral and forest resources typically intensified their extraction of these assets. Expansion of manufacturing often exacerbated pollution, while budget cuts simultaneously weakened or dismantled the governments' capacity to monitor and enforce environmental protection standards. In short, debt repayments were often financed by liquidating natural resource assets, by eroding soil fertility and air and water resource quality, by stripping the vegetative cover, and by further impoverishing the poor (Reed 1996).

These policies were problematic not only in their immediate impacts, but also in their larger effects on world markets. Simultaneous increases in natural resource production in many poor countries drove down world commodity prices, even as the uncounted environmental costs of supplying them mounted.[35] Competition in low-wage agriculture and manufacturing, similarly, drove prices below the real human costs of the production process and below wage levels necessary for workers' subsistence. The result was a classic tragedy of the commons in the making. Without some international mechanism to control such competition, many indebted countries might become trapped in a relentless downward spiral of competitive environmental destruction and impoverishment. By the time prices began to reflect the real costs involved, both the environmental resources and the human societies of the poorer countries might be seriously damaged, perhaps irreversibly (Reed 1996).

Neither the IMF nor other international lenders, however, took effective steps to incorporate protective measures against these impacts into their economic policies, nor did the United States and their other sponsoring countries require that they do so (Daly 1994; Reed 1996). Whatever lip service the countries themselves gave to the rhetoric of sustainable development in official United Nations conferences, the reality was that global economic policies, implemented by the international lending institutions and the workings of unfettered world trade, risked exacerbating both environmental destruction and economic disparities between rich and poor worldwide.

Trade Treaties: GATT and NAFTA

The global economy did not happen by chance, nor was it created by impersonal economic forces alone. It resulted in large part from a series of international policy agreements, led by the United States, to promote global trade liberalization.

The Bretton Woods agreement of 1944 created the World Bank, the International Monetary Fund, and subsequently the General Agreement on Tariffs and Trade (GATT) in 1947. The purpose of GATT was to establish universal principles of free trade in the emerging postwar world, gradually eliminating countries' use of import tariffs to protect domestic industries against foreign competitors. In principle this would increase overall economic efficiency, by allowing goods to be made whenever it was cheapest to do so. It would also increase global equity, by giving less-developed countries access to the previously protected markets of the industrialized ones; and it would prevent "trade wars" among countries that previously used tariffs to retaliate against one another.

The focus of GATT was solely on trade liberalization, and its rationale was rooted in a vision of unlimited material abundance rather than ecological limits. U.S. Treasury Secretary Henry Morgenthau, for instance, at Bretton Woods advocated "rapid material progress on an earth infinitely blessed with natural riches," and urged participants to embrace the "elementary economic axiom . . . that prosperity has no fixed limits" (Korten 1996, 15). Until 1994 GATT never even mentioned the environment as a concern, and the expertise of its dispute-resolution panels was limited to free-trade criteria rather than other implications such as environmental impacts. As early as 1971 the GATT secretariat created a Working Group on Environmental Measures and International Trade, but this group never even met until the 1990s (Vogel 1996, 352).

As tariffs were gradually reduced, however, the environmental era of the 1970s brought a wave of new regulatory programs for environmental protection as well as health and safety, both in the United States and elsewhere. One result was that trade experts became increasingly suspicious that some of these regulations were worded so as to serve as new "non-tariff barriers" to trade, as surrogates for the protectionist tariffs that were no longer allowed.[36] In 1979 a Standards Code was added to GATT to prevent such practices, and during the 1980s GATT staff began to look skeptically at environmental standards as potential trade barriers.

U.S. environmental groups generally paid little attention to trade policy before the 1990s, with the exception of policies pertaining to endangered species, exports of hazardous wastes and pesticides, and a twenty-year battle to reduce incidental killing of dolphins by commercial tuna fishing. In 1991, however, a GATT adjudication panel declared portions of the U.S. Marine Mammal Protection Act to be violations of U.S. obligations under GATT, triggering an immediate and continuing battle over conflicts between environmental-protection and free-trade policies (Vogel 1995, 103–25).

Dolphins often travel with schools of tuna, and thousands annually are killed incidentally in tuna nets unless the fishermen allow them to escape before harvesting the tuna. Under the Marine Mammal Protection Act of 1972, the United States imposed annual limits on dolphin mortality by all U.S. commercial tuna boats, reducing their dolphin kills by over 90 percent, and it authorized the U.S. government to ban imports of foreign tuna caught using the fishing methods that were now illegal for U.S. boats. It thus sought to prevent fishermen from Mexico and other countries from gaining a competitive advantage over U.S. boats by not using these practices and continuing to kill large numbers of dolphins.[37] This law was hailed at its passage as one of the most important pieces of wildlife legislation ever approved by Congress, and a model for other nations (Vogel 1995, 104).

The GATT trade panel ruled, however, that such U.S. action was not allowed. Under GATT, it ruled, each country could set reasonable rules for each *product,* so long as they were the same for both domestic and imported products, but it could control production *processes* only within its own borders. Thus the United States could impose labeling requirements for tuna that were caught by "dolphin-safe" practices, but it could not use trade sanctions to force Mexico to require dolphin-protection practices in tuna production (Vogel 1996, 348–50).

In essence, this decision thus appeared to confirm the legal right of any country to use environmental destruction as a competitive trade advantage, and to prohibit the importing country from protecting its own industries that were required to use safer practices. This was a serious threat, given the many countries whose ruling elites were willing, or driven by structural adjustment mandates, to trade environmental damage for short-term revenues. It was also a disaster for open-access resources, such as ocean fisheries, for which no other conservation regime existed. It even raised serious concerns that GATT-based challenges could be used to undermine international environmental agreements, such as the Montreal Protocol (controlling production of chemicals that damage the ozone layer), the Basel Convention on hazardous-waste trade, the London Convention on waste dumping, various fish and wildlife conservation treaties, and the Convention on International Trade in Endangered Species. It also had the potential to trigger challenges to a number of other U.S. environmental laws: the Endangered Species Act, various food safety laws, automobile fuel economy standards, and others (Athanasiou 1996, 171).[38]

Despite environmentalists' outrage at this decision, amendments to GATT which were signed in 1994 and ratified by the U.S. Congress in 1995 did not address either the specific issues of this case nor their broader implications for trade and the environment. The sole concessions in this "Uruguay Round" of GATT amendments, made under strong pressure from U.S. environmental groups, were to add the word "environment" to the preamble, and to allow each country to set its own environmental standards at levels it considered "appropriate." It also allowed countries to subsidize one-time capital investments to meet new environmental requirements, which could otherwise have been challenged as unfair trade advantages. At the same time, however, it created a World Trade Organization with significantly expanded powers to challenge "technical barriers to trade" such as national regulations, and it required that national standards "not be more trade-restrictive than necessary to fulfill a legitimate objective." In effect, it created new language for challengers to use against environmental restrictions (Esty 1994, 48–50). The World Trade Organization's dispute-resolution processes remained closed proceedings controlled by trade experts, with neither public accountability nor expertise in environmental issues. The report of the WTO's Committee on Trade and the Environment, released in November 1996, confirmed the organization's shortcomings: it reached agreements on several minor issues but failed to make significant progress on any of the major GATT-based conflicts between trade and the environment (Charnovitz 1997, 374).

The strengthening of GATT's position against regulatory barriers to trade raised additional concerns for environmental policy in the United States. A major policy goal of the 104th Congress, for instance, was to devolve environmental policy from the federal government to the states. But would the states' own environmental policy innovations then be attacked as barriers to trade? Or suppressed in advance by claims that they would damage the state's economic competitiveness in world markets, or by pressures for international "harmonization" of standards that would limit them to the lowest common denominator of existing approaches? Most fundamentally, would GATT undermine the United States' whole structure of strict standards by forcing open its markets to environmentally destructive competitors anywhere in the world? The answers to these questions remained disturbingly unclear.

One possible answer was to use another trade pact, the 1992 North American Free Trade Agreement (NAFTA), as a model for more detailed environmental-protection provisions in future amendments to GATT. NAFTA, a treaty intended to dramatically lower trade barriers among Canada, Mexico, and the United States, was a major goal of both the Bush and Clinton administrations, but was vulnerable to domestic opposition. It involved not simply an abstract commitment to free trade, but the visible consequences of job losses and severe pollution resulting from *"maquiladora"* industries operating in free-trade zones just across the Mexican border rather than in the United States.[39] The Clinton administration therefore negotiated further environmental language as well as a supplementary environmental "side agreement" to NAFTA before submitting it to Congress for ratification. Both these documents ultimately incorporated key provisions that could be models for future amendments to GATT (Vogel 1996, 356–58).

NAFTA's environmental provisions, limited though they were, made it the "greenest" trade agreement the United States had ever signed. It specifically stated that the provisions of key international environmental agreements took precedence over NAFTA, thus addressing the concern raised by the tuna-dolphin case. It also affirmed the right of each nation to enforce "generally agreed-upon international environmental or conservation rules and standards," so long as they were the least trade-restrictive necessary to achieve the environmental protection goal and did not appear to have trade-protectionist intent. Finally, the side agreement that accompanied the treaty contained several more far-reaching provisions.

This agreement established far more competent and accountable mechanisms than GATT for addressing the environmental impacts of trade decisions. One was a commission on environmental cooperation composed of senior environmental officials of each country, supported by a staff secretariat and advised by representatives of environmental organizations. This commission was authorized to consider the "environmental implications of products throughout their life cycles," including their production methods — a policy directly contrary to the GATT tuna-dolphin decision. Unlike GATT, the NAFTA side agreement also formalized the right of citizens to submit environmental concerns to the commission, and allowed some of the commission's reports to be made public. Finally, while the side agreement did not require any of the countries to enact new or more stringent environmental laws, it authorized each country to use both fines and trade sanctions against the others for failure to enforce their own environmental laws, a provision that went substantially beyond the principles of GATT and opened the way to effective sanctions against using environmental destruction as a trade advantage.

The actual results of NAFTA remain to be seen. It offers hope of increased international environmental cooperation between the United States and Mexico, and of some strengthening of Mexico's own environmental policies (Vogel 1996, 358–59). However, those policies remain far less protective than those of the United States, and acutely vulnerable to undermining by economic and political forces.

More generally, NAFTA and its side agreements provide one possible starting point for future amendments to GATT and other trade agreements. Given the years it took to negotiate the 1994 GATT amendments, however, further amendments do not appear likely in the near future.

Business Standards for Environmental Management

In the absence of effective environmental-protection provisions in world trade agreements, an alternate proposal was to incorporate standards for environmental management into the standards of businesses. They themselves, some business leaders argued, could develop reasonable norms for environmental practice, and incorporate them into their own requirements of their suppliers and customers, their investment and insurance criteria, and their corporate accounting procedures and performance assessments.

Businesses have long used "friendly" regulation, either by governments or by voluntary standard-setting organizations, to achieve greater efficiency, predictability, and profitability. Many businesses routinely seek government standards for such purposes as to guarantee the quality of their products, to disadvantage lower-quality competitors, and to limit their liability, and business-oriented expert panels have existed for decades to establish accepted standards for industrial hygiene, chemical exposures, and other purposes (Salter 1988). Interstate and international businesses also seek consistent national or international standards, in preference to diverse state or local standards, so that they can sell the same products, of the same quality and in the same packaging, in all markets.[40]

Since 1946 the Swiss-based International Organization for Standardization (ISO) has facilitated the development of hundreds of product standards for use by the international business community. With the rapid expansion of international trade in the 1980s, ISO undertook to develop *procedural* standards as well, first for quality control (ISO 9000) and then for environmental management systems (ISO 14000). The rationale for the ISO 9000 quality-control standards was that purchaser firms needed assurance that their suppliers kept defect rates within acceptable limits, and that this goal could be more effectively achieved by standardizing and certifying their quality-control procedures than by inspecting each shipment. The ISO 14000 standards for environmental management systems built on the logic of the quality-control standards: that purchasing firms had legitimate reasons to be concerned about the environmental management practices of their suppliers, and that certifying standardized systems for managing these practices was more efficient for everyone than verifying them in each transaction. Firms could "self-certify" or could seek the more meaningful certification of an approved independent auditing firm.

The ISO 14000 standards for certifying environmental management systems were finalized in 1996. They required each certified firm to have in place a formal environmental policy, measurable objectives and deadlines, and clear management responsibilities for implementation, monitoring, and correction of any problems or deficiencies. Significantly, they did not set substantive environmental standards, nor did they even require actual compliance with existing government standards as a precondition for certification. They merely required each firm that wished to become certified to set its *own* environmental goals, and to document explicit plans for implementing those goals. They also required a documented *commitment to achieving* compliance on the part of each certified firm, as well as commitments to pollution-prevention measures and to continuous improvement. Businesses were not required to make the contents of these certification reports public, however, out of deference to U.S. firms' fears of enforcement liability. Also, ISO technical subcommittees were charged with developing guidelines for environmental performance evaluation, environmental auditing, eco-labeling, environmental product standards, and other procedures for use by interested firms.[41]

The ISO 14000 standards claimed to use businesses' own interest in standardizing environmental management procedures to create an alternative to government regulations. The key to this claim, however, was the presumption that real business benefits would result from ISO certification. Certification itself could easily cost several thousand dollars or more, not counting corrective actions necessary to achieve it. For what firms would it be worth the money? And would it really produce commensurate environmental benefits?

For some businesses — such as auto manufacturers or firms dealing with governments that might require certification of their suppliers — such certification might become a necessary cost of doing business with their customers. For others it might offer a marketing advantage: some customers might prefer to buy from environmentally certified firms. It might also demonstrate their "due diligence" to banks and insurers, reducing risks and thus earning preferential rates on insurance and commercial loans, and it might similarly increase their attractiveness to investors.[42] From the perspective of transnational corporations, the ISO standards also offered a template for standardizing environmental management accountability across subsidiaries and suppliers worldwide: some leading firms in fact already had more sophisticated environmental management systems of their own, for just this reason.

Three more fundamental hopes motivated leading business advocates of the ISO standards, however. First, they hoped that business leadership could head off the possibility of more rigid and burdensome government standards, or could at least provide a basis for harmonizing them across national lines to better serve transnational firms' efficiency in a global economy. Second, they hoped that formal environmental management systems would actually make firms more efficient as well as more environmentally benign, by identifying cost-effective opportunities for pollution prevention, clean technologies, and good housekeeping that would reduce costs as well as environmental damage. Finally, many leading firms also saw the ISO standards — and the European Union's Eco Management and Auditing Scheme (EMAS), a similar but stricter procedure — as steps toward "upward harmonization" of worldwide environmental performance requirements, which would protect their own reputations while forcing competitors to commit to complying with environmental standards and continuing to improve as well.[43]

Within the United States, some leading firms also hoped to use ISO 14000 certification as a starting point for negotiating less burdensome federal and state regulatory requirements. In effect, they hoped to trade third-party certification of their environmental performance for relief from non-performance-related regulatory burdens, such as some control-technology requirements, permit-modification procedures, reporting and monitoring requirements, and inspections.[44] Several states and even some program offices within the EPA appeared open to such proposals, so long as they included not only ISO certification but also actual overcompliance with government standards and public verification of the result. However, many environmental groups and EPA enforcement officials remained wary of any changes that might reopen settled and enforceable legal precedents. By 1998 a multistate working group had painstakingly negotiated a set of ground rules with EPA for a series of ISO 14000 pilot projects with volunteer firms, but the results remained to be seen.

In short, the hope of many of the major corporations that participated in developing the ISO 14000 standards was that they would provide a framework for harmonizing environmental management practices in businesses worldwide, creating a new form of "voluntary regulation" rooted in businesses' own norms and incentives. They would thus avoid repetition of damaging disasters such as Bhopal and Seveso, as well as additional regulatory burdens. From the point of view of the leading firms, they might also prevent a destructive "race to the bottom" led by competitors using environmental destruction as a short-term advantage in world markets. Many developing countries, however, as well as many smaller firms worldwide, saw such standards as precisely what GATT forbade: a new form of trade barrier that would benefit the large transnational corporations at their expense, imposing expensive new overhead costs and thus excluding them from world markets.[45]

From an environmental perspective, the ISO and EMAS standards ultimately would succeed only if they eventually moved beyond mere management procedures to establish minimum substantive standards for environmental performance, and to provide for public verification of the results. Such provisions could never fully replace effective government standards, since self-interested businesses will always fail to adequately manage externalities and tragedies of the commons. However, negotiating such provisions could at least refocus debate from stalemated and ineffective national regulations toward worldwide norms for remedying the most environmentally damaging production practices (Roht-Arriaza 1995, 534–39).

Trade: Second Green Revolution, or Global Enclosure Movement?

Beyond the immediate issues of GATT, NAFTA, and ISO 14000 loomed a far more fundamental issue. Was the liberalization of world trade potentially a force for *improving* environmental management worldwide, or was it perhaps inherently in conflict with environmental protection and ecological sustainability? The basic function of world trade, after all, was to extract, transform, and transport more materials and energy, in a world that was already under severe environmental stress. In the process, it created greater and greater geographic separation between the environmental costs of these activities and their beneficiaries, displacing their impacts onto distant, poorer, and less powerful communities rather than preventing or reducing them. By its very nature world trade was driven by the aggregate of immediate financial self-interests, rather than by long-term sustainability or other values, and it would ultimately protect the environment only to the extent that short-term market advantages resulted.

Trade advocates argued, correctly, that many of the worst environmental impacts were caused by indigenously owned industries, and that transnational corporations (TNCs) often brought far more advanced technologies and practices with them. This was especially true after the Bhopal disaster, which led many TNCs to adopt U.S.- or European-level standards at all their facilities worldwide to minimize the risk of lawsuits.[46] Advocates also argued that the NAFTA treaty had in fact influenced Mexico to significantly improve its environmental policies and enforcement practices, and that many TNCs had greater stakes in harmonization of world standards upward to the level of most industrialized countries — especially for product standards, but also for consistency of management practices — than in risky short-term evasion of them. Some even argued that such a system would produce a "California effect," whereby an influential government with strict environmental standards and a large market — California or Germany, for instance — would force upward rather than downward competition in environmental performance worldwide, as exporters to it innovated to meet its requirements (Vogel 1995, 259–70).

These advocates acknowledged, however, that the California effect argument relied heavily on the sustained commitment of rich, powerful countries to strict environmental regulations, and thus on the preferences of those states' citizens and political elites. Real or perceived economic decline might weaken such commitments, and in any case their influence was limited to individual countries and to specific industries that wished to export to them. Even trade advocates acknowledged that the GATT agreement hampered efforts by the leading countries to promote stricter worldwide environmental standards for production processes, and that no further amendments to correct this problem were likely in the foreseeable future (Vogel 1995, 148–49).[47] Finally, trade advocates argued that trade competition had not caused downward competition in environmental standards because compliance costs were actually relatively modest in all but a handful of industries (Vogel 1995, 257). But it was of course precisely these few "dirty" industries, such as mining, smelting, logging, and some forms of energy production, that caused some of the most severe environmental damage.

Critics raised several fundamental concerns. First, they argued, free trade with countries that did not control the environmental and human costs of production was not truly economically efficient, let alone equitable or sustainable: it simply hid the environmental costs in different places and imposed them on less powerful populations (Daly 1993). This was especially true in countries where rapid population growth created an almost limitless supply of people seeking work for almost any wage or risk. Without enforceable minimum standards for environmental protection and subsistence wages, impersonal markets would simply redirect investments to those countries that had both the cheapest materials and energy and virtually unlimited pools of cheap labor. This would undermine the economies of those countries that had painstakingly created more sustainable environmental-protection laws and humanitarian "safety nets" for their populations — as some argued was now happening.

Second, critics argued, attempts to regulate and manage trade at the international level simply didn't work. There were no existing examples of effective international environmental protection regimes, and businesses and conservative nationalists passionately opposed them. The history of trade liberalization, in fact, demonstrated not the creation of global regulatory regimes but the *de*regulation of international commerce. In these critics' view, nation-states remained the highest level at which any semblance of community governance and accountability existed, and those that cared about environmental protection must therefore reassert their sovereignty on this issue, even if it required a less absolute commitment to trade liberalization (Daly 1993). The appropriate course of action, these critics implied, was to reaffirm the principles of nineteenth-century U.S. policy: limit foreign entanglements, and promote internal markets and self-sufficiency rather than a dangerous dependence on global economic forces.

Third, critics argued that the entire enterprise of trade liberalization amounted to a vast global "enclosure movement," in which global corporate and financial empires, aided by favorable government policies, were actively *destroying* more localized, self-sufficient communities and the institutions and resources that sustained them. Examples included fisheries and forests, but also, local businesses and even indigenous seed stocks and medicines, which corporations now sought to patent and sell back to local farmers and communities at higher prices (*The Ecologist* 1993).

For these critics, the only real solution was to mobilize grass-roots movements to resist further globalization of the economy, to reclaim communities' traditional commons from the forces of the world market, and to form global networks of similar grass-roots groups — and alliances with indigenous businesses seeking trade protection — for greater leverage against transnational corporations and financial institutions.

These criticisms underscored the serious unresolved environmental issues of the new global economy. The solutions they offered, however, also left serious problems unresolved. Even if the United States still possessed near-total economic autonomy, for instance — not to mention the political will — a retreat into economic nationalism would provide little help to the rest of the world's peoples and ecosystems, which would remain profoundly vulnerable to the impacts of economic globalization. The huge scale of the U.S. market remains one of the few forces that might still be powerful enough to influence global trade patterns for environmental benefit, though thus far it has often exacerbated them instead.

As a practical matter, moreover, the global economy has already become so pervasive that economic nationalism would be virtually impossible to recreate, even for the United States, short of world war or economic collapse. Given the risk of another unpredictable crisis in Middle Eastern oil supplies, it would have been prudent policy for the United States to reduce its dependence on this resource by aggressively promoting energy conservation and alternative fuels. Given the risk of some unpredictable future collapse in world financial markets, it would have been similarly prudent for the United States to reduce this vulnerability as well. It could still do this to some extent, if it had the political will to do so. The reality, however, is that the United States no longer has an economic identity that can be effectively disentangled from the world economy. Many U.S. firms' profits derive heavily from both exports and actual production in other countries, while many firms producing within the United States are now foreign-owned. Ordinary Americans depend on these trade relationships for a large fraction of their consumer purchases, and often for their savings and investments as well. National policies promoting economic self-sufficiency would reemerge as a matter of necessity if a collapse in world financial relationships should occur, but it is almost inconceivable, for better or worse, that they could be imposed by the U.S. government in the absence of such a crisis.

Needed: A Globalization of Environmental Politics

The reality is that the United States is now deeply enmeshed in a global economy, along with all other countries, and must seriously reassess its policy options to determine how it can sustain environmental and humanitarian as well as economic goals in this context. One possible tool might involve reducing U.S. dependence on foreign supplies of essential resources such as oil. Others might involve using U.S. market leverage to promote "upward harmonization" of worldwide environmental practices and promoting "greener production" both by U.S. and foreign firms. Still others might include continuing to disseminate to other countries innovations from domestic U.S. environmental policies, such as citizen access to information and legal procedures, disclosure requirements (the Toxics Release Inventory, for instance), tradable emission permits, and others. The United States might also borrow more freely from innovations that have emerged elsewhere, such as German product-stewardship requirements and the Dutch National Environmental Policy Plan.

The most important global environmental issues, however, require U.S. leadership and cooperation in multilateral initiatives rather than nationalist isolationism. Only the combined power of the governments of the world's largest economies might conceivably be sufficient to set environmental limits on the impersonal force of global economic opportunism, let alone the power and self-serving actions of transnational corporations and financial institutions. Environmental commons, as Garrett Hardin once said, ultimately can only be maintained by "mutual coercion, mutually agreed upon."

The political reality, however, is that neither the United States nor other governments are likely to take such initiative without either a global economic crisis or a more effective global mobilization of environmental politics. Strong U.S. environmental protection policies resulted only after a massive outpouring of public demand, followed by sustained, institutionalized pressure from organized environmental interest groups. Strong international policies will require no less.

In fact, the environmental era on a global scale has included a remarkable growth of nongovernmental organizations worldwide, and of global networking among environmental organizations and advocacy organizations for the poor, for protection of indigenous cultures, for human rights, and for other civic causes. In the 1960s few such organizations existed beyond the local level, if there; by 1992, some twenty-five hundred of them were represented at the U.N. Earth Summit alone, and far more existed and were in contact with one another, by electronic mail if not personal interaction.

Citizen environmental groups have gained limited but real influence in some international treaty negotiations, which previously had been conducted exclusively by subgovernments of government officials advised by interested businesses. In the United States, the NAFTA negotiations marked the first major involvement of environmental advocacy groups in trade policy, and while they were divided in their positions, they obtained important new provisions and had significant influence on the treaty's passage. Internationally, environmental NGOs have played important roles in developing many of the new environmental agreements, with the support of pro-environmental governments such as Norway's and others'.

The rise of global environmental NGOs is a significant and promising development, but their influence and potential power should not be overestimated, especially when measured against the far more rapid expansion of the global corporate and financial economy. Even in the United States, it remains far easier to mobilize civic pressure on local and national issues than on global ones: many environmental constituencies are no less parochial than their business counterparts, and mass public concern for the poor, at home let alone abroad, is rare and decreasing. As one recent commentator noted, "environmentalists have too often stood not for justice and freedom or even for realism, but merely for the comforts and aesthetics of affluent nature lovers. History will judge greens by whether they stand with the world's poor" (Athanasiou 1996, 304).

The internationalization of U.S. environmental policy has thus been a limited and uneven process so far, vastly outpaced by the globalization of business and trade-liberalization policies. It remains to be seen whether U.S. environmental groups and their counterparts elsewhere can mobilize enough influence to catch up.

16 Managing the Environment, Managing Ourselves

The rates, scales, kinds, and combinations of changes occurring now are fundamentally different from those at any other time in history. . . . We live on a human-dominated planet — and the momentum of human population growth, together with the imperative for further economic development in most of the world, ensures that our dominance will increase. . . . Maintaining populations, species, and ecosystems in the face of those changes, and maintaining the flow of goods and services they provide humanity, will require active management for the foreseeable future. — Peter Vitousek et al., in *Science,* July 1997

In July 1997, the journal *Science* devoted a special issue of over 40 pages to documenting the reality that the entire biosphere of planet Earth has now become dominated by human use. Like the U.S. Superintendent of the Census who in 1890 declared that the frontier was closed — that there were no longer any western lands empty of human settlement — so the *Science* authors reported that there are no longer any ecosystems on Earth that are not affected by human activities, and the aggregate impact is large and rising. Among other effects, human activities have now transformed over 40 percent of the planet's land surface, and increased atmospheric carbon dioxide concentrations by over 20 percent. Humans also use more than 50 percent of the world's accessible fresh surface water, have caused over 20 percent of the world's known bird species to become extinct, and have fully exploited, overexploited, or depleted over 60 percent of the world's marine fisheries (Vitousek et al. 1997, 495).

The common denominator of all these trends, and others, is the growing scale of the global human enterprise. The fundamental history of the past four hundred years, in short, is not simply the history of human societies and achievements — of technology and culture, of economics, politics, and wars — but a history of unprecedented expansion of the human species, and of its ever-growing capacity to manipulate the natural environment for its own material comfort and economic profit (Martin 1992, 120–30). The *Science* authors concluded that human societies must slow the rates at which their activities are now changing the Earth, to provide more time both for humans to understand and manage their impacts and for the ecosystems themselves to adapt to them. They urged that human societies invest more effort in understanding Earth's ecosystems and how they interact with the social, economic, cultural, and other factors that drive these changes. Finally, they asserted that humans must take responsibility for *managing* these changes — or more accurately, for managing the human activities that cause them — over the indefinite future.

American environmental policies have been prominent causes of these trends, in conjunction with the far larger forces of demographic, technological, and economic change that they have abetted. Throughout American history, the United States' dominant policies have been to promote the economic exploitation of natural resources, beginning with the seemingly inexhaustible abundance of the North American continent and expanding more recently — through the economic power of transnational corporations and capital markets — to include the accessible assets of the entire planet. The United States has not been unique in this: European trade and colonization began it, and most other governments have done likewise. But as the world's largest single market for material and energy resources, and a leading exporter of both production technologies and consumer lifestyles, its policies have been prominent influences and are central to any solution.

At times throughout this history, American environmental policies have included initiatives to manage the natural environment more directly and purposefully: to reduce risks to human life and health (diseases, floods), to provide services that markets by themselves did not (transportation infrastructure, multipurpose water management projects, urban water supply and waste management, outdoor recreation sites), to conserve resources for continuing future benefit (fisheries, forests, arable soils), to preserve nature's beauty and ecosystems (national parks, wetlands, endangered species), and to control environmentally damaging excesses of economic behavior (pollution, landscape destruction). In these policies too, the United States has often been a model for the rest of the world.

The net effect of these policies to date, even after more than a quarter-century of the modern environmental era, has been to provide unprecedented levels of material comfort to many people and extraordinary affluence to a few, and to reduce and even reverse some environmental damage, but only marginally to moderate the larger national and global forces of human population growth, landscape transformation, natural-resource use, and waste generation that define modern human history.

What then can we learn from the history of American environmental policy, from understanding the environmental era of the past three decades in the context of the previous four centuries?

Modern Label, Historical Reality

Environmental policy is not a phenomenon of the past three decades alone, but a constant thread throughout American history. More than most Americans often acknowledge or even realize, government policies were responsible for creating and maintaining much of the natural-resource-based wealth and power of the U.S. economy. They were also responsible for the United States' nationwide infrastructure of water-resource, energy, and transportation facilities and protected lands, its urban public services of water supply and wastewater and waste management, and the more recent control and cleanup of pollution discharges. The label is recent, but the fact of environmental policy runs throughout American history.

These policies included colonial and constitutional precedents that gave far greater deference to private property ownership, and imposed far more severe limits on government regulatory power, than in most other nations either then or now. They included extraordinary nineteenth-century incentives for rapid privatization and economic use of land and its resources, and for investment in canals and railroads. In a young country struggling to achieve economic viability and to defend itself against European empires, it was government policies that made public lands available for rapid occupation and economic use, and offered open immigration to settle and develop them. It was government policies too that provided land grants to leverage investment in transportation infrastructure — first canals, later railroads — building a transportation infrastructure that covered an entire continent in less than half a century. In a rapidly urbanizing society, it was government sanitation policies and public-health programs that dramatically reduced the great epidemics of diseases borne by air, water, food, and vectors to trivial levels, by providing clean water supplies, wastewater and waste management, and other public health services to cities and communities.

Later policies included the legacy of Progressive governance, which asserted the positive role of government both in municipal waste management and in national responsibility for conservation and efficient management of public lands and natural resources. Beginning in the early twentieth century, it was government policies that preserved the national forest lands from speculative development, developed a national system of publicly managed parks and forests, and offered public benefits — access for recreation and tourism, protection of wildlife habitat and wilderness areas, and preservation of cultural and historical sites — far beyond those that would have been provided by market forces alone.

Environmental policies also included the New Deal conservation programs, which used the powers of government to rebuild from economic and ecological collapse, to stabilize the agricultural and financial practices that caused this collapse, and even, briefly, to articulate a vision of conservation planning on the scale of entire river basins. It was government investments and management agencies that created a nationwide system of multipurpose water resource management facilities, providing controlled supplies of water for navigation, flood control, irrigation, urban water supplies, hydroelectric power, recreation, and other uses, and permitting human communities to flourish in otherwise arid regions.

Finally, American environmental policy includes the more recent policies of the environmental era: reducing urban and industrial pollution, curbing at least some of the federal projects and subsidy programs that were themselves causes of environmental impacts, and protecting additional natural lands and ecosystems in public management. Since 1970, government pollution-control regulations have required industries to radically reduce their emissions of air and water pollution, to reduce emissions from motor vehicles, and to end human exposure to airborne lead from fuel combustion. Government regulations and subsidies caused major cities and towns to clean up their wastewater discharges, and government reporting requirements forced industries to confront and reduce the immense quantities of toxic chemicals that they were releasing into the environment each year. Government regulations also compelled both industries and cities to clean up their waste-management practices: to stop open burning and close leaking dumps, separate hazardous industrial chemicals from ordinary wastes, control and stabilize contaminated sites, and dramatically increase the fraction of wastes that was recycled rather than merely discarded. New statutory requirements also opened government's own actions to public challenge based on their environmental impacts. Finally, government expenditures preserved larger expanses of especially valuable natural areas as public property for the future.

In short, public policies have played fundamental roles throughout American history in creating the material and economic conditions that freed most Americans from the day-to-day constraints and hardships of the natural environment, and allowed them to enjoy nature on their own terms, in comfort and relative affluence. They also have played essential roles in managing environmental resources to achieve larger and longer term public purposes than individuals and markets alone could have accomplished, and in controlling both the side effects and the cumulative overuse—the externalities and tragedies of the commons—that individuals, businesses, and other organizations often caused.

The Legacy of Past Policies

The purpose of American environmental policy has not always been to protect the environment, however, and government policies themselves have often caused severe impacts.

Throughout the nineteenth century, for instance, public-land policies promoted not only rapid settlement and economic use of natural resources, but also widespread deforestation, massive and wasteful slaughter of buffalo and other species, and pervasive fraud in the acquisition and exploitation of public resources. Public health and sanitation policies achieved major reductions in epidemic disease, but not before municipalities had first worsened health hazards by piping in water without providing for sewers to remove it, and then discharging it untreated into streams serving other communities' water supplies.

Federal conservation policies, meanwhile, preserved large areas of public lands and resources in government ownership, but also created powerful beneficiary constituencies that continued to defend their privileged access to public resources long past the eras in which the original subsidies may have seemed justified by their public benefits. The agencies created to manage these resources proved vulnerable to capture by those interests whose economic fortunes were most directly dependent on their actions: the Forest Service by the logging firms, the Bureau of Land Management by the livestock and mining industries, the fish and wildlife agencies first by agricultural predator-control interests and later by hunting and fishing groups. More generally, policies promoting the development of natural resources for economic use—mining and logging, farming and grazing, and federally subsidized water and energy development, for instance—created subsidies that distorted the market's own incentives for less intensive and less damaging uses of the environment.

In the mid-twentieth century, policies promoting all-out war production and postwar consumption were among the major causes not only of unprecedented economic prosperity but also of the severe levels of pollution and landscape destruction that accompanied it. The Cold War arms race promoted the development and use of new weapons that caused greatly increased environmental destruction, and U.S. policies promoting the globalization of trade also promoted a simultaneous globalization of resource extraction, industrial pollution, and urbanization that proceeded far more rapidly than any effective management of their environmental impacts.

Finally, the regulatory legacy of the most recent three decades achieved major successes in reducing pollution and in protecting natural lands and species, but left major environmental problems and trends unsolved and gradually degenerated into regulatory rigidity and political gridlock.

The history of American environmental policy is not therefore a history of triumphal progress, though important progress has clearly occurred. It is, rather, a history of constant tension between the continuing pressures and cumulative impacts of human use of the environment—encouraged and abetted by government policies facilitating and encouraging such use—and the intermittent punctuations of these patterns by policy reforms reaffirming common values of the environment that are at odds with immediate user interests. Government actions have been necessary to achieve many environmental purposes, but not always sufficient, and are vulnerable to failure and to producing their own forms of side effects.

Nor is this history consistently a record of an environmentalist public fighting for reform against corporate special interests, though that theme forms a strong undercurrent in modern American environmental politics and links conflicts over environmental issues to one of the most powerful and enduring morality plays of American politics. In some cases, such as the modern environmental movement, the reform impulse has resulted from grass-roots mobilization and the efforts of organized civic environmental groups. In other cases, such as Progressive conservation and the New Deal, it came primarily from strong executive leadership. In actuality, individuals' and small businesses' actions can sometimes be as damaging to the environment in their cumulative effects as those of big firms, and the recent "wise use" movement serves as a reminder that grass-roots public advocacy groups do not inevitably support environmental protection policies. Cloaking environmental politics in anticorporate rhetoric can be effective and appropriate for some environmental issues, but risks overlooking important opportunities for alliances with businesses whose own interests lie with greater environmental protection.

All too often, finally, reform has come only in response to a sense of impending or actual crisis, rather than from a willingness to support more stable government capability to forestall such crises and to provide for the common elements of a sustainable and equitable society.

The "Environmental Era" in Context

The United States entered the recent "environmental era" with widespread and serious environmental problems. These problems included high rates of fossil fuel combustion per capita and per unit of economic output, resulting from a history of cheap and abundant domestic supplies of fossil fuels and from policies promoting continued availability of cheap energy. They included serious air and water pollution — due especially to massive increases in industrial production and intensification of agriculture from World War II on — and high and rising rates of air pollution from motor vehicles. They included uncontrolled disposal practices for industrial wastes, and generally uncontrolled wastewater and waste management practices by cities and towns. They also included widespread destruction of natural landscapes and ecosystems, due especially to rapid suburbanization, coastal development, and large-scale public infrastructure projects such as dams and highways.

In 1970, the United States took a world leadership position in instituting far more authoritative national regulatory policies for environmental protection. These policies produced some clear benefits, but also imposed heavy burdens of compliance, and by the mid-1990s they were facing intensive political counterattack, as part of a broad pendulum swing against government regulation and spending. It is possible that the present debate will produce the moderate reforms that are widely acknowledged to be needed. It is equally possible, however, that it will produce merely a lingering erosion in policy effectiveness, or even a severe reduction of national environmental policy capacity if some of the most radical proposals should be enacted. Whether such changes will be offset by equal or better environmental results from policies at the subnational or international level, or will instead produce a fundamental reversal of commitment to environmental protection, remains to be seen.

Despite unprecedented policy initiatives and notable successes, moreover, many environmental problems remain unsolved. Smog continues to plague some cities, water pollution remains a problem despite major reductions in large industrial and municipal sources, and waste generation per capita continues to rise. The rate of energy use in the United States remains high, as does the production of polluting chemicals. Urbanization of the landscape, and related destruction of wetlands and other natural habitats, also continue with little policy guidance or control. Larger economic forces and technological changes, meanwhile, continue to develop in patterns that will pose new challenges as well as opportunities for environmental policy. Examples include vertical integration of livestock production, deregulation of electric utilities, the phaseout of agriculture price supports, and the continuing globalization of manufacturing and finance.

Most fundamentally, U.S. consumption of energy and material resources continues virtually undiminished, representing an "ecological footprint" whose imprint on the world's ecosystems extends far beyond the United States alone, drawing on an increasingly global economy whose environmental and social costs elsewhere remain largely invisible to Americans. Nor does there appear to be any significant political will to restrain U.S. consumption, to impose common minimum environmental standards for extraction and production worldwide, or to create effective international governance institutions to help solve environmental problems posed by the global economy.

It is possible, therefore, that some of the policy successes of the environmental era merely slowed, postponed, or displaced problems rather than producing permanent, sustainable solutions. In the late 1990s, environmental policy debate in the United States appears to be at a stalemate, between a Congress whose leadership is dominated by opponents of regulation and environmental advocacy groups who can still mobilize strong enough public opinion to block deregulation initiatives but not to achieve positive policy reforms. Neither of these sides appears ready to work together on a positive agenda for further environmental policy development.

Environment and Governance

As a matter of governance, environmental policy in the United States has developed in patterns that are far more uneven, adversarial, and vulnerable to political instability than is often recognized. Its distinctive features include a system of government that is constitutionally limited and divided, and imposes major restrictions on government power to restrict environmental exploitation by private property owners. However, it also provides unusually open citizen access to government decisions, including rights even to bring lawsuits against government itself as well as against businesses and other parties to compel environmental protection. These features produce policies that are perhaps more accountable but also more unstable than those in many other countries. Rather than a progressive maturation of policy capacity to manage environmental problems, the United States has experienced periodic "swings of the pendulum" between policy control by advocates and opponents of such a capacity, between initiatives to create and initiatives to destroy effective environmental governance.

The United States has developed probably the most extensive scientific and technical capacity of any country to support environmental policy-making. This is mainly due to its requirements that government agencies explicitly justify their regulatory proposals in public and in the courts, in part by including documentary records providing "substantial evidence" in support of proposed regulations. As a result, extensive capacity for scientific, engineering, and economic analysis of proposed policy initiatives has developed both in government agencies themselves and in consulting firms, regulated businesses and trade associations, applied research institutes, environmental advocacy groups, and universities.

Paradoxically, however, the United States' heavy investment in scientific and economic justification of environmental policy has been a barrier as well as a contributor to its success. It has extended scientific understanding but also diverted enormous professional effort and resources into analysis and documentation of particular decisions, and often delayed or prevented more immediate actions to improve environmental results: "paralysis by analysis." Much of the impetus for vigorous implementation of environmental protection policy came not so much from the use of more elaborate scientific analysis as from other changes in governance that empowered citizens to challenge the actions and inaction of government and businesses in the courts. Such litigation was arguably the leading force driving environmental protection policy throughout the environmental era, though it was itself an additional drain on professional effort and resources.

Today, U.S. environmental policy remains severely fragmented. The National Environmental Policy Act included a visionary statement of national policy to promote harmonization of human actions with the integrity of natural systems, as well as "action-forcing mechanisms" to promote implementation and a Council on Environmental Quality as a continuing institutional champion. However, it set no operational targets or timetables or "green plans" for the agencies, and did not ultimately succeed in integrating or superseding the agencies' more specific and conflicting mandates. The environmental impact statements mandated under the act helped block some of the worst specific proposals, but did not fundamentally redirect the agencies toward environmental goals. Even the Environmental Protection Agency continues to operate under multiple and largely separate statutory programs, so that most proposals for policy integration, innovations, or even changes in priorities remain personal initiatives of individual agency heads rather than institutionalized policy directions.

Since the 1980s, important new environmental protection incentives have been successfully inserted into the legislation of several sectors, such as agriculture, energy, and transportation, but it is not clear whether these will continue to be effective under the recent deregulation of agriculture and energy, nor whether the environmental incentives in transportation will survive reauthorization by the anti-environmental leadership of Congress. Proposals to privatize many functions, or to devolve them from federal to state and local governments, might exacerbate competitive market pressures at the expense of environmental protection. Environmental protection incentives are still largely absent from legislation affecting other sectors: trade in particular (the GATT treaty), but also mining, land development, and taxation.

In recent years, U.S. environmental agencies have been among the leaders in advocating further innovations in environmental policy. Some of these initiatives have been successfully introduced, but most only on a limited scale due to the constraints of existing laws. EPA has implemented risk-based decision-making in setting enforcement priorities and in recommending budget priorities, for instance, but it still must operate within the statutory limits and budget priorities set by Congress. The agency advocates pollution prevention in its official statements, but its legal requirements for control technology are still in effect. EPA has pioneered several market incentives, but most of these also remain experiments at the margins of the traditional paradigm rather than replacements for it.

Other policy innovations have been promoted far more widely than they have actually been implemented. Despite a large body of literature advocating unit-based pollution taxes and charges, for instance, the United States actually has almost none of them except at the level of local water and waste authorities, and even these are typically set at levels designed simply to generate revenues or to pay for environmental services rather than to promote waste reduction. Both EPA's own staff and citizen environmental groups have remained ambivalent over how much flexibility to allow state environmental agencies that propose innovative experiments in the administration of federal regulatory mandates — such as trading flexibility on some requirements for industries' promises to achieve equal or better environmental performance — out of fears that such precedents could open new loopholes in enforceability. Some leading business corporations, however, have made significant improvements in pollution prevention on their own, either because they discovered unexpected market benefits or because it was simply cheaper to reduce the costs of regulatory procedures — or to build in pollution prevention when modernizing their facilities.

Many U.S. states have greatly increased their capacity for environmental policy, in response both to public pressure and to federal requirements. Some leading states have acted far beyond federal requirements, serving as "laboratories of innovation" to be copied by others. Examples include California's tough air quality standards and carcinogen labeling requirements, New Jersey's "community right-to-know" and mandatory recycling laws, Massachusetts's Toxic Use Reduction Act, Wisconsin's negotiated siting law, and the Oregon benchmarks program for environmental policy planning. Others, however, have done only what was required of them, and some state legislatures have even explicitly prohibited any regulatory initiatives beyond those required by federal legislation.

For better or worse, however, the most powerful market incentives in U.S. environmental policy so far remain the greatly increased costs of economic liability for pollution cleanup (especially for hazardous waste contamination), of waste disposal (due to EPA regulations requiring safer design and operation of waste facilities), and of the regulatory process itself, especially reporting requirements and the opportunity costs of regulatory delays in competitive industries.

Since 1970 there has been an unprecedented increase in the number and effectiveness of citizen organizations advocating environmental protection. Many of these developed substantial staff capabilities to promote environmental protection, drawing on lawyers, economists, scientists, and publicists as well as political lobbyists. The continuing effectiveness of these groups remains critically dependent, however, on several key factors: their financial support, provided both by recruiting and retaining members and by obtaining grant support from foundations and other donors; their ability to arouse mass public opinion, and to attract favorable mass-media attention in order to do this; and their access to the courts, based on favorable interpretations both of the environmental laws themselves and of their own legal standing to bring litigation. Finally, they remain dependent on their skill in using all these factors to negotiate environmentally favorable outcomes with business, legislators, administrative agencies, and other stakeholders. All these factors have fluctuated substantially over time, and by the late 1990s their continued effectiveness is a matter of considerable uncertainty.

Environmental advocacy groups grew rapidly in the early 1970s, then eroded somewhat as the Arab oil embargo and economic fears displaced environmental concerns from the political agenda. Green groups' support grew again as fears of toxic chemicals and hazardous wastes reignited public concern, then softened once more in the late 1970s as a more pro-environment administration was elected, economic worries again dominated public attention, and business interests mobilized counterpressures against "overregulation." Membership grew dramatically again in the 1980s, in response to the Reagan administration's overreaching attempts to undermine national environmental policy mandates, but softened once more when these threats were averted.

In the early 1990s environmental proponents appeared poised for another major increase in effectiveness, with the rising visibility of global environmental issues (the ozone hole, global warming, the Rio Earth Summit, and others) and the appointment of many strong environmental leaders to influential positions in the Clinton administration. Instead, however, their memberships and media influence slipped once again, and they found themselves increasingly on the defensive against the most effectively organized adversaries they had yet faced. They succeeded once again in blocking major reversals of environmental policy proposed by the antigovernment 104th Congress in 1995–96, but by the late 1990s they appeared far more effective simply at protecting the existing system of statutes and regulations than at mobilizing support for significant reforms or new initiatives.

Even as environmental advocacy groups have continued to proliferate worldwide, in short, within the United States their membership, finances, and consequent effectiveness have increasingly fluctuated with economic anxiety and with changes in the visibility of environmental issues in the mass media. Public opinion can still be aroused by symbolic threats to the environmental laws, but otherwise environmental activists are vulnerable to being outmobilized — or at least stalemated — by antiregulatory interests in a political era of broad antigovernment cynicism.

Progress or Pendulum?

The 1994 congressional elections transferred control over Congress not only from the Democratic to the Republican party, but to an exceptionally ideological group of new legislators whose central priority was reducing the power and capacity of the national government. This came at a time when traditional opponents of regulation were joined by many small businesses — and ironically, by many local governments — that had been burdened by the prescriptive environmental laws passed in reaction to the Reagan attacks. In effect, U.S. environmental policy was repeating the political battles of the Reagan era only with roles reversed, with its opponents now in control of the legislature and its supporters in the White House. Opinion polls clearly showed continued public support for environmental protection, and opposition to weakening government capacity to assure it; but the polls also showed widespread public dissatisfaction with government regulation and spending in general, and environmental regulation was one of the most visible examples of such regulation. The future of U.S. environmental policy depended heavily on which of these forces would be most successful in framing the political choices between these preferences.

One possible outcome of this conflict could be a set of moderate reforms, which would increase flexibility in priorities and means of compliance but still maintain effective federal authority to assure that national environmental policy goals are achieved. A series of such reforms was recommended in early 1995 in a report commissioned by the congressional appropriations committees from the National Academy of Public Administration. This report recommended (among other things) that EPA should offer "accountable devolution" of major responsibilities to state governments, and greater operating flexibility to target companies willing to go "beyond compliance" in their own environmental improvements — somewhat like the Dutch covenants approach.

This "moderate reform" scenario, if supported by Congress, would probably lead to continued progress by those states and target firms with both the necessary commitment and the resources, but it might also lead to stagnation or regress in those that lacked either the resources or the will to continue without strong national pressure (Lester, 1995). Even leading states and firms might be undermined by opportunistic competition from others.

A second possible outcome, however, could be a radical weakening of national environmental policy capacity, if some of the more radical congressional proposals should be enacted. In early 1995, for instance, Congress enacted a budget amendment which reopened many national forests to far more intensive logging, and which included sweeping "supermandate" language stating that such logging is considered automatically in compliance with all environmental laws. Similarly damaging provisions were proposed to weaken other environmental policies, particularly the Endangered Species Act and wetland protection regulations. Others would require government compensation for any reduction of property values resulting from environmental regulations; require compensation for any additional federal mandates imposed on state and local governments; restrict EPA from regulating and enforcing against particular industries; and in some cases, rewrite and weaken the basic environmental laws themselves.

Finally, a third outcome could be simply a continued political stalemate, under which most of the current institutional capacity would be left in place, but its effectiveness would be reduced by congressional actions to cut budgets and increase paperwork burdens. This outcome is the actual result to date and appears most likely to continue for the foreseeable future.

The continuing political volatility of the U.S. experience therefore suggests caution in attributing any consistent pattern of "progress" to American environmental policy. Policymaking in the United States is more commonly described as a pendulum swinging periodically back and forth between pro- and anti-government dominance, rather than as a steady process of policy refinement or maturation, and this metaphor appears all too accurate for American environmental policy-making in the "environmental era."

Clinton: An Environmental President?

The election of Bill Clinton as president in 1992 raised widespread expectations of a return to active presidential leadership in environmental policy. George Bush had almost totally retreated from his early promises of an "environmental presidency," in deference to business interests and the conservative activist wing of the Republican party (Paarlberg 1996, 16). Clinton in contrast chose as his vice president Senator Al Gore, who had personally written a recent book-length call to arms on global environmental issues (*Earth in the Balance* 1992), and seemed willing to reassert strong initiatives in environmental policy.

Environmental protection was never Clinton's primary issue, and he had shown little interest in it as governor of Arkansas, but his early actions appeared to define a strong agenda. He appointed committed environmental protection advocates to key positions — former Arizona governor Bruce Babbitt as Interior Secretary, Florida environmental protection head Carol Browner as EPA administrator, former senator Tim Wirth as Assistant

Secretary of State for Environment — and many others to second-level policy positions. To Gore he assigned a far more authoritative role than was held by previous vice presidents, making him overall coordinator of environmental policy and overseer of the "reinvention" of government programs, and granting him other responsibilities.

Clinton almost immediately signed both the Biodiversity Convention and the Law of the Sea Treaty, though both also required Senate ratification, and he reaffirmed U.S. support for the United Nations' family planning programs: all actions reversing the policies of Reagan and Bush. He also issued an executive order on "environmental justice," ordering EPA and other federal agencies to correct any disproportionate environmental impacts of their actions on people of color.[1] He proposed a broad-based tax on energy use, to promote energy conservation while reducing the federal deficit; he ordered federal agencies to make special efforts to purchase energy-efficient, recycled, and other "green" products, to reduce their toxic emissions by one-half by 1999, and to disclose their own emissions to the public; and he launched an Environmental Technology Initiative intended to promote innovation, rapid diffusion, and exports of "green technology" by American businesses. He proposed legislation to make EPA a cabinet department, and appointed a blue-ribbon President's Commission on Sustainable Development to develop recommendations for implementing the Rio Earth Summit Declaration. Finally, through his appointees he launched a series of intensive negotiation processes — on federal grazing management, on management of the Everglades and of the remaining old-growth forests of the Pacific Northwest, on habitat-conservation plans for endangered species, and others — to seek consensus rather than continued political gridlock among the stakeholders in these high-profile environmental controversies (Wicker 1994).

Both Secretary Babbitt at Interior and Administrator Browner at EPA also launched highly publicized environmental policy initiatives. Babbitt proposed fundamental reforms in federal mining laws and grazing policies, arguing for market-based management rather than subsidized giveaways on both economic and environmental grounds, and created a National Biological Service to integrate scientific expertise across all Interior's agencies (Riebsame 1996; Wicker 1994). Browner announced the Common Sense Initiative to negotiate pollution reduction in six high-pollution industrial sectors, Project XL (for "excellence and leadership") to reward firms willing to go beyond mere compliance in exchange for regulatory flexibility, an "ecosystem management" approach to refocus environmental regulation on ecosystem-level results rather than just regulatory implementation, and a "performance partnership" approach to encouraging more flexible initiatives by state environmental agencies (Davies and Mazurek 1997a, b). Other Clinton appointees also seemed to take charge vigorously on environmental issues.

Clinton's commitment quickly proved to be shallower and more symbolic than it had initially seemed, however, limited almost entirely to issues for which easy consensual deals were possible without expenditure of hard bargaining or strong leadership (Wicker 1994; Paarlberg 1996; Rauber 1997). Faced with congressional opposition, he retreated almost immediately from a broad-based energy tax to a trivial levy on automobile fuel, and abandoned Babbitt's initiatives on grazing and mining reform without even forcing serious negotiation. He even proposed initially to abolish the Council on Environmental

Quality in favor of an enlarged White House environmental policy staff, retreating only after strong opposition from environmental advocates. Only on one environmental issue did Clinton expend serious political capital: the environmental side agreement to the 1994 North American Free Trade Agreement (NAFTA), which attracted environmentalists' support for the measure, making a key difference to an issue to which he was far more deeply committed, expanding free trade.

An increasingly conservative Congress, meanwhile, blocked funding for his Environmental Technology Initiative, calling it a government subsidy to favored industries, and blocked legislation to make EPA a cabinet department by attaching unacceptable risk-assessment and cost-benefit-analysis requirements to the legislation. The 1994 congressional elections then swept into office a far more ideologically conservative Republican majority, heavily supported by commodity user interests and committed to radical reductions of federal taxes and regulations, and with them to a far more constricted federal role in environmental protection. Their reading of environmental politics appeared to be that environmental issues were no longer major news stories for the American public as a whole, that membership in the environmental interest groups was declining substantially from its peak in the late 1980s, and that the environmental protection lobby was being clearly out-organized by the "wise use movement" and other antiregulatory forces (Paarlberg 1996, 28–29).

It was only after this new Congress proposed sweeping statutory reductions of environmental regulations and appropriations, and these prospects in turn galvanized another strong public backlash — and after Clinton himself faced a storm of public protest for signing a "Forest Health Act" mandating rapid expansion of logging on the public lands — that Clinton began to appear a strong environmental president once again. When Congress attached riders to budget bills that would limit EPA's enforcement powers and open the Arctic National Wildlife Refuge to oil exploration, for instance, Clinton allowed the federal government to shut down twice rather than sign the legislation, and he thus converted this into a potent political victory (Rauber 1997, 60). However, he seemed to remain content merely to settle for protecting the existing environmental laws rather than pushing for a positive environmental policy agenda of his own. It is a sobering commentary on the current limits of American environmental politics that Clinton so successfully captured public approval as an "environmental president" mainly for blocking radically anti-environmental congressional initiatives, when he had shown such limited commitment to leadership on positive initiatives of his own.

In the heat of the 1996 election campaign, Clinton and the Congress agreed to two important new environmental laws. One was the Food Quality Protection Act, which replaced the 1958 Delaney prohibition on carcinogenic food additives with new criteria based on risks to children, and required food stores to post information on agrichemical residues on their products — a "right to know" provision for consumers. The other was an amended Safe Drinking Water Act, which eased the burdens of regulating new contaminants on EPA and local water utilities, but also required them to disclose contaminant levels to their customers and to set up a revolving loan fund for drinking-water treatment facilities. Even during the campaign, however, Clinton's environmental record remained ambiguous. He set aside a huge new national monument in southern Utah (Grand Staircase-Escalante National Monument, totaling 1.7 million acres), for instance, but also directed the Agriculture Department to bail out cattle ranchers by opening up environmentally sensitive lands to grazing, ordered the sale of twelve million barrels of oil from federal reserves to drive down gasoline prices, and announced that he would be willing to discuss repealing even the modest increase in gasoline taxes he had won from Congress in 1993 as a substitute for a broad-based energy tax (*Raleigh News and Observer*, May 1, 1996).

In the wake of his reelection, Clinton asserted strong leadership on several new environmental initiatives: a noncontroversial initiative on environmental health protection for children, coupled with other children's initiatives in health and education, and a tightening of Clean Air Act regulations for particulates and ozone, which required a serious political battle. On other issues, however, both he and his appointees continued to temporize, and even the new particulate standards were compromised by delaying timetables for their implementation. His statements on global warming retreated from initial support of firm targets and timetables for control of greenhouse gases, to an ambivalence almost indistinguishable from that of George Bush: he proposed providing solar panels for one million homes, and offering new foreign-aid incentives for forest management to developing countries (which were likely to be rejected by the Senate in any case). He also refused to raise fuel-efficiency standards for automobiles, even though he could have done this without congressional approval, and did not contest a congressional provision that would end his power to do so (Rauber 1997, 61–62).

Meanwhile, EPA's highly touted innovation programs showed only limited results and provoked increasing frustration among participants. This was due to the continuing lack of statutory authority for these initiatives as well as deep distrust from environmentalists, stemming from the fact that some of the same industries that were proposing these initiatives were simultaneously supporting the antiregulatory radicals in Congress (Davies and Mazurek 1997a, 1997b). EPA's relationships with the states were often contentious, as it appeared alternately to encourage and then undermine state proposals for more flexible regulatory priorities and approaches. The report of Clinton's President's Commission on Sustainable Development also was disappointing: it contained anecdotal success stories and optimistic exhortation, but no serious policy proposals.

As of 1997, in short, the Clinton administration could take far more credit simply for blocking bad congressional proposals than for significant improvements in environmental policy. In fairness, the increasingly anti-environmental Congress substantially narrowed Clinton's opportunities for legislative achievements after 1994 (Paarlberg 1996). But this does not account for his failure to exert strong leadership before that election, or to use the "bully pulpit" of the presidency to arouse public support for a stronger agenda. In February 1998 Clinton announced a major new environmental initiative to clean up water pollution, especially runoff of nutrients and toxic chemicals from agriculture and urban stormwater that contaminate fish and shellfish habitat, beaches, and drinking water sources; the implementation and results of this program remain to be seen. Overall, Clinton's environmental policy has thus far been marked more deeply by symbols than substance, and by missed opportunities and lukewarm support than by strong leadership.

A "Next Generation" of Environmental Policies?

In 1997 a broad working group of environmental policy experts proposed a "next generation" of environmental policies, intended to move the debate over American environmental policy beyond its current stalemate (Esty and Chertow 1997). A pervasive theme of their recommendations was the need to shift the focus of discussion from the actions of government to the actions of the economic sectors that actually cause or remedy environmental impacts, and to think more creatively about how those sectors could be influenced to protect the environment, in ways that serve businesses' self-interests as well as that of the public.

In the industrial sector, for instance, production could be more efficiently organized along the principles of "clean production" and "industrial ecology." If industries were to be held responsible for materials and energy throughout their "life cycles" of human extraction and use, they might find it efficient to redesign their processes and to locate related industries together so as to make the most efficient use of all materials and energy, and to maximize recycling of unused materials into productive re-use, rather than discharging them as wastes. Examples of such highly efficient "eco-industrial parks" already exist, and could be more widely adopted. Other countries too have begun to demonstrate the effectiveness of these incentives, such as the extended product responsibility laws adopted by Germany, The Netherlands, and Sweden (Davis et al. 1997). Environmental policy innovations could encourage these practices in the United States as well: emission and waste fees to incorporate the full cost of waste management and environmental impacts into the costs of products, disclosure requirements to encourage both consumers and producers to confront the full environmental costs of their market choices, and "command and covenant" agreements that specify environmental performance targets and timetables for each firm but allow the firm itself to decide how it will achieve them.

Important opportunities for environmental progress also exist in the services sector, which has become the largest and fastest-growing sector of the American economy but has received little explicit attention from environmental policy. Major retailing chains now wield enormous influence over the manufacturers that supply them — Home Depot, for instance — and similarly influential firms exist in other sectors, such as Federal Express in shipping, key banks in commercial lending and investments, and insurance companies. The same is true of the controlling firms in vertically integrated industries such as automobile manufacturing and swine and poultry production, and of large-volume customers, including government agencies. To the extent that these influential organizations determine that positive environmental performance is important to their own goals, therefore, they could exert influence that is often far more powerful than government standard-setting and enforcement alone. Again, innovative environmental policy initiatives could encourage this result: disclosure requirements to force consideration of the environmental costs of these transactions, environmental criteria for investment and procurement decisions, international environmental codes of practice for production in key sectors, and waste-management and environmental-damage fees that incorporate full environmental costs into prices.

The "next generation" group offered similar advice for agriculture, energy, transportation, and other sectors: the goal of policy should not be to specify regulatory solutions to each problem, but to specify operational goals for environmental results and to identify and strengthen the economic incentives in each sector to promote their achievement. Their basic theme was that in order to succeed, environmental policy must link the public's environmental desires with their desires for other social goals as well, such as mobility, economic growth, jobs, competitive industries, and material comforts. They thus argued that environmental policies must be redesigned to "make environmental protection everybody's business," by building environmental considerations more fully into consumer prices and participatory decision-making procedures. To achieve this, they argued, advocates of environmental protection must focus not just on government regulatory agencies, but also on the rising roles of the private sector and on the effectiveness of nongovernment organizations for achieving environmental results. They also must build political and economic alliances with innovative businesses, rather than just controlling polluters and public-resource appropriators.

These recommendations offer some fresh ideas for further innovation in American environmental policy. Many environmental performance improvements make sense for both business and environmental reasons, and some of these are now occurring: the only reason they were not put into action years before was that no one stopped to think about them. The problem was simply old habits and routines, thoughtlessness, or simply lack of engineering attention to designing more efficient alternatives.

The reality of U.S. environmental policies in the late 1990s is that the dominant policy approach of the modern environmental era — federal standard-setting, permitting, and enforcement — is no longer sufficient to achieve significant further progress, and that other policies affecting the environment remain fragmented, inconsistent, and often counterproductive. The gap between the stated mandates of the regulatory agencies and their actual budget and staff capabilities to implement them are large and growing, and have been enlarged in particular by the increased burden of scientific and economic proof necessary to justify each regulatory decision. EPA's programs still operate by statute in separate statutory "stovepipes" — air, water, wastes, and toxic chemicals — rather than in integrated multimedia strategies aimed at the best overall means of reducing and preventing pollution. Coordination of environmental policy toward common aspirations across other agencies and sectors remains patchy and uneven.

The most hopeful recent development is that at least for leading firms in some economic sectors, the environment has finally been recognized as a legitimate and significant business issue, and even as a potential business opportunity rather than merely a costly annoyance to be left to lawyers and pollution-control engineers. For some, environmental audits of their processes have identified opportunities for major cost savings, for expansion into new markets, and for technological modernization that have improved the firm's competitive position in its own right: "ecological modernization."

The hope of many advocates is that these positive results will be widely replicated by other firms and in additional sectors, and will gradually replace practices that cause more severe environmental impacts. The unanswered question is whether such a hope is realistic, in the face of the impersonal, price-driven forces of global markets and the reality that even the "greenest" production processes still require the use of growing amounts of materials and energy and the continued transformation of the landscape for an expanding human population.

Managing the Environment, Managing Ourselves

By definition, however, even the most enlightened self-interest by itself will not correct the *externality* costs of pollution and other environmental impacts. These are the real social costs that businesses have inherent incentives to remove from their own cost calculus by imposing on others. Examples include waste disposal, accident and spill risks, and product risks, when such practices cost less than safer management or byproduct manufacture, and do not incur greater government-imposed liability. These incentives are not unique to business: governments face similar temptations to externalize social costs onto downwind or downstream jurisdictions, and onto politically weak constituencies, including future generations. Correcting such behavior requires that businesses (and others) be compelled to operate under the "polluter-pays principle": that is, that either through regulations, salable allowances, charges, liability principles, or other measures, they be required to pay the full costs that their practices impose on society and its environment.

Self-regulation also will not correct environmental tragedies of the commons, in which the cumulative effects of self-interested decisions by multiple users produce environmental destruction. By definition, such decisions by themselves will fail to incorporate the aggregate effects of all such decisions, leading to overuse and damage to the resource. Common-pool resources, such as air, water, public lands, and many other environmental resources, ultimately require some enforceable common regime for allocating their use, not simply good will by individual users. Such regimes may reflect either restrictions imposed by a higher authority or collective self-regulation ("mutual coercion, mutually agreed upon"), but one or the other is necessary.

Individual self-interest is not, therefore, a viable substitute for effective governance regimes for environmental protection. At best it may correct some private inefficiencies, and *may* contribute also to building broader support for fair and efficient regimes to manage externalities and common-pool resources.

The central and enduring challenge of environmental governance remains the fact that the human environment is in fundamental respects a common good. Managing and protecting it—particularly its common-good aspects—therefore requires governance, not merely the actions of individuals and businesses acting in their own perceived interests. Yet governance itself is vulnerable to all the imperfections and side effects noted in the first chapter, such as the entrenched power of organized beneficiaries of government action or inaction, free-riders and rent-seekers manipulating government for their own benefit, pork-barreling and log-rolling and "split-the-difference" compromises, displacement of impacts onto others, and the steep transaction costs of reaching collective agreements, resulting in rigidity even of imperfect or archaic policies. In the United States in particular, it is also vulnerable to the adverse side effects of the highly adversarial processes that have also achieved some of its greatest gains.

Can civic environmentalism then provide an effective, sustained force for environmental protection and sustainable development, especially in the newly dominant context of a global corporate economy? If not, then what? Was the environmental era simply an anomaly, a quirk of history during which mass middle-class affluence, a burgeoning college-student generation, and new legal and political opportunities for civic opposition led to a movement that managed temporarily to delay the relentless forces of economic exploitation of the environment? Do environmental concerns have a future in politics, or were they permanently supplanted in the 1980s — despite some occasional successes thereafter — by the globalization of corporate empires and the reemergence of pervasive economic insecurity even in the United States?

In a thoughtful book in 1989, Robert Paehlke argued that environmentalism offers the basis for a new political ideology, neither left nor right but allied with those advocating restoration of moderate progressivism as a response to 1990s neoconservatism. He noted that progressivism had served as a powerful and positive model for moderate centrist governance in the past — primarily through the use of government to soften the impacts of failure and misfortune by assuring reasonably equitable distribution of the benefits of economic growth — but that it collapsed in the absence of economic growth to distribute. Environmentalism, he argued, offers a new version of progressivism: neither "left" nor "right," but an agenda for sustainable development including both productivity enhancement *and* full employment, increased recycling and sustainable agriculture and forestry, restoration of urban infrastructures, strengthening of environmental protection as well as occupational health and safety, an increase in voluntary aid to poorer countries, and a linking of the agendas of the environmental movement with those of peace and socio-economic equity.

Al Gore's *Earth in the Balance,* written shortly before he was elected vice president, echoed Paehlke's vision. In Gore's view, free men and women who feel individual responsibility for a particular part of the earth are, by and large, its most effective stewards, both individually and through shared adoption of community responsibilities. Gore urged therefore the creation of a "Global Marshall Plan," to be financed jointly by the United States, Europe, Japan, and wealthy oil-producing states, in order to stabilize world population, promote rapid dissemination of environmentally appropriate technologies, incorporate environmental impacts explicitly into the economic accounting methods of world finance and trade, and establish social and political conditions conducive to the emergence of sustainable societies (1992, 295–307).

Paehlke's and Gore's visions, however, can only be achieved if the environmental policies of governments, both individually and collectively, can be focused effectively on the task of providing for ecologically sustainable and socially equitable development. The history of American environmental policy suggests that such policies are possible, if at all, only in the presence of unusual presidential leadership (and even then only for brief periods, as under each of the two Roosevelts) or intensively mobilized public demand (as in the recent environmental era), which is itself inherently difficult to sustain over time.

Other recent commentators have offered less sanguine assessments. Mark Dowie (1995) argues that the environmental era provides examples of what can be done with vastly expanded civic knowledge and mobilization, but that mainstream environmentalism has been "pushed to the brink of irrelevance" by its advocates' willingness to compromise and accommodate neoconservative business agendas. To Dowie, the hope for the future lies in a rejuvenated, angry, multicultural, grass-roots movement for environmental justice. Tom Athanasiou, most recently, argues that real environmentalism is fundamentally linked to issues of social justice, and that history will judge its advocates by whether they stand with the world's poor, fighting for justice and freedom rather than merely protecting the comforts and aesthetic pleasures of affluent nature lovers (1996, 304). To Athanasiou, markets left to their own devices persistently shift both ecological and social costs from the rich to the "commons," destroying both natural and human communities in the process: for "greens" to claim to be neither left nor right is therefore politically naive. Both Dowie and Athanasiou claim to be optimists, if only in a tragic sense of hoping for the best without fully expecting it.

What is missing from American environmental policy today is a coherent vision of the common environmental good that is sufficiently compelling to generate sustained public support for government action to achieve it. Such visions have emerged at several points in the past. Examples include those of the sanitation movement of the nineteenth century, the City Beautiful movement of the 1890s, the Progressive civic reform and conservation movements that followed it, and the New Deal vision of combining ecological, social, and economic recovery. They are largely absent today, however. The modern environmental movement, after the initial catharsis of Earth Day, has been far more effective as an opposition movement, rallying the public to arms against corporate polluters and government despoilers, than in articulating a coherent, positive vision of a desirable human society in harmony with its natural environment and building alliances with other political forces, such as progressive businesses and labor and civil rights groups, to achieve it. The Environmental Protection Agency's vision is limited to "risk management," reducing the most serious threats to health but not articulating a positive vision of its environmental protection goals. Free-market advocates offer a vision of freedom from taxation and government compulsion, implying that those with wealth can buy the environment they want, but this offers nothing to those less affluent and ignores the common-good elements of the environment that affect rich and poor alike. American society as a whole has become more and more casually cynical toward government, which bodes poorly for efforts to reaffirm its necessity or to rebuild its effectiveness for achieving the common good.

Currently, the closest approximation to such a vision is the idea of sustainable development, as articulated by the United Nations' World Commission for Environment and Development in 1987. The commission envisioned sustainable development as a pattern of development that would meet the needs of human communities today without jeopardizing those of the future, and their vision specifically included not only economic development and ecological sustainability but also social equity as essential and interdependent elements. Critics may attack such a vision by arguing that it merely papers over hard trade-offs behind a facade of coherence, and that possibility remains a continuing danger to be addressed. The value of the vision, however, is that it at least articulates these issues in a common framework, and proposes as a normative goal that they be solved jointly, in conscious relation with one another. Whatever the difficulty and need for trade-offs may be in practice, it articulates a worthwhile common vision and a frame of reference for evaluating more specific initiatives and policy proposals.

American environmental policy has moved an extraordinary distance over its history, from laissez-faire exploitation of natural resources and "dilution as the solution" for pollution to active public management and transformation of the environment and more recently to detailed national regulation of human impacts on it. It is now in a period of doldrums, marking time in a political environment in which self-interest, ideology, and mistrust combine to frustrate further cooperation in policy reform.

Yet some key elements of a new vision are present, and may well bear fruit. One is the recognition of environmental considerations as business issues, and discoveries that at least some of these offer opportunities for combining environmental and economic benefits. The ideas of full-cost accounting, clean production, industrial ecology, and ecological modernization are still just beginning to seep into the perspectives of many businesses, and hold at least the potential for more significant progress in harmonizing human activities with the environment than traditional regulation has achieved. Some businesses themselves have come to recognize that they will be far more successful if they build environmental considerations into their own strategic decision-making, by leading and innovating rather than merely complying.

A second promising development is the growing use of self-implementing policies, such as information disclosure requirements that compel reporting of data on businesses' environmental performances, cap-and-trade mechanisms that define overall limits on human use of environmental resources but allow reallocation of them among users, and liability policies that hold businesses responsible for the full environmental costs and consequences of their products and processes. These too offer hope of greater leverage on human actions that affect the environment than the relatively crude, labor- and cost-intensive instruments of direct regulation and enforcement by government.

Finally, a third glimmer of hope, though so far a more preliminary one, is offered by a variety of initiatives to manage human uses of environmental conditions more effectively on a regionwide basis rather than merely industry by industry and permit by permit. Watersheds and river basins, towns and urban regions, bays and estuaries, and "bioregions" of other sorts — these are the real places, the real environments, in which people live and in which communities of humans and other species function. Here and there one can see policy initiatives to manage both natural conditions and the human activities that affect them on the scale of such regions, rather than just to react to ad hoc crises or regulate individual sources through statewide or national standards. Most of these remain only occasional and tentative experiments, however.

To achieve any such vision, however, will require a far more widespread reaffirmation than is now evident both of public support for such a vision of the common good and of public and business acceptance of the necessity and positive power of collective action — governance — to achieve it. The enduring challenge for American environmental policy, in short, is to build and maintain public support for effective governance of the environment: for managing the environment by managing ourselves.

Chronology

<table>
<tr><td>1487–1600</td><td>Age of European exploration
Diaz finds sea route to India around Cape of Good Hope; Columbus discovers America; Verrazano and Cartier travel to North America; Cortez, Cabrillo, and Sir Francis Drake explore west coast of North America; Hernando DeSoto and Coronado explore interior of southern and southwestern North America; Spanish colonize Central and South America

"Columbian exchange" begins: worldwide intermingling of plant, animal, and human populations</td></tr>
<tr><td>1500–1700</td><td>Mercantile trade system develops; start of fur trade (1534–99)</td></tr>
<tr><td>1500–1650</td><td>European worldwide colonization begins
Charters drawn up of the British East India and Dutch West India Companies (1600), Virginia Company (1606), Dutch East India Company (1621)</td></tr>
<tr><td>1606–20</td><td>First permanent British settlements established in North America (Jamestown, Virginia; Massachusetts Bay; fishing settlements in Maine); royal grants of colonial lands to settlement companies</td></tr>
<tr><td>1608</td><td>Hugo Grotius's Mare Liberum (On Freedom of the Seas) establishes principles of open use of the seas, territorial waters limited to distance that countries can defend (three miles)</td></tr>
<tr><td>1630</td><td>Virginia first grants American land to settlers to protect its western frontier</td></tr>
<tr><td>1647</td><td>Local governments institute public-health quarantine laws

Massachusetts forbids pollution of Boston Harbor as a public health measure

Massachusetts establishes free public fishing rights in all bays, rivers, and "great ponds" and right of access across private lands to reach them; declares</td></tr>
</table>

closed seasons for fishing (1652) and for deer hunting (1691) as wildlife conservation measures

1654–1770   Virginia requires settlers to plant mulberry trees to promote silkworm culture and offers bounties for silk production

1658   First colonial laws to control forest fires drafted

1660s   Colonial towns appoint food inspectors to control adulteration and unsanitary packing of foods

1681   William Penn offers land for sale in Pennsylvania, requires one acre preserved as forest for every five acres cleared

1691   Colonial forest regulation: "Broad Arrow" policy reserves all large trees in American colonies for British navy (1691); 1705 law forbids cutting trees smaller than twelve inches in diameter to allow them time to grow; 1721 law forbids cutting white pines without royal license; 1741 law prohibits northern and middle colonies from unauthorized cutting of wood on public lands; 1743 law establishes royal forest reservations in North America

1702–84   Precursors of the Industrial Revolution: Thomas Newcomen invents the steam engine (1702); Boulton and Watt perfect it for pumps and locomotion (1763); Abraham Darby converts coal to coke as fuel for iron-making, replacing use of charcoal from wood (1709); Henry Cort's iron "puddling" process produces malleable decarbonized iron (1784), permits advances in manufacturing of industrial machinery

1709–71   Colonial water-resource policies: Massachusetts prohibits unauthorized dams blocking navigation and fish migration (1709), Connecticut forbids barriers to navigation on navigable rivers and lakes (1752), Pennsylvania declares its rivers "public highways" (1771)

1726   South Carolina prohibits pollution harmful to fish, targeting especially the use of fish poisoning as a harvesting method

1739   Massachusetts prohibits cutting vegetation from beaches and marshes

1763   Proclamation of 1763 forbids settlement west of Appalachian Mountains

1769–85   Beginnings of textile manufacturing industry: Richard Arkwright invents the water-frame spinning machine (1769), Edmund Cartwright invents the power loom (1785)

1775–89   Beginnings of scientific chemistry: Joseph Black identifies carbon dioxide (1775), Cavendish separates hydrogen from oxygen in water (1781), Ingenhousz identifies oxygen and demonstrates photosynthesis, Lavoisier publishes his *Elementary Treatise on Chemistry* (1789)

1776   Adam Smith's *Wealth of Nations* describes the "natural order" of economic markets, guided by the "invisible hand" of voluntary exchange with prices determined by supply and demand

Jeremy Bentham's utilitarianism proposes "greatest good for greatest number" as secular moral principle for human society

1776–81	**War of American Independence (Revolutionary War) and Confederation**
1777	Articles of Confederation drawn up (ratified 1781)
1780–1802	States cede land claims west of Allegheny Mountains to federal government as condition of confederation agreement
1783	Treaty of Paris ends Revolution, confirms Confederation's independence and boundaries
1784–95	Treaties of Fort Stanwix (1784), Fort MacIntosh (1785), and Greenville (1795) establish U.S. sovereignty over Native American lands of the "old Northwest"
1785	Land Ordinance of 1785 establishes Confederation policy for land disposal: lands to be surveyed in rectilinear sections, then sold at auction alternately in 640-acre lots and whole townships, with one section of every sixteen reserved for schools and government needs
1787	Northwest Ordinance establishes eventual statehood and terms of governance for western lands, affirms private property rights of landowners
1787	United States Constitution drafted (ratified 1791, including Bill of Rights)

1787–1860	**Westward settlement and "internal improvements"**
1789	U.S. government funds first "internal improvement": lighthouse at entrance to Chesapeake Bay
1793	U.S. government declares sovereignty over three-mile territorial sea
1796	First U.S. Land Act reaffirms terms of 1785 Land Ordinance, including survey process and terms of sale for public lands
1800	Harrison Frontier Land Act liberalizes terms of sale for public lands: allows four-year credit, reduces minimum price and purchase size, authorizes land offices in territories
1802	National road authorized, from Cumberland (Maryland) to Ohio River
1803	Louisiana Purchase adds 523 million acres of western Mississippi River basin to United States
1803–20	Early government-sponsored explorations of American West: Lewis and Clark travel up Missouri River and on to Oregon (1803–06), expeditions made by John Sibley (Red River valley), Zebulon Pike (southern Colorado, 1805–07), and Stephen Long (northern Colorado and New Mexico, 1819)
1807	Coast Survey established in Treasury Department
1808	Gallatin Report proposes national system of roads and canals
1812	General Land Office established under Treasury Department
1817–25	New York State constructs Erie Canal from Albany to Buffalo, reducing shipping costs by 85 percent and time by 70 percent; immediate success inspires federal funding of canals elsewhere (first federal canal grants to states, 1822)
1818	Calhoun Report proposes national plan for river navigation improvements
1819	Florida purchased from Spain

1819	Financial panic due to excessive land speculation collapses western land values and agricultural economy
1820	Land Act responding to financial crash requires all land purchases be made in cash (no credit), reduces minimum purchase price to $1.25 per acre
1824	Rivers and Harbors Act provides first of annual appropriations to Army Corps of Engineers for water-resource navigation improvements
	Supreme Court's decision in *Gibbons v. Ogden* confirms supremacy of federal regulatory powers over those of states under commerce clause of Constitution
1830	First of several Preemption Acts temporarily allows settlers to purchase lands at minimum prices without auction
	Indian Removal Act authorizes president to compel removal of eastern Native American tribes to reserved lands ("reservations") west of Mississippi; President Andrew Jackson uses it to remove Cherokees from Georgia, North Carolina, and Tennessee ("Trail of Tears")
1830–50	Industrialization advances: development of steam engines, steamboats, railroad locomotives, power weaving in textile manufacture, McCormick's reaper in agriculture, Colt's revolver
1836	Land speculation boom leads President Jackson to issue Specie Circular again requiring cash for all purchases of land; resulting economic contraction leads to financial panics in 1837, 1839
	Ralph Waldo Emerson publishes his essay *On Nature,* articulating transcendental vision of God in nature
1837	Supreme Court upholds principle that the "public interest" justifies regulation of private property (*Charles River Bridge* decision)
1841	Preemption Act permanently establishes right of preemption for settlers on all public lands, effectively opening the entire public domain to entry and land claims
1842	Public health movement begins: Chadwick report (England) — *The Sanitary Condition of the Labouring Population of England* — establishes basis for environmental sanitation as a public health program; inspires similar reports in New York (Griscom, *The Sanitary Condition of The Laboring Population of New York,* 1845), Boston (Shattuck, *Report of the Massachusetts Sanitary Commission,* 1850), and elsewhere
1842–60	"Great Reconnaissance": many state surveys of natural resources conducted, plus further federal explorations under John Fremont (1842–45)
1845	Texas annexed to United States
	"Manifest Destiny" phrase coined to express vision of settling entire continent
1846	England repeals its "Corn Laws" taxing U.S. grain imports, expanding export markets and sparking agricultural boom in upper Midwest

	Oregon Treaty obtains Pacific Northwest from Great Britain (180 million acres)
1848	Treaty of Guadalupe Hidalgo ends Mexican War (1846–48), secures U.S. sovereignty over California and Southwest (334 million acres)
1848	Gold discovered in California, California gold rush begins; others follow in Nevada (Comstock silver lode, 1858), Colorado (gold, 1859), elsewhere
1849	Department of the Interior created, General Land Office transferred to it
1850–70	Epidemics — typhus, typhoid, smallpox, diphtheria, yellow fever — hit New York, New Orleans, Cincinnati, St. Louis, New Orleans (nine thousand people die of yellow fever in 1853 in New Orleans); Asian cholera reaches United States in 1860s
	Swampland Acts promote cheap and often fraudulent sales of riparian lands supposedly "unfit for cultivation" for drainage and development
1850–60	First land grants given to railroad companies (Illinois Central R.R. 1850)
1851	Interior Department attempts to enforce timber trespass laws, forced to retreat by congressional pressure
1853	Gadsden Purchase adds southern Arizona (nineteen million acres) to United States
1854	Kansas-Nebraska Act abrogates U.S. agreements to leave western territories under control of Native American tribes
	Graduation Act reduces prices of public lands left unsold after specified number of years, creates another cheap way to claim public lands
1861–65	**Civil War**
	Southern states secede, Northern congressional majority passes sweeping new legislation on agrarian settlement, transcontinental railroads, and other issues that had previously been blocked
1862–73	Land grants given to transcontinental railroad companies
1862	Department of Agriculture founded, given mission to provide technical assistance to farmers
	Morrill Act provides land grants to support state "land grant" colleges for technical assistance to farmers
	Homestead Act offers public lands virtually free to settlers (160 acres for $26 after five-year residence, or for $1.25 per acre after six months)
1864	Yosemite Valley given to California as state park (re-ceded to federal government in 1905 after poor state management sparks campaign by John Muir and Sierra Club)
	George Perkins Marsh's *Man and Nature, Or Physical Geography as Modified by Human Activities* describes destructive environmental effects of earlier Mediterranean civilizations, warns of similar possibility in North America; sparks wider scientific and public concern over deforestation

Coal lands offered for sale at $25 per acre, in recognition of their higher value than ordinary lands

1865–1900   **Urbanization, industrialization, and resource management initiatives**

Transcontinental railroads trigger major expansion of logging, steelmaking, other industries; Bessemer steel process developed (1866–73); open-hearth process allows removal of sulfur and phosphorus from cruder ores, increasing air pollution (1881–90)

Petroleum industry develops (beginning with 1859 strike in Titusville, Pennsylvania): petroleum replaces whale oil, grows rapidly as fuel and booms with development of internal combustion engine in 1890s

1865–66   New York Citizens Association report urges creation of major municipal public health and sanitation program, New York City's Metropolitan Health Law (1866) establishes first municipal public health agency — model for other U.S. cities

1866–72   Mining laws established: Mining Act of 1866 declares mineral lands of public domain "free and open to public exploration and occupation" at $5 per acre; Placer Act (1870) allows miners to buy land for hydraulic (erosive surface) mining at $2.50 per acre in 160-acre lots, without royalties or cleanup requirements, and affirms "prior appropriation" principle for mining and water claims; General Mining Act (1872) extends open mining to all public lands

1867   Alaska purchased from Russia (365 million acres)

1867–78   Era of "Great Surveys" of American West: expeditions of Clarence King (1867–78), F. V. Hayden (1867–78), George Wheeler (1872–79), Major John Wesley Powell (1869–78)

1869   Massachusetts establishes first state board of health, beginning professionalization of state public health agencies (American Public Health Association founded 1872)

1872   Yellowstone Valley reserved from land claims as first national park

1873   Timber Culture Act allows additional 160-acre land claims if claimant promises to plant trees on 40 acres of them

1876   Forestry and Fisheries divisions created in the Department of Agriculture

1877   Desert Land Act allows land claims of 640 acres at $1.25 per acre based on unfulfillable promises to irrigate within three years

Carl Schurz appointed Secretary of Interior, begins professionalization of federal natural resource management (to 1881)

1878   John Wesley Powell's *Report on Lands of the Arid Region* recommends sweeping changes in settlement policies for arid western lands (small irrigated holdings along streams, far larger grazing lands away from them)

Timber and Stone Act allows purchase of forested public lands in 160-acre lots at $2.50 per acre (equal to one-tenth of their value at the time), eventually repealed in 1955; Free Timber Act allows free cutting of timber on public lands for agriculture, mining, and other "domestic uses"

1879   U.S. Geological Survey, first major government scientific agency, created in Interior Department to integrate data from the Great Surveys

1880s   Pasteur, Koch, Lister discover bacteria as disease organisms, discredit both contagionism and "miasma" theory underlying sanitation-based approach to public health; spark "new public health" based on microbiology, immunization, personal cleanliness

"Age of Enterprise": Era of business consolidation into holding companies, "pools," "trusts," integrated operating companies; Frederick Taylor develops "scientific management" of industrial production

Farmers mobilize agrarian political movement against eastern moneyed interests, railroads, middlemen, industrial monopolies; business interests counter by invoking "social Darwinism," economic "survival of the fittest"

1887   Dawes Act breaks up Indian reservations into individual allotments, opens the rest to claims by settlers; sparks Oklahoma land rush (1889)

1888–90   Irrigation surveys by U.S. Geological Survey identify promising sites for dams and irrigable lands; these lands temporarily reserved from land claims

1890–1920   "Age of Reform"

1890   Director of the Census declares end of meaningful concept of a western frontier

1891   General Revision Act revises public lands laws: repeals Timber Culture and Preemption Acts, limits homestead claims to 160 acres and total land claims to 320 acres

Forest Reserves Act (rider to General Revision Act) authorizes president to reserve forested lands from settlement, to protect irrigation dam sites from speculative land claims, and to control deforestation of watersheds; Presidents Cleveland and Benjamin Harrison use it to reserve millions of acres from further land claims

1892   Sierra Club founded by John Muir and others to advocate preservation of natural lands as national parks (and especially re-cession of Yosemite Valley from California to federal management)

1893   Columbian Exposition in Chicago (five hundredth anniversary) sparks "city beautiful" movement for urban design, beautification, and effective management

1890s   Research by bacteriologists, chemists, and sanitary engineers shows that typhoid is spread by exposure to pathogens in sewage; water-supply treatment processes introduced; some cities also pass smoke-control ordinances, though they are generally ineffective

1895	Col. George Waring introduces "Waring model" of waste management in New York City — first practical and comprehensive system of professional municipal waste management in the United States
1897	Forest Management Act authorizes permanent federal management of the forest reserve lands, including sale of dead and individually marked timber: statutory basis for federal management of the national forests
1898	Spanish-American War to end Spanish colonial rule in Cuba begins: first overseas commitment of American troops, far more casualties due to disease than to combat (yellow fever endemic in Cuba)
	Dr. Walter Reed, working with U.S. forces in Cuba, proves that yellow fever and other diseases are transmitted ecologically by insect vectors (mosquitoes)
1899	Refuse Act requires permit from Army Corps of Engineers for disposal of "refuse" into navigable waters — intended to prevent solid materials hazardous to shipping, reinterpreted by court decision in 1960s to include chemical pollutants as well
1900	Lacey Act prohibits interstate commerce in illegally captured wildlife, ends commercial hunting industry

1901–08	**Theodore Roosevelt's presidency: Progressivism and conservation**
1902	Newlands Reclamation Act creates federal revolving fund to finance irrigation projects, delegates management of water resource development projects to an administrative agency staffed by technical experts
1903	First national wildlife refuge created at Pelican Island, Florida
1903–10	"Muckraking" reporting exposes evils of business monopolies, substandard urban living conditions, unsanitary meat packing, political corruption
1905	Forest Transfer Act moves forest reserves from Interior Department to Agriculture Department, renames them national forests; U.S. Forest Service created to manage them
	Yosemite Valley re-ceded to federal government, becomes Yosemite National Park
1906	Pure Food and Drug Act and Meat Inspection Acts passed in response to reporting on unsanitary conditions
	American Antiquities Act allows president to set aside areas of special historic or cultural value as "national monuments"; Roosevelt and successors use it to set aside many larger areas as future national parks until Congress can act to designate them, including Mesa Verde, Grand Canyon, Death Valley, Katmai, and Glacier Bay
1907	Rider to Forest Service annual appropriation ends presidential power to reserve national forests without congressional approval; Roosevelt reserves over a hundred million acres more before signing it

	Roosevelt requires user fees for private hydropower dams
1908	Secretary of the Interior gives permit to San Francisco for water-supply reservoir in Hetch Hetchy Valley, adjacent to Yosemite, over strenuous objections of Sierra Club; permit ultimately approved in 1913
	Roosevelt hosts White House Governors Conference on Conservation
1909	Ballinger-Pinchot controversy erupts over federal management of Alaskan coal lands
1911	Weeks Act authorizes federal purchase of lands for reforestation — basis for eventual federal creation of eastern national forests
	Fur Seal Treaty signed
1912	U.S. Public Health Service created, authorized to conduct water-quality studies
1914	Public Health Service issues standards for drinking water quality on interstate carriers, creates Office of Industrial Hygiene and Sanitation
1916	National Park Service created

1917–18	**United States in World War I**
1918	Migratory Bird Treaty Act uses treaty power to authorize federal management of ducks, other migratory waterfowl across state lines, after previous legislation based on commerce clause declared unconstitutional
1920	Mineral Leasing Act establishes leasing system for fuel mineral extraction on public lands as alternative to sale of lands themselves: unlike hard-rock minerals under 1872 General Mining Act, it grants no free and open right to mine
	Water Power Act establishes federal regulation of hydroelectric power, creates Federal Power Commission
1924	Oil Pollution Control Act enacted; regulates oil pollution from seagoing vessels only, not from stationary sources
	Alaskan Fisheries Act establishes federal control over management of ocean fisheries
	Clarke-McNary Act creates federal-state cooperative forestry programs
	Teapot Dome scandal leads to criminal indictment of Secretary of the Interior on bribery charges over mismanagement of federal oil reserves
1928	Boulder Canyon Project Act authorizes first federal multipurpose water project (Hoover Dam), becomes model for others
	Corps of Engineers "308 reports" identify potential sites for multipurpose water control projects nationwide
1929–41	Stock market crash precipitates Great Depression: economic disaster compounded by natural disasters (droughts, giant dust storms, floods)

1933–41	**Franklin D. Roosevelt becomes president; New Deal conservation**
	Succession of attempts made to create presidential staff for policy integration and planning — National Planning Board (1933–34), National Resources Board (1934–45), National Resources Committee (1935–39), National Resources Planning Board (1939–43) — all finally superseded by war agencies (1941) and ended by Congress (1943)
1933	Civilian Conservation Corps created, employs over 2.5 million young men in conservation projects, soil erosion control, trail building (1933–41)
	Public Works Administration creates millions of jobs building water-resource projects and other major construction projects
	Tennessee Valley Authority created, first and only experiment in using a federal corporation to manage an entire river basin for natural resource conservation and economic development
1934	Duck Stamp Act permanently earmarks funding from hunting license tax for wildlife habitat conservation
	Taylor Grazing Act creates U.S. Grazing Service and formally designates rangelands for grazing and closes them to other uses, but puts effective control in hands of local rancher groups and sets grazing fees below market levels
	Fish and Wildlife Coordination Act requires water resource agencies to consult with fish and wildlife agencies on ways to minimize impacts of dams on fisheries
1935	Soil Conservation Service created in Department of Agriculture (based on previous Soil Erosion Service created in 1933 in Interior Department)
	Rural Electrification Administration begins bringing electrical service and related modernization to rural areas
	Connally Hot Oil Act controls interstate shipment of oil, strengthening state oil conservation laws
1936	Flood Control Act establishes federal authority for flood control projects, requires cost-benefit test for them
	Soil Conservation and Domestic Allotment Act offers price stabilization incentive for farmers in exchange for soil conservation measures
1937	Pittman-Robertson Act permanently earmarks funding for wildlife habitat conservation from tax on sporting goods and ammunition (modeled on Duck Stamp Act)
1938	Agricultural Adjustment Act establishes "parity" principle, market quotas, growing allotments for stabilizing farm prices
	Second Whaling Convention signed (first in 1931)
	Food, Drug and Cosmetics Act replaces 1906 Pure Food Act, prohibits misbranding and requires labeling of ingredients

1939   U.S. Fish and Wildlife Service created by merger of Biological Survey and
Bureau of Fisheries, transferred to Interior Department

1941–45   **World War II and postwar economic boom**
All-out industrial mobilization: automotive, aircraft, armaments, synthetic
chemicals, other industries undergo major expansions; government takes
over economy, establishes war-production and price controls

1944   Sustained-Yield Forest Management Act authorizes "cooperative
management units" combining cut-over private forest lands with uncut
federal lands

1945   World War II ends; Cold War begins
Bretton Woods Conference creates International Bank for Reconstruction
and Development (World Bank) and International Monetary Fund

United Nations charter drawn up (1945), United Nations created (1946)

President Truman proclaims U.S. sovereignty over soil resources of the outer
continental shelf—first challenge to Grotius's seventeenth-century doctrine
of limited national sovereignty over ocean resources

Los Angeles creates first county air pollution control agency

1946   Administrative Procedures Act spells out "due process" requirements for all
federal actions: notice and comment, hearings, reviewable record,
"substantial evidence," right of courts to overturn if "arbitrary and
capricious" or outside statutory authority

Atomic Energy Act creates the Atomic Energy Commission, transfers
control of all nuclear materials and weapons development to it from War
Department

Testing of nuclear weapons on Pacific islands begins

Bureau of Land Management created in Interior Department by merger of
Grazing Service and General Land Office

Fish and Wildlife Coordination Act amendments require water resource
agencies to minimize damage to fisheries from dam construction

International Whaling Commission created

1947   General Agreement on Tariffs and Trade (GATT) drawn up to end tariff
protectionism and promote international trade as disincentive to future
wars; four-year Marshall Plan for European economic recovery begins

California passes first statewide air pollution control law

Madison, Wisconsin, becomes first U.S. city to fluoridate its drinking water
to prevent tooth decay

1948   Beginnings of federal water pollution control policy: Federal Water
Pollution Control Act authorizes federal planning grants to local
governments for water quality management, authorizes federal lawsuits

against polluters of interstate rivers; 1956 amendments authorize federal grants for state water quality programs and construction of municipal wastewater treatment facilities and authorize federal government to call conferences to negotiate pollution control on interstate rivers

Donora, Pennsylvania, smog disaster and successive incidents (London's "killer smog," 1952) heighten public concern about air pollution hazards

Federal Insecticide, Fungicide and Rodenticide Act (FIFRA) requires registration of pesticides for each specific crop use

1949   United Nations sponsors scientific conference on conservation and utilization of natural resources

Aldo Leopold's *A Sand County Almanac* calls for a "land ethic" in natural resource use

1950   Mid-century conference on "Resources for the Future" promotes rise of natural resource economics

1950–65   Development of detailed cost-benefit standards for water project justification: "Green Book" (1950), Budget Circular A-47 (1952), Senate Document 97 (1962), Water Resource Council principles and standards (1965)

1951   President Truman creates President's Materials Policy Commission ("Paley Commission"); its five-volume report (*Resources for Freedom*) in 1952 documents heavy U.S. consumption of material and energy resources, increasing dependence on imports, and "free world" shortages of strategic materials

Dingell-Johnson Act earmarks funding for fishery conservation from fishing license fees

1953   Civilian nuclear power program created: President Eisenhower calls for international commitment to development of peaceful uses for atomic energy ("Atoms for Peace" speech, 1953); Civilian Nuclear Power Act (1954) authorizes electrical utilities to own nuclear materials and operate nuclear reactors for electric power production, directs Atomic Energy Commission to promote as well as regulate use of nuclear energy for this purpose and other civilian uses

Radioactive fallout discovered in upstate New York (1953), and sickens crew of Chinese fishing boat *Lucky Dragon* eighty miles downwind from nuclear test in Pacific (1954)

Eisenhower supports major increase in national-forest road construction to facilitate logging

Submerged Lands Act confirms riparian states' sovereignty over undersea lands for first three miles out from coast ("tidelands"); Outer Continental Shelf Act affirms federal sovereignty over the remainder out to limits of OCS (up to two hundred miles)

1954	Echo Park controversy: Sierra Club and other nature protection groups succeed in campaign to stop a water resource project that would have flooded canyons of Dinosaur National Monument (Colorado)
	Watershed Protection and Flood Prevention Act ("Small Watershed Act") authorizes Soil Conservation Service to subsidize water resource projects for local sponsoring organizations (farm owners, municipalities) in exchange for soil conservation measures
	Food for Peace Program donates U.S. agricultural surpluses to poorer countries
1955	Beginnings of federal air pollution control policy: 1954 act authorizes federal research and technical assistance
1956	National Park Service inaugurates "Mission 66," ten-year program of tourism infrastructure development aiming to increase its budget and political support by promoting "parks for people" rather than preservation alone
	Interstate highway system begun — 42,500-mile system, 90 percent subsidized by federal government, supported by a Highway Trust Fund with earmarked revenues from highway user taxes
	Vanishing Shoreline report documents rapid losses of shoreline to development, proposes federal funding to purchase remaining areas for public access and recreation
	Agriculture Department begins massive aerial pesticide spray campaigns against gypsy moth in Northeast and fire ant in Southeast
1958	Delaney Amendment to Food, Drug and Cosmetics Act bans use of any food additive shown to cause cancer in laboratory animals
	U.S. Scientific Committee on Effects of Atomic Radiation concludes that radiation exposure can be harmful even at smallest doses; United States and USSR begin voluntary moratorium on above-ground testing of nuclear weapons
	Outdoor Recreation Resources Review Commission created; 1962 reports projects tripling of demand by year 2000, urges federal program to acquire lands for outdoor recreation, create a Bureau of Outdoor Recreation in Interior Department
1959	"Cranberry scare" stirs public fears of exposure to carcinogens in agricultural chemical residues on foods
1960	Multiple Use Sustained Yield Act reaffirms multiple-use policy for national forests, adds recreation as an additional authorized use
1961–63	President Kennedy sponsors White House Conference on "New Conservation," adds $100 million to wastewater treatment construction grants program, creates Cape Cod National Seashore
1962	Rachel Carson's *Silent Spring* sparks widespread public awareness and concern about ecological effects of indiscriminate pesticide use

1963	Limited Nuclear Test Ban Treaty ends atmospheric testing of nuclear weapons: most important environmental agreement before 1970
1963–67	Development of federal air pollution policy: Clean Air Act (1963) provides federal support for state air pollution programs, authorizes federal regulation of motor vehicle emissions; Motor Vehicle Air Pollution Control Act (1965) authorizes federal emissions standards for cars, and federal enforcement; 1967 Air Quality Act establishes explicit national policy of air pollution control, authorizes federal regulation of stationary sources, directs federal development of scientific criteria documents for specified air pollutants
1964	Forest Service proposes massive timber sales including 8.75 billion board feet from Tongass National Forest in Alaska, clear-cutting of Monongahela National Forest in West Virginia
	Wilderness Act authorizes permanent protection of up to nine million acres of national forest lands as wilderness, directs Forest Service to review all roadless areas for potential designation
1965	President and Mrs. Lyndon Johnson sponsor White House Conference on Natural Beauty
	Land and Water Conservation Fund created, earmarks federal revenues for parkland acquisition by federal, state, and local governments, funded by revenues from offshore oil drilling, land sales, motorboat fuel taxes, and park entrance fees (eventually $2 billion per year)
1965–66	Development of federal water pollution policy: 1965 Water Quality Act sets first explicit national policy for prevention and control of water pollution, requires states to set standards subject to federal approval, expands construction grant program; Federal Water Pollution Control Administration created in Department of Health, Education and Welfare, then moved to Interior Department (1966) as Federal Water Quality Administration; presidential executive order (1966) mandates wastewater treatment for all federal facilities; 1966 Clean Water Restoration Act increases federal funding to $3.5 billion and federal share to 50 percent of construction costs
1966	National Historic Preservation Act passed
1967	Wreck of *Torrey Canyon* oil tanker causes massive oil spill off the coasts of England and Ireland
	Storm King v. Federal Power Commission decision affirms right of environmental groups to sue to challenge federal projects damaging to the environment
1968	Major new oil deposits discovered at Prudhoe Bay, Alaska
	United Nations Educational, Scientific, and Cultural Organization (UNESCO) sponsors Conference of Experts on the Biosphere

1969

Paul and Anne Ehrlich's *The Population Bomb* heightens public concern about global environmental impacts of human population growth
United Nations Fund for Population Activities founded at U.S. initiative

Oil rig blowout causes massive oil spill along California's Santa Barbara Channel

Cuyahoga River fire: Ohio river burns for eight days from industrial chemicals on surface

1970

"Environmental Era" begins
President Nixon signs National Environmental Policy Act (NEPA) on television on New Year's Day, declares 1970s the "decade of the environment"; begins annual environmental message to Congress, issues executive order on cleanup of pollution from federal facilities; NEPA creates Council on Environmental Quality, "environmental impact statement" requirement for federal actions

Clean Air Act establishes national minimum standards for ambient air pollution, mandates state implementation plans to achieve them; requires federal performance standards and technology-based permits for all new sources of air pollution and 90 percent reduction of auto emissions by 1975, establishes federal emissions standards for hazardous air pollutants; amendments in 1977 require prevention of significant deterioration in areas still cleaner than standards

Earth Day (April 22): massive nationwide public demonstrations held in support of environmental protection, turnout exceeded only by celebrations of end of World War II

President creates Environmental Protection Agency (EPA), National Atmospheric and Oceanic Agency

Water Quality Improvement Act passed in response to Santa Barbara oil spill authorizes federal government to clean up oil spills and bill the polluters, tightens liability, requires nuclear power plants to comply with state water quality standards

Public Land Law Review Commission ("Aspinall Commission") recommends many reforms of public land laws, but also advocates increased timber logging as "dominant use" of public lands

Bolle Report sharply criticizes Forest Service for clear-cut logging practices in Bitterroot National Forest (Montana)

1971

EPA begins intensive standard setting and permit writing, and aggressive enforcement of air and water pollution laws; Administrator William Ruckelshaus launches "Mission 5000" to close five thousand unsafe solid waste dumps, all are closed by late 1970s

Forest Service Roadless Area Review and Evaluation (RARE I) recommends wilderness designation for six million acres of national forest lands; environmental groups sue, RARE II (1977) subsequently recommends designating fifteen million acres

Joseph Sax's *Defending the Environment* urges allowing citizens to sue as "private attorneys general" under "public trust" doctrine to force agencies to enforce environmental laws

President Nixon calls for international negotiations to draft new Law of the Sea Treaty

1972   Federal Water Pollution Control Act ("Clean Water Act") sets national goals for water pollution control (all rivers fishable and swimmable by 1983, zero pollution discharge by 1985); requires federal wastewater discharge permits for all point sources of water pollution, based on best available technology, and federal standards for toxic water pollutants; increases federal construction grants for municipal wastewater treatment facilities to $6 billion; requires Corps of Engineers permits for draining or filling of wetlands

Federal Environmental Pesticide Control Act authorizes EPA to remove pesticides from use for "unreasonable adverse effects" on the environment

Coastal Zone Management Act promotes state planning and regulation of coastal development, requires that federal activities be consistent with these plans

Marine Mammal Protection Act passed

Dennis and Donella Meadows's *Limits to Growth* heightens awareness of interconnection between population growth, natural resource use, and pollution

First United Nations Conference on Human Environment held in Stockholm: increases worldwide concern for environmental problems, leads to creation of United Nations Environment Program, environmental ministries worldwide

1973   Endangered Species Act directs Fish and Wildlife Service to list endangered species, prohibits federal actions damaging them or their habitats, prohibits "taking" of these species by anyone

Convention on International Trade in Endangered Species drafted

Sherwood Rowland and Mario Molina hypothesize that chlorofluorocarbons (CFCs) could cause severe destruction of stratospheric ozone layer

Organization of Arab Oil Exporting Countries (OPEC) embargoes oil deliveries to United States in retaliation for Arab-Israeli War, causes sudden shortages and price increases; President Nixon responds by declaring "Project Independence" to rapidly develop U.S. energy resources

EPA begins phasedown of lead additives in gasoline to protect emission control devices, leading to 98 percent reduction in airborne exposures and blood-lead levels over next twenty years

1974   Safe Drinking Water Act directs EPA to set maximum contaminant levels for drinking water, requires local water authorities to monitor for them and meet EPA standards

Forest and Range Renewable Resources Planning Act (RPA) requires five- and ten-year management plans for national forests

Tennessee Valley Authority's Browns Ferry nuclear reactor disabled by fire

1975   Kepone pesticide spill into Virginia's James River causes major fish kill; high levels of polychlorinated biphenyls (PCB) measured in Hudson and other rivers; discoveries of "midnight dumping" of waste chemicals trigger pressures for hazardous waste regulation

Supreme Court halts clear-cutting on Monongahela National Forest as violation of 1897 Forest Management Act

1976   National Forest Management Act approves clear-cutting, but with strict guidelines; also requires Forest Service to open its administrative procedures to greater public input

Federal Lands Policy and Management Act for the first time confirms Bureau of Land Management authority for multiple-use management rather than disposal of public lands; triggers "Sagebrush Rebellion" (1977–81) by ranchers and other western commodity-use interests to intimidate the agency out of any shift to more active management

Fisheries Management and Conservation Act (Magnuson Act) bans foreign fleets from offshore fisheries, but also offers incentives to modernize and overbuild U.S. fleet

Resource Conservation and Recovery Act (RCRA) requires separate disposal of all hazardous industrial wastes, EPA standards and permits for all hazardous waste treatment, storage, and disposal facilities, "cradle-to-grave manifests" for all hazardous waste shipments by large-quantity generators, and EPA standards for all ordinary municipal waste landfills

Regulatory innovation: EPA introduces "offsets" policy to allow trading of air pollutant emissions in nonattainment areas; 1977 Clean Air Act amendments ratify this policy, 1979 "bubble policy" expands it

Toxic Substances Control Act requires premanufacturing notification to EPA before introduction of any new chemicals

Amory Lovins's article "The Road Not Taken" provides new economic arguments for energy conservation and small-scale, decentralized "soft path" for energy production

1977   President Jimmy Carter proposes "hit list" of water projects to stop as unjustified on both economic and environmental grounds; retreats in face of congressional opposition

Surface Mining Control and Reclamation Act requires rehabilitation of surface mine sites

Soil and Water Resource Conservation Act authorizes nationwide inventories of soil and water resource protection needs

1978   United States unilaterally bans "nonessential" uses of CFCs as aerosol propellants

Public Utilities Regulatory Policy Act (PURPA) requires electrical utilities to accept power generated by independent producers, pay fair market price for it

Michael Royston's article "Pollution Prevention Pays" argues that pollution is sign of business inefficiency, not just necessary cost of production

1979   Three Mile Island (Pennsylvania) nuclear reactor melts down in costly near disaster; orders for new U.S. nuclear reactors end

More OPEC oil price increases exacerbate worldwide economic recession

Alaska National Interest Lands Conservation Act protects large areas of Alaska as national parks after Interior Secretary Cecil Andrus threatens to invoke Antiquities Act and declare them national monuments in order to break Alaskan senators' filibuster

1980   Comprehensive Environmental Response, Compensation and Liability Act (CERCLA) creates federal "Superfund," financed mainly by tax on chemical industry, to pay for cleanup of contaminated sites; establishes strict joint and several liability for all parties responsible for contamination, directs EPA to create National Priority List and sue responsible parties to reimburse Superfund for cleanup costs

President Carter's Council on Environmental Quality publishes *Global 2000* report asserting U.S. national security interest in global environmental issues

1980s–90s   Reaction, counterreaction, and globalization

1981   Ronald Reagan becomes president, attempts to radically reverse growth of federal environmental regulations through budget cuts and administrative actions; also deregulates energy prices

1982   United Nations overwhelmingly passes "World Charter for Nature," with United States as sole vote against it; Law of the Sea Treaty concluded and signed by most nations after United States withdraws its support

1983–84   EPA Administrator Anne Gorsuch cited for contempt of Congress, dismissed with thirty to forty other senior environmental officials (Interior Secretary James Watt is dismissed the following year); William Ruckelshaus reappointed Administrator of EPA

1984   World Population Conference held in Mexico City: Reagan administration announces withdrawal of U.S. support for international population stabilization and family planning programs

Union Carbide pesticide plant in Bhopal, India releases toxic gas, killing or injuring thousands: worst industrial disaster in history, leads to "community right-to-know" legislation and federal Toxics Release Inventory legislation (1986)

Hazardous and Solid Waste Management Act applies hazardous waste requirements to "small-quantity generators," requires cleanup and replacement of all underground storage tanks that may be subject to leakage

1985   Vienna Convention drafts initial international agreement on control of ozone-depleting chemicals (CFCs and others); Antarctic stratospheric "ozone hole" discovered shortly thereafter

After international meeting at Villach (Austria), scientists announce consensus that human activities may be significantly accelerating warming of the global climate

Farm Security Act creates new Conservation Reserves program, adds "sodbuster" and "swampbuster" provisions denying federal benefits to farmers who start new production on erodible soils or wetlands

1986   Chernobyl nuclear reactor in Ukraine explodes, causing worldwide exposure to radiation

Superfund Act Reauthorization Amendments (SARA) tighten cleanup requirements, establish Toxic Release Inventory, national disclosure and right-to-know provisions for industrial chemical use and releases

Safe Drinking Water Act amendments require EPA to issue standards for twenty-five additional contaminants each year

Asbestos Hazard Emergency Response Act requires inspection for asbestos in all local schools, notification of parents

1987   Montreal Protocol establishes international agreements to phase out production of ozone-depleting chemicals, London Convention 1990 agrees to accelerate this process

United Nations' World Commission on Environment and Development (Brundtland Commission) issues report calling for "sustainable development" (*Our Common Future*)

EPA issues report on comparative risk assessment (*Unfinished Business*) calling for sweeping changes in the agency's program priorities

1988   Amendments to Federal Environmental Pesticide Control Act require EPA to re-register or cancel up to fifty thousand products that had been allowed to remain on the market ("grandfathered") under 1972 law

1989   *Exxon Valdez* shipwreck causes huge oil spill in Gulf of Alaska

Report on Alar by CBS's *60 Minutes* dramatizes EPA's inability to remove agricultural chemicals from market, sparks political battle over "regulatory protection of children's health" versus claims of "junk science"

1990   Pollution Prevention Act exhorts reduction of pollution at the source rather than treatment and disposal but leaves it to voluntary action, makes no changes in existing regulatory programs to encourage it

Clean Air Act amendments add automatic penalties for a nonattainment of goals, create national cap and tradable allowances for sulfur emissions to achieve 50 percent reduction from 1990 levels, require best technology (rather than just risk balancing) for reduction of hazardous air pollutants

1991   Iraq's invasion of Kuwait again exposes U.S. dependence on oil imports

Intermodal Surface Transportation Efficiency Act (ISTEA) allows some highway funds to be spent for congestion mitigation and air quality improvements, mitigation of wetland losses from highway construction, and promotion of integrated transport planning

GATT trade panel rules that U.S. regulations protecting dolphins under Marine Mammal Protection Act are inconsistent with GATT free-trade requirements

1992   United Nations sponsors "Earth Summit" in Rio de Janeiro (United Nations Conference on Environment and Development) on twentieth anniversary of Stockholm conference; produces "Agenda 21" for achieving sustainable development in twenty-first century

Energy Policy Act directs Department of Energy to develop a national energy strategy promoting conservation and efficient energy use, deregulates electrical utilities

1993   Bill Clinton becomes president, signs Biodiversity Convention and Law of the Sea Treaty (still unratified by Senate)

Interior Secretary Bruce Babbitt creates National Biological Service to integrate biological science expertise, proposes wide-ranging reforms in rangeland protection and mining laws; Clinton retreats in face of congressional opposition

1994   United States ratifies North American Free Trade Agreement (NAFTA) with environmental side agreement and expansion of GATT without environmental provisions, both with strong backing by President Clinton

1995   Conservative Republican majority takes office in Congress, proposes radical changes in many environmental laws; passes "Forest Health Act" mandating "salvage logging" on national forests and overriding environmental requirements and citizen-suit provisions, passes law limiting federal "unfunded mandates" on state and local governments

1996   Federal Agricultural Improvement and Reform Act begins seven-year phaseout of federal price supports for agricultural overproduction, along with related federal incentives for land conservation

Food Quality Protection Act replaces absolute ban on carcinogenic food additives (Delaney Amendment) with standards based on risks to children and other high-risk groups, requires posting of information on chemical residues in grocery stores

Amendments to Fishery Conservation and Management Act provide for government to buy back fishing boats, impose "individual transferable quotas" to ration declining stocks of fish

Amendments to Safe Drinking Water Act ease monitoring burdens on local water utilities, but require them to notify their customers of contamination problems, creating a revolving loan fund for improvement of water supply treatment, and promote pollution prevention measures for small utilities

Notes

Chapter 1: Environment and Governance

1 Many such programs, such as agricultural subsidies, below-cost logging and mining concessions, and underpriced use of water, fuels, and grazing lands, have been criticized on economic grounds as well.

2 Such regimes have been well documented among users of fisheries and pastures in subsistence societies, and their principles have been extended to some larger-scale environmental problems as well (Bromley 1992)

3 Two enduring problems complicate such claims, however. One is the existence of legitimate conflict among visions of the overall public interest itself, and of priorities within it, that are not merely differences in self-interest and that are not resolvable by increases in scientific knowledge. The other is the inevitable intermixture of private benefits with public goods. Even actions that serve an overall public interest benefit some private interests more than others, including not only businesses or property owners but the continued organizational success of advocacy groups. This circumstance inevitably tempts self-interested beneficiaries to cloak their own interests in those of the public, and self-interested opponents in turn to attack the identifiable beneficiaries rather than to discuss the merits of the action as it affects the overall public interest. These problems have no ultimate answers, except to acknowledge the legitimacy of differing visions and the reality of self-interests, and then to debate questions of what befits the public interest on the quality of evidence and reasoning of the arguments.

Chapter 2: Historical Context: European Colonization and Trade

1 Any contextual overview such as what follows can only touch on highlights from the work of others. This overview relies primarily on Weber (1971) and Stavrianos (1971); for more detailed treatment, see those sources or other texts on European history.

2 Jefferson and many other Enlightenment thinkers also professed interest in Deism, a religious position that conceived of God as having created the world but then left it to the workings of its own natural processes, like a cosmic "watchmaker." In this scheme, humans must rely on their own powers of reason to figure out how the world worked and to use it properly (Kline 1997, 8–9).

Chapter 3: Colonial Precedents: Environment as Property

1 The most systematic survey of this subject for the colonial period, and indeed for the entire period up to 1862, is Engelbert (1950), which regrettably was never published except as a doctoral dissertation and is therefore difficult to obtain. In this chapter I draw extensively and gratefully on Engelbert's work, as well as on Miller (1966), Sauer (1971), and others as noted in the text.

2 A constant irritant to the colonies was Britain's sometimes heavy-handed attempts to regulate trade patterns not just for its own benefit, but for the benefit of particular constituencies. One example is the Molasses Act of 1733, which attempted to protect the British West Indies planters against French competitors at the expense of the North American colonies (Stout 1973, 10–11).

3 Tobacco farming was prohibited in England for this reason, protecting Britain's own farmlands but creating a protected export market for the southern colonies as well.

4 Arguments of "natural rights" originated in the seventeenth century as a basis for English civil rights versus the Crown, but they also spread to America to become an important philosophical basis for American ideas of private property rights. Similar arguments were later used to justify settlers' squatting against the legal ownership of American land speculators.

Chapter 4: The Constitutional Framework

1 Massachusetts, Connecticut, New York, Virginia, North Carolina, South Carolina, and Georgia.

2 Influential land speculators in the Maryland legislature also expected that they would obtain better terms from the federal government than from Virginia (Jensen 1962).

3 *Martin v. Waddell,* 41 U.S. 234 (1842).

4 The broad scope of the commerce clause was confirmed by the Supreme Court in its 1824 decision in *Gibbons v. Ogden* (6 L. Ed. 23), which nullified a state-sanctioned monopoly on steamboat service in New York because it conflicted with federal licensing of coastal pilots (Futrell 1993, 13).

5 Firms might, for instance, simply document deliberate and criminal violations of the environmental laws in their environmental audits, and thus insulate them from prosecution on the grounds of self-incrimination.

6 *Charles River Bridge v. Warren Bridge,* 6 L. Ed. 773 (1837); *The License Cases,* 12 L. Ed. 256 (1847).

7 In the most extreme case, for instance, advocates of this principle could argue that *any* diminution of economic opportunity due to regulation requires compensation, thus negating the principle of regulation itself. A likely result would be blackmail of the taxpayers by interests demanding compensation for not polluting or for not performing other antisocial acts. The history of U.S. land development is full of examples of persons staking land claims in the path of government facilities so that they can then sell these lands back to the government at inflated prices; one would expect no less of compensation claims for regulatory takings.

8 The first of these decisions overturned a state coastal protection regulation that prohibited a beachfront owner from building a house; the second overturned a local land-use requirement that a business set aside floodplain land and grant public access for a bicycle path through it as conditions of receiving a permit to expand a store and parking lot. *Lucas v. South Carolina Coastal Council,* 424 S.E. 2d 484 (1992); *Dolan v. Tigard,* 114 S. Ct. 2309 (1994).

Chapter 5: Land and Transport: Commercial Development as Environmental Policy

1 The ownership of Alaskan lands was radically altered in the 1970s, by enactment of the Alaskan Native Claims Settlement Act in 1971 and the Alaska National Interest Lands Conservation Act in 1979. Federal land ownership in most other states remains more or less as stated.

2 For more detailed histories of the public lands, see especially Engelbert 1950, Gates 1968, Dick 1970, Hibbard 1965 [1924], Smith 1970 [1950], Dana and Fairfax 1980 [1956], Wilkinson 1992, and Worster 1985.

3 Jefferson also read Malthus's essays on the threat of overpopulation, and rejected his arguments on the grounds that continuous emigration to virgin territory in the West would render them irrelevant (McCoy 1980, 194–95).

4 The Cherokee confrontation also gave rise to one of the definitive confrontations between executive and judicial powers, as the Supreme Court under Chief Justice John Marshall ruled in favor of the Indians but President Andrew Jackson — a westerner himself, a general in the Indian Wars, and an advocate for the white settlers — refused to use federal troops to enforce the court's decision.

5 Perhaps the classic statement of this position was Crèvecoeur's *Letters from an American Farmer* (1957 [1782]), which presented American freehold farming as the bedrock of individual freedom and citizenship (Jones 1965, 328–29).

6 The Timber Culture Act of 1873, for instance, allowed settlers to claim an additional 160 acres if they would agree to plant and cultivate trees on 40 of them, though there was no effective way of enforcing the success or even cultivation of the plantations (Gates 1968, 399–401).

7 William Cronon notes for instance that for all its supposed "natural advantages" as a location for a major midwestern metropolis, the city of Chicago had equally severe disadvantages: substantial unstable lowlands both underlying it and in surrounding areas, a sandbar that virtually blocked its harbor, and substantial obstacles to shipping across land in the areas separating the several Great Lakes. These barriers were only overcome by major federal investments in transportation improvements (Cronon 1991, 55–74).

8 Interestingly, these grants also played an important role in the rise of modern business corporations. Corporations were initially chartered by special legislation specifically to serve the common good, such as the public purpose of building roads, canals, or other infrastructure projects. Their public charters allowed them to condemn land as needed for rights-of-way, using the government's power of eminent domain. In the famous *Dartmouth College* case in 1819, however, the Supreme Court held that corporations were in fact private entities whose charters, once granted, conferred contractual rights that could not subsequently be redefined unilaterally by state legislatures. By mid-century strictly private corporations had begun to proliferate under general laws of incorporation that no longer required specific public-interest responsibilities (Horwitz 1988, 53–55).

9 Not unlike airlines today, the nineteenth-century railroads engaged in price competition on lines between eastern cities, where they had to match competitors' fares, but made up their losses by charging higher rates to farmers in the West, where their lines were the only service available.

Chapter 6: Agencies and Experts: The Beginnings of Public Management

1 This was recommended by the Hoover commissions on government reorganization, and more recently in 1969 by President Nixon's Ash Commission on Government Reorganization. It has never occurred, however, due to the political opposition of the Corps's client constituencies and congressional protectors.

2 Several presidents and others had long advocated such a department, out of concern for the increasing burden of the government's business and the inability of existing departments to cope effectively with the new problems of national development. Opponents, however, preferred a minimalist approach to federal administration, and were supported in this by those who more specifically opposed expansion of federal subsidies for internal improvements and federal preemption of state prerogatives (Engelbert 1950, 200–202).

3 In 1969, the Nixon administration's Ash Commission on Government Reorganization recommended reorganizing it into a Department of Environment and Natural Resources, adding to it the Forest Service and the civilian water resource functions of the Army Corps of Engineers, but this proposal was never adopted.

4 These controversies also illustrate the "logic of collective action" described by political scientist Mancur Olson (1965), under which identifiable political minorities with personal economic interests in the outcomes can prevail over broader majority interests, since they can be mobilized more easily and have clearer personal stakes in the outcome.

5 Early land laws did provide for surveying of the lands, for reservation of one-third of all gold, silver, and lead mines for public revenue, and for reservation of some live-oak plantations in the South for naval shipbuilding, but these were not significant exceptions (Hibbard 1965 [1924], 494–96).

6 Hibbard deserves particular credit for noting the importance of resource classification as a step in the process of policy development for the public lands.

7 Typically a lease would run for three years, with operators paying the government about 10 percent of the output as a royalty in kind. Operators, however, complained that three years was too brief a period to make a profit on the capital investment of opening and working a mine. The administrative costs of the leasing system were often higher than the royalties in any case, especially since royalties often proved uncollectable. The actual process of mining also involved extensive unauthorized use of timber from adjacent public lands.

8 For instance, the immensely valuable iron- and copper-bearing lands of the Great Lakes states were simply offered for sale as ordinary agrarian lands and bought up by speculators.

9 The details of the prior appropriation system vary somewhat from state to state, with Colorado and others following a relatively pure version of the doctrine whereas California and some others developed a hybrid mix of riparian and appropriation principles (Dick 1970, 310–11).

10 The reserved water rights principle is founded in the constitutional powers of the federal government to manage public lands (under the property clause) and to provide for navigation (under the commerce clause). Supreme Court decisions have also held that water rights for Indian tribes were necessarily implied by the treaties setting aside reservations for them (*Winters v. United States,* 1908) and that reservations of public lands for other purposes also removed water sources on that land from appropriation under state laws (*Federal Power Commission v. Oregon,* 1955).

11 Schurz was also a leading advocate of civil service reform and professionalization of government administration more generally, and an architect of the landmark Pendleton Civil Service Act of 1883.

12 USGS earned its scientific respect in part by defining its mission as the production of scientific information, rather than the support of GLO's land sales survey process per se. It thus avoided the political pressures that were endemic to GLO's land disposal mission. This success bears comparison with the more problematic situation of science in the Environmental Protection Agency, whose research programs have frequently been criticized for being too narrowly tied to the ad hoc demands of its regulatory programs. See discussion in later chapters.

13 Indeed, the following year Congress extended this law to all the public land states, and serious frauds continued to be identified in the use of this law to appropriate public forest lands.

14 Several smaller sites were also reserved over the years, such as the Arkansas Hot Springs in 1832 and Michigan's Mackinac Island in 1875.

Chapter 7: Public Health and Urban Sanitation

1 For more detailed histories of public health and sanitation in the United States see especially Colten and Skinner 1996, Duffy 1990, Rosen 1958, Rosenau 1935, Selleck and Whitaker 1962, Smillie 1955, Starr 1982, and Winslow 1923.

2 Local governments from early on had authority under the police power to control and abate public "nuisances," which *Black's Law Dictionary* defines as "everything that endangers life or health, gives offense to the senses, violates the laws of decency, or obstructs reasonable and comfortable use of property." Butcheries, slaughterhouses, and tanneries were regulated as early as the mid-1600s, requiring them to operate and deposit their wastes only in designated areas away from residential neighborhoods (Bridenbaugh 1964, 85–86, 238–39). By the end of the eighteenth century the locations of privies, dumps, and wells were all regulated to varying degrees by many towns and cities (Bridenbaugh 1964, 475). A Boston ordinance as early as 1652, for instance, prohibited the construction of privies within twenty feet of highways or neighborhood houses unless they had vaults at least six feet deep (Bridenbaugh 1964, 86, 239).

3 The decision held unconstitutional a New York state law which would have given exclusive navigation privileges in New York waters to a particular firm (Robert Livingston and Robert Fulton), on grounds that it interfered with interstate commerce, which was a matter of federal authority. Later decisions also upheld state and local authority to regulate such activities as operation of slaughterhouses and fertilizing companies, garbage disposal, wastewater discharges, and emissions of noxious fumes and smoke. See the "slaughterhouse cases," 21 L. Ed. 702; *Fertilizing Company v. Hyde Park*, 97 U.S. 659; *California Reduction Company v. Sanitary Reduction Works*, 199 U.S. 306; *Gardner v. Michigan*, 199 U.S. 325; *Hutchinson v. Valdosta*, 227 U.S. 303; *Georgia v. Tennessee Copper Company*, 206 U.S. 230; and *Northwestern Laundry Company v. Des Moines*, 239 U.S. 486 (Tobey 1978 [1926], 51–53).

4 An example of these attacks was the published lecture of a Boston physician to the Suffolk District Medical Society in 1852, in which he claimed that both medical and business leaders agreed that quarantines had not worked. Diseases spread anyway, he argued, often among people who had had no obvious contact with those known to be afflicted, thereby discrediting the theory that contagion could in fact be the primary or sole cause of these diseases — even of plague, cholera, and yellow fever. Further, he argued that quarantine actually *concentrated* these diseases by keeping people locked up together. He went on to attack the quarantine system as "despotic," locking up rich and poor alike — as well as the doctors who treated them — until they recovered. He recommended therefore that the government abolish the quarantine system and substitute instead "the more rational and philosophical system of modern sanitary reform" which was then emerging in England (Clark 1972 [1852]).

5 The threat of fire was a serious concern in densely populated cities constructed largely of wood and heated and lighted by open flames. This may have been a greater motive for business support of water supply investments than health or even convenience (Duffy 1990, 30–31).

6 Waring was strongly influenced by the great landscape architect Frederick Law Olmsted, designer of Central Park, for whom he had worked as a young drainage engineer in the 1850s. Olmsted was one of the visionary advocates of humanizing the physical environment of cities and preserving scenic areas for public enjoyment. Waring also was one of the few strong advocates of separate sewer systems, so much so that in fact the separate systems of the time were often known as "Waring systems," and he had served both as a compiler of the 1880 Census report on urban sanitary conditions and as a member of the short-lived National Board of Health in the early 1880s. He served as New York City's street-cleaning commissioner during the same Progressive administration in which Theodore Roosevelt served as its police commissioner before going on to become governor, vice president, and then president within the following four years (Melosi 1981, 54–61).

7 Those who remember the *Mobro*, the famous "garbage barge" which carried Long Island garbage all the way to the Caribbean and back in 1987 before authorities were finally required to incinerate its cargo in New York, may be interested in a much earlier but similar incident in which barges carrying garbage from Washington, D.C., to a downstream dump were sunk by angry citizens of Alexandria (Armstrong et al. 1976, 435).

8 Pig-feeding of garbage remained a common practice up to the mid-1950s, and was only then abandoned after disease outbreaks (trichinosis and exanthema) led to health-mandated slaughters and state requirements that wastes be cooked before being fed to hogs. By the 1970s only about 4 percent of food wastes were still recycled as pig feed (Armstrong et al. 1976, 448).

9 An important issue here, however, is how much evidence should be required to justify government intervention. The cholera organism was not identified until the work of Koch in the 1880s, but during the 1854 London cholera epidemic Dr. John Snow, an English contagionist physician, identified the fact that nearly all his patients had consumed water from a particular public pump on Broad Street, and that other residents even in the same neighborhood who got water from different sources were not affected. He removed the handle from the pump, and new cases of the disease fell off dramatically within days. Subsequent investigation of the well showed clear evidence of contamination from the privy of a nearby house. This case is often cited as one of the forerunners of modern epidemiology (Rosen 1958, 314).

10 In retrospect this discrediting appears to have been too dismissive. Later research revealed the key roles of animal carriers in disease transmission, and many of these vectors thrived under unsanitary urban conditions. Modern assessments of the data suggest that sanitation measures did in fact bring about significant reductions in death and disease, even though the miasma theory itself was incorrect (Rosen 1958; Tesh 1981, 1989).

11 A key event was a clash between the City of Pittsburgh and Pennsylvania's State Board of Health in 1910 over Pittsburgh's application for temporary discharge permits for sewer extensions. The state required Pittsburgh to prepare a comprehensive plan for separating its sewage from its stormwater sewers and treating it; the city in response hired two leading sanitary engineering consultants who argued vigorously on cost-effectiveness grounds for continuation of the city's combined system of stormwater and sewage discharge. Faced with the combined opposition of the city and the engineering profession, the Board of Health backed down. Two years later, a report by the National Association for Preventing the Pollution of Rivers and Waterways — a group reportedly dominated by sanitary engineers — asserted more categorically that it was impossible to maintain or restore waterways to "their original and natural condition of purity," and that therefore "the discharge of raw sewage into our streams and waterways should not be universally prohibited by law" (Tarr and McMichael 1977, 57–59; Tarr et al. 1980, 73).

12 The use of coliform bacteria as an indicator of water purity was developed during this period, for instance, and was introduced as a basis for drinking water standards in interstate commerce by the Public Health Service in 1914 (Tarr 1985a, 1060).

13 An exception to this inattention was the U.S. Geological Survey, which was concerned with all aspects of water quality rather than merely its health effects. USGS produced reports as early as 1905 that noted the wide range of problems associated with industrial water pollutants: hazards to drinking water purity, habitat for vectors, and damage to fish and vegetation as well as to other natural processes. An important shift in perspective occurred in the 1920s, when a bacteriologist and a sanitary engineer working for the Public Health Service developed the Streeter-Phelps "oxygen sag" equation relating dissolved oxygen in streams to the biochemical oxygen demand of waste discharges, thus providing a common denominator for comparing the effects of municipal and industrial wastes on one important indicator of water quality (Tarr 1985a, 1060, 1064–65).

14 A 1912 investigation, for instance, estimated the economic cost of smoke pollution in Pittsburgh alone at $12 million per year. A 1911 USGS study estimated the nationwide cost at over $500 million, not even including the general inconvenience to individuals of living in it (Rosen 1993, 370–71). In St. Louis in 1905–06 smoke pollution killed an estimated one-third of the city's trees. In Milwaukee houses had to be repainted annually rather than just once every four to five years. In Pittsburgh a new American flag turned totally black within just two to three weeks. In many cities laundry could not even be hung out to dry without being dirtied once again (Grinder 1980, 87).

15 In the words of the New York Court of Appeals, for instance, "each member of society must submit to annoyances consequent upon the ordinary and common use of property, provided such use is reasonable . . . in view of the time, place and other circumstances" (*Cogswell v. New York, New Haven and Hartford Railroad,* 103 N.Y. 10 [1886]). In other cases, judges held that even though private property was "being invaded by this smoke . . . , 'public policy' is more important than private property," and that factories were both "legal and necessary." In urban areas, where pollution came from multiple industries and other sources, it was virtually impossible for an injured party to identify and successfully sue particular sources: no one source could be proven to have caused a measurable increase over the combined effects of all of them (Grinder 1980, 92–93).

16 In Milwaukee, for instance, the number of "smoky" days recorded by the weather bureau increased from 47 in 1916 to 212 in 1918 (Grinder 1980, 99).

17 These pipelines in turn were in part an unintended but beneficial result of energy policy incentives in the 1930s aimed at natural gas conservation. Natural gas occurred naturally with petroleum deposits, and had been widely wasted simply by producers flaring it off as they competed to pump oil as quickly as possible. Taxes imposed to correct this wasteful practice made other uses of natu-

ral gas more economically attractive, thus promoting the construction of pipelines to serve more distant interstate markets.

18 Note that this federal role in public health regulation, even though clearly limited to interstate commerce, emerged only after bitter opposition to it as a federal infringement of state and local police powers. Only after severe epidemics in 1878 in New Orleans and the Mississippi Valley did Congress finally act, and only after a decade of conflicts and further epidemics did the states finally accept the need for a stronger federal role (Duffy 1990, 167–72).

19 Most of the environmental regulations of the 1970s, in contrast, placed government in a clearly adversarial position toward industries, imposing unprofitable costs on them to control the environmental side effects of their production processes — though even in this period, industrial interests such as auto manufacturers and soft-coal producers actively influenced the regulatory laws in their own favor (Elliott et al. 1985). In the 1990s a hybrid version of this issue became more widely debated, as some industries sought to use environmental regulations as subtle "non-tariff barriers" to foreign competitors. See Chapters 11 and 15.

20 Note also that the Pure Food and Drug Act was not concerned strictly with health protection, but equally with product quality and efficacy, protecting consumers and businesses from changes in content by unscrupulous competitors. "Adulteration" in this sense included not only the addition of hazards to health, such as decomposed or otherwise unsanitary materials, but also substitution of cheaper ingredients or removal of valuable ones, or untruthful or deceptive labeling (Tobey 1926, 191).

21 34 Stat. 768. A federal pesticide law was passed in 1948, but contained only weak regulatory authority. The initial federal clean air and clean water laws were enacted in the 1950s and amended in the 1960s, but contained no significant federal regulatory authority. This changed only with the passage of the Clean Air Act in 1970. Previous laws limited federal authority to research, technical assistance, and coordinative responsibilities to encourage more active environmental protection programs on the part of the states. See more detailed discussion in later chapters.

Chapter 8: Progressivism: Conservation in the Public Interest

1 National Environmental Policy Act of 1969 (NEPA), 42 USCA 4321 *et seq.*

2 Among the few not created until much later were the Council on Environmental Quality, Environmental Protection Agency, National Oceanic and Atmospheric Administration, Department of Energy, and National Institute for Environmental Health Sciences.

3 Favorable policies included obvious gifts such as the railroad land grants but also more fundamental assets such as the legal concept of incorporation itself. "Corporations" would not even exist except that government policies allow individuals to pool assets in a single legal entity, then allow the individuals to limit their economic liability to the sum of those assets, and finally, allow the corporation itself to exercise the same rights and privileges as an individual citizen except with far greater economic power and influence (Horwitz 1988, 53–55; Handlin 1945).

4 This narrow view of its mission may seem surprising to modern readers, for whom the Corps has often been characterized as an ambitious agency, always seeking funds for all sorts of economically and environmentally questionable water projects (see e.g. Maass 1951; Laycock 1970). In the nineteenth century, however, its perspective was apparently shaped both by the limited expertise of its staff in navigation-related engineering and by the political conflicts through much of the century as to whether federal funding was even constitutional for purposes broader than navigation (Hays 1969 [1958], 8).

5 Note too that the Newlands Act was intended to provide irrigation water only to homesteaders, and to that end explicitly limited beneficiaries to 160 acres per landowner. In practice, however, larger farm operators systematically evaded this restriction, with the support of their political representatives and agency officials (Gates 1968, 655, 689–90).

6 The time required for congressional debate often allowed speculators to establish claims in the

meantime. Also, federal river and harbor projects were approved individually as earmarked line items, creating incentives for legislators to compete for them on purely selfish grounds rather than to approve those that were the most sensible and cost-effective.

7 Federal funding of river and harbor projects had long been advocated on the grounds that they would enhance interstate commerce; that they would be too costly for local or even state governments alone to finance, and their benefits shared too widely for states and localities to recoup; and that the federal government, therefore, was the only authority with jurisdiction broad enough both to finance them and to recoup their benefits. However, it was also obvious to any congressman or local booster that every federal expenditure provided concentrated benefits to the particular place where it was spent. The resulting pattern of legislative behavior, by which statutory appropriations are earmarked to benefit particular states and congressional districts, is commonly known as "pork-barrel" funding; the process by which such appropriations bills are passed, by assembling into a single bill enough such projects to attract the votes of a majority, is known as "logrolling." The appropriateness and even the constitutionality of such expenditures was debated throughout the early nineteenth century: for examples of the arguments on each side, see e.g. Smith 1971a, 176–253, 584–86.

8 This concern had already produced laws in 1890 and 1899 requiring federal approval of all proposed dams.

9 Policy disputes over public control of hydropower sites and coal-lands management were at the heart of the notorious "Ballinger-Pinchot affair" in 1909, in which Forest Service chief and former Roosevelt advisor Gifford Pinchot accused President Taft's Secretary of the Interior, Richard Ballinger, of misconduct in the approval of Alaskan coal land claims. Pinchot was ultimately fired for insubordination. The real issues concerned Ballinger's willingness to retreat from the Roosevelt/ Pinchot commitment to developing natural resources as public rather than private enterprises, particularly for hydropower development (Hays 1969 [1958], 147–74).

10 The provision allowing sale of timber was inserted as a compromise with mining interests who wanted continued access to timber from these lands, and the law also reopened these lands to mining claims even though they were reserved from other forms of entry (Hays 1969 [1958], 37; Gates 1968, 568–69). An important modern sequel to this act was an environmental lawsuit in the 1970s which challenged the Forest Service proposal for clear-cutting of the Monongahela National Forest in West Virginia on grounds that clear-cutting removed far more than the "dead, mature, or large growth trees" authorized by the 1897 law. The Supreme Court reluctantly agreed, leading Congress to pass a pivotal new forest management act in 1976. See discussion in Chapter 14.

11 Many were appointed based on political patronage, and the GLO was a long-standing target of criticism for abuses of the public land laws more generally.

12 Pinchot actually envisioned a more ambitious model for the Forest Service, as a largely self-financing public enterprise supported by commodity user fees, similar to the original idea of the Reclamation Service. The 1905 act provided for a special earmarked fund placing the proceeds of forest commodity sales under the discretionary control of the Secretary of Agriculture, but this fund was abolished in 1907 when Pinchot sought to have it made permanent (Hays 1969 [1958], 46).

13 Pinchot's primary example of "waste," for instance, was forest fires, which he argued were not part of the "natural order of things" but were rather a wasteful and destructive phenomenon "wholly within the control of men," which the human race had a duty to control (Pinchot 1910, 44–46). Scientists today would argue that forest fires are very much a part of the natural order, and even essential to the maintenance of prairies and the regeneration of some forest ecosystems. As to the appropriate time horizon for conservation, Pinchot was equally emphatic: "Conservation demands the welfare of this generation first, and afterwards the welfare of the generations to follow. . . . The development of our natural resources and the fullest use of them for the present generation is the first duty of this generation" (Pinchot 1910, 42, 44).

14 The peak year for national forest logging before World War II was 1907, with a cut of 960 million board feet, representing only 2 percent of the total national timber cut (Steen 1976, 90).

15 Pinchot actually wrote the charge himself.

16 Despite new statutory mandates, and growing criticism both from reputable outside studies and from within the Forest Service, the total annual cut has remained constant at about eleven billion board feet of timber per year. One possible reason is the power of logging interests, and of local communities which receive payments in lieu of taxes amounting to 25 percent of all federal timber sales revenues. Another is the bureaucratic interest of the agency itself, which since the Knutson-Vandenberg Act of 1930 has received discretionary funds, currently amounting to an estimated 20 percent of its budget, from the proceeds of timber sales (Wilkinson 1992, 168–71).

17 Some hydropower dam sites were reserved as potential "ranger stations."

18 During the ten days before signing it, however, Roosevelt added seventeen million more acres to the national forests.

19 The Weeks Act was the primary source of today's eastern national forests up and down the Appalachian Mountain chain, from New Hampshire to the Carolinas.

20 These prices were reduced in 1873 to $20 per acre, or $10 if more than fifteen miles distant from a rail line. Over six hundred thousand acres of coal lands were purchased under this system during the following fifty years, before the government changed its policy from sale to leasing of fuel mineral lands in the Mineral Leasing Act of 1920 (Gates 1968, 724–25; Hibbard 1924, 519).

21 Unlike other mining claims, under the Mineral Leasing Act the claimant has no vested right to mine. Permission must be granted by the government, and the government receives a royalty ranging from 10 to 25 percent of the proceeds. Leases are for fixed terms, usually five years for oil and gas and twenty years for coal, which can be renegotiated if renewed. The government can require reasonably prompt development, and cancel the lease if it is merely held or misused, and it can also require environmental standards and other restrictions in lease conditions (Wilkinson 1992, 53–54).

22 Roosevelt's ideas drew heavily on the rising movement for "scientific management" in business and industry, based on the principles of Frederick Taylor ("Taylorism"), who demonstrated through time-and-motion studies and other experiments the vastly superior performance of routinized production processes that were designed for optimum physical and economic efficiency (Hays 1969 [1958]).

23 Emerson and other Transcendentalists articulated the view that Earth is beautiful as an expression of its Creator, and that humans should therefore seek "the miraculous in the common," and find God in nature and wilderness (Emerson 1903 [1836]). His contemporary Henry David Thoreau argued that one must find *oneself* in nature, and thus learn how to live rather than merely to make a living. Consumed with human estrangement from nature, Thoreau rejected "getting and spending" as a model for life, distrusted the Industrial Revolution, and pleaded for national nature preserves in 1858, more than a decade before Yellowstone Park was first set aside. These voices articulated American versions of European Romanticism, but were well ahead of their time in the political sphere. Emerson wrote poetry and Thoreau a private journal; while they wrote the West was being settled, forests were cut over and stripped for agriculture or abandoned, the beaver and bison driven almost to extinction for their skins, the passenger pigeons hunted to extinction. But their ideas were to have important influence in later policy debates.

24 Other voices for non-commodity values included William Bartram (1996 [1791]), a naturalist contemporary of Thomas Jefferson and Daniel Boone; John James Audubon, a Haitian of the same period whose bird paintings heightened public interest in nature; Francis Parkman, historian of the westward migration (*The Oregon Trail*), who described the wilderness of the American West (Parkman 1969 [1849]); and George Catlin, whose paintings and travel writings documented the rapidly disappearing life of the Native American peoples of the Great Plains and of the "wilderness" west of white settlement. A scientific basis for environmental understanding was also emerging in the European literature, both in the traditions of German forestry and in Charles Darwin's exposition of the principles of evolution, natural selection, and the "web of life."

25 In retrospect, evidence suggests that the city's real motives had more to do with the profitability of hydroelectric power than with water needs, and the real beneficiary ultimately was the Pacific Gas and Electric Company (Wilkins 1995, 236–38).

26 According to Hays, Pinchot's opposition to "preservationists" revealed his basic view that the federal lands should be developed for commercial use rather than preserved from it. His major problem therefore was to restrain the influence of those who wished to leave them in their natural condition, untouched by lumberman or stockman. "The object of our policy," he told the Society of American Foresters in 1903, "is not to preserve the forests because they are beautiful . . . or because they are refuges for the wild creatures of the wilderness . . . but . . . [because they are] the making of prosperous homes. . . . Every other consideration comes as secondary" (Hays 1969 [1958], 41–42, 189–91).

27 Many national parks also were subject to preexisting claims and use rights, ranging from land claim "inholdings," which allowed privileged residences within the parks, to far more damaging mining operations still allowed to continue under the 1872 General Mining Act.

28 The first session of the National Conservation Congress in 1909, for instance, included speeches on the conservation of peace and friendship among nations, the conservation of the morals of youth, the conservation of children's lives through the elimination of child labor, the conservation of civic beauty, the elimination of waste in education and war, and the conservation of the Anglo-Saxon race (Hays 1969 [1958], 176).

Chapter 9: Administering the Environment: Subgovernments and Stakeholders

1 The regimentation of military life in both world wars exposed many young adults for the first time to organized recreational activities. Some historians credit this exposure for the subsequent dramatic rise in interest in recreation, parks, and leisure activities more generally (Armstrong et al. 1976, 562–70).

2 Herbert Hoover, an engineer and businessman, was director of the Food Administration during the First World War, and later Secretary of Commerce in the early 1920s before being elected president in 1928.

3 The widespread use of mass-market advertising also emerged in this period, spurred by the success of wartime propaganda for war bond purchases, by the incentives of large-scale producers to create larger national markets for mass-produced products, and by a new federal excess-profits tax — aimed at wartime profiteering — which created an incentive for businesses to redirect profits into market development expenditures.

4 The Mineral Leasing Act of 1920 arose in part from these wartime and postwar strategic concerns, as did the creation of Naval Petroleum Reserves on federal lands in the West.

5 Hoover was a more active president in some respects than Harding or Coolidge, such as in his support for water resource development: the Saint Lawrence and Mississippi waterways and Boulder Dam, for instance. Some historians have therefore viewed him as a constructive conservation leader who prepared the way for many of Franklin Roosevelt's New Deal conservation programs (Swain 1963, 165–66). His vision of governance, however, was limited to voluntary cooperation by businesses rather than formal regulation by "demon government," and to management of environmental assets by corporate trade associations rather than by government agencies. He was at odds both with Progressives in the Republican mold of Theodore Roosevelt and with Franklin Roosevelt's New Deal ideas of active national planning (Schlesinger 1986, 377–87).

6 The land-use case was double-edged in its impact, upholding government power to regulate in order to protect property owners against conflicting land uses, but in a situation where the proposed use was not a noxious industry but an apartment house. The mining case prevented the government from regulating land subsidence on the grounds that this took away without compensation the company's right to mine the coal underneath.

7 In the 1960s this pattern led political scientists to posit a "clientele capture" theory of administrative agency behavior, in place of their Progressive "public interest" image (e.g. McConnell 1966; Lowi 1969). Others argued that agencies worked *better,* and more pragmatically, if they interacted with their external political constituencies rather than relying on apolitical expertise ("partisan mutual adjustment": see Lindblom 1965).

8 A similar recent example was the policy strategy of EPA Administrator William Reilly under the Bush administration, which emphasized voluntary incentives for industries to adopt pollution prevention measures. Examples included the "33/50 Program," by which industries would pledge voluntary reductions in their toxic pollutant emissions by specified deadlines, and the "Green Lights" program, under which they would receive EPA recognition for voluntarily substituting more energy-efficient lighting.

9 The "Smokey the Bear" campaign to promote public forest fire awareness was considered one of the great success stories of Forest Service history. Ironically, however, later ecological research raised serious questions about the wisdom of this campaign, noting that many forest fires are of natural origin (particularly lightning), play essential roles in some ecosystems (allowing some valuable species to regenerate, and reducing competitor species), and even serve to burn off deadwood before it builds up to the point of a major conflagration (Schiff 1962; Pyne 1984).

10 The 1928 McSweeney-McNary Act, which culminated this effort, established continuing statutory authority for a forest research program in the USFS, as well as eleven forest experiment stations and a ten-year budget for each.

11 The Park Service also took advantage of wartime restrictions on foreign travel to promote park tourism, and of postwar nativist rhetoric — anti-immigration prejudice, the "Red scare," and conservative "Americanism" — to promote the parks as a fundamental manifestation of the national heritage (Swain 1963, 142).

12 Mather succeeded in capturing significant national forest lands for expansion of the national park system, including the Teton Mountains, Mount Whitney, and parts of the Kings Canyon area adjacent to Sequoia National Park. He also gained authorization for a new series of eastern national parks, including Shenandoah, Great Smoky Mountains, and Mammoth Cave National Parks (Swain 1963, 137).

13 By 1933 there were 102 federal wildlife refuges. Migratory waterfowl posed a particular sort of commons problem, since not only did their overall numbers need to be sustained against the cumulative effects of individual hunters and poachers, but they often were located in different states before and after their reproductive periods, leaving some states with the responsibility of protecting them to adulthood and others the benefits of then hunting them. An interesting footnote to the 1918 Migratory Bird Treaty Act was its predecessor, the 1913 Migratory Bird Act, which authorized federal jurisdiction over migratory waterfowl under the interstate commerce clause of the Constitution. This law was struck down by two federal courts, among the few rebuffs to expansionary use of the commerce clause to justify environmental regulation. As an alternative, the Wilson administration negotiated a similar treaty with Canada, and Congress and the Supreme Court approved it as an exercise of the federal treaty power (Bean 1983 [1977], 19–21; *Missouri v. Holland,* 252 U.S. 416, 1920).

14 The Norbeck-Anderson Act, passed in 1929, declared the refuges inviolate sanctuaries protected by federal wardens (Swain 1963, 41–43).

15 The Kaibab preserve (Grand Canyon National Game Preserve) was in fact on Forest Service land, and the hunting prohibition on it was invoked not by the Biological Survey but by the Arizona Game Commission. Its disastrous result, however, forced recognition that both ecological understanding and active management rather than merely preservation were necessary to a viable wildlife management policy (Leopold 1933).

16 The English grazing commons, which Hardin used as his example of destructive self-interest, were in fact managed sustainably for centuries by just such mutual controls at the local level. They were ultimately destroyed not by the self-interested decisions of the shepherds, but by landowners who enclosed them and converted them to other uses for market agriculture (Buck 1985).

17 Oil policy in the 1920s also produced one of the famous scandals of American political history, the so-called "Teapot Dome" affair, which ultimately sent a Secretary of the Interior to prison for accepting a bribe. Teapot Dome, Wyoming, was the site of one of several naval petroleum reserves established by Presidents Taft and Wilson to meet future military fuel needs. The Harding administration, however, took the position that they should be opened for development rather than

"locked up" for the future, and so transferred them to the Interior Department, whose secretary, Albert Fall, leased them without public notice to two personal friends. Fall was convicted of accepting a bribe when it was discovered in 1924 that these friends had concurrently made several hundred thousand dollars' worth of personal loans to him, and he became an election-year symbol of corruption and cronyism in the Harding administration. The real issue behind the scandal, however, was the outrage of Gifford Pinchot and other conservationists that Fall was reversing two decades of Progressive policy principles and reverting to laissez-faire policies of natural resource giveaways to influential businesses. Fall also had proposed to transfer the national forests from the Agriculture Department back to Interior (Noggle 1962; Swain 1963, 66–69).

18 Modern resource economists, for example, have argued that the only way to achieve sustainable rates of use of a non-renewable resource such as fossil fuels is to price them at the cost of both mitigating their environmental impacts and phasing in sustainable substitutes for them by the time they are exhausted (Tietenberg 1992, 131).

19 The energy crisis of the early 1970s provided a rare glimpse of the hazards of this policy, when a politically motivated cutoff of Middle Eastern oil caused serious shortages and sudden price increases. Energy conservation measures increased dramatically in response, and energy use rates slowed significantly over much of the following decade. By the 1990s, however, U.S. energy price levels (adjusted for inflation) had returned to historic low levels, along with even higher dependence on foreign suppliers and renewed complacency (Blair 1993, 11–13).

20 Related incentives to conserve natural gas may have encouraged the subsequent capital investments in gas pipelines that made this far cleaner fuel available as a substitute for coal in urban heating. Natural gas was found with oil and often simply vented in the process of oil pumping, until the Interior Department began charging five cents per one thousand cubic feet for all natural gas wasted (Swain 1963, 65).

21 FDR had not only a sentimental love of nature that dated back to his childhood, but over twenty years of practical personal experience in scientific forest management on his 1,250-acre Hyde Park estate. As a New York state senator (1911–13) he chaired the state Commission on Forest, Fish, and Game and helped create the state Department of Conservation. As New York's governor (1928–32) he championed state programs for reforestation and forest management, land utilization planning, water power protection and development, pollution control, and other initiatives which foreshadowed key elements of his New Deal programs (Owen 1983, 3–11).

22 A further difference was one of style of governance: TR emphasized efficient management by professional foresters, engineers and other specialists, while FDR's New Dealers were far more pragmatic generalists; "idea people" willing to innovate to achieve both socioeconomic and environmental goals and to use public policies as experiments (Schlesinger 1965, 18–19).

23 Another relief agency, the Works Progress Administration (WPA), built hundreds of schools, more than fifteen thousand parks and playing fields, and over eleven thousand swimming pools, golf courses, outdoor theaters, band shells and other outdoor-recreation facilities (Armstrong et al. 1976, 563–64). In addition, WPA provided jobs for unemployed scholars, teachers, and artists, among others, and from its support came important public art, photography, and historical scholarship projects. The Resettlement Administration also produced two classic films — *The Plow That Broke the Plains* and *The River* — portraying the Dust Bowl and floods of the Depression years as the consequences of human failure to conserve soil and water.

24 Despite his otherwise conservative Republican philosophy, Herbert Hoover as an engineer and former Secretary of the Navy and of Commerce was a strong advocate of waterway development projects: he was an active supporter of the Saint Lawrence Seaway and of completion of the "Lakes to the Gulf" system of deep-channel navigation.

25 Swain notes that once completed, Boulder Dam "watered more than a million acres of land; . . . generated in excess of 3,000,000 kilowatt-hours of hydroelectric power; and . . . regulated the flow of the Colorado River, providing both a constant supply of water and flood control for the Imperial Valley" (Swain 1963, 90).

26 Among the best-known examples are the projects that provided cheap water to convert Califor-

nia's Imperial and Central Valleys into large-scale, federally subsidized agribusiness operations (Gates 1968, 689–90; see also Worster 1985; Reisner 1986).

27 Bureaucratic rivalry and infighting were major features of this period, as the Corps and Bureau of Reclamation competed for hegemony over key river systems (the Missouri River basin conflict in particular was resolved only by a formal joint report to Congress in 1944, the Pick-Sloan Plan), and the SCS lobbied openly against both in favor of smaller headwater dams which it would build.

28 More recent extensions of such requirements, such as President Reagan's executive order requiring that environmental regulatory proposals be justified by economic benefits in excess of their cost, were even more problematic, since environmental regulations were intended to protect health and ecological processes rather than to promote economic development, and these costs were borne by regulated businesses — which were also the causes of the health and ecological damage — rather than by the government (see Executive Order 12,291, 1981; Smith 1984).

29 Chief protagonists were Henry Ford for private industry and Senator George Norris for the Progressives. Water-powered nitrate production was a process common to both explosives and fertilizers.

30 In Roosevelt's words, TVA would be "a corporation clothed with the power of government but possessed of the flexibility and initiative of a private enterprise. It should be charged with the broadest possible duty of planning for the proper use, conservation and development of the natural resources of the Tennessee River drainage basin and its adjoining territory for the general social and economic welfare of the nation" (Nixon 1957a, 151).

31 As stated in one of its publications, for instance, responding to political pressures to give greater priority to recreation in the operation of its reservoirs, "No matter how persuasively the claims of recreation may be pressed, the management of TVA must adhere to a plan of operation which achieves the benefits construction was undertaken to provide. . . . Priority was established in the law. . . . Power comes last of the three major objectives of TVA's existing system of reservoir control, but the requirements of all three must be met before the demands of other water uses are met" (TVA 1966, 47–48).

32 TVA was governed by a three-member board of directors. Its first chairman, Arthur Morgan, like FDR envisioned TVA as providing not merely a few specific services, such as water management and power and fertilizer production, but a comprehensive quasi-governmental program at a river-basin scale. In his vision it would be a true regional subgovernment, including self-help cooperatives, "subsistence homesteads," industrial development incentives, health and housing improvements, educational reform, and other initiatives. Co-directors Harcourt Morgan and David Lilienthal, however, were skeptical of this vision, and preferred limiting TVA more closely to grass-roots service and constituency-building. Their one exception was electric power production, as they did not trust the private electric power companies as partners (Schlesinger 1965, 327–34).

33 Tellico Dam eventually was built, due to political chicanery by Tennessee politicians, after a Supreme Court decision stopped it and several independent evaluations showed it to be unjustified economically as well as environmentally (Wheeler and McDonald 1986).

34 The Browns Ferry fire was a serious embarrassment to the nuclear power industry, occurring just after the release of a major risk assessment study, the Rasmussen report, which claimed to show that because of numerous independent safety systems a serious nuclear power accident was virtually inconceivable. The Browns Ferry fire, however, was caused by a workman using a candle to search for leaks in an area directly under the control room, where all these systems converged in a single vulnerable location.

35 The Forest Service had controlled grazing by permits and fees on the national forest lands since 1906, but no such management regime yet existed on the vast public lands remaining under the General Land Office in the Interior Department.

36 58 Stat. 887.

37 The six basic commodity crops were cotton, corn, wheat, rice, peanuts, and tobacco. Dairy products were soon added. Left out of this group were over one hundred other crops plus the livestock

sector (Paarlberg 1989, 42). The initial program was to be financed by excise taxes, but when these were invalidated by the Supreme Court, funding was provided from the general treasury (Schopsmeier 1986, 225).

38 Key statutes included the Soil Conservation and Domestic Allotment Act of 1936 and the Agricultural Adjustment Act of 1938 (Rasmussen et al. 1976, 4–8).

39 President Truman won a close election in 1948, for instance, in part by accusing Republicans of betraying the farmers (Schopsmeier 1986, 226).

40 Section 3 of the law, for instance, stated that "preference shall be given in the issuance of grazing permits to those within or near a district who are landowners engaged in the livestock business" (Gates 1968, 617).

41 Roosevelt's Agriculture Secretary, Henry Wallace, foresaw these risks and argued strenuously against the bill, but the president ultimately sided with Ickes and signed it (Nixon 1957a, 299–303, 306–14).

42 This user veto was ruthlessly applied during the 1940s in a vendetta by Senator Pat McCarran of Nevada against the Grazing Service. McCarran reacted to proposals for grazing fee increases with congressional investigations, draconian budget and staff cuts (totaling two-thirds of its staff in 1947), and systematic intimidation. Only a well-publicized counterattack by western historian Bernard DeVoto and others blocked the stockmen from destroying federal conservation policies and taking over the rangelands entirely (Gates 1968, 617–29). This controversy provided one of the starkest examples of interest-group capture of the agencies, which led political scientists in the 1950s and '60s to reject the Progressive "public interest" paradigm and replace it with the "interest-group pluralism" and "agency capture" theories of agency behavior (Foss 1960; McConnell 1966).

43 The Brownlow Commission recommendations foreshadowed the later creation of the Department of Health, Education, and Welfare, and the moving of the Bureau of Roads from Agriculture into a new Department of Transportation (Brownlow et al. had suggested a Department of Public Works).

44 President Nixon's Ash Commission, for instance, in 1969 unsuccessfully recommended reconfiguring the Interior Department into a Department of the Environment, with the addition of the Forest Service and the Army Corps of Engineers.

45 Ickes was a liberal Republican whose experience went all the way back to Theodore Roosevelt, and the longest-serving Interior Secretary in American history. He made major contributions to the expansion of the wildlife refuge and national park systems and to reform of the public land laws, among other initiatives. His ambition for a larger "Department of Conservation," however, ultimately antagonized too many opposing interests, and dissipated his effectiveness in bureaucratic infighting (Futrell 1993, 33–34).

Chapter 10: Superpower and Supermarket

1 An entire volume could and should be written on the overall impacts of war on the environment, especially the effects of technology-intensive modern mass warfare. Examples include not only the direct impacts of bombardment and destruction but also the more widespread if lesser impacts of troop movements and fortifications, and the pervasive and often irreversible consequences of mobilization, materiel production, postwar reconversion, and toxic wastes.

2 The massive hydroelectric power capacity generated by federal dams in the Columbia River basin, for instance, powerfully reshaped the environment and economy of the Pacific Northwest region during the war years. The Bonneville Power Administration grew rapidly into the second largest power system in the nation, and its cheap electricity powered the development of the aircraft and aluminum industries, the Hanford plutonium production facility for nuclear weapons and fuels, and many other West Coast defense production facilities. Both Cold War military pressures and postwar consumer demand promoted continued use of "free" water resources to keep electric rates cheap, both for manufacturers and customers and for government itself as a military purchaser (Armstrong et al. 1976, 360).

3 By one estimate, for example, it required three trees to equip each soldier: timber for barracks, bridge, and railroad construction, specialized light woods for aircraft, packing crates for war materiel, cellulose for explosives, resins for flamethrowers, and myriad other uses. Comparable pressures were imposed on minerals and other resources (Steen 1973, 246–50).

4 From 180 to 300 billion kilowatt-hours per year, and from under 20 to 30 quadrillion British thermal units respectively (U.S. Department of Commerce 1975, P40–57, Q565, S32, M83).

5 Similar raids were attempted during the Korean War: the Defense Department turned down proposals to use the Everglades National Park as a bombing range, and the National Park Service deflected a proposal for a reservoir in Capitol Reef National Monument in Utah (Richardson 1973, 59).

6 Federal expenditures for research and development increased ten times over from 1952 to 1970, from $1.5 to $15 million (U.S. Department of Commerce 1975, W126).

7 Both conservation and natural resource economics also emerged as explicit fields of study during the early postwar years, and a few prophetic books, such as Fairfield Osborn's *Our Plundered Planet* (1948), and William Vogt's *The Road to Survival* (1948), sounded alarms over global resource destruction and overpopulation. The University of Michigan, for instance, in 1952 became the first university to rename its School of Forestry a School of Natural Resources, creating in it a Department of Conservation distinct from its departments of forestry, fisheries, and wildlife management. Several major philanthropic foundations funded the creation of the distinguished resource economics research center Resources for the Future in Washington, D.C. In resource economics, see for instance the seminal work of Kapp (1950), Herfindahl (1961), Barnett and Morse (1963), and others during this period. These laid the foundations for the emergence of environmental economics in the 1960s (see especially Krutilla 1967; Kneese and Bower 1968, 1979).

8 As of 1952, for instance, the United States' largest supplier of chromium for steel-making was Turkey; it imported copper from Africa and South America, bauxite and petroleum from South America, and tin from Bolivia and Asia. It was totally dependent on foreign sources for three key materials (tin, quartz crystal, and industrial diamonds) and becoming increasingly import-dependent for twenty-five others; and it produced only 55 percent of the lead, 26 percent of the antimony, 10 percent of the cobalt, 9 percent of the mercury, and 8 percent of the manganese that it used (PCMP 1952, 156).

9 In the Pacific Northwest, for instance, demobilization policies encouraged growth in aluminum and other light-metals production by making wartime plants and electric power available at low cost (Armstrong et al. 1976, 360).

10 As early as the wartime mid-1940s, the United States had become increasingly dependent first on offshore oil extraction from the outer continental shelf—accompanying the development of new drilling platforms that made ocean oil wells feasible—and subsequently on foreign sources. With the dismantling of the British Empire worldwide resulting from World War II, American oil companies moved into the resulting vacuum in Iran, Saudi Arabia, and other oil-rich countries and began extracting growing quantities of oil at far lower cost than was possible in the now-declining known domestic oil fields.

11 Among these federal subsidies were the initial federal investments in developing nuclear technology itself, inexpensive charges for nuclear fuel refinement costs, liberal terms for treatment of nuclear power stations as "research" rather than commercial production facilities, underestimation of the full costs of the nuclear fuel cycle and of the future costs for reactor closure and decommissioning, and federal laws such as the Price-Anderson Act of 1957, which asserted statutory limits on the utilities' financial liability for any mishaps that might occur.

12 Most members of Congress in fact simply did not want to know what was being done in their name in the field of nuclear secrets, lest they either be held responsible for it or be accused of un-American disloyalty—the McCarthy era was then at its height—if they criticized it (Udall 1994, 7).

13 The AEC asserted preemptive jurisdiction over all regulation of radiation hazards per se, for instance, but until the enactment of the National Environmental Policy Act in 1970 it successfully

disclaimed any responsibility for nuclear reactors' non-radiation effects, such as thermal pollution of watercourses, aesthetic nuisance, or non-radiation-related conflicts with adjoining land uses (*State of New Hampshire vs. AEC,* 406 F. 2d 170 [1969], cert. denied 23 L. Ed. 748 [1969]). This policy left state environmental agencies angry and frustrated, since it allowed them no effective input during the design and construction process, and confronted them instead with faits accomplis when costly facilities were already fully constructed and poised to begin operation.

14 See further discussion in Chapter 11.

15 Annual U.S. birth rates had been as high as forty per thousand in the nineteenth century but were balanced by high infant mortality rates due to contagious disease (over 100 per thousand up to 1918). By World War II, birth rates had declined to about twenty per thousand, and death rates to less than fifty per thousand. Infant mortality rates continued to decline, to less than thirty per thousand by 1954 and to about twenty-one by 1970 (U.S. Department of Commerce 1975, B5, B181–82).

16 TVA's rationale for Tellico Dam, for instance, was a speculative industrial development area that did not yet exist. Others claimed inflated benefits for creating recreational lakes, even when other such areas already existed nearby.

17 Other influential opponents included the articulate western columnist Bernard DeVoto and a more self-interested California lobby group which stood to lose future water supplies from upper basin development (Richardson 1973). U.S. House Speaker Sam Rayburn was quoted as saying that congressmen received more mail in protest against Echo Park Dam than on any other subject (Sundquist 1968, 337).

18 The taxpayers of Massachusetts, New York, and other states, for instance, would each have had to pay larger shares of the cost than those of Colorado.

19 As Bernard DeVoto once advised his fellow westerners, "Don't snoot those unfortunate [easterners] too loudly or too obnoxiously. You might make them so mad that they would stop paying for your water development" (Richardson 1973, 61).

20 The Bureau of Reclamation failed to find new missions as the number of good unbuilt dam sites in the West diminished, and between 1950 and 1955 its appropriations dropped by more than 50 percent (Foresta 1984, 53). The Corps of Engineers continued, and thus became the main target for the rising environmental movement of the 1960s and '70s.

21 Another trigger was an act of crude bullying by the Internal Revenue Service, which in 1966 canceled the Sierra Club's tax-exempt status in retaliation for its successful campaigns against several water projects, thus threatening its donations and therefore its continued existence. This tactic, however, both radicalized the group's leadership and inadvertently pushed it into more overtly political tactics (Futrell 1993, 36–37).

22 Examples included Gateway National Recreation Area (New York), Cape Hatteras (North Carolina), Fire Island (New York), Indiana Dunes (Indiana), Pictured Rocks (Michigan), and others. One justification was to preserve these shorelines in their own right. A second was to meet burgeoning recreational demand, and a third was to relieve recreation pressures on the truly unique national parks by providing additional opportunities for mass recreation nearer to urban areas.

23 Ironically, however, this vigorous acquisition program catalyzed an opposition movement of self-interested landowners around the borders of existing parks, particularly those whose antecedents' historical land claims had given them ownership of privileged "inholdings" within the park boundaries, and who now resisted being bought out. These inholders became one of the principal constituencies of the so-called "Sagebrush Rebellion" of Western opposition to federal environmental management in the late 1970s, whose interests the Reagan administration represented. Reagan's notorious Secretary of the Interior, James Watt, actively supported the inholders' agenda, and ended the use of the Land and Water Conservation Fund for parklands acquisition (Culhane 1984, 308–10). Other important initiatives of the Johnson administration included the National Historic Preservation Act (1966), Wild and Scenic Rivers Act (1968), National Trails Act (1968), and a White House Conference on Natural Beauty in America.

24 The Forest Management Act of 1897, the statutory authority for management of the national forest reserves, had specifically authorized removal of dead, mature, or large-growth trees, individually marked and designated; clear-cutting at that time was considered forest destruction rather than good standard practice. By the 1950s, however, the Forest Service had adopted the industry's practices, arguing that clear-cutting and replacement with "even-aged management" ("tree farming") was the "modern" approach to forestry. Its position was challenged in court in the early 1970s in a lawsuit over clear-cutting on the Monongahela National Forest in West Virginia, which led to fundamental rewriting of the forest management laws in 1976.

25 On the first such cooperative sustained yield unit created, for instance, 60 percent of the land was private but 82 percent of the standing timber was federal, as the private land had already been heavily logged (Steen 1976, 251–52, 285).

26 Particularly controversial was the Forest Service practice of "sanitary" logging of dead and dying trees in recreation areas such as the Deadman Creek area of the California Sierra, where the Sierra Club was strongly active (Steen 1976, 303).

27 Wilderness areas were legally as well as poetically defined as areas "where the earth and its community of life are untrammeled by man, where man himself is a visitor who does not remain . . . an area of undeveloped Federal land retaining its primeval character and influence, without permanent improvements or human habitation, which is protected and managed so as to preserve its natural conditions."

28 As one noted political scientist pointed out, foresters were technically competent to identify resource problems and to propose an array of solutions, but lacked training that enabled them to choose between uses such as lumber and scenery: expertise in one aspect did not confer competence in all (Grant McConnell in the Sierra Club bulletin in 1958, quoted in Steen 1976, 306). Also, prior to the 1970s, the Forest Service asserted a more expansive view of this administrative discretion than did many other federal agencies, arguing that its land management was "proprietary" rather than sovereign — that is, that it was simply managing the government's property, like a post office or government office building — and therefore was not subject to the same degree of public participation and scrutiny as other agencies.

29 The growth of suburbs was not itself new: it became widespread in the nineteenth century, for instance, as new forms of transportation — steam ferries, omnibuses, commuter railroads, horsecars, elevated railroads, and cable cars — opened access to expanding residential areas on the edges of cities. Rising automobile ownership after World War I further encouraged the trend, coupled with government road-building programs financed by fuel taxes, and made possible for the first time suburbs of much lower densities remote from public transit. A federal aid program for highway construction was begun in 1916, and gasoline taxes were introduced by Oregon in 1919 and adopted by virtually every state by 1929 to finance road-building (Jackson 1985, 163–68, 172–77, 248–50).

30 Previous mortgages had been limited to one-half to two-thirds the value of the property, requiring far higher down payments and at substantially higher interest rates than those that became available once the federal government guaranteed the loans. Only in 1933, indeed, was the concept of long-term, self-amortizing mortgages with uniform monthly payments even introduced, by Roosevelt's Home Owners Loan Corporation (Jackson 1985, 195–97, 203–05).

31 During the 1950s FHA-insured single-family housing starts consequently exceeded multifamily starts by a ratio of seven to one. FHA appraisal standards placed heavy weight on a neighborhood's "relative economic stability" and "protection from adverse influences," both of which strongly favored affluent and uniformly white suburbs over minority or even integrated urban neighborhoods. They also prohibited any facilities that would allow dwellings to be used as stores, offices, or rental units (Jackson 1985, 206–08 ff.).

32 The highway system was ostensibly intended to promote dispersion of industries, so that large cities could not be as efficiently targeted by Russian missiles, and to speed evacuation of cities in the event of nuclear attack.

33 The American Road Builders Association was formed in 1943 under the leadership of General

Motors. It included automobile manufacturers and dealers, truckers, the oil, rubber, asphalt and construction industries, their labor unions, state highway administrators, and others who stood to gain economically from increased road construction and highway travel. Benefits claimed for the interstate system included reductions in traffic congestion, in safety hazards, and in business transportation costs. There appears to have been no serious discussion of its negative effects: the destruction of neighborhoods and parks in the paths of the highways, the promotion of suburban sprawl and concurrent decline of central cities and public transportation alternatives, nor even the implications of earmarking such major tax revenues solely for highways rather than for transportation as a whole or other public needs (Jackson 1985, 248–50).

34 The creation of the interstate highways also triggered a bitter battle to forbid the visual blight of uncontrolled commercial signs and billboards, as had already occurred along many existing roads. A 1958 law offered a bonus to states that controlled billboards on interstate highways, but by 1965 only 194 miles (1 percent) had been protected. Only a federal mandate, it appeared, could compete with the influence of the Outdoor Advertising Council on state legislators who received the group's contributions as well as their advertising services during election campaigns. President Lyndon Johnson sponsored a White House Conference on Natural Beauty in 1965, and proposed new legislation to withhold 10 percent of federal highway funds from states that did not prohibit off-premises billboards in noncommercial areas of federal highways, remove noncomplying signs by 1970, and remove or screen junkyards. The law required compensation for removal of signs that were legal when erected, however, and left determination of "commercial areas" to the states. Both these provisions invited perennial pressure for rezoning of additional business areas and for costly compensation, and in fact they even weakened some state laws.

Chapter 11: The Rise of Modern Environmentalism

1 Examples included New Jersey, Pennsylvania, and later New York on the Delaware River, the nine states of the Ohio River basin, and the Great Lakes states, all in the 1920s (Tarr et al. 1980, 74).

2 Key provisions of the 1948 Federal Water Pollution Control Act, for instance, had actually been proposed as early as 1936.

3 Opposition centered on two points: first, there was no guarantee that the states would actually use the proposed revenue source (a tax on telephone use) to build wastewater treatment facilities, and second, poorer states received greater amounts in federal grants than they would from the telephone tax anyway (Sundquist 1968, 326–28).

4 Muskie was a former governor of Maine, who had championed water quality improvement at the state level to protect the lobster industry (Sundquist 1968, 349).

5 The idea of comprehensive, basin-wide water quality planning was a long-standing ideal, which produced fifteen detailed river-basin reports and some sixty sub-basin plans by the early 1950s. However, basin-wide planning was ultimately preempted by project-by-project funding practices: construction grants for wastewater treatment plants were given out to municipalities as they received political support, while regional planning funds were those most often cut when budgets were tightened, leaving the basin-wide plans as after-the-fact paper exercises (Dworsky 1971, 364).

6 Before 1948 water pollution activities were one responsibility of the Division of Sanitary Engineering under the Public Health Service's Bureau of State Services (BSS). In 1948 a separate Division of Water Pollution Control was created to administer the growing responsibilities created by the new Water Pollution Control Act, but in 1953 the Eisenhower administration demoted it once again to branch status under BSS and secured congressional approval for deep cuts in its budget. This reversal reflected Eisenhower's philosophical opposition to the growing federal role in water pollution control. However, these reverses galvanized political pressures from municipalities and their congressional supporters, who in 1965 finally succeeded in upgrading the water pollution agency's status and removing it from the Public Health Service entirely (Dworsky 1971, 279–84, 364).

7 In 1961, the editor of the *American Journal of Public Health* called for a "new look at the environ-

ment" and expressed a need to "rescue the public health profession from its present state of indecision" on this issue.

8 Interior had numerous missions that were natural complements to those of the Federal Water Quality Administration, such as river basin planning, water resource development, fish and wildlife conservation, outdoor recreation, and water resources research.

9 At least one commentator has argued that this reorganization was a fundamental mistake, and that the Public Health Service should simply have been given broader legal authority and adequate budget resources for a more effective environmental health program (Eisenbud 1978, 352–53).

10 Studies as far back as 1910, for example, established most of what needed to be known to control smoke, soot, and ash, and studies in the 1920s began to document the health hazards of carbon monoxide from urban automobile emissions as well (Dworsky 1971, 544–48).

11 Very few of these local ordinances, in turn, went so far as to require permits for air pollution emissions (those that did included Los Angeles, St. Louis, Pittsburgh, and New York City). Only seven maintained enforcement bureaus, and most were limited to responding to complaints. Enforcement was also limited to visual standards for smoke (such as visual grading by Ringelmann chart), and did not address other pollutants such as dust, fumes, or sulfur dioxide (Stern 1951, 35–37; Tarr 1985b, 528).

12 Air quality research was done under the Public Health Services's Industrial Hygiene Division; it was limited primarily to studies of pulmonary health effects of occupational exposures in mining, garment-making, and the so-called "dusty trades" (Dworsky 1971, 545–46, 567–70).

13 Public laws 89–272 and 89–675. Initial automotive standards called for significant reductions in tailpipe emissions of hydrocarbons and carbon monoxide, and 100 percent control of crankcase emissions, beginning with the 1968 model year. They did not deal with other important motor vehicle emissions, such as nitrogen oxides and lead, nor did they address diesel emissions (Dworsky 1971, 647–48).

14 The amendments also provided federal grants for solid waste disposal facilities to replace the traditional open-burning dumps, which were major sources of urban air pollution (Sundquist 1968, 368).

15 Fluoridation consisted of adding about one part fluoride per million parts of water to public water supplies during its treatment.

16 Editorial, *American Journal of Public Health* 42:1304 (1952).

17 Nuclear scientists and engineers had grown up as an unusually cohesive and secret scientific community, bound together by unique expertise, by common background in the physical sciences, and by security clearances which proscribed public discussion and debate of much of their work. Given their backgrounds, they had assumed that the only significant radiation hazard would be from direct exposure, and were unfamiliar with the possibility of bioaccumulation. The issue was first noticed in 1953, when physicists in Troy, New York, identified sharply elevated levels of environmental "background" radiation during and after a rainstorm, and traced these pollutants to fallout of nuclear materials from atmospheric testing of nuclear weapons half a nation away. It was first publicized the following year, when the crew of a Japanese fishing boat in the Pacific, the *Lucky Dragon,* was afflicted with severe radiation sickness from the fallout of nuclear tests in the South Pacific, which attracted a sudden increase in attention by biologists (Commoner 1971, 50–60).

18 Public health professionals too, who in 1950 had praised the Atomic Energy Commission for its leadership in setting standards and assuring radiation protection, by 1956 noted more soberly the possible biological effects of even low-level exposure, and in 1959 called for a far more conservative approach, arguing that "anything less . . . may jeopardize life on this small planet." (Editorials, *American Journal of Public Health* 40:1441 [1950], 46:1147 [1956], and 49:804 [1959].)

19 SIPI's board of directors included such distinguished scientists as Rene Dubos and Margaret Mead, and overlapped extensively with the Committee on Science and the Promotion of Human Welfare of the American Association for the Advancement of Science. It inaugurated a widely distributed magazine, *Scientist and Citizen,* which in 1969 became the magazine *Environment.*

20 Only one animal study had been done, showing some thyroid tumors in rats that had been fed high doses over two years.

21 The Agriculture Department later estimated that even farmers who had *not* misapplied the chemical lost ten million dollars' worth of sales due to the scare (Bosso 1987, 99–100). In 1971 EPA banned 3-AT from use on food crops, though still — according to some critics — without strong evidence of any serious risk to human health (Wildavsky 1995, 18–19).

22 Editorial, *American Journal of Public Health* 36:657 (1946). From the standpoint of acute toxicity, DDT was in fact far less toxic than other insecticides already in use, such as nicotine and arsenical compounds, and than others which were later substituted for it, such as the organophosphates. None of these, however, carried the ecological risks of persistent toxicity through bioaccumulation.

23 Editorial, *American Journal of Public Health* 38:709 (1948).

24 New pests could rapidly expand into the ecological niches vacated by the ones destroyed, and even the target species often evolved rapidly into pesticide-resistant strains.

25 The thalidomide tragedy, the discovery that a drug prescribed in Europe for pregnant women caused severe birth defects, was a leading news story at the time *Silent Spring* was published.

26 An editorial in the *American Journal of Public Health* reviewing *Silent Spring* (52:2111 [1962]), acknowledged that Carson had "called attention to a problem that cannot be dismissed" and that "some of the results have been devastating." It nonetheless referred to her findings only as demonstrating an "alleged" threat to nature, based on hypothetical examples and on "the most obvious and extreme cases." It went on to remind the reader that pesticides were "essential" to food production and that "man will continue to intervene and will continue to upset ecological balances," and urged that action be taken only after more research rather than on the basis of "emotions and conjecture."

27 E.g. Selznick 1949 (TVA), Maass 1951 (the Army Corps of Engineers), Foss 1960 (the Bureau of Land Management), Morgan 1965 (the Soil Conservation Service), and McConnell 1966 (the Forest Service and BLM).

28 Theodore Lowi, for instance, argued in 1969 that "interest-group liberalism" cannot plan, cannot achieve justice, and weakens democratic institutions by substituting informal bargaining for formal procedures. He proposed a "juridical democracy" in which all delegations of administrative discretion not accompanied by clear legislative standards for implementation would be invalidated.

29 These guidelines included the "Green Book" of the Federal Interagency River Basin Committee (1950), the Budget Bureau's Budget Circular A-47 (1942), Senate Document 87–97 (1962), and the U.S. Water Resource Council's *Principles and Standards for Planning Water and Related Land Resources* (1965), all cited in Andrews 1976a. Unlike later requirements such as environmental impact statements, however, these guidelines were imposed only by administrative authority rather than by statute, and as such were enforceable only by presidential decisions and congressional appropriations, not by citizen challenges through the courts.

30 *Office of Communication, United Church of Christ v. Federal Communications Commission,* 359 F. 2d 994 (1966), 425 F. 2d 543 (1969).

31 The Wilderness Act, for example, took eight years to pass, and even then included undercutting amendments demanded by House Interior Committee chairman Wayne Aspinall (D-Colo.) to allow continued mining (Sundquist 1968, 518–20).

32 In the early 1970s, for instance, the longtime power broker of the public lands, Rep. Wayne Aspinall, was suddenly upset by a young environmentalist lawyer from Denver who had lived in his district for less than a year.

33 Similar patterns continued in the 1970s. In the 1971–72 Congress, 81 percent of the urban representatives voted for pro-environmental protection positions, while representatives from rural areas of the South, Midwest and Great Plains/intermountain West consistently resisted them (Martis 1976, 328–34).

34 Eisenhower proposed, for instance, to "give away" a variety of federal lands and functions to state and local governments, and in some cases to private businesses, and even to consider dismantling

some major federal New Deal initiatives such as TVA and agricultural production controls. His Kestnbaum Commission and second Hoover Commission were charged to identify as many federal functions as possible that could be turned back to the states. By 1955, however, his commitment to serious reform had been worn down: "In his 8 years Eisenhower learned that farmers did not want to face a free market, Tennessee Valley consumers of electricity did not prefer free enterprise to socialism, and no group currently subsidized welcomed a return to the jungles of competition" (Graham 1976, 119–23). He also was not philosophically consistent in his commitment: his record also included major expansions of public works programs for highways, forest road-building, and water projects, of nuclear power development, and the largest peacetime deficit in history up to that time.

35 Caldwell went on to assist Senator Henry Jackson (D-Wash.) and others in crafting the National Environmental Policy Act of 1969, which spelled out both principles and implementing procedures for such a national environmental policy.

36 The declaration is attributed to biologist Barry Commoner in his *Science and Survival* (1966, 12). It was repeated in Paul and Anne Ehrlich's *The Population Bomb* (1968) and widely quoted in the press in the late '60s. More precisely, heavy pollution of some areas of the lake by municipal sewage, industrial petrochemical discharges, and agricultural runoff was one important factor in the lake's decline, along with poor fishery management, and invasion of the lake by sea lampreys due to opening of the St. Lawrence Seaway. These conditions caused accelerated eutrophication of the lake, a major shift in fish populations from cold-water lake trout to warm-water species, concerns about possible concentration of poisons in fish through ecological food-chains, and periodic anaerobic conditions with resulting fish kills and blooms of toxic blue-green algae.

37 Popular books of the period, for instance, included such titles as *Famine 1975!* (Paddock 1967), *The Population Bomb* (Ehrlich 1968), *Future Shock* (Toffler 1970), *Our Plundered Planet* (Osborn 1970), *The Diligent Destroyers* (Laycock 1970), *Perils of the Peaceful Atom* (Curtis and Hogan 1970), *Vanishing Air* (Esposito 1970), *Water Wasteland* (Zwick and Benstock 1971), *Too Many* (Borgstrom 1971), *The Careless Atom* (Novick 1971), and *Limits to Growth* (Meadows 1972). Even conservative church denominations joined the chorus, with publications linking environmental pollution with pollution of the mind by pornography and other evils.

38 Nader was best known for his consumer advocacy on such issues as unsafe automobiles, but his staff also produced influential critiques of environmental issues: *Vanishing Air* (Esposito 1970), *Water Wasteland* (Zwick and Benstock 1971), and others.

39 A leading example was the Environmental Defense Fund, which by 1970 had already sued in three states to stop the widespread use of DDT. Other groups had brought suit to stop construction of a pumped-storage hydroelectric plant on a mountain overlooking the Hudson River (*Storm King v. Federal Power Commission*), the building of a highway through a Memphis park (the *Overton Park* case), and other projects.

40 President Nixon, for instance, in 1969 reportedly studied a poll showing that protection of the environment had become the third most important issue to voters nationwide (Quarles 1976, 12).

Chapter 12: Nationalizing Pollution Control

1 Presidential reorganization plans do not require legislation; they go into effect automatically if Congress does not disapprove them within sixty days. A separate but concurrent reorganization created the National Oceanic and Atmospheric Administration in the Department of Commerce, pulling together in one department the nation's major responsibilities for weather, climate, oceans, fisheries, and (later) coastal management.

2 EPA was actually a second-choice organizational proposal for environmental protection. The original idea was to create a federal Department of Environment and Natural Resources as one of four federal "mega-departments," starting with the Department of the Interior and adding related functions that had grown up in other agencies, such as the Forest Service and the Army Corps of Engineers. The goal was to permit unified policy-making and more efficient and effective integrated

management of the environment. Similar reorganizations had been proposed repeatedly in the past — by Harold Ickes (Franklin Roosevelt's Secretary of the Interior), by the 1949 Hoover Commission on Government Organization, by Stewart Udall (John Kennedy's Interior Secretary), and others — but had always been blocked by political opposition, chiefly from the Corps and Forest Service and their constituencies. Roy Ash, chairman of Nixon's reorganization commission, backed the idea of a Department of Environment and National Resources, but the commission's environmental protection subgroup (under Douglas Costle, later administrator of EPA in the Carter administration) opposed it, believing that it would require too much disruption of congressional subcommittee jurisdictions, that it would create too large and diverse an organization (like Interior, it would become just a holding company over more or less autonomous agencies), and that development constituencies would be likely to dominate environmental protection concerns. Also, a leaked letter from Interior Secretary Walter Hickel to President Nixon, deploring the administration's handling of an unrelated incident (shootings of student antiwar demonstrators at Kent State University) alienated the president from his Interior Secretary as this proposal was being considered (Landy et al. 1994, 31–32). The result was a proposal instead for a unified environmental *regulatory* agency, to integrate the environmental *protection* programs across air, water, land, and various pollution threats.

3 Congressional reforms of the early 1970s exacerbated this fragmentation of congressional committee jurisdictions. The reapportionments of the 1960s and 1970s brought in many new members, all of whom wanted immediate opportunities to show their effectiveness. Their reforms curbed the entrenched power of the old committee chairs, many of whom represented rural resource-use interests, but also greatly proliferated subcommittees to allow more members to exercise power and initiative. Increasingly the members also pursued individualistic reelection strategies based on individual television campaigns funded by political action committees rather than on party loyalty.

4 Most of these were water pollution cases referred under the authority of the 1899 Rivers and Harbors Act, since the 1972 Clean Water Act amendments had not yet been enacted. The 1899 Law prohibited discharge of "debris" into rivers and harbors without a permit, but a 1960s Supreme Court decision had reinterpreted it to cover chemical pollutants as well (Quarles 1976, 99; U.S. EPA 1993a, 13).

5 In general, they also produced more effective environmental results (see e.g. Harrison 1995; Jänicke and Weidner 1996).

6 As noted previously, the Public Health Service had had only nonregulatory functions and the FDA and Meat Inspection Service in effect protected the producers themselves from less scrupulous competitors. Other health and safety agencies — the Occupational Safety and Health Administration, and Consumer Product Safety Commission — were not created until the same year as EPA. The United States did have a number of economic regulatory agencies, beginning with the Interstate Commerce Commission in the 1880s, but these agencies functioned almost universally as "friendly" regulators to their industrial regulatees, stabilizing their markets and serving as guarantors of their market conditions (Horwitz 1988, 76).

7 Canceling a pesticide's regulation, moreover, was a less effective solution than it might seem: it could still be purchased, ostensibly for other approved uses, and then misapplied to nonapproved crops. Implementation also relied on county agricultural agents, who were not necessarily committed to enforcement of the new restrictions. Moreover, manufacturers could appeal each canceled use individually, and unlike initial approval, in cancellation proceedings the government bore the burden of proof for showing that the product was unsafe. The final lawsuits ending domestic use of DDT were not decided until 1973 (Bosso 1987, 154–56).

8 Note that each unit also lost some key expertise in the reorganization, as some staff members elected to take early retirement or stay with the departments in which they had already spent much of their careers (Eisenbud 1978, 352–53).

9 In 1995 EPA consisted of some nineteen thousand employees organized in four program offices (Air and Radiation; Water; Solid Wastes and Emergency Response; and Prevention, Pesticides, and Toxic Substances), five functional offices (Administration and Resource Management; Re-

search and Development; Enforcement and Compliance Assurance; International Activities; and Policy, Planning, and Evaluation), a General Counsel and Inspector General, and ten regions (National Academy of Public Administration 1995, 10–11).

10 Only the water program had any substantial previous regional structure; the others were primarily Washington-based.

11 The same historical moment also produced the Occupational Safety and Health Act, the Consumer Production Safety Act, and the National Highway Transportation Safety Act, all aimed at protecting the public from health and safety hazards at work and more generally.

12 The basis for the NAAQS was a series of scientific "criteria documents" that had been under development by the Public Health Service since the Clean Air Act of 1967. These had to be continually reviewed and updated.

13 This technology-forcing requirement was sponsored by Senator Edmund Muskie (D-Maine), author of the act and most of the air and water quality legislation of the 1960s. Muskie was considered the leading environmental protection advocate in the Senate, and a strong potential presidential candidate based on that record. Environmental advocates publicly embarrassed him in 1970, however, charging that his more moderate approaches had been ineffective, merely allowing intransigent industries to delay serious cleanup (Esposito 1970). Muskie therefore shifted his position and drafted far tougher demands on the automakers and other major polluting industries (Landy et al. 1994, 26–30). EPA in 1973 ultimately accepted a negotiated compromise with the industry of 85 percent reduction, based on the introduction of catalytic converters. This in turn required the introduction of unleaded gasoline to protect the converters, which ultimately proved to have major benefits of its own in reducing human inhalation of lead (Shy 1990). Later amendments to the law delayed the deadlines to the 1983 model year for most pollutants and 1985 for nitrogen oxides; and the 1990 amendments added new deadlines for a further 30 percent reduction in hydrocarbons and 60 percent reduction in nitrogen oxides by 1998, and an additional 50 percent reduction in emissions by 2003 (Findley and Farber 1992, 103–04).

14 These goals were widely ridiculed as unrealistic, particularly by economists. Industries also preferred to set water quality goals only in proportion to designated uses of the streams, which might include, for instance, use as an industrial wastewater sink. The federal goals were politically popular as symbolic commitments, however, especially in a presidential election year pitting Senator Muskie, their author, against President Nixon, who was seeking to position himself as an environmental president while still maintaining support from major industrial polluters.

15 The Clean Air Act required permits only for new sources or those modified to emit more pollution.

16 The Water Quality Improvement Act of 1970, passed in reaction to the major oil spills of the late 1960s, further required owners and operators of ships and offshore oil facilities to pay for cleanup of all spills. In addition, it prohibited sewage dumping from boats, restricted thermal pollution from power plants, and addressed acid mine drainage and pollution effects of pesticides (Armstrong et al. 1976, 419).

17 Amendments in 1987 required the states to identify water bodies in which ambient standards could not be met without controlling non-point sources, and to establish EPA-approved management programs, implementation milestones, and regulatory measures for them based on "total maximum daily loads" (TMDLs). They also authorized $400 million in federal subsidies for these programs. Results by the mid-1990s did not show major improvement, however, though some states began moving slowly toward more watershed-wide programs for reduction of water pollution.

18 Oil companies in particular began advertising campaigns to mobilize public support for rapid domestic oil development as a national security issue, and President Nixon, for instance, advocated a "Project Independence" to accelerate U.S. fuel minerals development.

19 EPA proposed, for instance, rationing parking lot capacity by permits in high-pollution cities, adding steep parking surcharges, and requiring dedicated bus and carpool lanes during rush hours.

20 NRDC, for instance, was founded in 1970 by Yale law students and experienced lawyers from the *Scenic Hudson* case, with a grant from the Ford Foundation; by 1990 it had a staff of 125 and mem-

bership of 70,000. Along with EDF, NRDC pioneered the use of lawsuits as an environmental strategy, particularly to compel vigorous implementation of the Clean Air and Clean Water Acts and other environmental laws. Between 1970 and 1975, 80 percent of NRDC's work was litigation and administrative proceedings against government agencies and utilities.

21 During the decade of the 1970s alone, philanthropic foundations contributed over $20 million to U.S. environmental advocacy groups. Conservative legislators several times considered ending the foundation's tax-exempt status in retaliation, but retreated in the expectation of public outcry. By the 1980s so many conservative foundations had copied these tactics that further challenges seemed unlikely (Bosso 1987, 147–48, 134).

22 The "Nader report" which helped shape the Clean Water Act, for instance, argued that "The major problem in pollution control is the vast economic and political power of large polluters. . . . As an essential first step toward making the nation's pollution control effort less vulnerable to political sabotage, pollution control officials must be deprived of the discretion to enforce or not, as they choose. Discretion invites pressure from polluters to see that it is exercised in their favor. . . . Aggrieved citizens need the right to go to court to compel pollution control officials to carry out their assigned duties . . . and to move against polluters themselves" (Zwick and Benstock 1971, 395–96).

23 These were the Clean Air Act, Clean Water Act, Resource Conservation and Recovery Act (RCRA, dealing with solid and hazardous wastes), and the Comprehensive Environmental Response, Compensation and Liability Act (CERCLA, or the Superfund Act).

24 Citizens could not use such suits to recover damages, but only to obtain injunctive relief to stop pollution or to compel agency action. This limitation was taken as assurance of altruistic motives by such plaintiffs. They could, however, recover attorneys' fees and other legal costs if they won the case (Gauna 1995, 43, 76), and some environmental law groups used this opportunity with growing effectiveness in the 1980s and '90s.

25 Melnick (1983) is more critical of the expanded role of the courts than are most environmentalists, arguing that the Clean Air Act preoccupied EPA with ad hoc mandates and deadlines at the expense of priorities. Gauna (1995) adds criticisms from the left, arguing that many of the key agency powers are discretionary and thus insulated from citizen suits, and that expanding access to the courts without providing for economic assistance or damage awards allows only relatively wealthy plaintiffs to present their concerns as representing the public interest. Citizen-suit provisions in the solid-waste statutes precluded suits against siting and permitting of hazardous-waste facilities, which blocked legal complaints against proposals that most concerned many low-income communities (Gauna 1995).

26 Many Vietnam veterans were concurrently returning home with health effects that appeared to be associated with their exposures to Agent Orange, a potent herbicide used in Vietnam which was often contaminated with dioxins (Wildavsky 1995).

27 The Public Health Service was even used as a pawn in this process: as early as 1937, farm-state congressmen used PHS field-survey data showing no acute effects on farm workers to discredit Food and Drug Administration experimental data on laboratory animals, which suggested risks of longer-term effects (Bosso 1987, 50–51).

28 This indemnification provision was not changed until 1988, when the liability for indemnity was moved from EPA to the Federal Judgment Fund, which relies on general appropriations rather than the EPA budget to pay claims against the government (Wellford 1972, 160; Findley and Farber 1992, 217).

29 As of 1990, for instance, there were an estimated seventy thousand chemicals in commercial production or being imported into the United States. Section 4 of TSCA allowed EPA to require industrial testing of any of these chemicals that might pose "unreasonable risks" to health or the environment. As of 1990, fourteen years after TSCA was enacted, EPA had considered less than 1 percent of these chemicals for possible testing. It had obtained complete test data for only 6 chemicals, and it had not yet finished assessing any of these to determine whether they should be regulated (Gottlieb 1995, 62–63).

30 These standards included, among others, site requirements, such as minimum depth to groundwater; construction standards, such as requirements for clay and plastic liners and leachate monitoring and collection systems; operating requirements, such as restrictions on liquids and monitoring of groundwater as well as air and water quality; and financial assurance requirements, to guarantee safe closure and post-closure monitoring.

31 By late 1989, for instance, there were 1,219 sites on EPA's National Priority List for remediation, but only 34 had been fully cleaned up (Findley and Farber 1992, 243). The reasons, however, included not simply bureaucratic and legal red tape, but also the slowness and sometimes impossibility of fully cleansing groundwater.

32 This practice undermined widely accepted principles of regulatory procedure; EPA Administrator Russell Train refused to comply with it, and the NIPCC was ultimately disbanded.

33 Landy et al. (1994, 240–41) are harshly critical of EPA's administrators, particularly Douglas Costle, for failing to lead more outspokenly in educating Congress and the public about the need for statutory reforms. They argue that only a Democrat could have done this, and that Costle had the political capital to do so but chose the easier path of bureaucratic security and self-aggrandizement instead. This assessment is debatable: Congress had shredded President Carter's attempt to cut funding for a "hit list" of water resource projects that were both environmentally and economically unjustified, it had frustrated many of his environmentally oriented energy initiatives, and it was threatening to block his proposals on Alaskan lands preservation. Carter was also bogged down in the Iran hostage crisis and other serious and divisive issues. It is not at all clear therefore that Costle had the political capital to open another whole agenda to rewrite EPA's laws. Whether or not he could have done this, however, the issue was clearly ripe for serious debate, and a substantial literature of proposals for regulatory reform was emerging (see e.g. Bardach and Kagan 1982).

Chapter 13: Reform or Reaction? The Politics of the Pendulum

1 Western natural-resource user interests had organized the Sagebrush Rebellion in the late 1970s to oppose more active federal management of the western public lands under the 1976 Federal Lands Policy and Management Act (FLPMA) and other reform statutes. This movement was led by western ranchers and cast itself in the role of grass-roots, anti-big-government populism, but it was also backed by major economic interests in the mining, petroleum, and forest products industries.

2 During his post-election transition in 1980–81 Reagan appointed a distinguished environmental "transition team" of experienced Republican advisors on environmental policy, who advised him explicitly of his opportunity for regulatory reform leadership. Reagan chose to ignore them, however, and to pursue instead the more aggressive deregulation agenda advocated by Stockman and Weidenbaum (Andrews 1984a).

3 A 1984 study by the Congressional Office of Technology Assessment identified over two hundred contaminants in groundwater used for drinking, many of them linked to cancer and other serious health effects, and documented serious contamination incidents in at least thirty-four states (Findley and Farber 1992, 226–27). A growing body of research was also documenting the possibility of cancer-causing chemicals in drinking water, caused ironically by byproducts of the disinfection process — chlorination — that had so dramatically reduced human mortality from infectious diseases (Okun 1996, 455–56).

4 The Natural Resources Defense Council, for instance, reacted to the decline of EPA enforcement under Gorsuch by bringing actions against more than one hundred companies in twenty-three states, obtaining millions of dollars in settlements for local groups allied with them. Many of these it filed under provisions of the Clean Water Act, in part because of the perceived laxity of EPA enforcement under the Reagan administration and in part because court settlements against polluters provided direct economic benefits in legal fees and funds for other environmental protection projects (Mahood 1990). During the 1980s, 50 percent of the Natural Resources Defense Council's

effort was devoted to public health issues (primarily toxic chemicals), while 25 percent was on conservation and 25 percent on international issues such as global warming, tropical deforestation, and arms control. In NRDC's own view, its most important accomplishments included lawsuits against EPA to phase out lead in gasoline (1973), to require EPA to write standards for toxic water pollutants (1976), and to remove ozone-depleting CFCs from nonessential aerosol uses (1978); lawsuits against Bethlehem Steel (1987) and Texaco (1991) leading to multimillion-dollar settlements for water pollution abatement; and a publicity campaign against the Uniroyal Company aimed at getting the firm to withdraw the growth-control chemical Alar from use on apples (1989).

5 Some acknowledged that pollution could also be prevented by process or input changes, but even the best still emphasized the expectation of exponentially increasing costs, and went on to devote the remainder of the text to control technologies (e.g. Stern et al. 1973, 401–05).

6 Interestingly, the core ideas behind "pollution prevention pays" — reassessing manufacturing processes from the perspective of materials and energy efficiency in light of their environmental impacts — had actually been advocated for over a decade by a few economists and engineers, and documented in a series of detailed industrial case studies involving beet-sugar processing, iron and steel making, fruit canning, and others. These studies showed how dramatically environmental pollution could be reduced by redesign of industrial processes to use materials and energy more efficiently. They did not capture as systematically the full range of cost savings involved, however, and their determinedly arcane label — "residuals-environmental quality management" — had none of the popular appeal of "pollution prevention pays." They therefore received far less attention than they deserved beyond a small community of specialists (Kneese and Bower 1979; and earlier works cited therein).

7 Industrial interests, for instance, argued for including off-site recycling as a form of waste reduction, since it converted one firm's wastes into another's economic inputs. Environmental advocates insisted on a more stringent definition, however, fearing a rise in "sham" recycling that would continue unsafe waste handling practices while evading regulation. Several reports by the Congressional Office of Technology Assessment sharply criticized EPA's adherence to the industry position (U.S. Congress 1986, 1987).

8 The Hazardous Waste Management Act of 1984, for instance, set a two-year deadline for deciding what chemicals to exclude from landfilling, and imposed an automatic ban on many of them if EPA did not act by that deadline. The Superfund act applied strict standards of liability for hazardous-waste cleanup costs to all parties that had any responsibility at all for contaminated sites, including subsequent owners. This greatly increased the financial exposure of those who had generated or dumped the wastes, and of their lenders and insurers as well.

9 These approaches differed in nuances, but shared a common emphasis on minimizing environmental problems throughout the entire life cycle of key materials and products, from extraction and primary processing through manufacturing, distribution, consumer use, recycling and reuse, and ultimate disposal of residuals. See e.g. National Academy of Engineering 1989, 1994.

10 Also known as the "CERES principles," these principles were developed by the Coalition for Environmentally Responsible Economics, a joint effort of several national environmental organizations and the Social Investment Forum.

11 Landy et al. (1994, 256) suggest that EPA strategically reemphasized ecology at a time when claims of chemical health risks were under increasingly skeptical attack, reflecting a judgment that sooner or later public opinion would catch up with the data and undermine the agency's position.

12 A study of EPA risk-assessment personnel, for instance, found that although most of those trained in the physical or social sciences, engineering, or law favored the use of risk assessment in policymaking, two-thirds of those trained in biomedical or environmental sciences — presumably those most familiar with its substance — opposed it (Andrews 1992, note 30).

13 In effect, this regulated the facilities as though both were enclosed under a common "bubble."

14 The six sectors were electronics, iron and steel, printing, metal plating, auto manufacturing, and petroleum refining.

15 As in the cases of several other environmental statutes cited in previous chapters, EPCRA ex-

emplified key industries' self-interest in uniform but "moderate" federal regulation that would pre-empt potentially stricter state or local statutes. EPCRA replaced and weakened stronger statutes in New Jersey and a few other leading states, but at the same time imposed right-to-know rules on many other states that might never have enacted such requirements themselves.

16 Some states went farther. California's "Proposition 65," for instance, required businesses to put warning labels on all products that contained significant levels of substances that could cause cancer or birth defects, and restricted disposal of them into drinking water sources. Massachusetts' Toxic Use Reduction Act mandated reduction of the use of toxic chemicals in industry and consumer products, and New Jersey required more detailed materials-balance studies of the chemicals entering and leaving industrial processes than did any federal laws.

17 The magnitude of these omissions was illustrated by an inadvertent disclosure by Kennecott Copper in 1987, which revealed that while its releases of copper from primary metals operations totaled 4 million tons, releases from its mining operations totaled more than thirty times that amount, some 130 million tons (Gottlieb 1995, 136–37).

18 The large basic-chemicals firms shared an interest not only in improving relations with their host communities, but also in reducing their vulnerability to being blamed for the actions of more marginal firms — many of which, such as firms that formulated pesticides and other dangerous products, were their own customers. The result was a gradual increase in pressure for better environmental management, not just from government but up and down the industrial supply chain itself.

19 As much as half or more of the salaries of some state environmental programs, for instance, were supported by federal program grants.

20 Between 1980 and 1985, state government organizations' budgets from federal sources were cut significantly: the National Governors Association by 29 percent, the National Conference of State Legislatures by 55 percent, and the Council of State Governments by 65 percent. For local governments the cuts were even deeper: the U.S. Conference of Mayors was cut by 47 percent, the National Association of Counties and International City Managers Association each by 73 percent, and the National League of Cities by 100 percent (Levine and Thurber 1986, 214–15).

21 New federal regulations for other purposes further exacerbated the municipalities' burden, particularly the Americans with Disabilities Act, which required access for the handicapped to all public buildings.

22 The intent of "takings" bills was to establish statutory criteria for interpreting the constitutional doctrine, stated in the Fifth Amendment, that property may not be taken for public use without due process and just compensation (see Chapter 4). Most traditional interpretations of this doctrine dealt with such issues as physical invasion of a piece of property, such as building a highway across it, but several cases in the late 1980s and '90s extended it to claims of "regulatory takings," in which the impact of an environmental regulation was alleged to have "taken" a piece of property by diminishing its economic value. The courts generally required compensation only in cases in which no reasonable economic use remained, but several congressional proposals in 1995 proposed to overturn this interpretation by requiring compensation whenever the economic value of a property was diminished by more than some specified percentage, such as 20 percent or 50 percent. Critics of such proposals argued that they were unworkable, rested on weak constitutional arguments, and in reality represented illegitimate attempts to use constitutional claims to hamstring or roll back environmental regulations (Byrne 1995).

23 Even these rates, however, were well below those of many other countries. By 1996 EPA claimed that the nation had reached an overall national goal of 25 percent recycling, and proposed a new goal of 35 percent by the year 2005.

Chapter 14: The Unfinished Business of National Environmental Policy

1 Its "impact statement" mechanism was widely emulated by advocates of other decision considerations: examples included "impact statements" for inflation, communities, economics, "regulatory flexibility" (small businesses), regulatory "takings," "family values," litigation, risks, and others.

2 The Army Corps of Engineers in fact adopted this position almost immediately, as authority to consider a wider range of environmental benefits to justify its projects. It was often far less scrupulous, however, in attempting to quantify all their environmental costs (Andrews 1976a). Environmental advocacy groups therefore became outspoken opponents of the agencies' uses of cost-benefit analysis. This was in a sense ironic, since cost-benefit analysis was an important tool of administrative reform. The Budget Bureau deliberately wrote narrow criteria of economic benefits to try to control many of the same pork-barrel projects for economic reasons that environmental groups wanted to stop because of their environmental impacts. An additional cause of environmentalists' opposition was the importance of some other issues on which economic-efficiency and environmental-protection goals were not congruent: federal highway projects, for instance, were required by economic criteria to be built on the least-cost path, and therefore were often routed through parks and low-income neighborhoods. Several of the early NEPA lawsuits involved just such cases, such as the *Overton Park* case in Memphis.

3 The Senate version of NEPA had envisioned the EIS as simply an addition "finding" by the official responsible for each federal decision: better actions, it assumed, would result from better ecological information within the normal decision process. The Senate-House conference version, however, redefined it as a "detailed statement," required explicit discussion of alternatives as well as environmental impacts, mandated interagency consultation and review, and required public review both of the statements and of the other agencies' comments on them. One other change was made at the insistence of House conferees, diluting Senate language that would have declared a "fundamental and inalienable right to a healthful environment" to a weaker statement that each person "should enjoy" such an environment — thus precluding lawsuits demanding that government provide a healthy environment (Andrews (1976a).

4 The basic principle that project benefits must exceed their costs was established by the 1936 Flood Control Act, at least for water projects, but the operational criteria were spelled out only in executive guidelines, which were not subject to citizen or judicial challenge (Andrews 1984b).

5 Political constituencies in favor of such projects remained powerful, however. President Carter tried to cut off funding for a "hit list" of water projects that were both economically and environmentally questionable, but was immediately blocked by congressional resistance.

6 Note that most federal actions subject to the requirement actually begin outside the federal agency, such as permit and grant requests. The agency is ultimately responsible for the decision, and for consideration of the action's environmental impacts, but the underlying environmental assessments are often prepared by the sponsors.

7 NEPA did require a onetime review by all agencies to identify any existing policies that prevented its implementation. This elicited few substantive issues, and in effect served only to foreclose subsequent legal claims that prior statutory missions prevented NEPA implementation.

8 EPA's Science Advisory Board identified cumulative loss of wildlife habitat as one of the gravest ecological risks facing the country, for example, and therefore an issue that should be central to national environmental policy. NEPA had no influence on this issue, however, except as it involved new action proposals on the federal lands (U.S. Environmental Protection Agency 1990).

9 President Nixon had in fact proposed a similar "Cabinet Council on Environmental Quality" in 1969, to be staffed by the White House, but Congress had purposefully created instead a separate CEQ subject to Senate confirmation in order to assure ongoing executive-level attention and policy continuity.

10 President Nixon ultimately withdrew his support for the legislation in the midst of the Watergate scandal, as the price of Arizona's congressional votes against his impeachment.

11 Examples of such actions included Army Corps of Engineers projects such as dredging of harbors and beach erosion control projects; offshore oil and gas development and building of other energy facilities; highway and bridge construction projects of the Department of Transportation; federal subsidies for port development projects and for housing and urban development in coastal cities; marine fisheries management programs; and in the Pacific Northwest, logging and land management on national forests and BLM lands along the coasts.

12 It was estimated that the United States had lost over half of its original wetlands, and that ten states had lost more than 70 percent (U.S. Council on Environmental Quality 1993, 96). The rate of annual loss from conversion of wetlands to agricultural uses, however, appeared to have decreased dramatically (from 600,000 acres per year between 1954 and 1974 to 31,000 acres per year from 1982 to 1992), while conversion to urban uses increased steeply, from 55,000 to over 88,000 acres per year (U.S. Council on Environmental Quality 1997, 462). President Bush in 1988 pledged to allow "no net loss of wetlands" during his administration, but then proposed to define "wetlands" so narrowly — based on hydrological criteria alone, rather than on the presence of wetland plant communities — that his pledge appeared meaningless or worse.

13 For instance, a regulation could be determined to be a compensable "taking" if it reduced the market value of the property by more than 20 percent, or 50 percent, or in some versions by any percentage at all, and the compensation would be taken from the budget of the regulatory agency. Such liabilities would clearly render the regulatory programs ineffectual, much as EPA's pesticide regulatory programs had been hamstrung by the requirement that EPA buy back unsold stocks of any pesticide it banned.

14 In many states, for instance, religious denominations had secured legislation prohibiting bars near churches: would the state now have to pay property owners not to open such establishments, or even for the hypothetical profits they might have received if they had?

15 Constitutionally, these powers derived from the treaty power for migratory species (the Migratory Bird Treaty Act of 1918), the commerce clause and its "navigation servitude" for migratory fisheries and federal water projects, and the property clause for federal lands and wildlife refuges.

16 Wildlife policy was one of the few areas in which the courts had historically limited the use of the commerce clause to justify federal intervention, and federal protection of migratory waterfowl had therefore been built instead on the treaty power.

17 A 1971 law, for instance, made federal land managers responsible for the well-being of wild horses and burros, populations that were not actually even native to the public lands but had become picturesque reminders of the frontier era. A 1972 law expanded federal protection of golden and bald eagles, which were visible symbols of natural beauty and national identity yet also were frequent victims of poisoning and shooting by sheep ranchers. Finally, the 1972 Marine Mammal Protection Act declared a moratorium on takings of whales, dolphins, and other marine mammals, which were often victims of harassment and commercial fishing practices (dolphins frequently travel with schools of tuna, for instance, and were frequently trapped in the nets unless fishermen released them before harvesting the tuna) (Bean 1983 [1977], 281–317).

18 In the Tellico Dam case, for instance, project advocates had the ESA amended to create a review process to balance the loss of endangered species against the economic benefits of proposed actions — a "God Committee," as it was called — yet this committee then found that the dam was unjustified on economic grounds as well. The dam was finally built when congressional supporters surreptitiously inserted a blanket exemption for it into an appropriations bill.

19 The decision was known as *Babbitt v. Sweet Home Chapter of Communities for a Great Oregon.*

20 In the 104th Congress this conflict extended even to an attempt to eliminate funding for the National Biological Service, an agency created in 1993 to consolidate and strengthen the biological science research programs from the Fish and Wildlife Service, National Park Service, Bureau of Land Management, and other Interior Department agencies. Congressional proposals went so far as to prohibit citizens from assisting the NBS as volunteers, lest its scientific activities identify additional endangered species unwelcome to landowners and developers.

21 Trawling for bottom-dwelling species, for instance, typically involves dragging heavy nets across the entire sea-bottom habitat, destroying its vegetation in the process. Indiscriminate trawling also incidentally kills many nontarget "by-catch" species: endangered sea turtles, dolphins migrating with tuna, and others. A particularly serious problem was the introduction of "drift nets," huge nets as many as thirty miles long which sometimes were lost at sea and drifted for months or years, trapping and killing fish indiscriminately.

22 See related discussion in Chapter 15.

23 The National Marine Fisheries Service was part of the National Oceanic and Atmospheric Administration, which President Nixon had created by reorganization in 1970 at the same time he created EPA, drawing together in the Department of Commerce many of the agencies that dealt with
oceans, weather, and climate.

24 Fishermen also resented and resisted other conservation measures, such as rules requiring "turtle
exclusion devices" to protect endangered sea turtles.

25 As the cheapest domestic oil fields were depleted during and after World War II, producers moved
offshore, both to the outer continental shelf (with the development of offshore oil drilling technology) and increasingly to foreign sources, such as the vast Arab oil fields of the Persian Gulf, where
U.S. economic influence moved rapidly into the vacuum left by postwar British retrenchment. U.S.
policies promoted this shift, allowing U.S. tax credits for taxes the oil firms paid to foreign
countries, and even toppling a prime minister in Iran who stood in the way of this process. By 1973
the United States represented only 5 percent of the world's population but consumed 35 percent of
its energy, and was increasingly dependent on imports for its oil supply (Davis 1993, 5; Kash and
Rycroft 1984, 6). Import quotas were introduced in 1959, limiting imports to 12.5 percent of domestic production, both to protect domestic producers and to limit overdependence on foreign
sources for security reasons. These quotas were removed by President Nixon in 1973, ironically just
months before the OPEC oil embargo demonstrated the legitimacy of the security concern.

26 Industries using large quantities of electricity received bulk-rate discounts, which allowed them to
pay lower rates the more they used. Such rates were based ostensibly on the economies of scale of
electricity production, and in reality on the risk that large users might build their own power
plants, but they also encouraged wasteful use rather than conservation.

27 In 1974, for instance, an accident caused by a workman searching for leaks with a candle disabled
TVA's Browns Ferry reactor for years, including most of its supposedly independent safety systems. The Three Mile Island (Pennsylvania) meltdown in 1979 destroyed that reactor permanently, producing multimillion-dollar costs even for relatively limited off-site impacts.

28 A major environmental-law precedent was the successful challenge to a proposed pumped-storage
plant that would have destroyed a scenic headland on the Hudson River to build a generating
plant. The plant would have used fossil fuels to pump water up to a reservoir in off-peak hours,
then release it to generate hydropower during peak hours, at a net loss of overall energy (*Scenic
Hudson Preservation Conference v. Federal Power Commission,* 1965). This case established the precedent that groups representing legally protected environmental interests rather than personal economic damage had standing to challenge federal agencies in court. Nuclear and coal-fired power
plants were among the most frequent targets of lawsuits under the environment impact statement
(EIS) requirement of the National Environmental Policy Act: examples included Vermont
Yankee, Calvert Cliffs (Maryland), Seabrook (New Hampshire), and others.

29 As one close observer put it, "The story of U.S. energy policy is largely an account of the failure of
genuinely free markets to appear and of the unwillingness of most market participants . . . to allow
a free market structure to develop" (Goodwin 1981, 666).

30 Nuclear reactor accidents in the 1970s and 1980s, such as a serious fire in the control room of
TVA's Browns Ferry reactor and the unanticipated pressure buildup and meltdown of the Three
Mile Island reactor in Pennsylvania, belied the history of one-sided safety reassurances by AEC officials, and revealed also the vast economic risks of nuclear accidents. Increasing operating experience showed the electric utilities themselves that the radiation stresses on materials might cause
much shorter operating lifetimes than anticipated for their reactors, as well as far higher costs of
closure and perpetual care. Finally, new access to declassified records in the 1990s provided evidence that the AEC had in fact known but deliberately suppressed evidence of radiation impacts of
its activities on possible victims, such as uranium miners and downwind human and animal populations (Armstrong et al. 1976, 390–97; U.S. Department of Commerce 1975, S65, S99; Udall
1994, 183–249; Gerber 1992). All this contributed to a decline in the U.S. nuclear power industry
that was almost as rapid as its rise, during which other countries continued to develop and utilize
nuclear power successfully. President Carter canceled plans for a "fast-breeder" reactor, which

would have reprocessed spent reactor fuel but also risked proliferation of weapons-grade nuclear materials. The 1986 Chernobyl disaster in the Ukraine, even though caused by flagrant human errors in operating an outmoded reactor of a type not used in the United States, further amplified public apprehension toward nuclear technology.

31 The CAFE standards, mandated by the Energy Policy and Conservation Act of 1975, required auto manufacturers to achieve an overall average of 27.5 miles per gallon for the cars they sold each year.

32 Technically this was not a national speed limit, but a condition of continuing to receive federal highway subsidies, which few states could afford to refuse. It was repealed by the 104th Congress in 1995.

33 President Clinton in 1993 proposed a broad-based tax on each BTU of energy production, intended both to lower the budget deficit and to reduce oil imports and environmental impacts. Congress, however, weakened it to a far more limited tax on motor vehicle fuels.

34 Examples included severe environmental and cultural destruction to the indigenous peoples of the Ecuadorian Amazon due to oil extraction concessions, and the 1995 execution of Nigerian poet/activist Ken Saro-wiwa by the Nigerian government for his organizing of opposition to oil extraction due to its impacts on his tribe in the Nigerian delta region.

35 EPA's "Green Lights" program also promoted substitution of low-energy light bulbs by businesses, to reduce the air-pollution impacts of electric power production.

36 The Congestion Mitigation and Air Quality Improvement Program provided a small fraction of transportation funds for transport-related air-quality improvements in nonattainment areas. Examples of such projects included transit and traffic flow improvements, ride-sharing and demand-management incentives, auto inspection and maintenance programs, and congestion-pricing pilot projects.

37 Wetland mitigation banking had the benefit of using highway funds to support purchases of wetlands for permanent preservation, but it also raised issues as to whether some of the wetlands purchased might have remained untouched anyway — "paper mitigation" — and whether they were ecologically equivalent to those destroyed.

38 The National Highway Designation Act of 1995.

39 In North Carolina, for instance, every town was required to treat its sewage before discharge, yet hog farms generating far more sewage than many towns were allowed simply to discharge it into open lagoons and spread it on fields without advanced treatment.

40 Not coincidentally, this followed the resurgence of the Democrat/environmentalist alliance in the 1984 elections, in reaction to the anti-environmental initiatives of the first Reagan administration. See discussion in Chapter 13.

41 From 1986 to 1993 the CRP temporarily retired 36.4 million acres, 96 percent of the program's goal. But these contracts were to begin expiring in 1995, and a 1993 survey indicated that 63 percent of these lands would be returned to some form of production when their contracts expired, depending on market conditions (U.S. Council on Environmental Quality 1993, 141–42).

42 Compliance with the Clean Water Act was also an issue, especially controlling erosion and sedimentation from cutover lands and logging roads.

43 The Alaskan Native Claims Settlement Act of 1971 had settled native claims to that the Trans-Alaska Pipeline could proceed, but also withheld eighty million acres for review as "national interest" lands for possible designation as national parks, national forests, wildlife refuges, and other federal protections (so-called "d-2 lands"). The Alaska National Interest Lands Conservation Act of 1979 confirmed these designations — after an intense political battle with Alaskan legislators, which ended only after Secretary of the Interior Cecil Andrus invoked the Antiquities Act of 1906, threatening to designate all these lands national monuments, to break a filibuster — and added fifty-six million acres to the wilderness system, tripling its size, as well as several new national parks (Mayer and Riley 1985, 264).

44 The "Bolle Report" was authored by the dean of the Montana State University Forestry School, Arnold Bolle.

45 This reflected a congressional reaction against Nixon's attempt to balance the budget by reducing funds for forest road building and reforestation.

46 The case was *West Virginia Division of the Izaak Walton League v. Butz.*

47 The Forest Service had long asserted an exemption from the public-participation requirements of the Administrative Procedures Act, on the grounds that its management of the national forests was a "proprietary" function under the property clause of the Constitution — that it was, in effect, just administering government property, as one would a government office building — rather than a "sovereign" function requiring public input on actions that affected citizens' rights. The NFMA nullified this claim.

48 Examples were documented in reports by the Natural Resources Defense Council in 1980, the U.S. General Accounting Office in 1984, and the *Atlantic Monthly* in 1991. In the forest planning model for the Pisgah-Nantahala National Forest in western North Carolina, for instance, environmental groups discovered a hidden constraint that blocked the model from producing any scenario in which timber cuts were reduced to less than 80 percent of current levels. When this constraint was removed, the model recommended dramatic reductions in timber cuts, reflecting the far greater productivity of those forests for recreational use than for timber production.

49 Critics often referred to it therefore as the "Bureau of Livestock and Mining."

50 Public land claims had been widely used for fraudulent and speculative profiteering, such as through "nuisance" claims in which speculators claimed land in order to force the government to buy it back from them for roads, settlements, and other purposes. A recent example was a $250,000 payment to buy out a claimant on the Yucca Mountain site for a proposed nuclear waste storage facility (Wilkinson 1992, 59).

51 In one example the Interior Department was compelled by law and court order to patent (sell) claims to land containing commercial quantities of oil shale for just $2.50 per acre, which the buyer then immediately resold for $2,000 per acre (Wilkinson, 1992, 62). In the 1980s a new gold extraction process was introduced which used liquid cyanide to leach gold particles out of open heaps of raw ore. One such mine in Colorado, owned by a Canadian firm, declared bankruptcy and closed in 1992, leaving behind a legacy of toxic contamination that destroyed seventeen miles of streams and cost EPA $40,000 per day to contain (*New York Times,* August 14, 1994). In 1996 the Secretary of the Interior was again forced by the courts to sell off over 1,800 acres in Nevada, worth an estimated $10 billion in gold deposits, for $5 per acre (*Washington Post,* May 17, 1994).

52 Created in 1964, the Land and Water Conservation Fund provided a new dedicated source of funding for national and state parkland acquisition. The original source of funds was a tax on motorboat fuel, which provided only modest revenues, but amendments in 1968 provided far greater revenues from a percentage of offshore oil royalties, sparking an ambitious parkland acquisition program over the following decade.

53 Key leaders included Ron Arnold, an industrial public relations consultant; Alan Gottlieb, a right-wing direct-mail expert; and Charles Cushman, the organizer of the National Inholders Association.

54 Examples included People for the West! the Alliance for America, the Environmental Conservation Association, the Endangered Species Reform Coalition, the Information Council on the Environment, Californians for Food Safety, the U.S. Council on Energy Awareness, and others (*National Wildlife,* October-November 1992, 9).

Chapter 15: Environmental Policy in a Global Economy

1 The theory of economic "comparative advantage," developed by the influential economist David Ricardo in the early nineteenth century, held that these relationships represented natural differences among the resources and labor-forces of the trading countries, and that it was to everyone's advantage to build on them. It was fitting for those countries that could mine valuable mineral deposits or grow coffee or bananas to do so, and trade them to other countries that lacked them but had other assets such as the technology to produce cheap manufactured goods. However, this theory over-

looked the significant inequalities in exchange that resulted, inasmuch as manufacturing generally produced greater profits than exporting of raw materials. It also was based on the presumption that capital and labor were relatively immobile, so that comparative advantages would not be broken down simply by moving manufacturing to societies with cheaper labor forces (Daly 1993).

2 There were a few other exceptions, though limited ones. An 1897 statute prohibited importation of wild animals or birds except by permit, and a 1905 law forbade imports of pest species that might injure crops or forests. In 1906 the United States prohibited imports of sponges from the Gulf of Mexico that had been harvested by methods that damaged the sponge beds, and the 1913 Underwood Tariff banned imports of feathers from some rare wild bird species. The Alaska Fisheries Act of 1926 prohibited imports of salmon caught in violation of U.S. fishery laws (Vogel 1995, 8–9).

3 U.S. oil firms, for instance, moved into Iran and the Middle East as the British withdrew, and the United States competed with the USSR for economic and political influence in the resource-rich countries of Africa.

4 The countries of Latin America clearly were capable of growing or buying their own food, but under the Reagan administration the value of Food for Peace shipments to that region increased from $20 million (1954–79) to $600 million (1980–87), as an element of Reagan's foreign policy strategy to increase U.S. political influence with the governments surrounding Sandinista-led Nicaragua (U.S. Congress 1990, 73, 149).

5 In 1972 President Nixon initiated a major shift in policy, commercializing crop surpluses in large-scale sales to the Soviet Union and others and rapidly reducing donation or below-cost "dumping" in the markets of less-developed countries. The Russian wheat sales triggered a rapid expansion of planting, especially on highly erodible lands of the Great Plains which were just ending their "Soil Bank" status, causing a serious new round of "sodbusting" and soil erosion.

6 U.S. AID studies in 1988, for instance, reportedly showed "saturation" of markets in several countries with U.S. food aid (Egypt, Honduras, and El Salvador), hurting local farmers (U.S. Congress 1990, 71, 147–48).

7 Far more foreign aid was distributed in the form of repayable loans than as grants: between 1985 and 1992 African countries reportedly paid over $80 billion in debt service, one-fourth of their total export earnings during that period (Athanasiou 1996, 157). Aid also was often tied to requirements that it be used to purchase goods and services from the "donor" country. More than half the World Bank's "aid" to the poorest countries in 1992–93, for instance, ended up in the world's ten richest countries, where it was spent on equipment and technical advice. Seventy percent of U.S. aid was spent on U.S. goods and services (Athanasiou 1996, 158).

8 *Limits to Growth* was widely attacked by economists for failing to incorporate market forces as compensating mechanisms, and thus implying that the only solution was government regulatory controls (cf. Cole et al. 1973). These attacks overshadowed the more important contribution of the book, which was to articulate for the first time in the popular literature the fundamental interdependence of population, resource use, and pollution. Previous publications had tended to treat these separately, focusing almost exclusively on one or another of them as a single cause of environmental problems. Paul and Anne Ehrlich's *The Population Bomb,* for instance, targeted population growth, while Barry Commoner blamed consumption per capita (Ehrlich 1968, Commoner 1971).

9 Its major speakers contrasted the apprehensive vision of Fairfield Osborn, president of the New York Zoological Society and the Conservation Foundation, who foresaw the fundamental challenges of the world's environmental problems, with the technological optimism of Australian economist Colin Clark, who confidently predicted an unlimited economic ability to expand food supplies as population grew (Caldwell 1990, 42–44).

10 All of these treaties were ratified and put into effect by 1983. Other agreements with more limited results included conventions on international wetlands, compensation for oil pollution damage, prohibition of environmental warfare, and conservation of living marine resources in the Antarctic (Caldwell 1990, 84–85).

11 These scientific discussions arose out of concern about a different issue, the potential stratospheric effects of a proposed fleet of "supersonic transport" (SST) aircraft. Sherwood Rowland and Mario Molina eventually were awarded the Nobel prize for their work on this problem.

12 International environmental agreements not only must be voluntarily accepted and ratified by national governments, but also must then be implemented through domestic legislation and enforcement. The only international sanctions available, if any, are against the country as a whole, not directly against the violators. This system thus provides only awkward and weak instruments for achieving environmental policy goals (Roht-Arriaza 1995, 483–85).

13 Based strongly in science rather than ideological rhetoric, the WCS stated three essential objectives — to maintain essential ecological processes and life support systems, preserve genetic diversity, and ensure sustainable utilization of species and ecosystems — and identified a series of obstacles to these goals in existing national and international policies.

14 The charter passed by a vote of 111 to 1 with 18 abstentions. The United States, under the Reagan administration, cast the single dissenting vote (Caldwell 1990, 90–93).

15 The latter was ultimately passed in a weakened form as a "Statement on Forest Principles."

16 The chair of Carter's Council on Environmental Quality, under whom this report was prepared, was Gus Speth, who went on to found the World Resources Institute and later to head the United Nations Development Program.

17 Reagan withdrew U.S. support rather than agree to compromises that would have shared revenues and technologies for seabed mining with developing countries under United Nations administration. Influential businesses as well as political conservatives particularly opposed efforts to define seabed resources as a "common world heritage" to be administered by a U.N.-affiliated "Enterprise." (Recall that it was a very similar concession, the requirement that all thirteen original states cede their western land claims to the federal government, that made the U.S. government a powerful national government rather than a merely federal one.) Most other major nations ratified the agreement, and Reagan apparently calculated that the U.S. could "free-ride" on the customary law of navigation rights which the other countries' agreement established, without having to accept the mineral-royalty principles it opposed (international courts often base their decisions not only on formal agreements such as treaties, but also on "customary law," meaning principles that appear to be generally accepted by most nations even though not formally ratified in treaties). President Clinton reversed Reagan's policy and signed the treaty just months before it was to go into force, but as of 1998 it still had not been ratified by the U.S. Senate.

18 A wedge issue is one that can be used to split other political alliances. In this case, Republican conservatives used an emotional issue on which the Roman Catholic church hierarchy had taken a dogmatic political position — abortion in particular, but also family-planning and fertility-reduction programs more generally — to try to split off blue-collar Roman Catholic voters from the Democratic party.

19 United Nations agencies played essential roles in disseminating information and organizing action on global issues of many kinds, from health, food and agriculture, trade, and the needs of children to development, the environment, and others. U.S. conservatives criticized some of them as unaccountable bureaucratic sinecures for political elites from poor and Communist countries, as at best wasteful and often ineffective, and as at worst organizational seedbeds for anti-U.S. agendas. Notwithstanding its positive contributions, moreover, the U.N. itself is ultimately a democracy of nondemocracies, accountable only to its member governments rather than to the people of their countries, and dependent on the financial support and political acquiescence of the United States and other financial and military powers.

20 Even this statement significantly overstates the real U.S. contribution to international development needs. The U.S. foreign aid budget is disproportionately allocated to a few countries for geopolitical strategic reasons, Israel and Egypt in particular, and to a few others for U.S. business interests, rather than to many others that have equal or greater development needs.

21 Once elected, he appointed his own vice president, Dan Quayle, chairman of a similar antiregulation commission.

22 Bush's support for new Clean Air Act amendments, considered his most important environmental legacy, was influenced by strong support from state and local governments. During the hot summer of 1989, over one hundred cities exceeded EPA smog standards, and a coalition of the eight northeastern states announced their intent to impose California's more rigorous standards for automotive emissions and requested federal help to reduce upwind sources in the Midwest (Kline 1997, 109–10).

23 Note the fundamental difference in this between Bush and President Nixon. Nixon had proven credentials with the right wing, and calculated that they had no one else to turn to except him, so he used this security to take a public leadership role in environmental protection and other more centrist political issues, as well as to reopen relations with mainland China. Reagan, in contrast, sought to radically shift public policy toward the right wing's agenda, rather than bring them closer to the center. Bush remained so insecure of the conservatives' support that for fear of offending them he avoided, abandoned, or even recanted many policies on which he could easily have taken leadership and claimed credit.

24 The United States was not the only country to weaken or undermine the Earth Summit negotiations, but it was clearly the public leader in doing so. Great Britain, Australia, Japan, and some others also preferred nonbinding targets for reducing greenhouse gas emissions (Athanasiou 1996, 202–03). Conversely, had the United States taken a pro-environmental leadership position it could have had a powerful influence in raising the commitment of other countries to serious negotiation.

25 The Biodiversity Convention was ultimately more concerned with establishing transnational corporations' "intellectual property rights" to genetic materials that might have commercial value than with preserving plant and animal species from extinction. It established, for instance, that genetic materials collected in poor countries became the property of the transnational companies that had collected them, rather than of the country or even the individual from whom they had been collected, and it eliminated any right of the country of origin to withhold them. It thus increased the control of transnational companies over a diminishing variety of naturally occurring seed stocks. Clinton signed the convention, but conditioned by an "interpretive statement" written by U.S. biotechnology firms that essentially mirrored President Bush's position (Athanasiou 1996, 205–11).

26 In its 1996 budget, for instance, Congress cut U.S. assistance for population and family planning programs in developing countries by 35 percent (Tobin 1996, 328).

27 Greenhouse gases such as carbon dioxide trap the heat of solar radiation in the earth's atmosphere; excess concentrations of them could therefore increase the average temperatures at the earth's surface, causing changes in the weather, melting of solar ice caps and consequent rises in sea level, and widespread changes in the environments of living organisms. In January 1998, climate researchers at the National Oceanic and Atmospheric Administration reported that 1997 had been the warmest on record for planet Earth, and that at least part of this effect was almost certainly due to emissions from human activities.

28 More balanced reporting might have noted that many of these problems were not uniquely severe under Communist governance. Many of the western industrial democracies had comparable environmental problems. Examples included air pollution in Athens and Rome, water pollution in the Rhine, agricultural groundwater pollution due to overfertilization in the Netherlands, and chemical and nuclear contamination around U.S. weapons-production facilities. To blame all these problems on Communist governance per se was as misleading as for the Communists to blame them all on capitalism (Andrews 1993a).

29 Many less-developed countries, for instance, depended on single crops such as coffee or cocoa for a large fraction of their hard-currency earnings, yet could easily be played off against other suppliers by the small number of transnational corporations (TNCs) that controlled the terms of trade. TNCs could also evade many national taxation policies by trading with themselves — "transfer pricing" among their operations in different countries — in ways that favored their own interests.

30 Sectors in which five or fewer companies controlled more than 50 percent of the world market included consumer durables, automotive products, airlines, aerospace technology, electronic components, electricity and electronics, and steel. Sectors where more than 40 percent of the market was similarly controlled included oil, personal computers, and the media. Some industries were even more concentrated: three global corporations controlled 70 percent of total exports and sales of bananas, leaving banana-exporting countries almost entirely at their mercy (Khor 1996, 19).

31 Leveraged buyouts allowed financial manipulators to buy firms using the firms' own assets as collateral. These policies allowed quick profits for investors, but in the process mortgaged the businesses' futures to debt service rather than modernization or stable employment. They also produced large-scale consolidation of business enterprises in pyramids of holding companies driven only by financial criteria rather than by the more diverse characteristics of particular lines of business. Consolidation was then followed by "downsizing" and "outsourcing": keeping only the most profitable core pieces, contracting out for other services, and selling off or simply eliminating the rest.

32 These figures excluded China, for which data were unavailable.

33 DDT, for instance, was banned from use in the United States in 1972, but neither its production nor export was ever prohibited. It remained in use worldwide along with other pesticides that had equal or greater hazards, both to farmworkers and to birds and other species (Athanasiou 1996, 27–28).

34 A 1991 survey by the World Health Organization found that of the fifty-nine moderately to rapidly industrializing countries, only ten had most of the components of an adequate environmental management program, twenty-nine had some, and twenty had little or none. Not one of the seventy-six less-industrialized countries had any significant institutional capacity for environmental management.

35 An IMF study in 1994, for instance, reported that real prices for commodities other than oil had fallen by about 45 percent over the previous ten years (Reed 1996).

36 U.S. "corporate average fuel efficiency" (CAFE) standards for cars, for instance, caused little difficulty for American auto manufacturers but imposed high taxes on European luxury cars whose manufacturers did not make fuel-efficient smaller cars as well. Also, some countries' recycling policies favored domestic manufacturers of bottled beverages over importers of disposable containers, and product sanitation standards could also be used to disadvantage imports (Vogel 1995, 131–34, 15–16, 41–49; Esty 1994, 44–45).

37 The U.S. market accounted for about half the annual world consumption of tuna.

38 GATT requirements for international "harmonization" of food safety regulations, for example, might be interpreted to require that U.S. standards for pesticide residues be no stricter than those of the Codex Alimentarius, an international set of standards set by an industry-based organization that was consistently far less strict than those of the United States and Europe (Athanasiou 1996, 171).

39 Trade agreements with Mexico allowed U.S. firms to operate some two thousand factories just across the Mexican border on a duty-free basis, providing jobs for Mexico and cheap labor for U.S. assembly plants. By law these plants were required to reexport their wastes to the United States as well as their products, but in practice lax enforcement allowed them to dump large quantities of hazardous wastes in Mexico (Vogel 1995, 234–35).

40 Local and domestic businesses also seek government regulations protecting them against outside competitors, such as local shops against Wal-Marts, or U.S. shoe manufacturers against foreign competitors. Some businesses owe their prosperity or even their existence to government regulations — those involved in recycling, hazardous waste disposal, tourist concessions in national parks, and environmental consulting, for instance — and would fight for their survival against proposals for deregulation.

41 The European Union had already developed its own somewhat stricter procedure, the Ecological Management and Auditing System (EMAS), as a "voluntary requirement" for E.U. firms. EMAS involved less paperwork than ISO 14000, but also more specific requirements as to which environ-

mental aspects must be considered and more explicit requirements for public disclosure, which U.S. firms resisted. Both the ISO and EMAS standards actually originated with a British standard (B.S. 7750) which was developed in the late 1980s for use in the United Kingdom.

42 A "clean" firm in a generally "dirty" sector, for instance, might gain significant benefits by differentiating itself from the potential liabilities of its competitors.

43 Most countries, for instance, had laws that nominally imposed environmental standards comparable at least to those of the World Health Organization, the European Union, or the United States. In many countries, however, these paper standards were never enforced. The ISO/EMAS standards required that the company demonstrate a verifiable commitment to compliance and continuous improvement. This was intended as a solution to the nonenforcement problem: one "leveling the playing field" in favor of companies operating in countries where compliance was in fact required.

44 Lucent Technologies (formerly AT&T), for instance, proposed to certify an entire division including plants in Florida, Pennsylvania, and Texas, and to use this certification to justify some regulatory relief.

45 Less-developed countries were also concerned that customer firms in the European Union and other developed countries would not accept their certifications, and would require costly certification by firms in the developed countries instead. They also feared proposals for product "eco-labeling" requirements, which might be subject to highly variable, subjective, and potentially protectionist criteria mandated by the developed countries.

46 The majority owner of the Bhopal facility was actually the government of India, but it was the U.S. firm Union Carbide that faced lawsuits and public blame for the incident.

47 Environmental groups, for instance, proposed a new GATT provision to guarantee "environmental conditionality" — that is, that countries might not be penalized for taking measures in conflict with GATT rules if their main purpose was to protect the environment (Vogel 1995, 135).

Chapter 16: Managing the Environment, Managing Ourselves

1 A grass-roots alliance of environmental groups advocating for environmental justice emerged in the early 1980s, sparked by discoveries that chemical waste dumps — such as Love Canal in upstate New York, the Warren County, North Carolina PCB landfill, and other contaminated sites — were most often located in or near communities of low-income people and people of color. These groups were rooted in blue-collar and ethnic minority communities, and formed a network that was almost entirely separate from and often critical of "mainstream" national environmental membership groups such as the Sierra Club, Environmental Defense Fund, and Natural Resources Defense Council. Motivated initially by opposition to contaminated sites in their own neighborhoods and communities, they rapidly broadened their strategy to link the agendas of environmental protection and civil rights, and of people of color and low-income white communities, under the banner of environmental justice. A 1991 People of Color Environmental Leadership Summit mobilized political pressure for federal attention to their grievances in the 1992 election campaign, and in 1994 President Clinton issued an executive order directing all federal agencies to identify and correct any disproportionate negative impacts of their actions on such communities. Like other environmental issues, the momentum of this campaign was blocked in 1994 by the election of an actively hostile Republican Congress. In 1998, EPA announced a new and more stringent interim policy threatening state agencies with loss of federal funds if they issued pollution permits that might contribute to disproportionate impacts on minority communities, but business groups and state and local governments opposed it on the grounds that such a threat might simply force many businesses out of minority communities, reversing efforts to bring jobs and investments to them.

References

Abelson, Philip H. 1994. Risk Assessments of Low-Level Exposures. *Science* 265:1507.

Ackerman, Bruce A., and William Hassler. 1981. *Clean Coal/Dirty Air.* New Haven: Yale University Press.

Ackerman, Bruce A., and Richard B. Stewart. 1985. Reforming Environmental Law. *Stanford Law Review* 37:1333–65.

———. 1988. Reforming Environmental Law: The Democratic Case for Market Incentives. *Columbia Journal of Environmental Law* 13:171–99.

Administrative Conference of the United States. 1991. *A Guide to Federal Agency Rulemaking.* 2nd ed. Washington, D.C.: Administrative Conference of the United States.

Albion, Robert G. 1926. *Forests and Seapower: The Timber Problem of the Royal Navy, 1652–1862.* Cambridge: Harvard University Press.

Allen, David. 1990. Preventing Pollution. Chap. 10 in *Fighting Toxics,* edited by G. Cohen and J. O'Connor. Washington, D.C.: Island.

Ambrose, Stephen E. 1996. *Undaunted Courage: Meriwether Lewis, Thomas Jefferson, and the Opening of the American West.* New York: Simon & Schuster.

American Chemical Society. 1969. *Cleaning Our Environment: The Chemical Basis for Action.* Washington, D.C.: American Chemical Society.

Ames, Bruce; Renae Magaw; and Lois Swirsky Gold. 1987. Ranking Possible Carcinogenic Hazards. *Science* 236:271–80.

Anderson, Terry L. 1997. Dances With Myths. *Reason* 29 (February): 45–50.

Andrews, Richard N. L. 1976a. *Environmental Policy and Administrative Change.* Lexington, Mass.: Lexington Books.

———. 1976b. NEPA in Practice: Environmental Policy or Administrative Reform? *Environmental Law Reporter* 6:50001–09.

———. 1980. Class Politics or Democratic Reform: Environmentalism and American Political Institutions. *Natural Resources Journal* 20:221–41.

———. 1984a. Deregulation: The Failure at EPA. Chap. 7 in *Environmental Policy in the 1980s: Reagan's New Agenda,* edited by Norman Vig and Michael Kraft. Washington, D.C.: CQ.

———. 1984b. Economics and Environmental Decisions, Past and Present. Chap. 2 in *Environmental Policy Under Reagan's Executive Order: The Role of Benefit-Cost Analysis,* edited by V. Kerry Smith. Chapel Hill: University of North Carolina Press.

———. 1992. Pollution Prevention: Heading Off Potential Problems. *EPA Journal* 18(2):40–45.

———. 1993a. Environmental Policy in the Czech and Slovak Republic. Chap. 2 in *Environment and Democratic Transition: Policy and Politics in Central and Eastern Europe,* edited by Anna Vari and Pal Tamas. Boston: Kluwer.

———. 1993b. Long-Range Planning in Environmental and Health Regulatory Agencies. *Ecology Law Quarterly* 20:515–82.

———. 1996. Risk-Based Decisionmaking. Chap. 10 in *Environmental Policy in the 1990s,* edited by Norman Vig and Michael Kraft. 3rd ed. Washington, D.C.: CQ.

Andrews, Richard N. L.; Lubomir Paroha; Jan Vozab; and Petr Sauer. 1994. Decentralized Environmental Management in the Formerly Communist States: A Case Study of Decin, Czech Republic. *Environmental Impact Assessment Review* 14(2):111–36.

Armstrong, Ellis L.; Michael C. Robinson; and Suellen Hoy, eds. 1976. *History of Public Works in the United States.* Chicago: American Public Works Association.

Ashton, T. S. 1964 [1948]. *The Industrial Revolution, 1760–1830.* New York: Oxford University Press.

Athanasiou, Tom. 1996. *Divided Planet: The Ecology of Rich and Poor.* Boston: Little, Brown.

Ausubel, Jesse H. 1996. The Liberation of the Environment. *Daedalus* 125(3):1–17.

Ayres, Robert U. 1989. Industrial Metabolism. In National Academy of Engineering, *Technology and the Environment.* Washington, D.C.: National Academy Press, pp. 23–49.

Bailar, John C. III; Edmund A. C. Crouch; Rashid Shaikh; and Donna Speigelman. 1988. One-Hit Models of Carcinogenesis: Conservative or Not? *Risk Analysis* 8:485–97.

Bardach, Eugene, and Robert Kagan, eds. 1982. *Social Regulation: Strategies for Reform.* San Francisco: Institute for Contemporary Studies.

Barnes, Harry E. 1935. *Society in Transition: Problems of a Changing Age.* Englewood Cliffs, N.J.: Prentice-Hall.

Barnett, Harold, and Chandler Morse. 1963. *Scarcity and Growth.* Baltimore: Johns Hopkins University Press.

Barnett, Harold C. 1994. *Toxic Debts and the Superfund Dilemma.* Chapel Hill: University of North Carolina Press.

Bartlett, Richard A. 1974. *The New Country: A Social History of the American Frontier, 1776–1890.* New York: Oxford University Press.

Bartlett, Robert. 1984. The Budgetary Process and Environmental Policy. In *Environmental Policy in the 1980s: Reagan's New Agenda,* edited by Norman Vig and Michael Kraft. Washington, D.C.: CQ, pp. 121–41.

Bartram, William. 1996 [1791]. *Travels Through North and South Carolina.* New York: Library of America.

Bean, Michael J. 1983 [1977]. *The Evolution of National Wildlife Law.* New York: Praeger.

Beardsley, Dan; Terry Davies; and Robert Hersh. 1997. Improving Environmental Management: What Works, What Doesn't. *Environment* 39(7):6–9, 28–35.

Beer, George L. 1893. *The Commercial Policy of England Toward the American Colonies.* Vol. 3 of *Studies in History, Economics and Public Law.* New York: Columbia College.

Begley, Ronald. 1997. Electric Power Deregulation: Will It Mean Dirtier Air? *Environmental Science & Technology* 31(10):462A–465A.

Benbrook, Charles M. 1996. *Pesticides at the Crossroads.* Yonkers, N.Y.: Consumers Union.

Bennett, G. 1991. The History of the Dutch National Environmental Policy Plan. *Environment* 33(7):6–9, 31–33.

Berkhofer, Robert. 1972. Jefferson, the Ordinance of 1784, and the Origins of the American Territorial System. *William and Mary Quarterly* 29:231–62.

Berry, Michael A. 1984. *A Method for Examining Policy Implementation: A Study of Decision-*

Making for National Ambient Air Quality Standards, 1964–1984. Ph.D. diss., University of North Carolina at Chapel Hill.

Blair, Peter D. 1993. U.S. Energy Policy Perspectives for the 1990s. In *Making National Energy Policy,* edited by Hans H. Landsberg. Washington, D.C.: Resources for the Future, pp. 7–40.

Blake, John B. 1959. *Public Health in the Town of Boston, 1630–1822.* Cambridge: Harvard University Press.

Borgstrom, Georg. 1971. *Too Many.* New York: Collier.

Bosso, Christopher J. 1987. *Pesticides and Politics: The Life Cycle of a Public Issue.* Pittsburgh: University of Pittsburgh Press.

Breyer, Stephen. 1993. *Breaking the Vicious Circle.* Cambridge: Harvard University Press.

Brick, Phil. 1995. Determined Opposition: The Wise Use Movement Challenges Environmentalism. *Environment* 37(8):17–20, 36–42.

Bridenbaugh, Carl. 1964. *Cities in the Wilderness: The First Century of Urban Life in America, 1625–1742.* New York: Capricorn.

———. 1952. *Myths and Realities: Societies of the Colonial South.* Baton Rouge: Louisiana State University Press.

Bromley, Daniel M., ed. 1992. *Making the Commons Work.* San Francisco: Institute for Contemporary Studies.

Bronowski, Jacob. 1973. *The Ascent of Man.* Boston: Little, Brown.

Bryner, Gary C. 1987. *Bureaucratic Discretion: Law and Policy in Federal Regulatory Agencies.* New York: Praeger.

———. 1993. *Blue Skies, Green Politics: The Clean Air Act of 1990.* Washington, D.C.: CQ.

Buck, Susan J. 1985. No Tragedy on the Commons. *Environmental Ethics* 7:49–61.

Burtraw, Dallas; Alan J. Krupnick; and Karen L. Palmer. 1996. Air Quality and Electricity: What Competition May Mean. *Resources* 123 (Spring 1996): 6–8.

Byrne, J. Peter. 1995. Ten Arguments for the Abolition of the Regulatory Takings Doctrine. *Ecology Law Quarterly* 22:89–142.

Caldwell, Lynton K. 1963. Environment: A New Focus for Public Policy? *Public Administration Review* 22:132–39.

———. 1984. The World Environment: Reversing U.S. Policy Commitments. Chap. 15 in *Environmental Policy in the 1980s: Reagan's New Agenda,* edited by Norman Vig and Michael Kraft. Washington, D.C.: CQ.

———. 1990. *International Environmental Policy: Emergence and Dimensions.* 2nd ed. Durham, N.C.: Duke University Press.

———. 1997. Implementing NEPA: A Non-Technical Political Task. In *Towards a National Environmental Policy: The First 25 Years,* edited by Ray Clark and Larry Canter. Delray Beach, Fla.: St. Lucie.

Carp, E. Wayne. 1984. *To Starve the Army at Pleasure: Continental Army Administration and American Political Culture, 1775–1783.* Chapel Hill: University of North Carolina Press.

Carson, Rachel. 1962. *Silent Spring.* Boston: Houghton Mifflin.

Charnovitz, Steve. 1997. A Critical Guide to the WTO's Report on Trade and the Environment. *Arizona Journal of International and Comparative Law* 14(2):341–79.

Chaterjee, Pratap, and Mathias Finger. 1994. *The Earth Brokers.* New York: Routledge.

Christy, Francis T., Jr. 1975. Property Rights in the World Ocean. *Natural Resources Journal* 15:695–712.

Citizens' Association of New York. Council of Hygiene and Public Health. 1970 [1865, 1866]. *Sanitary Condition of the City.* New York: Arno.

Clark, Henry G. 1972 [1852]. Superiority of Sanitary Measures Over Quarantines. *Origins of Public Health in America: Selected Essays, 1820–1855.* New York: Arno.

Clinton, William J. 1993. Remarks Announcing a New Environmental Policy. *Weekly Compilation of Presidential Documents* 29 (February 15, 1993): 159–60.

Colborn, Theodora; Frederick vom Saal; and Ana M. Soto. 1993. Developmental Effects of Endocrine Disrupting Chemicals in Wildlife and Humans. *Environmental Health Perspectives* 101:378–84.

Cole, H. S. D.; Christopher Freeman; Marie Jahoda; and K. L. R. Pavitt. 1973. *Models of Doom: A Critique of the Limits to Growth.* New York: Universe.

Colten, Craig E., and Peter N. Skinner. 1996. *The Road to Love Canal.* Austin: University of Texas Press.

Commoner, Barry. 1966. *Science and Survival.* New York: Viking.

——. 1971. *The Closing Circle.* New York: Knopf.

Conniff, Richard. 1994. Federal Lands: New Showdowns in the Old West. *National Geographic* 185:2–39.

Covello, Vincent, and Joshua Menkes. 1985. *Risk Assessment and Risk Assessment Methods: The State-of-the-Art.* Washington, D.C.: National Science Foundation, Division of Policy Research and Analysis.

Crenson, Matthew A. 1971. *The Un-Politics of Air Pollution: A Study of Non-Decisionmaking in the Cities.* Baltimore: Johns Hopkins University Press.

Cronon, William. 1983. *Changes in the Land: Indians, Colonists, and the Ecology of New England.* New York: Hill and Wang.

——. 1991. *Nature's Metropolis: Chicago and the Great West.* New York: Norton.

Crosby, Alfred W. 1986. *The Columbian Exchange: Biological and Cultural Consequences of 1492.* Westport, Conn.: Greenwood.

Culhane, Paul J. 1984. Sagebrush Rebels in Office: Jim Watt's Land and Water Politics. In *Environmental Policy in the 1980s: Reagan's New Agenda,* edited by Norman Vig and Michael Kraft. Washington, D.C.: CQ, pp. 293–317.

Curtis, Richard, and Elizabeth Hogan. 1970. *The Perils of the Peaceful Atom: The Myth of Safe Nuclear Power Plants.* London: V. Gollancz.

Dales, J. H. 1968. *Pollution, Property, and Prices.* Toronto: University of Toronto Press.

Daly, Herman E. 1993. The Perils of Free Trade. *Scientific American* 269(5):50–57.

——. 1994. Fostering Environmentally Sustainable Development: Four Parting Suggestions for the World Bank. *Ecological Economics* 10:183–87.

Dana, Samuel T. and Sally K. Fairfax. 1980 [1956]. *Forest and Range Policy.* New York: McGraw-Hill.

Davies, J. Clarence III, and Barbara Davies. 1975. *The Politics of Pollution.* Indianapolis: Bobbs-Merrill.

Davies, J. Clarence III. 1995. Congress Discovers Risk Analysis. *Resources* 118 (Winter): 5–8.

Davies, J. Clarence III, and Jan Mazurek. 1997a. *Industry Incentives for Environmental Improvement: Evaluation of U.S. Federal Initiatives.* Washington, D.C.: Global Environmental Management Initiative.

——. 1997b. *Regulating Pollution: Does the U.S. System Work?* Washington, D.C.: Resources for the Future.

Davis, David H. 1993. *Energy Politics.* 4th ed. New York: St. Martin's.

Davis, Gary A.; Catherine A. Wilt; and Jack N. Barkenbus. 1997. Extended Product Responsibility: A Tool for a Sustainable Economy. *Environment* 39(7):10–15, 36–38.

de Nevers, Noel H.; Robert Neligan; and Herschel Slater. 1977. Air Quality Management, Pollution Control Strategies, Modeling, and Evaluation. Chap. 1 in *Air Pollution,* vol. 5, edited by Arthur Stern. New York: Academic.

de Saillan, Charles. 1993. In Praise of Superfund. *Environment* 35(8):42–44.

Degler, Carl N. 1970 [1959]. *Out of Our Past: The Forces that Shaped Modern America.* New York: Harper & Row.

Dick, Everett. 1970. *The Lure of the Land: A Social History of the Public Lands from the Articles of Confederation to the New Deal.* Lincoln: University of Nebraska Press.

Dippie, Brian W. 1991. American Wests: Historiographical Perspectives. Chap. 9 in *Trails: Toward a New Western History,* edited by Patricia N. Limerick, Clyde A. Milner II, and Charles E. Rankin. Lawrence: University Press of Kansas.

Dobson, Andy. 1997. "Hot Spots" and Endangered Species: New Directions for Public Policy. *The Chronicle of Higher Education* (31 October 1997): B6–7.

Doll, Richard, and Richard Peto. 1981. The Causes of Cancer: Quantitative Estimates of Avoidable Risks of Cancer in the United States Today. *Journal of the National Cancer Institute* 66:1191–1285.

Dowie, Mark. 1995. *Losing Ground: American Environmentalism at the Close of the Twentieth Century.* Cambridge: MIT Press.

Downs, Anthony. 1972. Up and Down With Ecology: The Issue-Attention Cycle. *The Public Interest* 28 (Summer): 38–50.

Dubos, Rene. 1959. *Mirage of Health: Utopias, Progress, and Biological Change.* New York: Harper.

Duffy, John. 1990. *The Sanitarians: A History of American Public Health.* Urbana: University of Illinois Press.

Dunn, Richard S. 1959. *Seventeenth-Century America: Essays in Colonial History.* Edited by James M. Smith. Chapel Hill: University of North Carolina Press, pp. 195–225.

Dworsky, Leonard B. 1971. *Conservation in the United States: Water and Air Pollution.* New York: Chelsea House/Van Nostrand Reinhold.

Ecologist, The. 1993. *Whose Common Future? Reclaiming the Commons.* London: Earthscan.

Edelman, Murray. 1971. *The Politics of Symbolic Action.* Chicago: Markham.

Efron, Edith. 1984. *The Apocalyptics: Cancer and the Big Lie.* New York: Simon & Schuster.

Ehrlich, Paul, and Anne Ehrlich. 1968. *The Population Bomb.* New York: Ballantine.

Eisenbud, Merril. 1978. *Environment, Technology, and Health: Human Ecology in Historical Perspective.* New York: New York University Press.

Elkins, Stanley, and Eric McKitrick. 1993. *The Age of Federalism.* New York: Oxford University Press.

Elliott, E. Donald; Bruce A. Ackerman; and John C. Millian. 1985. Toward a Theory of Statutory Evolution: The Federalization of Environmental Law. *Journal of Law, Economics and Organization* 1:313–40.

Emerson, Ralph Waldo. 1903 [1836]. *Nature.* In *The Complete Works of Ralph Waldo Emerson,* edited by Edward W. Emerson. Boston: Houghton Mifflin.

Engelbert, Ernest A. 1950. *American Policy for Natural Resources: An Historical Survey to 1862.* Ph.D. diss., Harvard University.

Environment Canada. 1990. *Canada's Green Plan.* Ottawa, Canada: Environment Canada.

Epstein, Samuel; Lester Brown; and Carl Pope. 1982. *Hazardous Waste in America.* San Francisco: Sierra Club Books.

Esposito, John. 1970. *Vanishing Air.* New York: Grossman.

Esty, Daniel. 1994. *Greening the GATT.* Washington, D.C.: Institute for International Economics.

——. 1996. Revitalizing Environmental Federalism. *Michigan Law Review* 95:570–653.

——, and Marion Chertow. 1997. *Thinking Ecologically: The Next Generation of Environmental Policy*. New Haven: Yale University Press.

Faeth, Paul. 1995. *Growing Green: Enhancing the Economic and Environmental Performance of American Agriculture*. Washington, D.C.: World Resources Institute.

Faeth, Paul; Robert Repetto; Kim Kroll; Qi Dai; and Glenn Helmers. 1991. *Paying the Farm Bill: U.S. Agricultural Policy and the Transition to Sustainable Agriculture*. Washington, D.C.: World Resources Institute.

Farvar, M. Taghi, and John P. Milton. 1972. *The Careless Technology: Ecology and International Development*. Garden City, N.Y.: Natural History.

Findley, Roger W., and Daniel A. Farber. 1992. *Environmental Law in a Nutshell*. St. Paul, Minn.: West.

Finkel, Adam. 1994. A Second Opinion on an Environmental Misdiagnosis: The Risky Prescriptions of *Breaking the Vicious Circle. NYU Environmental Law Journal* 3:295–381.

Finkel, Adam M., and Dominic Golding, eds. 1995. *Worst Things First? The Debate Over Risk-Based National Environmental Priorities*. Baltimore: Johns Hopkins University Press.

Fiorino, Daniel. 1988. Regulatory Negotiation as a Policy Process. *Public Administration Review* 46:764–72.

Flader, Susan. 1974. *Thinking Like a Mountain: Aldo Leopold and the Evolution of an Ecological Attitude Toward Deer, Wolves, and Forests*. Columbia: University of Missouri Press.

Foresta, Ronald A. 1984. *America's National Parks and Their Keepers*. Washington, D.C.: Resources for the Future.

Fortrey, Samuel 1663. *England's Interest and Improvement*. Cambridge.

Foss, Philip. 1960. *Politics and Grass*. Seattle: University of Washington Press.

Fumento, Michael. 1993. *Science Under Siege*. New York: William Morrow.

Futrell, J. William. 1993. The History of Environmental Law. Chap. 1 in *Sustainable Environmental Law: Integrating Natural Resource and Pollution Abatement Law From Resources to Recovery*, edited by Celia Campbell-Mohn, Barry Breen, J. William Futrell, James M. McElfish, Jr., and Paula Grant. St. Paul, Minn.: West.

Galenson, David W. 1996. Settlement and Growth of the Colonies: Population, Labor, and Economic Development. Chap. 4 in *The Colonial Era*. Vol. 1 of the *Cambridge Economic History of the United States,* edited by Stanley L. Engerman and Robert E. Gallman. New York: Cambridge University Press.

Garrett, Laurie. 1994. *The Coming Plague: Newly Emerging Diseases in a World Out of Balance*. New York: Penguin.

Gates, Paul W. 1968. *History of Public Land Law Development*. Prepared for the U.S. Public Land Law Review Commission. Washington, D.C.: Government Printing Office.

Gauna, Eileen. 1995. Federal Environmental Citizen Provisions: Obstacles and Incentives on the Road to Environmental Justice. *Ecology Law Quarterly* 22:1–88.

Gerber, Michele S. 1992. *On the Home Front: The Cold War Legacy of the Hanford Nuclear Site*. Lincoln: University of Nebraska Press.

Getches, David H. 1990. *Water Law in a Nutshell*. St. Paul, Minn.: West.

Glicksman, R., and Christopher Schroeder. 1991. EPA and the Courts: Twenty Years of Law and Politics. *Law and Contemporary Problems* 54(4):249–309.

Goetzmann, William H. 1993 [1967]. *Exploration and Empire: The Explorer and the Scientist in the Winning of the American West*. Austin: Texas State Historical Association.

Goodwin, Craufurd D., ed. 1981. *Energy Policy in Perspective: Today's Problems, Yesterday's Solutions*. Washington, D.C.: Brookings Institution.

Gore, Al. 1992. *Earth in the Balance*. Boston: Houghton Mifflin.

Gottlieb, Robert. 1993. *Forcing the Spring: The Transformation of the American Environmental Movement*. Washington, D.C.: Island.

———, ed. 1995. *Reducing Toxics: A New Approach to Policy and Industrial Decisionmaking*. Washington, D.C.: Island.

Graham, Frank, Jr. 1970. *Since Silent Spring*. Boston: Houghton Mifflin.

Graham, John D.; Laura C. Green; and Marc J. Roberts. 1988. *In Search of Safety: Chemicals and Cancer Risk*. Cambridge: Harvard University Press.

Graham, Otis L., Jr. 1976. *Toward a Planned Society: From Roosevelt to Nixon*. New York: Oxford University Press.

———. 1996. *A Limited Bounty: The United States Since World War II*. New York: McGraw-Hill.

Greene, Jack P. 1993. *The Intellectual Construction of America*. Chapel Hill: University of North Carolina Press.

Greenwood, Ted. 1984. *Knowledge and Discretion in Government Regulation*. New York: Praeger.

Grinder, R. Dale. 1980. The Battle for Clean Air: The Smoke Problem in Post–Civil War America. In *Pollution and Reform in American Cities, 1870–1930*, edited by Martin V. Melosi. Austin: University of Texas Press, pp. 83–103.

Hacker, Louis M. 1940. Economic and Social Origins of the American Revolution. In his *The Triumph of American Capitalism*. New York: Simon & Schuster, pp. 145–70.

Handlin, Oscar. 1959. The Significance of the Seventeenth Century. Chap. 1 in *Seventeenth Century America: Essays in Colonial History*, edited by James M. Smith. Chapel Hill: University of North Carolina Press.

———, and Mary Handlin. 1945. Origins of the American Business Corporation. *Journal of Economic History* 5:1–23.

Hardin, Garrett. 1968. The Tragedy of the Commons. *Science* 162:1243–48.

Harlow, Ralph. 1929. Aspects of Revolutionary Finance. *American Historical Review* 35:46–68.

Harris, Marshall. 1953. *Origins of the Land Tenure System in the United States*. Ames: Iowa State University Press.

Harrison, Kathryn. 1995. Is Cooperation the Answer? Canadian Environmental Enforcement in Comparative Context. *Journal of Public Policy Analysis and Management* 14:221–44.

Hays, Samuel P. 1969 [1958]. *Conservation and the Gospel of Efficiency*. New York: Atheneum.

———. 1987. *Beauty, Health, and Permanence: Environmental Politics in the United States, 1955–1985*. New York: Cambridge University Press.

Heclo, Hugh. 1978. Issue Networks and the Executive Establishment. In *The New American Political System*, edited by Anthony King. Washington, D.C.: American Enterprise Institute, pp. 87–124.

Herfindahl, Orris. 1961. What Is Conservation? In *Three Studies in Mineral Economics*. Washington, D.C.: Resources for the Future.

Hibbard, Benjamin H. 1965 [1924]. *A History of the Public Land Policies*. New York: Macmillan.

Higginbotham, Don. 1971. *The War of American Independence: Military Attitudes, Policies, and Practices, 1763–1789*. New York: Macmillan.

Hirt, Paul W. 1994. *A Conspiracy of Optimism: Management of the National Forests Since World War Two*. Lincoln: University of Nebraska Press.

Hobbes, Thomas. 1996 [1651]. *Leviathan*. New York: Oxford University Press.

Hobsbawm, E. J. 1968. *Industry and Empire*. Baltimore: Penguin.

Hofstadter, Richard. 1955. *The Age of Reform*. New York: Vintage.

Hornstein, Donald. 1992. Reclaiming Environmental Law: A Normative Critique of Comparative Risk Analysis. *Columbia Law Review* 92:562–633.

——. 1993. Lessons From Federal Pesticide Regulation on the Paradigms and Politics of Environmental Law Reform. *Yale Journal on Regulation* 10:369–446.

Horwitz, Robert B. 1988. *The Irony of Regulatory Reform.* New York: Oxford University Press.

Hoy, Suellen. 1995. *Chasing Dirt: The American Pursuit of Cleanliness.* New York: Oxford University Press.

Jackson, Kenneth T. 1985. *Crabgrass Frontier: The Suburbanization of the United States.* New York: Oxford University Press.

Jänicke, Martin, and Helge Jörgens. 1996. National Environmental Policy Plans and Long-Term Sustainable Development: Learning from International Experiences. Berlin: Fachbereich Politische Wissenschaft, Freie Universität Berlin, FFU report 96-5.

Jänicke, Martin, and Helmut Weidner, eds. 1996. *National Environmental Policies: A Comparative Study of Capacity Building.* New York: Springer Verlag.

Jefferson, Thomas. 1955 [1787]. *Notes on the State of Virginia.* Edited by William Peden. Chapel Hill: University of North Carolina Press.

Jensen, Merrill. 1969. The American Revolution and American Agriculture. *Agricultural History* 43:107–27.

——. 1974. *The American Revolution Within America.* New York: New York University Press.

——. 1939. The Creation of the Public Domain, 1781–1784. *Mississippi Valley Historical Review* 26:323–42.

——. 1962. *The New Nation: A History of the United States During The Confederation, 1781–1789.* New York: Knopf.

Jones, Charles O. 1975. *Clean Air: The Policies and Politics of Pollution Control.* Pittsburgh: University of Pittsburgh Press.

Jones, E. L. 1996. The European Background. Chap. 3 in *The Colonial Era.* Vol. 1 of the *Cambridge Economic History of the United States,* edited by Stanley L. Engerman and Robert E. Gallman. New York: Cambridge University Press.

Jones, Howard M. 1965. *O Strange New World.* London: Chatto & Windus.

Judah, Charles B., Jr. 1933. *The North American Fisheries and British Policy to 1713.* Urbana: University of Illinois Press.

Kapp, K. William. 1950. *The Social Costs of Business Enterprise.* New York: Schocken.

Kash, Don E., and Robert W. Rycroft. 1984. *U.S. Energy Policy: Crisis and Complacency.* Norman: University of Oklahoma Press.

Kayden, Jerold S. 1996. Private Property Rights, Government Regulation, and the Constitution: Searching for Balance. In *Land Use in America,* edited by H. Diamond and P. Noonan. Washington, D.C.: Island, pp. 257–77.

Keller, Morton. 1994. *Regulating a New Society: Public Policy and Social Change in America, 1900–1933.* Cambridge: Harvard University Press.

Kempton, Willett; James Boster; and Jennifer Hartley. 1995. *Environmental Values in American Culture.* Cambridge: MIT Press.

Kerwin, Cornelius M. 1994. *Rulemaking: How Government Agencies Write Law and Make Policy.* Washington, D.C.: CQ.

Khor, Martin. 1996. Colonialism Redux. *The Nation* 263(3):18–20.

Kline, Benjamin. 1997. *First Along the River: A Brief History of the U.S. Environmental Movement.* San Francisco: Acada.

Klosterman, R. 1980. A Public Interest Criterion. *Journal of the American Planning Association* 46:323–32.

Klyza, Christopher M. 1996. *Who Controls the Public Lands?* Chapel Hill: University of North Carolina Press.

Kneese, Allen V., and Blair T. Bower. 1968. *Managing Water Quality: Economics, Technology, and Institutions.* Baltimore: Johns Hopkins University Press.

———. 1979. *Environmental Quality and Residuals Management.* Baltimore: Johns Hopkins University Press.

Korten, David C. 1996. The Limits of the Earth. *The Nation* 263(3):14–18.

Kotov, Vladimir, and Elena Nikitina. 1993. Russia in Transition: Obstacles to Environmental Protection. *Environment* 35(10):11–19.

Krech, Shepard III. 1994. Ecology and the American Indian. *Ideas from the National Humanities Center* 3(1):4–22.

Krimsky, Sheldon, and Alonzo Plough. 1989. *Environmental Hazards: Communicating Risks as a Social Process.* Dover, Mass.: Auburn House.

Krutilla, John V. 1967. Conservation Reconsidered. *American Economic Review* 57:777–86.

Kupperman, Karen O., ed. 1995. *America in European Consciousness, 1492–1750.* Chapel Hill: University of North Carolina Press.

Lacey, Michael J. 1979. *The Mysteries of Earth-Making Dissolve: A Study of Washington's Intellectual Community and the Origins of American Environmentalism in the Late Nineteenth Century.* Ph.D. diss., George Washington University.

Landy, Marc K.; Marc J. Roberts; and Stephen R. Thomas. 1994. *The Environmental Protection Agency: Asking the Wrong Questions.* 2nd ed. New York: Oxford University Press.

Lash, Jonathan; Katherine Gillman; and David Sheridan. 1984. *A Season of Spoils: The Story of the Reagan Administration's Attack on the Environment.* New York: Pantheon.

Latin, Howard. 1985. Ideal Versus Real Regulatory Efficiency: Implementation of Uniform Standards and 'Fine-Tuning' Regulatory Reforms. *Stanford Law Review* 37:1267–1332.

Lawson, Murray G. 1943. *Fur: A Study in English Mercantilism, 1700–1775.* Toronto: University of Toronto Press.

Laycock, George. 1970. *The Diligent Destroyers.* New York: Ballantine.

Lazarus, Richard. 1991. The Tragedy of Distrust in the Implementation of Federal Environmental Law. *Law and Contemporary Problems* 54(4):311–74.

Lele, Sharachandra M. 1991. Sustainable Development: A Critical Review. *World Development* 19:607–21.

Leonard, Eugenie A. 1950. Paper as a Critical Commodity. *Pennsylvania Magazine of History and Biography* 74:488–99.

Leopold, Aldo. 1933. *Game Management.* New York: Charles Scribner's Sons.

———. 1966 [1949]. *A Sand County Almanac.* New York: Ballantine.

Lester, James P. 1995. Federalism and State Environmental Policy. Chap. 3 in *Environmental Politics and Policy: Theories and Evidence,* edited by James P. Lester. Durham, N.C.: Duke University Press.

Leuchtenberg, William E. 1995. *The FDR Years: On Roosevelt and His Legacy.* New York: Columbia University Press.

Levine, Charles, and James Thurber. 1986. Reagan and the Intergovernmental Lobby: Iron Triangles, Cozy Subsystems, and Political Conflict. Chap. 11 in *Interest Group Politics,* edited by Allan Cigler and Burdett Loomis. 2nd ed. Washington, D.C.: CQ.

Lewis, Thomas A. 1992. Cloaked in a Wise Disguise. *National Wildlife,* October–November, 4–9.

Lindblom, Charles E. 1965. *The Intelligence of Democracy.* New York: Free Press.

Linden, Eugene. 1996. The Exploding Cities of the Developing World. *Foreign Affairs* 75(1) (January–February): 52–65.

Lipset, Seymour M. 1963. *The First New Nation.* New York: Basic.

Liroff, Richard A. 1986. *Reforming Air Pollution Regulation: The Toil and Trouble of EPA's Bubble.* Washington, D.C.: The Conservation Foundation.

Loomis, Burdett, and Allan Cigler. 1986. "Introduction: The Changing Nature of Interest Group Politics." Chap. 1 in *Interest Group Politics,* edited by Allan Cigler and Burdett Loomis. 2nd ed. Washington, D.C.: CQ.

Lovins, Amory. 1976. Energy Strategy: The Road Not Taken. *Foreign Affairs* 55:65–96.

Lowi, Theodore. 1969. *The End of Liberalism.* New York: Norton.

Lowitt, Richard. 1984. *The New Deal and the West.* Bloomington: Indiana University Press.

Lowrie, Walter, and Matthew St. Clair Clarke, eds. 1832. Public Lands. In *American State Papers.* Vol. 1. Washington, D.C.: U.S. Government Printing Office.

Lund, Thomas A. 1975. British Wildlife Law Before the American Revolution: Lessons from the Past. *Michigan Law Review* 74:49–74.

Maass, Arthur. 1950. Congress and Water Resources. *American Political Science Review* 44:576–93.

———. 1951. *Muddy Waters: The Army Engineers and the Nation's Rivers.* Cambridge: Harvard University Press.

———. 1970. Public Investment Planning in the United States: Analysis and Critique. *Public Policy* 18:213–16.

Mahood, H. R. 1990. *Interest Group Politics in America: A New Intensity.* Englewood Cliffs, N.J.: Prentice-Hall.

Marcus, Alfred. 1980. *Promise and Performance: Choosing and Implementing Environmental Policy.* Westport, Conn.: Greenwood.

Marsh, George Perkins. 1965 [1864]. *Man and Nature: Or, Physical Geography as Modified by Human Action.* Cambridge: Harvard University Press.

Martin, Calvin L. 1992. *In the Spirit of the Earth.* Baltimore: Johns Hopkins University Press.

Martis, Kenneth C. 1976. *The History of Natural Resources Roll Call Voting in the United States House of Representatives.* Ph.D. diss., University of Michigan.

Marx, Leo. 1964. *The Machine in the Garden: Technology and the Pastoral Ideal in America.* New York: Oxford University Press.

Matson, Cathy. 1996. The Revolution, the Constitution, and the New Nation. Chap. 9 in *The Colonial Era.* Vol. 1 of the *Cambridge Economic History of the United States,* edited by Stanley L. Engerman and Robert E. Gallman. New York: Cambridge University Press.

Mayer, Carl J., and George A. Riley. 1985. *Public Domain, Private Dominion: A History of Public Mineral Policy in America.* San Francisco: Sierra Club Books.

Mazmanian, Daniel, and Jeanne Nienaber. 1979. *Can Organizations Change? Environmental Protection, Citizen Participation and the Corps of Engineers.* Washington, D.C.: Brookings Institution.

McCloskey, Robert G. 1964 [1951]. *American Conservatism in the Age of Enterprise.* New York: Harper.

McConnell, Grant. 1966. *Private Power and American Democracy.* New York: Vintage.

McCoy, Drew R. 1980. *The Elusive Republic: Political Economy in Jeffersonian America.* Chapel Hill: University of North Carolina Press.

McCusker, John J., and Russell R. Menard. 1985. *The Economy of British America, 1607–1789.* Chapel Hill: University of North Carolina Press.

McElfish, James, and Elissa Parker. 1995. *Rediscovering the National Environmental Policy Act: Back to the Future.* Washington, D.C.: Environmental Law Institute.

McElvaine, Robert. 1993 [1984]. *The Great Depression, America 1929–1941.* New York: Times Books.

McGarity, Eileen M. 1997. From NIMBY to Civil Rights: The Origins of the Environmental Justice Movement. *Environmental History* 2(3):301–23.

McGarity, Thomas. 1991. The Internal Structure of EPA Rulemaking. *Law and Contemporary Problems* 54(4):57–111.

McHarg, Ian. 1969. *Design with Nature.* Garden City, N.Y.: Natural History Press.

McKenzie, James J.; Roger C. Dower; and Don Chan. 1992 *The Going Rate: What It Really Costs to Drive.* Washington, D.C.: World Resources Institute.

McNickle, D'Arcy. 1975 [1949]. *They Came Here First.* New York: Harper and Row.

Meadows, Donella H.; Dennis L. Meadows; Jørgen Randers; and William W. Behrens III. 1972. *The Limits to Growth.* New York: Universe.

Meinig, D. W. 1986. *Atlantic America, 1492–1800.* Vol. 1 of *The Shaping of America: A Geographical Perspective on 500 Years of History.* New Haven: Yale University Press.

———. 1993. *Continental America, 1800–1867.* Vol. 2 of *The Shaping of America: A Geographical Perspective on 500 Years of History.* New Haven: Yale University Press.

Melnick, R. Shep. 1983. *Regulation and the Courts: The Case of the Clean Air Act.* Washington, D.C.: Brookings.

Melosi, Martin V. 1980. Environmental Crisis in the City: The Relationship Between Industrialization and Urban Pollution. In *Pollution and Reform in American Cities,* edited by Martin V. Melosi. Austin: University of Texas Press, pp. 3–31.

———. 1981. *Garbage in the Cities: Refuse, Reform, and the Environment, 1880–1980.* Chicago: Dorsey.

Miles, Rufus. 1976. *Awakening from the American Dream.* New York: Universe.

Miller, Joseph A. 1973. *Congress and the Origins of Conservation: Natural Resource Policies, 1865–1900.* Ph.D. diss., University of Minnesota.

Miller, John C. 1966. *The First Frontier: Life in Colonial America.* New York: Dell.

Morell, James B. 1992. *The Law of the Sea.* London: McFarland.

Morgan, Robert J. 1965. *Governing Soil Conservation: Thirty Years of the New Decentralization.* Baltimore: Johns Hopkins University Press.

Mossman, B. T.; J. Bignon; M. Corn; J. Seaton; and J. B. L. Gee. 1990. Asbestos: Scientific Developments and Implications for Public Policy. *Science* 247:294–301.

Mowry, George E. 1962 [1958]. *The Era of Theodore Roosevelt and the Birth of Modern America.* New York: Harper & Row.

Mullan, Fitzhugh. 1989. *Plagues and Politics: The Story of the United States Public Health Service.* New York: Basic.

Nader, Ralph; Ronald Brownstein; and John Richard. 1981. *Who's Poisoning America: Corporate Polluters and Their Victims in a Chemical Age.* San Francisco: Sierra Club Books.

Nash, Roderick E. 1982 [1967]. *Wilderness and the American Mind.* New Haven: Yale University Press.

National Academy of Engineering. 1989. *Technology and the Environment.* Washington, D.C.: National Academy Press.

———. 1994. *The Greening of Industrial Ecosystems.* Washington, D.C.: National Academy Press.

National Academy of Public Administration. 1995. *Setting Priorities, Getting Results: A New Direction for EPA.* Washington, D.C.: National Academy of Public Administration.

National Research Council. 1994. *Science and Judgment in Risk Assessment.* Washington, D.C.: National Academy Press.

Nelson, Robert H. 1986. Private Rights to Government Actions: How Modern Property Rights Evolve. University of Illinois Law Review 1986:361–86.

———. 1991. *Reaching for Heaven on Earth.* Lanham, Md.: Littlefield Adams.

Netherlands Ministry of Housing, Physical Planning and Environment. 1990. *Highlights of the Dutch National Environmental Policy Plan.* The Hague: Netherlands Ministry of Housing, Physical Planning and Environment.

Nettels, Curtis P. 1962. *The Emergence of a National Economy, 1775–1815.* New York: Holt, Rinehart and Winston.

Nixon, Edgar B., ed. 1957. *Franklin D. Roosevelt and Conservation, 1911–1945.* Washington, D.C.: U.S. Government Printing Office.

Noggle, Burl. 1962. *Teapot Dome: Oil and Politics in the 1920s.* Baton Rouge: Louisiana State University Press.

Novick, Sheldon. 1972. *The Careless Atom.* New York: Dell.

Okun, Daniel A. 1996. From Cholera to Cancer to Cryptosporidiosis. *Journal of Environmental Engineering* 122(6):453–58.

Olson, Mancur. 1965. *The Logic of Collective Action.* Cambridge: Harvard University Press.

Onuf, Peter S. 1987. *Statehood and Nation: A History of the Northwest Ordinance.* Bloomington: Indiana University Press.

Opie, John. 1994 [1987]. *The Law of the Land.* Lincoln: University of Nebraska Press.

Oregon Progress Board. 1991. *Oregon Benchmarks: Setting Measurable Standards for Progress.* Report to the 1991 Oregon Legislature. Salem: Oregon Progress Board.

Organisation for Economic Co-operation and Development (OECD). 1996. *Environmental Performance Review: United States.* Paris: OECD.

Osborn, Fairfield. 1970 [1948]. *Our Plundered Planet.* New York: Pyramid.

Owen, Anna Lou Riesch. 1983. *Conservation Under F.D.R.* New York: Praeger.

Paarlberg, Don. 1989. Tarnished Gold: Fifty Years of New Deal Farm Programs. Chap. 2 in *The New Deal and Its Legacy: Critique and Reappraisal,* edited by Robert Eden. Westport, Conn.: Greenwood.

Paarlberg, Robert L. 1996. A Domestic Dispute: Clinton, Congress, and International Environmental Policy. *Environment* 38(8):16–20, 28–33.

Paddock, William, and Paul Paddock. 1967. *Famine 1975! America's Decision: Who Will Survive?* Boston: Little, Brown.

Paehlke, Robert C. 1989. *Environmentalism and the Future of Progressive Politics.* New Haven: Yale University Press.

Parkman, Francis. 1969 [1849]. *The Oregon Trail.* Madison: University of Wisconsin Press.

Pearce, David; Neil Adger; David Maddison; and Dominic Moran. 1995. Debt and the Environment. *Scientific American* 272(6):52–56.

Percival, Robert. 1991. Checks Without Balance: Executive Office Oversight of the Environmental Protection Agency. *Law and Contemporary Problems* 54(4):127–204.

Peterson, John M., and Ralph Gray. 1969. *Economic Development of the United States.* Homewood, Ill.: Irwin.

Petulla, Joseph M. 1988. *American Environmental History.* 2nd ed. Columbus, Ohio: Merrill.

Pinchot, Gifford. 1967 [1910]. *The Fight for Conservation.* Seattle: University of Washington Press.

Polanyi, Karl. 1944. *The Great Transformation.* New York: Farrar and Rinehart.

Portney, Paul, ed. 1990. *Public Policies for Environmental Protection.* Washington, D.C.: Resources for the Future.

Potter, David M. 1954. *People of Plenty: Economic Abundance and the American Character.* Chicago: University of Chicago Press.

Pyne, Stephen J. 1984. *Introduction to Wildland Fire: Fire Management in the United States.* New York: Wiley.

Quarles, John. 1976. *Cleaning Up America: An Insider's View of the Environmental Protection Agency.* Boston: Houghton Mifflin.

Rabe, Barry. 1996. Power to the States: The Promise and Pitfalls of Decentralization. Chap. 2 in *Environmental Policy in the 1990s,* edited by Norman Vig and Michael Kraft. 3rd ed. Washington, D.C.: CQ.

Rakove, Jack N. 1979. *The Beginnings of National Politics: An Interpretive History of the Continental Congress.* New York: Knopf.

Rasmussen, Wayne D., and Gladys L. Baker. 1986. The New Deal Farm Programs: The Myth and the Reality. In *The Roosevelt New Deal: A Program Assessment Fifty Years Later,* edited by Wilbur J. Cohen. Austin: Lyndon B. Johnson School of Public Affairs, University of Texas, pp. 201–19.

Rasmussen, Wayne D.; Gladys L. Baker; and James S. Ward. 1976. *A Short History of Agricultural Adjustment, 1933–75.* Agriculture Information Bulletin No. 391. Washington, D.C.: U.S. Department of Agriculture. Economic Research Service.

Rauber, Paul. 1997. The Great Green Hope. *Sierra* 82(4):40–43, 60–63.

Raup, P. 1982. An Agricultural Critique of the National Agricultural Lands Study. *Land Economics* 58:260–74.

Raushenbush, Stephen. 1968. Conservation in 1952. *Annals of the American Academy of Social and Political Science* 281:1–9.

Rawls, John. 1971. *A Theory of Justice.* Cambridge: Belknap Press of Harvard University Press.

Reed, David. 1996. *Structural Adjustment, the Environment, and Sustainable Development.* London: Earthscan.

Regenstein, Lewis. 1982. *America the Poisoned.* Washington, D.C.: Acropolis.

Reilly, William. 1990. Aiming Before We Shoot: The Quiet Revolution in Environmental Policy. *Northern Kentucky Law Review* 18:159–74 (Speech to the National Press Club, September 26, 1990, USEPA Document No. 20Z-1011).

Reisner, Marc. 1986. *Cadillac Desert.* New York: Viking.

Repetto, Robert. 1995. *Jobs, Competitiveness, and Environmental Regulation: What Are the Real Issues?* Washington, D.C.: World Resources Institute.

Repetto, Robert, and Malcolm Gilles. 1988. *Public Policies and the Misuse of Forest Resources* Washington, D.C.: World Resources Institute.

Richardson, Elmo. 1973. *Dams, Parks and Politics: Resource Development and Preservation in the Truman-Eisenhower Era.* Lexington: University Press of Kentucky.

Riebsame, William E. 1996. Ending the Range Wars? *Environment* 38(4):4–9, 27–29.

Ringquist, Evan J. 1993. *Environmental Protection at the State Level: Politics and Progress in Controlling Pollution.* Armonk, N.Y.: M. E. Sharpe.

Roht-Arriaza, Naomi. 1995. Shifting the Point of Regulation: The International Organization for Standardization and Global Lawmaking on Trade and the Environment. *Ecology Law Quarterly* 22:479–539.

Rosen, Christine. 1993. Differing Perceptions of the Value of Pollution Abatement Across Time and Place: Balancing Doctrine in Pollution Nuisance Law. *Law and History Review* 11:303–81.

Rosen, George. 1958. *A History of Public Health.* New York: MD Publications.

Rosenau, Milton J. 1935 [1913]. *Preventive Medicine and Hygiene.* New York: D. Appleton & Co.

Rostow, Walt W. 1960. *The Stages of Economic Growth.* New York: Cambridge University Press.

Royston, M. 1979. *Pollution Prevention Pays.* London: Pergamon.

———. 1980. Making Pollution Prevention Pay. *Harvard Business Review* 58 (November-December): 6–27.

Rubin, Charles T. 1994. *The Green Crusade: Rethinking the Roots of Environmentalism*. New York: Free Press.

Ruckelshaus, William D. 1992. The Role of the Medical Profession in the Environmental Arena. *Academic Medicine* 67:146–50.

Rushefsky, Mark. 1986. *Making Cancer Policy*. Albany: State University of New York Press.

Russell, Milton, and Michael Gruber. 1987. Risk Assessment in Environmental Policy-Making. *Science* 236:286–90.

Safina, Carl. 1994. Where Have All the Fishes Gone? *Issues in Science and Technology* 10(3): 37–43.

St. John de Crèvecoeur, J. Hector. 1957 [1782]. *Letters from an American Farmer*. New York: E. P. Dutton.

Sale, Kirkpatrick. 1993. *The Green Revolution: The American Environmental Movement, 1962–1992*. New York: Hill and Wang.

Salisbury, Neal. 1996. History of Native Americans from Before the Arrival of the Europeans until the American Civil War. Chap. 1 in *The Colonial Era*. Vol. 1 of the *Cambridge Economic History of the United States,* edited by Stanley L. Engerman and Robert E. Gallman. New York: Cambridge University Press.

Salomon, Lester M. 1989. *Beyond Privatization: The Tools of Government Action*. Washington, D.C.: Urban Institute.

Salter, Liora. 1988. *Mandated Science: Science and Scientists in the Making of Standards*. Boston: Kluwer.

Sarokin, David J.; Warren R. Muir; Catherine G. Miller; and Sebastian R. Sperber. 1985. *Cutting Chemical Wastes*. New York: INFORM.

Sauer, Carl O. 1971. *Sixteenth Century North America*. Berkeley: University of California Press.

Savas, Edward S. 1982. *Privatizing the Public Sector*. Chatham, N.J.: Chatham House.

Sax, Joseph L. 1971. *Defending the Environment*. New York: Knopf.

Schaeffer, Janet. 1972. Solid Wastes. In *Nixon and the Environment: The Politics of Devastation,* edited by James Rathlesberger. New York: Village Voice/Taurus Communications, pp. 239–56.

Schapsmeier, Edward L., and Frederick H. Schapsmeier. 1986. Henry A. Wallace as Agricultural Secretary and Agrarian Reformer. In *The Roosevelt New Deal: A Program Assessment Fifty Years Later,* edited by Wilbur J. Cohen. Austin: Lyndon B. Johnson School of Public Affairs, University of Texas, pp. 221–33.

Schiff, Ashley. 1962. *Fire and Water: Scientific Heresy in the Forest Service*. Cambridge: Harvard University Press.

Schlesinger, Arthur M. 1965 [1958]. *The Coming of the New Deal*. Boston: Houghton Mifflin.
——. 1986. *The Cycles of American History*. Boston: Houghton Mifflin.

Schneider, Keith. 1993. What Price Cleanup? *New York Times,* 21–26 March 1993.

Schnoor, Jerald L.; James N. Galloway; and Bedrich Moldan. 1997. East Central Europe: An Environment in Transition. *Environmental Science & Technology* 31(9):412A–416A.

Scott, William B. 1977. *In Pursuit of Happiness: American Conceptions of Property from the Seventeenth to the Twentieth Century*. Bloomington: Indiana University Press.

Scoville, Warren J. 1953. Did Colonial Farmers "Waste" Our Land? *Southern Economics Journal* 20:178–81.

Sedjo, Roger A. 1995. Ecosystem Management: An Uncharted Course for Public Forests. *Resources* 121 (Fall): 10, 18–20.

Selleck, Henry B., and Alfred H. Whittaker. 1962. *Occupational Health in America*. Detroit: Wayne State University Press.

Selznick, Philip. 1949. *TVA and the Grass Roots*. Berkeley: University of California Press.

Shabecoff, Philip. 1993. *A Fierce Green Fire: The American Environmental Movement*. New York: Hill and Wang.

Shy, Carl M. 1990. Progress and Public Health: Lessons from Environmental Lead. *Environmental Impact Assessment Review* 10:417–31.

Sinclair, Upton. 1906. *The Jungle*. New York: Doubleday, Page & Co.

Smillie, Wilson G. 1955. *Public Health: Its Promise for the Future, 1607–1914*. New York: Macmillan.

Smith, Adam. 1933 [1776]. *The Wealth of Nations*. New York: E. P. Dutton.

Smith, Frank E. 1966. *The Politics of Conservation*. New York: Harper.

———, ed. 1971a. *Conservation in the United States: Land and Water, 1492–1900*. New York: Chelsea House.

———, ed. 1971b. *Conservation in the United States: Land and Water, 1900–1970*. New York: Chelsea House.

Smith, Henry Nash. 1970 [1950]. *Virgin Land: The American West as Symbol and Myth*. Cambridge: Harvard University Press.

Smith, V. Kerry. 1984. *Environmental Policy Under Reagan's Executive Order: The Role of Cost-Benefit Analysis*. Chapel Hill: University of North Carolina Press.

Smythe, Robert. 1994. *Renewing NEPA: NEPA Effectiveness Study*. A Report to the U.S. President's Council on Environmental Quality. Chevy Chase, Md.: Potomac Resource Consultants.

Soper, Philip. 1974. The Constitutional Framework of Environmental Law. In *Federal Environmental Law*, edited by Erica Dolgin and Thomas Guilbert. Minneapolis, Minn.: West, pp. 20–125.

Sorenson, David S. 1979. Food for Peace — Or for Defense and Profit? The Role of P.L. 480, 1963–73. *Social Science Quarterly* 60:62–71.

Soroos, Marvin S. 1996. From Stockholm to Rio and Beyond: The Evolution of Global Environmental Governance. Chap. 13 in *Environmental Policy in the 1990s*, edited by Norman Vig and Michael Kraft. 3rd ed. Washington, D.C.: CQ.

Sosin, Jack M. 1961. *Whitehall and the Wilderness: The Middle West in British Colonial Policy, 1760–1775*. Lincoln: University of Nebraska Press.

Starr, Paul. 1982. *The Social Transformation of American Medicine*. New York: Basic.

Stavrianos, Leften Stavros. 1971. *The World Since 1500*. Englewood Cliffs, N.J.: Prentice-Hall.

Steen, Harold K. 1976. *The U.S. Forest Service: A History*. Seattle: University of Washington Press.

Stephenson, Orlando W. 1925. The Supply of Gunpowder in 1776. *American Historical Review* 30:271–81.

Stern, Arthur C. 1951. Air Pollution: The Status Today. *American Journal of Public Health* 41:27–37.

Stern, Arthur C.; Henry C. Wohlers; Richard W. Boubel; and William P. Lowry. 1973. *Fundamentals of Air Pollution*. New York: Academic.

Stewart, Richard B. 1975. The Reformation of American Administrative Law. *Harvard Law Review* 88:1667–1815.

Stout, Neil R. 1973. *The Royal Navy in America*. Annapolis, Md.: Naval Institute Press.

Sundquist, James L. 1968. *Politics and Policy: The Eisenhower, Kennedy, and Johnson Years*. Washington, D.C.: Brookings Institution.

Swain, Donald. 1963. *Federal Conservation Policy 1921–1933*. Berkeley: University of California Publications in History.

Swift, Byron. 1997. The Acid Rain Test. *Environmental Forum* 14(3):17–25.

Tarr, Joel A. 1971. Urban Pollution—Many Long Years Ago. *American Heritage* 22 (October):65–69, 106.

———. 1985a. Industrial Wastes and Public Health. *American Journal of Public Health* 75:1059–67.

———. 1985b. The Search for the Ultimate Sink: Urban Air, Land and Water Pollution in Historical Perspective. In *Environmental History: Critical Issues in Comparative Perspective,* edited by Kendall Bailes. New York: University Press of America, pp. 516–52.

———. 1996. *The Search for the Ultimate Sink.* Akron, Ohio: University of Akron Press.

Tarr, Joel A., and Francis McMichael. 1977. Decisions About Wastewater Technology: 1850–1932. *Journal of the Water Resources Planning and Management Division, American Society of Civil Engineers* 103 (May): 47–61.

Tarr, Joel A.; James McCurley; and Terry F. Yosie. 1980. The Development and Impact of Urban Wastewater Technology: Changing Concepts of Water Quality Control, 1850–1930. In *Pollution and Reform in American Cities, 1870–1930,* edited by Martin V. Melosi. Austin: University of Texas Press, pp. 59–82.

Taylor, Serge. 1984. *Making Bureaucracies Think: The Environmental Impact Strategy of Administrative Reform.* Stanford, Calif.: Stanford University Press.

Teitelbaum, Michael S. 1992/93. The Population Threat. *Foreign Affairs* 71(5):63–78.

Tesh, Sylvia. 1981. Disease Causality and Politics. *Journal of Health Politics, Policy and Law* 6:369–90.

———. 1988. *Hidden Arguments: Political Ideology and Disease Prevention Policy.* New Brunswick, N.J.: Rutgers University Press.

Tietenberg, Tom. 1992. *Environmental and Natural Resource Economics.* New York: Harper-Collins.

Tobey, James A. 1978. *The National Government and Public Health.* New York: Arno.

Toffler, Alvin. 1970. *Future Shock.* New York: Random House.

Toynbee, Arnold, 1956 [1884]. *The Industrial Revolution.* Boston: Beacon.

Tuchman, Barbara. 1978. *A Distant Mirror: The Calamitous 14th Century.* New York: Knopf.

Turner, Frederick Jackson. 1962. *Rise of the New West, 1819–1829.* New York: Collier.

Turner, Frederick. 1985. *Rediscovering America: John Muir in His Time and Ours.* New York: Viking.

Udall, Stewart. 1963. *The Quiet Crisis.* New York: Holt, Rinehart & Winston. Reprinted with additional material, *The Quiet Crisis and the Next Generation,* Salt Lake City: Gibbs-Smith, 1988.

———. 1994. *The Myths of August.* New York: Pantheon.

United Nations Industrial Development Organization. 1989. *Industry and Development: Global Report, 1988–89.* Vienna: UNIDO.

———. 1991. *Industry and Development: Global Report, 1990–91.* Vienna: UNIDO.

U.S. Congress. House Committees on Agriculture and on Foreign Affairs. 1990. *Review of U.S. International Food Assistance Programs.* Joint hearing, 1 November 1989, Serial 101-32. Washington, D.C.: Government Printing Office.

U.S. Congress. House Committee on Government Operations. 1971. *Stream Channelization.* Hearings, June 1971, part 2. Washington, D.C.: Government Printing Office.

U.S. Congress. House Committee on Science and Astronautics. 1968. *Managing the Environment.* Washington, D.C.: Government Printing Office.

U.S. Congress. Office of Technology Assessment. 1986. *Serious Reduction of Hazardous Waste.* Washington, D.C.: Government Printing Office.

———. 1987. *From Pollution to Prevention: A Progress Report on Waste Reduction.* Washington, D.C.: Government Printing Office.

U.S. Council on Environmental Quality. 1971. *Toxic Substances.* Washington, D.C.: Government Printing Office.

———. 1977. *National Wildlife Law.* Washington, D.C.: Government Printing Office.

———. 1978. *Off-Road Vehicles on Public Lands.* A Report to the President's Council on Environmental Quality. Washington, D.C.: Government Printing Office.

———. 1980a. *National Agricultural Lands Study.* Washington, D.C.: Government Printing Office.

———. 1980b. *The Global 2000 Report to the President, Entering the Twenty-First Century.* Washington, D.C.: Government Printing Office.

———. 1990. *Environmental Quality 1990.* Washington, D.C.: Government Printing Office.

———. 1993. *Environmental Quality 1993.* Washington, D.C.: Government Printing Office.

———. 1997. *Environmental Quality: 25th Annual Report, 1994–95.* Washington, D.C.: Government Printing Office.

U.S. Department of Commerce. 1975. *Historical Statistics of the United States.* 1975. Washington, D.C.: Government Printing Office.

U.S. Department of Energy. Office of Environmental Management. 1995. *Estimating the Cold War Mortgage: The 1995 Baseline Environmental Management Report.* Report No. DOE/EM-0232. Washington, D.C.: U.S. Department of Energy.

U.S. Department of Health, Education, and Welfare. 1969. *Report of the Secretary's Commission on Pesticides and Their Relationship to Environmental Health.* Washington, D.C.: Government Printing Office.

U.S. Department of the Interior. Bureau of Land Management. 1973. *Public Land Statistics.* Washington, D.C.: Government Printing Office.

U.S. Environmental Protection Agency. 1987. *Unfinished Business: A Comparative Assessment of Environmental Problems.* Washington, D.C.: U.S. Environmental Protection Agency.

———. 1993a. *Oral History Interview-1: William D. Ruckelshaus.* Document No. EPA 202-K-92-003. Washington, D.C.: U.S. Environmental Protection Agency.

———. 1993b. *Oral History Interview-2: Russell E. Train.* Document No. EPA 202-K-93-001. Washington, D.C.: U.S. Environmental Protection Agency.

———. 1997. *Managing for Better Environmental Results.* Report No. EPA 100-R-97-004. Washington, D.C.: U.S. Environmental Protection Agency.

U.S. Environmental Protection Agency. Science Advisory Board. 1990. *Reducing Risk: Strategies for Environmental Protection.* Washington, D.C.: U.S. Environmental Protection Agency.

U.S. Federal Interagency River Basin Committee. Subcommittee on Benefits and Costs. 1950. *Proposed Practices for Economic Analysis of River Basin Projects* ("Green Book"). Washington, D.C.: Government Printing Office.

U.S. General Accounting Office. 1994. *Toxic Substances Control Act: EPA's Limited Progress in Controlling Toxic Chemicals.* Report No. GAO/T-RCED-94-212. Washington, D.C.: General Accounting Office.

———. 1996. *Water Pollution: Many Violations Have Not Received Adequate Enforcement Attention.* Report No. GAO/RCED-96-23. Washington, D.C.: General Accounting Office.

U.S. President's Commission on Materials Policy. 1952. *Resources for Freedom.* Washington, D.C.: Government Printing Office.

U.S. Public Land Law Review Commission. 1970. *One Third of the Nation's Land.* Washington, D.C.: Government Printing Office.

U.S. Senate. 1962. *Policies, Standards and Procedures in the Formulation, Evaluation and Review of*

Plans for Use and Development of Water and Related Land Resources. Senate Document 87-97. Washington, D.C.: Government Printing Office.

U.S. Tennessee Valley Authority. 1966. *Nature's Constant Gift.* Knoxville: Tennessee Valley Authority.

U.S. Water Resource Council. 1965. *Principles and Standards for Planning Water and Related Land Resources.* Washington, D.C.: Government Printing Office.

Vig, Norman. 1984. The President and the Environment. In *Environmental Policy in the 1980s: Reagan's New Agenda,* edited by Norman Vig and Michael Kraft. Washington, D.C.: CQ, pp. 77–95.

Vitousek, Peter M.; Harold A. Mooney; Jane Lubchenco; and Jerry M. Melillo. 1997. Human Domination of Earth's Ecosystems. *Science* 277:494–99.

Vogel, David. 1995. *Trading Up: Consumer and Environmental Regulation in a Global Economy.* Cambridge: Harvard University Press.

———. 1996. International Trade and Environmental Regulation. Chap. 16 in *Environmental Policy in the 1990s,* edited by Norman Vig and Michael Kraft. 3rd ed. Washington, D.C.: CQ.

Vogt, William. 1948. *The Road to Survival.* New York: W. Sloane Associates.

Walsh, John. 1978. EPA and Toxic Substances Law: Dealing With Uncertainty. *Science* 202:598–602.

Ward, Barbara. 1962. *The Rich Nations and the Poor Nations.* New York: Norton.

Ward, Barbara, and Rene Dubos. 1972. *Only One Earth: The Care and Maintenance of a Small Planet.* New York: Norton.

Wargo, John. 1996. *Our Children's Toxic Legacy: How Science and Law Fail to Protect Us from Pesticides.* New Haven: Yale University Press.

Warner, Sam Bass. 1972. *The Urban Wilderness: A History of the American City.* New York: Harper & Row.

Washburn, Wilcomb E. 1959. The Moral and Legal Justifications for Dispossessing the Indians. Chap. 2 in *Seventeenth Century America: Essays in Colonial History,* edited by James M. Smith. Chapel Hill: University of North Carolina Press.

Weber, Eugen J. 1973. *A Modern History of Europe.* London: Robert Hale & Co.

Wellford, Harrison. 1972. Pesticides. In *Nixon and the Environment: The Politics of Devastation,* edited by James Rathlesberger. New York: Village Voice / Taurus Communications, pp. 146–62.

Wengert, Norman. 1962. The Ideological Basis of Conservation and Natural Resource Policies. *Annals of the American Academy of Political and Social Sciences* 344:65–75.

Wheeler, William B., and M. J. McDonald. 1986. *TVA and the Tellico Dam, 1939–1979.* Knoxville: University of Tennessee Press.

Whelan, Elizabeth. 1985. *Toxic Terror.* Ottawa, Ill.: Jameson.

Whitaker, John. 1976. *Striking a Balance: Environment and Natural Resources in the Nixon-Ford Era.* Washington, D.C.: American Enterprise Institute.

White, Lynn, Jr. 1962. *Medieval Technology and Social Change.* New York: Oxford University Press.

Wicker, Tom. 1994. Waiting for an Environmental President. *Audubon* 96(5):49–54, 102–03.

Wildavsky, Aaron. 1964. *The Politics of the Budgetary Process.* Boston: Little, Brown.

———. 1995. *But Is It True? A Citizen's Guide to Environmental Health and Safety Issues.* Cambridge: Harvard University Press.

Wilkins, Thurman. 1995. *John Muir: Apostle of Nature.* Norman: University of Oklahoma Press.

Wilkinson, Charles F. 1992. *Crossing the Next Meridian: Land, Water, and the Future of the West.* Washington, D.C.: Island.

Williams, Dennis C. 1993. *The Guardian: EPA's Formative Years.* Document No. EPA-202-K-93-002. Washington, D.C.: U.S. Environmental Protection Agency.

Winslow, Charles-Edward A. 1923. *The Evolution and Significance of the Modern Public Health Campaign.* New Haven: Yale University Press.

Wolf, Charles. 1979. A Theory of Non-Market Failures. *The Public Interest* 55 (Spring): 114–33.

Wolman, Abel. 1965. The Metabolism of Cities. In *Cities: A Scientific American Book.* New York: Knopf, pp. 156–74.

World Bank. 1992. *Development and Environment.* World Development Report 1992. Washington, D.C.: World Bank.

World Health Organization. 1991. *Combatting Environmental Pollution: National Capabilities for Health Protection.* Report No. WHO/PEP/91.14. Geneva: World Health Organization.

World Commission on Environment and Development. 1987. *Our Common Future.* New York: Oxford University Press.

Worster, Donald M. 1985. *Rivers of Empire: Water, Aridity, and the Growth of the American West.* New York: Pantheon.

Worster, Donald. 1991. Beyond the Agrarian Myth. Chap. 1 in *Trails: Toward a New Western History,* edited by Patricia N. Limerick, Clyde A. Milner II, and Charles E. Rankin. Lawrence: University Press of Kansas.

Zwick, David, and Marcy Benstock. 1971. *Water Wasteland.* New York: Grossman.

Index

Managing the Environment, Managing Ourselves

A History of American Environmental Policy

Richard N. L. Andrews

American environmental policy is not just a product of late-twentieth-century concerns about the environment, says Richard Andrews in this important book. It is also rooted in America's nearly four-hundred-year history of government actions to promote or control human uses of nature. This book tells that rich history and shows how it affects environmental issues today and in the future.

Andrews traces the interplay between environmental policies and broader patterns of economic, social, and political history, and he shows not only what is unique about recent environmental policy but also how it emerged from earlier patterns and precedents. Andrews explores enduring questions about the nature and implications of American environmental governance then sums up the legacy of American environmental policy and poses its central challenges.

"Easily the most comprehensive history of American environmental policy I have ever seen. It will serve as an excellent reference book for policy historians, environmental historians, and environmental policy analysts." — Robert Paehlke, author of *Environmentalism and the Future of Progressive Politics*

Richard N. L. Andrews is professor of environmental policy in the Department of Environmental Sciences and Engineering, Department of City and Regional Planning, Curriculum in Public Policy Analysis, and Curriculum in Ecology at the University of North Carolina at Chapel Hill.